Theory and Applications of ECONOMIC INDICES

Proceedings of an International Symposium
Held at the University of Karlsruhe April–June 1976

Edited by
W. Eichhorn, R. Henn, O. Opitz, R.W. Shephard
at the Universities of Karlsruhe and Berkeley

Physica-Verlag · Würzburg
1978
ISBN 3 7908 0191 7

CIP-Kurztitelaufnahme der Deutschen Bibliothek

Theory and applications of economic indices:
proceedings of an internat. symposium held at the
Univ. of Karlsruhe, April – June 1976 / ed. by
W. Eichhorn . . . – Würzburg, Vienna : Physica-
Verlag, 1978.
ISBN 3-7908-0191-7

NE: Eichhorn, Wolfgang [Hrsg.]; Universität
⟨Karlsruhe⟩

Printed in Germany by repro-druck „Journalfranz" Arnulf Liebing GmbH + Co., Würzburg
ISBN 3 7908 0191 7

Preface

An international symposium on economic indices was held at the University of Karlsruhe April, May, and June of 1976, involving participants from Belgium, Canada, Finland, Great Britain, Luxembourg, Sweden, Switzerland, and the USA. Also many participants from German universities and other German institutions made contributions. Karlsruhe supplied the predominant part of the German contributors.

This symposium was a follow-on of a similar symposium held during May, June, and July of 1973 on production theory, stimulated by the results there obtained. (The proceedings of the 1973 symposium were published under the title PRODUCTION THEORY, with the same editors, by Springer-Verlag, Berlin-Heidelberg-New York 1974, Lecture Notes in Economics and Mathematical Systems, Vol. 99).

For the discussions of the seminar 32 papers spanning a large part of the field of economic indices were presented and these papers are herewith published as a coherent collection under the title: THEORY AND APPLICATIONS OF ECONOMIC INDICES.

Part I on methodological topics contains three papers involving an axiomatic foundation for economic indices, the relationship of cluster analysis to the theory of economic indices and a philosophcal discussion of object and number logic for price indices.

Part II on price indices contains several papers with an axiomatic approach to various issues in the formation of price indices, and papers dealing with cost of living indices, purchasing power parity methods, comparisons of price indices, stochastic and dynamic price indices, and a paper on an extension of Gorman's price aggregation theorem.

Part III on other economic indices contains a paper on a true wage index as kind of a counterpart to the true cost of living index, a treatment of indices of income inequality, a paper on indices of preference inequality, an application of a new definition of the degree of monopoly, a treatment of a household production function as a measure of satisfaction, a dynamic formulation of indices for the theory of cost and production, a treatment of index properties of ray-homothetic dynamic production structures and a paper considering the sensitivity of key sector indices.

Part IV on topics related to economic indices contains a variety of papers, which include problems of aggregation in various fields of research and an investigation of neutral changes in utility and tastes which is useful for defining both taste-dependent true cost of living indices and wage indices.

It is interesting that nearly one half of the 32 papers deal with or contain functional equations or systems of them, pointing perhaps to new roles of mathematics in index number theory.

We take this opportunity to acknowledge indebtedness to Stiftung Volkswagenwerk (Volkswagen Foundation) for financial means to carry out the symposium, and express our sincere appreciation for this support.

Karlsruhe and Berkeley
October 1977

W. Eichhorn, R. Henn,
O. Opitz, R.W. Shephard
Editors

TABLE OF CONTENTS

PART I

Methodological Topics Concerning Economic Indices

PART II

Price Indices

PART III

Other Economic Indices

PART IV

Topics Related to Economic Indices

List of Contributors

J. ACZÉL, Faculty of Mathematics, University of Waterloo, Waterloo, Ontario, Canada.

S.N. AFRIAT, Department of Economics, University of Ottawa, Ottawa, Ontario, Canada K1N 6N5.

MARTIN J. BECKMANN, Department of Economics, Brown University, Providence, Rhode Island, 02912, U.S.A., and: Institut für Angewandte Mathematik, Technische Universität München, D-8000 München, Germany.

KARL-HEINZ BERTSCH, Fachbereich Rechts- und Wirtschaftswissenschaften, Universität Mainz, D-6500 Mainz, Federal Republic of Germany.

CHARLES BLACKORBY, Department of Economics, University of British Columbia, British Columbia, Canada V6T 1W5.

RALPH BÜRK, Institut für Wirtschaftstheorie und Operations Research, Universität Karlsruhe, D-7500 Karlsruhe, Federal Republic of Germany.

KLAUS CONRAD, Sonderforschungsbereich 21, Universität Bonn, D-5300 Bonn, Federal Republic of Germany.

HELMUT DIEHL, Office Statistique des Communautés Européennes, Boîte Postale 1907, Luxembourg.

WOLFGANG EICHHORN, Institut für Wirtschaftstheorie und Operations Research, Universität Karlsruhe, D-7500 Karlsruhe, Federal Republic of Germany.

ROLF FÄRE, Department of Economics, University of Lund, S-22005 Lund 5, Sweden.

SUSANNE FUCHS-SELIGER, Institut für Wirtschaftstheorie und Operations Research, Universität Karlsruhe, D-7500 Karlsruhe, Federal Republic of Germany.

HELMUT FUNKE, Institut für Wirtschaftstheorie und Operations Reserach, Universität Karlsruhe, D-7500 Karlsruhe, Federal Republic of Germany.

WILHELM GEHRIG, Institut für Wirtschaftstheorie und Operations Research, Universität Karlsruhe, D-7500 Karlsruhe, Federal Republic of Germany.

BERND GOLDSTEIN, Lehrstuhl für Statistik und Ökonometrie, Gesamthochschule Siegen, D-5900 Siegen, Federal Republic of Germany.

GÜNTER HACKER, Institut für Wirtschaftstheorie und Operations Research, Universität Karlsruhe, D-7500 Karlsruhe, Federal Republic of Germany.

ERICH HÄRTTER, Fachbereich Rechts- und Wirtschaftswissenschaften, Universität Mainz, D-6500 Mainz, Federal Republic of Germany.

GEORG HASENKAMP, Sonderforschungsbereich 21, Universität Bonn, D-5300 Bonn, Federal Republic of Germany.

RAINER HECKER, Philips GmbH, Apparatefabrik Krefeld, D-4150 Krefeld 12, Federal Republic of Germany.

CLAUS HILD, Lehrstuhl für Statistik und Ökonometrie, Gesamthochschule Siegen, D-5900 Siegen, Federal Republic of Germany.

HARTMUT KOGELSCHATZ, Institut für Statistik und Mathematische Wirtschaftstheorie, Universität Karlsruhe, D-7500 Karlsruhe, Federal Republic of Germany.

GÜNTER MENGES, Lehrstuhl für Wirtschafts- und Sozialstatistik, Universität Heidelberg, D-6900 Heidelberg, Federal Republic of Germany.

BERND MUNDLOS, Lehrstuhl für Statistik und Ökonometrie, Technische Universität Braunschweig, D-3300 Braunschweig, Federal Republic of Germany.

OTTO OPITZ, Institut für Entscheidungstheorie und Unternehmensforschung, Universität Karlsruhe, D-7500 Karlsruhe, Federal Republic of Germany.

LOUIS PHLIPS, Center for Operations Research and Econometrics, Universite Catholique de Louvain, B-1348 Louvain-La-Neuve, Belgium.

FRITZ POKROPP, Institut für Statistik und Ökonometrie, Universität Hamburg, D-2000 Hamburg 13, Federal Republic of Germany.

DANIEL PRIMONT, Department of Economics, University of Massachusetts, Boston, Massachusetts, U.S.A.

KLAUS REEH, Seminar für Ökonometrie und Statistik der Universität München, D-8000 München 22, Federal Republic of Germany.

R. ROBERT RUSSELL, Department of Economics, University of California, San Diego, La Jolla, California 92093, U.S.A.

JOCHEN SCHWARZE, Lehrstuhl für Statistik und Ökonometrie, Technische Universität Braunschweig, D-3300 Braunschweig, Federal Republic of Germany.

RONALD W. SHEPHARD, Department of Industrial Engineering and Operations Research, University of California, Berkeley, Berkeley, California 94720, U.S.A.

KLAUS SPREMANN, Institut für Wirtschaftstheorie und Operations Research, Universität Karlsruhe, D-7500 Karlsruhe, Federal Republic of Germany.

FRANK STEHLING, Institut für Wirtschaftstheorie und Operations Research, Universität Karlsruhe, D-7500 Karlsruhe, Federal Republic of Germany.

GÖTZ UEBE, Institut für Angewandte Mathematik, Technische Universität München, D-8000 München, Federal Republic of Germany.

YRJÖ O. VARTIA, The Research Institute of the Finnish Economy, SF-00100 Helsinki 10, Finland.

JOACHIM VOELLER, Institut für Wirtschaftstheorie und Operations Research, Universität Karlsruhe, D-7500 Karlsruhe, Federal Republic of Germany.

ARTHUR VOGT, Eidgenössisches Statistisches Amt, CH-3003 Bern, Switzerland.

PART I

Methodological Topics Concerning Economic Indices

What is an Economic Index ?

An Attempt of an Answer

by Wolfgang Eichhorn [1)]

O. Introduction

This volume considers so many different economic indices that the question of a common origin may reasonably be asked. Moreover, the question arises immediately: what kind of mechanism produces an economic index from a set of economic figures or objects ?

In what follows, we try to give an answer to these questions. After presenting a variety of examples and studying some axiomatics as well as many functional equations we get to the following answer:

An *economic index is an economic measure, i.e., a function*

(0.1) $$F : D \to \mathbb{R}$$

which maps, on the one hand, a set D *of economically interesting objects into the set* $\mathbb{R}$ *of real numbers and which satisfies, on the other hand a system of economically relevant conditions (for instance, monotonicity and homogeneity or homotheticity conditions).*

The form of these conditions depends on the economic information which we want to obtain from the particular measure.

The function values of an economic index F are *economic index numbers*. We point out here that an index is a *mapping* (0.1), *not*

1) I am indebted to Janos Aczél, Ronald Shephard, and to my colleagues and friends of the Institut für Wirtschaftstheorie und Operations Research for helpful comments and suggestions.

a real number, whereas *an index number is an element of the range* $\mathbb{R}$ *of an index.*

PFANZAGL's book "Theory of Measurement" [1971] could serve as a most suitable methodological foundation of a theory of economic indices. Many of the examples of economic indices contained in this paper could illustrate PFANZAGL's theoretical treatment similarly well as it is done by his own examples that are mainly taken from psychophysics and psychology.

As we shall see, the problems of defining certain classes of economic indices can only be treated by paying attention to the "parallelism of object logic and formal (or mathematical) logic"; see, in this connection, the contribution by MENGES to this volume. If we forget about the mathematical logic, the system of conditions which must be satisfied by the desired index may turn out to be *inconsistent* (see the examples of inconsistent sets of conditions in section 3). If we neglect the object logic, the index thus obtained may not provide us with the economic information we are looking for.

With the aid of indices we aggregate data of the same (or of a similar) kind in order to gain better insight into complex data. To put it in other words, we use indices for simplifying complex data systems. So far, there is a relationship to *numerical taxonomy (taxonometry, multivariate analysis, data analysis)* that contains a variety of techniques for data simplification. OPITZ emphasizes this relationship in his contribution to this volume.

Obviously, a single economic index may not be sufficient to provide *full* insight into the quantitative aspects of an economic structure (e.g., an economy or a firm). For this purpose *systems* of economic indices have to be considered (see, for instance, HECKER's contribution to this volume). At the conclusion we will show that *every system of* k *economic indices can be interpreted as a vector-valued function or mapping*

(0.2) $$\underline{F} : D \to \mathbb{R}^k$$

whose components $F_1, F_2, \ldots, F_k$ *are economic indices.*

1. Economic Quantities and Functions of these Quantities

Let $z_1, z_2, \ldots, z_p$ be quantities which are of interest for economists, such as GNP (= gross national product), profit, investment, prices, input quantities, output quantities, and so on.

In order to obtain particular information from such a vector $\underline{z} = (z_1, z_2, \ldots, z_p)$ of quantities we very often apply some kind of mechanism, F say, which assigns a real number $F(z_1, z_2, \ldots, z_p)$ to the vector $\underline{z}$. If, for instance, z_1 = GNP, z_2 = population, and we are interested in GNP per capita, then

(1.0) $$F(z_1, z_2, \ldots, z_p) = \frac{z_1}{z_2} .$$

In this case, the mechanism F is a real-valued function which satisfies the following conditions.

(1.1) Monotonicity:

$$z_1 \mapsto F(\underline{z}) \text{ is strictly increasing}$$

$$z_2 \mapsto F(\underline{z}) \text{ is strictly decreasing}$$

$$z_i \mapsto F(\underline{z}) \text{ is constant } (i = 3, \ldots, p).$$

(1.2) Homogeneity of degree 0:

$$F(\lambda \underline{z}) = F(\underline{z}) \text{ for all real } \lambda > 0.$$

(1.3) Homogeneity of degree 1 with respect to z_1:

$$F(\lambda z_1, z_2, \ldots, z_p) = \lambda F(\underline{z}) \text{ for all } \underline{z} \text{ and all } \lambda > 0.$$

(1.4) Normalization:

$$F(1,1,z_3,\ldots,z_p) = 1 \qquad \text{for all } z_3,\ldots,z_p.$$

We emphasize that, conversely, *the conditions* (1.1) to (1.4) *imply the form* (1.0) *of* F, *i.e., characterize* F .

Proof:

$$\begin{aligned} F(\underline{z}) &= F\left(z_2\frac{z_1}{z_2},\ z_2\cdot 1,\ z_2\frac{z_3}{z_2},\ldots,z_2\frac{z_p}{z_2}\right) \\ &= F\left(\frac{z_1}{z_2},1,\frac{z_3}{z_2},\ldots,\frac{z_p}{z_2}\right) && \text{(by (1.2))} \\ &= \frac{z_1}{z_2}F\left(1,1,\frac{z_3}{z_2},\ldots,\frac{z_p}{z_2}\right) && \text{(by (1.3))} \\ &= \frac{z_1}{z_2} && \text{(by (1.4))} \blacksquare \end{aligned}$$

As a byproduct of this proof we note that the conditions (1.1) to (1.4) are *dependent* in the following sense: conditions (1.2), (1.3), (1.4) imply condition (1.1).

Are the conditions (1.2), (1.3), (1.4) independent ?
The answer is *yes* for $p \geqq 3$, since F given by

$$F(\underline{z}) = \frac{z_1 z_3 z_4 \cdots z_p}{z_2^{p-1}}$$

satisfies (1.2) and (1.3), but not (1.4),

$$F(\underline{z}) = \left(\frac{z_1}{z_2}\right)^{1/2}$$

satisfies (1.2) and (1.4), but not (1.3), and

$$F(\underline{z}) = z_1/z_2^2$$

satisfies (1.3) and (1.4), but not (1.2) $\blacksquare$

Note that in the foregoing reasoning our starting point was a well-known economic index, namely GNP per capita. We *characterized* it by some of its properties. Hence, we can *define* it by these properties. We point out here that the properties (1.1) to (1.4) of F can be motivated easily if it is our aim to use F to measure GNP relative to population.

This example gives a first hint how to answer the question we asked in the title: *An economic index is an economic measure, i.e., a real-valued function whose domain is a set of vectors of economic figures and which satisfies a system of economically motivated conditions. The form and the content of these conditions depends on what we want to measure.*

What, then, is an *economic index* <u>*number*</u> ? It is the *value* of an economic index. This definition implies that every economic quantity is an economic index number (provided, we agree that, given any economic quantity z_i, the function F_i given by $F_i(\underline{z})=z_i$ for all $\underline{z}$, can be considered as an economic index).

The following sections of this article will provide us with a variety of systems of conditions for various indices. It is *not* the aim of these sections to create *new* systems of conditions or axioms for certain economic indices. We rather study the systems in order to corroborate both the adequacy and usefulness of our definition of an economic index.

2. What is a Price Level ?

The economic meaning of the term price level rests on the idea that there exists a nonnegative-valued function which measures the prices of the goods (commodities and services) under consideration such that the ratio of two function values determined at two different price situations indicates the change of the prices.

Let

$$\underline{p} = (p_1,\dots,p_n) \in \mathbb{R}^n_+ \qquad (\mathbb{R}_+ \text{ the nonnegative reals, } n \geqq 2)$$

be the price vector of n goods.

(2.0) Definition. *A function*

$$L : \mathbb{R}^n_+ \to \mathbb{R}_+, \quad \underline{p} \mapsto L(\underline{p})$$

is called a *price level* *if* L *satisfies the following two axioms for all* $\underline{p} \in \mathbb{R}^n_+$. *Then the value* $L(\underline{p})$ *represents the* *value of the price level at the price situation* $\underline{p}$.

(2.1) Monotonicity Axiom. The function L is strictly increasing:

$$L(\underline{p}) > L(\bar{\underline{p}}) \quad \text{if } \underline{p} \geq \bar{\underline{p}}\,.$$ [1)]

(2.2) Linear Homogeneity Axiom. If all prices change λ-fold ($\lambda \in \mathbb{R}_+$), then the value of L is multiplied by λ:

$$L(\lambda\underline{p}) = \lambda L(\underline{p}) \qquad (\lambda \in \mathbb{R}_+).$$

Examples of price levels, i.e., of functions L satisfying axioms (2.1) and (2.2) are given by:

(2.3) $L(\underline{p}) = c_1p_1+\dots+c_np_n$ $\quad\left\{\begin{array}{l} c_1 > 0,\dots,c_n > 0 \text{ arbitrary} \\ \text{real constants;}\end{array}\right.$

(2.4) $L(\underline{p}) = C\,p_1^{\alpha_1}\,p_2^{\alpha_2}\cdots p_n^{\alpha_n}$ $\quad\left\{\begin{array}{l} C,\alpha_1,\dots,\alpha_n \text{ arbitrary positive} \\ \text{real constants, } \Sigma\alpha_\nu = 1;\end{array}\right.$

---

1) We write $\underline{x} = (x_1,\dots,x_n) > (y_1,\dots,y_n) = \underline{y}$ if $x_1 > y_1,\dots,x_n > y_n$, and $\underline{x} \geq \underline{y}$ if $x_1 \geqq y_1,\dots,x_n \geqq y_n$ but $\underline{x} \neq \underline{y}$, and $\underline{x} \geqq \underline{y}$ if $x_1 \geqq y_1,\dots,x_n \geqq y_n$.

(2.5) $L(\underline{p}) = \left(\beta_1 p_1^{-\rho} + \ldots + \beta_n p_n^{-\rho}\right)^{-\frac{1}{\rho}}$ $\begin{cases} \beta_1 > 0, \ldots, \beta_n > 0, \rho \neq 0 \\ \text{arbitrary real constants.} \end{cases}$

(2.6) Remark. *If* $L_1, \ldots, L_k$ *are price levels according to definition (2.0), then*

(2.7) $\left(\gamma_1 L_1^{\delta} + \ldots + \gamma_k L_k^{\delta}\right)^{\frac{1}{\delta}}$ $\begin{cases} \delta \neq 0, \gamma_1 \geqq 0, \ldots, \gamma_k \geqq 0 \\ \textit{arbitrary real constants}, \Sigma\gamma_k = 1 \end{cases}$

and

(2.8) $L_1^{\delta_1} L_2^{\delta_2} \ldots L_k^{\delta_k}$ $\begin{cases} \delta_1 \geqq 0, \ldots, \delta_k \geqq 0 \textit{ arbitrary} \\ \textit{real constants}, \Sigma\delta_k = 1 \end{cases}$

are also price levels. Here L^{σ} *is defined by*

$$\underline{p} \mapsto [L(\underline{p})]^{\sigma}.$$

Each of the price levels given by (2.3), (2.4), and (2.5) can be characterized by adding appropriate conditions to the axioms (2.1) and (2.2). Examples of such conditions are given by the following 'tests'.

(2.9) Additivity Test. A price level L is called *additive* if every additive change in the prices from $\underline{p}$ to $\underline{p} + \bar{\underline{p}}$ yields an additive change of the value of L from $L(\underline{p})$ to $L(\underline{p}) + L(\bar{\underline{p}})$:

$$L(\underline{p} + \bar{\underline{p}}) = L(\underline{p}) + L(\bar{\underline{p}}) .$$

(2.10) Multiplicativity Test. A price level L is called *multiplicative* if the value of L at the price vector $(\lambda_1 p_1, \ldots, \lambda_n p_n)$ $(\lambda_1 \in \mathbb{R}_+, \ldots, \lambda_n \in \mathbb{R}_+)$ is equal to the value of L at the price vector $\underline{p} = (p_1, \ldots, p_n)$ multiplied by a nonnegative real number ρ depending on the λ_i's:

$$L(\lambda_1 p_1, \ldots, \lambda_n p_n) = \rho(\lambda_1, \ldots, \lambda_n) L(\underline{p}) \quad (\lambda_i \in \mathbb{R}_+,\ i = 1, \ldots, n).$$

(2.11) Quasilinearity Test. A price level L is called *quasilinear* if there exist real constants $a_1, a_2, \ldots, a_n, b$ with $a_1 a_2 \ldots a_n \neq 0$ and a continuous and strictly monotonic function

$$f : \mathbb{R}_{++} \to \mathbb{R} \qquad (\mathbb{R}_{++} \text{ the positive reals})$$

with the inverse f^{-1} such that, for the restriction of L to $\mathbb{R}^n_{++}$,

$$L(\underline{p}) = f^{-1}\left[a_1 f(p_1) + a_2 f(p_2) + \ldots + a_n f(p_n) + b\right].$$

(2.12) Theorem *(Characterization of the price levels (2.3), (2.4), (2.5)). A function* $L: \to \mathbb{R}^n_+ \to \mathbb{R}_+$ *satisfies the axioms (2.1) and (2.2) and the*

(i) Additivity Test if and only if it is given by (2.3)

(ii) Multiplicativity Test if and only if it is given by (2.4)

(ii) Quasilinearity Test if and only if it is either given by (2.4) or by (2.5).

For the proofs of this theorem and of the theorems of the next section see EICHHORN and VOELLER [1976].

3. What is a Price Index ?

If we only require that a price index shall measure the change of a price level (value) as the price vector changes then we have

Definition A of a price index. *A price index is a function*

$$P : \mathbb{R}^{2n}_{++} \to \mathbb{R}_{++}, \quad ^{1)} \qquad (\underline{p}^o, \underline{p}) \mapsto P(\underline{p}^o, \underline{p})$$

1) In what follows, we assume, for technical reasons, the positivity of both the domains of definition and ranges.

given by

$$(3.0) \qquad P(\underline{p}^o,\underline{p}) = \frac{L(\underline{p})}{L(\underline{p}^o)} \qquad \begin{cases} \underline{p}^o = \textit{base period price vector} \\ \underline{p} = \textit{comparison period price vector,} \end{cases}$$

where L *is a price level (see definition (2.0)).*

Since L satisfies axioms (2.1) and (2.2), the price index P given by (3.0) has, among others, the following four properties which we call axioms.

(3.1) Monotonicity Axiom. The function P is strictly increasing with respect to $\underline{p}$ and strictly decreasing with respect to $\underline{p}^o$:

$$P(\underline{p}^o,\underline{p}) > P(\underline{p}^o,\bar{\underline{p}}) \qquad \text{if} \quad \underline{p} \geq \bar{\underline{p}} \quad ,$$

$$P(\underline{p}^o,\underline{p}) < P(\bar{\underline{p}}^o,\underline{p}) \qquad \text{if} \quad \underline{p}^o \geq \bar{\underline{p}}^o \quad .$$

(3.2) Linear Homogeneity Axiom. If all comparison prices change λ-fold ($\lambda \in \mathbb{R}_{++}$), then the value of P is changed by λ :

$$P(\underline{p}^o,\lambda\underline{p}) = \lambda P(\underline{p}^o,\underline{p}) \qquad (\lambda \in \mathbb{R}_{++}).$$

(3.3) Identity Axiom. If all prices remain constant, then the value of P equals unity:

$$P(\underline{p}^o,\underline{p}^o) = 1.$$

(3.4) Dimensionality Axiom. A dimensional change in the unit of the currency does not change the value of the function P:

$$P(\lambda\underline{p}^o,\lambda\underline{p}) = P(\underline{p}^o,\underline{p}) \qquad (\lambda \in \mathbb{R}_{++}).$$

A second interpretation of this axiom is the following: If two economies are identical except for the definition of the unit of money, then the values of the respective price indices are the same.

We point out here that there exist functions P satisfying axioms (3.1) to (3.4) which cannot be written in the form (3.0). Take, for instance,

$$(3.5)\qquad P(\underline{p}^o,\underline{p}) = \left[\beta_1\left(\frac{p_1}{p_1^o}\right)^{-\rho} + \ldots + \beta_n\left(\frac{p_n}{p_n^o}\right)^{-\rho}\right]^{-\frac{1}{\rho}} \qquad \begin{cases} \rho \neq 0, \beta_1 > 0, \ldots, \beta_n > 0 \\ \text{arbitrary real} \\ \text{constants}, \Sigma\beta_\nu = 1. \end{cases}$$

According to definition A, the function P given by (3.5) is *not* a price index. But in our opinion, axioms (3.1) to (3.4) constitute a set of axioms sufficient for a price index to serve as a quantitative measure responsive to any price change (but not necessarily responsive to utility functions of households). By 'sufficient' we mean that it is not necessary to add one or more independent axioms to axioms (3.1) to (3.4) in order to exclude inappropiate solutions of (3.1) to (3.4), of which there are none.

In this connection, it is interesting to note:

(3.6) Theorem. *Every function* $P : \mathbb{R}^{2n}_{++} \to \mathbb{R}_{++}$ *which satisfies axioms (3.1), (3.2), and (3.3) also satisfies the so-called Mean Value Test:*

$$\min\{\frac{p_1}{p_1^o},\ldots,\frac{p_n}{p_n^o}\} \leqq P(\underline{p}^o,\underline{p}) \leqq \max\{\frac{p_1}{p_1^o},\ldots,\frac{p_n}{p_n^o}\} .$$

(3.7) Theorem. *Axioms (3.1) to (3.4) are independent in the following sense: Any three of these axioms can be satisfied by a function* P *which does not satisfy the remaining axiom.*

The foregoing considerations lead us to:

Definition B of a price index. *A function*

$$P : \mathbb{R}^{2n}_{++} \to \mathbb{R}_{++}, \qquad (\underline{p}^o, \underline{p}) \mapsto P(\underline{p}^o, \underline{p})$$

is called a price index if P *satisfies the Mononoticity Axiom (3.1), the Linear Homogeneity Axiom (3.2), the Identity Axiom (3.3), and the Dimensionality Axiom (3.4). Then the value* $P(\underline{p}^o, \underline{p})$ *represents the value of the price index at the price situation* $(\underline{p}^o, \underline{p})$.

We emphasize that the following problem is still *unsolved.*

(3.8) Problem. *Determine all price indices in the sense* B*, i.e., determine all functions* P *satisfying the axioms (3.1) to (3.4).*

Since we can generate new price indices (in the sense B) by convex combination of k $\geq$ 2 price indices (in the sense B) in an analogous matter as done with the price levels in remark (2.6), it *may* be possible to solve problem (3.8) by applying a theorem of KREIN and MILMAN [1940] on convex sets.

Well-known examples of price indices (in the sense B), i.e., of functions P satisfying axioms (3.1) to (3.4), are given by (3.5) and

$$(3.9) \qquad P(\underline{p}^o, \underline{p}) = \frac{\underline{c}\,\underline{p}}{\underline{c}\,\underline{p}^o} \qquad \begin{cases} (\underline{c} = (c_1, \dots, c_n) \\ c_\nu > 0 \text{ real constants}; \end{cases}$$

$$(3.10) \qquad P(\underline{p}^o, \underline{p}) = \left[\frac{\underline{a}\,\underline{p}}{\underline{a}\,\underline{p}^o} \; \frac{\underline{b}\,\underline{p}}{\underline{b}\,\underline{p}^o}\right]^{\frac{1}{2}} \qquad \begin{cases} \underline{a} = (a_1, \dots, a_n), \underline{b} = (b_1, \dots, b_n) \\ a_\nu > 0,\ b_\nu > 0 \text{ real constants}; \end{cases}$$

$$(3.11) \qquad P(\underline{p}^o, \underline{p}) = \left(\frac{p_1}{p_1^o}\right)^{\alpha_1} \left(\frac{p_2}{p_2^o}\right)^{\alpha_2} \cdots \left(\frac{p_n}{p_n^o}\right)^{\alpha_n} \qquad \begin{cases} \alpha_1 > 0, \dots, \alpha_n > 0 \text{ real} \\ \text{constants}, \ \Sigma\alpha_\nu = 1. \end{cases}$$

$$(3.12)\quad P(\underline{p}^{o},\underline{p}) = \frac{[\beta_1 p_1^{-\rho}+\ldots+\beta_n p_n^{-\rho}]^{-1/\rho}}{[\beta_1 (p_1^{o})^{-\rho}+\ldots+\beta_n (p_n^{o})^{-\rho}]^{-1/\rho}} \qquad \begin{cases} \beta_1>0,\ldots,\beta_n>0,\rho\neq 0 \\ \text{real constants ,} \\ \Sigma\beta_\nu = 1. \end{cases}$$

Characterizations of these indices by adding further conditions to the axioms (3.1) to (3.4) are due to GEHRIG [see this volume] in the case (3.5), (3.11), to ACZÉL and EICHHORN [1974a], [1974b] in the case (3.9), to FUNKE and VOELLER [see this volume] in the case (3.10), and to EICHHORN and VOELLER [1976] in the case (3.11). Obviously, (3.12) can be characterized by applying (2.11), (2.12), and (3.0). For a generalization of the papers by ACZÉL and EICHHORN [1974a], [1974b] see ACZÉL [this volume].

So far, we have given definitions of the term price index without bringing into play the *quantities* of the goods considered. Taking into consideration the quantity vector or *basket of goods* consumed by a household with a given budget in a certain period is a first step towards the so-called *economic* theory of the price index in which consumer preferences play an important role. Nevertheless, what we will develop next up to theorem (3.24), still belongs to the so-called *atomistic* (see FRISCH [1936] or HASENKAMP, this volume) or *statistical* (see FRISCH [1936] or ALLEN [1975, p. 47]) or *mechanical* (see SAMUELSON and SWAMY [1974]) approach to the theory of the price index. This approach is chosen in (parts of) the contributions to this volume by DIEHL, FUNKE and VOELLER, GEHRIG, HILD and HACKER, VARTIA, and by MUNDLOS and SCHWARZE who define the price index not as a deterministic function but as a random variable. HASENKAMP's contribution compares atomistic and economic indices.

Let

$$\underline{q}^{o} = (q_1^{o},\ldots,q_n^{o}) \in \mathbb{R}^n_{++} \text{ and } \underline{q} = (q_1,\ldots,q_n) \in \mathbb{R}^n_{++}$$

be the quantity vectors of n goods in a base period and in a comparsion period, respectively, and let $\underline{p}^{o} \in \mathbb{R}^n_{++}$ and $\underline{p} \in \mathbb{R}^n_{++}$ represent the corresponding price vectors. Then, P given by

(3.9) is the LASPEYRES [1871] price index if $\underline{c} = \underline{q}^o$;

(3.9) is the PAASCHE [1874] price index if $\underline{c} = \underline{q}$;

(3.9) is the MARSHALL-EDGEWORTH price index if $\underline{c} = \underline{q}^o + \underline{q}$;

(3.10) is I. FISHER's [1922] ideal index if $\underline{a} = \underline{q}^o, \underline{b} = \underline{q}$.

The following definition extends definition B to the case, where the quantities are involved also.

Definition C of a price index. *A function*

$$P : \mathbb{R}^{4n}_{++} \to \mathbb{R}_{++}, \qquad (\underline{q}^o,\underline{p}^o,\underline{q},\underline{p}) \mapsto P(\underline{q}^o,\underline{p}^o,\underline{q},\underline{p})$$

is called a price index (depending on prices and quantities) if P *satisfies the following five axioms for all* $(\underline{q}^o,\underline{p}^o,\underline{q},\underline{p}) \in \mathbb{R}^{4n}_{++}$.[1)] *Then the value* $P(q^o,p^o,q,p)$ *represents the value of the price index at the price-quantity situation* $(\underline{q}^o,\underline{p}^o,\underline{q},\underline{p})$.

(3.13) Monotonicity Axiom

$$P(\underline{q}^o,\underline{p}^o,\underline{q},\underline{p}) > P(\underline{q}^o,\underline{p}^o,\underline{q},\bar{\underline{p}}) \qquad \text{if } \underline{p} \geq \bar{\underline{p}},$$

$$P(q^o,p^o,q,p) < P(\underline{q}^o,\bar{\underline{p}}^o,\underline{q},\underline{p}) \qquad \text{if } \underline{p}^o \geq \bar{\underline{p}}^o.$$

(3.14) Linear Homogeneity Axiom

$$P(\underline{q}^o,\underline{p}^o,\underline{q},\lambda\underline{p}) = \lambda P(\underline{q}^o,\underline{p}^o,\underline{q},\underline{p}) \qquad (\lambda \in \mathbb{R}_{++}).$$

(3.15) Identity Axiom

$$P(\underline{q}^o,\underline{p}^o,\underline{q},\underline{p}^o) = 1.$$

(3.16) Dimensionality Axiom

$$P(\underline{q}^o,\lambda\underline{p}^o,\underline{q},\lambda\underline{p}) = P(\underline{q}^o,\underline{p}^o,\underline{q},\underline{p}) \qquad (\lambda \in \mathbb{R}_{++}).$$

1) The first four axioms are analogous to axioms (3.1) to (3.4).

(3.17) Commensurability Axiom. A change in the units of measurement of goods does not change the value of the function P:

$$P\left(\frac{q_1^o}{\lambda_1},\ldots,\frac{q_n^o}{\lambda_n},\lambda_1 p_1^o,\ldots,\lambda_n p_n^o,\frac{q_1}{\lambda_1},\ldots,\frac{q_n}{\lambda_n},\lambda_1 p_1,\ldots,\lambda_n p_n\right)=P(\underline{q}^o,\underline{p}^o,\underline{q},\underline{p})$$

$(\lambda_1 \in \mathbb{R}_{++},\ldots,\lambda_n \in \mathbb{R}_{++})$.

(3.18) Theorem. *Axioms (3.13) to (3.17) are independent in the sense of theorem (3.7).*

We note that from axioms (3.13), (3.14), and (3.15) we obtain, as in theorem (3.6),

$$(3.19) \qquad \min\left\{\frac{p_1}{p_1^o},\ldots,\frac{p_n}{p_n^o}\right\} \leqq P(\underline{q}^o,\underline{p}^o,\underline{q},\underline{p}) \leqq \max\left\{\frac{p_1}{p_1^o},\ldots,\frac{p_n}{p_n^o}\right\}.$$

Axioms (3.14) and (3.15) imply the so-called

(3.20) Proportionality Test. If all base period prices change λ-fold ($\lambda \in \mathbb{R}_{++}$), then the value of P equals λ:

$$P(\underline{q}^o,\underline{p}^o,\underline{q},\lambda\underline{p}^o)=\lambda \qquad (\lambda \in \mathbb{R}_{++}).$$

Whereas axioms (3.13) to (3.17) are independent and *consistent* in the sense that there are functions P satisfying all of them [1)], I. FISHER's *famous system of tests for assessing the quality of a potential price index is inconsistent.* His system consists, among others, of the Proportionality Test (3.20), the Commensurability Test (i.e., our Commensurability Axiom (3.17)), and the following tests.

[1)] Note that the process of generating new price levels from given ones as described in remark (2.6) can also be applied to price indices in the sense of Definition C.

(3.21) Circular Test. If in a first time period all quantities and prices change from $\underline{q}^o,\underline{p}^o$ to $\underline{q}^1,\underline{p}^1$ and in a subsequent time period they change from $\underline{q}^1,\underline{p}^1$ to $\underline{q},\underline{p}$ then the value of P for the entire time period is the product of the values of P for the two time periods:

$$P(\underline{q}^o,\underline{p}^o,\underline{q}^1,\underline{p}^1)P(\underline{q}^1,\underline{p}^1,\underline{q},\underline{p})=P(\underline{q}^o,\underline{p}^o,\underline{q},\underline{p}).$$

(3.22) Factor Reversal Test. In P, interchange, $\underline{q}^o$ and $\underline{p}^o$ as well as $\underline{q}$ and $\underline{p}$. The resulting $P(\underline{p}^o,\underline{q}^o,\underline{p},\underline{q})$ can be regarded as the value of a quantity index if $P(\underline{q}^o,\underline{p}^o,\underline{q},\underline{p})$ is the value of a price index. The product of the two values is the ratio of the values of the two baskets of goods in question, i.e.,

$$P(\underline{q}^o,\underline{p}^o,\underline{q},\underline{p})P(\underline{p}^o,\underline{q}^o,\underline{p},\underline{q}) = \frac{\underline{q}\,\underline{p}}{\underline{q}^o\underline{p}^o}.$$

(3.23) Determinateness Test. If any scalar argument in P tends to zero, then $P(\underline{q}^o,\underline{p}^o,\underline{q},\underline{p})$ tends to a unique positive real number (which depends on the values of the other components of $(\underline{q}^o,\underline{p}^o,\underline{q},\underline{p})$).

(3.24) Theorem. *Tests (3.17), (3.20), (3.21), (3.22), and (3.23) are inconsistent in the sense that there does not exist any function* P *satisfying them all. There exist even inconsistent subsets of these tests, the smallest being* {(3.20), (3.21), (3.22)} *and* {(3.17), (3.20), (3.21), (3.23)}.

For the proof of this and for inconsistency of systems of similar but weaker tests, see EICHHORN and VOELLER [1976, sections 3.2 to 3.5].

It is interesting to note that the famous DIVISIAindex, which is reconsidered by VOGT in this volume, does *not* meet our definition C of a price index.

(3.25) Definition D of a price index. *Let* $\mathcal{C}$ *be a path*[1] *from the point* $(\underline{q}^o,\underline{p}^o) \in \mathbb{R}^{2n}_{++}$ *to the point* $(\underline{q},\underline{p}) \in \mathbb{R}^{2n}_{++}$ *such that the following line integral exists. The function*

$$P_{\mathcal{C}} : \mathbb{R}^{4n}_{++} \to \mathbb{R}_{+}$$

given by

$$(3.26) \quad P_{\mathcal{C}}(\underline{q}^o,\underline{p}^o,\underline{q},\underline{p}) = \exp \int_{\mathcal{C}} \frac{q_1 dp_1 + \ldots + q_n dp_n + 0 \cdot dq_1 + \ldots + 0 \cdot dq_n}{q_1 p_1 + \ldots + q_n p_n} =: \exp \int_{\mathcal{C}} \frac{\underline{q}\, d\underline{p}}{\underline{q}\,\underline{p}}$$

is called the DIVISIA price index with respect to the path $\mathcal{C}$.

We emphasize that the value (3.26) of $P_{\mathcal{C}}$ *depends on the path* $\mathcal{C}$ *from* $(\underline{q}^o,\underline{p}^o)$ *to* $(\underline{q},\underline{p})$ whereas definitions A, B, and C only depend on $\underline{p}^o$ and $\underline{p}$ or on $(\underline{q}^o,\underline{p}^o)$ and $(\underline{q},\underline{p})$, respectively.

Obviously, the DIVISIA index satisfies the following modifications of the Circular Test (3.21) and the Factor Reversal Test (3.22):

$$(3.27) \qquad P_{\mathcal{C}_o}(\underline{q}^o,\underline{p}^o,\underline{q}^1,\underline{p}^1)\,P_{\mathcal{C}_1}(\underline{q}^1,\underline{p}^1,\underline{q},\underline{p}) = P_{\mathcal{C}}(\underline{q}^o,\underline{p}^o,\underline{q},\underline{p}) \, ,$$

where $\mathcal{C}_o$ and $\mathcal{C}_1$ run from $(\underline{q}^o,\underline{p}^o)$ to $(\underline{q}^1,\underline{p}^1)$ and from $(\underline{q}^1,\underline{p}^1)$ to $(\underline{q},\underline{p})$, respectively, and $\mathcal{C}$ is the union of $\mathcal{C}_o$ and $\mathcal{C}_1$; and

$$(3.28) \qquad P_{\mathcal{C}}(\underline{q}^o,\underline{p}^o,\underline{q},\underline{p})\,Q_{\mathcal{C}}(\underline{q}^o,\underline{p}^o,\underline{q},\underline{p}) = \frac{\underline{q}\,\underline{p}}{\underline{q}^o\underline{p}^o}$$

for all smooth paths $\mathcal{C}$, where $Q_{\mathcal{C}}$ given by

$$(3.29) \qquad Q_{\mathcal{C}}(\underline{q}^o,\underline{p}^o,\underline{q},\underline{p}) = \exp \int_{\mathcal{C}} \frac{\underline{p}\, d\underline{q}}{\underline{p}\,\underline{q}}$$

is the DIVISIA "quantity index".

---

[1] We may consider $\mathcal{C}$ as the path along which the quantity-price vector has run from the quantity-price situation of the base period to that of the comparison period.

We note that for certain paths $\mathcal{C}$ from $(\underline{q}^o,\underline{p}^o)$ to the same $(\underline{q}^o,\underline{p}^o)$,

$$P_{\mathcal{C}}(\underline{q}^o,\underline{p}^o,\underline{q}^o,\underline{p}^o) \neq 1$$

is possible. Nevertheless, we call the DIVISIA index a *price index* for the following reason: It is not the aim of the DIVISA index to compare two price-quantity situations but instead to reflect the price and quantity changes at all times *between* two situations.

Sometimes a household may prefer the information given by the DIVISIA index to that offered by a price index in the sense of definition C. But there is a third kind of information, and probably the most important one, which a household would like to get about the price changes. It is the information on how the price changes have influenced its standard of living, this standard depending on changes of both quality and taste.

Clearly, we now have arrived at the central problem of what FISHER and SHELL [1972], in the title of their book, call the economic theory of price indexes. At this point, preferences or utility functions of households will be indispensable.

Definition E of a price index: The cost-of-living index.
Let $\underline{p}^o \in \mathbb{R}^m_{++}$ and $\underline{q}^o \in \mathbb{R}^m_+$ be the vectors of prices and quantities of the m goods in which a household with a budget $y^o \in \mathbb{R}_{++}$ was interested in a base period, and let $\underline{p} \in \mathbb{R}^n_{++}$ and $\underline{q} \in \mathbb{R}^n_+$ be the vectors of prices and quantities of the n goods being of interest for the same household in a comparison period. Let U^o and U be sets of cardinal utility functions

$$u^o : \mathbb{R}^m_+ \to \mathbb{R}_+ , \qquad \underline{q}^o \mapsto u^o(\underline{q}^o)$$

and

$$u : \mathbb{R}^n_+ \to \mathbb{R}_+ , \qquad \underline{q} \mapsto u(\underline{q}) ,$$

respectively, for which the following extrema and function values exist and are positive. *A function*

$$P : \mathbb{R}^m_{++} \times \mathbb{R}^n_{++} \times \mathbb{R}_{++} \times U^o \times U \to \mathbb{R}_{++}$$

given by

$$(\underline{p}^o, \underline{p}, y^o, u^o, u) \mapsto P(\underline{p}^o, \underline{p}, y^o, u^o, u) = \frac{y}{\bar{y}^o} ,$$

where

$$\bar{y}^o = \inf \{\bar{\underline{q}}^o \underline{p}^o \mid \bar{\underline{q}}^o \varepsilon \mathbb{R}^m_+ \text{ solves } \max \{u^o(\underline{q}^o) \mid \underline{q}^o \varepsilon \mathbb{R}^m_+ , q^o p^o \leqq y^o \}\}$$

and

$$y = \inf \{\underline{q}\underline{p} \mid \underline{q} \varepsilon \mathbb{R}^n_+, u(\underline{q}) = \max \{u^o(\underline{q}^o) \mid q^o \varepsilon \mathbb{R}^m_+, \underline{q}^o \underline{p}^o \leqq y^o \}\}$$

is called a <u>*cost-of-living index*</u>.

According to this definition, a price index for a household does not only depend on the prices of the base and comparison period but also on the utility function and the budget of the household during the base period and on its utility function during the comparison period. Roughly speaking, the index compares the budget of the base period with the smallest budget necessary in the comparison period in order to attain that level of utility, or standard of living, which was at best possible with the budget y^o in the base period. Clearly, $\bar{y}^o = y^o$ if u^o is strictly increasing. Note that definition E takes into consideration changes of both quality and taste. Similar definitions without assuming cardinality of the utility functions have been proposed by VOELLER [1974].

Most of the literature on the economic theory of the price index considers an important special case of definition E, where

(i) $m = n$,

(ii) the set of the goods in consideration does not change from the base to the comparison period (the quantities do !),

(iii) $U^o = U$, $u^o = u$.

Then assuming the cardinality of the utility functions is not necessary. If, in addition to (i), (ii), and (iii),

(iv) $u^o = u$ is homothetic,

the price indices so defined satisfy certain modifications of FISHER's tests; see, for instance, SAMUELSON and SWAMY [1974]. In this volume, the contributions by AFRIAT; BLACKORBY, PRIMONT, and RUSSELL; FUCHS-SELIGER; HASENKAMP; and VARTIA deal with or contain certain aspects of the economic theory of the price index; BECKMANN's contribution, which is not directly directed to price index theory, analyses special types of change in utility functions; the paper by PHLIPS on a true wage index is kind of a counterpart to the true cost of living index.

4. What is the Effectiveness of a Production Process?

The definitions B and C of a price index contained several *functional equations*, e.g., the equations (3.2), (3.4), (3.14), (3.15), (3.16), and (3.17).

Systems of functional equations also play an important role in previous attempts of defining the *effectiveness* [1] of a production process.

[1] We speak of effectiveness, rather than efficiency, since the phrase "efficient production process" does not have the meaning of an index in the literature on production theory; see, e.g., SHEPHARD [1970, p. 180], or the concluding remark of this section.

A *production process* can be considered as a quadruple

(4.1) $$(K,t,\underline{x},\underline{u}) \in \mathbb{R}_+^{2+n+m}$$

where $K \in \mathbb{R}_+$ is the capital necessary for setting up and running the production, and $t \in \mathbb{R}_+$ is the time period required to produce the output vector $\underline{u} \in \mathbb{R}_+^m$ with the aid of the input vector $\underline{x} \in \mathbb{R}_+^n$.

In the following we will define two different notions of the effectiveness of a production process: *technical effectiveness* and *economic effectiveness*.

Let $\underline{p} \in \mathbb{R}_+^n$ be the (given, constant) vector of the prices of the inputs. Then the variable cost $k \in \mathbb{R}_+$ of process (4.1) is $k = \underline{x}\,\underline{p}$. If we are interested only in the variable cost and the time period required to produce the output vector $\underline{u}$, then we will consider, instead of the quadruple (4.1), only the triple

(4.2) $$(t,k,\underline{u}) \in \mathbb{R}_+^{2+m} ,$$

which can also be called a production process.

In EICHHORN [1972], [1978] we proposed:

(4.3) Definition. *By the* *technical effectiveness* T *of production process (4.2) we mean a function*

(4.3) $$T : \mathbb{R}_+^{2+m} \to \mathbb{R}_+ , \quad (t,k,\underline{u}) \mapsto T(t,k,\underline{u})$$

that is strictly decreasing with respect to t *and* k, *strictly increasing with respect to* $\underline{u}$, *and, in addition, satisfies the following seven functional equations for all* $\lambda \in \mathbb{R}_{++}$, $t \in \mathbb{R}_{++}$, $k \in \mathbb{R}_{++}$, $\underline{u} \in \mathbb{R}_+^n$:

(4.4) $T(\lambda t,\lambda k,\lambda \underline{u}) = T(t,k,\underline{u})$,

(4.5) $T(t,\lambda k,\lambda \underline{u}) = \phi(\lambda)T(t,k,\underline{u})$, $\phi: \mathbb{R}_{++} \to \mathbb{R}_{++}$, strictly increasing, $\phi(1) = 1$,

(4.6) $T(\lambda t,k,\lambda \underline{u}) = \psi(\lambda)T(t,k,\underline{u})$, $\psi: \mathbb{R}_{++} \to \mathbb{R}_{++}$, strictly increasing, $\psi(1) = 1$,

(4.7) $T(\lambda t,\lambda k,\underline{u}) = \chi(\lambda)T(t,k,\underline{u})$, $\chi: \mathbb{R}_{++} \to \mathbb{R}_{++}$, strictly decreasing, $\chi(1) = 1$,

(4.8) $T(t,k,\lambda \underline{u}) = \rho(\lambda)T(t,k,\underline{u})$, $\rho: \mathbb{R}_{++} \to \mathbb{R}_{++}$, strictly increasing, $\rho(1) = 1$,

(4.9) $T(t,\lambda k,\underline{u}) = \sigma(\lambda)T(t,k,\underline{u})$, $\sigma: \mathbb{R}_{++} \to \mathbb{R}_{++}$, strictly decreasing, $\sigma(1) = 1$,

(4.10) $T(\lambda t,k,\underline{u}) = \tau(\lambda)T(t,k,\underline{u})$, $\tau: \mathbb{R}_{++} \to \mathbb{R}_{++}$, strictly decreasing, $\tau(1) = 1$.

A special case of the system (4.4) to (4.6), namely (4.4), (4.5), and

(4.6') $$T(\lambda t,k,\lambda u) = \lambda T(t,k,u) \qquad (u \in \mathbb{R}_{+}),$$

was considered by VINCZE [1960]. ACZÉL [section 8 of his contribution to this volume] analysed assumptions (4.5) to (4.8).

Let us call assumptions (4.4) to (4.10) axioms. They are easily motivated. For instance, axiom (4.4) says that the effectiveness of a process $(t,k,\underline{u})$ is not changed if the process is multiplied by $\lambda \in \mathbb{R}_{++}$. Multiplication by λ may (but need not) mean that the same machinery is operating in the time period λt as in t.

Among others, it was shown by EICHHORN [1972], [1978]:

(4.11) Theorem. *The axioms (4.4) to (4.10) are consistent, but not independent. Any two of them are independent. There exist subsets of four independent equations from (4.4) to (4.10), but any five of them are dependent. Examples of independent quadruples are {4.5, 4.6, 4.7, 4.9}, {4.5, 4.6, 4.7, 4.10}, {4.5, 4.6, 4.9, 4.10}. There exist triples but no pairs among the axioms (4.4) to (4.10) from which the remaining axioms follow in the sense that a function satisfying each axiom of the triple also satisfies the entire set of axioms. Examples of such triples are {4.4, 4.5, 4.6}, {4.4, 4.5, 4.9}, {4.4, 4.6, 4.10}, {4.4, 4.9, 4.10}. Each of these triples is independent. Let* T *be any function (4.3) satisfying axioms (4.4) to (4.10) or one of the above-mentioned triples. Then there exist constants* $\alpha \in \mathbb{R}_{++}$, $\beta \in \mathbb{R}_{++}$, *and a function* $f : \mathbb{R}_+^m \to \mathbb{R}_+$ *that is homogeneous of degree* $\alpha + \beta$, *such that, for* $t \in \mathbb{R}_{++}$ *and* $k \in \mathbb{R}_{++}$, T *is given by*

$$(4.12) \qquad T(t,k,\underline{u}) = \frac{f(\underline{u})}{t^\alpha k^\beta} .$$

Every function of this kind satisfies axioms (4.4) to (4.10).

If, in this theorem, T is taken to be the technical effectiveness of the production process (4.2), that is, if T, in addition to satisfying (4.4) to (4.10), is supposed to be strictly increasing with respect to $\underline{u}$, then f of (4.12) must be strictly increasing. If only one commodity is produced, that is, if $\underline{u} = u \in \mathbb{R}_+$, then, clearly, (4.12) becomes

$$T(t,k,u) = \frac{C u^{\alpha+\beta}}{t^\alpha k^\beta}$$

where C is a positive real constant. The determination of α and β or of the ratio α/β is an empirical matter (see VINCZE [1960, p.38]).

We turn now to the notion of *economic* effectiveness of a production process as it has been introduced in EICHHORN [1972], [1978].

(4.13) **Definition.** *We define the economic effectiveness of the production process (4.1) to be a function* E *that depends on* K, t, *and the "measures of profitability", that is,*

$$\frac{\underline{u}\,\underline{\pi}}{\underline{x}\,\underline{p}} =: \xi \quad \text{and} \quad \underline{u}\,\underline{\pi} - \underline{x}\,\underline{p} =: \eta \quad \begin{cases} \underline{\pi} \in \mathbb{R}^m_{++} & \text{price vector of the outputs} \\ \underline{p} \in \mathbb{R}^n_{++} & \text{price vector of the inputs,} \end{cases}$$

$$\underline{x} \geq \underline{0},$$

and which satisfies the following assumptions (4.14) to (4.18) for all possible values of the variables:

$$(4.14) \qquad E(K,t,\xi,\eta) = \begin{cases} E_+(K,t,\xi,\eta) > 0 & \text{if} \quad \eta > 0 \\ 0 & \text{if} \quad \eta = 0 \\ E_-(K,t,\xi,\eta) < 0 & \text{if} \quad \eta < 0, \end{cases}$$

where

$$E_+ : \mathbb{R}^2_+ \times \,]1,\infty[\, \times \mathbb{R}_{++} \to \mathbb{R}_{++}$$ [1)]

and

$$E_- : \mathbb{R}^2_+ \times [0,1[\, \times \mathbb{R}_{--} \to \mathbb{R}_{--}$$

$$(4.15) \qquad E(K,\lambda t,\xi,\lambda\eta) = E(K,t,\xi,\eta) \qquad \textit{for all } \lambda \in \mathbb{R}_{++}$$

$$(4.16) \qquad E(\lambda K,t,\xi,\lambda\eta) = E(K,t,\xi,\eta) \qquad \textit{for all } \lambda \in \mathbb{R}_{++}$$

[1)] In the following, $\mathbb{R}_{--} := \{x \mid x \in \mathbb{R},\ x < 0\}$,
$]a,b[\; := \{x \mid a < x < b\}$, $\quad [a,b[\; := \{x \mid a \leqq x < b\}$,
$]a,b] := \{x \mid a < x \leqq b\}$, $\quad [a,b] := \{x \mid a \leqq x \leqq b\}$.

$$(4.17)\quad \begin{cases} E_+(K,t,\xi,\lambda\eta) = \mu(\lambda)E_+(K,t,\xi,\eta) \\ \textit{for all } \lambda \in \mathbb{R}_{++} \textit{ with strictly increasing } \mu:\mathbb{R}_{++}\to\mathbb{R}_{++}, \mu(1)=1 \\ E_-(K,t,\xi,\lambda\eta) = \mu^*(\lambda)E_-(K,t,\xi,\eta) \\ \textit{for all } \lambda \in \mathbb{R}_{++} \textit{ with strictly increasing } \mu^*:\mathbb{R}_{++}\to\mathbb{R}_{++}, \mu^*(1)=1 \end{cases}$$

$$(4.18)\quad \begin{cases} E_+(K,t,\lambda\xi,\eta) = \nu(\lambda)E_+(K,t,\xi,\eta) \\ \textit{for all } \lambda \in]1,\infty[\textit{ with strictly increasing } \nu:]1,\infty[\to\mathbb{R}_{++} \\ E_-(K,t,\lambda\xi,\eta) = \nu^*(\lambda)E_-(K,t,\xi,\eta) \\ \textit{for all } \lambda \in [0,1[\textit{ with strictly decreasing } \nu^*: [0,1[\to\mathbb{R}_{++}. \end{cases}$$

Let us consider the assumptions (4.14) to (4.18) a bit further. Assumption (4.14) is a normalizing condition, and seems to be quite natural. Assumption (4.15) says in particular that the production processes

$$(K,t,\underline{x},\underline{u}) \quad\text{and}\quad (K,\lambda t,\lambda\underline{x},\lambda\underline{u}) \qquad (\lambda \in \mathbb{R}_{++})$$

are equally effective. This means, for instance, that the economic effectiveness of a machinery is not changed if it operates λt time units instead of t time units. As to assumption (4.16) , the economic effectiveness of the production processes

$$(K,t,\underline{x},\underline{u}) \quad\text{and}\quad (\lambda K,t,\lambda\underline{x},\lambda\underline{u}) \qquad (\lambda \in \mathbb{R}_{++})$$

is identical. For instance, two identical production processes operating in parallel have the same economic effectiveness as each of them operating alone. This requirement is reasonable from the point of view of return on investment. Assumption (4.17) says the following: If

$$K^* = K,\ t^* = t,\ \frac{\underline{u}^*\underline{\pi}}{\underline{x}^*\underline{p}} = \frac{\underline{u}\ \underline{\pi}}{\underline{x}\ \underline{p}},\ \underline{u}^*\underline{\pi} - \underline{x}^*\underline{p} = \lambda(\underline{u}\ \underline{\pi} - \underline{x}\ \underline{p}) \quad (\lambda \in \mathbb{R}_{++})$$

is valid for the two production processes

$$(K,t,\underline{x},\underline{u}) \quad \text{and} \quad (K^*,t^*,\underline{x}^*,\underline{u}^*)$$

then the economic effectiveness of $(K^*,t^*,\underline{x}^*,\underline{u}^*)$ is a multiple of the economic effectiveness of $(K,t,\underline{x},\underline{u})$, where this multiple depends on (and increases strictly with) λ. Assumption (4.18) can be interpreted in a similar manner.

(4.19) <u>Theorem.</u> *Every function* E *that satisfies the assumptions (4.14) to (4.18) can be represented by* [1)]

$$(4.20) \qquad E(K,t,\xi,\eta) = \begin{cases} c\xi^{\alpha}\left(\frac{\eta}{Kt}\right)^{\beta} & \text{for } (K,t,\xi,\eta) \in \mathbb{R}^2_+ \times]1,\infty[\times \mathbb{R}_{++} \\ 0 & \text{for } (K,t,\xi,\eta) \in \mathbb{R}^2_+ \times \{1\} \times \{0\} \\ -c^*\xi^{-\alpha^*}\left|\frac{\eta}{Kt}\right|^{\beta} & \text{for } (K,t,\xi,\eta) \in \mathbb{R}^2_+ \times [0,1[\times \mathbb{R}_{--}, \end{cases}$$

where the constants c, c^*, α, α^*, β, β^* *are positive real numbers. Every function* E *given by (4.20) with positive constants* c, c^*, α, α^*, β, β^* *satisfies the assumptions (4.14) to (4.18).*

For the proof see EICHHORN [1978].

(4.21) <u>Corollary.</u> *Let the economic effectiveness* E *of the production process* $(K,t,\underline{x},\underline{u}) \in \mathbb{R}^{2+n+m}_+$ *be given, where* $\underline{x} \neq \underline{0}$. *Let* $\underline{p} \in \mathbb{R}^n_{++}$ *and* $\underline{\pi} \in \mathbb{R}^m_{++}$ *be the vectors of the prices of the inputs and the outputs, respectively. If* $\underline{u}\ \underline{\pi} - \underline{x}\ \underline{p} \geq 0$, *then there exist constants* $c > 0, \alpha > 0, \beta > 0$ *such that*

---

1) In the following formula, $x^{-\gamma} := \infty$, if $x = 0$, $\gamma > 0$.

$$(4.22)\qquad E\left(K,t,\frac{\underline{u}\ \underline{\pi}}{\underline{x}\ \underline{p}},\underline{u}\ \underline{\pi}-\underline{x}\ \underline{p}\right)=c\left(\frac{\underline{u}\ \underline{\pi}}{\underline{x}\ \underline{p}}\right)^{\alpha}\left(\frac{\underline{u}\ \underline{\pi}-\underline{x}\ \underline{p}}{Kt}\right)^{\beta}.$$

If $\underline{u}\ \underline{\pi}-\underline{x}\ \underline{p}<0$, *then there exist real constants* $c^*>0$, $\alpha^*>0$, $\beta^*>0$ *such that*

$$(4.23)\qquad E\left(K,t,\frac{\underline{u}\ \underline{\pi}}{\underline{x}\ \underline{p}},\underline{u}\ \underline{\pi}-\underline{x}\ \underline{p}\right)=-c^*\left(\frac{\underline{u}\ \underline{\pi}}{\underline{x}\ \underline{p}}\right)^{-\alpha^*}\left|\frac{\underline{u}\ \underline{\pi}-\underline{x}\ \underline{p}}{Kt}\right|^{\beta^*}.$$

According to (4.22), the economic effectiveness of a (profitable) production process is a power $\alpha>0$ of the "profitability" $\underline{u}\ \underline{\pi}\ /\ \underline{x}\ \underline{p}$ of the process times a power $\beta>0$ of the gross profit $\underline{u}\ \underline{\pi}-\underline{x}\ \underline{p}$ per capital and time unit, times a positive constant c. For comparing the economic effectivenes of two different processes the magnitude of the quotient α/β is essential. It has to be chosen depending on what is more important in the particular situation, the value of $\underline{u}\ \underline{\pi}\ /\ \underline{x}\ \underline{p}$ or the value of $(\underline{u}\ \underline{\pi}-\underline{x}\ \underline{p})/Kt$. If $c=1$, $\alpha=1$, $\beta\to 0$, or $c=1$, $\beta=1$, $\alpha\to 0$, the economic effectiveness tends to well-known economic indices.

Let S be a set of production processes. A process $(K^*,t^*,\underline{x}^*,u^*)\in S$ is called *efficient* if there is no process $(K,t,\underline{x},\underline{u})\in S$ with

$$(-K,-t,-\underline{x},\underline{u})\geq(-K^*,-t^*,-\underline{x}^*,\underline{u}^*).$$

From the strict monotonicity properties of E it follows that *every production process with maximum economic effectiveness is efficient.*

5. What is the Profitability of an Investment ?

An *investment* can be considered to be a vector

$$(5.1)\qquad (\underline{x},\underline{y})\in\dot{\mathbb{R}}^{n+1}_{+}\times\mathbb{R}^{n+1}_{+}$$

where $\underline{x} = (x_o, x_1, \dots, x_{n-1}, x_n) \in \dot{\mathbb{R}}_+^{n+1} := \{\underline{r} \mid \underline{r} \in \mathbb{R}_+^{n+1}, \underline{r} \neq \underline{0}\}$ is the vector of the expected expenditures during the years $0,1,\dots,n-1$, n and $\underline{y} = (y_1, y_2, \dots, y_n, y_{n+1}) \in \mathbb{R}_+^{n+1}$ is the vector of the expected returns during the years $1,2,\dots,n$, as well as of the salvage value at the end of the n-th year.

If the investor assumes a constant interest rate of i per cent, then the index

$$(5.2) \qquad \Pi : \dot{\mathbb{R}}_+^{n+1} \times \mathbb{R}_+^{n+1} \to \mathbb{R}_+$$

given by

$$(5.3) \qquad \Pi(\underline{x},\underline{y}) = \frac{y_1 q^n + y_2 q^{n-1} + \dots + y_n q + y_{n+1}}{x_o q^{n+1} + x_1 q^n + \dots + x_{n-1} q^2 + x_n q} \qquad \left(q = 1 + \frac{i}{100}\right)$$

is well known as the *profitability* of the investment (5.1). If this value is $\leqq 1$, then, clearly, the investment does not yield any profit.

Obviously, this index satisfies the following conditions:

$$(5.4) \qquad \Pi(\underline{x},\underline{y}) \begin{cases} = 0 \text{ for } (\underline{x},\underline{0}) \in \dot{\mathbb{R}}_+^{n+1} \times \mathbb{R}_+^{n+1} \\ > 0 \text{ otherwise.} \end{cases}$$

(5.5) Additivity Tests:

$$\Pi(\underline{x},\underline{y}+\bar{\underline{y}}) = \Pi(\underline{x},\underline{y}) + \Pi(\underline{x},\bar{\underline{y}}) \text{ for all } \underline{x} \in \dot{\mathbb{R}}_+^{n+1}, \underline{y} \in \mathbb{R}_+^{n+1}, \bar{\underline{y}} \in \mathbb{R}_+^{n+1}$$

$$\frac{1}{\Pi(\underline{x}+\bar{\underline{x}},\underline{y})} = \frac{1}{\Pi(\underline{x},\underline{y})} + \frac{1}{\Pi(\bar{\underline{x}},\underline{y})} \text{ for all } \underline{x} \in \dot{\mathbb{R}}_+^{n+1}, \bar{\underline{x}} \in \dot{\mathbb{R}}_+^{n+1}, \underline{y} \in \dot{\mathbb{R}}_+^{n+1}.$$

Let us forget for a moment the form (5.3) of Π. *We are interested in the general solution of the functional equations (5.5) with (5.2), (5.4), that is, in all indices (5.2) which satisfy (5.4) and (5.5).*

By repeated application of the first equation (5.5) we obtain:

$$\Pi(\underline{x},N\underline{z}) = N\Pi(\underline{x},\underline{z}) \text{ for all positive integers } N$$

or, with $\underline{z} = (M/N)\underline{y}$ (M also a positive integer),

$$\Pi(\underline{x},\frac{M}{N}\underline{y}) = \frac{1}{N}\Pi(\underline{x},M\underline{y}) = \frac{M}{N}\Pi(\underline{x},\underline{y}) , \tag{5.6}$$

that is,

$$\Pi(\underline{x},\lambda\underline{y}) = \lambda\Pi(\underline{x},\underline{y}) \text{ for all positive rational } \lambda . \tag{5.7}$$

Similarly, the second equation (5.5) implies

$$\Pi(\lambda\underline{x},\underline{y}) = \frac{1}{\lambda}\Pi(\underline{x},\underline{y}) \text{ for all positive rational } \lambda. \tag{5.8}$$

From (5.7) and (5.8) it follows that

$$\Pi(\lambda\underline{x},\lambda\underline{y}) = \Pi(\underline{x},\underline{y}) \text{ for all positive rational } \lambda. \tag{5.9}$$

Also, (5.8) follows from (5.7) and (5.9) [and (5.7) from (5.8) and (5.9)].

As will become clear from the theorem below every solution of (5.5) with (5.2) and (5.4) is a solution of equation (5.7) to (5.9) with arbitrary positive *real* λ. The converse is not true.

Note that properties (5.4), (5.7), and (5.9) make sense if one wishes to introduce an index "profitability of an investment" axiomatically: (5.4) The profitability is zero if all returns are zero, otherwise it is positive. (5.7) If the expenditures remain unchanged then a μ per cent increase (decrease) of all returns yields a μ per cent increase (decrease) of the profitability. (5.9) If all expenditures and returns increase (decrease) with the same percentage then the profitability remains unchanged.

As has been shown in connection with the theory of price and productivity indices (ACZÉL and EICHHORN [1974a], [1974b], EICHHORN and VOELLER [1976]) the following holds without any continuity assumption.

(5.10) Theorem. *A function (5.2) satisfies (5.4) as well as the functional equations (5.5) if and only if it is given by*

$$(5.11) \qquad \Pi(\underline{x},\underline{y}) = \frac{b_1y_1+b_2y_2+\ldots+b_ny_n+b_{n+1}y_{n+1}}{a_ox_o+a_1x_1+\ldots+a_{n-1}x_{n-1}+a_nx_n}$$

with positive real constants $a_o,\ldots,a_n,b_1,\ldots,b_{n+1}$.

In other words, *the indices given by (5.11) are characterized by (5.2), (5.4), and (5.5).*

The index given by (5.11) is a bit more general than the index given by (5.3). It is well suited to replace (5.3) for the following reasons: The interest rate may vary or the returns in the year ν may be, for a certain reason, much more important than those in other years.

6. How Can we Measure the Concentration of the Industry, the Income Inequality, and the Societal Income?

In this section we shall consider things as different as a market with n firms and a society with n income recipients. The vector

$$(6.0) \qquad \underline{x} = (x_1,\ldots,x_n) \in \dot{\mathbb{R}}^n_+ := \{\underline{r} \mid \underline{r} \in \mathbb{R}^n_+,\ \underline{r} \neq \underline{O}\}$$

will represent the vector of turnovers of the n firms or the distribution of income, respectively. More precisely, x_i will be the turnover of firm i or the incomce of recipient i, respectively (i = 1,...,n).

In what follows, we use the notation

$$y_i := \frac{x_i}{x_1+\dots+x_n} \quad \text{and} \quad S^n := \{\underline{y} \mid \underline{y} \in \mathbb{R}^n_+ , \Sigma y_i = 1\}.$$

Every index

$$I_n : S^n \to \mathbb{R}_+ \qquad (n = 2,3,\dots)$$

measuring the inequality (or concentration) of the above-mentioned income distribution or the concentration of the above-mentioned industry should at least satisfy the following four axioms which can be interpreted easily.

(6.1) Symmetry Axiom:

$$I_n(y_1,\dots,y_n) = I_n(y_{\pi(1)},\dots,y_{\pi(n)})$$

for all permutations π of $(1,2,\dots,n)$.

(6.2) Monotonicity Axiom:

$$I_n(y_1,\dots,y_i+\varepsilon,\dots,y_j-\varepsilon,\dots,y_n) > I_n(\underline{y})$$

for all i,j $(i \neq j)$ with $y_i > y_j$ and all $\varepsilon \epsilon]0,y_j]$.

(6.3) Expansibility Axiom:

$$I_n(\underline{y}) < I_{n+1}(\underline{y},0).$$

(6.4) Normalization Axiom:

$$I_n\left(\frac{1}{n},\dots,\frac{1}{n}\right) = 0 \ (\text{or} = 1).$$

The following properties of the system (6.1) to (6.4) corroborate that it is well chosen.

Axioms (6.1) and (6.2) imply:

(6.5) Mean Value Test:

$$I_n\left(\frac{1}{n},\ldots,\frac{1}{n}\right) \leqq I_n(\underline{y}) \leqq I_n(1,0,\ldots,0) \text{ for all } \underline{y} \in S^n.$$

(6.6) Theorem. *Axioms (6.1) to (6.4) are independent and consistent.*

Proof. Each of the functions given by

(6.1*) $$I_n^*(\underline{y}) = y_1^2 + \ldots + y_n^2 - \frac{1}{n} + \begin{cases} y_1^2 & \text{if } y_1 > y_i \quad (i = 2,\ldots,n) \\ 0 & \text{otherwise} \end{cases}$$

(6.2*) $$I_n^*(\underline{y}) = \sqrt{y_1}\log y_1 + \ldots + \sqrt{y_n}\log y_n + \sqrt{n}\log n$$

(6.3*) $$I_n^*(\underline{y}) = y_1^2\log y_1 + \ldots + y_n^2\log y_n + \frac{\log n}{n}$$

(6.4*) $$I_n^*(\underline{y}) = y_1^2 + \ldots + y_n^2 + n$$

satisfies three of the axioms (6.1) to (6.4), but the function given by (6.k*) does not satisfy axiom (6.k), k = 1,2,3,4. Hence, axioms (6.1) to (6.4) are independent. The functions given by

(6.7) $$I_n(\underline{y}) = y_1\log y_1 + \ldots + y_n\log y_n + \log n$$

(6.8) $$I_n(\underline{y}) = y_1^\alpha + \ldots + y_n^\alpha - n^{1-\alpha} \qquad (\alpha > 1)$$

satisfy the system (6.1) to (6.4). This proves the consistency of (6.1) to (6.4) with $I_n\left(\frac{1}{n},\ldots,\frac{1}{n}\right) = 0$

We point out here that (6.7) is THEIL's *index* (see BÜRK and GEHRIG, this volume). Examples of functions satisfying (6.1) to (6.4) with $I_n\left(\frac{1}{n},\ldots,\frac{1}{n}\right) = 1$ are given by

(6.9) $$I_n(\underline{y}) = n\, y_1^{y_1} y_2^{y_2} \cdots y_n^{y_n}$$ [1]

(6.10) $$I_n(\underline{y}) = n\left(y_1^{\alpha}+\ldots+y_n^{\alpha}\right)^{\frac{1}{\alpha-1}} \qquad (\alpha > 1).$$

Note that (6.10) is a multiple of the *generalized exponential mean of oder* α and that (6.10) tends to (6.9) for $\alpha \to 1$. Obviously, (6.7) is the logarithm of (6.9). If $\alpha = 2$ in (6.10) we have a multiple of HERFINDAHL's *index* which originally had been used to measure industrial concentration (see BÜRK and GEHRIG, this volume).

We emphasize that the indices given by (6.7) to (6.9) are closely related to the measures of entropy in information theory; see ACZÉL and DARÓCZY [1975], and ACZÉL [section 6 of his contribution to this volume]. They are not the only solutions of the system (6.1) to (6.4): If, for instance, the functions $I_n^1,\ldots,I_n^k$ satisfy (6.1) to (6.4) and $F: \mathbb{R}_+^k \to \mathbb{R}_+$ is a strictly increasing function with

$$F(x_1,\ldots,x_k) = 0 \quad \text{for all } (x_1,\ldots,x_k) \neq \underline{0}$$

then the function

$$I_n: S^n \to \mathbb{R}_+ \text{ given by } I_n(\underline{y}) = F\left(I_n^1(\underline{y}),\ldots,I_n^k(\underline{y})\right)$$

also satisfies (6.1) to (6.4).

The solutions of the following problems seem to be unknown.

---

[1] We define: $y^r \log y = 0$ for $y = 0$ $(r \in \mathbb{R}_{++})$,
$y^y = 1$ for $y = 0$.

(6.11) Problems. *Determine all functions I_n that satisfy axioms (6.1) to (6.4). Characterize each of the functions (6.7) to (6.10) by adding one or more further conditions to (6.1) to (6.4).*

In their contribution to this volume, BÜRK and GEHRIG call the above type of approaches to the measurement of industry concentration or income inequality *mechanistic* approaches (as distinguished from *economic* approaches). Nevertheless, functions of vectors of turnovers or incomes satisfying (6.1) to (6.4) can still be considered as *economic* indices: as they are measuring systems of data describing *economic* situations.

For economic approaches to income inequality and the concentration of the industry or, rather, the degree of monopoly, see in this volume BÜRK and GEHRIG, and SPREMANN, respectively.

From now on, let the vector (6.O) represent the vector of the (real) incomes of the n income recipients of a society. Slightly different from BÜRK and GEHRIG [this volume] we propose to define the (mechanistic) *indices of societal income* to be a system of functions

(6.12) $$S_n: \dot{\mathbb{R}}^n_+ \to \mathbb{R}_+ \qquad (n = 1,2,...)$$

that satisfies the following axioms for all $\underline{x} \in \dot{\mathbb{R}}^n_+$, $\underline{x}^* \in \dot{\mathbb{R}}^n_+$, $x \in \mathbb{R}_{++}$, $\lambda \in \mathbb{R}_{++}$.

(6.13) Identiy Axiom:

$$S_n(x,...,x) = x.$$

(6.14) Linear Homogeneity Axiom:

$$S_n(\lambda \underline{x}) = \lambda S_n(\underline{x}).$$

(6.15) Monotonicity or Sensitivity Axiom:

$$\underline{x} \geq \underline{x}^* \text{ implies } S_n(\underline{x}) > S_n(\underline{x}^*).$$

(6.16) Symmetry Axiom:

$$S_n(x_1,\ldots,x_n) = S_n(x_{\pi(1)},\ldots,x_{\pi(n)})$$

for all permutations π of $(1,\ldots,n)$.

(6.17) Aggregation Axiom:

Define $\xi_k := S_k(x_1,\ldots,x_k)$, $k = 1,2,\ldots;$

$$S_n(\xi_k,\ldots,\xi_k,x_{k+1},\ldots,x_n) = S_n(\underline{x}) \text{ for each } k \leqq n.$$

Axioms (6.13) to (6.16) can be interpreted easily. For an elucidating interpretation of axiom (6.17) see BÜRK and GEHRIG [this volume].

Since the system of functions given by

(6.18) $$S_n(\underline{x}) = \left[\frac{1}{n}(x_1^{\varepsilon}+\ldots+x_n^{\varepsilon})\right]^{1/\varepsilon} \quad (\varepsilon \in \mathbb{R}_{++};\ n = 1,2,\ldots)$$

satisfies axioms (6.13) to (6.17), we have a *consistent* set of axioms. At this point the following problems arise.

(6.19) Problems. *Are the axioms (6.13) to (6.17) independent?* (Conjecture: Yes). *Determine all systems of functions* S_n *that satisfy (6.13) to (6.17).*

Note that BÜRK's and GEHRIG's theorem 13 does *not* solve the second problem, since their definition of the (mechanistic) indices of societal income is slightly different from the one considered here.

7. General Definition of an Economic Index. Systems of Economic Indices

The economic indices considered in this paper thus far, have mostly been certain real-valued functions of vectors of economic quantities *that could be represented by real numbers.*

We emphasize that there exist very interesting economic indices whose domains of definition *are not at all sets of real vectors.* For instance, STEHLING's [this volume] indices I of preference inequality are mappings

$$I : \mathcal{R}(\mathcal{A}) \times \mathcal{R}(\mathcal{A}) \to \mathbb{R}_+$$

satisfying the conditions of a metric as well as a certain additional condition, *where* $\mathcal{R}(\mathcal{A})$ *is the set of all strict preference relations on the set* $\mathcal{A}$ *(of a finite number) of distinct abstract alternatives.*

Let us now summarize what we have learned from the (incomplete list of) examples of indices presented in this paper:

(7.1) Definition. *Let* D *be a set of economically interesting objects, for instance, the*

- *set of the vectors of the prices of a commodity set (2)* [1)]
- *set of the vectors of both the prices and the quantities of a set of goods (in two different time periods) (3)*
- *set of the production processes that is at a firm's disposal (4)*
- *set of the vectors of both the expected expenditures and returns on investments during a series of years (5)*
- *set of the vectors of the turnovers of a number of firms (6)*

---

1) The numbers in brackets refer to the respective sections or formulae of this paper.

- *set of the vectors of the incomes of a set of persons (6)*
- *Cartesian product* $\mathcal{R}(\mathcal{A}) \times \mathcal{R}(\mathcal{A})$, *where* $\mathcal{R}(\mathcal{A})$ *is the above-mentioned set of preference relations.*

An <u>*economic index*</u> *is an economic measure, i.e., a function*

$$F : D \to \mathbb{R}$$

which maps, on the one hand, the set D *into the set* $\mathbb{R}$ *of real numbers and which satisfies, on the other hand, a system of economically relevant conditions. The form of these conditions depends on the economic information which we want to obtain from the particular measure. Examples of such conditions are properties as*

- *monotonicity or sensitivity* ((1.1), (2.1), (3.1), (3.13), (4.5)-(4.10), (4.17), (4.18), (5.4) *together with* (5.5), (6.2), (6.15))
- *homogeneity* ((1.2), (1.3), (2.2), (3.2), (3.14), (4.4), (4.15), (4.16), (6.14))
- *homotheticity* ((iv) *in section* 3)
- *normalization* ((1.4), (3.3), (3.15), (6.4), (6.13))
- *additivity* ((2.9), (5.5))
- *multiplicativity* ((2.10))
- *quasilinearity* ((2.11))
- *dimensionality* ((3.4), (3.16))
- *internality* ((3.6), (3.19), (6.5))
- *commensurability* ((3.17))
- *proportionality* ((3.20))
- *circularity* ((3.21))
- *reversibility* ((3.22))
- *determinateness* ((3.23))
- *continuity* ((3.23))
- *symmetry* ((6.1), (6.16))
- *expansibility* ((6.3))
- *aggregation* ((6.17)).

The reason why indices are defined and applied is the practical impossibility of judging or comparing complex or extensive systems of data. Using an index means *aggregating* a well-defined system of data. At the same time, a lot of information about the data system is lost. Thus far, a single economic index only provides a certain quantitative aspect of the economic structure (e.g., (part of) an economy or a firm) in which one is interested. In order to gain a better insight, one is often anxious to consult various other indices with respect to the economic structure under consideration. To say it in other words, *systems of indices* provide more information about a data system than a single index.

Let

$$\begin{array}{llll} F_1 : D_1 \to \mathbb{R}, & d_1 \mapsto F_1(d_1), & d_1 \in D_1 \\ \vdots & \vdots & \\ F_k : D_k \to \mathbb{R}, & d_k \mapsto F_k(d_k), & d_k \in D_k \end{array}$$

be such a system of economic indices. We point out here that *any such system can be interpreted as a vector-valued function or mapping*, namely

$$\underline{F} : D \to \mathbb{R}^k, \quad \underline{d} \mapsto \underline{F}(\underline{d}), \quad \underline{d} \in D.$$

Obviously,

$$D := D_1 \times \ldots \times D_k, \quad \underline{d} := (d_1, \ldots, d_k)$$

$$\underline{F} := (\bar{F}_1, \ldots, \bar{F}_k)$$

$$\bar{F}_\kappa(d_1, \ldots, d_k) := F_\kappa(d_\kappa) \qquad (\kappa = 1, \ldots, k).$$

References

ACZÉL, J.: Some Recent Applications of Functional Equations to Combinatorics, Probability Distributions, Information Measures and to the Theory of Index Numbers in Mathematical Economics. This volume.

ACZÉL, J., and Z. DARÓCZY: On Measures of Information and Their Characterizations. Mathematics in Science and Engineering Series, Vol. 115. Academic Press, New York-San Francisco-London 1975.

ACZÉL, J., and W. EICHHORN: A Note on Additive Indices. Journal of Economic Theory 8, 1974a, 525-529.

ACZÉL, J., and W. EICHHORN: Systems of Functional Equations Determining Price and Productivity Indices. Utilitas Mathematica 5, 1974b, 213-226.

AFRIAT, S.N.: On Wald's "New Formula" for the Cost of Living. This volume.

ALLEN, R.G.D.: Index Numbers in Theory and Practice. The Macmillan Press, London 1975.

BECKMANN, M.J.: Neutral Changes in Tastes and Utility. This volume.

BLACKORBY, Ch., D. PRIMONT, and R.R. RUSSELL: An Extension and Alternative Proof of Gorman's Price Aggregation Theorem. This volume.

BÜRK, R., and W. GEHRIG: Indices of Income Inequality and Societal Income. An Axiomatic Approach. This volume.

DIEHL, H.: Examination of Purchasing-Power-Parity Methods with a View to Choosing the Most Appropriate Method for a European-Community Purchasing-Power-Parity Model. This volume.

EICHHORN, W.: Effektivität von Produktionsverfahren. Operations Research-Verfahren 12, 1972, 98-115.

EICHHORN, W.: Functional Equations in Economics. Applied Mathematics and Computation Series, Vol. 11. Addison-Wesley, Reading 1978.

EICHHORN, W., and J. VOELLER: Theory of the Price Index. Fisher's Test Approach and Generalizations. Lecture Notes in Economics and Mathematical Systems, Vol. 140. Springer-Verlag, Berlin-Heidelberg-New York 1976.

FISHER, F.M., and K. SHELL: The Economic Theory of Price Indexes - Two Essays on the Effect of Taste, Quality and Technological Change. Academic Press, New York-London 1972.

FISHER, I.: The Making of Index Numbers. Houghton Mifflin, Boston 1922. Third Edition, Revised 1927. Reprinted by Augustus M. Kelley, New York 1967.

FRISCH, R.: Annual Survey of General Economic Theory: The Problem of Index Numbers. Econometrica 4, 1936, 1-38.

FUCHS-SELIGER, S.: Revealed Preference and the Economic Theory of Index Numbers. This volume.

FUNKE, H., and J. VOELLER: A Note on the Characterization of Fisher's "Ideal Index". This volume.

GEHRIG, W.: Price Indices and Generalized Associativity. This volume.

HASENKAMP. G.: Economic and Atomistic Index Numbers. Contrasts and Similarities. This volume.

HECKER, R.: A System of Indices for the External Analysis of the Earning Capacity Standard and Financial Power of Industrial Joint Stock Companies. This volume.

HILD, C., and G. HACKER: A Note on Criteria for Price Index Systems. This volume.

KREIN, M., and D. MILMAN: On Extreme Points of Regular Convex Sets. Studia Mathematica 9, 1940, 133-138.

LASPEYRES, E.: Die Berechnung einer mittleren Waarenpreissteigerung. Jahrbücher für Nationalökonomie und Statistik 16, 1871, 296-314.

MENGES, G.: Semantics and "Object Logic" of Price Indices. This volume.

MUNDLOS, B., and J. SCHWARZE: Basic Ideas on Stochastic Indices. This volume.

OPITZ, O.: On the Relationship Between Numerical Taxonomy and the Theory of Economic Indices. This volume.

PAASCHE, H.: Über die Preisentwicklung der letzten Jahre, nach den Hamburger Börsenentwicklungen. Jahrbücher für Nationalökonomie und Statistik 23, 1874, 168-178.

PFANZAGL, J.: Theory of Measurement. 2nd revised edition. Physica-Verlag, Würzburg-Wien 1971.

PHLIPS, L.: A Taste-Dependent True Wage Index. This volume.

SAMUELSON, P.A., and S. SWAMY: Invariant Economic Index Numbers and Canonical Duality: Survey and Synthesis. The American Economic Review 64, 1974, 566-593.

SHEPHARD, R.W: Theory of Cost and Production Functions. Princeton University Press, Princeton 1970.

SPREMANN, K.: The Degree of Monopoly and Multivariable Sales Policies. This volume.

STEHLING, F.: Indices of Preference Inequality and the Construction of Social Preference Relations. This volume.

VARTIA, Y.O.: Fisher's Five Tines Fork and Other Quantum Theories of Index Numbers. This volume.

VINCZE, E.: Über das Problem der Berechnung der Wirtschaftlichkeit. Acta Technica Academiae Scientiarum Hungaricae 28, 1960, 33-41.

VOELLER, J.: Theorie des Preis- und Lebenshaltungskostenindex. Dissertation, Karlsruhe 1974.

VOGT, A.: Divisia Indices on Different Paths. This volume.

Semantics and "Object Logic" of Price Indices

by Günter Menges

1. Introductory Notes

In this short communication I shall try to identify and clarify those problems in the framework of price indices which arise apart from the mathematical problems, i.e. I concern myself today with the non-mathematical or semantic problems. Of course, this can neither be done without mathematics nor can it be done truly independently of the mathematical problems. Likewise the mathematical problems are not treatable independently of the semantic ones which led Flaskämper to the formulation of a

Parallelismus von Sach- und Zahlenlogik

or, better and in English, of a

parallelism of object logic and formal (or mathematical) logic.

2. Semantics

In modern logic, semantics means non-linguistic statements and considerations, namely those which are not pure consequences of axioms but which have, on the one hand, a relationship to the linguistic structure, and on the other hand a meaning; more precisely, an empirical (extra-linguistic) meaning.

Semantics can be considered as consisting of two closely related concepts, that of interpretation and that of validity (better: real validity) of a mathematical statement.

In any case, semantics is that part of scientific work which can not be done by a machine but which is bound to a human being.

This indicates a pretty general view of the notion of semantics. A somewhat special view which is not common but "tritt - zumindest in dieser Form - aus meiner Leier zum ersten Mal ans Licht", is the subdivision of semantics in (causal) explanation and (teleological) understanding. I hold that the interpretation as well as the validity of a mathematical statement is quite different according as the phenomenon is either to be explained or to be understood. Furthermore, I hold that this distinction is fundamental for price indices. More about that later.

3. Object Logic

The expression "object logic" (Sachlogik) was introduced by Flaskämper [1949] to denote

> notions which allow the measurement of genuinely "qualitative" social objects and
>
> the interpretation of the meaning of quantitative results and
>
> the choice of adequate mathematical tools.

Furthermore, Flaskämper [1933, 1940] stated the parallelism of object logic and mathematical logic, and he understood this parallelism mainly (though not solely) with respect to statistical comparisons, and he had the conception that the main statistical problem on hand or even the problem as such manifests itself in object logic while the "mathematical logic" part is of a mere subsidiary nature, the part which has to "parallel" the object logic. In any case, the justification of a notion or a method has to be granted by the object logic only.

In a modern model- or measure-theoretical framework one may pose the problem as follows [Menges - Skala 1973, S. 309 f]:

There are k sets of mathematical objects

$$A_1, \ldots, A_k$$

and, for the sake of simplicity, likewise k sets of empirical phenomena

$$B_1, \ldots, B_k .$$

The cartesian product of the sets of mathematical objects A_i is the superset of a mathematical system

$$S \subset A_1 \times \ldots \times A_k .$$

On the other hand, the cartesian product of the set of empirical objects B_i is the superset of an empirical system R

$$R \subset B_1 \times \ldots \times B_k .$$

It is not possible, to represent the empirical system R properly and exactly but it exists nevertheless in the form of a certain network of empirical meaning. It is, however, possible to observe certain partial aspects or patterns R_T with

$$R_T \subset R.$$

The parallelism of object logic and mathematical logic is represented by an isomorphism of the kind

$$R_T (b_1, \ldots, b_k) \Leftrightarrow S_T (I(b_1), \ldots , I(b_k)) ;$$

$$b_i \in B_i .$$

If such an isomorphism is recognized (pattern recognition) at all one will try to extend it so as to cover

$$\bar{R} (b_1, \ldots , b_k) \Leftrightarrow \bar{S} (I(b_1), \ldots , I(b_k))$$

with

$$R_T \subset \bar{R} \subseteq R \quad \text{and} \quad S_T \subset \bar{S} \subseteq S .$$

One may consider $\bar{R}$ as a theory which fits the observed pattern R_T. The theory bridges the gap between the observed pattern R_T and the"higher" network of empirical meaning R. One could call $\bar{R}$ the specification of a theory, within a similar framework as in econometric theory. The specification is good, i.e. the pattern is well-specified within R_T, if it comes close to R, since the "validity" of the mathematical system $\bar{S}$ is the greater the closer $\bar{R}$ comes to R. In any case, the specification task can be seen in the object logical interpretation of as many and as great parts of the mathematical system as possible.

In the framework of index theory there is a certain network of empirical meaning (Sinnzusammenhang). Out of this network R a theory $\bar{R}$ is to be developed which allows the recognition of the pattern R_T. Within this pattern there is the notion of a certain standard of life, the notion of a base period etc. And then, within the corresponding mathematical system $\bar{S}$, we define the proper index formula.

These short considerations may suffice in order to give you an idea of the possibilities of the formal treatment of the parallelism of object logic and mathematical logic.

A main point of the considerations to which I turn now, is the network R . It is, as I indicated already, comprehensible only in a vague and more intuitive way. But this natural vagueness is accompanied by a clear and distinct fixing of the aim of the whole setup. We must define as exactly and as clearly as possible what is intended. It is not the question of cause and effect we are concerned with here but the "telos". It is what H. von Wright, in his book Explanation and Understanding [1971], calls the aristotelian epistemology. He even goes so far as to claim a teleological or practical syllogism of the following kind

A wants Z
A thinks that he can produce Z only by doing a
A does a.

From this syllogism alone, there follows, in v. Wright's view, the (practical) substantiation of the understanding of behaviour (Verstehen in Max Weber's sense). It has nothing at all to do with causality.

With respect to price indices, there can be said: Z is the aim of households, e.g. to get as many goods or utility or whatever out of the money as possible. Households think that they can produce Z only by purchasing the goods 1, 2, ..., n in the quantities $q_1, \ldots, q_n$. Therefore, the households consume

$$\begin{bmatrix} q_1 \\ \cdot \\ \cdot \\ \cdot \\ q_n \end{bmatrix} .$$

$q_1, \ldots, q_n$ is not to be thought of as the effect of a certain cause, Z or anything else. But, by understanding the aim Z , we can - as statisticians - try to find proper q's within the network of meaning (Sinnzusammenhang).

And from this knowledge of the aim Z and the proper q's we deduce a theory, e.g. the Laspeyres one with proper q's of a proper base period etc., and we then define a mathematical system, the index formula (in vector notation)

$$\frac{p_I' q_O}{p_O' q_O} ,$$

where $p' = (p_1, \ldots, p_n)$ is the corresponding price vector; the subscript O refers to the base period, the subscript I to the "current" period. It can also be the case that we have, within the network R , two competing theories, as we indeed have them in price index theory, namely the theory "Paasche" as opposed to the theory "Laspeyres".

We may find that there are some considerations which speak in favor of theory "Paasche". The latter may be considered to be better suited for the purpose of transforming nominal values into real values, since - via the corresponding mathematical system S -:

$$\frac{\text{nominal value}}{\text{price index Paasche}} = \text{quantity index Laspeyres}$$

since

$$\frac{p_I' q_I}{p_O' q_O} : \frac{p_I' q_I}{p_O' q_I} = \frac{p_O' q_I}{p_O' q_O} .$$

But, are we still in the frame of the same network of meaning? Apparently not!
We have instead quite a new setup with another aim. The new

aim of the households reads as follows:

Households want constancy of prices
(if this is true) etc.

We have then, for this new aim, to look for a corresponding theory, and this theory may be seen in the theory "Paasche". And the theory "Paasche" with proper q's of a proper period (the current one) leads - as a corresponding mathematical system - to the index formula

$$\frac{p_I' \, q_I}{p_0' \, q_I} .$$

And so on.

Certainly, the theories "Laspeyres" and "Paasche" lie so close together that it may be useful to look for a joint super network of meaning.

It may then and only then be reasonable to establish criteria for the judgement of theories within the super network.

In my opinion, this is the only reasonable task of index criteria.

If this is so, a mathematical orientation of the index criteria, as in the sense of Irving Fisher [1927] , is completely misleading, since the mathematical orientation is a consequence rather than a reason for the judgement of index theories.

On the other hand, those proper criteria can be of a more or less mathematical nature, or better: can be more or less well-suited for a mathematical formulation.

The main criteria which are well-suited for mathematical formulation are the following:

1) time reversal test (not in Fisher's but in Flaskämper's [1928] interpretation: exchange of the direction of comparison)
2) multiplication (see above) - same in Fisher's, v. Bortkiewicz's [1924], and Flaskämper's interpretation
3) "Interkalierbarkeit" (v. Bortkiewicz and Flaskämper advocated it, Fisher refused it).

I hold, that v. Bortkiewicz's interpretation of "Interkalierbarkeit" is too narrow. He had in mind "Interkalierbarkeit" only with respect to the mathematical operation of multiplication, that means indices which fulfill his Interkalierbarkeitskriterium belong to a scale unique up to similarity transformations. A proper interpretation would be such that the corresponding mathematical system includes an interval scale (uniqueness up to positive-linear transformations).

If this interpretation is adopted, the Laspeyres index still fulfills the criterion, while the Paasche index does not.

Many other aspects could be added. But I leave this matter now in order to say a few words about quite another basic interpretation or semantics of price index numbers, namely in the framework of what v. Wright calls the causal explanation or "galilean espistemology".

Here we have also semantic problems but no longer object logical ones. Instead, a price index number in this context is interpreted as part of a causal system. No longer the question of understanding and meaning and teleology is of concern but the questions of what causes price changes and what effects have price changes. Here we consider the price index number as a random variable. It is this interpretation which presumably has been the leading or even the only one at this symposion, questions of imbedding of the price index in an econometric model.

As fas as I can see, this imbedding can be carried out in either of the three following kinds

1) price index as an endogenous variable

2) price index as an exogenous variable

(these two forms are common in econometric work). But we have a very specific third kind

3) price index as deflator.

Let me start with the third kind:
As is well-known, price indices are used for the transformation of nominal values into real ones, or of values at current prices into values at constant prices.

We have met this task already in our "aristotelian" considerations. I believe, it is one of the basic misconceptions, perhaps the very misconception in index theory, to believe that both tasks could be fulfilled by one and the same index number, i.e. that one and the same index number can equally well serve both purposes, that of understanding (description, aristotelian epistemology) and that of causal explanation (galilean epistemology).

If we use a price index as a deflator we have an aim, but it is by no means the "telos" with respect to households, as in the descriptive context, it is rather an instrumental aim. What we really want is to find - within a causal context - a measure which allows the transformation of actually observed values into fictitious ones. This task is governed by completely different principles. We do not ask for a notion of household or of behavior of households or of aims of households, or the like.

We have rather to define an economic aggregate, say private consumption or disposable income etc., split this well-defined aggregate into parts - goods or establishments etc. - observe prices of those and compile an index as a measure for the transformation into the fictitious "constant prices values". By doing this we have always the hope that the fictitious values are either better explanators or better to be explained as compared with the values at current prices.

The quality or easiness of causal explanation is therefore the only reasonable yardstick for this task. It is subordinated to the two main aims, namely either as exogenous or endogenous variable, the corresponding aggregate functions within the econometric model.

Now, turning to No. 2, the index number as an exogenous variable. This task is closely related to the third one; the difference is only that in case No. 3 the exogenous character of the price index is implicit, in case No. 2 the exogenous character is explicit. I admit that there are other tasks possible as well, take the terms of trade as an example or the price index of an aggregate A explaining an aggregate B , say the price index of private consumption as an explaining variable for the labor income. But I am convinced that the problems then differ only gradually and not principally, i.e. the principle of quality and easiness of causal explanation retains, though its realization may be somewhat more difficult.

The most interesting case from a methodological point of view is case No. 1: the price index as an endogenous variable. Here we face the task to explain price changes or inflation altogether, and it is this case in which the "galilean" epistemology in v. Wright's sense becomes most prominent.

First of all we define the price index not only mentally or implicitely as a random variable but explicitely and with all consequences.

We now subordinate the price index under the etiality principle and suggest the following epistemological relationship:

The observed price index p is the effect of a certain cause. Which cause? Not a single cause, but a general cause c which produces different possible effects p_i with certain probabilities $f(p_i)$

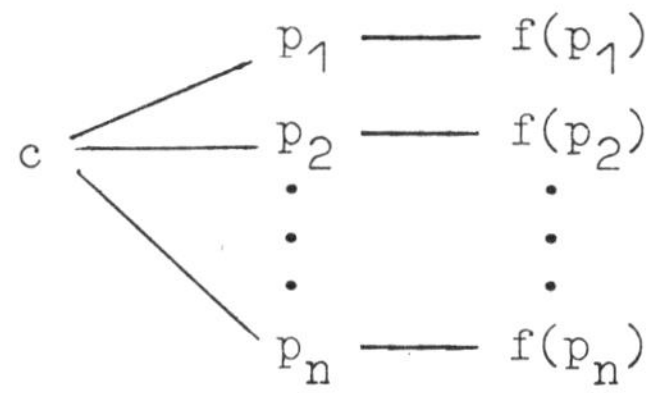

But there is a basic difficulty to overcome, common to all causal (better: etial) explanation in economics; namely the problem that there exist different competing general causes.

The only answer for the solution of this problem which has so far been given, is the confirmation logic by Carnap [1953].

Without entering into details, I would claim here that the measurement problem of index numbers in the framework of case No. 1 is to be subjected to the principles of etiality and of confirmation logic in Carnap's sense. And this principle will in general lead to other measurement procedures and other index formulae, as compared with the ones mentioned before.

Here we need measurement procedures and index formulae with a discriminatory capacity, so as to confirm different causal hypotheses with different degrees of confirmation, ultimately under a certain acceptance or decision rule which tells us which hypothesis is most confirmed under the given empirical evidence.

References

v. Bortkiewicz, L. [1924]: Zweck und Struktur einer Indexzahl. Nordisk Statistic Tidskrift, B. 2 (1924), S. 369-408; 3 (1924), S. 208-251.

Carnap, R. [1953]: On the comparative concept of confirmation. The British Journal for the Philosophy of Science, vol.3, 1953, pp.311-318.

Fisher, I. [1927]: The Making of Index Numbers. Boston 1927.

Flaskämper, P. [1928]: Theorie der Indexzahlen. Beitrag zur Logik des statistischen Vergleichs. Berlin - Leipzig 1928.

Flaskämper, P. [1939]: Die Bedeutung der Zahl für die Sozialwissenschaften. Allgemeines Statistisches Archiv, Bd. 23, 1933, S.58-71.

Flaskämper, P. [1940]: Mathematische und nichtmathematische Statistik. In: Die Statistik in Deutschland nach ihrem heutigen Stand (Ehrengabe für Friedrich Zahn). Hrsg.: F. Burgdörfer, Bd. I, Berlin 1940.

Flaskämper, P. [1949]: Allgemeine Statistik. Hamburg 1944, 2. Aufl. 1949.

Menges, G. und H. Skala [1973]: Grundriß der Statistik. Teil 2: Daten, ihre Gewinnung und Verarbeitung. Opladen 1973.

v.Wright,H.[1971]: Explanation and Understanding. London 1971.

On the Relationship Between Numerical Taxonomy and the Theory of Economic Indices

by Otto Opitz

Numerical taxonomy (taxonometry, multivariate analysis, data analysis) encompasses many diverse techniques for data simplification. Well-defined similarities between different objects (applications in social sciences may relate to: individuals, groups, products, industries, regions, informations, data etc.) characterized by certain features or characters are analysed. With the aim of compressing, aggregating, grouping and identifying characters or objects the basic problems of numerical taxonomy are divided into object representation, object classification, and object identification. Methods of numerical taxonomy for applications originated in biology. In the meantime they have been applied in ecology, psychology, linguistics, archaeology, and social sciences.

1. Characterization of Objects

Let us start from a set of objects $Q = \{1,...,q\}$ described by a set of certain characters $M = \{1,...,p\}$. Defining A_k as the set of possible sample observations of the character $k \in M$ the description of the objects can be determined by p mappings $a_k: Q \to A_k$ $(k=1,...,p)$. The sample results may be expressed in the data matrix (see [5], section 2.1)

$$(1.1) \qquad A := (a_k(i))_{i\in Q, k\in M} =: (a_{ik})_{i\in Q, k\in M}.$$

If all matrix elements are real numbers we have a quantitative, otherwise a qualitative or mixed data matrix. The rows $a_1^{`},...,a_q^{`}$ of the matrix are called the object vectors.

For analysing similarities of objects we define a <u>distance index</u>

(1.2) $d: Q \times Q \to \mathbb{R}_+$

with $d(i,i) = 0 \quad (i \in Q)$, $d(i,j) = d(j,i) \quad (i,j \in Q)$.

The mapping d sometimes satisfies metric or ultrametric properties (see [5], section 2.1) and is strictly increasing with the dissimilarity of pairs of objects, that is

(1.3) $d(i,j) < d(i',j') \Longleftrightarrow i,j$ "more similar" than i',j'.

The distance indices form the so-called <u>distance matrix</u>

(1.4) $D := (d(i,j))_{i,j \in Q} =: (d_{ij})_{i,j \in Q}$.

The distance matrix is evaluated either by an empirical comparison of objects in pairs or by the data matrix A. For quantitative data matrices we often make use of a <u>L_r-metric</u> (see [1], p. 29 or [5], section 2.2)

(1.5) $d^r(i,j) = \left(\sum_{k \in M} |a_{ik} - a_{jk}|^r \right)^{1/r} \qquad (r=1,2,\ldots)$.

Qualitative or mixed data matrices generally contain several qualitative data types with nominal, ordinal or cardinal structures. Furthermore Schader([5], section 2.2) discusses topological, hierarchical, and algebraic data. For these cases we are able to determine distance indices $d_k: Q \times Q \to \mathbb{R}_+$ for each character $k \in M$, essentially invariant with respect to strictly monotonic transformations. Finding a real function $f: \mathbb{R}_+^p \to \mathbb{R}_+$ which connects the d_k's in an appropriate manner we have

(1.6) $d(i,j) = f(d_1(i,j),\ldots,d_p(i,j))$,

that is the <u>aggregated distance index</u> for Q.

Eichhorn defines in his contribution to this volume an economic index as "a function $F:D \to \mathbb{R}$, which maps, on the one hand, a set D of economically interesting objects into the set $\mathbb{R}$ of real numbers and which satisfies, on the other hand, a system of economically relevant conditions (for instance, monotonicity and homogeneity or homotheticity conditions)". We emphasize that it is important requiring strict monotonicity of f in any variable. Furthermore, for quantitative data we may define $d_k(i,j) = |a_{ik}-a_{jk}|$ according to (1.5) and then we obtain

$$d(i,j) = f(d_1(i,j),\dots,d_p(i,j)) = \left(\sum_{k\in M}[d_k(i,j)]^r\right)^{1/r} \quad \text{for any } r \in \mathbb{N}.$$

Then we have homogeneity of degree 1 for the function f. For qualitative or mixed data and comparable d_k's we choose

$$\text{(1.6i)} \qquad d(i,j) = \sum_k \alpha_k d_k(i,j) \text{ with the weights } \alpha_k \geqq 0,$$

and for incomparable d_k's

$$\text{(1.6ii)} \qquad d(i,j) = \sum_{(i',j')} |\{k \in M: d_k(i',j') < d_k(i,j)\}|.$$

In (1.6i) we have homogeneity of degree 1, in (1.6ii) homogeneity of degree 0. For other forms of aggregation see, for instance, Schader ([6], chapter 3).

With the distance indices for object pairs we get compatible distance indices for sets of objects or systems of sets. We call the mappings $h^s:P^sQ \to \mathbb{R}_+$ (s=1,2)[1] the homogeneity index and $v^s:P^sQ\times P^sQ \to \mathbb{R}_+$ (s=1,2)[1] the dissimilarity index for subsets of Q(s=1) or for subsets of P^1Q (s=2). Corresponding to (1.3) the relation $h^s(K) < h^s(L)$ means "K is more homogeneous than L" and $v^s(K,L) < v^s(K',L')$ means "K,L are more similar than K',L'". Often further assumptions for h^s, v^s (s=1,2) are made, for instance:

---

1) P^1Q is the power set, P^2Q the power set of the power set of Q.

$$(1.7)\quad \begin{cases} 0 = d(i,i) = h^1(\{i\}) = h^2(\{K\}) & (i \in Q,\ K \in P^1Q) \\ v^1(\{i\},\{j\}) = d(i,j)\ (i,j \in Q),\ v^2(\{K\},\{L\}) = v^1(K,L) & (K,L \in P^1Q) \\ v^s(K,K) = 0,\ v^s(K,L) = v^s(L,K) & (K,L \in P^sQ,\ s=1,2). \end{cases}$$

These further assumptions are satisfied, for instance, by

$$(1.8)\quad \begin{cases} h^1(K) = \sum_{i,j \in K} d(i,j),\ v^1(K,L) = \sum_{i \in K, j \in L} d(i,j) & (K \neq L) \\ h^2(\mathcal{K}) = \sum_{K,L \in \mathcal{K}} v^1(K,L),\ v^2(\mathcal{K},\mathcal{L}) = \sum_{K \in \mathcal{K}, L \in \mathcal{L}} v^1(K,L) & (\mathcal{K},\mathcal{L} \subset P^1Q,\ \mathcal{K} \neq \mathcal{L}). \end{cases}$$

2. The Basic Problems of Numerical Taxonomy and Some Properties of Economic Indices

Explaining the basic problems of numerical taxonomy with the aim of compressing, aggregating, grouping and identifying characters or objects we shall see various connections between numerical taxonomy and the theory of economic indices (see the contribution of Eichhorn in this volume).

So object representation is given, if we represent the objects described by a data matrix or a distance matrix in a minimal dimensional space $\mathbb{R}^m$ so, that the arrangement of the points in $\mathbb{R}^m$ reasonably characterizes the similarity of the objects (for instance, with the L_2-metric). Then we look for a mapping

$$(2.1)\quad \rho: Q \to \mathbb{R}^m \text{ with } m \leqq p \text{ minimal}$$

$$d(i,j) \underset{(=)}{<} d(i',j') \Longrightarrow \hat{d}^2(\rho(i),\rho(j)) \underset{(=)}{<} \hat{d}^2(\rho(i'),\rho(j'))$$

With $\rho(i) = u_i \in \mathbb{R}^m$ we define

$$(2.2)\quad \hat{d}^r(\rho(i),\rho(j)) = \left(\sum_{k=1}^{m} |u_{ik}-u_{jk}|^r\right)^{1/r} \quad \text{for } r \in \mathbb{N}$$

analogously to (1.5).

In this case it is not significant to assume monotonicity conditions for the mapping ρ, because we cannot specify a reasonable order for Q. On the other hand, defining

(2.3) $\delta: Q \times Q \to \mathbb{R}^m \times \mathbb{R}^m$,

orders for $Q \times Q$ or $\mathbb{R}^m \times \mathbb{R}^m$ are induced by d or $\hat{d}^2$, respectively (see (2.1)). Solving the problem of object representation we treat the optimization problem

(2.4) $\min \sum_{(i,j)} |\delta(i,j) - \hat{d}^2(\rho(i), \rho(j))|$,

where δ is a strictly monotonic transformation of d and m is minimal in the sense, that the error of the original data is adequate.

For quantitative data we may replace the set of objects Q by their p-dimensional object vectors and according to (2.1) we obtain the mapping

(2.1i) $\hat{\rho}: \mathbb{R}^p \to \mathbb{R}^m$ with $m \leqq p$ minimal

together with a monotonicity condition corresponding to (2.1).

Furthermore, in linear representation we define

(2.1ii) $\hat{\rho}(a_i) = A\, f_i \qquad (i \in Q)$,

where A is the quantitative data matrix (see (1.1)) and where the so-called factor loadings f_i are orthonormal.

For this case $\hat{\rho}$ is homogeneous of degree 1. For quantitative, ordinal, or nominal data matrices problems of the type (2.4) are treated in factor analysis ([5], chapter 3), for distance matrices in multidimensional scaling ([5], section 3.2, [7]). For quantitative data the Lagrange multipliers are applied usually, otherwise gradient methods.

Object classification is the problem of finding a partition or covering of the sets of objects in classes so that the objects of a class are as similar as possible and/or the objects of different classes are as dissimilar as possible. Then we look for a mapping

(2.5) $\kappa : Q \to P^s Q \ (s=1,2)$[1] with $|\kappa(Q)| \leqq q$ given or minimal in a certain sense

$d(i,j) \leqq d(i',j') \Longrightarrow v^s(\kappa(i),\kappa(j)) \leqq v^s(\kappa(i'),\kappa(j'))$.

Corresponding to object representation we have monotonicity relative to the orders for QxQ induced by d or for P^sQxP^sQ induced by v^s.

Solving the problem of object classification with maximal different classes and given the number of classes we maximize the term $\sum_{(i,j)} v^s(\kappa(i), \kappa(j))$ with given $|\kappa(Q)|$. This is equivalent to the optimization problem (see (2.4))

(2.6) $\min \left(\sum_{(i,j)} |\delta(i,j) - v^s(\kappa(i), \kappa(j)|\right)$,

where δ is a strictly monotonic transformation of d and $|\kappa(Q)|$ is given.

Whereas in object representation it is intended to reduce the number of characters with an adequate loss of information (see (2.1) and (2.1i)), in object classification we intend to reduce the number of objects by classifying the set of objects, or in other words, we try to comprehend the objects to classes representing types of objects with monotonicity conditions (see (2.5)), but without significant homogeneity conditions because of the qualitative kind of the procedure.

---

1) For s=1 we get a partition of Q: to every $i \in Q$ there is attached a subset of Q (disjunct classification). For s=2 to every object $i \in Q$ there is attached a system of subsets of Q (nondisjunct classification).

For any type of data matrices or distance matrices such problems are treated in cluster analysis ([1], paragraph 22-24, 36-42, [5], section 4.3).

For completeness let us make some remarks on the inversion of the classification procedure determining the essential characters and their weights which reproduce the classification result.
Object identification is given, if we try to determine for a disjunct classified set of objects described by characters, the weight of characters such that the given classification is reproduced in the best possible way. Then we look for a mapping

(2.7) $\gamma: P^1Q \to P^1Q$

with $v^1(K,L) \leqq v^1(K',L') \Longrightarrow v^1(\gamma(K), \gamma(L)) \leqq v^1(\gamma(K'),\gamma(L'))$
and $\varphi: \mathbb{R}_+^p \to \mathbb{R}_+$ with $\varphi(v_1^1(K,L),\dots,v_p^1(K,L)) = v^1(\gamma(K), \gamma(L))$
(Here, the dissimilarities $v_1^1,\dots,v_p^1$ correspond to the distances $d_1,\dots,d_p$ (see (1.6), (1.7), (1.8)), and the function φ corresponds to f in (1.6)).

In order to solve the problem of object identification with a best classification reproduction we maximize the term

$$\sum_{(K,L)} v^1(\gamma(K), \gamma(L))^{1)} = \sum_{(K,L)} \varphi(v_1^1(K,L),\dots,v_p^1(K,L)).$$

This is equivalent to the optimization problem (see (2.4) or (2.6))

(2.8) $$\min_{\varphi} \sum_{(K,L)} |v^1(K,L) - \varphi(v_1^1(K,L),\dots,v_p^1(K,L))| .$$
with $\varphi \in \phi$.

1) For quantitative data $\sum v^1(\gamma(K), \gamma(L))$ corresponds to the discriminant criterion of discriminant analysis.

For ϕ being the set of linear functions we have a linear optimization problem.
An object identification in connection with a disjunct classification yields hints for the stability of the classes relative to the weights of characters. For the classification $K \subset P^1Q$ with $i \in K(i) \in K$ and

(2.9) $$\varphi_{iK} := \varphi(v_1^1(\{i\},K) - v_1^1(\{i\}, K(i)),\ldots,v_p^1(\{i\},K) - v_p^1(\{i\}, K(i)))$$
for all $i \in Q,\ K \in K$

we obtain with

(2.10) $$B = \{\varphi \in \phi:\ \varphi_{iK} \geqq 0,\ i \in Q,\ K \in K\}$$

a criterion for the stability of K relative to f if K was found with $d(i,j) = f(d_1(i,j),\ldots,d_p(i,j))$ (see (1.6)).
For a given data matrix, a classification K and the result

(2.11) $$\max\ \{\beta:\ \varphi_{iK} - \beta \geqq 0,\ \varphi \in \phi\} > 0$$

we are able to reproduce the classification K by the sample comprehended in the data matrix.
For these cases reproducing a classification we look for the essential characters resp. their weights receiving the monotonicity conditions of (2.7).

References

[1] Bock, H.H. (1974): Automatische Klassifikation, Vandenhoeck & Ruprecht, Göttingen.

[2] Eichhorn, W. (1977): What is an Economic Index? An Attempt of an Answer. This volume.

[3] Gower, J.C. (1971): A General Coefficient of Similarity and Some of its Properties, Biometrics, 27.

[4] Jardine, N. and Sibson, R. (1971): Mathematical Taxonomy, J. Wiley & Sons, London, New York, Sydney, Toronto.

[5] Opitz, O. (Editor) (1977): Numerische Taxonomie in der Marktforschung, mit Beiträgen von K. Ambrosi, Th. Burdelski, W. Dub, W. Lauwerth, O. Opitz, M. Schader. F. Vahlen, München.

[6] Schader, M. (1977): Anordnung und Klassifikation von Objekten bei qualitativen Merkmalen, Dissertation, Universität Karlsruhe.

[7] Shepard, R.N. (1974): Representation of Structures in Similarity Data: Problems and Prospects, Psychometrica, 39.

[8] Sneath, P.H.A. and Sokal, R.R. (1973): Numerical Taxonomy, Freeman & Co., San Francisco.

PART II

Methodological Topics Concerning Economic Indices

On Wald's "New Formula" for the Cost of Living

by S.N. Afriat

Introduction

Wald (1939) used a pair of linear expansion loci as a basis for deciding the relation between incomes which, at the different prices in two periods, have the same purchasing power. He remarked that the expansion loci, or loci of consumption when prices are fixed, which are associated with a quadratic utility function are linear. This opened the possibility that the two given loci could be associated simultaneously with some quadratic utility. Points on the loci which were indifferent with such a utility would then correspond to incomes which, at the associated prices, had the same purchasing power. Though the utility was not determined, and might not exist, and would not be fully determinate even if it should exist, Wald proved the relation nevertheless to be determinate and he showed a way to calculate it.

While this is the basis for Wald's "New Formula", there has been no enquiry about the existence of the quadratic utility which gave the principle for the derivation of the formula, and is still needed for its interpretation. If none exists his conclusion, though still true, is vacuous. It will appear that decisive to the existence question is a qualification that the range of incomes in view for comparison should fall within a certain limited range.

The expansion loci of a quadratic generally are linear, but possibly the dimension is greater than one. For them simply to be lines the quadratic must be regular, that is have a regular matrix of second derivatives. But in this case the lines are all concurrent in a single point. Thus if Wald intended the given lines to be complete expansion loci of a quadratic, and not just parts of those loci, they must intersect. By introducing the point of intersection, Wald's proposition on determinacy has a very simple proof, and also the formula for equivalent incomes is greatly simplified. But should the lines be intended just as parts of complete loci of higher dimension, they need not intersect. Instead of the intersection the calculation, in what will be distinguished as the regular case, will involve a unique pair of "critical points" determined on the lines. When the lines do intersect the critical points coincide with the point of intersection.

The critical points, besides giving an especially concise form for the formula, have a necessary part in the resolution of the existence question. They divide the loci into pairs of half-lines, and no quadratic can admit both. This shows a necessary vacuity in Wald's proposition if it is left as originally offered, without specific confinement of the loci to limited parts of the lines. A pair of halves of the loci will admit a quadratic, and incomes must correspond to points of these if they are to have comparison. The identification of which pair of halves corresponds to a distinction of cases, elliptical and hyperbolic. The threshold between these, the non-regular parabolic case, is where the critical points do not exist, or are "at infinity". This case requires the loci to be parallel.

A further qualification needed to avoid vacuity, beside confinement of the loci to particular halves bounded by the critical points, arises because generally a quadratic has limited application as a utility function. It applies only in the region of the commodity space where it is non-decreasing and quasiconcave. Just the requirement that it admit the loci locally can force this region to be smaller than the entire commodity space. There is escape from this conflict if Wald's utility function is not required altogether to be quadratic, but instead is required just to admit representation by a quadratic in a neighbourhood of the parts of the loci where incomes are to be compared. As already remarked, for valid comparisons the location of those parts relative to the critical points is limited by the character of the case, elliptical or hyperbolic, if the case if regular, though this limitation lapses in the parabolic case.

Wald described the expansion loci as lines, and used them to compare incomes. But in the way now described, the range of incomes to which comparisons is to apply is critical to the consistency question, and it should be made specific. Correspondingly the expansion loci should not be offered simply as lines but as specific line segments. The complete lines which are their extension can then be distinguished as the carrier lines. The segments lie within the commodity space but the carrier lines lie partly outside. The critical points are determined on the carrier lines and there is no necessity for them to lie in the commodity space. Rather, constraint to the commodity space has no part in the theory of Wald's formula. The circumstance that a line segment which represents an actual locus of consumption for a range of incomes must lie within the commodity space is for purposes of mathematics, if not of economics, accidental.

All that is important is where the segments lie in regard to the critical points on their carrier lines.

Wald's theorem generalizes the theorem of Buscheguennce (1925) that Fisher's price-index is 'exact' on the hypothesis that demand is governed by a homogeneous quadratic. A discussion of the connection between the two theorems is in Afriat (1976); in particular, when the expansion loci intersect, as they must if the expansion loci of the quadratic are identical with, and not larger than, the given lines, and in which case the critical points coincide in the point of intersection, Wald's theorem is a simple corollary.

A generalization of Wald's formula is shown in Afriat (1956) and is taken further in Afriat (1961), and reproduced in Afriat (1967) (appearing in Shubik (1967)).

The expression for the "New Formula" in terms of critical points is nowhere visible in the original derivation of Wald, of which expositions have been given by Ulmer (1949) and Banerjee (1975). An outline of theory where the critical points enter in a broader context involving the "incremental price-index" concept and "limits" propositions is given by Afriat (NBER 1970 Conference, Proceedings 1972). This theory directly generalizes price-index theory shown in Afriat (1976).

1. Critical Points

Consider a linear expansion (L, p), $L \subset \Omega^n$ being a line in the commodity space, a segment K of which gives the locus of consumption when prices are fixed at $p \in \Omega_n$ and incomes have some range I. The line is specified by any one of its points $a \in L$, and any displacement d on it. Then any point $x \in L$ is given by

$$x = a + dt$$

for some value of the parameter t.

Any bundle of goods $x \in L$ on the locus has associated with it an income $M \in \Omega$ given by

$$px = M.$$

Points of L and incomes are to be in a 1-1 correspondence, so x must be the unique point of L thus associated with M. Since the relation is $M = pa + (pd)t$ the condition for this is that $pd \neq 0$, and without loss in generality d, being any displacement on the line, can be chosen so that

$$pd > 0.$$

The relation between incomes and parameters of associated points is then monotonic increasing.

Let (L_0, p_0), (L_1, p_1) be two given linear expansions, where L_0, L_1 are described by

$$x_0 = a_0 + d_0t_0, \quad x_1 = a_1 + d_1t_1,$$

with

$$p_0d_0 > 0, \quad p_1d_1 > 0.$$

Points $c_0 \in L_0$, $c_1 \in L_1$ are a pair of *critical points* on the loci if

$$p_0c_0 = p_0c_1, \quad p_1c_0 = p_1c_1.$$

The condition on the parameters of such points is

$$p_0a_0 + p_0d_0t_0 = p_0a_1 + p_0d_1t_1,$$
$$p_1a_0 + p_1d_0t_0 = p_1a_1 + p_1d_1t_1,$$

that is

$$\begin{pmatrix} p_0d_0 & -p_0d_1 \\ -p_1d_0 & p_1d_1 \end{pmatrix} \begin{pmatrix} t_0 \\ t_1 \end{pmatrix} = \begin{pmatrix} p_0a_1 - p_0a_0 \\ p_1a_1 - p_1a_0 \end{pmatrix}.$$

It appears from here that the condition

$$p_0d_1p_1d_0 \neq p_0d_0p_1d_1$$

is necessary and sufficient for the existence of a unique pair of critical points. This will define the *regular case*. In this case c_0, c_1 can replace the arbitrary points a_0, a_1 so L_0, L_1 are described by

$$x_0 = c_0 + d_0t_0, \quad x_1 = c_1 + d_1t_1.$$

The incomes corresponding to points on the loci are given by

$$p_0x_0 = M_0, \quad p_1x_1 = M_1.$$

The *critical incomes* are those corresponding to the critical points, given by

$$p_0c_0 = E_0, \quad p_1c_1 = E_1.$$

Then the correspondence between incomes and parameters of points can be stated

$$M_0 - E_0 = (p_0d_0)t_0, \quad M_1 - E_1 = (p_1d_1)t_1.$$

Ranges I_0, I_1 of incomes correspond to segments K_0, K_1 on the lines.

The regular case permits two possibilities

$$p_0d_1p_1d_0 > \text{ or } < p_0d_0p_1d_1,$$

and these will be distinguished as the *hyperbolic* and *elliptical cases*, for reasons which will appear.

THEOREM 1. *Let* (L_0, p_0), (L_1, p_1) *be a pair of linear expansions, and* d_0, d_1 *any displacements on the lines. Then necessary and sufficient for the existence and uniqueness of critical points* c_0, c_1 *on the lines, such that*

$$p_0c_0 = p_0c_1, \quad p_1c_0 = p_1c_1,$$

is that

$$p_0d_1p_1d_0 \neq p_0d_0p_1d_1.$$

For any M_0, M_1 *there exist unique* $x_0 \in L_0$, $x_1 \in L_1$ *such that*

$$p_0x_0 = M_0, \quad p_1x_1 = M_1,$$

if and only if

$$p_0d_0 \neq 0, \quad p_1d_1 \neq 0.$$

FIGURE 1.

The Critical Points

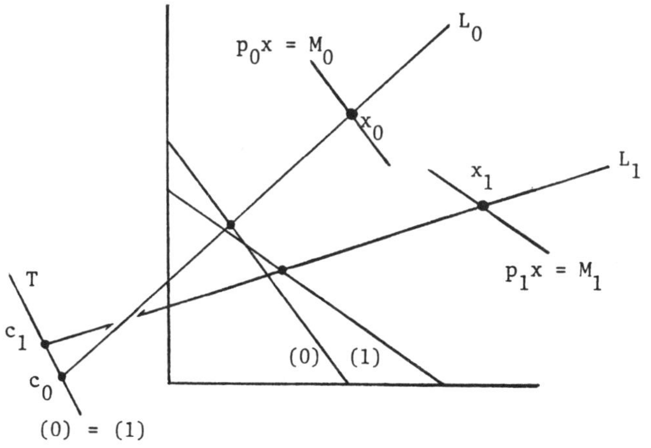

2. Admissible Utility

A utility function $\phi : \Omega^n \to \Omega$ *admits*, or is admitted by a demand (x, p), of quantities x at prices p, or the two are *compatible*, if ϕ represents x as a bundle of goods giving maximum utility among all those which cost no more at the prices, and giving minimum cost among all those which have as much utility, that is

(i) $py \leqq px \Rightarrow \phi(y) \leqq \phi(x)$

(ii) $py < px \Rightarrow \phi(y) < \phi(x)$.

Any budget constraint $px = M$, with $M > 0$, can be stated $ux = 1$, where $u = M^{-1}p$. The utility associated with the budget constraint is the maximum utility attainable under it, that is

$$\psi(u) = \max[\phi(x) : ux \leqq 1],$$

ψ being the adjoint of ϕ, or the associated indirect utility function.

The conditions for ϕ to admit (x, p), with $M = px$, are now stated

(i)' $\phi(x) = \psi(M^{-1}p)$

(ii)' $N < M \Rightarrow \psi(N^{-1}p) < \psi(M^{-1}p)$

A utility function ϕ admits a linear expansion (K, p), K being a linear segment with carrier line L, is that it admit every demand (x, p) for $x \in K$. If $x = a + dt$ is a parametric description of L, with $pd > 0$, the correspondence of incomes with parameters, and hence with points, is $M = pa + (pd)t$. Then the segments of points K corresponds to a range of parameters T, and a range of incomes I.

The condition for ϕ to admit (K, p) is now that, for all $x = a + dt$, $M = pa + (pd)t$ and $t \in T$, (i)' and (ii)' should hold. Thus $\psi(M^{-1}p)$ is an increasing function of $M \in I$; equivalently $\phi(x)$

with $x = a + dt$ is an increasing function of $t \in T$, since, with $pd > 0$, M is an increasing function of t.

FIGURE 2.

Admissible Utility

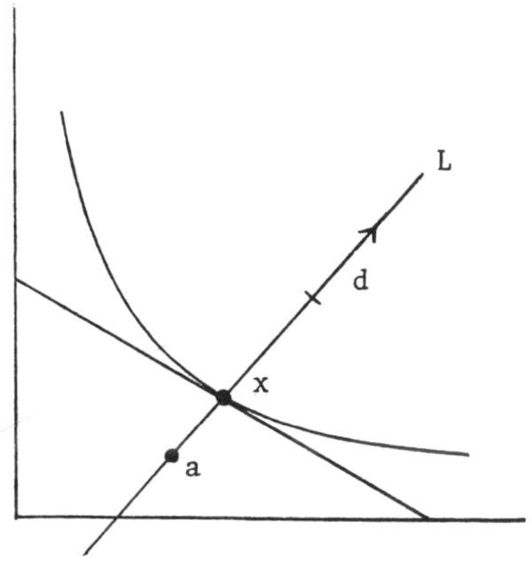

(p, L) a given linear expansion

line L specified by any point a and displacement d

described parametrically by $x = a + dt$

correspondence between points x and incomes M

determined by budget condition $px = M$

which gives $t = (M - pa)/pd$

ϕ a utility function admitted by (p, L)

provided that for all M

$$py \lesssim px \Rightarrow \phi(y) \leqq \phi(x)$$

$$py < px \Rightarrow \phi(y) < \phi(x)$$

3. General Comparison

For any incomes M_0, M_1 at different prices p_0, p_1 to have the same purchasing power, as decided by a utility ϕ with adjoint ψ, the condition is

$$\psi(M_0^{-1}p_0) = \psi(M_1^{-1}p_1).$$

With $\psi(M^{-1}p)$ is monotonic increasing in M, this condition determines a relation between equivalent incomes which is monotonic increasing.

Let a pair of linear expansions (K_0, p_0), (K_1, p_1) be given, where K_0, K_1 are linear segments with carrier lines L_0, L_1 having critical points c_0, c_1 and displacements d_0, d_1 such that

$$p_0d_0 > 0, \quad p_1d_1 > 0.$$

Thus the lines are described parametrically by

$$x_0 = c_0 + d_0t_0, \quad x_1 = c_1 + d_1t_0$$

where

$$p_0c_0 = p_0c_1, \quad p_1c_0 = p_1c_1$$

and the regularity condition

$$p_0d_1p_1d_0/p_0d_0p_1d_1 \neq 1$$

assures that such c_0, c_1 exist and are unique. The correspondences between incomes M_0, M_1 and points $x_0 \in L_0$, $x_1 \in L_1$ such that $p_0x_0 = M_0$, $p_1x_1 = M_1$ in terms of parameters t_0, t_1 of the points are

$$M_0 - E_0 = (p_0d_0)t_0, \quad M_1 - E_1 = (p_1d_1)t_1,$$

where

$$E_0 = p_0c_0, \quad E_1 = p_1c_1$$

are the critical incomes, and these relations between incomes and parameters are monotonic increasing. The segments K_0, K_1 on the lines correspond to ranges T_0, T_1 of the parameters and ranges I_0, I_1 of incomes.

Also let it be assumed that

$$p_0 d_1 \neq 0, \quad p_1 d_0 \neq 0.$$

This scheme of data is to be used to establish purchasing power comparisons between incomes in the ranges I_0, I_1 at the prices p_0, p_1. Such comparison is based on utility, and the use of the data is to impose on the utility function the requirement of compatibility with the expansions (K_0, p_0), (K_1, p_1). With such utility, comparison of incomes M_0, M_1 in I_0, I_1 becomes the same as comparison of correspondi points x_0, x_1 in K_0, K_1 since admissibility of ϕ requires

$$\phi(x_0) = \psi(M_0^{-1} p_0), \quad \phi(x_1) = \psi(M_1^{-1} p_1).$$

Consider such a comparison in which points $x_0 \in K_0$, $x_1 \in K_1$ with parameters t_0, t_1 have been established as indifferent, that is

$$\phi(x_0) = \phi(x_1).$$

Let $\check{x}_1$, $\hat{x}_1$ L_1 with parameters $\check{t}_1$, $\hat{t}_1$ be determined so that

$$p_0 x_0 = p_0 \check{x}_1, \quad p_1 x_0 = p_1 \check{x}_1.$$

Thus,

$$p_0(c_0 + d_0 t_0) = p_0(c_1 + d_1 \check{t}_1),$$

$$p_1(c_0 + d_0 t_0) = p_1(c_1 + d_1 t_1),$$

which, since c_0, c_1 are critical points, are equivalent to

$$p_0 d_0 t_0 = p_0 d_1 \check{t}_1, \quad p_1 d_0 t_0 = p_1 d_1 \hat{t}_1,$$

which, since $p_0 d_1 \neq 0$, $p_1 d_1 \neq 0$, determine unique $\check{t}_1$, $\hat{t}_1$.

Now

$$p_0 x_0 = p_0 \check{x}_1 \Rightarrow \phi(x_0) \geqq \phi(\check{x}_1)$$

and, assuming K_1 large enough to contain $\hat{x}_1$,

$$p_1 x_0 = p_1 \hat{x}_1 \Rightarrow \phi(\hat{x}_1) \geqq \phi(x_0).$$

Thus, since $\phi(x_0) = \phi(x_1)$,

$$\phi(\hat{x}_1) \geqq \phi(x_1) \geqq \phi(\check{x}_1),$$

and because utility increases along K_1 this is equivalent to

$$\hat{t}_1 \geqq t_1 \geqq \check{t}_1.$$

It will now be seen that

$$\hat{t}_1 > \check{t}_1,$$

unless $t_0 = t_1 = 0$. Thus suppose $\hat{t}_1 = \check{t}_1$. Then $\hat{t}_1 = t_1 = \check{t}_1$, so t_0 and t_1 satisfy

$$p_0 d_0 t_0 = p_0 d_1 t_1, \quad p_1 d_0 t_0 = p_1 d_1 t_1.$$

But the regularity condition assures that the only solution to these equations is $t_0 = t_1 = 0$.

Taking $t_0 = t_1 = 0$, another conclusion is that

$$\phi(c_0) = \phi(c_1),$$

for any ϕ compatible with both (c_0, p_0), (c_1, p_1).

Now take $t_0 \neq 0$, so equivalently $t_1 \neq 0$. Then, as has been seen,

$$\check{t}_1 < \hat{t}_1 \text{ and } \check{t}_1 \leqq t_1 \leqq \hat{t}_1.$$

It will now be seen also that, with ϕ differentiable, it is necessary that

$$\check{t}_1 < t_1 < \hat{t}_1.$$

For suppose $\check{t}_1 = t_1$. Then ϕ is constant on the segment $\langle x_0, \check{x}_1 \rangle$, so the gradient is perpendicular to this segment, while at $\check{x}_1$ it has the direction of p_1. But, since $\phi(x_0) = \phi(\check{x}_1)$, it is impossible that $p_1\check{x}_1 \leqq p_1 x_0$, unless also $p_0 x_0 = p_0 \hat{x}_1$. But this is impossible, since it would imply $\check{x}_1 = \hat{x}_1$, contradicting $\check{t}_1 < \hat{t}_1$. Hence $p_1 \check{x}_1 > p_1 x_0$, so p_1 is not perpendicular to $\langle x_0, \check{x}_1 \rangle$. Thus $\check{t}_1 = t_1$ is impossible, and so similarly is $\hat{t}_1 = t_1$.

Introducing the expressions for $\check{t}_1$, $\hat{t}_1$ it has appeared that

$$(p_0d_0/p_0d_1)t_0 < t_1 < (p_1d_0/p_1d_1)t_0.$$

By the same argument with 0, 1 interchanged,

$$(p_1d_1/p_1d_0)t_1 < t_0 < (p_0d_1/p_0d_0)t_1.$$

A first conclusion from these relations is that

$$p_0d_1 > 0, \quad p_1d_0 > 0.$$

For, since $p_1d_1 > 0$, $p_1d_0 < 0$ gives $p_1d_1/p_1d_0 < 0$, and this by multiplication with

$$(p_1d_1/p_1d_0)t_1 < t_0 \text{ gives}$$

$$t_1 > (p_1d_0/p_1d_1)t_0,$$

so there is a contradiction. Thus $p_0d_1 > 0$, and similarly $p_1d_0 > 0$. Now with this an immediate further conclusion is that either $t_0, t_1 > 0$ or $t_0, t_1 < 0$, equivalently

$$t_0t_1 > 0,$$

and also

$$t_0 < (p_0d_1p_1d_0/p_0d_0p_1d_1)t_0$$

and the same with 0, 1 interchanged. Thus in the hyperbolic case

$$p_0d_1p_1d_0/p_0d_0p_1d_1 > 1$$

it follows that $t_0 > 0$, and again $t_1 > 0$; and similarly in the elliptical case $t_0, t_1 < 0$.

THEOREM 2. *Let* (L_0, p_0), (L_1, p_1) *be a pair of linear expansions and* d_0, d_1 *any displacements on the lines, with directions in which* $M_0 = p_0x_0$, $M_1 = p_1x_1$ *increase so that*

$$p_0d_0 > 0, \quad p_1d_1 > 0.$$

$$p_0d_1p_1d_0 \neq p_0d_0p_1d_1,$$

so the lines have a unique pair of critical points c_0, c_1 *such that*

$$p_0c_0 = p_0c_1, \quad p_1c_0 = p_1c_1,$$

determining critical incomes

$$E_0 = p_0c_0, \quad E_1 = p_1c_1.$$

Let K_0, K_1 *be segments of* L_0, L_1 *which include* c_0, c_1 *and let* ϕ *be a utility function compatible with* $(K_0, p_0), (K_1, p_1)$. *For the existence of such* ϕ *it is necessary that*

$$p_0d_1 > 0, \quad p_1d_0 > 0$$

and that c_0, c_1 *be end-points of* K_0, K_1; *in the hyperbolic case*

$$p_0d_1p_1d_0 > p_0d_0p_1d_1$$

they must be lower end points, that is $x_0 \in K_0 \Rightarrow M_0 \geqq E_0$, $x_1 \in K_1 \Rightarrow M_1 \geqq E_1$, *and in the elliptical case*

$$p_0d_1p_1d_0 < p_0d_0p_1d_1$$

they must be upper end points, that is $x_0 \in K_0 \Rightarrow M_0 \leqq E_0$, $x_1 \in K_1 \Rightarrow M_1 \leqq E_1$. *With any such* ϕ, *and* $x_0 \in K_0$, $x_1 \in K_1$, *such that* $p_0x_0 = M_0$, $p_1x_1 = M_0$, *a necessary condition that* $\phi(x_0) = \phi(x_1)$ *is that*

$$\frac{p_1d_1}{p_0d_1} \leqq \frac{M_1 - E_1}{M_0 - E_0} \leqq \frac{p_1d_0}{p_0d_0}$$

in the hyperbolic case with $M_0 \geqq E_0$, $M_1 \geqq E_1$, *or*

$$\frac{p_1d_1}{p_0d_1} \geqq \frac{M_1 - E_1}{M_0 - E_0} \geqq \frac{p_1d_0}{p_0d_0}$$

in the elliptical case with $M_0 \leqq E_0$, $M_1 \leqq E_1$. *In either case*

$$\frac{M_1 - E_1}{M_0 - E_0} = \left(\frac{p_1d_0p_1d_1}{p_0d_0p_0d_1}\right)^{\frac{1}{2}}$$

is a correspondence between M_0, M_1 *which satisfies these conditions.*

It will appear that this last correspondence must be identical with Wald's "New Formula". For by computing with reference to a quadratic utility this formula is going to be produced again. But here it has been arrived at without any dependence on quadratics, or any regard at all to the form of the utility function. Also it has been established in a framework of qualifications which, because of the generality, must apply equally in Wald's context.

FIGURE 3.

Hyperbolic and Elliptical Cases

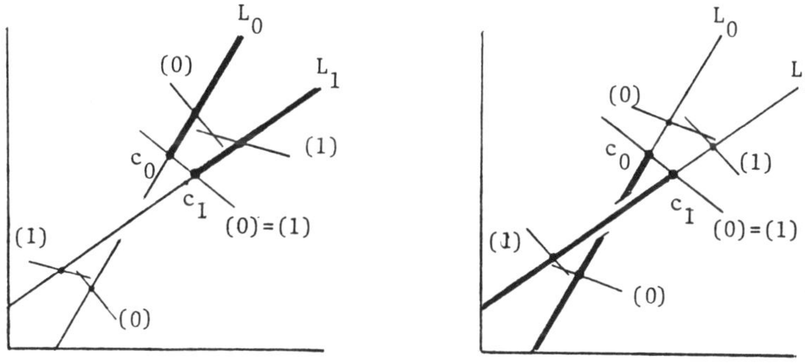

Hyperbolic

$p_0 d_1 p_1 d_0 > p_0 d_0 p_1 d_1$

Elliptical

$p_0 d_1 p_1 d_0 < p_0 d_0 p_1 d_1$

4. Quadratics

Let $\phi(x)$ be a function, $g(x)$ the gradient with elements $g_j(x) = \partial\phi/\partial xj$ and $h(x)$ the Hessian with elements $h_{ij} = \partial^2\phi/\partial x_i \partial x_j$. Then ϕ is a quadratic if the Hessian, or matrix of second derivatives, is a constant $h(x) = h$. Then h must be symmetric, $h' = h$, and also

(i) $$\phi(x) = \phi(o) + g(o)x + \tfrac{1}{2}x'hx$$

(ii) $$g(x) = g(o) + x'h.$$

A *centre* of the quadratic is any point c where $g(c) = 0$, so

$$0 = g(o) + c'h.$$

A *central quadratic* is one for which a centre exists. In this case

(ii)' $$g(x) = (x - c)'h$$

and

(i)' $$\begin{aligned}\phi(x) &= \phi(o) - c'hc + \tfrac{1}{2}(x - c)'A(x - c)\\ &= \phi(c) + \tfrac{1}{2}(x - c)'A(x - c)\\ &= \phi(c) + \tfrac{1}{2}g(x)(x - c).\end{aligned}$$

For a *homogeneous quadratic*

$$\phi(x\lambda) = \phi(x)\lambda^2,$$

which requires

$$\phi(x) = \tfrac{1}{2}x'hx,$$

and then

(ii)" $$g(x) = x'h,$$

so

$$\phi(o) = 0, \quad g(o) = 0$$

and

(i)'' $\phi(x) = \frac{1}{2}g(x)x.$

Thus a homogeneous quadratic is a central quadratic for which the origin is a centre at which its value is zero.

If ϕ is a centre quadratic and c a centre then

$$\phi(z) = \phi(z + c) - \phi(c)$$

is a homogeneous quadratic, and

$$\phi(x) = \phi(c) + \phi(z - c),$$

that is, the central quadratics are just translations of the homogeneous quadratics, obtained by translations of the origin of the arguments and the origin of the value.

For any quadratic,

(iii) $g(x) - g(a) = (x - a)'h$

so that, by symmetry of h,

(iv)
$$\begin{aligned}(g(x) - g(a))(y - b) &= (x - a)'h(y - b)\\ &= (y - b)'h(x - a)\\ &= (g(y) - g(b))(x - a).\end{aligned}$$

Also

(v)
$$\begin{aligned}\phi(y) - (x) &= g(x)(y - x) + \tfrac{1}{2}(y - x)'h(y - x)\\ &= g(x)(y - x) + \tfrac{1}{2}(g(y) - g(x))(y - x)\\ &= \tfrac{1}{2}(g(x) + g(y))(y - x)\\ &= g((x + y)\tfrac{1}{2})(y - x).\end{aligned}$$

In particular, for a central quadratic, with c as a centre, so that $g(c) = 0$,

(iv)' $g(x)(y - c) = g(y)(x - c)$

and for a homogeneous quadratic

(iv)'' $g(x)y = g(y)x.$

Any function ϕ is concave if

$$\phi(x\alpha + y\beta) \geqq \phi(x)\alpha + \phi(y)\beta$$

for $\alpha, \beta \geqq 0$, $\alpha + \beta = 1$.

For any quadratic, if $\alpha + \beta = 1$ then

$$\phi(x)\alpha + \phi(y)\beta - \phi(x\alpha + y\beta) = (g(x) - g(y))(x - y)\alpha\beta.$$

Thus, let $z = x\alpha + y\beta$. Then from (iv),

$$\begin{aligned}
&\phi(x)\alpha + \phi(y)\beta - \phi(z) \\
&= (\phi(x) - \phi(z))\alpha + (\phi(y) - \phi(z))\beta \\
&= \tfrac{1}{2}(g(x) + g(z))(x - z)\alpha + \tfrac{1}{2}(g(y) + g(z))(y - z)\beta \\
&= \tfrac{1}{2}g(x)(x - z)\alpha + \tfrac{1}{2}g(y)(y - z)\beta \\
&= \tfrac{1}{2}g(x)(x - y)\alpha\beta + \tfrac{1}{2}g(y)(y - x)\beta\alpha \\
&= (g(x) - g(y))(x - y)\alpha\beta
\end{aligned}$$

It follows that for a quadratic to be concave it is necessary and sufficient that

$$(g(x) - g(y))(x - y) \leqq 0.$$

By (iii) this is the condition that h be non-positive definite.

Alternatively, for any function $\phi(x)$ with gradient $g(x)$ to be concave a necessary and sufficient condition is

$$\phi(y) \leqq \phi(x) + g(x)(y - x).$$

Then from (v) it follows that for a quadratic to be concave a necessary and sufficient condition is that h be non-positive definite, that is $z'hz \leqq 0$ for all h. From (i)', for a central quadratic this condition is $\phi(x) \leqq \phi(c)$ for all x, and for a homogeneous quadratic it is $\phi(x) \leqq 0$.

5. Quadratic Comparison

THEOREM 3. *Let* (L_0, p_0), (L_1, p_1) *be a pair of linear expansions with a unique pair of critical points* c_0, c_1. *Let* $\phi(x)$ *be a quadratic which is non-constant on* L_0 *and on* L_1, *with gradient* $g(x)$ *which has the direction of* p_0 *at two distinct points of* L_0 *and of* p_1 *at two distinct points of* L_1. *Then*

$$g(c_0) = 0, \; g(c_1) = 0,$$

$$\phi(c_0) = \phi(c_1),$$

and for any $x_0 \varepsilon L_0$, $x_1 \varepsilon L_1$,

$$\phi(x_0) = \phi(x_1)$$

is equivalent to

$$p_0(x_0 - c_0)p_1(x_0 - c_0) = p_0(x_1 - c_1)p_1(x_1 - c_1).$$

Since ϕ is quadratic,

(i) $$g(x\lambda + y\mu) = \lambda g(x) + \mu g(y) \quad \text{if} \quad \lambda + \mu = 1$$

(ii) $$\phi(x) - \phi(c) = \tfrac{1}{2}(g(x) + g(c))(x - c)$$

so that

(ii)' $$\phi(x) - \phi(c) = \tfrac{1}{2}g(x)(x - c) \quad \text{if} \quad g(c) = 0$$

and

(iii) $$(g(x_0) - g(c_0))(x_1 - c_1) = (g(x_1) - g(c_1))(x_0 - c_0)$$

so that

(iii)' $$g(x_0)(x_1 - c_1) = g(x_1)(x_0 - c_0) \quad \text{if} \quad g(c_0) = g(c_1) = 0.$$

By hypothesis

$$g(a_0) = \alpha p_0, \; g(b_0) = \beta p_0$$

for some $a_0, b_0 \varepsilon L_0$ and α, β. Then for any $x_0 \varepsilon L_0$, that is $x_0 = a_0\rho + b_0\sigma$ where $\rho + \sigma = 1$, by (i),

$$\begin{aligned} g(x_0) &= g(a_0\rho + b_0\sigma) \\ &= \rho g(a_0) + \rho g(b_0) \\ &= \rho\sigma p_0 + \sigma\beta p_0 \\ &= (\rho\alpha + \sigma\beta)p_0 \\ &= \lambda p_0 \end{aligned}$$

where $\lambda = \rho\sigma + \sigma\beta$, which, if it is not always zero, is zero for at most one point of L_0, and similarly with 1 in place of 0. Thus, for all $x_0 \in L_0$, $x_1 \in L_1$

$$\text{(iv)} \qquad g(x_0) = \lambda_0 p_0, \quad g(x_1) = \lambda_1 p_1$$

for some λ_0, λ_1 not always zero. In particular

$$\text{(v)} \qquad g(c_0) = \mu_0 p_0, \quad g(c_1) = \mu_1 p_1$$

for some μ_0, μ_1. Then by (ii) with (v)

$$\begin{aligned} \phi(c_0) - \phi(c_1) &= \tfrac{1}{2}(g(c_0) + g(c_1))(c_0 - c_1) \\ &= \tfrac{1}{2}(\mu_0 p_0 + \mu_1 p_1)(c_0 - c_1). \end{aligned}$$

But, because c_0, c_1 are critical points,

$$p_0(c_0 - c_1) = 0, \quad p_1(c_0 - c_1) = 0,$$

so it follows that

$$\text{(vi)} \qquad \phi(c_0) = \phi(c_1).$$

Then further, again by (ii), with (iv) and (v),

$$\begin{aligned} \phi(x_0) - \phi(c_0) &= \tfrac{1}{2}(\lambda_0 p_0 + \mu_0 p_0)(x_0 - c_0), \\ \phi(x_0) - \phi(c_1) &= \tfrac{1}{2}(\lambda_0 p_0 + \mu_1 p_1)(x_0 - c_1) \end{aligned}$$

Again because c_0, c_1 are critical points,

$$\begin{aligned} p_0(x_0 - c_0) &= p_0(x_0 - c_1), \\ p_1(x_0 - c_1) &= p_1(x_0 - c_0), \end{aligned}$$

so these relations, with (vi), give

$$\mu_0 p_0(x_0 - c_0) = \mu_1 p_1(x_0 - c_0).$$

By the same argument with 0, 1 interchanged,

$$\mu_0 p_0(x_1 - c_1) = \mu_1 p_1(x_1 - c_1).$$

Hence either $\mu_0 = \mu_1 = 0$ or

$$p_0(x_1 - c_1)p_1(x_0 - c_0) = p_0(x_0 - c_0)p_1(x_1 - c_1).$$

But the uniqueness of the critical points excludes the second possibility. For any other critical points would have the form

$$c_0{}^* = c_0 + (x_0 - c_0)s_0, \quad c_1{}^* = c_1 + (x_1 - c_1)s_1$$

for s_0, s_1 such that

$$p_0(x_0 - c_0)s_0 = p_0(x_1 - c_1)s_1$$
$$p_1(x_0 - c_0)s_0 = p_1(x_1 - c_1)s_1$$

and the condition for $s_0, s_1 = 0$ to be the only solution is equivalent to the denial of the second possibility. Thus $\mu_0 = \mu_1 = 0$, showing that

(vii) $\qquad g(c_0) = 0, \quad g(c_1) = 0.$

Hence by (ii)', with (iv),

(viii) $$\phi(x_0) - \phi(c_0) = \tfrac{1}{2}\lambda_0 p_0(x_0 - c_0)$$
$$\phi(x_1) - \phi(c_1) = \tfrac{1}{2}\lambda_1 p_1(x_1 - c_1)$$

so, by (vi), $\phi(x_0) = \phi(x_1)$ is equivalent to

(ix) $\qquad \lambda_0 p_0(x_0 - c_0) = \lambda_1 p_1(x_1 - c_1).$

But by (iii)' with (iv) and (vii),

(x) $\qquad \lambda_0 p_0(x_1 - c_1) = \lambda_1 p_1(x_0 - c_0).$

Unless $\lambda_0, \lambda_1 = 0$, elimination gives that

$$p_0(x_0 - c_0)p_1(x_0 - c_0) = p_0(x_1 - c_1)p_1(x_1 - c_1)$$

is equivalent to (ix). It remains to see that $\lambda_0, \lambda_1 \neq 0$. It has been remarked that λ_0 and λ_1 are each either always zero or zero for at most one point. They have been proved zero at their respective critical points. By hypothesis ϕ is non-constant on the lines, so they are not always zero. Therefore they are zero just at the critical points. Consequently, for $x_0 \in L_0$, $\phi(x_0) = \phi(c_0)$ only for $x_0 = c_0$. For, as already stated,

$$\phi(x_0) - \phi(c_0) = \tfrac{1}{2}\lambda_0 p_0(x_0 - c_0)$$

for $x_0 \in L_0$, so ϕ is non-constant if and only if $p_0(x_0 - c_0)$ is not always zero, which, as will be made explicit, is if and only if this is zero only for $x_0 - c_0$. The same holds on L_1.

The last argument is just that if d_0 is any displacement on L_0, so any point is $x_0 = c_0 + d_0 t_0$, then

$$p_0(x_0 - c_0) = (p_0 d_0) t_0,$$

which is always zero if $p_0 d_0 = 0$ and otherwise is zero just for $t_0 = 0$, that is $x_0 = c_0$.

A consequence, which has relevance for the following Corollary, is that for the existence of a ϕ such as enters in the Theorem, $p_0 d_0 \neq 0$ is necessary. The same applies to L_1. Thus with $\phi(x_0) = \phi(x_1)$, $x_0 = c_0$ if and only if $x_1 = c_1$. In this case there is nothing more to prove. Otherwise $x_0 \neq c_0$ and $x_1 \neq c_1$, so $\lambda_0, \lambda_1 \neq 0$.

COROLLARY (i). *Let* d_0, d_1 *be any displacements on* L_0, L_1 *and let*

$$p_0 d_0 \neq 0, \quad p_1 d_1 \neq 0,$$

as is required for the existence of ϕ *such as appears in the theorem, and which assures that for any* M_0, M_1 *there exist unique* $x_0 \in L_0$, $x_1 \in L_1$ *such that*

$$p_0 x_0 = M_0, \quad p_1 x_1 = M_1.$$

Then for any such ϕ *if* x_0, x_1 *have the relation*

$$\phi(x_0) = \phi(x_1)$$

then the corresponding M_0, M_1 *have the relation*

$$\frac{p_1d_0(M_0 - p_0c_0)^2}{p_0d_0} = \frac{p_0d_1(M_1 - p_1c_1)^2}{p_1d_1}.$$

Any points on L_0, L_1 are

$$x_0 = c_0 + d_0t_0, \quad x_1 = c_1 + d_1t_1$$

where, if

$$p_0x_0 = M_0, \quad p_1x_1 = M_1,$$

the parameters t_0, t_1 are determined from

$$M_0 - p_0c_0 = (p_0d_0)t_0, \quad M_1 - p_1c_1 = (p_1c_1)t_1.$$

By the theorem, if $\phi(x_0) = \phi(x_1)$ then

$$p_0d_0t_0p_1d_0t_0 = p_0d_1t_1p_1d_1t_1.$$

Substitution for t_0, t_1 then gives

$$p_0d_0p_1d_0\left(\frac{M_0 - p_0c_0}{p_0d_0}\right)^2 = p_0d_1p_1d_1\left(\frac{M_1 - p_1c_1}{p_1d_1}\right)^2,$$

as required.

COROLLARY (ii). *If there exists* ϕ *such as appears in the theorem then*

$$p_1d_0p_0d_1/p_0d_0p_1d_1 > 0.$$

Since ϕ varies on L_0, L_1 this relation between M_0, M_1 and the corresponding x_0, x_1 must require one to vary when the other does. For this it is necessary that

$$p_1d_0 \neq 0, \quad p_0d_1 \neq 0.$$

But then for this relation to hold anywhere except at c_0, c_1 as it must, the required conclusion is necessary.

On either of the lines, the quadratic has the same value at points symmetrically displaced from the critical point. Thus it has two branches on L_0, according to which side of the critical point c_0 is chosen, and similarly on L_1, in combination giving four possibilities. The choice affects only the sign of $M_0 - p_0c_0$, and leaves $(M_0 - p_0c_0)^2$ and $\phi(x_0)$ unaffected; and similarly on L_1. Correspondingly, the given relation between M_0, M_1 gives a fixed value for

$$\left(\frac{M_1 - p_1c_1}{M_0 - p_0c_0}\right)^2,$$

assuring that $\phi(x_0) = \phi(x_1)$, but at every level ϕ leaves four possibilities, since the signs of $M_0 - p_0c_0$ and $M_1 - p_1c_1$ remain indeterminate. These two signs can be fixed in two ways to give a monotonic increasing relation between M_0, M_1. These ways give

$$\frac{M_1 - p_1c_1}{M_0 - p_0c_0} > 0$$

leaving the numberator and denominator with signs which are the same but otherwise indeterminate, and result in the relation

$$M_1 - E_1 = P_{10}(M_0 - E_0)$$

where

$$E_0 = p_0c_0, \quad E_1 = p_1c_1$$

are the critical incomes and, as permitted by the conclusion in Corollary (ii), $P_{10} > 0$ is given by

$$P_{10} = \left(\frac{p_1d_0p_1d_1}{p_0d_0p_0d_1}\right)^{\frac{1}{2}}.$$

The interpretation of ϕ as a utility function requires such a monotonic increasing relation, and it has been seen, as a result of Corollary (ii), that it is possible to have one. But from the discussion in Section 4, such an interpretation brings an additional requirement that $M_0 - E_0$ and $M_1 - E_1$ not only must have the same sign but also have a specific sign, positive or negative according as the case is hyperbolic or elliptical.

The uniqueness of the critical points corresponds to the regular case, for which the condition is

$$p_1 d_0 p_0 d_1 / p_0 d_0 p_1 d_1 < 1 \quad \text{or} \quad > 1,$$

the distinctions in this being for the hyperbolic and elliptical cases.

FIGURE 4.

Income Purchasing Power

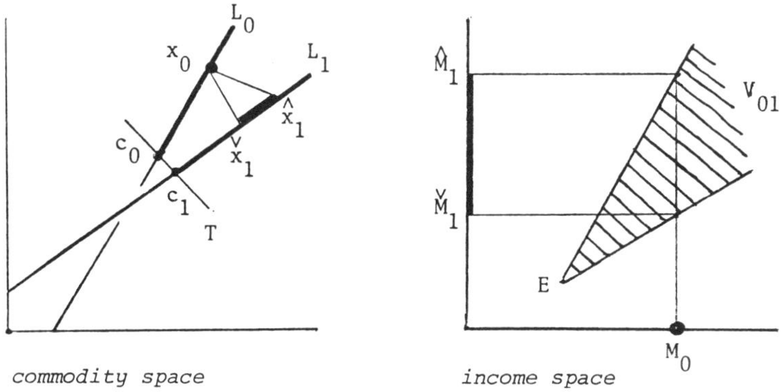

commodity space *income space*

FIGURE 5.

Wald's "New Formula"

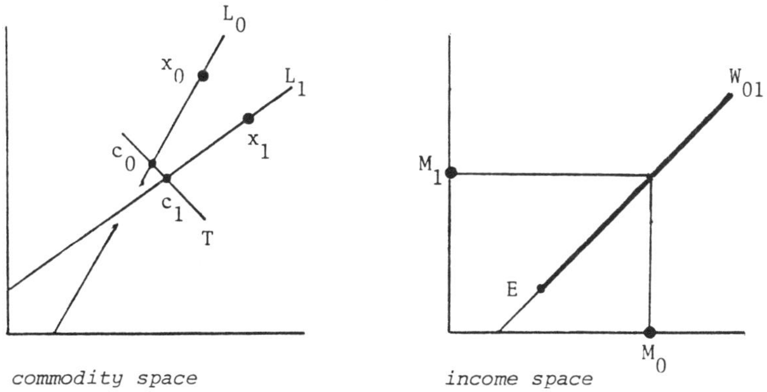

commodity space *income space*

6. Expansion Loci of Quadratics

A function ϕ is quasiconcave if

$$t \leqq \phi(x), \phi(y) \Rightarrow t \leqq \phi(x\alpha + y\beta)$$

for $\alpha, \beta \geqq 0, \alpha + \beta = 1$.

THEOREM 4. *A necessary and sufficient condition for a homogeneous quadratic* ϕ, *with gradient* g, *to be quasiconcave on a convex cone* V *is that*

$$g(x)yg(y)x \geqq g(x)xg(y)y \quad (x, y \in V),$$

provided

$$\phi(x) \geqq 0 \quad (x \in V),$$

and that

$$g(x)yg(y)x \leqq g(x)xg(y)y \quad (x, y \in V)$$

provided

$$\phi(x) \leqq 0 \quad (x \in V).$$

Any concave function is quasiconcave, and so is the transform $\omega(\phi)$ of a quasiconcave function by an increasing function ω. For a linearly homogeneous function ϕ, on a convex cone V, it is quasiconcave if and only if it is concave, and this is if and only if it is superadditive, that is

$$\phi(x + y) \geqq \phi(x) + \phi(y) \quad (x, y \in V).$$

If it has gradient g, this is if and only if

$$g(y)x \geqq \phi(x) \quad (x, y \in V).$$

Thus for a homogeneous quadratic ϕ, in a convex cone V where $\phi \geqq 0$, $\Phi = \phi^{\frac{1}{2}}$ is a linearly homogeneous increasing transform, with gradient $G = \frac{1}{2}\phi^{-\frac{1}{2}}g$. Then the condition for Φ, and equivalently ϕ, to be quasi-concave is

$$G(y)x \geqq \phi(x),$$

that is

$$\tfrac{1}{2}(\phi(y))^{-\frac{1}{2}}g(y)x \geqq \phi(x)^{\frac{1}{2}}.$$

Since

$$\phi(x) = \tfrac{1}{2}g(x)x \quad \text{and} \quad g(x)y = g(y)x,$$

that is

$$(g(x)y\ g(y)x)^{\frac{1}{2}} \geqq (g(x)x\ g(y)y)^{\frac{1}{2}},$$

equivalently

$$g(x)y\ g(y)x \geqq g(x)x\ g(y)y.$$

Replacing ϕ by $-\phi$, this must also be the condition for ϕ to be quasiconvex on a convex cone where it is non-positive.

Similarly, for ϕ to be quasiconcave on a convex cone where it is non-positive, the condition is

$$g(x)y\ g(y)x \leqq g(x)x\ g(y)y.$$

This is moreover the condition that it be non-positive and quasiconcave everywhere on the linear space through the cone.

By contrast, when ϕ is non-negative and quasiconcave on a convex cone, the property does not extend thus. This case, where the extension of the quadratic has a necessary inversion of such characteristics, is distinguished as *hyperbolic*, and the former is the *elliptical* case, where the character of the quadratic on the cone is preserved in its extension on the linear space through the cone.

COROLLARY. *A necessary and sufficient condition for a central quadratic* ϕ, *with* c *as a centre, and gradient* $g(x)$, *so* $g(c) = 0$, *to be quasiconcave on a convex cone* V *with* c *as a vertex is that*

$$g(x)(y - c)g(y)(x - c) \geqq g(x)(x - c)g(y)(y - c)(x, y \in V)$$

provided

$$\phi(x) \geqq 0 \quad (x \in V)$$

and that

$$g(x)(y - c)g(y)(x - c) \leqq g(x)(x - c)g(y)(y - c)(x, y \in V)$$

provided

$$\phi(x) \leqq 0 \quad (x \in V).$$

For the central quadratics are translations of the homogeneous quadratics (section 5), and any translation of a quasiconcave function is quasiconcave.

Since the Hessian h of a quadratic is symmetric, the range and null space

$$R = [g : g = x'h], \quad N = [x : hx = 0]$$

are orthogonal complements, whose dimensions , are the rank and nullity of h, such that $\rho + \nu = n$. The linear manifolds which are any translations of them are the *sectional* and *axial manifolds* of the quadratic.

The gradient of a quadratic is the same at two points if and only if the points lie on the same axial manifold. For

$$\begin{aligned} g(x) = g(y) \quad &\Leftrightarrow \quad h(x - y) = 0 \\ &\Leftrightarrow \quad x - y \in N \\ &\Leftrightarrow \quad x + N = y + N. \end{aligned}$$

The gradient describes a linear manifold

$$G = [u : u = g(x)],$$

the *gradient manifold,* which is a particular sectional manifold. There is a unique element $d \in G$ of minimum length, the *central gradient,* perpendicular to G and thus in N. Any point c where it is attained, such that $g(c) = d$, is an *epicentre* of the quadratic.

The locus of epicentres is a particular axial manifold, the *central axis* C. For a central quadratic the central gradient is null and the epicentres are centres. This is necessarily the case for a regular quadratic. A singular central quadratic is distinguished as *cylindrical*, since in this case the quadratic is constant on every axial manifold, so it is completely described by its values in any sectional manifold, where it appears as a regular quadratic with a unique centre. The contrary non-central case where $d \neq 0$ is described as *parabolic*. In this case every gradient $g(x)$ is resolved into two orthogonal components, one of which is constant and equal to $d \in N$ and the other lies in R. If a quadratic is regular, the hessian being a regular matrix, then a centre, which is a point where the gradient vanishes, always exists. Also if a centre exists it is unique if and only if the quadratic is regular.

The values of the gradient of a parabolic quadratic at two points have the same direction only if they are identical. For let the gradient by g_0, g_1 at two points, and let the direction be the same, so $g_0 = \lambda g_1$ for some λ. Then

$$g_0 = \bar{g}_0 + d, \quad g_1 = \bar{g}_1 + d$$

where $\bar{g}_0$, $\bar{g}_1$ are the orthogonal projections on R, and are orthogonal to d. Hence

$$dd' = (\bar{g}_0 + d)d' = \lambda(\bar{g}_1 + d)d' = \lambda dd'.$$

But $dd' > 0$ since $d \neq 0$. It follows that $\lambda = 1$, and $g_0 = g_1$.

For a utility function ϕ with gradient g, the expansion locus corresponding to prices p is described by points x near which

ϕ is quasiconcave and

$$g(x) = \lambda p \quad \text{for some} \quad \lambda > 0.$$

A local sense is understood, because if a given function happens to have a definition everywhere then in having regard also to values elsewhere such points need not be on the locus. But if the function is admitted as representing utility only near the points, and representation elsewhere is undetermined, it is possible to complete the function so such points are on the locus. The need for this distinction is pointed out in the Introduction. A quadratic function, though defined everywhere as such, is applicable as a utility function in a limited region, which here is required to include certain points which are in view, and outside that region the utility function is undetermined.

Expansion loci of a utility function being loci where the gradient has a fixed direction, determined by the prices, for a parabolic quadratic they are loci where the gradient is constant. But for any quadratic the loci where the gradient is constant are a family of parallel linear manifolds, the axial manifolds which are translations of the null-space of the Hessian, and therefore of the central axis. Hence *for a parabolic quadratic utility function the expansion loci are the parallel linear manifolds which are translations of the central axis.*

In Wald's problem, that is the problem presented by his formula, two expansion lines are given and a quadratic has to be found. The existence of critical points on the lines excludes the parabolic possibility, and implies any such quadratic is central. Then to find any quadratic, the complete lines cannot be retained, but must be truncated on one side of the critical points, which side being decided by the case being elliptical or hyperbolic. In the parabolic case there is a difference in that no such truncation of the lines is involved, and a quadratic will admit them completely if at all. This is because a parabolic quadratic is quasiconcave everywhere if it is anywhere, and this is if and only if it is concave. But no such admitting quadratic need exist. The given expansion lines can force any admitting quadratic to be quasiconvex near them, and therefore everywhere. But such an admitting quadratic also must be quasiconcave, making impossibility.

Since it is the regular case in which critical points exist which is being treated, any admitted quadratics must be central, so the parabolic case is excluded. But it can be remarked that the condition for this case to be admitted is that the expansion lines, if they are to be accepted as complete loci and not just parts of manifolds of higher dimension, must be parallel. Otherwise they must be at least enlarged by taking the 2-manifold through each which contains a secant line parallel to the other. Involved with this is that if

$$p_0d_1p_1d_0 = p_0d_0p_1d_1$$

then

$$p_0dp_1d = p_0dp_1d$$

for all d in the span of d_0, d_1. This is the case where the "Laspeyres" MPI, or price index, equals the "Paasche" MPI.

THEOREM 5. *The expansion loci of a central quadratic are convex cones with the central axis as the vertex manifold, so for a regular quadratic they are rays with the unique centre as their common vertex. The demand sets, in which they cut budget sets at corresponding prices, are translations of the central axis, these being single points for a regular quadratic.*

Let ϕ be a central quadratic, with gradient g, and central axis C, so $g(c) = 0$ for any $c \in C$. Let L be the expansion locus of ϕ for prices p, so for any $x \in L$, ϕ is quasiconcave near x, and

$$g(x) = \lambda p \text{ for some } \lambda > 0.$$

Consider any point

$$y = c + (x - c)t$$

on the line joining c and x. If $t > 0$ it is on the open ray E through x with vertex c, and if $t < 0$ it is on the opposite open ray. It has to be seen that, for any $c \in C$ and $x \in L$, the ray E is part of L, but no point of the opposite ray is.

Since ϕ is quasiconcave near x it is quasiconcave near every point on the line joining c to x, excepting possibly c. This appears from the above Corollary, and because

$$\phi(y) = \tfrac{1}{2}g(y)(y - c) = \tfrac{1}{2}g(x)(x - c)t^2 = \phi(x)t^2,$$

so ϕ has a fixed sign near points of this line except c. Hence for any point y on this line to belong to L, it suffices that

$$g(y) = \mu p \text{ for some } \mu > 0.$$

But

$$g(y) = g(x)t$$

so $\mu = \lambda t$. Thus $\mu > 0$ if and only if $t > 0$, that is y is in E.

Since the gradient is constant on the translation of the central axis C through x, also this linear manifold belongs to L. So do the translations of C through every point of the ray through x from any $c \in L$, and these cover all points of L.

7. Existence Theorem

THEOREM 6. *A necessary and sufficient condition that vectors* g_0, g_1 *be the gradients of some homogeneous quadratic at points* x_0, x_1 *is that*

(i) $$g_0x_1 = g_1x_0,$$

provided

(ii) $$\begin{vmatrix} g_0x_0 & g_0x_1 \\ g_1x_0 & g_1x_1 \end{vmatrix} \neq 0.$$

Then the values of all such quadratics at any point $x_0\alpha_0 + x_1\alpha_1$ *in the space spanned by* x_0, x_1 *are the same, and equal to*

(iii) $$\tfrac{1}{2}(\alpha_0g_0 + \alpha_1g_1)(x_0\alpha_0 + x_1\alpha_1).$$

One such quadratic is

(iv) $$\Phi(x) = \tfrac{1}{2}x'Hx$$

where

$$H = G'(GX)^{-1}G$$

and

(v) $$X = (x_0, x_1), \quad G = \begin{pmatrix} g_0 \\ g_1 \end{pmatrix},$$

the matrix GX *being symmetric by (i) and regular by (ii). This quadratic has the property*

(vi) $$\Phi(x) = \Phi(ex)$$

where

(vii) $$e = X(GX)^{-1}G$$

is such that $e^2 = e$ *and is the projector onto the space* X *spanned by* x_0, x_1 *parallel to the orthogonal complement of the space* G *spanned by* g_0, g_1.

The necessity of (i) and the conclusion (iii) are immediate

from general properties of a homogeneous quadratic.

The gradient of the quadratic $\Phi(x)$ given by (iv) is

$$G(x) = x'H.$$

It will be shown that

$$G(x_0) = g_0, \quad G(x_1) = g_1.$$

For any $\alpha = \begin{pmatrix} \alpha_0 \\ \alpha_1 \end{pmatrix}$, denote

$$x_\alpha = x_0\alpha_0 + x_1\alpha_1 = X\alpha,$$

$$g_\alpha = \alpha_0 g_0 + \alpha_1 g_1 = \alpha' G.$$

Then it suffices to show that

$$G(x_\alpha) = g_\alpha.$$

Thus, by (i) GX is symmetric, so

$$GX = (GX)' = X'G'.$$

and hence

$$\begin{aligned} G(x_\alpha) &= x_\alpha' H \\ &= \alpha' X' G' (GX) \quad G \\ &= \alpha' GX (GX) \quad G \\ &= \alpha' G \\ &= g_\alpha, \end{aligned}$$

as required.

It is immediate that e given by (vii) is idempotent, $e^2 = e$. Therefore it is the projector onto its range R_e parallel its null space N_e. But

$$\begin{aligned} R_e &= [x : x = ey] \\ &= [x : x = X(GX)^{-1}Gy] \\ &\subset [x : x = Xz] = X. \end{aligned}$$

Thus $R_e \subset X$. But also

$$e_X = X(GX)^{-1}GX$$
$$= X,$$

which shows that $X \subset R_e$. Hence $R_e = X$. Also

$$N_e = [x : ex = 0]$$
$$= [x : x(GX)^{-1}Gx = 0]$$
$$\subset [x : Gx = 0] = \bar{G}$$

where $\bar{G}$ is the orthogonal complement of G. Thus $N_e \subset \bar{G}$. But R_e is of dimension 2, so N_e is of dimension $n - 2$, and $\bar{G}$ has the same dimension since G is of dimension 2. But a linear space has no proper subspaces of equal dimension, so it follows that $N_e = \bar{G}$.

Finally, with GX symmetric, it is verified directly that $e'He = H$ and from this (vi) follows.

THEOREM 7. *For* $x_0, x_1 \in R^n$ *and* $g_0, g_1 \in R_n$, *and*

$X = (x_0, x_1)$, $G = \begin{bmatrix} g_0 \\ g_1 \end{bmatrix}$, *let*

$$GX = \begin{pmatrix} g_0x_0 & g_0x_1 \\ g_1x_0 & g_1x_1 \end{pmatrix}$$

be symmetric and regular and such that $GX > 0$ *or* $GX < 0$. *Then there exists a homogeneous quadratic which is quasiconcave near* x_0, x_1 *and at* x_0, x_1 *has gradient* g_0, g_1 *if and only if*

$$\Phi(x) = \tfrac{1}{2}x'Hx,$$

where

$$H = G'(GX)^{-1}G,$$

is one such quadratic, and this is if and only if

$$|GX| < 0, \quad \textit{if} \quad GX > 0,$$

and

$$|GX| > 0, \quad if \quad GX < 0.$$

The gradient of Φ is $G(x) = x'H$, so the values at x, x are given by $X'H$. But since GX is symmetric this is G. Thus

$$G(x_0) = g_0, \quad G(x_1) = g_1.$$

For $\alpha = \begin{pmatrix} \alpha_0 \\ \alpha_1 \end{pmatrix}$, let

$$x_\alpha = x_0\alpha_0 + x_1\alpha_1 = X\alpha,$$

$$g_\alpha = \alpha_0 g_0 + \alpha_1 g_1 = \alpha' G,$$

so now

$$G(x_\alpha) = g_\alpha = \alpha' G$$

$$\Phi(x_\alpha) = \tfrac{1}{2}G(x_\alpha)x_\alpha = \tfrac{1}{2}\alpha' GX\alpha.$$

Let

$$V = [x_\alpha : \alpha \geqq 0],$$

so this is the convex cone generated by x_0, x_1 excluding the origin. Also let W be the carrier linear space. Then

$$\Phi(x) > 0 \quad \text{or} \quad < 0 \quad (x \in V)$$

according as

$$GX > 0 \quad \text{or} \quad < 0.$$

The same condition is preserved in some neighbourhood N of any point of V. Hence (section 7), Φ is quasiconcave in N if and only if for all $x, y \in N$

$$D(x, y) < 0 \quad \text{or} \quad > 0.$$

Correspondingly, where

$$D(x, y) = \begin{vmatrix} G(x)x & G(x)y \\ G(y)x & G(y)y \end{vmatrix}$$

$$= \left| \begin{pmatrix} G(x) \\ G(y) \end{pmatrix} (x, y) \right|.$$

Now, for any

$$C = (\alpha, \beta) = \begin{pmatrix} \alpha_0, & \beta_0 \\ \alpha_I, & \beta_1 \end{pmatrix},$$

$$D(x_\alpha, x_\beta) = \left| \begin{pmatrix} \alpha'G \\ \beta'G \end{pmatrix} (x\alpha, x\beta) \right|$$

$$= \left| \begin{pmatrix} \alpha' \\ \beta' \end{pmatrix} GX(\alpha, \beta) \right|$$

$$= |C|^2 |GX|,$$

so, provided $|C| \neq 0$, which is the condition for x_α, x_β to be independent

$$D(x, y) < 0 \quad \text{or} \quad > 0 \quad (x, y \in W)$$

if and only if

$$|GX| < 0 \quad \text{or} \quad > 0$$

correspondingly.

The required condition can now be deduced near any point of V, or in a neighbourhood N which can be chosen to include any closed set in N.

With $e = X(GX)^{-1}G$, for any x

$$ex = X\alpha = x_\alpha, \quad \text{where} \quad \alpha = (GX)^{-1}Gx,$$

so $ex \in V$. Then also

$$\Phi(x) = \Phi(ex) = \Phi(x_\alpha),$$

so

$$G(x) = G(ex) = G(x_\alpha),$$

and further

$$G(x)y = G(ex)ey = G(x_\alpha)x_\beta$$

where similarly $ey = x_\beta$. Thus for any x, y

$$D(x, y) = D(ex, ey) \text{ and } ex, ey \in W.$$

Thus the condition on D in respect to W holds also everywhere. Therefore it holds in N. Hence Φ is quasiconcave in N as required.

THEOREM 8. *A necessary and sufficient condition for the quadratic consistency of a pair of linear expansion segments* (K_0, p_0), (K_1, p_1) *with a unique pair of neutral points* c_0, c_1 *is that, with*

$$D = \begin{pmatrix} p_0(x_0 - c_0), & p_0(x_1 - c_1) \\ p_1(x_0 - c_0), & p_1(x_1 - c_1) \end{pmatrix},$$

either $D > 0$, $|D| < 0$ *for all* x_0, x_1 *in* K_0, K_1 *or* $D < 0$, $|D| > 0$ *for all* x_0, x_1 *in* K_0, K_1.

The conditions have been seen to be necessary, so it remains to show the sufficiency.

Let R be the span of p_0, p_1 and N its orthogonal complement. Then $c_0 - c_1$ belongs to N; equivalently, a translation C of N contains c_0, c_1 and hence also the line joining them. Thus p_0c, p_1c have fixed values for all $c \in C$. Let x_0, x_1 be any points in K_0, K_1 different from c_0, c_1 and let c be any point of C. Quadratic consistency requires

$$p_0(x_1 - c)p_1(x_0 - c) > 0.$$

Then it is possible to determine $\lambda_0, \lambda_1 > 0$ such that

$$\lambda_0 p_0(x_1 - c) = \lambda_1 p_1(x_0 - c)$$

independent of the particular c in C. Let

$$g_0 = \lambda_0 p_0, \quad g_1 = \lambda_1 p_1$$

and

$$G = \begin{pmatrix} g_0 \\ g_1 \end{pmatrix}, \quad X = (x_0, x_1), \quad I = (1, 1)$$

so

$$X - cI = (x_0 - c, \quad x_1 - c).$$

Then

$$|G(X - cI)| = \lambda_0 \lambda_1 |D|$$

so $G(X - cI)$ is regular since $\lambda_0, \lambda_1 > 0$ and $|D| \neq 0$. Also it is symmetric by the choice of λ_0, λ_1. Hence

$$H = G'(G(X - cI))^{-1}G$$

is defined and symmetric, and the range and null space are R and N. Then the quadratic

$$\Phi(x) = \tfrac{1}{2}(x - c)'H(x - c),$$

with gradient

$$G(x) = (x - c)'H,$$

is independent of the choice of $c \in C$ and has C as its central axis. Also

$$G(x_0) = g_0, \quad G(x_1) = g_1$$

and

$$\Phi(x_0) = \Phi_0, \quad \Phi(x_1) = \Phi_1$$

where

$$\Phi_0 = \tfrac{1}{2}\lambda_0 p_0(x_0 - c), \quad \Phi_1 = \tfrac{1}{2}\lambda_1 p_1(x_1 - c).$$

If the elements of $G(X - cI)$ are negative and its determinant is positive then it is negative definite, so H is negative definite and $\Phi(x)$ is concave. Also

$$x \in K_0 \Rightarrow G(x) = \lambda p_0, \quad \lambda > 0 \Rightarrow G(x) \geqq 0$$

and similarly

$$x \in K_1 \Rightarrow G(x) \geqq 0.$$

It follows that $\Phi(x)$ is compatible with (K_0, p_0), (K_1, p_1). In the other case $G(X - cI)$ has its elements positive and its determinant negative. This is necessary and sufficient that $\Phi(x)$ be quasiconcave in a convex neighbourhood containing x_0, x_1 and hence also in the cone projecting x_0, x_1 from C, which includes K_0, K_1 so again $\Phi(x)$ is compatible with (K_0, p_0), (K_1, p_1).

Bibliography

Afriat, S.N. *Theory of Economic Index Numbers.* Department of Applied Economics, Cambridge, 1956 (mimeograph).

__________ The Cost of Living Index. Research Memoranda Nos. 24 (March 1961), 27 (April 1961), and 29 (August 1961). Econometric Research Program, Princeton University. Presented at the Stillwater Meeting of the Econometric Society, August 1961. Partial abstract in *Econometrica* 30, 2 (1962): 357. No. 29 published in *Studies in Mathematical Economics in Honor of Oskar Morgenstern,* ed. by Martin Shubik, Chapter 23, 335-365. Princeton University Press, 1967.

__________ The Theory of Comparisons of Real Income and Prices. In D.J. Daly (ed.), *International Comparisons of Prices and Output,* Proceedings of the National Bureau of Economic Research Conference at York University, Toronto, 1970. Studies in Income and Wealth, Vol. 37, 13-84. Columbia University Press, 1972.

__________ *The Price Index.* 1976; Cambridge University Press, forthcoming.

Banerjee, Kali S.: *Cost of Living Index Numbers.* New York: Marcel Dekker, 1975.

Buscheguennce, S.S.: Sur une classe des hypersurfaces: à propos de 'l'index idéal' de M. Irving Fischer. *Recueil Mathématique* (Moscow) 32 (1925), 625-631. (Russian title: Byushgens, S.S., Ob odnom klasse giperpoverkhnostey: po povodu 'idealnovo indeksa' Irving Fischer' a pokupatelnoi sili deneg. *Mathematischeskii Sbornik* 32 (1925), 625-631.)

Shubik, M. (editor): *Studies in Mathematical Economics in Honor of Oskar Morgenstern.* Princeton University Press, 1967.

Ulmer, M.J. *The Economic Theory of Cost of Living Index Numbers.* New York: Columbia University Press, 1949.

Wald, A.: A New Formula for the Index of the Cost of Living. *Econometrica* 7, 4 (1939), 319-335.

Additions to bibliography:

Afriat, S.N. *Combinatorial Theory of Demand.* London: Input-Output Publ. Co., 1976 (Occasional Paper No. 1).

An Extension and Alternative Proof of Gorman's Price Aggregation Theorem

by Charles Blackorby, Daniel Primont, and R.Robert Russell

1. Introductory Remarks

In his classic paper on price aggregation, Gorman [1959] established necessary and sufficient conditions for the existence of ("perfect") price aggregates -- i.e., price indices, $\Pi^1(P^1),\ldots,\Pi^m(P^m)$, satisfying

$$\text{(i)} \qquad y_r = \hat{\Theta}^r(\Pi^1(P^1),\ldots,\Pi^m(P^m),y), \quad r=1,\ldots,m,$$

where P^r, y_r, and $\hat{\Theta}^r$ are, respectively, the price vector, expenditure allocation, and allocation function for the rth sector and y is total expenditure. Gorman's conditions exploit the structure,

$$\text{(ii)} \qquad U(X) = \sum_{r=1}^{d} U^r(X^r) + \hat{U}(U^{d+1}(X^{d+1}),\ldots,U^m(X^m)),$$

where X^r is the quantity vector in the rth sector, the aggregator functions U^r, $r=1,\ldots,d$, have the "generalized Gorman polar form",

$$\underset{X^r}{\text{Max}} \{U^r(X^r) | P^r \cdot X^r \leq y_r\} = \Psi^r\left(\frac{y_r}{\Pi^r(P^r)}\right) + \Lambda^r(P^r),$$

and the functions U^r, $r=d+1,\ldots,m$, are homothetic ($\Lambda^r(P^r) \equiv 0$, $r=d+1,\ldots,m$).

Gorman shows (given certain maintained regularity assumptions) that the structure (ii) is sufficient for price aggregation (i) for arbitrary d and m. He also shows that, if U is weakly separable, if there are at least three groups in the partition ($m \geq 3$), and if not precisely m-1 of the aggregator functions are homothetic ($d \neq 1$), price aggregation implies that the utility function can be written with the structure (ii). Gorman [1959, p. 478] concludes that the structure (ii) and the concomitant restrictions on the aggregator functions "<u>are a set of sufficient conditions for perfect price aggregates</u> though they may not be necessary in the two special cases cited."

The "two special cases" are, of course, the two-group case ($m=2$) and the case where all but one of the aggregator functions is homothetic ($d=1$). In fact, both of these exceptions are attributable to the two-group anomaly in the relationship between strong separability and (groupwise) additivity.* It is well known that, if there are only two groups, weak and strong separability coincide and the equivalence of strong separability and additivity is breached. For this reason, Gorman's necessity proof, which establishes strong separability and hence (given $m \geq 3$ and $d \neq 1$) additivity, does not

---

*If $d=1$, the structure (ii) entails two group additivity:

$$U(X) = U^1(X^1) + \tilde{U}(X^2,\ldots,X^m)$$

where, of course,

$$\tilde{U}(X^2,\ldots,X^m) = \hat{U}(U^2(X^2),\ldots,U^m(X^m)).$$

go through in either of the two-group cases (m=2 and d=1).

The principal purpose of this note is to extend Gorman's results to both of these two-group cases. Our (necessity) proof cannot, in the two-group cases, exploit the properties of strong separability. Rather, the properties of the functional structure itself are exploited. Consequently, our proof is quite different from Gorman's and may be instructive in and of itself.

Section II lays out our notation, fundamental definitions, and assumptions. Section III develops the notions of direct and indirect conditional utility functions, which play an important role in the proofs that follow. Section IV states and proves our basic theorem on the existence of price aggregates and Section V states and proves a dual theorem on quantity aggregation. Section VI concludes the paper.

II. PRELIMINARIES

Let Ω^n and Ω^n_+ be the nonnegative and strictly positive Euclidean n-orthants, respectively. Denote commodity bundles by $X = [x_1,\ldots,x_n] \in \Omega^n$, and corresponding price vectors by $P = [p_1,\ldots,p_n] \in \Omega^n_+$. Letting the strictly positive scalar y represent consumer expenditure, $P/y \in \Omega^n_+$ is the normalized price vector.

The variable indices of X and P form the set $I = \{1,\ldots,n\}$. Partition I into m subsets or sectors, $\{I^1,\ldots,I^m\}$. Correspondingly, the vectors X and P have decompositions, $X = [X^1,\ldots,X^m]$ and $P = [P^1,\ldots,P^m]$. Similarly, Ω^n and Ω^n_+ have Cartesian decompositions

$\Omega^n = \Omega^{(1)} \times \ldots \times \Omega^{(m)}$ and $\Omega_+ = \Omega_+^{(1)} \times \ldots \times \Omega_+^{(m)}$ where, of course, the dimensionality of $\Omega^{(r)}$ and $\Omega_+^{(r)}$ is given by the cardinality of I^r. When the kth good or price is in the rth sector, x_k is a component of $X^r \in \Omega^{(r)}$ and p_k is a component of $P^r \in \Omega_+^{(r)}$.

Let $U: \Omega^n \to \mathbb{R}$ be a continuous, semi-strictly quasi-concave,* nondecreasing utility function, and let $V: \Omega_+^n \to \mathbb{R}$, defined by

$$V(P/y) = \max_X \{U(X) \,|\, \tfrac{P}{y} \cdot X \le 1\},$$

be the corresponding indirect utility function. Given the properties of U, V is necessarily continuous, semi-strictly quasi-convex, and nonincreasing.

Partition I into I^r and I^c by letting $I^c = \bigcup_{s \neq r} I^s$ and define the mapping, $\beta^r: \Omega^n \to \mathcal{P}(\Omega^{(r)})$, by**

$$\beta^r(X^r, X^c) = \{\hat{X}^r \in \Omega^{(r)} \,|\, U(\hat{X}^r, X^c) \ge U(X^r, X^c)\}.$$

---

*Semi-strict quasi-concavity is defined by

$$U(X) > U(\hat{X}) \Rightarrow U(\lambda X + (1-\lambda)\hat{X}) > U(\hat{X}),\ \forall \lambda \in (0,1),\ \forall (X, \hat{X}) \in \Omega^n \times \Omega^n.$$

This assumption implies that upper level sets are convex (but not necessarily strictly convex). It also precludes "thick" indifference sets except possibly for a single thick indifference set corresponding to an unconstrained maximal utility level. Semi-strict quasi-convexity is defined by reversing the above inequalities.

**$\mathcal{P}(\Omega^{(r)})$ is the power set of $\Omega^{(r)}$.

This correspondence therefore defines a set of points in $\Omega^{(r)}$ for each fixed reference vector (X^r, X^c) such that each point in $\beta^r(X^r, X^c) \times \{X^c\}$ is "no worse than" (X^r, X^c). The set of variables, I^r, is <u>separable</u> from the kth variable in U if $\beta^r(X^r, X^c)$ is invariant with respect to the value of the kth variable, x_k. This separability condition - due to Stigum [1967] - is equivalent to Gorman's [1968] condition that "the conditional ordering on $[\Omega^{(r)}]$ is the same for all" values of x_k.

Similarly, the set I^r is separable from the kth variable in V, $k \notin I^r$, if the mapping, $\alpha^r\colon \Omega^n_+ \to P(\Omega^{(r)}_+)$, defined by

$$\alpha^r\left(\frac{P^r}{y}, \frac{P^c}{y}\right) = \left\{\frac{\hat{P}^r}{y} \in \Omega^{(r)}_+ \,\middle|\, V\left(\frac{\hat{P}^r}{y}, \frac{P^c}{y}\right) \leq V\left(\frac{P^r}{y}, \frac{P^c}{y}\right)\right\},$$

is independent of the value of the kth normalized price p_k/y.

Consumer preferences are <u>directly strongly separable</u>* if every proper subset of the partition $\hat{I} = \{I^1, \ldots, I^m\}$ is separable from its complement in U; i.e., the union of any number of sectors is separable from the variables in the remaining sectors. Preferences are <u>directly weakly separable</u> if every sector, I^r, is separable in U from the variables in all the other sectors.

---

*That is, strongly separable "in the indicated partition of I." This phrase is implicitly included in all of our discussion of separable structures.

Results of Debreu [1959] and Gorman [1968] characterize the forms of the utility functions implied by these symmetric structures. If $m > 2$,* preferences are directly strongly separable if and only if there exist continuous, semi-strictly quasi-concave functions, $\tilde{U}, U^1, U^2, \ldots, U^m$, such that the utility function image can be written as

$$U(X^1, \ldots, X^m) = \tilde{U}(U^1(X^1) + \ldots + U^m(X^m)),$$

where U is increasing in its single argument and each U^r is non-decreasing in X^r. Of course, U can be normalized so that

$$U(X) = U^1(X^1) + \ldots + U^m(X^m).$$

Preferences are directly weakly separable if and only if there exist continuous, semi-strictly quasi-concave functions, $\hat{U}, U^1, \ldots, U^m$, such that the utility function image can be written as

$$U(X^1, \ldots, X^m) = \hat{U}(U^1(X^1), \ldots, U^m(X^m))$$

where $\hat{U}$ is increasing in each of its m arguments and each U^r is non-decreasing in X^r. If a function is weakly separable and each of the category functions is homothetic, the function is said to be <u>homothetically separable</u>. If the function is homothetically separable, each category felicity function may be trivially normalized to be positively linearly homogeneous (PLH).

---

*If m=2, weak and strong separability coincide and the following additive representation does not go through.

Indirect weak and strong separability are defined analogously to direct weak and strong separability by replacing the direct utility function U with the indirect utility function V and X with P/y. Thus, if m > 2, indirect strong separability is equivalent to the existence of continuous, semi-strictly quasi-concave, nondecreasing functions, $V^1,\ldots,V^m$, and a continuous, decreasing function $\tilde{V}$ such that

$$V(P/y) = \tilde{V}\left(\sum_{r=1}^{m} V^r(P^r/y)\right) .^*$$

Indirect weak separability is equivalent to the existence of continuous, semi-strictly quasi-concave, nondecreasing functions, $V^1,\ldots,V^m$, and a continuous, semi-strictly quasi-convex, decreasing function, $\hat{V}$, such that

$$V(P/y) = \hat{V}(V^1(P^1/y),\ldots,V^m(P^m/y)).$$

The notion of indirect homothetic separability is analagous to direct homothetic separability discussed above.

In general, direct and indirect separability do not imply one another. However, U is homothetically separable if and only if V is negatively homothetically separable.**

---

*Obviously the representation could be renormalized so that $\hat{V}$ is increasing and each V^r is nonincreasing.

**See Blackorby, Primont, and Russell [1975] for a proof of this result, which was previously proved under stronger regularity conditions by Lau [1969].

III. CONDITIONAL UTILITY FUNCTIONS

In our proof of the extended Gorman theorem, we exploit a representation of the preference ordering in which a conditional optimization is imbedded. This function, which we refer to as a conditional (indirect) utility function, is closely related to the aggregate utility function of Hicks' [1946] "composite commodity" theorem and has been analyzed by Gorman [1953], Diewert [1973], and Epstein [1975]. In our analysis of quantity aggregation in Section V, we exploit the dual to this function, referred to as the conditional direct utility function.

The conditional indirect utility function, $H:\Omega^m \times \Omega_+^n \to \mathbb{R}$, is defined by

$$H({}_1y,P) = \{\text{Max } U(X)\,|\,P^r \cdot X^r \leq y_r,\ r=1,\ldots,m\}, \tag{1}$$

where ${}_1y=[y_1,\ldots,y_m]$ is a vector of (undetermined) "category incomes." The conditional utility function inherits the properties of U in ${}_1y$ and the properties of V in P^r, r=1,...,m. Furthermore, H is continuous in $({}_1y,P)$ and homogeneous of degree zero (HDO) in each pair (y_r,P^r). Finally, to any H with these properties there corresponds a utility function satisfying the above stated regularity conditions. (See Diewert [1973] and Epstein [1975] for proofs of these duality results.) In addition note that if the sectors $I^2, I^3,\ldots,I^m$ are empty, H becomes, as a special case, the indirect utility function.

Solving the problem

$$\underset{{}_1y}{\text{Max}}\ H({}_1y,P) \text{ s.t. } \sum_{r=1}^{m} y_r \leq y \wedge {}_1y \in \Omega^m$$

yields the vector valued income allocation correspondence $\Theta = (\Theta^1,\ldots,\Theta^m)$, with images

$$y_r = \Theta^r(P,y),\ r=1,\ldots,m.$$

Substituting these images into H generates the indirect utility function (in nonnormalized prices and expenditure),*

$$W(P,y) = H(\Theta(P,y),P).$$

Just as H is dual to U, we can define the conditional direct utility function, $G:\Omega^m\times\Omega^n\to \mathbb{R}$, which is dual to $\overset{*}{V}$, the extension by lower continuity of the indirect utility function to Ω^n, by**

$$(2)\qquad G({}_1y/y,X) = \underset{P/y}{\text{Min}}\{\overset{*}{V}(P/y)\,|\,(P^r/y)\cdot X^r \leq (y_r/y),\ r=1,\ldots,m\}.$$

The conditional direct utility function inherits the properties of V in ${}_1y/y$ and the properties of U in X^r, r=1,...,m. In addition G is jointly continuous in $({}_1y/y,X)$ and homogeneous of degree zero in each pair $(y_r/y,X^r)$. The proofs of these assertions parallel the arguments of Diewert [1973] and Epstein [1975] for the properties of H.

---

*If $\Theta(P,y)$ is a nondegenerate set, an arbitrary element of the image will do.

**This extension is required in order to compactify the constraint set in the optimization problem that defines G. See Diewert [1974] for a discussion of extension by lower continuity of the indirect utility function.

If m=1, in which case $y_1/y=1$, G is the direct utility function.

Solving

$$\text{(3)} \qquad \operatorname*{Min}_{{}_1y/y} \; G({}_1y/y,X) \text{ s.t. } \sum_r \frac{y_r}{y} \leq 1$$

yields the "share imputation" correspondences γ^r, r=1,...,m, with images

$$\text{(4)} \qquad \frac{y_r}{y} = \gamma^r(X), \quad r=1,\ldots,m.$$

Substituting arbitrary elements of these images into (3) yields the direct utility function. We can alternatively write

$$\text{(5)} \qquad y_r = y\gamma^r(X) = \eta^r(X,y), \quad r=1,\ldots,m,$$

where η^r, the rth sector imputation correspondence, is PLH in y.

In order to examine separability properties of the direct and indirect conditional utility functions, it is useful to introduce the notation $R = \{1,\ldots,m\}$ for the set of group (and group expenditure) indices. Further, $\hat{RI} = \{\{1\}\cup I^1,\ldots,\{m\}\cup I^m\}$ is a partition of $R\cup I$ that is induced by the partition $\hat{I}$ of I. Separability of $\{r\}\cup I^r$ from a variable in its complement (relative to $R\cup I$) is defined analogously to separability in the direct and indirect utility functions. Structures induced by separability -- all with respect to the partition $\hat{RI}$ -- in the direct and indirect conditional utility functions are as follows:

Weak separability of H:

$$\text{(6)} \qquad H({}_1y,P) = \hat{H}(h^1(y_1,P^1),\ldots,h^m(y_m,P^m)).$$

Strong separability of H (m>2):

$$H({}_1y,P) = \tilde{H}\left(\sum_{r=1}^{m} h^r(y_r,P^r)\right). \tag{7}$$

Weak separability of G:

$$G({}_1y/y,X) = \hat{G}(g^1(y_1/y, X^1),\ldots,g^m(y_m/y,X^m)). \tag{8}$$

Strong separability of G (m>2):

$$G({}_1y/y,X) = \tilde{G}\left(\sum_{r=1}^{m} g^r(y_r/y,X^r)\right). \tag{9}$$

The h^r and g^r (r=1,...,m) functions in the above representations inherit the properties of H and G, respectively, and $\hat{H}$, $\tilde{H}$, $\hat{G}$, and $\tilde{G}$ are continuous, semi-strictly quasi-concave, and increasing.

The following theorem has been proved by Blackorby, Primont, and Russell [1977a].

Theorem 1: Suppose that U is continuous, semi-strictly quasi-concave, and nondecreasing. The indirect (respectively direct) conditional utility function is weakly (respectively strongly) separable in the partition $\hat{RI}$ if and only if the direct (indirect) utility function is weakly (strongly) separable in the corresponding partition $\hat{I}$.

The direct and indirect conditional utility functions and their properties are very instrumental in proving the theorems on price and quantity aggregation. For the same purpose, it will be useful to consider additional restrictions on these functions. If the functions h^r, $r=1,\ldots,m$, satisfy

$$h^r(y_r, P^r) = \Psi^r\left(\frac{y_r}{\Pi^r(P^r)}\right) + \Lambda^r(P^r) \tag{10}$$

where Π^r is PLH, Λ^r is HDO, and Ψ^r is increasing, we say that the aggregator function U^r has the generalized Gorman polar form (Gorman [1959]).* Note that the properties of Π^r and Λ^r imply that

$$h^r(y_r/y, P^r/y) = \Psi^r\left(\frac{y_r/y}{\Pi^r(P^r/y)}\right) + \Lambda^r(P^r/y). \tag{11}$$

Similarly, treating P^r/y as dual to X^r and y_r/y as self-dual, we say that the indirect utility aggregator V^r has the generalized Gorman form if

$$g^r(y_r/y, X^r) = \Xi^r\left(\frac{y_r/y}{\Gamma^r(X^r)}\right) + \chi^r(X^r), \tag{12}$$

where Γ^r is PLH, χ^r is HDO, and Ξ^r is decreasing. We refer to (11) and (12) as "structural duals" since they are obtained by imposing the same structure on the dual functions G and H (with respect to the dual variables $(X, {}_1y/y)$ and $(P/y, {}_1y/y)$). They are not duals in the sense of representing the same class of preferences; the Gorman polar form structure does not have the same implications for consumer preferences as does the Gorman form structure.

---

*The ordinary Gorman polar form is generated by letting Ψ be the identity function (Gorman [1961]).

IV. PRICE AGGREGATION

In the spirit of Gorman's classic paper [1959], we formally define Gorman price aggregation with respect to the partition $\hat{I}$ as the existence of PLH functions,

$$\Pi^r : \Omega_+^{(r)} \to \Omega_+^1, \; r=1,\ldots,m,$$

and PLH income allocation functions,

$$\hat{\Theta}^r : \bigtimes_{r=1}^{m} R(\Pi^r) \times \Omega_+^1 \to \Omega^1, \; r=1,\ldots,m,^*$$

such that

$$y_r = \hat{\Theta}^r(\Pi^1(P^1),\ldots,\Pi^m(P^m),y), \; r=1,\ldots,m. \tag{13}$$

Proof of the price aggregation theorem requires a preliminary result. Price aggregation concerns solutions to the problem

$$\underset{{}_1y}{\text{Max}} \; H({}_1y,P) \text{ s.t. } \sum_{r=1}^{m} y_r = y$$

and the conditions under which they have the form in (13). To lighten the notation let

$$f(q,z) = H({}_1y,P) \text{ for } q\varepsilon\Omega^m, \; z\varepsilon\Omega^n,$$

and consider the slightly more general problem:

$$\underset{q\varepsilon\Omega^m}{\text{Max}} \; f(q,z) \text{ s.t. } b\cdot q = c \tag{14}$$

where $b = (b_1,\ldots,b_m)\varepsilon\Omega_+^m$ and $c\varepsilon\Omega_+^1$.

$^*R(\Pi^r)$ is the range of Π^r.

Suppose the solution to (14) has the form

$$q = \phi(b,c,\rho^1(z^1),\ldots,\rho^m(z^m)) = \phi(b,c,\rho(z)) \tag{15}$$

(where $\rho(z)$ is the m-tuple of images $(\rho^1(z^1),\ldots,\rho^m(z^m))$. In this case the choice function, ϕ, for fixed values of b and c, is weakly separable in some partition of the set of n variable indices of z. Intuitively, this must mean that the maximand f possesses some structural property that is reflected in the form of the choice function. Our intuition is justified in the following:

Lemma: Suppose the (indirect) function $v:\Omega^{m+1} \times \Omega^n \to \mathbb{R}$ defined by

$$v(b,c,z) = f(\phi(b,c,\rho(z)),z) = \max_q\{f(q,z) \mid b\cdot q = c\},$$

is continuously differentiable in b and c. Then the solution to (14) has the form in (15) if and only if there exist functions, $g:\Omega^m \times \Omega^m \to \mathbb{R}$ and $h:\Omega^n \to \mathbb{R}$, such that

$$f(q,z) = g(q,\rho(z)) + h(z). \tag{16}$$

Proof:* Maximizing (16) subject to $b\cdot q = c$ clearly gives (15) since the optimal solution for q is independent of the value of h(z). To prove the converse, apply Roy's Theorem to the indirect function v for a fixed point $\rho(z)\in\Omega^m$ to get

$$q_i = \phi_i(b,c,\rho(z)) = \frac{-\partial v(b,c,a)/\partial b_i}{\partial v(b,c,a)/\partial c}, \quad i = 1,\ldots,m.$$

---

*This proof appears in Blackorby, Primont, and Russell [1977a] but, because of its shortness and the importance of the result in what follows, we repeat it here for completeness.

Hence gradients of level sets of v have components

$$\frac{\partial v/\partial b_i}{\partial v/\partial b_j} = \frac{\phi_i(b,c,\rho(z))}{\phi_j(b,c,\rho(z))} .$$

Integration over b and c yields

$$v(b,c,z) = w(b,c,\rho(z)) + h(z)$$

where h(z) is a constant of integration which, in general, depends on z. Noting that v is homogeneous of degree zero in (b,c), we can write

$$v(b,c,z) = \hat{v}(b/c,z)$$

and

$$w(b,c,\rho(z)) = \hat{w}(b/c,\rho(z)).$$

Finally,

$$f(q,z) = \underset{b/c}{\text{Min}}\{\hat{v}(b/c,z)|\frac{b}{c}\cdot q \leqq 1\}$$

$$= \underset{b/c}{\text{Min}}\{\hat{w}(b/c,\rho(z)) + h(z)|\frac{b}{c}\cdot q \leqq 1\}$$

$$= g(q,\rho(z)) + h(z).||$$

We are now prepared to state and prove our main result.

Theorem 2: Suppose that the utility function U is continuous, semi-strictly quasi-concave, and nondecreasing. Then price aggregation is possible if the image of U can be written

(17) $$U(X) = \overset{*}{U}\left(\sum_{r=1}^{d} U^r(X^r) + \hat{U}(U^{d+1}(X^{d+1}),\ldots,U^m(X^m))\right)$$

where each U^r, r=1,...,d has the generalized Gorman polar form and each U^r, r=d+1,...,m, is homothetic. Moreover, if U is weakly separable with respect to $\hat{I}$ and the conditional indirect utility function H is twice differentiable, then the structure is necessary for strong price aggregation.

Proof: We first prove sufficiency of the structure (17). First note that the homothetic functions, U^r, r=d+1,...,m, can be normalized to be PLH; thus, assume that they have already been thusly normalized. The conditional indirect utility function has the image

$$H({}_1y,P) = \max_X \left\{ \overset{*}{U}\left(\sum_{r=1}^{d} U^r(X^r) + \hat{U}(U^{d+1}(X^{d+1}),\ldots,U^m(X^m))\right) \;\middle|\; X\varepsilon\Omega^n \wedge P^r\cdot X^r \leq y_r,\ r=1,\ldots,m \right\}$$

$$= \overset{*}{U}\left(\sum_{r=1}^{d} h^r(P^r,y_r) + \hat{U}(h^{d+1}(P^{d+1},y_{d+1}),\ldots,h^m(P^m,y_m))\right),$$

where, of course,

$$h^r(P^r,y_r) = \max_{X^r} \{U^r(X^r)\,|\,X^r \varepsilon\ \Omega^{(r)} \wedge P^r\cdot X^r \leq y_r\},\ r=1,\ldots,m,$$

and each h^r, r=d+1,...,m, is negatively linearly homogeneous (NLH).*
Moreover, by hypothesis, we can write

$$(18)\qquad H({}_1y,P) = \overset{*}{U}\left(\sum_{r=1}^{d} \Psi^r\left(\frac{y_r}{\Pi^r(P^r)}\right) + \Lambda^r(P^r) + \hat{U}(y_{d+1}/\Pi^{d+1}(P^{d+1}),\ldots,y_m/\Pi^m(P^m))\right)$$

where Π^r, r=d+1,...,m, are PLH functions defined by

---

*A function, f, is NLH if $f(tX) = t^{-1}f(X)$ for all $t > 0$.

$$\Pi^r(P^r) = \frac{y_r}{h^r(P^r,y_r)} = \frac{1}{h^r(P^r,1)} .$$

As $\overset{*}{U}$ is increasing, maximizing (18) subject to

$$(19) \qquad \sum_{r=1}^{m} y_r \leq y$$

is equivalent to maximizing

$$\sum_{r=1}^{d} \Psi^r\left(\frac{y_r}{\Pi^r(P^r)}\right) + \Lambda^r(P^r) + \hat{U}(y_{d+1}/\Pi^{d+1}(P^{d+1}),\ldots,y_m/\Pi^m(P^m))$$

subject to (19). But this latter problem gives the same solution as maximizing

$$\sum_{r=1}^{m} \Psi^r\left(\frac{y_r}{\Pi^r(P^r)}\right) + \hat{U}(y_{d+1}/\Pi^{d+1}(P^{d+1}),\ldots,y_m/\Pi^m(P^m))$$

subject to (19). The solution is clearly of the form

$$y_r = \hat{\Theta}^r(\Pi^1(P^1),\ldots,\Pi^m(P^m),y), \quad r=1,\ldots,m.$$

To prove the necessity condition, suppose that we are given

$$(20) \qquad y_r = \hat{\Theta}^r(\Pi^1(P^1),\ldots,\Pi^m(P^m),y), \quad r=1,\ldots,m,$$

where each $\hat{\Theta}^r$ is PLH in its m+1 arguments $\{\Pi^1(P^1),\ldots,\Pi^m(P^m),y\}$ and each Π^r is PLH in P^r. (20) is the solution to the problem

$$\max_{_1y} H(_1y,P) \quad \text{s.t.} \quad \sum_{r=1}^{m} y_r = y$$

where H is the conditional indirect utility function. By the Lemma there exist functions, say $\hat{h}$ and Λ, such that

$$H({}_1y,P) = \hat{h}(\Pi^1(P^1),\ldots,\Pi^m(P^m),{}_1y) + \Lambda(P) \tag{21}$$

By Theorem 1, weak separability of U in $\hat{I}$ implies that H is weakly separable in the corresponding partition $\widehat{RI}$; hence

$$H({}_1y,P) = \hat{H}(h^1(P^1,y_1),\ldots,h^m(P^m,y_m)). \tag{6}$$

Moreover, the aggregator functions can be taken as

$$h^r(P^r,y_r) = H(\underline{0}_1,\ldots,y_r,\ldots,\underline{0}_m,\underline{0}^1,\ldots,P^r,\ldots,\underline{0}^m), \quad r=1,\ldots,m,$$

where the $\underline{0}_s$ and $\underline{0}^s$, $s=1,\ldots,m$, $s\neq r$, are appropriate reference vectors (as described in the Gorman [1968] representation theorem). Using (21), we can also write

$$\begin{aligned} h^r(P^r,y_r) &= \hat{h}(\Pi^1(\underline{0}^1),\ldots,\Pi^r(P^r),\ldots,\Pi^m(\underline{0}^m),\underline{0}_1,\ldots,y_r,\ldots,\underline{0}_m) \\ &\quad + \Lambda(\underline{0}^1,\ldots,P^r,\ldots,\underline{0}^m) \\ &= \hat{h}(\Pi^1(\underline{0}^1),\ldots,1,\ldots,\Pi^m(\underline{0}^m),\underline{0}_1,\ldots,y_r/\Pi^r(P^r),\ldots,\underline{0}_m) \\ &\quad + \Lambda(\underline{0}^1,\ldots,P^r,\ldots,\underline{0}^m) \\ &= \Psi\left(\frac{y_r}{\Pi^r(P^r)}\right) + \Lambda^r(P^r) \end{aligned} \tag{22}$$

where the second identity follows from first degree homogeneity of Π^r and homogeneity of degree zero of H in the pair (P^r,y_r)* and where the functions, Ψ^r and Λ^r, are defined by the last identity.

---

*It is easy to show that zero degree homogeneity of H implies that Λ is HDO.

Substituting (22) into (6) yields

$$H({}_1y,P) = \hat{H}\left(\Psi^1\left(\frac{y_1}{\Pi^1(P^1)}\right) + \Lambda^1(P^1),\ldots,\Psi^m\left(\frac{y_m}{\Pi^m(P^m)}\right) + \Lambda^m(P^m)\right). \tag{23}$$

It remains to show that H implies the structure of (17). In order to show this, we first note that necessary conditions for solving

$$\max_{{}_1y} H({}_1y,P) \quad \text{s.t.} \quad \sum_{r=1}^{m} y_r \leq y$$

are

$$\frac{\partial H({}_1y,P)/\partial y_r}{\partial H({}_1y,P)/\partial y_s} = 1 \quad \forall\ r,s.$$

Because of (23), these conditions are equivalent to*

$$\frac{\hat{H}_r(\psi^1+\lambda^1,\ldots,\psi^m+\lambda^m)\cdot\Psi^{r\prime}\left(\frac{y_r}{\Pi^r(P^r)}\right)\cdot\frac{1}{\Pi^r(P^r)}}{\hat{H}_s(\psi^1+\lambda^1,\ldots,\psi^m+\lambda^m)\cdot\Psi^{s\prime}\left(\frac{y_s}{\Pi^s(P^s)}\right)\cdot\frac{1}{\Pi^s(P^s)}} = 1 \quad \forall\ r,s,$$

or

$$\frac{\hat{H}_r(\psi^1+\lambda^1,\ldots,\psi^m+\lambda^m)}{\hat{H}_s(\psi^1+\lambda^1,\ldots,\psi^m+\lambda^m)} = \frac{\Pi^r(P^r)}{\Pi^s(P^s)}\cdot\frac{\Psi^{s\prime}\left(\frac{y_s}{\Pi^s(P^s)}\right)}{\Psi^{r\prime}\left(\frac{y_r}{\Pi^r(P^r)}\right)} \quad \forall\ r,s, \tag{24}$$

where, of course,

$$\psi^r = \Psi^r\left(\frac{y_r}{\Pi^r(P^r)}\right), \quad r=1,\ldots,m,$$

$$\lambda^r = \Lambda^r(P^r), \quad r=1,\ldots,m,$$

*For a proof that $\hat{H}$ can be chosen to be differentiable (given that H is), see Blackorby, Primont, and Russell [1977b, Corollary 4.1.1].

$\hat{H}_r$ is the derivative of $\hat{H}$ with respect to the rth argument, and $\Psi^{r'}$ is the derivative of Ψ^r with respect to its one argument. Substituting in (24) for y_r and y_s using

$$y_r = \hat{\Theta}^r(\Pi^1(P^1),\ldots,\Pi^m(P^m),y), \tag{20}$$

it is apparent that the ratios in (24) are independent of $\Lambda^r(P^r)$, $r=1,\ldots,m$.

Without loss of generality, suppose that $\Lambda^r(P^r) \neq 0$, $r=1,\ldots,d$, and $\Lambda^r(P^r) = 0$, $r=d+1,\ldots,m$. As the ratios in (24) are independent of $\Lambda^r(P^r)$ for all r, it is apparent that for all r and s such that $r > d$ and $s > d$, the ratio must be independent of the qth argument in $\hat{H}$ for all $q \leq d$. Thus, the set of variables $\{d+1,\ldots,m\}$ is separable in H from the components of $\{1,\ldots,d\}$ and we can therefore aggregate over this separable set:

$$H({}_1y,P) = \bar{H}(\psi^1+\lambda^1,\ldots,\psi^d+\lambda^d,\bar{U}(\psi^{d+1},\ldots,\psi^m)). \tag{25}$$

We now consider successively four cases: (i) d=0, (ii) d=1, (iii) d=m=2, and (iv) $d \geq 2$. Establishing the structure (17) from (25) requires a somewhat different mode of argument in each case.

Case (i)(d=0): In this case, because U is weakly separable,

$$U(X) = \hat{H}(U^1(X^1),\ldots,U^m(X^m)) \tag{26}$$

where

$$U^r(X^r) = \underset{P^r}{\text{Min}}\left\{\Psi^r\left(\frac{1}{\Pi^r(P^r)}\right) \mid P^r \varepsilon \Omega_+^{(r)} \wedge P^r \cdot X^r \leq 1\right\}.^*$$

---

*This duality argument is carried out at unit category income rather than normalizing prices by y_r (exploiting the homogeneity property of h^r) since y_r could be zero, in which case P^r/y_r is undefined.

As Π^r is PLH, U^r is PLH and (26) belongs to the class (17).

Case (ii) (d=1): In this case

$$H({}_1y,P) = \bar{H}(\psi^1+\lambda^1,\ \bar{U}(\psi^2,\ldots,\psi^m)) = \bar{H}(\psi^1+\lambda^1,\mu)$$

where

$$\mu = \bar{U}(\psi^2,\ldots,\psi^m).$$

We will show that $\bar{H}$ must satisfy the Sono [1961] condition for additivity, as extended by Blackorby, Primont, and Russell [1977b]. In the notation of this theorem with d=1, we need to show that

$$(27)\qquad \frac{\partial}{\partial\psi^s}\left(\frac{\hat{H}_1(\psi^1+\lambda^1,\psi^2,\ldots,\psi^m)}{\hat{H}_r(\psi^1+\lambda^1,\psi^2,\ldots,\psi^m)}\right)\frac{\hat{H}_r(\psi^1+\lambda^1,\psi^2,\ldots,\psi^m)}{\hat{H}_1(\psi^1+\lambda^1,\psi^2,\ldots,\psi^m)} = \sigma^{rs}(\psi^2,\ldots,\psi^m),$$

$$r,s=2,\ldots,m.$$

However, from the above arguments, we know that the ratios

$$\frac{\hat{H}_1(\psi^1+\lambda^1,\psi^2,\ldots,\psi^m)}{\hat{H}_r(\psi^1+\lambda^1,\psi^2,\ldots,\psi^m)},\quad r=2,\ldots,m,$$

are themselves independent of $\psi^1+\lambda^1$. Hence (27) is trivially satisfied. Thus there exist functions, $\overset{*}{H}$, ζ, and $\hat{U}$ such that

$$H({}_1y,P) = \overset{*}{H}(\zeta(\psi^1+\lambda^1)+\hat{U}(\psi^2,\ldots,\psi^m)).$$

Moreover, as

$$\frac{\overset{*}{H}'(\zeta(\psi^1+\lambda^1)+\hat{\mu})\cdot\zeta'(\psi^1+\lambda^1)}{\overset{*}{H}'(\zeta(\psi^1+\lambda^1)+\hat{\mu})\cdot\hat{U}_r(\psi^2,\ldots,\psi^m)}$$

(where $\hat{U}_r$ is the rth partial derivative of U) is independent of λ^1, ζ must be linear. Thus, we can in fact write

$$H({}_1y,P) = \overset{*}{H}(\psi^1+\lambda^1+\hat{U}(\psi^2,\ldots,\psi^m)).$$

A construction analogous to that in case (i) yields a direct objective function which belongs to the class (17).

Case (iii) ($d = m = 2$): In this case,

$$H({}_1y,P) = \bar{H}(\psi^1+\lambda^1, \psi^2+\lambda^2)$$

and an argument much the same as that in case (ii) establishes the structure

$$H({}_1y,P) = \overset{*}{H}(\psi^1+\lambda^1+\psi^2+\lambda^2)$$

which implies the structure (17).

Case (iv) ($d \geq 2$): Note that in this case certain ratios of derivatives of $\hat{H}$ and $\bar{H}$ are related by

$$(28)\qquad \frac{\hat{H}_r(\psi^1+\lambda^1,\ldots,\psi^d+\lambda^d,\psi^{d+1},\ldots,\psi^m)}{\hat{H}_s(\psi^1+\lambda^1,\ldots,\psi^d+\lambda^d,\psi^{d+1},\ldots,\psi^m)}$$

$$= \frac{\bar{H}_r(\psi^1+\lambda^1,\ldots,\psi^d+\lambda^d,\mu)}{\bar{H}_\mu(\psi^1+\lambda^1,\ldots,\psi^d+\lambda^d,\mu)\cdot \bar{U}_s(\psi^{d+1},\ldots,\psi^m)}\ ;\ r=1,\ldots,d;s=d+1,\ldots,m,$$

where, in this case,

$$\mu = \bar{U}(\psi^{d+1},\ldots,\psi^m)$$

and $\bar{H}_\mu$ and $\bar{U}_s$ are derivatives of $\bar{H}$ and $\bar{U}$ with respect to μ and ψ^s, respectively.* From the above, we know that the left-hand side of (28) is independent of $\psi^t+\lambda^t$, $t=1,\ldots,d$; hence the right-hand side is independent of the same arguments. As $\bar{U}_s(\psi^{d+1},\ldots,\psi^m)$ is trivially independent of these arguments for all $s > d$, so are

*If $m=d\geq 2$, a simplification of this argument goes through.

$$\frac{\bar{H}_r(\psi^1+\lambda^1,\ldots,\psi^d+\lambda^d,\mu)}{\bar{H}_\mu(\psi^1+\lambda^1,\ldots,\psi^d+\lambda^d,\mu)};\ r=1,\ldots,d;\ t=1,\ldots,d;$$

hence all pairs $\{r,d+1\}$, where $d+1$ indexes μ, are separable from their complements in $\{1,\ldots,d,\ d+1\}$. Consider, for example, the pairs, $\{1,\ d+1\}$ and $\{2,\ d+1\}$, whose intersection is $\{d+1\}$. Applying the Gorman [1968] theorem on additive structures, we can write

$$\bar{H}(\psi^1+\lambda^1,\ldots,\psi^d+\lambda^d,\mu) = \tilde{H}(\psi^1+\lambda^1+\psi^2+\lambda^2+\mu,\psi^3+\lambda^3,\ldots,\psi^d+\lambda^d).$$

Note that every argument of $\tilde{H}$ is a term containing some λ^r. Hence the ratio of partial derivatives with respect to any two arguments must be independent of all other variables in $\tilde{H}$. This means that $\tilde{H}$ is strongly separable in the coordinate-wise partition of its variables. Therefore, we can write

$$H({}_1y,P) = \overset{*}{H}\left(\sum_{r=1}^{d}(\psi^r+\lambda^r) + \hat{\mu}\right)^*$$

$$=\overset{*}{H}\left(\sum_{r=1}^{d}\ \psi^r\left(\frac{y_r}{\Pi^r(P^r)}\right) + \Lambda^r(P^r)\ + \hat{U}\left(\psi^{d+1}\left(\frac{y_{d+1}}{\Pi^{d+1}(P^{d+1})}\right),\ldots,\right.\right.$$

$$\left.\left.\psi^m\left(\frac{y_m}{\Pi^m(P^m)}\right)\right)\right).$$

Finally, a construction analagous to (27) above yields the structure

$$\text{(17)}\qquad U(X) = \overset{*}{H}\left(\sum_{r=1}^{d} U^r(X^r) + \hat{U}(U^{d+1}(X^{d+1}),\ldots,U^m(X^m))\right)$$

where each

---

* $\hat{\mu} = g(\mu)$, say, and each $g^r(\psi^r+\lambda^r)$ can be assumed to be linear by the argument given in case (i) for ζ.

$$U^r(X^r) = \left\{ \underset{P^r}{\text{Min}} \ \Psi^r\left(\frac{1}{\Pi^r(P^r)}\right) + \Lambda^r(P^r) \,|\, P^r \in \Omega_+^{(r)} \wedge P^r \cdot X^r \leq 1 \right\}, \quad r=1,\ldots,d,$$

clearly has the generalized Gorman polar form and each

$$U^r(X^r) = \underset{P^r}{\text{Min}} \left\{ \Psi^r\left(\frac{1}{\Pi^r(P^r)}\right) \,|\, P^r \in \Omega_+^{(r)} \wedge P^r \cdot X^r \leq 1 \right\}, \quad r=d+1,\ldots,m,$$

is PLH, hence homothetic.||

The salient condition involving (17) in Theorem 2 is essentially a functional structure but not necessarily a separability condition. This is because of the anomalous binary partition case which arises when m=d=2 or d=1 in Equation (17). If m=d=2, (17) becomes

(29) $$U(X) = \overset{*}{U}(U^1(X^1) + U^2(X^2))$$

where U^1 and U^2 have the generalized Gorman polar forms. Assuming nonhomothetic separability in the binary partition, this structure is necessary and sufficient for price aggregation (maintaining the regularity conditions, differentiability, and weak separability) but is <u>not</u> implied by strong (equals weak) separability. Similarly, if d=1, (17) has the form (29) where U^1 has the generalized Gorman polar form and U^2 is homothetic. Again, this structure cannot be characterized by ι separability condition. If these two cases are excluded by assumption the necessary and sufficient conditions for price aggregation can be characterized by separability conditions:

<u>Corollary 2.1</u> (Gorman [1959]): Suppose that H is differentiable and that U satisfies the regularity conditions and is weakly separable in the partition $\hat{I}$ where $\hat{I}$ contains more than two elements and not

precisely m-1 of the aggregator functions of the weakly separable representation of U are homothetic. Suppose furthermore that the partition I is ordered such that all nonhomothetic sectors (if any) precede the homothetic sectors (if any). Then strong price aggregation is possible if and only if (i) U is strongly separable in the partition

$$\{I^1, \ldots, I^d, \bigcup_{r=d+1}^{m} I^r\}$$

where d is the number of nonhomothetic sectors, and each aggregator U^r, $r=1,\ldots,d$, has the generalized Gorman polar form, and (ii) the aggregator over $\bigcup_{r=d+1}^{m} I^r$ is itself weakly separable in the partition $\{I^{d+1}, \ldots, I^m\}$.

Two special cases of the sufficiency part of Theorem 2 which are perhaps most likely to be applied in practice are obtained by letting d=0 and d=m respectively.

Corollary 2.2: If U satisfies the regularity conditions, homothetic weak separability implies price aggregation.

Corollary 2.3: If U satisfies the regularity conditions, strong separability of U in a partition with more than two groups where each aggregator has the generalized Gorman polar form implies price aggregation.

V. QUANTITY AGGREGATION

Price aggregation arises naturally in an organizational structure in which a fixed total expenditure is first allocated (perhaps by a central planner) to m sectors (or divisions) and the sectoral expenditure allocations are then used to purchase commodities (or inputs) for use or consumption in the appropriate sector. The existence of Gorman price aggregates economizes on information required for the execution of the central planning problem. An alternative organizational structure is one in which the central planner announces sectoral input valuation levels and the division managers compute shadow prices, given their input allocations, to be used by the central planner in adjusting input quotas. The existence of quantity aggregates -- dual to Gorman price aggregates -- economizes on the information required for the central planning problem (see Blackorby, Primont, and Russell [1977a]).

Treating P as dual to X and ${}_1y$ and y as self-dual, the dual to Gorman price aggregation is the existence of PLH functions,

$$\Gamma^r : \Omega^{(r)} \to \Omega^1, \quad r=1,\ldots,m,$$

and imputation correspondences,

$$\eta^r : \bigtimes_{r=1}^{m} R(\Gamma^r) \times \Omega_+^1 \to \Omega^1, \quad r=1,\ldots,m,$$

such that

$$y_r = \eta^r(\Gamma^1(X^1),\ldots,\Gamma^m(X^m),y), \quad r=1,\ldots,m, \tag{30}$$

where η^r is PLH in y.

The following theorem is dual to Theorem 2:

Theorem 3: Suppose that the direct objective function U is continuous, semi-strictly quasi-concave, and nondecreasing. Then quantity aggregation is possible if the image of the indirect function V can be written

$$V(P/y) = \overset{*}{V}\left(\sum_{r=1}^{d} V^r(P^r/y) + \hat{V}(V^{d+1}(P^{d+1}/y),\ldots,V^m(P^m/y)) \right) \tag{31}$$

where each V^r, $r=1,\ldots,d$, has the generalized Gorman form (12) and each V^r, $r=d+1,\ldots,m$, is homothetic. Moreover, if V is weakly separable and the direct conditional utility function G is differentiable, the structure (31) is necessary for quantity aggregation.

Proof: The homogeneity property of η^r and Γ^r, $r=1,\ldots,m$, makes (30) equivalent to

$$\frac{y_r}{y} = \hat{\eta}^r(\Gamma^1(X^1),\ldots,\Gamma^m(X^m)), r=1,\ldots,m.$$

Thus, exploiting the duality between the direct and indirect conditional utility functions, in which X is dual to P/y and ${}_1y/y$ is self-dual to ${}_1y$, the theorem follows by duality from Theorem 2.||

Duals to Corrollaries 2.1-2.3 also hold. In particular, homothetic separability suffices for quantity aggregation as does indirect strong separability where each aggregator has the (nonhomothetic) Gorman form if there are more than two groups.

VI. CONCLUDING REMARKS

The issue of price aggregation arose in the context of the two-stage budgeting procedure introduced by Strotz [1957]. In the first stage the consumer allocates total expenditure among m groups of commodities; in the second stage he allocates each of the group expenditures, y_r, $r=1,\ldots,m$, among the commodities in that group. If the consumer can carry out the second stage for each group knowing only expenditure and prices for that group, then each of the intra-sector allocation correspondences (or conditional demand correspondences) have images:

$$X^r = \phi^r(P^r, y_r), \quad r=1,\ldots,m. \tag{32}$$

Given optimal group expenditures, these second stage allocations are optimal if and only if the utility function is weakly separable (Gorman [1971], see also Blackorby, Primont, and Russell [1977b, Theorem 5.4]). In this case the second stage is decentralizable and (32) is the solution to:

$$\max_{X^r} U^r(X^r) \text{ s.t. } P^r \cdot X^r \leq y_r, r=1,\ldots,m.$$

It is for this reason that weak separability is assumed throughout the analysis of the first stage of the budgeting process; inter-sector expenditure allocation correspondences which yield optimal sectoral expenditures would be less than appealing if these optimal sectoral expenditures were then squandered within each sector.

Decentralizability of the utility maximization problem is very useful for the purpose of econometric estimation of systems of demand equations. If the number of commodities is large,* the estimation of the complete system of (typically nonlinear) demand equations is computationally infeasible. Weak separability, and therefore decentralizability, rationalizes the estimation of a set of smaller sectoral demand systems (32).** This approach has been exploited by,

---

*If is is not, separability and aggregation are implicitly being invoked (see Blackorby, Primont, and Russell [1977b, Chapter 8]).

**Of course, the estimators of the parameters of systems of sectoral demand systems retain their optimal properties only if very restrictive assumptions are made about the error structure.

among others, Phlips [1971], Heien [1974], Pinard [1975], McMenamin [1975], Conrad [1976], and Anderson [1976]. Estimation of the remaining parameters of the complete system can then be accomplished by estimating the expenditure allocation functions of the first stage of the budgeting process, conditional upon the estimated values of the parameters of the intra-sectoral demand systems.

These first stage allocation functions in general are of the form

$$y_r = \Theta^r(P,y), \quad r=1,\ldots,m;$$

i.e., the allocations depend on all prices and on total expenditure. However, if the conditions for perfect price aggregates are met, the allocation functions have the form in (13), so that optimal sectoral expenditures depend only on total expenditure and on m sectoral price indices.

One unattractive aspect of the price aggregation concept characterized by equation (13) is that it is really nothing more than a structural characteristic of the sectoral allocation functions. The role played by the price indices in the optimization (or, more descriptively, in the organizational decision process) is not explicated by this characterization. For example, it is not necessarily true that the multiple of the rth sector price index $\Pi^r(P^r)$ and the associated quantity index $U^r(X^r)$ (evaluated at the optimal level of X^r, given P^r and y) equals the sectoral expenditure, y_r. It is well known, however, that if the sufficiency condition of Corollary 2.1 -- homothetic separability -- is satisfied, $\Pi^r(P^r)\cdot U^r(\overset{*r}{X}) = y_r$ (where $\overset{*r}{X}$ is optimal at (P^r, y_r)) for all r (Gorman [1959]).* In this case, an evocative optimization algorithm employing price and quantity indices is rationalized:

$$\text{(33)} \qquad \underset{{}_1u}{\text{Max}}\ \hat{U}(u_1,\ldots,u_m) \text{ s.t. } \sum_{r=1}^{m} \Pi^r(P^r)\cdot u_r \leq y$$

where ${}_1u = [u_1,\ldots,u_m]$. Optimal expenditure on the rth sector is then given by

$$y_r = \Pi^r(P^r)\cdot \mu^r(\Pi^1(P^1),\ldots,\Pi^m(P^m),y) = \hat{\Theta}^r(\Pi^1(P^1),\ldots,\Pi^m(P^m),y)$$

where $\mu^r(\Pi^1(P^1),\ldots,\Pi^m(P^m),y), r=1,\ldots,m$, solves (33).

Alternatively, solving

$$\text{(34)} \qquad \underset{{}_1\pi}{\text{Min}}\ V(\pi_1,\ldots,\pi_m) \text{ s.t. } \sum_{r=1}^{m} \pi^r\cdot U^r(X^r) \leq 1,$$

where ${}_1\pi = [\pi_1,\ldots,\pi_m]$, yields the structured imputation functions,

$$y_r = \nu^r(U^1(X^1),\ldots,U^m(X^m),y)\cdot U^r(X^r) = \eta^r(U^1(X^1),\ldots,U^m(X^m),y)$$
$$r=1,\ldots,m,$$

where $\nu^r(U^1(X^1),\ldots,U^m(X^m),y)$, $r=1,\ldots,m$, solves the optimization problem (34).

---

*Blackorby, Lady, Nissen, and Russell [1970] showed that (maintaining weak separability of U) homothetic separability is necessary as well as sufficient for this "adding-up" condition.

References

Anderson, R. W. [1976], Commodity Aggregation and Price Indices in Demand Analysis, Ph.D. dissertation, University of Michigan.

Blackorby, C., G. Lady, D. Nissen, and R. R. Russell [1970], "Homothetic Separability and Consumer Budgeting," Econometrica, 38, 468-472.

Blackorby, C., D. Primont, and R. R. Russell [1975], "Some Simple Remarks on Duality and the Structure of Utility Functions," Journal of Economic Theory, 11, 155-160.

_____________ [1977a], "Dual Price and Quantity Aggregation," Journal of Economic Theory, forthcoming.

_____________ [1977b], Duality, Separability, and Functional Structure; Theory and Applications, New York, American Elsevier/North Holland.

Brown, M., and D. Heien [1972], "The S-Branch Utility Tree; a Generalization of the Linear Expenditure System, Econometrica, 40, 737-747.

Conrad, K. [1976], "Dynamic Utility and Aggregator Functions for the Allocation of Private Consumption in Input-Output Models -- An Econometric Analysis", this volume.

Debreu, G. [1959], "Topological Methods in Cardinal Utility Theory," in Mathematical Methods in the Social Sciences (K. Arrow, S. Karlin, and P. Suppes, eds.), Palo Alto, Stanford University Press.

Diewert, E. W. [1973], "Hicks' Aggregation Theorem and the Existence of a Real Value Added Function," Department of Manpower and Immigration, Ottawa, forthcoming in An Econometric Approach to Production Theory (D. McFadden and M. Fuss, eds.).

Diewert, E. W. [1974], "Applications of Duality Theory," in Frontiers of Quantitative Economics, II (M. Intriligator and D. Kendrick, eds.), Amsterdam, North Holland.

Epstein, L. [1975], "A Disaggregate Analysis of Consumer Choice Under Uncertainty," Econometrica, 43, 877-892.

Gorman, W. M. [1953], "Community Preference Fields," Econometrica, 21, 63-80.

____________ [1959], "Separable Utility and Aggregation," Econometrica, 27, 469-481.

____________ [1961], "On A Class of Preference Fields," Metroeconomica, 13, 53-56.

____________ [1968], "The Structure of Utility Functions," Review of Economic Studies, 35, 369-390.

____________ [1971], "Two Stage Budgeting," unpublished paper, London School of Economics and Political Science.

Heien, D. [1974], "Some Further Results on the Estimation of the S-Branch Utility Tree," Research Discussion Paper Number 10, Price Research Division, U.S. Bureau of Labor Statistics.

Hicks, J. R. [1946], Value and Capital, Oxford.

Lau, L. J. [1969], "Duality and the Structure of Utility Functions," Journal of Economic Theory, 5, 394-396.

McMenamin, S. [1975], A Disaggregated International Linkage Model: The Supply Price Approach, Ph.D. dissertation, University of California, San Diego.

Phlips, L. [1971], "Substitution, Complementarity, and the Residual Variation Around Dynamic Demand Equations," American Economic Review, 61, 586-597.

Pinard, J. P. [1975], A Disaggregated International Linkage Model: The Profit Function Approach, Ph.D. dissertation, University of California, San Diego.

Sono, M. [1961], "The Effect of Price Changes on the Demand and Supply of Separable Goods," International Economic Review, 2, 239-271.

Stigum, B. P. [1967], "On Certain Problems of Aggregation," International Economic Review, 8, 349-367.

Strotz, R. H. [1957], "The Empirical Implications of a Utility Tree," Econometrica, 25, 269-280.

Examination of Purchasing-Power-Parity-Methods with a View to Choosing the Most Appropriate Method for a European-Community Purchasing-Power-Parity Model

by Helmut Diehl

1. Preliminary Remarks

For some time the Statistical Office of the European Communities (SOEC) has been concerned with the problem of developing a European-Community (EC) purchasing-power-parity model.[1)] From the very beginnings this model has undergone several changes in its basic conception, technical organisation, practical execution and especially in its methodology.

The most recent significant innovation was provided by the accession of the United Kingdom, Ireland and Danmark to the European Community.
The SOEC saw this event as an opportunity to rethink and modify the whole model. In this revision the methodology played an important part. The main aspects and results of the studies, which

---

[1)] A more detailed description of this model and its historical development is given by: H. Diehl: "Die Berechnung von Kaufkraftparitäten für private Verbraucher durch das Statistische Amt der Europäischen Gemeinschaften", Sonderhefte zum Allgemeinen Statistischen Archiv, Heft 10 (1976), S. 47-67.

have been undertaken in order to find the most appropriate method of price-parity calculation for the new EC-model, are reported in the present paper.[1]

II. Some Conventions, Definitions and Explanations

For the sake of simplicity the notion "price-parity" will be used in the following instead of "purchasing-power-parity" or "spatial price-index".
The basic subject "price-parity" needs some definitional clarification.

1) Elementary price-parity

In its simplest form the price parity is defined as follows: Being given 2 countries A and B with respective prices p_{iA} and p_{iB} for a specific product i, the ratio p_{iA}/p_{iB} is called the elementary price-parity of the product i for country A with respect to country B.

2) Bilateral (overall) price-parity

If there are still 2 countries A and B, but N products ($i = 1,\ldots,N$), one has N elementary price parities p_{iA}/p_{iB} ($i = 1,\ldots,N$).
In order to obtain one single measure $P_{A/B}$ for the relative overall price level of country A with respect to country B - such a measure is called a "bilateral price-parity" - one has to find an appropriate aggregation of the N elementary price-parities. This aggregation requires suitable auxiliary parameters, usually available in form of the consumption quantities q_i of each product.

---

[1] Similar studies from different viewpoints have been undertaken by:
- I.B.Kravis et al.: "A system of international comparisons of gross product and purchasing power", John Hopkins University Press (1975).
- L.Drechsler: "Weighting of index numbers in international comparisons", Review of Income and Wealth (March 1973), pp.17-34.

3) Multilateral price-parities

Having M(M>2) countries involved, one can establish a system of $\frac{1}{2}$ (M^2-M) independent bilateral price-parities, if one considers independently each possible pair of countries. This kind of consideration may be called a multiple-bilateral one.

If however one wants to have for the M countries a consistent set of only M-1 independent price-parities, one speaks of the multilateral price-parity problem. In the following we will deal with this latter multilateral form of the price-parity problem.

III. The Framework of the EC-Price-Parity-Model

The aim of the following investigation is to find for the EC-price-parity-model the most appropriate method for the price-parity calculation.

This requires the specification of the framework of the model with all its particular features and aspects which are relevant for judging the adequacy of the available methods. For this reason we formulate the following 4 families of criteria, in the light of which the various methods will be examined:

1. The basic conditions imposed by the concrete circumstances of the project.
2. Certain required properties for the price-parities, which ensure some indispensable fundamental qualities and operational consistencies.
3. Some desirable properties, the existence of which can provide certain technical facilities or theoretical elegance.
4. Some further special properties inherent to the construction principles of the methods.

1. Basic conditions: There are two basic conditions arising from the practical circumstances:

   1.1. The number of countries involved is 9 and we will deal with this situation from the multilateral viewpoint.

   1.2. As regards the list of products, for which the prices are to be surveyed, we are confronted with the fact of "missing products". This situation requires that we must operate with a system of so-called binary lists combined with a 9-countries-common list:
   The common list consists of all the products and services existing in identical or quasi-identical form in all countries. The binary lists on the other hand include products and services, which do not exist for all countries, but at least for two of them (therefore "binary lists"). This principle is adopted as a compromise in order to reconcile three incompatible requirements:

   - having a common list for the 9 countries
   - this list should be representative for all countries
   - the products and services of this list must have a high degree of comparability between the various countries.

2. Required properties: The following two properties represent strong requirements, which the price-parity-system has to fulfil absolutely. Their implications result in a more precise definition of what we called above the multilateral price-parity problem.

   2.1. The price-parity-system must be a multilateral-closed-fullscale one.

   This means: The number of countries involved (more than two) is fixed in advance; no other country can join this set and no country can leave it without disturbing the system. The comparison will be a joint and simultaneous one between all countries. Each comparison within any subgroup of countries is of the same interest.

2.2. The price-parity-system must fulfil the properties of country-reversibility (sometimes called base-country-invariance) and transitivity (also called circularity).

Country-reversibility: For any two countries A and B the price-parity $P_{A/B}$ for A with respect to B must satisfy the condition

$$(1) \quad P_{A/B} = \frac{1}{P_{B/A}} .$$

Transitivity: For any 3 countries A, B, C the condition

$$(2) \quad P_{A/B} \cdot P_{B/C} = P_{A/C}$$

must hold.

This condition ensures the existence of an overall-consistent set of only M-1 independent price parities for M countries.

3. Desirable properties: The following two properties can be fulfilled in exceptional cases only and are therefore formulated as desirable properties.

3.1 Factor-reversibility

One speaks of the existence of factor-reversibility, if for a given price-parity $P_{A/B}$ there exists an associated explicit quantity-parity $Q_{A/B}$ and both together fulfil the following two conditions:

(3) $P_{A/B}\ (p;q) = Q_{A/B}\ (q;p)$ (price-quantity-symmetry), where p and q stand for the respective price- and quantity vectors,

(4) $P_{A/B} \cdot Q_{A/B} = V_{A/B}$, where $V_{A/B}$ is the value ratio

$$\sum_i p_{iA} q_{iA} \Big/ \sum_i p_{iB} q_{iB} .$$

Factor-reversability ensures in an elegant form operational consistencies between price-parities, quantity-parities and value-ratios.

3.2. Additivity

Let the total set of products G be subdivided into k disjoint subsets $g_1,\dots,g_k$, the union of which is G. If the corresponding "total price-parity" $P_{A/B}^{(G)}$, which is calculated for the total set G, and the "partial price-parities" $P_{A/B}^{(g_r)}$, which are calculated independently for each subset g_r $(r = 1,\dots,k)$, fulfil for any pair (A,B) and any subdivision of G the condition

$$(5)\quad \sum_{i\varepsilon G} p_{iA}q_{iA} \Big/ P_{A/B}^{(G)} = \sum_{r=1}^{k} \left[\sum_{i\varepsilon g_r} p_{iA}q_{iA} \Big/ P_{A/B}^{(g_r)} \right] ,$$

one says the price parities are additive.

This property ensures that partial "deflation" of the aggregates $\sum_{i\varepsilon g_r} p_{iA}q_{iA}$ of the subset g_r and summation of the results lead to the same result as direct "deflation" of the aggregate $\sum_{i\varepsilon G} p_{iA}\,q_{iA}$ of the total set G.

Additivity is especially relevant for detailed "deflation" operations in National-Accounts-Systems and Input-Output-Tables as it provides certain internal consistencies for the corresponding transformations.

4. Special properties: The following properties can neither be formulated as required nor as desirable ones as they represent particular features of the methods resulting from their construction principles. But there is some interest in studying them carefully, because they can provide valuable indications as to the suitability of a price-parity-system for specific uses.

4.1 Does the method involve parameters, which respect the size or importance of the various countries ?

4.2 What are the particular features of the methods from economic and mathematical viewpoints ?

IV. Relevant Price-Parity-Methods for the EC-Model

The final aim of the investigations is to find among the available price-parity-methods the best one for the EC-model.

As a first step those methods have to be selected, which are relevant in the sense that they respect the basic conditions and fulfil the required properties decribed above.

For this purpose a systematic study of various methods or families of methods is undertaken with respect to the criteria 1.1., 1.2., 2.1., 2.2. of chapter III.

1. The classical methods Laspeyres, Paasche and Fisher

   are non suited in the multilateral case, since they cannot provid transitive price-parities; they are therefore irrelevant to the EC-model (criterion 2.2 is not satisfied).

2. Methods based on constant average (international) quantities q_i^*, like

   $$(6) \quad P_{A/B} = \frac{\sum_i p_{iA} q_i^*}{\sum_i p_{iB} q_i^*},$$

   cannot be applied in the case of "binary lists" and are therefore irrelevant to the EC-model (criterion 1.2. is not satisfied).

3. Method based on averaged price-relatives with constant (international) weighting coefficients.

   3.1 The arithmetic mean of price-relatives,

   $$(7) \quad P_{A/B} = \sum_i \frac{p_{iA}}{p_{iB}} \cdot \alpha_i, \quad (\sum_i \alpha_i = 1),$$

   does not fulfil the country-reversability and transitivity requirements and is therefore an irrelevant method for the EC-model (criterion 2.2. is not satisfied).

3.2. The geometric mean of price-relatives,

$$(8)\ P_{A/B} = \prod_i \left(\frac{p_{iA}}{p_{iB}}\right)^{\beta_i}, \quad (\sum_i \beta_i = 1),$$

known as the Walsh-method, conflicts with the "binary-list principle" and is therefore irrelevant to the EC-model (criterion 1.2. is not satisfied).

4. The central-country-method, which makes one country (the central-country) the focus of interest and performs all the comparisons on the base of the bilateral comparisons of each country with the central-country, does not respect the multilateral-closed-fullscale requirement. It is therefore irrelevant to the EC-model (criterion 2.1. is not satisfied).

5. The Van Yzeren-method[1)], which has formerly been applied by the SOEC, does not meet the "binary-list-condition" and becomes therefore irrelevant to the new EC-model (criterion 1.2. is not satisfied).

In addition to these five methods or families of methods, which proved to be irrelevant to the EC-model, there are however two relevant methods satisfying the basic conditions 1.1. and 1.2. as well as the required properties 2.1. and 2.2.:

- the method of Geary-Khamis (GK)
- and the method of Eltetö-Köves-Szulc (EKS).

Here follows a short presentation of these two methods:

[1)] For a detailed description see: J. Van Yzeren: "Three methods of Comparing the purchasing power of currencies", Netherlands Central Bureau of Statistics, Statistical Studies, (December 1956), pp. 3-34.

6. Geary-Khamis-method:[1)]

Basic elements and notation:

- N products $i = 1,\dots,N$
- M countries $j = 1,\dots,M$
- known prices p_{ij} $(i = 1,\dots,N \;;\; j = 1,\dots,M)$
- known quantities q_{ij} $(i = 1,\dots,N \;;\; j = 1,\dots,M)$
- unknown exchange rates e_j $(j = 1,\dots,M)$ between country j and a fictitious "international-price-country"
- unknown international average prices $\bar{p}_i$ $(i = 1,\dots,N)$.

A homogeneous system of simultaneous linear equations describes the interrelations between the unknown variables and the known parameters p_{ij}, q_{ij}, e_j, $\bar{p}_i$:

$$
(9)\quad
\begin{aligned}
\bar{p}_i &= \sum_{j=1}^{M} e_j p_{ij} q_{ij} \Big/ \sum_{j=1}^{M} q_{ij}, \quad i = 1,\dots,N \\
e_j &= \sum_{i=1}^{N} \bar{p}_i q_{ij} \Big/ \sum_{i=1}^{N} p_{ij} q_{ij}, \quad j = 1,\dots,M.
\end{aligned}
$$

The solutions of this system have to be found by means of the standard techniques for systems of homogeneous linear equations.

The system (9) defines the following (implicit) price-parity between countries j = A and j = B:

$$
(10)\quad P_{A/B} = \frac{e_B}{e_A} = \frac{\sum_i p_{iA} q_{iA}}{\sum_i \bar{p}_i q_{iA}} \Bigg/ \frac{\sum_i p_{iB} q_{iB}}{\sum_i \bar{p}_i\, q_{iB}} .
$$

This version of the system shows, how the price-parity $P_{A/B}$ can be explained by means of the price-parity between A and

---

[1)] See also: S.H.Khamis: "A new system of index numbers for national and international purposes", Journal of the Royal Statistical Society 135 (1972), pp. 96-121.

the "international-price-country" on the one hand and the price-parity between B and the "international-price-country" on the other hand.

It is interesting to indicate the result for the case M = 2 :

$$(11)\quad P_{A/B} = \frac{\sum_i p_{iA} \frac{q_{iA}\, q_{iB}}{q_{iA}+q_{iB}}}{\sum_i p_{iB} \frac{q_{iA}\, q_{iB}}{q_{iA}+q_{iB}}} \; ;$$

this corresponds with the "average-quantity-principle" (see method 2, above), if the average consists in a harmonic mean.

The associated quantity-parity is given by:

$$(12)\quad Q_{A/B} = \frac{\sum_i \bar{p}_i q_{iA}}{\sum_i \bar{p}_i q_{iB}} \; .$$

<u>Proof of the relevance of the GK-method:</u>

Criterion 1.1. is satisfied: M can be any integer greater than 1.

Criterion 1.2. is satisfied: The GK-method is applicable in the case of "binary lists". Khamis indicates sufficient conditions[1)] for the existence of unique and positive solutions of the system of equations (9). These conditions allow rather extreme cases of missing products.

Criterion 2.1. is satisfied: The conception of the system of equations (9) respects the multilateral-closed-fullscale requirement.

---

1) See: S.H. Khamis: "A new system of index numbers for national and international purposes", Journal of the Royal Statistical Society 135 (1972), pp. 96-121.

Criterion 2.2. is satisfied: The country-revers bility and transitivity requirements are obviously fulfilled if (10) is applied.

7. Eltetö-Köves-Szulc-method (EKS)[1]

There are M countries and for each pair (j,k) of them the Fisher-price-parity

$$(13)\quad F_{j/k} = \left[\frac{\sum_i p_{ij}q_{ik}}{\sum_i p_{ik}q_{ik}} \cdot \frac{\sum_i p_{ij}q_{ij}}{\sum_i p_{ik}q_{ij}}\right]^{1/2}, \quad F_{j/k} = \frac{1}{F_{k/j}},$$

is known. This indicates a set of $\frac{1}{2}(M^2-M)$ intransitive bilateral price-parities. By means of a projection based on the least-square-principle this set can be transformed into a set of M-1 transitive parities. They are obtained by minimizing the expression

$$(14)\quad \sum_j \sum_k \left[\log E_{j/k} - \log F_{j/k}\right]^2 \qquad (j,k = 1,\ldots,M;\ j > k)$$

with respect to $E_{j/k}$ under the (transitivity) conditions

$$E_{j/m} \cdot E_{m/k} = E_{j/k} \quad \text{(m being any other country).}$$

One obtains as solutions the EKS-price-parities

$$(15)\quad E_{j/k} = \left[\prod_{m=1}^{M} F_{j/k}^{(m)}\right]^{\frac{1}{M}}, \quad \text{with } F_{j/k}^{(m)} = F_{j/m} \cdot F_{m/k}\,.$$

The associated quantity-parities are obtained by starting with the Fisher-quantity-parities instead of the Fisher-price-parities.

[1] The original publications describing this method are not in English, but see: L. Drechsler: "Weighting of index numbers for international comparisons", Review of Income and Wealth (March 1973), pp. 17-34.

Proof of the relevance of the EKS-method:

Criterion 1.1. is satisfied: M can be any integer greater than 1.

Criterion 1.2. is satisfied: For binary lists the bilateral Fisher-price-parities can be calculated without any difficulty. By means of the intermediate role of the Fisher-price-parities the EKS-method overcomes the binary-list-problem.

Criterion 2.1. is satisfied: The approach (14) embodies the multilateral-closed-fullscale requirement.

Criterion 2.2. is satisfied: The country-reversibility and transitivity requirements are ensured by the construction (14).

V. Comparison between the Geary-Khamis-method and the Eltetö-Köves-Szulc-method in the light of the desirable and the special properties

Being given that GK and EKS are essentially of identical quality in what regards the basic conditions and the required properties, one has to undertake more detailed investigationsin the light of the desirable and special properties in order to find out, which one is better suited for the purposes of the EC-model.

1. Factor-reversibility (criterion 3.1.)

   The GK-method does not fulfil the factor-reversibility property, since the symmetry-condition (3) between the price-parity (10) and the quantity-parity (12) does not hold (relation (4) however holds for (10) and (12), as can easily be verified).

   The EKS-method fulfils the factor-reversibility property. This becomes clear even without mathematical demonstration: the Fisher-price-and quantity-parities satisfy the factor-reversibility in the form of the conditions (3) and (4); the EKS-parities being geometric means of the Fisher-parities satisfy it as well.

2. Additivity (criterion 3.2.)

The EKS-method does not fulfil the additivity property, since it is fundamentally based on the geometric mean.

The GK-method does not fulfil the additivity property either, at least not in the strict sense of condition (5). In order to show this we consider the simplest case of the price-parity for a country A with respect to the fictitious "international-price-country" denoted by E.
This price-parity is given by $P_{A/E} = \sum_i p_{iA}q_{iA} / \sum_i \bar{p}_i / q_{iA}$.
The additivity condition (5) would then require that

$$(16) \quad \sum_{i\varepsilon G} p_{iA}q_{iA} \Big/ P_{A/E}^{(G)} = \sum_{r=1}^{k} \left[\sum_{i\varepsilon g_r} p_{iA}q_{iA} \Big/ P_{A/E}^{(g_r)} \right]$$

$$\text{or} \quad (17) \quad \sum_{i\varepsilon G} \bar{p}_i q_{iA} = \sum_{r=1}^{k} \sum_{i\varepsilon g_r} \bar{p}_i q_{iA}$$

for any country A and any subdivision $(g_1,\ldots,g_k)$ of G.

Relation (17) does, however, not hold for the following reason: As a consequence of (5) and (9), the international prices $\bar{p}_i$ on the right-hand side of (17) depend via the conversion rates $e_1,\ldots,e_M$ on the group g_r, to which the product i belongs:

$$(18) \quad \bar{p}_i = \bar{p}_i \left[e_1(g_r),\ldots,e_M(g_r) \right] ,$$

if i is an element of $g_r (r=1,\ldots,k)$.

The international prices $\bar{p}_i$ on the left-hand side of (17) depend on the total G:

(19) $\bar{p}_i = \bar{p}_i \left[e_1(G), \ldots, e_M(G) \right]$ for each i.

Consequently, for any fixed i, the left-hand $\bar{p}_i$ and the right-hand $\bar{p}_i$ are in general different from each other and the summations on both sides cannot lead to the same result.

But there exists a possibility of establishing the equality of (17) by using on the right side the $\bar{p}_i$ calculated for the total G as described in (19). This implies that the corresponding "partial price-parities" for g_r are

$$(20) \quad P_{A/E}^{(g_r)} = \frac{\sum_{i \varepsilon g_r} p_{iA} q_{iA}}{\sum_{i \varepsilon g_r} \bar{p}_i q_{iA}}, \quad (r=1,\ldots,k),$$

with $\bar{p}_i = \bar{p}_i \left[e_1(G), \ldots, e_M(G) \right]$ for each product i.

This kind of additivity of the GK-method may be called a quasi-additivity. It must, however, be emphasized, that this quasi-additivity is only valid for operations between a country A and the "international-price-country" E.

This crucial behaviour of the GK-method in respect to additivity has not yet been pointed out in the literature.

3. Respect of the importance of the countries (criterion 4.1)

The EKS-method does not respect the importance of the various countries.

The GK-method on the other hand respects the importance of the countries by means of the quantities q_i entering as weights into the international-price-concept (see (9)). But this approach leads to a rather curious effect:

Let A be a very small and B be a very large country in regard to their importances concerning the quantities q_i, so that we may assume that q_{iA}/q_{iB} is very small for each i. From formula (11) we obtain

$$(21) \quad P_{A/B} = \frac{\sum_i p_{iA}\left[\frac{q_{iA}}{\frac{q_{iA}}{q_{iB}}+1}\right]}{\sum_i p_{iB}\left[\frac{q_{iA}}{\frac{q_{iA}}{q_{iB}}+1}\right]} .$$

This expression tends towards

$$(22) \quad P_{A/B} = \frac{\sum_i p_{iA}q_{iA}}{\sum_i p_{iB}q_{iA}}$$

as q_{iA}/q_{iB} tends towards zero.

That means: the price-parity between A and B is determined by the quantity-structure of the very unimportant country A. On the other hand it is the price-structure of the important country B that determines the quantity-parity between both countries.

This illogical distortion becomes relevant in the EC-model, where there is a constellation of countries with very different economic importance. In order to eliminate this effect one should operate with per-capita-quantities.

4. Particular features (criterion 4.2)

Geary-Khamis-method: The construction principle of the GK-method is in a sense a synthesis between the central-country philosophy (see IV, 4) and the Paasche approach. The fictitious "international-price-country" plays the role of the central-country, from which (as the base-country) the other countries are looked at from a Paasche viewpoint, i.e. the quantities of the other countries are used (see (9)). The bilateral comparisons are realized via the "international-price-country" (see (10)). The conflict between the central-country approach and the multilateral-closed-fullscale requirement is avoided in this construction by the fact, that the international-price-country as central-country is an "average-country" which embodies all the countries involved.

From the economic viewpoint it can be said, that the GK-approach shows a high degree of plausibility. From the mathematical viewpoint, however, it must be said, that there is little analytical transparency in the relationship between the final results (price-parities) and the initial elements (prices and quantities). The computational effort of the GK-method is rather high.

EKS-method: The construction principle (application of the least-square approach) is a pure mathematical manipulation in order to change an intransitive set of price-parities into a transitive one. The result of this purely technical procedure is quite astonishing: the EKS-price-parities are geometric means of the basic Fisher-price-parities, which themselves are also geometric means of the Paasche- and Laspeyres-price-parities. With some logic one can interprete the EKS-price-parities as higher-order-Fisher-price-parities.

From the economic viewpoint one misses the direct plausibiliy in this approach. But on the other hand the clear relationship between the basic elements and the final results provides a high degree of analytical transparency. The mathematical simplicity of the formula (15) and the clearly structured hierarchy Paasche-Laspeyres-Fisher-EKS ensure some practial advantages, especially if one wants to perform specific investigations for subgroups of products or subgroups of countries. The computational effort for the EKS-method is rather low.

VI. Conclusion

One can draw the following conclusions from the results of the above investigations:

Of the method examinedsfor calculating price-parities the Geary-Khamis-method and the Eltetö-Köves-Szulc-method have proved as the only relevant ones for the EC-model, since they alone fulfil its basic conditions and requirements.
A more detailed examination showed that there exist some essential differences between them with regard to further properties and specific features:

- the EKS-method satisfies the factor-reversability, the GK-method does not.
- the GK-method possesses a "quasi-additivity" property, the EKS-method has no additivity property at all.
- the GK-method embodies an economic approach, whereas the EKS-method is a mathematical-statistical one.
- there are still other differences concerning further criteria like "characteristicity" and "unbiasedness" , which have not been considered in the present paper but have been thoroughly studied by L. Drechsler in his above-mentioned article.

In spite of all these differences it is impossible, even for the purposes of the EC-model, to attribute a clear superiority to one of them - there is no universally best method for the EC-model. The choice between the GK-method and the EKS-method should be made with regard to specific applications and practical advantages, for instance:

If, in the concrete case of National-Accounts-Systems, international comparisons of real values are to be made for detailed subaggregates, then the GK-price-parities are preferable on account of their quasi-additivity, which can provide a certain consistency for the corresponding operations.

If, however, this particular additivity-property becomes irrelevant, for instance in the case of real wage comparisons or other specific uses, the EKS-method seems to be more appropriate, as it offers some useful practical advantages resulting from its mathematical simplicity.

Revealed Preference and the Economic Theory of Index Numbers

by Susanne Fuchs-Seliger

Introduction

This paper deals with the relationship of the economic theory of price index numbers to the theory of revealed preference. This theory, pioneered by Samuelson and developed by Houthakker represents a model of consumer behavior. Samuelson's basic assumptions had been influenced considerably by the economic theory of price index numbers. If we assume that each member of a group of households has the same utility function u which he tries to maximize subject to his budget constraint, then the economic price index, i.e. the cost of living index, can be stated as follows:

Definition 1: The economic price index is a functional such that

$$P: \mathbb{R}^{2n}_{++} \times \mathbb{R}_{++} \to \mathbb{R}_{+};\ P(p^0,p^1;M^0) = \frac{M^1}{M^0},\ \text{with } M^1 = \min_{x \in \mathbb{R}^n_+} p^1 \cdot x \text{ and}$$

$$u(x) = u(x^0), \text{ where } x^0 \varepsilon \{x \mid p^0 \cdot x \leqq M^0\} := K(p^0,M^0) \text{ and } u(x^0) \geqq u(y)$$
for all $y \in K(p^0,M^0)$.

Less formally we can say: The economic price index equals the ratio of the minimum costs of a given standard of living in two price situations. The idea of economic price index numbers is based on the strong hypothesis that every household of the group has the same utility function . But even if we assume that they all have the same scale of preferences represented by the utility function the preferences are not known and cannot even be determined by observation. By observing the behavior of the individuals, only an approximation of the cost of living index can be found.

However, in the following analysis we do not consider these problems and assume that every individual has his utility function which conforms to the utility function of any other member of the group and that this function can be determined by observing the actions of the individuals We suppose that we have a record of their behavior in various price-income situations.

The economic theory of price index numbers is concerned with rational individuals, who act according to their scale of preferences.

Hicks postulates that under these assumptions the behavior of the consumers satisfies the following two conditions, which he calls the indifference tests [2], i.e.: If x^o and x^1 are two commodity bundles purchased by the individual at prices p^o and p^1, respectively, and if they are elements of the same indifference class, then the following conditions must be satisfied:

$$(1) \quad p^o x^o \leqq p^o x^1$$

and

$$(2) \quad p^1 x^1 \leqq p^1 x^o.$$

The meaning of the first inequality is the following: If the consumer buys x^o in the price situation p^o, then x^o must be cheaper or at most as expensive as x^1, for if this were not the case, he would buy x^1 instead of x^o which he appreciates as much as x^o and still would have some money left for other purchases or saving. In an analogous way the second inequality can be interpreted.

Hicks derived, by multiplying the inequalities (1) and (2):

$$(p^o x^1) \cdot (p^1 x^o) \geqq (p^o x^o) \cdot (p^1 x^1).$$

He calls this relation the "Index-Number Theorem", because it contains that the Laspeyres index is greater than or equal to the Paasche index. This holds both for the quantity and for the price index.

If the commodity bundles x^o and x^1 are not elements of the same but of different indifference surfaces, then, since the individuals are expected to act rationally, it is impossible that the indifference tests

$$p^o x^1 \geqq p^o x^o \text{ and } p^1 x^o \geqq p^1 x^1$$

are satisfied. Therefore we must have

$$\neg(p^o x^1 \geqq p^o x^o \wedge p^1 x^o \geqq p^1 x^1) \quad ^{1)}$$

---

1) $\neg$ means "it is not true that...."

Hicks calls this formula the "consistency test". As can be seen below the consistency test is closely related to Samuelson's Weak Axiom of Revealed Preference which is fundamental for the theory of revealed preference.

In accordance with the traditional theory of index numbers the revealed preference approach assumes that the consumer has a constant scale of preferences that can be determined by observing his behavior in various price-income situations. As we mentioned above, a fundamental hypothesis of this theory is the Weak Axiom of Revealed Preference, which can be stated formally by

$$p^o x^o \geqq p^o x^1 \Longrightarrow p^1 x^1 < p^1 x^o.$$

Its relationship to Hicks' tests is obvious.[1)] The Weak Axiom can be interpreted as follows:

If the consumer purchases x^o in the price situation p^o at income $p^o x^o$ although x^1 is also available, then in the price situation p^1 where both x^o and x^1 are also available, he chooses x^1 because at market prices $p^1 x^o$ exceeds his income.

In the next section we will show that in the theory of revealed preference the economic price index can always be determined although the utility function of the consumer may not be continuous but only upper semicontinuous.

Existence of the cost of living index in the theory of Revealed Preference

Since our proof is based on results due to Houthakker [3] and Uzawa [8] we are first going to state Uzawa's axioms which are a reformulation of Houthakker's postulates.

---

1) Only in the case where the equality holds in the indifference tests we get a contradiction to the Weak Axiom. The reason for this is the fact that Hicks supposes the indifference surfaces to be convex to the origin, whereas the Weak Axiom implies that the indifference surfaces are strict convex to the origin.

Uzawa's axioms are the following:

DI : $h: \mathbb{R}^n_{++} \times \mathbb{R}_+ \to \mathbb{R}^n_+$, $x = h(p,M)$, is a continuous demand function,

where $x = (x_1,\ldots,x_n)$ denotes a commodity vector,
$p = (p_1,\ldots,p_n)$ a price vector and M stands for the income of the individual.

DII : $\forall\, x \in \mathbb{R}^n_{++}\ \exists (p,M) : x = h(p,M)$.

DIII : $p \cdot h(p,M) = M$.

DIV : Let $p^o, p^1 \in \mathbb{R}^n_{++}$ and $p(t) = p^o + t(p^1 - p^o)$ with $t \in [0,1]$: then there exists a $K \in \mathbb{R}_{++}$ such that for all $M', M'' \in \mathbb{R}_{++}$ and for all $t \in [0,1]$: $\|h(p(t),M') - h(p(t),M'')\| \leqq K|M'-M''|$ [2].

In accordance with Houthakker, Uzawa assumes the Strong Axiom of Revealed Preference because the Weak Axiom of Revealed Preference can be applied only in those cases where there exist price-income situations in which x^o and x^1 are both available and one of them is chosen. The Strong Axiom, however, establishes an assumption on the behavior of the consumer if he can only "indirectly compare" two commodity bundles. The meaning of this will be clear after we have introduced the definition of the relation "x is indirectly revealed preferred to y".
In order to state the Strong Axiom formally we state the next definitions.

Definition 2: Let $x^o = h(p^o,M^o)$ and $x^1 = h(p^1,M^1)$. Then:
$x^o R x^1 :\Longleftrightarrow x^o \neq x^1 \wedge p^o x^o \geqq p^o x^1$.

1) In contrary to Uzawa we assume the continuity of h, because we need it in the proof of Lemma 3.
2) Instead of the local Lipschitz condition assumed by Uzawa ([8], p.10) we use a modification of this introduced by Stigum (see [7], p. 412), and also [1]).

Definition 3: $xR^*y :\iff xRy \vee \exists\, x^1 \ldots x^n : x^0Rx^1 \wedge \ldots \wedge x^nRy.$

xRy is read "x is revealed preferred to y", whereas xR^*y is read "x is indirectly revealed preferred to y".
Now the Strong Axiom of Revealed Preference will be formulated in terms of the relation R^*.

DV : Strong Axiom of Revealed Preference:

$$xR^* y \Longrightarrow \neg(yR^*x).$$

If we replace R^* by R we get

$$xRy \Longrightarrow \neg(yRx).$$

This is the Weak Axiom of Revealed Preference in terms of R. As can be seen immediately, the Strong Axiom implies the Weak Axiom.

Rose found out that both axioms are equivalent for two-dimensional commodity vectors [5].
In view of our theorem on the cost of living index and revealed preference theory we remember that we have to determine the commodity bundle x^1 which at prices p^1 is equivalent to x^0 at market prices p^0. We will show that such a commodity bundle x^1 exists on the Engel curve corresponding to p^1. By this we mean the following:

Definition 4: Let $p^1 \in \mathbb{R}^n_{++}$. Then the set $\{x \mid x \in \mathbb{R}^n_+ \wedge x = h(p^1,M)$ for any $M \geqq 0\}$ is called the "Engel curve corresponding to p^1".

We continue our analysis by defining two functions due to Uzawa.

Definition 5: Let $p^a, p^b \in \mathbb{R}^n_{++}$ and $M^a \in \mathbb{R}_{++}$. Then $\rho_{b,a}(M^a) := \sup\{M \mid h(p^a,M^a)\ R^* h(p^b,M)\}$.

This definition implies that the consumer considers $x^b = h(p^b, \rho_{b,a}(M^a))$ at most as good as x^a. We will show later that $x^b = h(p^b, \rho_{b,a}(M^a)$ is the only commodity bundle of the Engel curve corresponding to p^b which is indifferent to x^a. The term $\frac{\rho_{b,a}(M^a)}{M^a}$ characterizes the cost of living index at prices p^b.

Next, we shall prove some properties of the function $\rho_{b,a}$.

Lemma 1: If DI-DIII and DV are assumed, then $\rho_{b,a}(M^a)$ is finite for any M^a.

Proof: Suppose to the contrary that there exists a sequence $<M^n>_{n\in\mathbb{N}}$ such that

(1) $\lim_{n\to\infty} M^n = \infty$ and $h(p^a,M^a)\ R^*h(p^b,M^n)$ for all n.

From DV we get $\neg(h(p^b,M^n)\ R^*h(p^a,M^a))$ and therefore $\neg(h(p^b,M^n)Rh(p^a,M^a))$. From this we can conclude $M^n \leqq h(p^a,M^a)\cdot p^b$ for all M^n. This contradicts (1).

Lemma 2: Under assumption of DI-DIII and DV the function $\rho_{b,a}$ is monotonically increasing.

Proof: For any $\varepsilon > 0$ we have:

$$M^a + \varepsilon = h(p^a, M^a + \varepsilon)p^a > M^a = h(p^a,M^a)\cdot p^a.$$

From this we can conclude:

for any $\bar{M} \in \{M|h(p^a,M^a)\ R^*h(p^b,M)\} \equiv A$ we have

$$\bar{M} \in \{M|h(p^a,M^a + \varepsilon)\ R^*h(p^b,M)\} \equiv B.$$

This implies $A \subset B$ and therefore

$\sup A \leqq \sup B$. q.e.d.

Obviously, the statements of the previous lemmas also hold if instead of the Strong Axiom the Weak Axiom is assumed. In order to prove the continuity we are going now to define a function which-as can be seen below-stands in a close relationship to $\rho_{b,a}$.

<u>Definition 6:</u> Let $p^a, p^b \in \mathbb{R}^n_{++}$. Then
$\rho'_{b,a}(M^a) = \inf \{M | h(p^b,M)\ R^* h(p^a,M^a)\}$.

If we define the set $W^+(x^a)$ by

<u>Definition 7:</u> Let $x^a = h(p^a,M^a)$.
$W^+(x^a) := \{x/x \in \mathbb{R}^n_+ \wedge x R^* x^a\}$,

this implies that the commodity bundle determined by $h(p^b,\rho'_{b,a}(M^a))$ is an element of the boundary of $\overline{W^+(x^a)}$. Uzawa could prove that the axioms DI-DV imply that the functions $\rho_{b,a}$ and $\rho'_{b,a}$ are equal. In Theorem 1 we shall state this important result.

<u>Theorem 1:</u> Under assumption of DI-DV, we get for any $M^a \in \mathbb{R}_{++}$:

$$\rho_{b,a}(M^a) = \rho'_{b,a}(M^a).$$

The proof will not be repeated here. It only should be noted that the upper and lower income sequences which are defined according to Houthakker's upper and lower sequences of offer curves play an important part there. The idea of the proof will be obvious by the definition of these sequences which shall be stated next, and by the following illustration.

<u>Definition 8:</u> (recursive definition of the lower and upper income sequences):
Consider any price vectors p^a, p^b and any positive income M^a. Let $p(t)$ be defined by $p(t) = p^a + t(p^b - p^a)$ with $t \in [0,1]$.

Then for any positive integer s the "upper income sequence" $\langle \bar{M}^{k,s} \rangle_{k<s}$ and "lower income sequence" $\langle M^{k,s} \rangle_{k<s}$ are defined by the following:

I : If $k = 0$, then $\bar{M}^{0,s} = M^a$ and $M^{0,s} = M^a$.

II : Suppose $\bar{M}^{k,s}$ and $M^{k,s}$ are already defined for all $k < s$, $k \in \mathbb{N} \cup \{0\}$. Then $\bar{M}^{k+1,s}$ and $M^{k+1,s}$ are defined by:

1) $\bar{M}^{k+1,s} = p(\frac{k+1}{s})\bar{x}^{k,s}$ with $\bar{x}^{k,s} = h(p(\frac{k}{s}), \bar{M}^{k,s})$

2) $M^{k,s} = p(\frac{k}{s})\ x^{k+1,s}$ with $x^{k+1,s} = h(p(\frac{k+1}{s}), M^{k+1,s})$.

For the last step we have to give an explanation. Suppose $M^{k,s}$ is already determined. Then we have to find an x on the Engel curve corresponding to $p(\frac{k+1}{s})$ which solves the equality $M^{k,s} = p(\frac{k}{s})\cdot x$.
But since by DI , $h : \mathbb{R}_+ \to \mathbb{R}^n_+$, $x = h(p(\frac{k+1}{s}), M)$ is continuous with respect to M, x changes continuously with M. We therefore can fix such an income which we denote by $M^{k+1,s}$. The corresponding commodity vector will be denoted by $x^{k+1,s}$.
The following figure will illustrate the definition of the upper and lower income sequences (see [8], p.15).

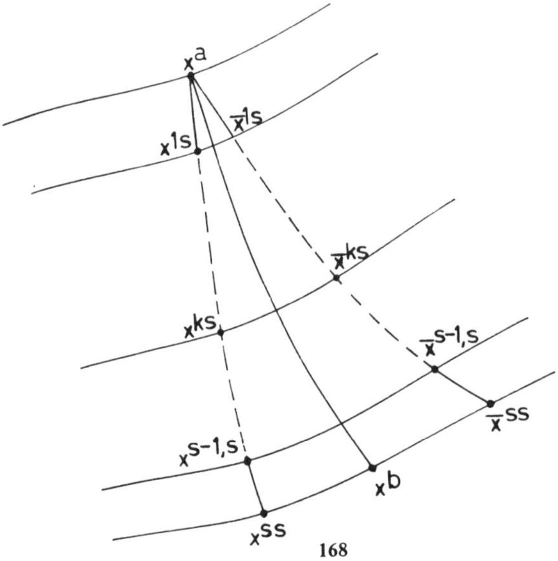

By DI-DV it can be shown that the upper and lower income sequences converge to the same function. Therefore we have $\rho'_{b,a}(M^a) = \rho_{b,a}(M^a)$ for any M^a. This ensures that we don't have indifference classes with thick portions. As a simple corollar to Theorem 1 we immediately obtain the next theorem ([8], p.14).

Theorem 2: DI-DV imply:

For all $M < \rho_{b,a}(M^a) : h(p^a,M^a)R^*h(p^b,M)$.

For all $M > \rho_{b,a}(M^a) : h(p^b,M)\ R^*h(p^a,M^a)$.

Since the preceding theorem does not exclude the possibility that $h(p^a,M^a)R^*h(p^b, \rho_{b,a}(M^a))$ or $h(p^b, \rho_{b,a}(M^a))R^*h(p^a,M^a)$ is true, the next lemma will show that this cannot happen if DI-DV are assumed.

Lemma 3: Suppose $h(p^a,M^a)R^*h(p^b,M^b)$ 1) holds. Then under DI-DV there exist

(i) an $\varepsilon_1 > 0$ such that $h(p^a,M^a - \varepsilon_1)R^*h(p^b,M^b)$

and

(ii) an $\varepsilon_2 > 0$ such that $h(p^a,M^a)R^*h(p^b,M^b + \varepsilon_2)$.

Proof for (i): By the definition of R^* we have:

$$x^aRx^b \vee \exists x^1 \ldots x^n\ [x^aRx^1 \wedge \ldots \wedge x^nRx^b]$$

If x^aRx^b, then the definition of R implies:

$$x^ap^a > x^bp^a \vee x^ap^a = x^bp^a.$$

1) By $(p^\cdot,M^\cdot)$ we denote the price-income situation corresponding to $x^\cdot$.

If $x^a p^a > x^b p^a$ then because of the continuity of h with respect to M (which is implied by DI) the proof is obvious. Now let $x^a p^a = x^b p^a$. Since $x^a \neq x^b$, by the continuity of h, there exists a $p(t^o)$ with $p(t^o) = p^b + t^o(p^a - p^b)$ and $0 < t^o < 1$, such that

$$x^d = h(p(t^o),\ p(t^o)\cdot x^b) \neq x^b.$$ 1)

For suppose that for all $t \in]0,1[, h(p(t),p(t)x^b) = x^b$ then since h is continous, $\lim_{t\to 1} h(p(t),\ p(t)x^b) = h(p^a,p^a x^b) = x^b$. But as $p^a x^b = p^a x^a$, this involves that $h(p^a,p^a x^b) = x^a$, contradicting the assumption that $x^a \neq x^b$.

From $p(t^o)\ x^d = p(t^o)x^b$ follows

$$(1)\ x^d R x^b,$$

and thus by the Strong Axiom, $p^b x^b < p^b x^d$.

Therefore we have

$$\begin{aligned} p^a x^d &= p(t^o)x^d + (1-t^o)(p^a-p^b)x^d \\ &< p(t^o)x^b + (1-t^o)(p^a-p^b)x^b \\ &= p^a x^b = p^a x^a. \end{aligned}$$

If we choose $x^c = h(p^a,p^a x^d)$ the above inequality implies

$$x^c = h(p^a,M^a - \varepsilon_1),$$

with $\varepsilon_1 = p^a x^a - p^a x^d > 0$.

Therefore we have $x^c = x^d \vee x^c R x^d$ and thus, by the definition of $R^*$and (1), $x^c R^* x^b$. 2)

Suppose $x^a R^* x^b$ but not $x^a R x^b$. Then by definition, $\exists x^1,\dots,x^n\ [x^a R x^1 \wedge \dots \wedge x^n R x^b]$. As $x^a p^a \geqq x^1 p^a$, we get by the same arguments as in the previous case

$$\exists \tilde{\varepsilon}^1 > 0 \text{ such that } h(p^a,M^a - \tilde{\varepsilon}^1)R^* x^1$$

and thus by the transitivity of R^*, $h(p^a,M^a - \tilde{\varepsilon}^1)R^* x^b$.

---

1) For this conclusion here we first time apply the assumption that h is continuous.

2) The method of this proof is due to Stigum (see [7], p. 417).

Proof for (ii):
Suppose $x^a R^* x^b$. Then if $x^a R x^b$, we proceed as in case (i):
If $x^a p^a > x^b p^a$, the proof is established by the continuity of h with respect to M.
Suppose $x^a p^a = x^b p^a$. Let $x^c = \frac{1}{2} x^a + \frac{1}{2} x^b$, then $x^a \neq x^c$ and

$$(2) \quad x^a p^a = x^c p^a.$$

Hence by DV:

$$p^c x^c < p^c x^a.$$

From this inequality and from

$$p^c x^c = p^c \cdot \frac{x^a}{2} + p^c \cdot \frac{x^b}{2}$$

we can conclude that $p^c x^c > p^c x^b$. The continuity of h with respect to M ensures that there is an x^d such that $x^d = h(p^b, M^b + \varepsilon_2)$, with $\varepsilon_2 > 0$, and $p^c x^c > p^c x^d$. This implies, $x^c R x^d$. Since by (2), $x^a R x^c$ we have, $x^a R^* x^d$. If $x^a R^* x^b$ but not $x^a R x^b$ we proceed as in case (i). From $x^a R x^1 \wedge \ldots \wedge x^n R x^b$ we can conclude that there exists a $\delta_1 > 0$ such that $x^n R^* h(p^b, M^b + \delta_1)$. Therefore by the transitivity of R^* we obtain $x^a R^* h(p^b, M^b + \delta_1)$. q.e.d.

As noted from the proof, the statements of Lemma 3 also hold if instead of the Strong Axiom the Weak Axiom is assumed. Now, with the help of the preceding lemma we can prove our next theorem.

Theorem 3: If conditions DI-DV are satisfied, then $\rho_{b,a}$ is continuous on $\mathbb{R}_{++}$.

Proof: We show first that $\rho_{b,a}$ is right continuous. Therefore let $\langle M^{a_n} \rangle_{n \in \mathbb{N}}$ be a monotonically decreasing sequence such that $M^{a_n} \neq M^a$ and $\lim_{n\to\infty} M^{a_n} = M^a$.

By Lemma 2, the sequence $\langle\rho_{b,a}(M^{a_n})\rangle_{n\in\mathbb{N}}$ is also monotonically decreasing and bounded by $\rho_{b,a}(M^a)$. This ensures $\lim_{n\to\infty}\rho_{b,a}(M^{a_n})$ exists and

$$\lim_{n\to\infty}\rho_{b,a}(M^{a_n}) \geqq \rho_{b,a}(M^a).$$

Suppose $\lim_{n\to\infty}\rho_{b,a}(M^{a_n}) > \rho_{b,a}(M^a)$. Then there exists a $\hat{M}$ such that

$$(1)\quad \lim_{n\to\infty}\rho_{b,a}(M^{a_n}) > \hat{M} > \rho_{b,a}(M^a).$$

By (1) and Lemma 3, there exists an $\varepsilon_1 > 0$ such that

$$h(p^b,\hat{M})R^*h(p^a,M^a + \varepsilon_1).$$

Thus by the continuity of h with respect to M we can conclude for sufficiently large n,

$$(2)\quad h(p^b,\hat{M})R^*h(p^a,M^{a_n}).$$

As by (1) we have $h(p^a,M^{a_n})\ R^*h(p^b,\hat{M})$, this together with (2) ensures

$$h(p^b,\hat{M})R^*h(p^b,\hat{M}),$$

contradicting the irreflexivity of R^*. Therefore we have

$$\lim_{n\to\infty}\rho_{b,a}(M^{a_n}) = \rho_{b,a}(M^a).$$

The proof for left continuity follows analogously. q.e.d.

These results will help us to establish the following equivalence.

Theorem 4: DI-DV imply:

$$h(p^a,M^a)R^*h(p^b,M^b) \iff M^b < \rho_{b,a}(M^a)$$
$$h(p^b,M^b)R^*h(p^a,M^a) \iff M^b > \rho_{b,a}(M^a).$$

Proof for "$\Longleftarrow$" see Theorem 2.

Proof for "$\Longrightarrow$":

1) Let $h(p^a,M^a)R^*h(p^b,M^{b_1})$. By Lemma 3 we conclude that there exists an $\varepsilon_1 > 0$ such that $h(p^a,M^a)R^*h(p^b,M^{b_1} + \varepsilon_1)$. Thus, by the definition of $\rho_{b,a}(M^a)$, we cannot have $M^{b_1} = \rho_{b,a}(M^a)$. It is also impossible that $M^{b_1} > \rho_{b,a}(M^a)$, for this would imply that $h(p^b,M^{b_1})R^*h(p^a,M^a)$ and thus, by the transitivity of R^*, $h(p^b,M^{b_1})R^*h(p^b,M^{b_1})$, in contradiction to the irreflexivity of R^*, which is implied by the Strong Axiom.

2) Let $h(p^b,M^{b_2})R^*h(p^a,M^a)$. Suppose that $M^{b_2} = \rho_{b,a}(M^a)$, then Lemma 3 ensures that there exists an $\varepsilon_2 > 0$ such that

$$h(p^b, \rho_{b,a}(M^a) - \varepsilon_2)R^*h(p^a,M^a).$$

Since $\rho'_{b,a}(M^a) = \rho_{b,a}(M^a)$ we get,

$$h(p^b,\rho'_{b,a}(M^a) - \varepsilon_2)R^*h(p^a,M^a),$$

contradicting the definition of $\rho'_{b,a}(M^a)$. q.e.d.

If we introduce the relation "revealed indifferent" by

<u>Definition 9:</u> $xI^*y :\Longleftrightarrow \neg(xR^*y) \wedge \neg(yR^*x)$,

then by combining this definition and the preceding result, we can conclude the next theorem.

<u>Theorem 5:</u> If conditions DI-DV are satiesfied then for any $x^a = h(p^a,M^a)$ and $x^b = h(p^b, \rho_{b,a}(M^a))$, $x^aI^*x^b$.

$x^aI^*x^b$ means that the individual has shown by his actions that he neither prefers x^a to x^b nor x^b to x^a.

As a corollary to Theorem 4 and 5 we obtain the following result.

Theorem 6: If in a model of consumer behavior conditions DI-DV are satisfied, then for any given x^a, at price situation p^b there exists only one commodity vector, namely $x^b = h(p^b, \rho_{b,a}(M^a))$, such that $x^a I^* x^b$.

If we recall the definition of the Engel curve, we may also say, that there exists one element of the Engel curve corresponding to p^b, which is indifferent to x^a. This commodity bundle is determined by $x^b = h(p^b, \rho_{b,a}(M^a))$.

At last we establish the relationship of the cost of living index and conditions DI-DV.

Theorem 7: Under the assumptions DI-DV the cost of living index $P(p^a,p^b;M^a)$ equals the ratio $\frac{\rho_{b,a}(M^a)}{M^a}$.

Proof: The axioms DI-DV imply the existence of an upper semicontinuous utility function u such that

$$u(x) > u(y) \iff xR^* y, \quad \forall\, x,y \in \mathbb{R}^n_{++}$$

(see Uzawa [8] , pp. 14-18). Therefore by Theorem 6 we can immediately conclude that

$$P(p^a,p^b;M^a) = \frac{\rho_{b,a}(M^a)}{M^a}.$$

However, the conditions DI-DV do not imply the existence of a continuous utility function generating the given demand function. This was shown by a counterexample constructed by Hurwicz and Richter (see [4], pp. 65-66).

Summary:

In the last section we have shown that Uzawa's preference axioms ensure the existence of the cost of living index at any market prices, although there need not exist a continuous utility function representing the consumer's preference scale.

This index is given by the term $\frac{\rho_{b,a}(M^a)}{M^a}$, where $\rho_{b,a}$ is a continuous, monotonically increasing real valued function, which determines the income M^b at which for the market prices p^b the commodity vector $x^b = h(p^b, M^b)$ is indifferent to any given x^a.

References

[1] Fuchs-Seliger, S.: "Bemerkungen zur Widerspruchsfreiheit der Axiome in der Theorie der Revealed Preference", "Contributions to Mathematical Economics and Game Theory in Honor of O. Morgenstern ed. by R. Henn and O. Moeschlin, Berlin,Heidelberg, New York: Springer-Verlag, 1977

[2] Hicks, J.R.: A Revision of Demand Theory, Oxford: At the Clarendon Press, 1956

[3] Houthakker, H.S.: "Revealed Preference and the Utility Function", Economica, N.S. 17 (1950), 159-174

[4] Hurwicz, L.; M.K. Richter: "Revealed Preference Without Demand Continuity Assumptions" in "Preferences, Utility and Demand" ed. by J.S. Chipman, L. Hurwicz, M.K. Richter, and H.F. Sonnenschein. New York: Harcourt Brace Jovanovich, Inc. 1971

[5] Rose, H.: "Consistency of Preference: The Two-Commodity-Case", Review of Economic Studies, 25 (1958), pp.124-125

[6] Samuelson, P.A.: Foundations of Economic Analysis. Cambridge: Harvard University Press, 1948

[7] Stigum, B.P.: "Revealed Preference - A Proof of Houthakker's Theorem", Econometrica, 41 (1973), 411-423

[8] Uzawa, H.: "Preference and Rational Choice in the Theory of Consumption" in "Preferences, Utility,and Demand", see [4].

A Note on the Characterization of Fisher's "Ideal Index"

by Helmut Funke and Joachim Voeller

If the deduction of a certain index from a set of given conditions is stated in the form of an "if and only if theorem", then we speak of a characterization of the particular index. That is, the index in question not only satisfies the required conditions but also represents the only index which can be deduced from these conditions.

Mainly for two reasons characterizations of indices deserve attention. First, the conditions needed for a characterization can be regarded as properties of a clearly defined index. Second, a characterization might be helpful to the statistician. It offers him a catalog of attributes of a certain index the usefulness and characteristics of which he can now judge more accurately.

A characterization of Fisher's "ideal index" may prove particularly interesting since this index satisfies Fisher's tests for price and quantity indices except for the Circular Test. Still, Irving Fisher called it the best index available.- For a detailed analysis as well as a comprehensive bibliography on Fisher's test approach in the theory of the price index, see EICHHORN-VOELLER [1976].

In EICHHORN-VOELLER [1976, p. 42-43] a first characterization of Fisher's "ideal index" was published. There one of Fisher's original tests, the Factor Reversal Test, was used together with an additional requirement to accomplish the characterization. In the following, we require two of Fisher's tests and add a new condition which we call Weight Property.

Let

$$\underline{q}^o = (q_1^o,\ldots,q_n^o) \in \mathbb{R}^n_{++},$$

$$\underline{q} = (q_1,\ldots,q_n) \in \mathbb{R}^n_{++}$$

be the quantities of n commodities in a base year and in a comparison year, respectively, and let

$$\underline{p}^o = (p_1^o,\ldots,p_n^o) \in \mathbb{R}^n_{++},$$

$$\underline{p} = (p_1,\ldots,p_n) \in \mathbb{R}^n_{++}$$

represent the corresponding prices for the commodities. Then we consider index functions of the form

$$P:\ \mathbb{R}^{4n}_{++} \to \mathbb{R}_{++},\quad (\underline{q}^o,\underline{p}^o,\underline{q},\underline{p}) \mapsto P(\underline{q}^o,\underline{p}^o,\underline{q},\underline{p})$$

satisfying certain conditions. The value $P(\underline{q}^o,\underline{p}^o,\underline{q},\underline{p})$ represents the value of the price index at the price-quantity situation $(\underline{q}^o,\underline{p}^o,\underline{q},\underline{p})$. For technical reasons, only positive components of the four vectors occuring in P are permitted.

The following relations are stated as functional equations which are valid for all $(\underline{q}^o,\underline{p}^o,\underline{q},\underline{p}) \in \mathbb{R}^{4n}_{++}$:

Time Reversal Test:

If in a first time period all quantities and prices change from $\underline{q}^o$, $\underline{p}^o$ to $\underline{q}$, $\underline{p}$ and in a subsequent time period they change back from $\underline{q}$, $\underline{p}$ to $\underline{q}^o$, $\underline{p}^o$, then the value of P for the entire period is the product of the values of P for the two time intervals and equals one:

$$(1)\qquad P(\underline{q}^o,\underline{p}^o,\underline{q}^o,\underline{p}^o) = P(\underline{q}^o,\underline{p}^o,\underline{q},\underline{p})\,P(\underline{q},\underline{p},\underline{q}^o,\underline{p}^o) = 1.$$

Factor Reversal Test:

In P, interchange $\underline{q}^o$ and $\underline{p}^o$ as well as $\underline{q}$ and $\underline{p}$. The resulting $P(\underline{p}^o,\underline{q}^o,\underline{p},\underline{q})$ can be regarded as the value of a quantity index if $P(\underline{q}^o,\underline{p}^o,\underline{q},\underline{p})$ is the value of a price index. The product of the two values is the ratio of the values of the two baskets of goods in question:

(2) $$P(\underline{q}^o,\underline{p}^o,\underline{q},\underline{p})\ P(\underline{p}^o,\underline{q}^o,\underline{p},\underline{q}) = \frac{\underline{qp}}{\underline{q}^o\underline{p}^o}\ .^{*)}$$

Weight Property:

An interchange of the quantities $\underline{q}^o$ and $\underline{q}$ which can be interpreted as weights for the corresponding prices $\underline{p}^o$ and $\underline{p}$ does not change the value of P:

(3) $$P(\underline{q}^o,\underline{p}^o,\underline{q},\underline{p}) = P(\underline{q},\underline{p}^o,\underline{q}^o,\underline{p})\ .$$

(4) Theorem:

The conditions given by (1), (2), and (3) are independent in the following sense: Any two of these conditions can be satisfied by a function $P\colon \mathbb{R}^{4n}_{++} \to \mathbb{R}_{++}$ which does not satisfy the remaining condition.

Proof:

The function given by

$$P(\underline{q}^o,\underline{p}^o,\underline{q},\underline{p}) = \left[\frac{\underline{qp}}{\underline{q}^o\underline{p}^o}\right]^{\frac{1}{2}}$$

satisfies (1) and (2), but not (3).

---

*) $\underline{q}^o\underline{p}^o := q_1^o p_1^o + q_2^o p_2^o + \ldots + q_n^o p_n^o$,

$\underline{qp} := q_1 p_1 + q_2 p_2 + \ldots + q_n p_n$.

The function represented by

$$P(\underline{q}^o,\underline{p}^o,\underline{q},\underline{p}) = \frac{(\underline{q}^o+\underline{q})\underline{p}}{(\underline{q}^o+\underline{q})\underline{p}^o} \quad \text{("Marshall-Edgeworth-Index")}$$

meets (1) and (3), but not (2).

Finally, the function given by

$$P(\underline{q}^o,\underline{p}^o,\underline{q},\underline{p}) = \left[\frac{\underline{q}^o\underline{p}}{\underline{q}^o\underline{p}^o}\,\frac{\underline{q}\underline{p}}{\underline{q}\underline{p}^o}\right]^{\frac{1}{2}} \frac{\underline{p}^o\underline{p}}{\underline{q}^o\underline{q}}$$

satisfies (2) and (3), but not (1).

■

(5) Theorem:
A function $P\colon \mathbb{R}^{4n}_{++} \to \mathbb{R}_{++}$ satisfies the Time Reversal Test, the Factor Reversal Test, and the Weight Property if and only if P is Fisher's "ideal index", i.e.,

$$P(\underline{q}^o,\underline{p}^o,\underline{q},\underline{p}) = \left[\frac{\underline{q}^o\underline{p}}{\underline{q}^o\underline{p}^o}\,\frac{\underline{q}\underline{p}}{\underline{q}\underline{p}^o}\right]^{\frac{1}{2}} .$$

Proof:

"$\Leftarrow$": is trivial.

"$\Rightarrow$": By interchanging $\underline{p}^o$ and $\underline{p}$ in (2), we obtain

$$P(\underline{q}^o,\underline{p},\underline{q},\underline{p}^o)\; P(\underline{p},\underline{q}^o,\underline{p}^o,\underline{q}) = \frac{\underline{q}\underline{p}^o}{\underline{q}^o\underline{p}} .$$

By applying (3), this equation becomes

$$P(\underline{q},\underline{p},\underline{q}^o,\underline{p}^o)\; P(\underline{p}^o,\underline{q}^o,\underline{p},\underline{q}) = \frac{\underline{q}\underline{p}^o}{\underline{q}^o\underline{p}} .$$

Dividing (2) by the last equation, we derive

$$\frac{P(\underline{q}^o,\underline{p}^o,\underline{q},\underline{p})}{P(\underline{q},\underline{p},\underline{q}^o,\underline{p}^o)} = \frac{\underline{qp}}{\underline{q}^o\underline{p}^o}\,\frac{\underline{q}^o\underline{p}}{\underline{qp}^o} .$$

Multiplying this equation with (1) finally yields

$$\left[P(\underline{q}^o,\underline{p}^o,\underline{q},\underline{p})\right]^2 = \frac{\underline{qp}}{\underline{q}^o\underline{p}^o}\,\frac{\underline{q}^o\underline{p}}{\underline{qp}^o} ,$$

that is,

$$P(\underline{q}^o,\underline{p}^o,\underline{q},\underline{p}) = \left[\frac{\underline{q}^o\underline{p}}{\underline{q}^o\underline{p}^o}\,\frac{\underline{qp}}{\underline{qp}^o}\right]^{\frac{1}{2}} .$$

■

Reference

EICHHORN,W. and J. VOELLER: Theory of the Price Index - Fisher's Test Approach and Generalizations. Lecture Notes in Economics and Mathematical Systems, Vol. 14o, Springer Verlag, Berlin - Heidelberg - New York,1976.

Price Indices and Generalized Associativity

by Wilhelm Gehrig

0. Introduction[1]

In the axiomatic theory one considers a price index as a positive-valued function, which depends either

(i) on the prices of n commodities of a base year and of the current year or

(ii) on both the prices and quantities of n commodities of a base year and of the current year,

and satisfies several properties (see section 1), which are called a x i o m s, because they are in a certain sense natural.

1. Price Indices of Type (i): Definition, Examples, Axiomatics

Let $\mathbb{R}$ denote the set of real numbers.

Then the sets $\mathbb{R}^n_+$, $\mathbb{R}^n_{++}$ are defined by

$$\mathbb{R}^n_+ := \{\underline{x}=(x_1,..,x_n)\,|\,x_i \geq 0, x_i \in \mathbb{R}, i=1,..,n\} ,$$

$$\mathbb{R}^n_{++} := \{\underline{x}=(x_1,..,x_n)\,|\,x_i > 0, x_i \in \mathbb{R}, i=1,..,n\} ,$$

respectively.

---

1) I am indebted to Prof.W.EICHHORN for his helpful comments.

We further denote by

(0) $\underline{p}^o=(p_1^o,\dots,p_n^o)\in\mathbf{R}^n_{++}$, $\underline{p}=(p_1,\dots,p_n)\in\mathbf{R}^n_{++}$

the vectors of the prices of n commodities of a base year and of the current year, respectively.

By a price index depending on the vectors (0), we understand a function

(1) $$F:\begin{cases}\mathbf{R}^{2n}_{++}\to\mathbf{R}_{++}\\(\underline{p}^o,\underline{p})\mapsto F(\underline{p}^o,\underline{p}),\end{cases}$$

satisfying the following axioms (A1) - (A4).

(A1) MONOTONICITY AXIOM: For all $\underline{p}^o,\overline{\underline{p}}^o,\underline{p},\overline{\underline{p}}\in\mathbf{R}^n_{++}$:

$$F(\underline{p}^o,\underline{p}) > F(\underline{p}^o,\overline{\underline{p}}) \text{ if } \underline{p}\geq\overline{\underline{p}} \qquad (\underline{p}\geq\overline{\underline{p}}:\Longleftrightarrow\underline{p}\geqq\overline{\underline{p}}\wedge\underline{p}\neq\overline{\underline{p}})$$

and

$$F(\underline{p}^o,\underline{p}) < F(\overline{\underline{p}}^o,\underline{p}) \text{ if } \underline{p}^o\geq\overline{\underline{p}}^o.$$

(A2) LINEAR HOMOGENEITY AXIOM:

$$F(\underline{p}^o,\lambda\underline{p}) = \lambda F(\underline{p}^o,\underline{p}) \qquad \forall\underline{p}^o,\underline{p}\in\mathbf{R}^n_{++},\forall\lambda\in\mathbf{R}_{++}.$$

(A3) IDENTITY AXIOM:

$$F(\underline{p}^o,\underline{p}^o) = 1 \qquad \forall\underline{p}^o\in\mathbf{R}^n_{++}.$$

(A4) DIMENSIONALITY AXIOM:

$$F(\lambda\underline{p}^o,\lambda\underline{p}) = F(\underline{p}^o,\underline{p}) \qquad \forall\underline{p}^o,\underline{p}\in\mathbf{R}^n_{++},\forall\lambda\in\mathbf{R}_{++}.$$

Among others, the functions F given by (2)-(4) can be regarded as price indices:

(2) $$F(\underline{p}^o,\underline{p}) = \frac{\underline{c}\cdot\underline{p}}{\underline{c}\cdot\underline{p}^o} \qquad (\underline{c}=(c_1,\dots,c_n)\in\mathbf{R}^n_{++}\text{ constant}),$$

(3) $$F(\underline{p}^o,\underline{p}) = \{\sum_{i=1}^n\beta_i(p_i/p_i^o)^{\alpha}\}^{\frac{1}{\alpha}} \qquad (\alpha\neq0,\beta_i>0\text{ real const.},\sum_{i=1}^n\beta_i=1),$$

(4) $$F(\underline{p}^o,\underline{p}) = \prod_{i=1}^n(p_i/p_i^o)^{\alpha_i} \qquad (\alpha_i>0,\text{real constants},\sum_{i=1}^n\alpha_i=1).$$

Depending on the interpretation of the c_i's, the formula (2) may be the price index of LASPEYRES or PAASCHE.The functions given by (3) and (4) are well-known to be of the ACMS-type or COBB-DOUGLAS-(CD-) type, respectively.[1)]

[1)] See K.J.ARROW-H.B.CHENERY-B.S.MINHAS-R.M.SOLOW [1961], C.W.COBB-P.H.DOUGLAS [1928], respectively.

2. Characterization of the CD- and ACMS- Price Indices by Generalized Associativity

A characterization of the price index given by (2) is due to J.ACZÉL-W.EICHHORN [1974a], [1974b]. Characterizations of (4) can be found in W.EICHHORN [1977] and W.EICHHORN-J.VOELLER [1976].

In this paper we will show that a function F satisfying the following system (5) of functional equations is always a price index of the CD- or of the ACMS-type.

We consider the following system for $n \geqq 3$:

$$(5)\quad F(\underline{p}^o,\underline{p})=\Psi^1\{G(p_1^o,p_1),H^1(G(p_2^o,p_2),\ldots\ldots\ldots,G(p_n^o,p_n))\}=$$
$$\vdots$$
$$=\Psi^i\{G(p_i^o,p_i),H^i(G(p_1^o,p_1),..,G(p_{i-1}^o,p_{i-1}),G(p_{i+1}^o,p_{i+1}),..,G(p_n^o,p_n))\}=$$
$$\vdots$$
$$=\Psi^n\{G(p_n^o,p_n),H^n(G(p_1^o,p_1),\ldots\ldots\ldots,G(p_{n-1}^o,p_{n-1}))\},$$

where

$$(V_1)\begin{cases}\Psi^i:\ \mathbf{R}_{++}^2\to\mathbf{R}_{++},\ H^i:\ \mathbf{R}_{++}^{n-1}\to\mathbf{R}_{++},\ G:\ \mathbf{R}_{++}^2\to\mathbf{R}_{++},\\ \Psi^i\varepsilon C^1(\mathbf{R}_{++}^2),\ H^i\varepsilon C^1(\mathbf{R}_{++}^{n-1}) \qquad (\forall i=1,..,n).\\ \Psi_j^i(w_1,w_2):=\frac{\partial}{\partial w_j}\Psi^i(w_1,w_2)>0\ (\forall w_1,w_2>0;\forall i=1,..,n;\forall j=1,2).\\ H_k^i(z_1,..,z_{n-1})>0\quad(\forall z_1,..,z_{n-1}>0;\forall i=1,..,n;\forall k=1,..,n-1).^{1)}\\ \Psi^i(\lambda x,\lambda y)=\lambda\Psi^i(x,y)\quad(\forall x,y,\lambda>0;\forall i=1,..,n).\\ H^i(\lambda z_1,..,\lambda z_{n-1})=\lambda H^i(z_1,..,z_{n-1})\ (\forall z_1,..,z_{n-1},\lambda>0;\forall i=1,..,n).\\ G(p_i^o,\lambda p_i)=\lambda G(p_i^o,p_i)\ \text{ and }\ G(\lambda p_i^o,p_i)=\frac{1}{\lambda}G(p_i^o,p_i)\quad(\forall p_i^o,p_i,\lambda>0).\\ G(p_i^o,p_i^o)=1\ (\forall p_i^o>0).\\ \Psi^i(1,1)=H^i(1,..,1)=1\quad(\forall i=1,..,n).\end{cases}$$

---

1) We always denote by f_j the partial derivative with respect to the jth argument of a (partially differentiable) function $f:\ D\subseteq\mathbf{R}^n\to\mathbf{R}$ (D open in $\mathbf{R}^n$)

In (5) we require from a price index, that its value is always the same no matter whether it is regarded as a function of the change of the first price and an index of the changes of all remaining prices or whether it is a function of the change of the second price and an index of the changes of all remaining prices,.., or whether it is a function of the change of the nth price and an index of the changes of all remaining prices.

LEMMA I: Every function $F: \mathbb{R}^{2n}_{++} \rightarrow \mathbb{R}_{++}$ of the form (5) with functions G, Ψ^i and H^i satisfying (V_1) is a price index.

Proof: We have to show that F satisfies (A1) - (A4).

Since Ψ^i and H^i are strictly increasing and G is strictly increasing in the second and strictly decreasing in the first argument, it follows for all $\underline{p}^o, \overline{\underline{p}}^o, \underline{p}, \overline{\underline{p}} \in \mathbb{R}^n_{++}$ that

(i) $$F(\underline{p}^o,\underline{p}) > F(\underline{p}^o,\overline{\underline{p}}) \qquad \text{if } \underline{p} \geq \overline{\underline{p}}$$
and
$$F(\underline{p}^o,\underline{p}) < F(\overline{\underline{p}}^o,\underline{p}) \qquad \text{if } \underline{p}^o \geq \overline{\underline{p}}^o ,$$

that is (A1).

(ii) $$F(\underline{p}^o,\lambda\underline{p})=\Psi^i\{\lambda G(.),H^i(\lambda G(.),..,\lambda G(.))\}=\Psi^i\{\lambda G(.),\lambda H^i(G(.),..,G(.))\}=$$
$$=\lambda\Psi^i(.,.)=\lambda F(\underline{p}^o,\underline{p}) \qquad (\forall\lambda>0,\forall\underline{p}^o,\underline{p}\in\mathbb{R}^n_{++}) ,$$

that is (A2).

(iii) $$F(\underline{p}^o,\underline{p}^o)=\Psi^i\{G(p_i^o,p_i^o),H^i(G(p_1^o,p_1^o),..,G(p_{i-1}^o,p_{i-1}^o),G(p_{i+1}^o,p_{i+1}^o),..,G(p_n^o,p_n^o))\}$$
$$=\Psi^i\{1,H^i(1,..,1)\}=$$
$$=\Psi^i(1,1) = 1 \qquad (\forall\underline{p}^o\in\mathbb{R}^n_{++}),$$

that is (A3).

(iv) $$F(\lambda\underline{p}^o,\lambda\underline{p})=\Psi^i\{G(p_i^o,p_i^o),H^i(G(p_1^o,p_1),..,G(p_{i-1}^o,p_{i-1}^o),G(p_{i+1}^o,p_{i+1}^o),..,G(p_n^o,p_n^o))\}$$
$$=F(\underline{p}^o,\underline{p}) \qquad (\forall\lambda>0,\forall\underline{p}^o,\underline{p}\in\mathbb{R}^n_{++}),$$

that is (A4) ■

LEMMA II: For arbitrary, but constant $x_i=\tilde{x}_i>0$ $(i=2,..,n)$ the following two assertions are true:

(A) The equations

(6) $$y_1=H^1(x_2,\tilde{x}_3,..,\tilde{x}_n) \text{ and } y_i=H^i(x_1,\tilde{x}_2,..,\tilde{x}_{i-1},\tilde{x}_{i+1},..,\tilde{x}_n) \quad (i=2,..,n)$$

are uniquely solvable with respect to x_2 and x_1 for $y_1 \varepsilon I^{y_1}$ and $y_i \varepsilon I^{y_i}$, respectively. I^{y_k} $(k=1,..,n)$ are open and non-empty intervals in $\mathbb{R}_{++}$.

(B) The "inverses" θ^k $(k=1,..,n)$ of (6), which satisfy

(7) $$x_2=\theta^1(y_1) \text{ and } x_1=\theta^i(y_i) \quad (i=2,..,n) \quad (y_k \varepsilon I^{y_k}; k=1,..,n)$$

are continuously differentiable and have positive derivatives.

Proof: From $H^i \varepsilon C^1(\mathbb{R}^{n-1}_{++})$, $H^i(\mathbb{R}^{n-1}_{++})=\mathbb{R}_{++}$ and $H^i_1>0$ [1)] it follows that the functions

$$x_2 \mapsto h^1(x_2) := H^1(x_2,\tilde{x}_3,..,\tilde{x}_n) \text{ and}$$

$$x_1 \mapsto h^i(x_1) := H^i(x_1,\tilde{x}_2,..,\tilde{x}_{i-1},\tilde{x}_{i+1},..,\tilde{x}_n) \quad (i=2,..,n)$$

are continuously differentiable with $h^{k'}>0$ $(k=1,..,n)$. Therefore the image sets

$$I^{y_1} := \{y_1 \mid y_1=h^1(x_2), x_2>0\}; I^{y_i} := \{y_i \mid y_i=h^i(x_1), x_1>0\} \quad (i=2,..,n)$$

are open and non-empty intervals in $\mathbb{R}_{++}$.

Moreover, the inverse functions

$$\overset{-1}{h^k}: \begin{cases} I^{y_k} \to \mathbb{R}_{++} \\ h^k(x_j) \mapsto x_j, \; x_j \varepsilon \mathbb{R}_{++} \end{cases} \quad \begin{matrix} (k=1,..,n; \\ j=2 \text{ if } k=1; \\ j=1 \text{ if } k>1\;) \end{matrix}$$

exist and are continuously differentiable with $\overset{-1}{h^k}{}'>0$.

We denote these inverses by $\theta^k := \overset{-1}{h^k}$ ■

---

1) By writing $f>0$ for a function $f: D \subseteq \mathbb{R}^n \to \mathbb{R}$ we always mean that $f(\underline{x})>0$ for all $\underline{x} \varepsilon D$.

We will prove now, that the assumptions made on G in (V_1) imply

(8) $$G(p_i^o, p_i) = \frac{p_i}{p_i^o} .$$

From $$G(p_i^o, \lambda p_i) = \lambda G^i(p_i^o, p_i)$$

it follows that

(9) $$G(p_i^o, p_i) = p_i H(p_i^o) \qquad \text{with } H(x) := G(x,1).$$

On the other hand, we have from

$$G(\lambda p_i^o, p_i) = \frac{1}{\lambda} G(p_i^o, p_i),$$

setting $\lambda = \frac{1}{p_i^o}$,

(10) $$G(p_i^o, p_i) = \frac{1}{p_i^o} L(p_i) \qquad \text{with } L(y) := G(1,y).$$

Equating (9) and (10), we obtain

(11) $$\frac{1}{p_i^o} L(p_i) = p_i \, H(p_i^o).$$

Setting succesively $p_i^o=1, p_i=1$, we obtain

$$L(p_i) = cp_i,$$
$$H(p_i^o) = c/p_i^o \qquad \text{with } c := H(1) = L(1),$$

that is

(12) $$G(p_i^o, p_i) = c \frac{p_i}{p_i^o} .$$

The additional assumption $G(p_i^o, p_i^o)=1$ requires $c=1$, that is (8) ■

If we set $x_i = p_i/p_i^o$, then (5) becomes (for $\underline{x} \varepsilon \mathbb{R}^n_{++}$)

(13) $$\Psi^1(x_1, H^1(\underline{x}^{\cdot 1})) = \Psi^2(x_2, H^2(\underline{x}^{\cdot 2})) = \cdots = \Psi^i(x_i, H^i(\underline{x}^{\cdot i})) = \cdots = \Psi^n(x_n, H^n(\underline{x}^{\cdot n})).$$ [1)]

This system of functional equations is an extension of the so-called "generalized associativity equation"

$$G^1(x, F^1(y,z)) = G^2(z, F^2(x,y))$$

(see J.AZCÉL [1966],p.327).

---

1) $\underline{x}^{\cdot i} := (x_1, \ldots, x_{i-1}, x_{i+1}, \ldots, x_n)$.

We consider

$$(14)\qquad \Psi^1(x_1,H^1(x_2,..,x_n)) = \Psi^2(x_2,H^2(x_1,x_3,..,x_n)).$$

By partial differentiation of (14) with respect to x_1 and x_n,

$$(15)\quad \begin{cases} \Psi^1_1(x_1,H^1(x_2,..,x_n)) = \Psi^2_2(x_2,H^2(x_1,x_3,..,x_n))\cdot H^2_1(x_1,x_3,..,x_n) \\ \Psi^1_2(x_1,H^1(x_2,..,x_n))\,H^1_{n-1}(x_2,..,x_n) = \Psi^2_2(x_2,H^2(x_1,x_3,..,x_n))H^2_{n-1}(x_1,x_3,..,x_n) \end{cases}$$

We set $x_i=\tilde{x}_i$ $(i=3,..,n)$ and divide the first of the above equations by the second. This yields

$$(16)\qquad \frac{\Psi^1_1(x_1,H^1(x_2,\tilde{x}_3,..,\tilde{x}_n))}{\Psi^1_2(x_1,H^1(x_2,\tilde{x}_3,..,\tilde{x}_n))} = \frac{H^2_1(x_1,\tilde{x}_3,..,\tilde{x}_n)}{H^2_{n-1}(x_1,\tilde{x}_3,..,\tilde{x}_n)}\,H^1_{n-1}(x_2,\tilde{x}_3,..,\tilde{x}_n)\ .$$

From Lemma II we know that $y_1=H^1(x_2,\tilde{x}_3,..,\tilde{x}_n)$ is uniquely solvable for $y_1\varepsilon I^{y_1}$ such that $x_2=\theta^1(y_1)$ with continuously differentiable θ^1 with $\theta^{1'}>0$. Defining the functions m^1 and k^1 by

$$(17)\quad m^1(y_1):=\int\frac{dy_1}{H^1_{n-1}(\theta^1(y_1),\tilde{x}_3,..,\tilde{x}_n)}\quad ;\ k^1(x_1):=\int\frac{H^2_1(x_1,\tilde{x}_3,..,\tilde{x}_n)}{H^2_{n-1}(x_1,\tilde{x}_3,..,\tilde{x}_n)}\,dx_1\quad ,$$

m^1 and k^1 are continuously differentiable with $k^{1'},m^{1'}>0$.
Equations (16) and (17) imply the partial differential equation

$$(18)\qquad m^{1'}(y_1)\Psi^1_1(x_1,y_1) - k^{1'}(x_1)\Psi^1_2(x_1,y_1) = 0 \qquad (x_1>0,y_1\varepsilon I^{y_1}),$$

whose general solution is given by

$$(19)\qquad \Psi^1(x_1,y_1) = h(k^1(x_1)+m^1(y_1)) \qquad (x_1>0,y_1\varepsilon I^{y_1})$$

with an arbitrary continuously differentiable function h satisfying $h'>0$.

We insert (19) in (13) in order to get

$$(20)\qquad \Psi^1(x_1,H^1(\underline{x}^{\cdot 1})) = h(k^1(x_1)+m^1(H^1(\underline{x}^{\cdot 1}))) =$$

$$= \Psi^2(x_2,H^2(\underline{x}^{\cdot 2})) =$$

$$\vdots$$

$$= \Psi^i(x_i,H^i(\underline{x}^{\cdot i})) =$$

$$\vdots$$

$$= \Psi^n(x_n,H^n(\underline{x}^{\cdot n})).$$

Equation (20) is valid for $x_1>0$ and $(x_2,.,x_n)\varepsilon M^1:=\overset{-1}{H^1}(I^{y_1})$, that is

$$M^1:=\{(x_2,.,x_n)\,|\,(x_2,.,x_n)\varepsilon \mathbb{R}^{n-1}_{++},H^1(x_2,.,x_n)\varepsilon I^{y_1}\}.$$

Since I^{y_1} is an open interval in $\mathbb{R}_{++}$ and H^1 is continuous, the set M^1 is open in $\mathbb{R}^{n-1}_{++}$.

It is also true, that $(x_2,\tilde{x}_3,.,\tilde{x}_n)\varepsilon M^1$ for all $x_2>0$ (see Lemma II).

Since M^1 is open in $\mathbb{R}^{n-1}_{++}$, it contains an open, (n-1)-dimensional interval

$$Z^1:=I_1^{x_2}\times\cdots\times I_1^{x_n}$$

with $\tilde{x}_2\varepsilon I_1^{x_2},\ldots,\tilde{x}_n\varepsilon I_1^{x_n}$.

For $x_1>0$ and $(x_2,.,x_n)\varepsilon M^1$ we obtain from (20)

(21) $\psi^i(x_i,H^i(x_1,.,x_{i-1},x_{i+1},.,x_n)) = h(k^1(x_1)+m^1(H^1(x_2,.,x_n)))$ (i=2,..,n).

We set

$$x_2=\tilde{x}_2,\ldots,x_{i-1}=\tilde{x}_{i-1},x_{i+1}=\tilde{x}_{i+1},.,x_n=\tilde{x}_n ,$$

Thereafter we solve

$$y_i=H^i(x_1,\tilde{x}_2,.,\tilde{x}_{i-1},\tilde{x}_{i+1},.,\tilde{x}_n) \qquad (i=2,..,n)$$

with respect to x_1 and obtain (see Lemma II)

$$x_1=\theta^i(y_i)$$

and then, with (21)

(22) $\psi^i(x_i,y_i) = h(k^1(\theta^i(y_i))+m^1(H^1(\tilde{x}_2,.,\tilde{x}_{i-1},x_i,\tilde{x}_{i+1},.,\tilde{x}_n)))$.

From (22) we obtain, with

$$m^i(y_i):= k^1(\theta^i(y_i))$$

and

$$k^i(x_i):= m^1(H^1(\tilde{x}_2,.,\tilde{x}_{i-1},x_i,\tilde{x}_{i+1},.,\tilde{x}_n))$$

(23) $\psi^i(x_i,y_i) = h(k^i(x_i)+m^i(y_i))$ $(x_i\varepsilon I_1^{x_i},y_i\varepsilon I^{y_i})$.

We remark further that m^i and k^i are continuously differentiable with $m^{i'},k^{i'}>0$.

Inserting (23) into (13), it follows that

$$(24)\qquad \Psi^i(x_i, H^i(\underline{x}^{\cdot i})) = h(k^i(x_i)+m^i(H^i(\underline{x}^{\cdot i}))) \qquad (i=2,..,n).$$

These equations are valid for $x_i \varepsilon I_1^{x_i}$ and $(x_1,..,x_{i-1},x_{i+1},..,x_n)\varepsilon M^i$, where

$$M^i := \overset{-1}{H^i}(I^{y_i}) \cap (\mathbf{R}_{++} \times I_1^{x_2} \times \cdot \times I_1^{x_{i-1}} \times I_1^{x_{i+1}} \times \cdot \times I_1^{x_n}) \neq \emptyset ,$$

that is

$$M^i := \{\underline{x}^{\cdot i} \mid x_1 > 0, x_j \varepsilon I_1^{x_j} (j=2,..,i-1,i+1,..,n), H^i(\underline{x}^{\cdot i}) \varepsilon I^{y_i}\}.$$

Since H^i is continuous and I^{y_i} is open in $\mathbf{R}_{++}$, $\overset{-1}{H^i}(I^{y_i})$ is open in $\mathbf{R}_{++}^{n-1}$. Hence M^i is open in $\mathbf{R}_{++}^{n-1}$, because it is the intersection of two open sets. As M^1, all M^i contain an open, (n-1)-dimensional interval

$$Z^i := I_i^{x_1} \times \cdot \times I_i^{x_{i-1}} \times I_i^{x_{i+1}} \times \cdot \times I_i^{x_n} \qquad (i=2,..,n)$$

with $\tilde{x}_k \varepsilon I_i^{x_k}$ $(i,k=2,..,n; i \neq k)$.

Especially the $I_i^{x_1}$ can be chosen in such a way that $I_2^{x_1} = I_3^{x_1} = \cdots = I_n^{x_1}$, since $(x_1, \tilde{x}_2,.., \tilde{x}_{i-1}, \tilde{x}_{i+1},.., \tilde{x}_n)\varepsilon M^i$ for all $x_1 > 0$.

Summarizing, the equations (20) and (24) are valid for $(x_1,..,x_n)$ from

$$\begin{aligned}
i=1:&\quad \mathbf{R}_{++} \times I_1^{x_2} \times \cdots\cdots \times I_1^{x_n}\\
&\quad \vdots\\
i=j:&\quad I_j^{x_1} \times I_j^{x_2} \times \cdot \times I_j^{x_{j-1}} \times I_1^{x_j} \times I_j^{x_{j+1}} \times \cdot \times I_j^{x_n}\\
&\quad \vdots\\
i=n:&\quad I_n^{x_1} \times I_n^{x_2} \times \cdots\cdots \times I_n^{x_{n-1}} \times I_1^{x_n},
\end{aligned}$$

respectively.

We define (for $j=1,..,n$) I^{x_j} (with $I_1^{x_1} = \mathbf{R}_{++}$) by

$$I^{x_j} := \bigcap_{i=1}^{n} I_i^{x_j} \quad .$$

and remark that all I^{x_j} are non-empty and open, since all $I_i^{x_j}$ contain a whole (one-dimensional) neighbourhood of $\tilde{x}_j$ and the intersection of finitely many open sets is again an open set.

Let
$$T:=I^{x_1}\times\cdots\times I^{x_n}$$
.

Then we obtain, for $\underline{x}\varepsilon T$, by inserting (20) and (24) into (13),

(25)
$$h(k^1(x_1)+m^1(H^1(\underline{x}^{\cdot 1}))) = \cdots = h(k^i(x_i)+m^i(H^i(\underline{x}^{\cdot i}))) = \cdots = h(k^n(x_n)+m^n(H^n(\underline{x}^{\cdot n}))).$$

Since $h'>0$, it is further true that

(26) $k^1(x_1)+m^1(H^1(\underline{x}^{\cdot 1}))=\cdots=k^i(x_i)+m^i(H^i(\underline{x}^{\cdot i}))=\cdots=k^n(x_n)+m^n(H^n(\underline{x}^{\cdot n}))$.

Now we consider succesively

(27)
$$k^i(x_i)+m^i(H^i(\underline{x}^{\cdot i}))=k^{i+1}(x_{i+1})+m^{i+1}(H^{i+1}(\underline{x}^{\cdot i+1})).$$

Since $m^{i\,'}>0$, we obtain from (27)

(28)
$$H^i(\underline{x}^{\cdot i}) = \overset{-1}{m^i}\{m^{i+1}(H^{i+1}(\underline{x}^{\cdot i+1}))+k^{i+1}(x_{i+1})-k^i(x_i)\}$$

The left side in (28) does not depend on x_i.Hence, with $x_i=\tilde{x}_i$ and

$$g(\underline{x}^{\cdot i,i+1}):=m^{i+1}(H^{i+1}(x_1,..,\tilde{x}_i,x_{i+2},..,x_n))-k^i(\tilde{x}_i)$$

(29)
$$H^i(\underline{x}^{\cdot i}) = \overset{-1}{m^i}(g^i(\underline{x}^{\cdot i,i+1})+k^{i+1}(x_{i+1})).$$

We have proved:

THEOREM I : Let (13) be given, where the functions Ψ^i and H^i satisfy (V_1). Then

$$\Psi^1(x_1,y_1) = h(k^1(x_1)+m^1(y_1)) \quad (x_1>0,y_1\varepsilon I^{y_1}),$$

$$\Psi^j(x_j,y_j) = h(k^j(x_j)+m^j(y_j)) \quad (x_j\varepsilon I_1^{x_j},y_j\varepsilon I^{y_j};j=2,..,n),$$

and

$$H^i(\underline{x}^{\cdot i}) = \overset{-1}{m^i}\{g^i(\underline{x}^{\cdot i,i+1})+k^{i+1}(x_{i+1})\} \quad (x_j\varepsilon I^{x_j};i,j=1,..,n;i\neq j).$$

Here, the functions h,k^i and m^i are continuously differentiable and have positive derivatives.The functions g^i are continuously differentiable, and, moreover, all their partial derivatives are positive-valued.

Inserting (29) into (25) yields for $\underline{x}\varepsilon T$,

$$(30)\qquad h(k^1(x_1)+k^2(x_2)+g^1(\underline{x}^{\cdot 2,3})) = \vdots$$
$$= h(k^i(x_i)+k^{i+1}(x_{i+1})+g^i(\underline{x}^{\cdot i,i+1})) = \vdots$$
$$= h(k^n(x_n)+k^1(x_1)+g^n(\underline{x}^{\cdot n,1})).$$

Equation (30) shows that we still have (2n+1) unknown functions, by which F is given.But so far, we didn't make use of the additional assumption that the functions Ψ^j (j=1,..,n) are linearly homogeneous.This property enables us, in connection with the strict monotonicity of the Ψ^i's in both arguments, to determine the explicit form of h,k^j and m^j.

By Theorem I, we know that

$$\Psi^i(x_i,y_i) = h(k^i(x_i)+m^i(y_i)) \qquad (x_i\varepsilon I_1^{x_i}, y_i\varepsilon I^{y_i}; I_1^{x_1}=\mathbb{R}_{++}).$$

Since Ψ^i is linearly homogeneous,

$$(31)\qquad \Psi^i(\lambda x_i,\lambda y_i)=h(k^i(\lambda x_i)+m^i(\lambda y_i))=\lambda h(k^i(x_i)+m^i(y_i))=\lambda\Psi^i(x_i,y_i),$$

where λ must be chosen so that

$$\lambda x_i\varepsilon I_1^{x_i} \quad \underline{\text{and}} \quad \lambda y_i\varepsilon I^{y_i}.$$

To ensure this we consider (31) for $x_i\varepsilon\bar{I}^{x_i}$ and $y_i\varepsilon\bar{I}^{y_i}$ where

$$\bar{I}^{x_i} c I^{x_i} \underline{c} I_1^{x_i} \quad \text{and} \quad \bar{I}^{y_i} c I^{y_i} \;{}^{1)}$$

with $\tilde{x}_i\varepsilon\bar{I}^{x_i}$ and $\tilde{y}_i = H^i(\tilde{x}_1,..,\tilde{x}_{i-1},\tilde{x}_{i+1},..,\tilde{x}_n)\varepsilon\bar{I}^{y_i}$ ($\tilde{x}_1\varepsilon I^{x_1}$)

are open intervals.Then we determine two open intervals $I_\lambda^{x_i}$ and $I_\lambda^{y_i}$ such that

$$\lambda x_i\varepsilon I_1^{x_i} \;(\lambda\varepsilon I_\lambda^{x_i}, x_i\varepsilon\bar{I}^{x_i}) \quad \text{and} \quad \lambda y_i\varepsilon I^{y_i} \;(\lambda\varepsilon I_\lambda^{y_i}, y_i\varepsilon\bar{I}^{y_i}).$$

It can be easily seen that $1\varepsilon I_\lambda^{x_i}$ and $1\varepsilon I_\lambda^{y_i}$.

In what follows, we consider (31) for

$$x_i\varepsilon\bar{I}^{x_i}, \; y_i\varepsilon\bar{I}^{y_i}, \; \lambda\varepsilon I^{\lambda_i} \quad , \text{where } I^{\lambda_i}:=I_\lambda^{x_i}\cap I_\lambda^{y_i}.$$

---

1) This means for $I_a:=(a,a'), I_b:=(b,b'): I_a c I_b$ such that a>b and a'<b'.

<u>Remark:</u> In the case of k^1 and m^1 we determine first $\overline{I}^{y_1} \subset I^{y_1}$ as described and then $I_\lambda^{y_1}$. Since x_1 varies then furthermore in $\mathbb{R}_{++}$, we have $\overline{I}^{x_1} = \mathbb{R}_{++}$.

From (31) we obtain, because of the strict monotonicity of h

$$k^i(\lambda x_i)+m^i(\lambda y_i) = \bar{h}^{-1}\{\lambda h(k^i(x_i)+m^i(y_i))\} \quad (x_i \in \overline{I}^{x_i}, y_i \in \overline{I}^{y_i}, \lambda \in I^{\lambda_i}).^{1)} \tag{32}$$

With

$$\left\{\begin{array}{l} u_i := k^i(x_i) \\ z_i := m^i(y_i) \\ \bar{h}_\lambda^{-1}(x) := \bar{h}^{-1}(\lambda x) \\ \overset{-1}{k}{}^i_\lambda(u_i) := \lambda \overset{-1}{k}{}^i(u_i) \\ \overset{-1}{m}{}^i_\lambda(z_i) := \lambda \overset{-1}{m}{}^{i}(z_i) \end{array}\right. , \tag{33}$$

it follows from (32) that

$$\bar{h}_\lambda^{-1}(h(u_i+z_i)) = k^i(\overset{-1}{k}{}^i_\lambda(u_i)) + m^i(\overset{-1}{m}{}^i_\lambda(z_i)). \tag{34}$$

Now we define functions d_λ, e_λ^i and n_λ^i by

$$\left\{\begin{array}{l} d_\lambda(x) := \bar{h}_\lambda^{-1}(h(x)) \\ e_\lambda^i(x) := k^i(\overset{-1}{k}{}^i_\lambda(x)) \\ n_\lambda^i(x) := m^i(\overset{-1}{m}{}^i_\lambda(x)) \end{array}\right. . \tag{35}$$

The functions d_λ, e_λ^i and n_λ^i are continuously differentiable with $d_\lambda', e_\lambda^{i\,\prime}, n_\lambda^{i\,\prime} > 0$, since the functions $\overset{-1}{h}_\lambda, h, k^i, \overset{-1}{k}{}^i_\lambda, m^i, \overset{-1}{m}{}^i_\lambda$ have these properties.

By (34), this leads to

$$d_\lambda(u_i+z_i) = e_\lambda^i(u_i) + n_\lambda^i(z_i). \tag{36}$$

---

1) With $I^{\lambda_1} = I_\lambda^{y_1}$, since $I_\lambda^{x_1} = \mathbb{R}_{++}$.

Functional equation (36) is only valid for

$$u_i \varepsilon I^{u_i} := \{\bar{u}_i \mid \exists\ x_i \varepsilon \bar{I}^{x_i} \text{ such that } k^i(x_i) = \bar{u}_i\},$$

$$z_i \varepsilon I^{z_i} := \{\bar{z}_i \mid \exists\ y_i \varepsilon \bar{I}^{y_i} \text{ such that } m^i(y_i) = \bar{z}_i\}.$$

Since m^i and k^i are continuous and strictly increasing functions and $\bar{I}^{x_i}$ and $\bar{I}^{y_i}$ are open intervals, I^{u_i} and I^{z_i} are likewise open intervals. F.STEHLING [1974,p.83-85] has proved that (36) implies

$$e^i_\lambda(u_i) = c^i(\lambda)u_i + a^i(\lambda) \qquad (u_i \varepsilon I^{u_i}), \tag{37}$$

$$n^i_\lambda(z_i) = c^i(\lambda)z_i + \bar{a}^i(\lambda) \qquad (z_i \varepsilon I^{z_i}). \tag{38}$$

Backward substitution with (35) and (33) leads to

$$k^i(\lambda x_i) = c^i(\lambda)k^i(x_i) + a^i(\lambda) \qquad (x_i \varepsilon \bar{I}^{x_i}, \lambda \varepsilon I^{\lambda_i}), \tag{39}$$

$$m^i(\lambda y_i) = c^i(\lambda)m^i(y_i) + \bar{a}^i(\lambda) \qquad (y_i \varepsilon \bar{I}^{y_i}, \lambda \varepsilon I^{\lambda_i}). \tag{40}$$

We take $\tilde{x}_i$ and $\tilde{y}_i$ and determine the intervals[1)]

$$I^{x_i}_{\lambda_i} := (1/\tilde{x}_i)\bar{I}^{x_i} \cap I^{\lambda_i} \quad \text{and} \quad I^{y_i}_{\lambda_i} := (1/\tilde{y}_i)\bar{I}^{y_i} \cap I^{\lambda_i}.$$

Clearly, $I^{x_i}_{\lambda_i}$ and $I^{y_i}_{\lambda_i}$ are open intervals with $1 \varepsilon I^{x_i}_{\lambda_i}, 1 \varepsilon I^{y_i}_{\lambda_i}$.

Since $I^{x_i}_{\lambda_i}, I^{y_i}_{\lambda_i} \subseteq I^{\lambda_i}$, $\tilde{x}_i I^{x_i}_{\lambda_i} \subseteq \bar{I}^{x_i}$ and $\tilde{y}_i I^{y_i}_{\lambda_i} \subseteq \bar{I}^{y_i}$, the functional equations (39) and (40) are also valid for $\lambda \varepsilon I^{x_i}_{\lambda_i}, x_i \varepsilon \tilde{x}_i I^{x_i}_{\lambda_i}$ and $\lambda \varepsilon I^{y_i}_{\lambda_i}, y_i \varepsilon \tilde{y}_i I^{y_i}_{\lambda_i}$, respectively. We denote $\tilde{x}_i I^{x_i}_{\lambda_i}$ by $I^{x_i}_i$ and $\tilde{y}_i I^{y_i}_{\lambda_i}$ by $I^{y_i}_i$.

The solution of (39) for $\lambda \varepsilon I^{x_i}_{\lambda_i}, x_i \varepsilon I^{x_i}_i$ and of (40) for $\lambda \varepsilon I^{y_i}_{\lambda_i}, y_i \varepsilon I^{y_i}_i$ has been determined by the author [1976,p.100-106].

---

1) For $a \varepsilon \mathbf{R}$ and $I \subset \mathbf{R}$ we define aI by $aI := \{z \mid z = ax, x \varepsilon I\}$.

We obtain either

$$(41)\quad \begin{cases} k^1(x_1)=\gamma_1\log x_1+\delta_1\ , & m^1(y_1)=\overline{\gamma}_1\log y_1+\overline{\delta}_1\ \ (x_1>0,\ y_1\varepsilon I_{\lambda_1}^{y_1}\cdot I_1^{y_1})^{1)},\\ k^i(x_i)=\gamma_i\log x_i+\delta_i\ , & m^i(y_i)=\overline{\gamma}_i\log y_i+\overline{\delta}_i\ \ (x_i\varepsilon I_{\lambda_i}^{x_i}\cdot I_i^{x_i},\ y_i\varepsilon I_{\lambda_i}^{y_i}\cdot I_i^{y_i}\ ,\\ & \qquad\qquad i=2,..,n) \end{cases}$$

or

$$(42)\quad \begin{cases} k^1(x_1)=\varepsilon_1 x_1^{\alpha_1}+\eta_1\ , & m^1(y_1)=\overline{\varepsilon}_1 y_1^{\alpha_1}+\overline{\eta}_1\qquad (x_1,y_1 \text{ as in (41)}),\\ k^i(x_i)=\varepsilon_i x_i^{\alpha_i}+\eta_i\ , & m^i(y_i)=\overline{\varepsilon}_i y_i^{\alpha_i}+\overline{\eta}_i\qquad (x_i,y_i \text{ as in (41)},\\ & \qquad\qquad i=2,..,n). \end{cases}$$

Since k^i and m^i are strictly increasing, the constants $\overline{\varepsilon}_i,\varepsilon_i,\overline{\alpha}_i,\alpha_i,\overline{\gamma}_i$ and γ_i satisfy: $\overline{\gamma}_i,\gamma_i,\overline{\varepsilon}_i\alpha_i,\varepsilon_i\alpha_i>0$.

We set
$$\tilde{I}^{y_i}:=I_{\lambda_i}^{y_i}\cdot I_i^{y_i}\ (i=1,..,n)\ \text{and}\ \tilde{I}^{x_i}:=I_{\lambda_i}^{x_i}\cdot I_i^{x_i}\ (i=2,..,n).$$

The sets T (see page 10) and $\tilde{T}$, which is defined by

$$\tilde{T}:=\mathbf{R}_{++}\times\tilde{I}^{x_2}\times\cdots\times\tilde{I}^{x_n}$$

are not disjoint, since $\tilde{x}_i\varepsilon I_i^{x_i}$, and therefore we have, because of $1\varepsilon I_{\lambda_i}^{y_i}$, that $\tilde{x}_i\varepsilon\tilde{I}_i^{x_i}$.

Therefore
$$\tilde{\tilde{I}}^{x_i}:=I^{x_i}\cap\tilde{I}^{x_i}\neq\emptyset\ .^{2)}$$

We set
$$\tilde{\tilde{T}}:=T\cap\tilde{T}$$

and notice, that $\tilde{\tilde{T}}$ is an open, non-empty interval in $\mathbf{R}_{++}^{n-1}$ with $\tilde{\underline{x}}\varepsilon\tilde{\tilde{T}}$.

Next we determine the explicit form of the function h on subintervals of the intervals

$$(43)\qquad I^i:=\{k^i(x_i)+k^{i+1}(x_{i+1})+g^i(\underline{x}^{\cdot i,i+1})\,|\,\underline{x}\varepsilon\tilde{\tilde{T}}\}\qquad (i=1,..,n)\ ,$$

because then we can, with the aid of (30), locally determine the explicit form of F.

---

1) For $I_1,I_2\subset R$ we define $I_1\cdot I_2$ by $I_1\cdot I_2:=\{z\,|\,z=xy,x\varepsilon I_1,y\varepsilon I_2\}$.

2) $\tilde{\tilde{I}}^{x_1}=I^{x_1}$, since $\tilde{I}^{x_1}=\mathbf{R}_{++}$.

Case 1: k^1 and m^1 from (41).

We obtain, with (19) and (41)

(44) $$\Psi^1(x_1,y_1) = h(\gamma_1 \log x_1+\bar{\gamma}_1 \log y_1+\delta_1+\bar{\delta}_1) \qquad (x_1>0, y_1 \varepsilon \tilde{I}^{y_1}).$$

Now we determine $I^{*y_1} c \tilde{I}^{y_1}$ and $I^{*\lambda_1}$ with $1 \varepsilon I^{*\lambda_1}$ such that $I^{*\lambda_1} \cdot I^{*y_1} = \tilde{I}^{y_1}$. From (44) it follows, because of the linear homogeneity of Ψ^1, that for all $\lambda \varepsilon I^{*\lambda_1}, y_1 \varepsilon I^{*y_1}$ and $x_1>0$

(45) $$\lambda h(\gamma_1 \log x_1+\bar{\gamma}_1 \log y_1+\bar{\delta}_1+\delta_1)=h(\gamma_1 \log x_1+\bar{\gamma}_1 \log y_1+(\gamma_1+\bar{\gamma}_1)\log \lambda+\delta_1+\bar{\delta}_1).$$

It is true that

(46) $$\{\gamma_1 \log x_1+\bar{\gamma}_1 \log y_1+\delta_1+\bar{\delta}_1 \mid x_1>0, y_1 \varepsilon I^{*y_1}\}=\mathbb{R}.$$

We choose now $\underset{\approx}{\tilde{x}} \varepsilon T$ and define

(47) $$\tilde{C}^i := k^i(\tilde{x}_i)+k^{i+1}(\tilde{x}_{i+1})+g^i(\underline{\tilde{x}}^{\cdot i,i+1}) \qquad (i=1,..,n).$$

Then we determine in each of these n cases x_1 in such a way, that

$$\gamma_1 \log x_1+\bar{\gamma}_1 \log y_1+\delta_1+\bar{\delta}_1=\tilde{C}^i ,$$

which is, because of (46),always possible.We obtain

$$x_1 = \exp\{\frac{\tilde{C}^i-\delta_1-\bar{\delta}_1}{\gamma_1}\}\cdot y_1^{-\bar{\gamma}_1/\gamma_1} \qquad (y_1 \varepsilon I^{*y_1}).$$

Let

$$w_i := (\gamma_1+\bar{\gamma}_1)\log \lambda+ \tilde{C}^i \iff \lambda = \exp\{\frac{w_i-\tilde{C}^i}{\gamma_1+\bar{\gamma}_1}\}$$

In view of (45) we obtain

(48) $$h(w_i) = C^i \cdot \exp\{\frac{w_i}{\gamma_1+\bar{\gamma}_1}\} \quad , \text{ where } C^i := h(\tilde{C}^i)\cdot \exp\{\frac{-\tilde{C}^i}{\gamma_1+\bar{\gamma}_1}\}>0.$$

The w_i's are elements of the open intervals

$$W^i := \{\bar{w}_i \mid \bar{w}_i=(\gamma_1+\bar{\gamma}_1)\log \lambda+\tilde{C}^i, \lambda \varepsilon I^{*\lambda_1}\}.$$

Since $1 \varepsilon I^{*\lambda_1}$, it is true that $\tilde{C}^i \varepsilon W^i$ $(i=1,..,n)$.

Since $\underline{x} \mapsto k^i(x_i)+k^{i+1}(x_{i+1})+g^i(\underline{x}^{\cdot i,i+1})$ is a continuous function, there exists for each i=1,..,n an open sphere $U_{\varepsilon_i}(\tilde{\underline{x}})$, which is mapped by this function into W^i.

We set

$$U_\varepsilon(\tilde{\underline{x}}):=\bigcap_{i=1}^{n} U_{\varepsilon_i}(\tilde{\underline{x}}).$$

For all $\underline{x}\varepsilon T':=\tilde{\tilde{T}}\cap U_\varepsilon(\tilde{\underline{x}})$ we obtain, in view of (48) and (30),

$$(49)\quad h(k^i(x_i)+k^{i+1}(x_{i+1})+g^i(\underline{x}^{\cdot i,i+1}))=C^i\cdot\exp\{\frac{k^i(x_i)+k^{i+1}(x_{i+1})+g^i(\underline{x}^{\cdot i,i+1})}{\gamma_1+\bar{\gamma}_1}\}$$

for i=1,..,n.Next we show, that, if h is of the form (48), <u>all</u> k^i are of the form (41).

For $\tilde{\underline{x}}\varepsilon\tilde{\tilde{T}}$ we defined $\tilde{C}^i:=k^i(\tilde{x}_i)+k^{i+1}(\tilde{x}_{i+1})+g^i(\tilde{\underline{x}}^{\cdot i,i+1})$.

By (29), it follows from this definition that

$$\tilde{C}^i = k^i(\tilde{x}_i) + m^i\{H^i(\tilde{\underline{x}}^{\cdot i})\}.$$

With

$$\tilde{y}_i = H^i(\tilde{\underline{x}}^{\cdot i})$$

we obtain

$$\tilde{C}^i = k^i(\tilde{x}_i) + m^i(\tilde{y}_i).$$

Because of the continuity of $(x_i,y_i) \mapsto k^i(x_i)+m^i(y_i)$ and the fact, that $\tilde{C}^i$ is an inner point of W^i, it is true that the image set of a certain open sphere $U_{\delta_i}(\tilde{x}_i,\tilde{y}_i)$ lies entirely in W^i.

Let $I''^{x_i}\times I''^{y_i}$ be an open cube with $I''^{x_i}\times I''^{y_i} \subset U_{\delta_i}(\tilde{x}_i,\tilde{y}_i)$.

We suppose, that any one of the k^i (i=2,..,n) is of the form (42).Then it follows, by (48) and Theorem I, that

$$(50)\quad \Psi^i(x_i,y_i) = C^i\cdot\exp\{\frac{1}{\gamma_1+\bar{\gamma}_1}\cdot(\varepsilon_i x_i^{\alpha_i}+\bar{\varepsilon}_i y_i^{\alpha_i}+\eta_i+\bar{\eta}_i)\}\ (x_i\varepsilon I''^{x_i},y_i\varepsilon I''^{y_i}).$$

But Ψ^i given by (50) is not linearly homogeneous as opposed to our assumptions in (V_1).

To prove this, one takes open intervals $I'^{x_i}\subset I''^{x_i}$, $I'^{y_i}\subset I''^{y_i}$ and determines an open interval I'^{λ} such that $\lambda x_i\varepsilon I''^{x_i}$ $(\lambda\varepsilon I'^{\lambda},x_i\varepsilon I'^{x_i})$ and $\lambda y_i\varepsilon I''^{y_i}$ $(\lambda\varepsilon I'^{\lambda},y_i\varepsilon I'^{y_i})$.

The linear homogeneity of Ψ^i requires that for all $\lambda\varepsilon I'^{\lambda}$, $x_i\varepsilon I'^{x_i}$ and $y_i\varepsilon I'^{y_i}$

$$(51)\quad \exp\{\frac{\lambda^{\alpha_i}\cdot(\varepsilon_i x_i^{\alpha_i}+\bar{\varepsilon}_i y_i^{\alpha_i})}{\gamma_1+\bar{\gamma}_1}\} = \lambda\cdot\exp\{\frac{\varepsilon_i x_i^{\alpha_i}+\bar{\varepsilon}_i y_i^{\alpha_i}}{\gamma_1+\bar{\gamma}_1}\} .$$

But (51) is valid for <u>at most one</u> $\lambda\varepsilon I'^{\lambda}$.

From (41), (48) and Theorem I we obtain therefore for the ith equation of our system

$$(52)\quad \Psi^i(x_i,H^i(\underline{x}^{\cdot i}))=C^i\cdot\exp\{\frac{\gamma_i\log x_i+\delta_i+\gamma_{i+1}\log x_{i+1}+\delta_{i+1}+g^i(\underline{x}^{\cdot i,i+1})}{\gamma_1+\bar{\gamma}_1}\}\quad (\underline{x}\varepsilon T')$$

and from (52) with

$$\xi_i := \frac{\gamma_i}{\gamma_1+\bar{\gamma}_1} >0 \ ,\ \tilde{g}^i(\underline{x}^{\cdot i,i+1}):=C^i\cdot\exp\{\frac{\delta_i+\delta_{i+1}+g^i(\underline{x}^{\cdot i,i+1})}{\gamma_1+\bar{\gamma}_1}\},$$

$$(53)\qquad \Psi^i(x_i,H^i(\underline{x}^{\cdot i})) = x_i^{\xi_i}\cdot x_{i+1}^{\xi_{i+1}}\cdot\tilde{g}^i(\underline{x}^{\cdot i,i+1}).$$

<u>Case 2:</u> k^1 and m^1 from (42).

Here we assume, in addition to (V_1), that it is for all $\tilde{C}^i$ (see (47)) possible to choose $x_1>0$ so that

$$(V_2)\qquad \varepsilon_1 x_1^{\alpha_1}+\bar{\varepsilon}_1 y_1^{\alpha_1}+\eta_1+\bar{\eta}_1 = \tilde{C}^i \qquad (i=1,..,n).$$

Since Ψ^i is linearly homogeneous we must have, for all $\lambda\varepsilon I^{*\lambda_1}$, $y_1\varepsilon I^{*y_1}$ and $x_1>0$,

$$(54)\quad \lambda\cdot h(\varepsilon_1 x_1^{\alpha_1}+\bar{\varepsilon}_1 y_1^{\alpha_1}+\eta_1+\bar{\eta}_1) = h(\lambda^{\alpha_1}\{\varepsilon_1 x_1^{\alpha_1}+\bar{\varepsilon}_1 y_1^{\alpha_1}\}+\eta_1+\bar{\eta}_1) .$$

We set $y_1=y_1^o\varepsilon I^{*y_1}$ and denote by $x_1^{i_o}$ the (unique) solution of

$$(*)\qquad \varepsilon_1 x_1^{\alpha_1}+\bar{\varepsilon}_1 (y_1^o)^{\alpha_1}+\eta_1+\bar{\eta}_1 = \tilde{C}^i.$$

We define

$$w_i:=\eta_1+\bar{\eta}_1+\lambda^{\alpha_1}\cdot\{\varepsilon_1(x_1^{i_o})^{\alpha_1}+\bar{\varepsilon}_1(y_1^o)^{\alpha_1}\} \iff \lambda=\left[\frac{w_i-\eta_1-\bar{\eta}_1}{\varepsilon_1(x_1^{i_o})^{\alpha_1}+\bar{\varepsilon}_1(y_1^o)^{\alpha_1}}\right]^{\frac{1}{\alpha_1}} .$$

From this it follows that

$$\varepsilon_1,\bar{\varepsilon}_1 \gtrless 0 \iff w_i \gtrless \eta_1+\bar{\eta}_1 .$$

The variables w_i vary in the open intervals $W^{i'}$

(55) $$W^{i'}:=\{\overline{w}_i|\overline{w}_i=\lambda^{\alpha_1}\cdot(\varepsilon_1(x_1^{i_o})^{\alpha_1}+\overline{\varepsilon}_1(y_1^o)^{\alpha_1})+\eta_1+\overline{\eta}_1;\lambda\varepsilon I^{*\lambda_1}\} \qquad (i=1,..,n).$$

Since $1\varepsilon I^{*\lambda_1}$, it follows that $\tilde{C}^i\varepsilon W^{i'}$. (Note that $\overline{w}_i=\tilde{C}^i$ iff $\lambda=1$).

From (54),

(56) $$h(w_i) = \overline{\beta}_i\cdot\{\frac{w_i-\eta_1-\overline{\eta}_1}{\beta_i}\}^{1/\alpha_1} \qquad (w_i\varepsilon W^{i'};i=1,..,n),$$

where

$$\overline{\beta}_i:=h(\tilde{C}^i)>0 \text{ and } \beta_i:=\varepsilon_1(x_1^{i_o})^{\alpha_1}+\overline{\varepsilon}_1(y_1^o)^{\alpha_1}.$$

It is further valid that $\beta_i \gtrless 0 \Longleftrightarrow w_i\gtrless\eta_1+\overline{\eta}_1$ and sign β_i = sign ε_1 = sign $\overline{\varepsilon}_1$.

The continuity of $\underline{x} \mapsto k^i(x_i)+k^{i+1}(x_{i+1})+g^i(\underline{x}^{\cdot i,i+1})$ and $\tilde{C}^i\varepsilon W^{i'}$ ensure that the image set of an open sphere $U_{\varepsilon_{i'}}(\underline{\tilde{x}})$ lies entirely in $W^{i'}$.

We define

$$U_{\varepsilon'}(\underline{\tilde{x}}):=\bigcap_{i=1}^{n} U_{\varepsilon_{i'}}(\underline{\tilde{x}}).$$

For all $\underline{x}\varepsilon T'':=\tilde{\tilde{T}}\cap U_{\varepsilon'}(\underline{\tilde{x}})$, we obtain in view of (56) and (30),

(57) $$h(k^i(x_i)+k^{i+1}(x_{i+1})+g^i(\underline{x}^{\cdot i,i+1}))=\overline{\beta}_i\cdot\{\frac{k^i(x_i)+k^{i+1}(x_{i+1})+g^i(\underline{x}^{\cdot i,i+1})-\eta_1-\overline{\eta}_1}{\beta_i}\}^{1/\alpha}$$

In what follows, we show that

(58) $$\alpha_1=\alpha_2=\cdots\alpha_n=:\alpha.$$

According to (47) and (29),

$$\tilde{C}^i = k^i(\tilde{x}_i) + m^i(\tilde{y}_i).$$

We consider an open cube

$$T''^{x_i}\times T''^{y_i} \subset U_{\overline{\delta}_i}(\tilde{x}_i,\tilde{y}_i),$$

where $U_{\overline{\delta}_i}(\tilde{x}_i,\tilde{y}_i)$ is an open sphere which is mapped into $W^{i'}$ by k^i+m^i.

In view of Theorem I, (42) and (56) we have for $x_i \varepsilon \bar{I}''^{x_i}, y_i \varepsilon \bar{I}''^{y_i}$

(59) $$\Psi^i(x_i,y_i) = (\rho_i x_i^{\alpha_i} + \bar{\rho}_i y_i^{\alpha_i} + \omega_i)^{1/\alpha_1},$$

where

$$\omega_i := \frac{\bar{\beta}_i^{\alpha_1}}{\beta_i} \cdot (\eta_i + \bar{\eta}_i - \eta_1 - \bar{\eta}_1), \quad \rho_i := \frac{\bar{\beta}_i^{\alpha_1}}{\beta_i} \cdot \varepsilon_i > 0, \quad \bar{\rho}_i := \frac{\bar{\beta}_i^{\alpha_1}}{\beta_i} \cdot \bar{\varepsilon}_i > 0.$$

Since Ψ^i is positive-valued,

$$(\rho_i x_i^{\alpha_i} + \bar{\rho}_i y_i^{\alpha_i} + \omega_i)^{1/\alpha_1} > 0.$$

Because of $\Psi_1^i, \Psi_2^i > 0$ it is further true that sign α_i=sign α_1 $(i=2,..,n)$. Again we take open intervals $\bar{I}'^{x_i} c \bar{I}''^{x_i}$, $\bar{I}'^{y_i} c \bar{I}''^{y_i}$ and $\bar{I}'^{\lambda}$ such that $\lambda x_i \varepsilon \bar{I}''^{x_i}$ $(\lambda \varepsilon \bar{I}'^{\lambda}, x_i \varepsilon \bar{I}'^{x_i})$ and $\lambda y_i \varepsilon \bar{I}''^{y_i}$ $(\lambda \varepsilon \bar{I}'^{\lambda}, y_i \varepsilon \bar{I}'^{y_i})$. The linear homogeneity of Ψ^i requires, for all $x_i \varepsilon \bar{I}'^{x_i}, y_i \varepsilon \bar{I}'^{y_i}$ and $\lambda \varepsilon \bar{I}'^{\lambda}$,

(60) $$\{\lambda^{\alpha_i} \cdot (\rho_i x_i^{\alpha_i} + \bar{\rho}_i y_i^{\alpha_i}) + \omega_i\}^{1/\alpha_1} = \lambda \cdot \{\rho_i x_i^{\alpha_i} + \bar{\rho}_i y_i^{\alpha_i} + \omega_i\}^{1/\alpha_1}.$$

Then it is also valid that

(61) $$\frac{1}{\alpha_1} \cdot \ln\{\lambda^{\alpha_i} \cdot (\rho_i x_i^{\alpha_i} + \bar{\rho}_i y_i^{\alpha_i}) + \omega_i\} = \ln \lambda + \frac{1}{\alpha_1} \cdot \ln\{\rho_i x_i^{\alpha_i} + \bar{\rho}_i y_i^{\alpha_i} + \omega_i\}.$$

We set $x_i = x_i^o \varepsilon \bar{I}'^{x_i}$, $y_i = y_i^o \varepsilon \bar{I}'^{y_i}$ and define $\bar{C}_i^o := \rho_i (x_i^o)^{\alpha_i} + \bar{\rho}_i (y_i^o)^{\alpha_i}$.

Then

(62) $$g(\lambda) := \frac{1}{\alpha_1} \cdot \ln(\bar{C}_i^o \lambda^{\alpha_i} + \omega_i) = \ln \lambda + \frac{1}{\alpha_1} \cdot \ln(\bar{C}_i^o + \omega_i) =: f(\lambda) \quad (\lambda \varepsilon \bar{I}'^{\lambda}).$$

For all $\lambda \varepsilon \bar{I}'^{\lambda}$ it follows that

(63) $$g'(\lambda) = f'(\lambda),$$

that is

(64) $$\alpha_i \bar{C}_i^o \lambda^{\alpha_i} = \alpha_1 \bar{C}_i^o \lambda^{\alpha_i} + \alpha_1 \omega_i \qquad (i=2,..,n).$$

Formula (64) is valid for all $\lambda \varepsilon \bar{I}'^{\lambda}$ iff

(65) $$\alpha_i = \alpha_1 \text{ and } \omega_i = 0 \quad (i=2,..,n).$$

Conversely, (65) is also sufficient for Ψ^i to be linearly homogeneous.

Furthermore, it is possible to prove, that, if h is of the form (56), all k^i are of the form (42).This proof runs analogously to its counterpart in the case, where h is of the form (48) and all k^i are of the form (41). From (58), (56) and Theorem I we obtain, for the ith equation of our system,

(66) $$\Psi^i(x_i,H^i(\underline{x}^{\cdot i})) = (\phi_{ii}x_i^\alpha+\phi_{ii+1}x_{i+1}^\alpha+\bar{g}^i(\underline{x}^{\cdot i,i+1}))^{1/\alpha} \qquad (\underline{x}\varepsilon T''),$$

where

$$\bar{g}^i(\underline{x}^{\cdot i,i+1}):=\frac{\bar{\beta}_i^\alpha}{\beta_i}\cdot(g(\underline{x}^{\cdot i,i+1})+\eta_i+\eta_{i+1}-\eta_1-\bar{\eta}_1),\phi_{ii}:=\frac{\bar{\beta}_i^\alpha}{\beta_i}\cdot\varepsilon_i>0,\phi_{ii+1}:=\frac{\bar{\beta}_i^\alpha}{\beta_i}\cdot\varepsilon_{i+1}>0.$$

From (53) and (66) we can now derive the explicit form of our price index F.

Let us write (53) and (66) in full detail:

(53) $$\begin{aligned} &x_1^{\xi_1}\cdot x_2^{\xi_2}\cdot\tilde{g}^1(\underline{x}^{\cdot 1,2}) = \\ &= x_2^{\xi_2}\cdot x_3^{\xi_3}\cdot\tilde{g}^2(\underline{x}^{\cdot 2,3}) = \\ &\vdots \\ &= x_i^{\xi_i}\cdot x_{i+1}^{\xi_{i+1}}\cdot\tilde{g}^i(\underline{x}^{\cdot i,i+1})) = \\ &\vdots \\ &= x_n^{\xi_n}\cdot x_1^{\xi_1}\cdot\tilde{g}^n(\underline{x}^{\cdot n,1}) \qquad (\underline{x}\varepsilon T'). \end{aligned}$$

(66) $$\begin{aligned} &(\phi_{11}x_1^\alpha+\phi_{12}x_2^\alpha+\bar{g}^1(\underline{x}^{\cdot 1,2}))^{1/\alpha} = \\ &= (\phi_{22}x_2^\alpha+\phi_{23}x_3^\alpha+\bar{g}^2(\underline{x}^{\cdot 2,3}))^{1/\alpha} = \\ &\vdots \\ &= (\phi_{ii}x_i^\alpha+\phi_{ii+1}x_{i+1}^\alpha+\bar{g}^i(\underline{x}^{\cdot i,i+1}))^{1/\alpha} = \\ &\vdots \\ &= (\phi_{nn}x_n^\alpha+\phi_{n1}x_1^\alpha+\bar{g}^n(\underline{x}^{\cdot n,1}))^{1/\alpha} \qquad (\underline{x}\varepsilon T''). \end{aligned}$$

For all i=1,..,n we obtain from (53)

(67) $$\Psi^i(x_i,H^i(\underline{x}^{\cdot i})) = C\cdot x_1^{\xi_1}\cdot x_2^{\xi_2}\cdot\dots\cdot x_n^{\xi_n} \qquad (C>0\text{ const.};\underline{x}\varepsilon T')$$

and from (66)

(68) $$\Psi^i(x_i,H^i(\underline{x}^{\cdot i})) = (b_1x_1^\alpha+\dots+b_nx_n^\alpha)^{\frac{1}{\alpha}} \qquad (b_i>0\text{ const.};\underline{x}\varepsilon T'').$$

The formulae (67) and (68) can be obtained by simple substitutions. We demonstrate the first step:

By (53),

$$x_1^{\xi_1} \cdot x_2^{\xi_2} \cdot \tilde{g}^1(\underline{x}^{\cdot 1,2}) = x_2^{\xi_2} \cdot x_3^{\xi_3} \cdot \tilde{g}^2(\underline{x}^{\cdot 2,3}) \qquad (\underline{x} \varepsilon T').$$

Let $x_1 = \tilde{x}_1$. Then

$$\tilde{g}^1(\underline{x}^{\cdot 1,2}) = x_3^{\xi_3} \cdot \frac{1}{\tilde{x}_1^{\xi_1}} \cdot \tilde{g}^2(\tilde{x}_1, x_4, .., x_n).$$

Now, if we define a new function $\tilde{\tilde{g}}^1$ by

$$\tilde{\tilde{g}}^1(x_4, ..., x_n) = \frac{1}{\tilde{x}_1^{\xi_1}} \cdot \tilde{g}^2(\tilde{x}_1, x_4, ..., x_n),$$

this leads to

$$\tilde{g}^1(x_3, .., x_n) = x_3^{\xi_3} \cdot \tilde{\tilde{g}}^1(x_4, ..., x_n).$$

This procedure can be continued for all $\tilde{g}^i$ and the remaining (n-3) steps.

By (66),

$$\phi_{11} x_1^\alpha + \phi_{12} x_2^\alpha + \bar{g}^1(x_3, ..., x_n) = \phi_{22} x_2^\alpha + \phi_{23} x_3^\alpha + \bar{g}^2(x_1, x_4, .., x_n) \quad (\underline{x} \varepsilon T'').$$

Setting $x_1 = \tilde{x}_1$, $x_2 = \tilde{x}_2$ we obtain

$$\bar{g}^1(x_3, ..., x_n) = \phi_{23} x_3^\alpha + \bar{g}^2(\tilde{x}_1, x_4, ..., x_n) + (\phi_{22} - \phi_{12})\tilde{x}_2^\alpha - \phi_{11}\tilde{x}_1^\alpha,$$

that is,

$$\bar{g}^1(x_3, .., x_n) = \phi_{23} x_3^\alpha + \bar{\bar{g}}_1(x_4, .., x_n)$$

with

$$\bar{\bar{g}}^1(x_4, .., x_n) := \bar{g}^2(\tilde{x}_1, x_4, .., x_n) + (\phi_{22} - \phi_{12})\tilde{x}_2^\alpha - \phi_{11}\tilde{x}_1^\alpha.$$

Formulae (67) and (68) are valid for a certain open sphere $U_\tau(\underline{\tilde{x}})$ of any arbitrary $\underline{\tilde{x}} \varepsilon \mathbf{R}^n_{++}$. This follows from our construction. Now, by the continuity of the function

$$\underline{\Psi}: (\underline{p}^o, \underline{p}) \varepsilon \mathbf{R}^{2n}_{++} \rightarrow \underline{\Psi}(\underline{p}^o, \underline{p}) = \left(\frac{p_1}{p_1^o}, ..., \frac{p_n}{p_n^o}\right) \varepsilon \mathbf{R}^n_{++},$$

there exist for each such $U_\tau(\underline{\tilde{x}})$ open spheres $U_\kappa(\underline{\tilde{p}}^o, \underline{\tilde{p}})$ such that

$$\underline{\Psi}(U_\kappa(\underline{\tilde{p}}^o, \underline{\tilde{p}})) \subset U_\tau(\underline{\tilde{x}}),$$

that is, for every point $(\underline{p}^o, \underline{p}) \varepsilon \mathbf{R}^{2n}_{++}$ we have a certain neighbourhood for which the explicit form of our price index F is either given by

(67)' $$F(\underline{p}^o, \underline{p}) = C \cdot \prod_{i=1}^n (p_i / p_i^o)^{\xi_i} \qquad (\xi_1 + \dots + \xi_n = 1 \text{ by (A2)})$$

or by

(68)' $$F(\underline{p}^o, \underline{p}) = \{\sum_{i=1}^n b_i (p_i / p_i^o)^\alpha\}^{1/\alpha}.$$

If $U_\kappa(\underline{p}^o,\underline{p})$ is such that at least one $(\underline{p}^o,\underline{p}^o)\varepsilon U_\kappa(\underline{p}^o,\underline{p})$, then by $F(\underline{p}^o,\underline{p}^o)=1$, we have an additional restriction for the constants C, $b_1,..,b_n$, namely:

$$C=1 \text{ and } b_1+b_2+..+b_n=1.$$

Now we can formulate our main Theorem by summarizing our results.

THEOREM II: 1) Let a function $F:\mathbf{R}^{2n}_{++}\rightarrow\mathbf{R}_{++}$ satisfy (5) with (V_1). Then F is a price index (see Lemma I).

2) If, in addition to (V_1), the assumption (V_2) is valid, then F is locally (that means: in sufficiently small neighbourhoods[1] of each $(\underline{p}^o,\underline{p})\varepsilon\mathbf{R}^{2n}_{++}$) either of the form

(69) $$F(\underline{p}^o,\underline{p}) = C\cdot\prod_{i=1}^{n}(p_i/p_i^o)^{\xi_i} \quad (\xi_i>0;\xi_1+\cdots+\xi_n=1;C>0)$$

or of the form

(70) $$F(\underline{p}^o,\underline{p}) = \{\sum_{i=1}^{n} b_i(p_i/p_i^o)^{\alpha}\}^{\frac{1}{\alpha}} \quad (\alpha\neq 0;b_i>0).$$

3) If, for any $(\underline{p}^o,\underline{p})\varepsilon\mathbf{R}^{2n}_{++}$, $U_\kappa(\underline{p}^o,\underline{p})$ is such that $(\underline{p}^o,\underline{p}^o)\varepsilon$ $\varepsilon U_\kappa(\underline{p}^o,\underline{p})$, then, by the identity axiom (A3), the constants $C,b_1,..,b_n$ can further be specified, namely:

$$C=1 \text{ and } b_1+b_2+\cdots+b_n=1.$$

---

[1] We denote these neighbourhoods by $U_\kappa(\underline{p}^o,\underline{p})$.

References

ACZÉL,J.: Lectures on Functional Equations and Their Applications. Academic Press, New York and London, 1966.

ACZÉL,J., EICHHORN,W.: A Note on Additive Indices. Journal of Economic Theory, Vol.8, No.4, 1974a, 525-529.

ACZÉL,J., EICHHORN,W.: Systems of Functional Equations Determining Price and Productivity Indices. Utilitas Mathematica 5, 1974b, 213-226.

ARROW,K.,J., CHENERY,H.,B., MINHAS,B.,S., SOLOW,R.,M.: Capital-Labour Substitution and Economic Theory. Review of Economics and Statistics 43, 1961, 225-250.

COBB,C.W., DOUGLAS,P.H.: A Theory of Production. American Economic Review 18, 1928, 139-165.

EICHHORN,W.: Functional Equations in Economics. Addison Wesley, Reading, 1977.

EICHHORN,W., VOELLER,J.: Theory of the Price Index. Lecture Notes in Economics and Mathematical Systems, Vol.140, Springer-Verlag, Berlin-Heidelberg-New York, 1976.

GEHRIG,W.: Neutraler technischer Fortschritt und Produktionsfunktionen mit beliebig vielen Produktionsfaktoren. Mathematical Systems in Economics, Vol.20. Verlag Anton Hain, Meisenheim am Glan, 1976.

STEHLING,F.: Neutral Inventions and CES Production Functions. In: Eichhorn,W., Henn,R., Opitz,O., Shephard.R.,W. (eds.): Production Theory. Lecture Notes in Economics and Mathematical Systems, Vol.99, Springer-Verlag, Berlin-Heidelberg-New York, 1974.

Economic and Atomistic Index Numbers: Contrasts and Similarities

by Georg Hasenkamp

1. Introduction

The problem of index numbers is one of the oldest, yet still one of the most vexing challenges in economics. The political significance attached to the "cost-of-living" index, or to "price inflation" is in no way matched by the ability of the economist to provide measures for such numbers. Furthermore, virtually all empirical work in economics -- like macro-economic models -- involves data that has been generated by applying index numbers for either deflation procedures and/or aggregation purposes.

Frisch (1936), in one of the most important papers on index numbers, distinguished between the atomistic (or statistical) approach, and the economic (or functional) approach to index numbers. Virtually all index numbers which are actually constructed from economic data have their foundation within the atomistic approach. Criteria for this atomistic approach to index numbers are traditionally provided by the so called Fisher's Test Criteria -- see Fisher (1922). Within the more recent work on index numbers, the atomistic approach was given a contemporary framework by Eichhorn (1976, 1977), and Eichhorn and Voeller (1976). There are certainly some advantages to this approach:
a) Atomistic index numbers satisfy a set of (mathematically) "plausible" axioms, and b) Most of the index numbers are easy to compute. Still, an uneasy feeling remains: it involves the

question why -- for economic data -- the economic approach to index numbers is not more frequently used.

In this paper we shall contrast one particular class of atomistic index numbers with one particular class of economic index numbers. Even though both approaches rest on different criteria, we shall see that the economic approach in our example assigns in essence a proper weighting scheme for an unspecified weighting scheme within the atomistic approach. The economic approach furthermore permits a wide variety of index numbers, depending on the exact definition. Each such case will be accompanied by an example involving actual economic data, in order to illustrate the sensitivity of the index number value under the different assumptions.

Underlying the concept of an index number is a well defined economic unit for which measurements on a set of (positive) prices $p \in R^n_{++}$, and on a set of (positive) quantities $x \in R^n_{++}$ are available under two alternative periods (or situations) "0" and "1". The period is denoted by a superscript, and the individual element by a subscript on elements in p and x.

Two index numbers are generally considered: a) A price index which is supposed provide a scalar measure on the "movement" of a set of prices from a period to another, and b) A quantity index which is supposed to provide a scalar measure on the "movement" of a set of quantities from one period to another. Often the concept of a quantity index is entirely analogous to that of a price index; in this case we shall discuss only the price index in greater detail.

II. Atomistic Index Numbers

Suppose only one price p_1 is involved. The price index may then be defined on heuristic or intuitive grounds by the ratio of prices

$$r^{01} = p_1^1 \; / \; p_1^0 \quad . \tag{1}$$

Whenever several prices are involved, we propose -- in analogy to equation (1) -- some "combination" of the individual price ratios $p_i^1 \; / \; p_i^0$.[1)] In particular, we shall consider the weighted <u>mean of order</u> ρ of these price ratios:

$$r^{01}(\rho) = [\Sigma_i w_i (p_i^1/p_i^0)^{\rho}]^{1/\rho} \; , \tag{2}$$

where the w_i are a set of given (positive) "weights" w_i , such that $\Sigma \, w_i = 1$, and $-\infty<\rho<\infty$, for $\rho \neq 0$; however the limit as ρ approaches zero is defined below, so that we shall write the mean without a special comment to its value "at" $\rho = 0$.

We note a few special cases for (2) under alternative values for ρ ; see also Hardy, Littlewood and Polya (1934):

a) Take $\rho=1$, then (2) becomes the weighted linear mean

$$r^{01}(1) = \Sigma \; w_i (p_i^1/p_i^0) \quad . \tag{3}$$

b) Take the limit $\rho\to 0$, then (2) becomes a weighted geometric mean

$$r^{01}(0) = \Pi (p_i^1/p_i^0)^{w_i} \; . \tag{4}$$

c) Take the limit $\rho\to-\infty$, then the price index in (2) approaches

$$\underline{r}^{01} = \min \; [(p_1^1/p_1^0), \ldots, (p_n^1/p_n^0)] \; . \tag{5}$$

d) Take the limit $\rho\to\infty$, then the price index in (2) approaches

$$\bar{r}^{01} = \max \; [(p_1^1/p_1^0), \ldots, (p_n^1/p_n^0)] \; . \tag{6}$$

For a particular ρ , the price index (2) may be considered as a function of price ratios $s = (s_1,\ldots,s_n)'$, where $s_i = p_i^1 / p_i^0$, conditional on a set of "weights" $w = (w_1,\ldots,w_n)'$. This function we denote by $P_\rho(\cdot;w)$, so that

$$P_\rho(s;w) = (\Sigma w_i s_i^{\rho})^{1/\rho} . \tag{7}$$

This function satisfies the following axioms, and is therefore an atomistic index number; see Eichhorn (1977) and Eichhorn and Voeller (1977) for the foundation of these axioms:

<u>Axiom 1:</u> Identity Axiom.
Let all $s_i = 1$, then

$$P_\rho(s;w) = 1 ,$$

since the (positive) weights w_i sum to unity.

<u>Axiom 2:</u> Monotonicity Axiom.
Let $s_i \geq \bar{s}_i$ for all i , but for at least one j , $s_j > \bar{s}_j$, then

$$P_\rho(s;w) > P_\rho(\bar{s};w).$$

<u>Axiom 3:</u> Linear Homogeneity Axiom.
Let $s_i^* = \lambda s_i = \lambda p_i^1/p_i^0$ for all i and some positive scalar λ , then

$$P_\rho(s^*;w) = P_\rho(\lambda s;w) = \lambda P_\rho(s;w) .$$

<u>Axiom 4:</u> Dimensionality Axiom.
Let the units of measurement be changed to $p_i^* = \lambda_i p_i$ for some positive scalar λ_i . This leaves the value of the price index unchanged, since

$$s_i^* = p_i^{*\,1}/p_i^{*\,0} = \lambda_i p_i^1/\lambda_i p_i^0 = s_i .$$

The limits obtained in equations (3) and (4) are atomistic indices since they satisfy the four axioms listed above. However, the limit $\underline{r}^{01}$ in equation (5), and the limit $\bar{r}^{01}$

in equation (6) do not satisfy the Monotonicity Axiom, hence they may not be considered as atomistic indices.

In Eichhorn (1977) and Eichhorn and Voeller (1976) the following was shown (in a somewhat more general form): Let $\hat{s}$ be an m×1 vector of elements with price indices

$$\hat{s}_j = P_{\rho_j}(s,w^j) \tag{8}$$

for all particular ρ_j satisfying $-\infty<\rho_j<\infty$ and appropriate weights w^j ; also let $\hat{w}$ be an m×1 vector of positive weights, $\Sigma \hat{w}_j = 1$:

$$P_\rho(\hat{s};\hat{w}) = [\Sigma\hat{w}_j\hat{s}_j^\rho]^{1/\rho} = [\Sigma\hat{w}_j(\Sigma w_i^j s_i^{\rho_j})^{\rho/\rho_j}]^{1/\rho} \tag{9}$$

also satisfies the above four Axioms, and hence is an atomistic price index. This gives us

Theorem 1:
A weighted mean of order ρ of atomistic price indices $P_{\rho_j}(s,w^j)$ is again an atomistic index.

Proof: An elementary exercise.

The following Theorem plays some important role in section III dealing with economic index numbers, but it also fits within the present context.

Theorem 2:
If $\rho' \leq \rho''$ in the weighted mean of order ρ , equation (2) for given $w = (w_1,\ldots,w_n)'$ and $s = (s_1,\ldots,s_n)'$ then

$$r^{01}(\rho') = [\Sigma w_i s_i^{\rho'}]^{1/\rho'} \leq [\Sigma w_i s_i^{\rho''}]^{1/\rho''} = r^{01}(\rho'') . \qquad (10)$$

Proof: For a proof of Theorem 2 we need to make use of the following:

i) $r^{01}(\rho)$ is continuous on ρ, $-\infty<\rho<\infty$.

ii) $f(y) = y \log(y), y\varepsilon R_{++}$, is convex.

iii) Jensen's Inequality: Let $g(\cdot)$ be a convex function, let $\Sigma\alpha_i = 1$, all scalars α_i positive, and let $y_i \varepsilon R$, then $g(\Sigma\alpha_i y_i) \leq \Sigma\alpha_i g(y_i)$.

Now it suffices to show that $dr^{01}(\rho)/d\rho \geq 0$. Take any $\rho \neq 0$, then

$$\begin{aligned} dr^{01}(\rho)/d\rho &= d \exp \{(1/\rho) \log (\Sigma w_i s_i^{\rho})\}/d\rho \\ &= r^{01}(\rho)\{(-1/\rho^2) \log (\Sigma w_i s_i^{\rho}) + \\ &\quad + (1/\rho)(\Sigma w_i s_i^{\rho})(\Sigma w_i s_i^{\rho} \log s_i)\} . \end{aligned}$$

Since $\rho^2 r^{10}(\rho)(\Sigma w_i s_i^{\rho})>0$ for $r^{10}(\rho) = 1/r^{01}(\rho)$, we can multiply the derivative by this term without changing its sign. This then gives us a function $h(\cdot)$ of ρ

$$\begin{aligned} h(\rho) &= -\Sigma(w_i s_i^{\rho}) \log (\Sigma w_i s_i^{\rho}) + \rho(\Sigma w_i s_i^{\rho} \log s_i) \\ &= -(\Sigma w_i s_i^{\rho}) \log (\Sigma w_i s_i^{\rho}) + (\Sigma w_i s_i^{\rho} \log s_i^{\rho}) . \end{aligned}$$

But, using $w_i = \alpha_i, s_i^{\rho} = y_i$, and $g(y) = y \log y$ from above, we see that $h(\rho) \geq 0$ by Jensen's Inequality. This, and the continuity of $r^{01}(\cdot)$ at $\rho = 0$, implies $dr^{01}(\rho)/d\rho \geq 0$; thus the theorem follows.

By combining the conclusion of Theorem 2 with the limits obtained in equations (5) and (6) we obtain the inequality

$$\underline{r}^{01} \leq r^{01}(\rho) \leq \overline{r}^{01} , \qquad (11)$$

for any given set of prices and set of weights, by picking either arbitrary small or large values for ρ . Equality will hold in (11) whenever all $s_i = c$, a positive constant. [See also the mean value test in Eichhorn (1977) and Eichhorn and Voeller (1977)].

Since ρ is arbitrary (in $-\infty < \rho < \infty$) within the atomistic approach to index numbers, one could in essence pick any number between $\underline{r}^{01}$ and $\overline{r}^{01}$ as the value for the price index. This is a simple procedure, but certainly unsatisfactory to the economist who would like to attach some reasoning to the choice of ρ .

In addition to specifying a value for ρ , the computation of a price index (7) requires a specification for the set of weights. While the atomistic approach does not justify the particular choices for ρ and w , we shall list below the most popular atomistic price indices:

a) Take $\rho = 1$ and $w_i^0 = p_i^0 x_i^0 / \Sigma p_j^0 x_j^0 = p_i^0 x_i^0 / p^{0'} x^0$ then the price index becomes

$$La^{01} = \Sigma w_i^0 (p_i^1 / p_i^0) = p^{1'} x^0 / p^{0'} x^0 \quad ; \tag{12}$$

this is the widely used Laspeyres index.

b) Take $\rho = 1$ and $w_i^{01} = p_i^0 x_i^1 / p^{0'} x^1$ then the price index becomes

$$Pa^{01} = \Sigma w_i^{01} (p_i^1 / p_i^0) = p^{1'} x^1 / p^{0'} x^1 \; ; \tag{13}$$

this is the Paasche index. We note that $Pa^{01} = 1/La^{10}$.

c) Take $\rho = 0$ and $\overline{w}_i = 1/2 (w_i^0 + w_i^1)$ for $w_i^1 = p_i^1 x_i^1 / p^{1'} x^1$, then the price index becomes

$$T^{01} = \Pi \, (p_i^1 / p_i^0)^{\overline{w}_i} \; ; \tag{14}$$

this is the Törnqvist (1936) index.

d) Take $\rho = 0$ and $w_1 = w_2 = 1/2$, and apply Theorem 1 to La^{01} and Pa^{01} then the price index becomes

$$F^{01} = (La^{01})^{1/2}(Pa^{01})^{1/2}$$
$$= [(p^{1'}x^{0}/p^{0'}x^{0})(p^{1'}x^{1}/p^{0'}x^{1})]^{1/2} \; ; \qquad (15)$$

this is the Fisher's (1922) "ideal" index.

Now we shall turn to the economic approach to index numbers. For the particular example illustrated, we shall see that economic theory does in fact provide a clue to the choice of ρ and the set of weights w.

III. Economic Index Numbers

Typically one distinguishes between the consumer and the producer as the underlying economic unit. However, instead of using the term utility function for the consumer, or production function for the producer, we shall combine the two cases under the (neutral) terminology of an aggregator function $u(\cdot)$ defined on quantities x:

$$u = u(x) \; , \qquad (16)$$

where u is either "utility" or "output" depending on the case. From the outset, we shall assume the usual regularity conditions: $u(\cdot)$ is continuous, strictly (quasi-) concave, nondecreasing, and strictly increasing in at least one quantity. Later, in our example, we shall assume a further condition, namely homotheticity or affine homotheticity.

The pure theory of economic index numbers has received sufficient attention in recent years -- e.g., Afriat (1972), Diewert (1976), Fisher and Shell (1972), Muellbauer (1975), Phlips (1974), Phlips and Sanz-Ferrer (1975), Pollak (1971, 1975), Samuelson and Swamy (1974), and Theil (1975). Therefore, after a short review of the basic concepts, we will pay attention to more special problems, some of which might be of more interest for empirical work.

1. Price Index

The price index -- or cost-of-living index -- is formally defined as the ratio of minimum expenditures, in the two periods (or situations) compared, in order to attain a (base) level of the aggregator function (16). It is important to notice that -- in addition to the aggregator function -- a behavioral assumption is needed, namely the one of a constrained optimization behavior. Basic to the price index is therefore the concept of a <u>cost function</u> defined on prices and the level of the aggregator function:[2)]

$$C(p;\bar{u}) = \min_x \{p'x \mid u(x) = \bar{u}\} \qquad (17)$$
$$= p'\hat{x} \quad ,$$

where $\hat{x} = \hat{x}(p,\bar{u})$ is the solution to the minimization problem (17), the system of (Hicksian) demand functions. Let total expenditures be $p'\hat{x} = \hat{m}$ in (17) then

$$u(\tilde{x}) = \max_x \{u(x) \mid p'x = \hat{m}\} \qquad (18)$$
$$= \bar{u} \;,$$

where $\tilde{x} = \tilde{x}(p,\hat{m})$ is the solution to the problem (18), the system of (Marshallian) demand functions. The price index is then the ratio of two cost functions for given $\bar{u}$:

$$c^{01}(p^1,p^0;\bar{u}) = C(p^1;\bar{u})/C(p^0;\bar{u}) \;. \qquad (19)$$

Whenever $\bar{u} = u(\tilde{x}^0)$, so $p^{0'}\tilde{x}^0 = p^{0'}\tilde{x}(p^0,m^0) = m^0$, the price index may be written as

$$c^{01} = p^{1'}\hat{x}^1/m^0 \;, \qquad (20)$$

where $\hat{x}^1 = \hat{x}(p^1,\bar{u})$. The denominator of (20) is -- in principle -- observable; however, the numerator is <u>not</u> observable, since $\hat{x}^1$ is the solution to a hypothetical situation. Thus, neither the value of $\hat{x}^1$, nor c^{01} can be computed --unless we know the system of demand functions $\hat{x}(\cdot,\cdot)$; this is equivalent to a knowledge of the aggregator function $u(\cdot)$.

The parameters of a pre-specified analytic form of an aggregator function can be estimated via the system of derived (Hicksian or Marshallian) demand functions.[3] This, however, requires the availability of a sufficiently long time series (or a large cross-section) of price and quantity data with (necessary) variations in <u>relative</u> prices.

In the price index (19) we have implicitly assumed that the cost function, and hence the underlying aggregator function, is not changing over the periods compared.[4] If it were, so that we attach superscripts "0" and "1" to the cost function, the ratio

$$\hat{c}^{01} = C^1(p^1;\bar{u})/C^0(p^0;\bar{u}) \tag{21}$$

might be interpreted as a <u>cardinal</u> price index. The identity

$$\hat{c}^{01} = [C^1(p^1;\bar{u})/C^0(p^1;\bar{u})][C^0(p^1;\bar{u})/C^0(p^0;\bar{u})] = r_1^{01}\cdot c_0^{01} \tag{22}$$

relates the <u>ordinal</u> price index with base "0", namely

$$c_0^{01} = C^0(p^1;\bar{u})/C^0(p^0;\bar{u}) \tag{23}$$

to the cardinal index via an "<u>efficiency</u>" <u>measure</u> at prices p^1

$$r_1^{01} = C^1(p^1;\bar{u})/C^0(p^1;\bar{u}) \quad . \tag{24}$$

Alternative to the identity (22) is the identity

$$\hat{c}^{01} = r_0^{01}c_1^{01} \quad , \tag{22'}$$

where

$$c_1^{01} = C^1(p^1;\bar{u})/C^1(p^0;\bar{u}) \qquad (23')$$

is the ordinal price index with base "1" , and

$$r_0^{01} = C^1(p^0;\bar{u})/C^0(p^0;\bar{u}) \qquad (24')$$

is the efficiency measure at prices p^0 . We note that $c_0^{01} \neq c_1^{01}$ in general.

Another question of interest is the independence of the price index (19) of the level $\bar{u}$: Suppose the aggregator function $u(\cdot)$ in (16) is homogeneous of degree 1 in quantities x . The cost function then factors as

$$\begin{aligned} C(p;\bar{u}) &= \min_x \{ p'x \mid u(x) = \bar{u} \} \\ &= \bar{u} \min_{x^*}\{ p'x^* \mid u(x^*) = 1 \} \\ &= \bar{u}h(p) \ , \end{aligned} \qquad (25)$$

say, where $x^* = \bar{u}^{-1}x$. Thus, under (25), the price index becomes

$$c_h^{01} = h(p^1)/h(p^0) \ , \qquad (26)$$

which is independent of $\bar{u}$. Furthermore we note that $c_h^{10} = 1/c_h^{01}$, the fundamental point made by Samuelson and Swamy (1974).

2. Quantity Index

It appears that a clear concept of an economic quantity index exists only in the case of a homogeneous (of degree 1) aggregator function $u(\cdot)$ -- e.g., see Afriat (1972), Pollak (1971), and Samuelson and Swamy (1974). Formally defined, it is the ratio of expenditures on observed,optimal quantities at a constant "price level". The condition of observed, optimal quantities implies that these are given by the (Hicksian) demand functions in the two periods, namely $x^0 = \hat{x}(p^0,\bar{u}^0)$ and

$x^1 = \hat{x}(p^1, \bar{u}^1)$. For $u(\cdot)$ homogeneous of degree 1 in x , we have, according to equation (25), the identity

$$p^{0\prime}x^0 = u(x^0)h(p^0) \quad . \tag{27}$$

The demand functions in $\hat{x}(\cdot, \bar{u})$ are homogeneous of degree 0 in prices, thus we can write $x^1 = \hat{x}(p^1, \bar{u}^1) = \hat{x}(p^{*1}, \bar{u}^1)$, where $p^{*1} = c_h^{10}p^1$, and

$$p^{*1\prime}x^1 = u(x^1)h(p^{*1})$$

$$= u(x^1)h(p^0) \quad , \tag{28}$$

since $h(p^{*1}) = c_h^{10}h(p^1) = h(p^0)$. Thus, the quantity index at price level $h(p^{*1}) = h(p^0)$ is given by

$$s_n^{01} = p^{*1\prime}x^1/p^{0\prime}x^0 = u(x^1)/u(x^0) \quad , \tag{29}$$

this is equivalent to "deflating" the ratio of actual expenditures $m^1/m^0 = p^{1\prime}x^1/p^{0\prime}x^0$ by the price index c_h^{01} .

This deflation procedure of actual expenditures by a price index is also maintained in the more general case, where $u(\cdot)$ is <u>not</u> necessarely homothetic -- or homogeneous of degree 1 in x, to give an <u>index</u> of <u>real</u> <u>expenditures</u>

$$t^{01} = [c^{01}]^{-1} \, m^1/m^0 \quad . \tag{30}$$

3. An Example

i) Homogeneous CES-type aggregator function

The homogeneous (of degree 1) Constant-Elasticity-of-Substitution (CES)-type aggregator function is of the form

$$u = u(x) = [\Sigma\alpha_i^* x_i^{\rho*}]^{1/\rho*} \quad , \tag{31}$$

where $0<\alpha_i^*<1$, $\Sigma\alpha_i^* = 1$, and in order to ensure concavity, ρ satisfies $-\infty<\rho<1$ for $\rho \neq 0$; however, the limit $\rho \to 0$ is defined below.[5] The elasticity of substitution

$$\sigma_{ij} = -\frac{d \log (x_i/x_j)}{d \log u_i(x)/u_j(x)} = \sigma = 1/(1-\rho) , \qquad (32)$$

where $u_i(x) = \partial u(x)/\partial x_i$, is a constant for all pairs x_i and x_j.[6] For $\rho = 1$ the aggregator function reduces to a weighted linear mean

$$u(x) = \Sigma\alpha^*_i x_i , \qquad (33)$$

in which the quantities are perfect substitutes, $\sigma = \infty$. By taking the limit $\rho \to 0$, so $\sigma = 1$, the aggregator function becomes a weighted geometric mean

$$u(x) = \Pi x_i^{\alpha^*_i} , \qquad (34)$$

which is referred to as a Cobb-Douglas (CD)-type aggregator function. By taking the limit $\rho \to -\infty$ the aggregator function reduces to

$$u(x) = \min [(x_1/\alpha_1),\ldots,(x_n/\alpha_n)] , \qquad (35)$$

where $\sigma = 0$.[7]

The cost function (17) corresponding to (31) is given by

$$C(p;\bar{u}) = \bar{u}[\Sigma\alpha_i p_i^{\rho}]^{1/\rho} \qquad (36)$$

where $\alpha_i = \alpha_i^{*\,-1/(\rho-1)}$ and $\rho = \rho^*/(\rho^*-1) = 1-\sigma$.
By Shephard's Lemma -- see Shephard (1970, Chapter 8), the Hicksian system of demand functions is

$$\hat{x}(p,\bar{u}) = \bar{u}\partial h(p)/\partial p \qquad (37)$$

where

$$h(p) = [\Sigma\alpha_i p_i^{\rho}]^{1/\rho} . \tag{38}$$

By using the identity $m = \bar{u}h(p)$, the Marshallian system of demand functions follows by substitution in (37) as

$$\tilde{x}(p,m) = [m/h(p)][\partial h(p)/\partial p] , \tag{39}$$

$$= m \{\alpha_i p_i^{\rho-1}/(\Sigma\alpha_j p_j^{\rho})\} \tag{40}$$

for our example. Thus, the budget share $p_i\tilde{x}_i/p'\tilde{x}=p_i\tilde{x}_i/m=w_i$ is in its parametric form given by

$$w_i = \alpha_i p_i^{\rho}/ (\Sigma\alpha_j p_j^{\rho}) \tag{41}$$

For the CES-type utility function, the price index c_h^{01} of (26) specializes to

$$c_h^{01}(\rho) = (\Sigma\alpha_i p_i^{1^{\rho}})^{1/\rho}/(\Sigma\alpha_j p_j^{0^{\rho}})^{1/\rho} \tag{42}$$

$$=[\Sigma\, w_i^0 (p_i^1/p_i^0)^{\rho}]^{1/\rho} , \tag{43}$$

where the base period budget shares are given by

$$w_i^0 = \alpha_i p_i^{0^{\rho}}/(\Sigma\alpha_j p_j^{0^{\rho}}) \tag{44}$$

in their parametric form, which is equivalent to

$$w_i^0 = p_i^0\tilde{x}_i^0/m^0 , \tag{45}$$

for quantities determined by demand functions $\tilde{x}(p,m)$.

At this point we pause to note that the economic price index (43) resembles the atomistic price index given in equation (2). Economic theory, however, determines

a) the weights w_i in (2) by the base period budget shares w_i^0 in (43), and

b) links the parameter ρ with the elasticity of substitution σ as $\rho = 1 - \sigma$.

Thus, for $-\infty < \rho \leq 1$ the economic index (43) also satisfies the four axioms underlying atomistic indices. For $\rho = 1$, so $\sigma = 0$, we have

$$c_h^{01}(1) = \bar{c}^{01} = \Sigma w_i^0 (p_i^1 / p_i^0) \ , \tag{46}$$

which is the Laspeyres index; this is in view of the parameter restrictions on ρ an upper bound on $c_h^{01}(\rho)$. Thus, the proper interpretation of the Laspeyres index rests with the fixed proportion aggregator function (35).[8) 9)]

Theorem 2 is now of fundamental importance: Given prices p^1 , p^0 , and budget shares w_i^0 , it follows for $\rho' \leq \rho''$ in our example,

$$c_h^{01}(\rho') \leq c_h^{01}(\rho'') \tag{47}$$

-- i.e., a larger elasticity of substitution, which follows from $\rho = 1 - \sigma$, implies a lower (or not greater) value for the price index; this does make sense!

Finally, we note that we may use equation (29) for our example to obtain the quantity index

$$s_h^{01}(\rho^*) = [\Sigma \alpha_i^* x_i^{1\,\rho^*}]^{1/\rho^*} / [\Sigma \alpha_j^* x_j^{0\,\rho^*}]^{1/\rho^*} \tag{48}$$

$$= [\Sigma w_i^0 (x_i^1 / x_i^0)^{\rho^*}]^{1/\rho^*} \ , \tag{49}$$

where the weights w_i^0 are given by

$$w_i^0 = \alpha_i^* \tilde{x}_i^{0\,\rho^*} / (\Sigma \alpha_j^* \tilde{x}_j^{0\,\rho^*}) \tag{50}$$

in their parametric form, which is equivalent to

$$w_i^0 = p_i^0 \tilde{x}_i^0 / p^{0\prime} \tilde{x}^0 \tag{51}$$

for quantities determined by demand functions $\tilde{x}(p,m)$.[10)]

ii) Affine homogeneous CES-type aggregator function

The aggregator function is now specified to be homogeneous in transformed (and unobservable) quantities $x^* = (x_1^*, \ldots, x_n^*)' = (x_1 - z_1, \ldots, x_n - z_n)' = x - z$. The (unobservable) quantity z_i is the predetermined share of quantity x_i , and only the share x_i^* of x_i is endogenously determined via an optimizing behavior:

$$u(x^*) = u(x-z) = [\Sigma \alpha_i^* x_i^{*\rho^*}]^{1/\rho^*} = [\Sigma \alpha_i^* (x_i - z_i)^{\rho^*}]^{1/\rho^*} . \tag{52}$$

The cost function corresponding to (52) is of the form

$$C(p;\bar{u},z) = p'z + \bar{u}h(p) , \tag{53}$$

where $h(\cdot)$ is given by (38), so that the Hicksian system of demand function is of the form

$$\hat{x}(p,\bar{u},z) = z + \bar{u}\,\partial h(p)/\partial p . \tag{54}$$

By substituting the identity for supernumerary expenditures m^*,

$$m^* = m - p'z = \bar{u}h(p) , \tag{55}$$

into (54), the Marshallian system of demand functions follows as

$$\tilde{x}(p,m,z) = z + [m^*/h(p)][\partial h(p)/\partial p] \ , \tag{56}$$

$$= z + (m-p'z)\{\alpha_i p_i^{\rho-1}/(\Sigma\alpha_j p_j^{\rho})\} \tag{57}$$

$$= z + \tilde{x}^*(p,m^*)$$

in our example. Thus, the marginal budget share $w_i^* = p_i x_i^*/m^*$ is given by the parametric form

$$w_i^* = \alpha_i p_i^{\rho} / (\Sigma\alpha_j p_j^{\rho}) \ ,$$

whenever x_i^* is determined by $\tilde{x}^*(p,m^*)$, equation (57). For the demand system (57) the expenditure elasticity η_i for quantity x_i is

$$\eta_i = \partial \log \tilde{x}_i(p,m,z)/\partial \log m = w_i^*/w_i \ , \tag{58}$$

where $w_i = p_i x_i/m$. Finally we note that the elasticity of substitution -- under a cost minimizing behavior -- is not a constant, it is given by

$$\sigma_{ij} = - \partial \log (\hat{x}_i/\hat{x}_j)/\partial \log (p_i/p_j)$$

$$= \sigma[(x_i^*/x_i)a_{ji} + (x_j^*/x_j)a_{ij}] \ , \tag{59}$$

where $a_{ji} = w_j/(w_j+w_i)$, so $a_{ji}+a_{ij} = 1$, and $\sigma = 1/(1-\rho)$; c. f. Hasenkamp (1976) for a derivation of this elasticity.[11)]

For the affine homogeneous CES-type utility function we have to distinguish between the cardinal price index -- where the z-quantities are allowed to vary in the cost functions -- and the ordinal price index -- where the z-quantities are treated as if they are constant.

A) The cardinal price index [Phlips (1974), and Phlips and Sanz-Ferrer (1975)]:

The cardinal price index is given by

$$c^{01} = [p^{1'}z^{1}+\bar{u}h(p^{1})]/[p^{0'}z^{0}+\bar{u}h(p^{0})] . \tag{60}$$

Whenever $\bar{u} = u(x^{*0})$, we can utilize the identity $h(p^0)\bar{u} = p^{0'}x^{*0} = m^0-p^{0'}z^0$, and rewrite (60) as

$$\begin{aligned} c^{01} &= (p^{0'}z^0/m^0)(p^{1'}z^1/p^{0'}z^0) + [(m^0-p^{0'}z^0)/m^0]h(p^1)/h(p^0) \\ &= \mu q^{01} + (1-\mu)c^{01}_{h^*} , \end{aligned} \tag{61}$$

where $\mu = p^{0'}z^0/m^0$, $q^{01} = p^{1'}z^1/p^{0'}z^0$, and

$$c^{01}_{h^*} = h(p^1)/h(p^0) , \tag{62}$$

$$= [\Sigma\alpha_i w_i^{*0}(p_i^1/p_i^0)^{\rho}]^{1/\rho} \tag{63}$$

for our particular example.[12)] The index c_{h*}^{01} of (62) is termed the <u>marginal price index</u> by Theil (1975) and Afriat (1974). By using the identity in (58) we rewrite the marginal budget share w_i^{*0} in (63) to obtain

$$c_{h*}^{01} = [\Sigma\alpha_i(\eta_i^0 w_i^0)(p_i^1/p_i^0)^{\rho}]^{1/\rho} \tag{64}$$

-- i.e., the weights w_i^{*0} are budget shares w_i^0 corrected by the expenditure elasticity η_i^0 ; $w_i^{*0} = \eta_i^0 w_i^0$. By defining $z^1 = z^0 + \Delta z$, the term q^{01} in (61) is rewritten as

$$q^{01} = L_p(p^1,p^0;z^0) + p^{1'}\Delta z/p^{0'}z^0 \quad , \tag{65}$$

where $L_p(p^1,p^0;z^0)$ is a Laspeyres price index (with quantities z^0), so that (61) becomes

$$c^{01} = \bar{c}^{\,01} + (p^{1'}\Delta z)/m^0 \quad , \tag{66}$$

where

$$\bar{c}^{\,01} = \mu\ Lp(p^1,p^0;z^0) + (1-\mu)c_{h*}^{01} \quad . \tag{67}$$

B) The ordinal price index [Fisher and Shell (1972)]
For either period "0" or "1" the ordinal price index uses either z^0 or z^1 as a fixed reference; thus four alternative definitions of an ordinal price index are possible. We shall only discuss the two indices with base period "0" and

reference z^0 or z^1 ; the other two indices follow by a symmetric argument.

For the case with base period "0" and reference z^0 , the ordinal price index becomes

$$c^{01}_{z^0} = [p^{1'}z^0+\bar{u}h(p^1)]/[p^{0'}z^0+\bar{u}h(p^0)] \quad . \tag{68}$$

Under the condition $\bar{u} = u(x^{*0})$ this index specializes to

$$c^{01}_{z^0} = \mu(p^{1'}z^0/p^{0'}z^0)+(1-\mu)[h(p^1)/h(p^0)]$$

$$= \bar{c}^{01} \quad , \tag{69}$$

from equation (67).[13)]

For the case with base period "0" and reference z^1 , the ordinal price index becomes

$$c^{01}_{z^1} = [p^{1'}z^1+\bar{u}h(p^1)]/[p^{0'}z^1+\bar{u}h(p^0)] \quad . \tag{70}$$

Fisher and Shell specify $\bar{u}$ as follows: Maximize $u(x^*)$ s.t. $p^{0'}z^1+p^0x^* = m^0$, p^0 and m^0 exogenous, actual prices and total expenditures in period "0" . This yields $\bar{u} = u(x^{*10})$, say. Quantities x^{*1} of the reference period "1" are determined by minimizing $p^{1'}x^*$ s.t. $u(x^*) = \bar{u}$. The index $c^{01}_{z^1}$ we rewrite as

$$c^{01}_{z^1} = \{[p^{0'}z^1+\bar{u}h(p^0)]/[p^{1'}z^1+\bar{u}h(p^1)]\}^{-1}$$

$$= \{\mu L_p(p^0,p^1;z^1)+(1-\mu)c^{10}_{h^*}\}^{-1} \quad , \qquad (71)$$

whenever $\bar{u} = u(x^{*10})$, and where $\mu = p^{1'}z^1/m^1$; here $m^1 = p^{1'}z^1+\bar{u}h(p^1)$ refers to the hypothetical expenditure level implied by the price index (70).

C) Comments

At this point we pause in order to summarize and note the following points.

a) The ordinal price indices $c^{01}_{z^0}$ in equation (69) -- or (67) and $c^{01}_{z^1}$ in equation (71) involve convex combinations of a Laspeyres price index and a marginal price index.

b) The cardinal price index c^{01} in equation (66) equals the ordinal price index $c^{01}_{z^0}$, corrected by a term which measures changes in predetermined quantities namely $(p^{1'}\Delta z)/m^0$

c) Since the Laspeyres index and the marginal price index of (64) with $-\infty<\rho\leq 1$ satisfy the four axioms for atomistic price indices, the ordinal indices serve as an economic illustration for Theorem 1.

d) The marginal price index $c^{01}_{h^*}$ of equation (64) resembles the atomistic index in equation (2). Economic theory, however, determines weights w_i in (2) by the base period marginal budget shares $w_i^{*O} = \eta_i^O w_i^O$ in (64). Furthermore, economic theory links the parameter ρ with the elasticity of substitution between the x^* quantities σ, as $\rho = 1-\sigma$.

D) Real expenditure index

For the real expenditure index t^{01} -- defined in equation (30) -- we have the choice of using either one of the ordinal (or cardinal) price indices, or the marginal price index c_{h*}^{01} for deflation purposes.

The marginal price index does not involve (in essence) an arbitrary choice for the z-specification, as in either price index, and therefore appears more convenient:

$$t^{01} = [c_h^{01}]^{-1} m^1/m^O$$

$$= [\bar{p}^{1'} z^1 + h(\bar{p}^1) u(x^{*1})]/[p^{O'} z^O + h(p^O) u(x^O)]$$

$$= \mu \bar{s}^{01} + (1-\mu) s_{h*}^{01} \tag{72}$$

where $\mu = p^{O'} z^O/m^O$, $\bar{s}^{01} = \bar{p}^{1'} z^1/p^{O'} z^O$, for $\bar{p}^1 = [c_{h*}^{01}]^{-1} p^1$, so $h(\bar{p}^1) = h(p^O)$, and

$$s_{h*}^{01} = u(x^{*1})/u(x^{*O}), \text{ or} \tag{73}$$

$$= [\Sigma w_i^{*O} (x_i^1/x_i^{*O})^{\rho^*}]^{1/\rho^*}$$

$$= [\Sigma(\eta_i^0 w_i^0)(x_i^{*\,1}/x_i^{*\,0})^{\rho^*}]^{1/\rho^*} \tag{74}$$

in our example of a CES-type function for $u(\cdot)$.

iii) Empirical Illustration

We shall provide an illustration for the economic index numbers with W-German (per capita) expenditure data (of private households) for the years 1954-1967. The quantities are confined to "industrial products", in order to dramatize the differences between the cardinal and ordinal indices; during the years 1954-1967 W-Germany enjoyed economic growth, and its influence on predetermined z-quantities might be substantial. The four quantities are categorized as:

x_1 = chemical products,

x_2 = machine products,

x_3 = electro and optical products,

x_4 = metal products.

Two different data bases were used: In the data base D1, imports and domestically produced quantities of the four industrial products were aggregated according to the CD-type aggregator function (34), so that their prices were also aggregated via a (weighted) geometric mean.[14] The advantage of this aggregation scheme is simple estimation of parameters; the disadvantage is confining the elasticity of substitution σ to unity for such "similar" quantities. In the data base D2, a CES-type aggregator function (31) was used, which resulted in a high elasticity of substitution, but required more estimation efforts. For all industrial quantities, the predetermined z-quantities were specified to be of the form

$$z_{i_t} = \delta_{0_i} + \delta_{1_i} x_{i_{t-1}} \quad , \tag{75}$$

following the suggestion of Pollak (1970), Phlips (1974), and Phlips and Sanz-Ferrer (1975). In the resulting (Marshallian) demand system we have specified an additive disturbance term ε_i in each of the four demand functions, with zero mean and covariance $E(\varepsilon_{i_t} \varepsilon_{j_{t'}} | \cdot) = \omega_{ij}$ for $t = t'$ (zero for $t \neq t'$). Since the data satisfy the restriction $\Sigma p_i x_i = m$, the disturbances are restricted as $\Sigma \varepsilon_i = 0$ in each period. This implies a singular covariance matrix Ω. The (joint) normal distribution for the ε_i's is then defined by using the Pseudo-Inverse Ω^+ in the density function. As is well known, this implies that one demand function is dropped from the system in the process of obtaining maximum-likelihood estimates of parameters; c.f. Barten (1969). We have used the iterative method described in Malinvaud (1970, Chapter 9) to obtain maximum-likelihood estimates. The most relevant parameters and statistical indicators are summarized in Table 1. Model D2-CES refers to using a CES-type aggregator function to data base D2; a similar interpretation is used for Model D2-CD, Model D1-CES, and Model D1-CD. For all four models rather implausible estimates resulted whenever δ_{0_1} and δ_{0_2} were not restricted to zero; hence we set $\delta_{0_1} = \delta_{0_2} = 0$.

Table 1

In Table 2 we present budget shares and expenditure elasticities for the models used, and in Table 3 the relevant price ratios are presented.

Table 2

Table 3

In Table 4 we present the indices for the different models. A comparison of the results can be made along three different lines: i) For a given model, among the different indicies, ii) For a given data base, among the different aggregator functions, and iii) For a given aggregator function, among the different data bases.

Table 4

For a given model, we note that differences among the marginal price index, the various ordinal indices, and the statistical indices are only at most .2 per-cent of the per-cent inflation rate. This is, given the various different concepts and definitions, rather surprising. However, we note that the ordinal index $c_{z^1}^{01}$ tends to be on the lower side. The cardinal indices are -- given the growth in consumption -- consistently larger than any ordinal indices.

Except again for the cardinal indices, the differences between the indices corresponding to different aggregator function, for given data base, are also rather small -- at most .2 per-cent of the rate. A word of caution is needed to compare the marginal price index: Theorem 2 does not apply, since different (fitted) budget shares and expenditure elasticities are involved. Thus, even though the σ-estimate in the CES-type aggregator function is smaller than unity, the CES-type $c_{h^*}^{01}$ < CD-type $c_{h^*}^{01}$.

The differences of indices corresponding to the different data bases is substantial. Data base D2 -- via a CES-type aggregation of imports and domestically produced quantities -- reflects the more plausible price movement of elementary prices in the data base. Thus, while a CD-type aggregation for the data base overstates price increases, the predominant practice of "aggregation" via Laspeyres price indices would magnify this overstatement even more.[15)] The point of this illustration is that <u>no</u> empirical study in economics is able to reflect more meaning than the care used to generate the underlying data: This <u>is</u> a problem of index numbers!

Footnotes

*SFB 21, University of Bonn, Adenauerallee 24-42, D-5300 Bonn.

Contribution to the International Seminar on Index Numbers, Karlsruhe 1976. Members of the Seminar and in particular W. Eichhorn and J. Voeller, commented on, and thus helped to improve aspects of the paper. Jan Kemta was so kind and commented on an earlier version; his insistance on clarity lead to several reformulations of sections. Remaining errors or shortcommings are to blame on the author alone.

1) Alternatively, we could require the "existence" of a price level function h(p), such that -- in analogy to equation (1) -- the price index becomes the ratio of these price levels,

$$r^{01} = h(p^1)/h(p^0) \ .$$

There is no need to introduce the concept of a "price level" at this stage; instead, we refer to section III on economic index numbers.

2) This cost function is clearly homogeneous of degree 1 in prices p; furthermore, concavity in prices is also evident. For a detailed reference on cost and aggregator functions see Shephard (1970).

3) The Marshallian system of demand functions typically allows the estimation of parameters in the aggregator function -- or cost function -- only up to a monotonic transformation of u(•): The returns to scale parameter, or a multiplicative "efficiency" parameter can be estimated via the Hicksian system, but not via the Marshallian system of demand functions -- see the analytic example illustrated in section III-3. However, the (sub-) set of parameters estimable in a Marshallian system is sufficient to compute ordinal indices.

4) Familiar concepts of changing aggregator functions are technological progress in production, and taste change in utility analysis.

5) The efficiency parameter α_0 and the returns to scale parameter r are incorporated into the measure for output, so that in the the conventional way of writing a production function, "output" equals $u = \alpha_0[u(x)]^r$.

6) Of course, the restriction of a constant $\sigma_{ij} = \sigma$ is not very realistic. One possible generalization is the affine CES-type aggregator function in which σ_{ij} is variable over the quantities.

7) Before taking the limit $\rho \to -\infty$, one should rewrite (31) in its "equivalent" form

$$u(x) = [\Sigma\alpha_i(p_i/\alpha_i)^{\rho}]^{1/\rho} ,$$

where $\alpha_i = \alpha_i^{-1/(\rho-1)}$, and then fix α_i .

8) We could take the limit $\rho\to-\infty$ in (43) to obtain

$$\underline{c}^{01} = \min[(p_1^1/p_1^0),\ldots,(p_n^1/p_n^0)] .$$

However, this is not -- in general -- the price index corresponding to an aggregator function with $\lim \rho^* \to 1$ -- i.e., the aggregator function (33). Under (33), which allows perfect substitution among quantities, only <u>one</u> quantity will be purchased in each period; this depends on relative prices. Thus, given that x_j^0 units are purchased during the base period, yielding a level $\alpha_j^* x_j^0 = u^0$, base period expenditures are $p_j^0 x_j^0 = m^0$. If x_i is purchased in the reference period, $x_i^1 = (\alpha_j^* / \alpha_i^*) x_j^0$ units are required to attain $u^1 = u^0$. This gives a price index of the form

$$c^{01} = p_i^1 x_i^1 / p_j^0 x_j^0$$

$$= (\alpha_j/\alpha_i)(p_i^1/p_j^0) \;;$$

we note that for $i=j$, $c^{01} = \underline{c}^{01}$.

9) Perhaps a short example for a cardinal index: In the production function $u = \alpha_0(t)u(x)$, $u(\cdot)$ given by (31), the efficiency parameter $\alpha_0(t)$ measures technological change over time t . Then the cardinal index factors as

$$\hat{c}^{01} = [\alpha_0(0)/\alpha_0(1)]c_h^{01}(\rho) \quad ,$$

where $c_h^{01}(\rho)$ is given by (43). For $\alpha_0(1)>\alpha_0(0)$, the case of a technological progress, the cardinal index $\hat{c}^{01}<c_n^{01}(\rho)$, the ordinal index.

10) This follows by substituting for x_i^0 in $\alpha_i^* x_i^{0\rho*}$ the demand function (40), and for $(\Sigma\alpha_j^* x_j^{0\rho*})$ the expresssion $m^{\rho*}/(\Sigma\alpha_j p_j^{\rho})^{-\rho*/\rho}$ by using the factorization $m = h(\mathbf{p})u(x)$. It is now a matter of algebra to show

$$\alpha_i^* x_i^{0\rho*}/(\Sigma\alpha_j^* x_j^{0\rho*}) = \alpha_i p_i^{0\rho}/(\Sigma\alpha_j p_j^{0\rho}) = w_i^0 \quad .$$

11) One also obtains this elasticity of substitution by using definition (32) for a total output/utility defined by

$$U = \min\,[z_1/a_1,\ldots,z_n/a_n] + u(x-z) \quad ,$$

where the a_i are (positive constants, and $u(\cdot)$ is defined in (52).

12) The form (61) of the cardinal index is valid for any unit cost function $h(p)$ corresponding to an affine aggregator function $u(x-z)$. This generalization is also valid for

ordinal indices.

13) The function $h(\cdot)$ in these ordinal indices is given by (38) whenever $u(\cdot)$ is of the CES-type.

14) This claim follows by taking the limit $\rho \to 0$ in (38).

15) We have not constructed a third data base by using the Laspeyres price index "aggregation" of imports and domestically produced quantities. Perhaps this would have demonstrated our argument in more detail.

Table 1

Summary of Estimation Results

Parameter, Statistic \ Model	D2-CES	D2-CD	D1-CES	D1-CD
δ_{11}	.5049 (.1686)	.6085 (.1481)	.4954 (.1400)	.6262 (.1293)
δ_{12}	.2254 (.1676)	.2945 (.1483)	.1427 (.1410)	.2949 (.1607)
δ_{13}	.3332 (.1676)	.4353 (.1413)	.2328 (.1563)	.3796 (.1564)
δ_{14}	.2861 (.2546)	.2299 (.2037)	.0186 (.0165)	.2009 (.2965)
ρ	.3463 (.2297)	0.	.2931 (.1871)	0.
σ	.6537	1.	.7069	1.
L	- 1.99	-2.09	- 1.87	- 1.96
R_1^2	.9940	.9927	.9943	.9935
R_2^2	.9979	.9977	.9981	.9979
R_3^2	.9970	.9964	.9970	.9964
R_4^2	.9721	.9725	.9713	.9729

Below parameter estimates we present (asymptotic) standard errors in parentheses. The value of the log-likelihood function is denoted by L ; the "fit measure" R_i^2 was computed as unity less the ratio of residual variance to the variance of dependent variable.

Table 2

Budget Shares and Expenditure Elasticities

Model / Variable	D2-CES		D2-CD		D1-CES		D2-CD	
	1967	1955	1967	1955	1967	1955	1967	1955
w_1	.3422	.2765	.3464	.2727	.3421	.2786	.3465	.2809
w_2	.3215	.2473	.3183	.2510	.3205	.2468	.3178	.2479
w_3	.3167	.4421	.3158	.4425	.3180	.4407	.3161	.4376
w_4	.0196	.0341	.0196	.0338	.0194	.0339	.0190	.0336
η_1	.8697	1.1240	.8229	1.0450	.8405	1.0730	.8089	.9979
η_2	1.3500	1.6970	1.4330	1.8180	1.4200	1.8100	1.4680	1.8830
η_3	.8002	.5751	.7589	.5416	.7473	.5286	.7356	.5314
η_4	.7620	.4521	.9787	.5672	1.0190	.6246	1.0480	.6097

Budget shares are "fitted" shares -- i.e., parametric budget shares, evaluated with parameter estimates.

Table 3

Price Ratios

Price Ratios \ Data Base	D2	D1
p_1^1/p_1^0	.9972	1.1379
p_2^1/p_2^0	1.2438	1.3845
p_3^1/p_3^0	1.1176	1.3918
p_4^1/p_4^0	1.0365	1.0365

Here "O" = 1955 and "1" = 1967.

The original date are taken from: W. Frerichs und K. Kübler:"Die Datenbasis des Disaggregierten Prognosesystems" - Dokumentation - Institut für Gesellschafts- und Wirtschaftswissenschaften, Universität Bonn, Juni 1976.

Table 4

Indices

Indices \ Model		D2-CES	D2-CD	D1-CES	D1-CD
$c_{h^*}^{01}$	equ. (63)	1.129	1.134	1.301	1.304
$\mu^0 = p^{0'} z^0 / m^0$		.517	.578	.512	.596
$\mu^1 = p^{1'} z^1 / m^1$		.429	.513	.399	.527
c^{01}	equ. (61)	1.970	2.183	1.960	2.278
$1/c^{10}$	equ. (61)	1.477	1.612	1.564	1.754
$c_{z^0}^{01}$	equ. (69)	1.111	1.112	1.305	1.304
$1/c_{z^1}^{10}$	equ. (69)	1.109	1.109	1.288	1.287
$c_{z^1}^{01}$	equ. (71)	1.088	1.084	1.275	1.273
$1/c_{z^0}^{10}$	equ. (71)	1.124	1.129	1.302	1.304
t^{01}	equ. (72)	2.943	2.930	2.553	2.547
$s_{h^*}^{01}$	equ. (74)	3.483	3.380	3.142	2.979
La^{01}	equ. (12)	1.113	1.114	1.307	1.307
$1/La^{10} = P_a^{01}$	equ. (13)	1.106	1.105	1.283	1.282

Here "0" = 1955 and "1" = 1967. The Laspeyres Index and the Paasche Index were computed by using "fitted" budget shares; hence these indices should differ for the models used.

References

Afriat, S.N. (1972): "The Theory of International Comparison of Real Income and Prices", in D.J. Daly, editor, International Comparison of Prices and Output, NBER, New York, 1972.

Afriat, S.N. (1974): Measurement of the Purchasing Power of Incomes with Linear Expansion Data", Journal of Econometrics, Vol. 2, 1974, pp. 343-364.

Barten, A.P. (1969): "Maximum Likelihood Estimation of a Complete System of Demand Equations", European Economic Review, Vol. 1, 1969, pp. 7-73.

Diewert, W.E. (1976): "Exact and Superlative Index Numbers", Journal of Econometrics, Vol. 4, No.2,May 1976.

Eichhorn, W. (1976): "Fisher's Test Revisited", Econometrica, Vol. 44, 1976, pp. 247-256.

Eichhorn, W. (1977): Functional Equations in Economics, Addison-Wesley, Reading, 1977.

Eichhorn, W. and J. Voeller (1976): Theory of the Price Index Fisher's Test Approach and Generalizations, Lecture Notes in Economics and Mathematical Systems, Berlin-Heidelberg-New York, 1976.

Fisher, F.M. and K. Shell (1972): The Economic Theory of Price Indices, Academic Press, New York 1972.

Fisher, I. (1922): The Making of Index Numbers,Mifflin, Boston, 1922.

Frish, R. (1936): "Annual Survey of General Economic Theory: The Problem of Index Numbers", Econometrica, Vol. 4, 1936, pp. 1-38.

Hardy, G.H., J.E. Littlewood, and G. Pólya (1934): Inequalities, Cambridge University Press, Cambridge 1934.

Hasenkamp, G. (1976): "Elasticity of Substitution: The case of an Affine Homothetic Aggregator Function", SFB 21 paper, University of Bonn, October 1976.

Malinvaud, E. (1970): Statistical Methods of Econometrics, North-Holland, Amsterdam 1970.

Muellbauer, J. (1975): "The Cost of Living and Taste and Quality Change", Journal of Economic Theory, Vol. 10, 1975, pp. 269-283.

Phlips, L. (1974): Applied Consumption Analysis, North-Holland, Amsterdam 1974.

Phlips, L. and R. Sanz-Ferrer (1975): "A Taste-Dependent True Index of the Cost of Living", Review of Economics and Statistics, Vol. 57, 1975, pp. 495-501.

Pollak, R. A. (1970): "Habit Formation and Dynamic Demand Functions", Journal of Political Economy, Vol. 78, 1970, pp. 745-763.

Pollak, R. A. (1971): "The Theory of the Cost of Living", U. S. Bureau of Labor Statistics, Washington D.C., paper No. 11, 1971.

Pollak, R. A. (1975): "Subindices in the Cost of Living Index", International Economic Review, Vol. 16, 1975, pp. 135-150.

Samuelson, P. A. and S. Swamy (1974): "Invariant Economic Index Numbers and Canonical Duality: Survey and Synthesis", American Economic Review, Vol. 64, 1974, pp. 566-593.

Shephard, R. W. (1970): "The Theory of Cost and Production Functions", Princeton University Press, Princeton, 1970; first edition 1953).

Theil, H. (1975): _Theory and Measurement of Consumer Demand_, Vol. 1, North-Holland, Amsterdam 1975.

Törnqvist, L. (1936): "The Bank of Finland's Consumption Price Index", _Bank of Finland Monthly Bulletin_, No. 10, 1936, pp. 1-8.

A Note on Criteria for Price Index Systems

by Claus Hild and Günter Hacker[1)]

When using index numbers, such as price indices, there are different formulae which can be applied, so that the question arises which of them is better than the others for certain purposes. A way to answer this question is to consider so-called index number systems which encompass the price development and computation of indices over a certain period of time, or the price structure of all regional units (countries, regions, etc.) to be compared. The aim then is to determine a price index system which best describes the given observation. This article deals with an attempt made by Pfouts in (1972) [2)]: A geometrical aspect of his criterion is given, and another criterion is suggested.

1. Introduction

The formulation of price index systems used in this paper rests on an article by Pfouts (1966) where an axiomatic approach to index numbers is given, but where no attention is paid to the economic theory of price index numbers. Pfouts states that most of the commonly used index number formulae may be written as the inner product of a vector of price observations and a vector of weights:

$$(1.1) \qquad \pi_{t_o t}(\underline{q}_{t_o}, \underline{p}_{t_o}, \underline{q}_t, \underline{p}_t) = \langle \underline{w}_{t_o t}, \underline{p}_t \rangle ,$$

where $\pi_{t_o t}: \mathbb{R}_+^{4K} \to \mathbb{R}_+$ is the price index function with $\underline{q}_{t_o}$, $\underline{q}_t$,

1) The authors are indebted to Professor Dr. W. Eichhorn and Professor Dr. R. Henn of Karlsruhe University for stimulating discussions and helpful comments; but the authors alone are responsible for any errors.

2) In this paper we treat price indices only.

$\underline{p}_{t_o}$, $\underline{p}_t$ denoting the vectors of K quantities and K prices, resp., and where t_o represents the base year and t the current year [1].
The k-th element of the weighting vector $\underline{w}_{t_o t}$ is given by

$$w_{t_o t,k} = f_k(\underline{q}_{t_o}, \underline{p}_{t_o}, \underline{q}_t)$$

as the value of the weighting functions

$$f_k\colon \mathbb{R}_+^{3K} \to \mathbb{R}_+ \,, \quad k=1,\ldots,K \;^{2)}.$$

From (1.1) it is clear that only price index functions are considered which are linear in $\underline{p}_t$. Therefore we omit the term "linear" from now on.

When a certain price index formula with a fixed base year t_o is chosen, the price indices of the form (1.1), calculated over a certain period of time $\mathcal{T}: = \{1,\ldots,T\}$ by means of the observed price vectors $\underline{p}_1,\ldots,\underline{p}_T$, may be considered as a whole (Pfouts (1972)):

$$(1.2) \qquad \begin{pmatrix} \pi_1 \\ \vdots \\ \pi_T \end{pmatrix} = \begin{pmatrix} \langle \underline{w}_1, \underline{p}_1 \rangle \\ \vdots \\ \langle \underline{w}_T, \underline{p}_T \rangle \end{pmatrix} = \begin{pmatrix} \underline{w}_1' & \cdots & 0 \\ \vdots & \ddots & \vdots \\ 0 & \cdots & \underline{w}_T' \end{pmatrix} \begin{pmatrix} \underline{p}_1 \\ \vdots \\ \underline{p}_T \end{pmatrix} \quad \text{or} \quad \underline{\pi} = W\underline{p}$$

where $\underline{p} = (\underline{p}_1',\ldots,\underline{p}_T')' \in \mathbb{R}_+^{TK}$ is the price vector (of all goods in all periods), $\underline{\pi} = (\pi_1,\ldots,\pi_T)' \in \mathbb{R}_+^T$ the price index vector and $W = \operatorname{diag}(\underline{w}_1',\ldots,\underline{w}_T')$ is the bloc diagonal matrix of weights, called weighting matrix, on the right hand side of (1.2) [3]. In order to simplify notation we write $\underline{w}_t : = \underline{w}_{t_o t}$ where t_o, the indication of

---

1) We restrict ourselves to price indices to compare the prices of different periods t_o and t, but the symbol t could also refer to a geographical unit.

2) We point out that we have slightly changed the notation used by Pfouts (1966, 1972) because of the fact that, if a certain index formula is chosen, the kind of function is the same for all t, only the argument changes.

3) Prime ' denoting matrix or vector transposition.

the base year is deleted, as t_o is kept fix for the whole period in consideration. Both $t_o \in \mathcal{T}$ or $t_o \notin \mathcal{T}$ may be valid. Relation (1.2) is called price index system.

Let us consider two representations of such price index systems:

a) For the price index formula of Paasche the weights and indices are given by

$$w_{tk}^P = \frac{q_{tk}}{\langle \underline{q}_t, \underline{p}_{t_o} \rangle} \qquad t \in \mathcal{T},\ k=1,\dots,K$$

$$\pi_t^P = \langle \underline{w}_t^P, \underline{p}_t \rangle = \frac{\langle \underline{q}_t, \underline{p}_t \rangle}{\langle \underline{q}_t, \underline{p}_{t_o} \rangle} .$$

b) For the price index formula of Laspeyres we have

$$w_{tk}^L = \frac{q_{t_o k}}{\langle \underline{q}_{t_o}, \underline{p}_{t_o} \rangle} = : w_k \qquad \text{for all } t \text{ and } k$$

$$\pi_t^L = \langle \underline{w}_t^L, \underline{p}_t \rangle = \langle \underline{w}, \underline{p}_t \rangle = \frac{\langle \underline{q}_{t_o}, \underline{p}_t \rangle}{\langle \underline{q}_{t_o}, \underline{p}_{t_o} \rangle}$$

with $\underline{w} = (w_1, \dots, w_K)$. Thus, a Laspeyres price index system takes the simple form

$$\underline{\pi}^L = (I \otimes \underline{w}')\underline{p}$$ [1].

Notations:

1. By $\mathcal{W}$ we denote the set of weighting matrices of the price index formulae in consideration (e.g. $\mathcal{W} = \{W^L, W^P\}$).
2. By $\overline{\mathcal{W}}$ we denote the class of all weighting matrices having constant weights, i.e., $\underline{w}_t = :\underline{w}$ for all t (W^L, the Laspeyres weighting matrix is clearly an element of $\overline{\mathcal{W}}$).

After having formulated a price index system, Pfouts (1972) is confronted with the problem of developing a criterion for judging whether it is better to use $W_* \in \mathcal{W}$ instead of $W \in \mathcal{W}$, i.e., whether

1) The symbol "$\otimes$" denotes the Kronecker product $A \otimes B = (a_{ij}B)$ of two matrices.

one should use the price index formula associated with W_* rather than the one associated with W.

2. Pfouts' Criterion; a Geometrical Aspect

In his article "price index systems" Pfouts (1972) considers (1.2) as a system of linear equations in the $\underline{p}$ vector, the general solution of which is given by

$$(2.1) \qquad \underline{\tilde{p}} = W^{+}\underline{\pi} + (I-W^{+}W)\underline{z} \ , \qquad \underline{z} \in \mathbb{R}^{TK} \text{ arbitrary} \ ,$$

where W^{+} is the pseudo-inverse of W [1], which is easily seen to be $W^{+} = W'(WW')^{-1}$ as obviously $rk(W) = T$, if no period occurs to have zero weights for all goods, which reasonably can be assumed.

Considering (2.1) means to look for all prices $\underline{\tilde{p}}$ which may be different from the observed price vector $\underline{p}$ but yield the same vector of indices $\underline{\pi}$, for $W\underline{\tilde{p}} = WW^{+}\underline{\pi} + W(I-W^{+}W)\underline{z} = WW^{+}W\underline{p} = W\underline{p} = \underline{\pi}$.

The (price) vector $W^{+}\underline{\pi} = W^{+}W\underline{p} =: \underline{\hat{p}}$ is the one that satisfies (1.2) possessing a minimum (Euclidian) norm, because for all $\underline{\tilde{p}}$ with $W\underline{\tilde{p}} = \underline{\pi}$ we have $\|\underline{\tilde{p}}\|^2 = \|W^{+}\underline{\pi}+(I-W^{+}W)\underline{z}\|^2 = \|W^{+}\underline{\pi}\|^2 + \|(I-W^{+}W)\underline{z}\|^2 \geqslant \|W^{+}\underline{\pi}\|^2 = \|W^{+}W\underline{p}\|^2 = \|\underline{\hat{p}}\|^2$, where the second equation is valid because of $\langle W^{+}\underline{\pi}, (I-W^{+}W)\underline{z}\rangle = 0$. As $\|\underline{\hat{p}}\|^2 = \sum_{t=1}^{T} \sum_{k=1}^{K} \hat{p}_{tk}$ is minimal Pfouts denotes $\underline{\hat{p}}$ as least squares prices (LS-prices) [2].

---

1) By a pseudo-inverse A^{+} of any matrix A we mean the uniquely existing generalized inverse that satisfies
(i) $AA^{+}A = A$ (ii) $A^{+}AA^{+} = A^{+}$ (iii) $(AA^{+})' = AA^{+}$ (iv) $(A^{+}A)' = A^{+}A$.

2) Originally, Pfouts' notation of least squares prices results from the point of view of minimizing $\|\underline{\pi}-W\underline{p}\|^2$ which is the least squares problem of approximating an inconsistent equation; but $\underline{\pi} = W\underline{p}$ is consistent, so $\|\underline{\pi}-W\underline{p}\|^2 = 0$.

Example:

For a Laspeyres price index system we have

$$\hat{\underline{p}}^L = (I_T \otimes \underline{w}')^+ (I_T \otimes \underline{w}')\underline{p} = (I_T \otimes \underline{w}'^+)(I_T \otimes \underline{w}')\underline{p} =$$
$$= (I_T \otimes \underline{w}'^+ \underline{w}')\underline{p} = (I_T \otimes \underline{w}\underline{w}^+)\underline{p} = (I_T \otimes \frac{\underline{w}\underline{w}'}{\|\underline{w}\|^2})\underline{p} \ .$$

By means of (2.1) Pfouts defines a criterion in the following way: For two different price index functions $\pi_{t_o t}$ and $\pi^*_{t_o t}$ (same base year, different formulae) or $\pi_{t_o t}$ and $\pi_{t^*_o t}$, $t_o \neq t^*_o$ (same formula, different base years), associated with the price index systems $\underline{\pi} = W\underline{p}$ and $\underline{\pi}_* = W_* \underline{p}$, resp., if the relation

(2.2) $\quad \| \underline{p} - \hat{\underline{p}}(W) \| \geqslant \| \underline{p} - \hat{\underline{p}}(W_*) \|$

holds, Pfouts suggests to use W_* rather than W, where $\hat{p}(W)$ and $\hat{p}(W_*)$ denote the "LS"-prices of the two alternative price index systems.

For this suggestion we give a geometrical illustration of the procedure applied. Let $\mathcal{M}(W')$ denote the T-dimensional linear subspace of $\mathbb{R}^{TK}$ spanned by the rows of W, then $\hat{\underline{p}} \in \mathcal{M}(W')$ is exactly the orthogonal projection of $\underline{p}$ on $\mathcal{M}(W')$. In words this means: "The price development is measured by its projection on $\mathcal{M}(W')$". From the projection theorem we know that $\underline{p}$ may be uniquely written as

(2.3) $\quad \underline{p} = \hat{\underline{p}} + \underline{d} \quad$ with $\hat{\underline{p}} \in \mathcal{M}(W')$ and $\underline{d} \in \mathcal{M}^{\perp}(W') = \mathcal{K}(W)$,

where $\mathcal{K}(W)$ is the kernel of W. This yields the result $\hat{\underline{p}} \perp \underline{d}$ which Pfouts states, letting $\underline{d} = (I - W^+W)\underline{p}$.

From the geometrical point of view the criterion proposed by means of (2.2) is to choose the weighting matrix whose row space lies nearer to the price vector $\underline{p}$. We realize here that no attention is paid to the index vectors $\underline{\pi}$ and $\underline{\pi}_*$.

It is easy to prove that

$$(2.4) \qquad \| \underline{p} - \hat{\underline{p}}(W_*) \| \leqslant \| \underline{p} - \hat{\underline{p}}(W) \| \iff \| \hat{\underline{p}}(W_*) \| \geqslant \| \hat{\underline{p}}(W) \|$$

so one may restrict oneself to the consideration of the projections (or LS-prices) only.

Thus, the way Pfouts purposes to find a criterion for the choice of a price index function (i.e. weighting matrix) is centered around his interest in a price vector having minimum norm. In connection with that one might ask the question for the economic sense of such a price vector. We therefore dedicate our subsequent work to the aim of suggesting another criterion which takes care of the economic aspect.

3. A Criterion for Prices Measured by Deviations from Their Means

A price index system may be concerned with price observations over time (e.g. years) as well as with price observations in different geographical units (e.g. countries). Because its purpose is to aggregate the informations about prices, it seems to be reasonable to take account of the price fluctuation over time or between countries.

Thus, we construct a mean price of each good as arithmetic mean of its prices [1)] over all periods:

$$(3.1) \qquad \bar{p}_k = \frac{1}{T} \sum_{t=1}^{T} p_{tk} \quad (k=1,\ldots,K) \quad \text{or} \quad \bar{\underline{p}} = \frac{1}{T} L'\underline{p} \ ,$$

---

1) The use of mean prices points out the connection with those problems that deal with the determination of purchasing powers of money between different countries or sections of population within a country; for example in the Geary-Khamis approach (e.g. (1958)) average prices (or international prices) are defined, the calculation of which is very different from our mean prices and much more complicated.

where $\bar{\underline{p}} = (\bar{p}_1,\dots,\bar{p}_K)'$, $L' = (\underbrace{I_K,\dots,I_K}_{T\text{-times}})$. So, if the prices are the same for all t, we have $\underline{p} = \underline{\iota} \otimes \bar{\underline{p}}$, with $\underline{\iota} = (1,1,\dots,1)'$.

Next we define the price deviations as the difference of the individual prices $\underline{p}_t$ and the mean price vector $\bar{\underline{p}}$:

$$(3.2) \qquad \underline{a}_t := \underline{p}_t - \bar{\underline{p}} \quad (t=1,\dots,T) \qquad \text{or} \quad \underline{a} = \underline{p} - L\bar{\underline{p}} \ ,$$

where $\underline{a} = (\underline{a}_1',\dots,\underline{a}_T')' \in \mathbb{R}^{TK}$. As a well-known measure for the degree of variation of the prices we consider

$$(3.3) \qquad \| \underline{a} \|^2 = \| \underline{p} - L\bar{\underline{p}} \|^2 = \sum_{t=1}^{T} \| \underline{p}_t - \bar{\underline{p}} \|^2 = \sum_{t=1}^{T} \sum_{k=1}^{K} (p_{tk} - \bar{p}_k)^2 .$$

With respect to (3.2) we rewrite a price index system $\underline{\pi} = W\underline{p}$, where $\underline{p} = L\bar{\underline{p}} + \underline{a}$, as

$$(3.4) \qquad \underline{\pi} = W\underline{p} = (WL)\bar{\underline{p}} + W\underline{a} = \bar{W}\bar{\underline{p}} + W\underline{a} = \hat{\underline{\pi}} + W\underline{a} \ .$$

We denote the $(T\times K)$-matrix $\bar{W} = WL$ as consolidated weighting matrix, as the vectors of weights are put together as rows of the new matrix $\bar{W}$. The vector $\hat{\underline{\pi}}$ may be denoted as medium price index vector which gives the values of the price indices if no price fluctuation appears. So, if constant weights are used, all components of $\hat{\underline{\pi}}$ are the same and equal to the arithmetic mean of the price indices [1].

From the construction of mean prices and price deviations it is clear that $L\bar{\underline{p}}$ is the projection of $\underline{p}$ on the column space of L, $\mathcal{M}(L)$, and $\underline{a}$ is the projection of $\underline{p}$ on $\mathcal{K}(L')$, for $L\bar{\underline{p}}$ may be writ-

1) $\hat{\pi}_t = \sum_{k=1}^{K} w_k \bar{p}_k = \sum_{k=1}^{K} w_k (\frac{1}{T} \sum_{\tau=1}^{T} p_{\tau k}) = \frac{1}{T} \sum_{\tau=1}^{T} \sum_{k=1}^{K} w_k p_{\tau k} = \frac{1}{T} \sum_{\tau=1}^{T} \pi_\tau = \bar{\pi}$.

ten as $LL^+\underline{p}$, and $\underline{a} = (I-LL^+)\underline{p}$ [1].

For a given price index system there may exist price developments with the same mean price and with less fluctuation (that means that the price deviations are of smaller norm) but still yielding the same index vector. Indeed there are many deviations which generate the same vector of price indices. All these are given by the general solution of $\underline{\pi}-\underline{\hat{\pi}} = W\underline{a}$, which is

$$(3.5) \qquad \underline{\tilde{a}} = W^+(\underline{\pi}-\underline{\hat{\pi}}) + (I-W^+W)\underline{z} \qquad (\underline{z} \in \mathbb{R}^{TK}).$$

The deviation vector $\underline{\hat{a}} := W^+(\underline{\pi}-\underline{\hat{\pi}}) = W^+W(\underline{p}-L\underline{\bar{p}}) = W^+W\underline{a}$ is the one having minimum norm; indeed this can be shown analogously to the minimum norm property of the LS-prices (c.f. section 2 of this article).

So we formulate the new criterion

$$(3.6) \qquad C(W) := \min_{\underline{\pi}=W\underline{p}} \|\underline{a}\| = \min_{\underline{\pi}-\underline{\hat{\pi}}=W\underline{a}} \|\underline{a}\| = \|\underline{\hat{a}}(W)\| \qquad W \in \mathcal{W}.$$

That means, that one should look for a price structure with a smaller fluctuation than the observed one. If they lie far away from each other, there is plenty of range for price developments forming the same indices. This might lead to a wrong impression of what is going on in economy. So we are forced to minimize this range or, geometrically, we look for that weighting matrix $W \in \mathcal{W}$ whose row space $\mathcal{R}(W')$ lies nearest to the $\underline{a}$ vector, i.e., we minimize $\|\underline{a}-\underline{\hat{a}}(W)\|$.

Definition 1:

Let W_*, $W \in \mathcal{W}$. Then the weighting matrix W_* is called "better" than W, written $W_* \succsim W$, if $C(W_*) \geq C(W)$ (or equivalently if $\|\underline{a}-\underline{\hat{a}}(W_*)\| \leq \|\underline{a}-\underline{\hat{a}}(W)\|$), where $\underline{\hat{a}}(W_*)$, $\underline{\hat{a}}(W)$ are the projections of $\underline{a}$ on the row space of W_*, W, resp.

---

[1] Note that $L^+ = (L'L)^{-1}L' = \frac{1}{T}L'$.

Definition 2:

A weighting matrix W_* is said to be optimal with respect to a given set $\mathcal{W}$ if

(3.7) $$\max_{W \in \mathcal{W}} C(W) = \max_{W \in \mathcal{W}} \min_{\underline{\pi} = Wp} \| \underline{a} \| = \| \hat{\underline{a}}(W_*) \|.$$

Theorem 1:

Given $W \in \overline{\mathcal{W}}$, then the projection $\hat{\underline{a}}$ of the price deviation $\underline{a}$ on $\mathcal{M}(W')$ belongs also to $\mathcal{K}(L')$.

Proof:

As the weights are constant for all periods we write them as $\underline{w}$ for all $t \in \mathcal{T}$.

In order to show that $\hat{\underline{a}} \in \mathcal{K}(L')$ we have to prove that $\sum_{t \in \mathcal{T}} \hat{\underline{a}}_t = 0$.

Now, the projections $\hat{\underline{a}}_t$ for all t=1,...,T are given by:

(3.8) $$\hat{\underline{a}}_t = \frac{\underline{w}}{\| \underline{w} \|^2} \langle \underline{w}, \underline{a}_t \rangle = \frac{\underline{w}\underline{w}'}{\| \underline{w} \|^2} \underline{a}_t .$$

So, from $L'\underline{a} = \sum_{t=1}^{T} \underline{a}_t = 0$ we have

(3.9) $$\sum_{t=1}^{T} \hat{\underline{a}}_t = \sum_{t=1}^{T} \frac{\underline{w}\underline{w}'}{\|\underline{w}\|^2} \underline{a}_t = \frac{\underline{w}\underline{w}'}{\|\underline{w}\|^2} \sum_{t=1}^{T} \underline{a}_t = 0 . \square$$

Obviously, not for all sets $\mathcal{W}$ of weighting matrices the orthogonal projection $\hat{\underline{a}}(W)$ has this property. Consider the realistic case, where $T \leqslant K$. If the weights are linearly dependent, so $rk(\bar{W}) < T$ [1), a different projection $\hat{\hat{\underline{a}}}(W)$ of $\underline{a}$ on $\mathcal{M}(W')$ is available such that $L'\hat{\hat{\underline{a}}} = 0$.

---

1) In the case where the Paasche formula is used, dependence of vectors of quantities and of weights is equivalent:

Let $d_t := 1/\langle \underline{q}_t, \underline{p}_{t_o} \rangle$, $\Delta := \text{diag}(d_1,\dots,d_T)$, $Q := (q_{tk})$;

If $\underline{\lambda} \neq 0$ with $Q'\underline{\lambda} = 0 \iff \Delta Q'\underline{\lambda} = 0 \iff \bar{W}'\underline{\lambda} = 0$ as $\Delta Q = \bar{W}$.

Theorem 2:

Let $rk(\bar{W}) < T$, then a projection $\hat{\hat{\underline{a}}}(W) \in \mathcal{M}(W')$ with the property $\hat{\hat{\underline{a}}}(W) \in \mathcal{K}(L')$ is given by

$$(3.10) \qquad \hat{\hat{\underline{a}}}(W) := W^{+}MW\underline{a} ,$$

where $M := I - \bar{W}[\bar{W}'(WW')^{-1}\bar{W}]^{-} \bar{W}(\bar{W}\bar{W}')^{-1}$ 1).

Proof:

A projection $\hat{\hat{\underline{a}}}(W)$ is element of $\mathcal{M}(W')$, i.e., it can be written as $\hat{\underline{a}} = W'\underline{c}$ for some $\underline{c} \in \mathbb{R}^{T}$. In addition we want to have that $\hat{\hat{\underline{a}}} \in \mathcal{K}(L')$, then $L'\hat{\hat{\underline{a}}} = (WL)'\underline{c} = \bar{W}'\underline{c} = 0$ must be valid. From the assumption $rk(\bar{W}) < T$ we conclude that there exists a $\underline{c} \neq 0$ with $\underline{c} \in \mathcal{K}(\bar{W}') = \mathcal{M}^{\perp}(\bar{W})$. If we chose $\underline{c}$ as orthogonal projection of $\underline{\pi}$ on $\mathcal{M}^{\perp}(\bar{W})$ under norm $\|\underline{x}\|_{WW'} := \sqrt{\underline{x}'(WW')^{-1}\underline{x}}$, $\underline{x} \in \mathbb{R}^{T}$, so $\underline{c} = (WW')^{-1}M\underline{\pi} = (WW')^{-1}MW\underline{p} = (WW')^{-1}MW\underline{a}$. It is easy to check that $W^{+}MW$ is (symmetric) idempotent and therefore a projection matrix. □

It is very interesting to notice that in this case both the projections of $\underline{p}$ and $\underline{a}$ on $\mathcal{M}(W')$ are the same. But there is some defect. As $W^{+}M$ is no generalized inverse of W, hence $\hat{\hat{\underline{a}}}$ is no solution of $\underline{\pi}-\hat{\underline{\pi}} = W\underline{a}$, but it is one of $\underline{\pi}-\bar{W}\hat{\hat{\underline{p}}} = W\underline{a}$, where $\hat{\hat{\underline{p}}} := (\bar{W}'(WW')^{-1}\bar{W})^{-} \bar{W}'(WW')^{-1}\underline{\pi}$ is an "approximated" mean price determined by generalized least squares methods from $\underline{\pi}$ on $\bar{W}$.

Theorem 3:

Given a weighting matrix W then for the two projections $\hat{\hat{\underline{a}}}(W)$ (from Theorem 2) and $\hat{\underline{a}}(W)$ (from (3.6)) we have:

$$(3.11) \qquad \|\hat{\hat{\underline{a}}}(W)\| \leq \|\hat{\underline{a}}(W)\| \leq \|\underline{a}\| .$$

---

1) A^{-} denotes any generalized inverse of a matrix A, i.e., $AA^{-}A = A$.

Proof:

We have seen above that we have $\|\underline{\tilde{a}}\| \geqslant \|\underline{\hat{a}}(W)\|$ for all $\underline{\tilde{a}}$ with $W\underline{\tilde{a}} = \underline{\pi}-\underline{\hat{\pi}}$, especially for $\underline{\tilde{a}} = \underline{a}$; and we have: $\|W^{+}W\underline{a}\|^2 = \|W\underline{a}\|^2_{WW'} =$
$= \|W(p-L\bar{p})\|^2_{WW'} = \|\underline{\pi}-\bar{W}\bar{p}\|^2_{WW'} \geqslant \|\underline{\pi}-\bar{W}\hat{\bar{p}}\|^2_{WW'} = \|M\underline{\pi}\|^2_{WW'} = \|MW\underline{a}\|^2_{WW'} =$
$= \|W^{+}MW\underline{a}\|^2$. □

On the basis of $\underline{\hat{\hat{a}}}$ for the set of weighting matrices with $rk(\bar{W}) < T$, one may formulate a criterion analogous to Definition 1. It is trivial that for the case $T \geqslant K$ such a projection always exists.

References

Geary, R.C. (1958): A Note on the Comparison of Exchange Rates and Purchasing Powers Between Countries, I.R.S.S., Vol. 121, Part 1, pp. 97 - 99.

Pfouts, R.W. (1966): An Axiomatic Approach to Index Numbers, Reviews of the International Statistical Institute, Vol. 34, 2, pp. 174 - 185.

Pfouts, R.W. (1972): Index Number Systems, Econometrica, Vol. 40, 5, pp. 931 - 934.

Rao, C.R. and Mitra, S.K. (1971): Generalized Inverse of Matrices and Its Applications, New York - London - Sydney - Toronto, 1971.

Basic Ideas on Stochastic Indices

by Bernd Mundlos and Jochen Schwarze

1. Introduction

Since the classical definitions of Price Index Numbers by LASPEYRES and PAASCHE this theory has been extended by new, more complicated and refined expressions for meaningful index formulas. Furthermore methods to test the properties of such formulas were developed. In particular, FISHER's tests such as the Proportionality-, the Circular- and the Factor-Reversal-Test are notable, having caused far-reaching discussions in the literature on index numbers.
WALD [10] proved that no index formula satisfies the three mentioned tests simultaneously. Other work on satisfaction of the tests has been done by ACZEL-EICHHORN [1], EICHHORN-VOELLER [5] and the detailed examination by VOELLER [9]. For the best known index, the Cost of Living Index (CLI), which is mainly a price-index, and which we want to consider here, the index formulas and the variables used to compute the index will be discussed. This ultimately involves an intensive discussion about utility, (see e.g. [6],[10]), but this matter is not in the scope of this paper.

The practical use of index formulas raises fundamental problems. They are caused mainly by the following facts:
An index has to be a representative characteristic for a more or less heterogeneous population. For the cost of living index this means:
The individual prices and quantities are generally different. They are caused by a great number of influences of which a certain part is randomness. Thus one can interpret the index as the expectation of a random variable.

The data of an index are based in general on sampling. Accordingly prices and quantities are statistics and the index becomes a function of statistics and a statistic itself. Therefore we have two independent reasons to define an index not as a deterministic function but as a random variable.
In literature one can hardly find such treatment.

WALD [10] made some reflections on this subject, based on the indices of LASPEYRES and PAASCHE. He mentioned that the ratios of prices $\frac{p(t)}{p(0)}$ can be interpreted as a random variable with corresponding expectation. But then he discarded this concept, since the expectations need to be considered different for each commodity because of different influences.

In another context ANDERSON [2], [3] draws attention to some "sore points" of the empirical research of index numbers which point to a stochastic index. He shows that an index should not be regarded as a unique, deterministic quantity, but it is necessary to have a critical examination of the errors involved. ANDERSON's examples show clearly the necessity, at least, to estimate the error band of indices.

BANERJEE [4] examines stratified random sampling with respect to the commodity-scheme of the CLI.

A hint to the necessity to understand the index as a statistic can also be found by MENGES and SKALA [7], p. 337.

In the following some inital ideas of a stochastic index are set forth.

2. General Definition of a Deterministic Index

Vectors of prices are given (for the basis period 0 and the current period t) by

$$p(0) \quad , \quad p(t) \in \mathbb{R}_+^N$$

with

$$\mathbb{R}_+^N = \{x \mid x = (x_1, \ldots , x_N) \; ; \; x_\nu \in \mathbb{R}^1 \; ; \; x_\nu \geq 0 \; ; \; \nu = 1, \ldots , N\}.$$

A price - index is a function

(1) $$I(p(0), p(t)) : \mathbb{R}_+^{2N} \longrightarrow \mathbb{R}_+^1 \quad , \quad p(0) \neq 0$$

with the following properties:

(2a) $I(p(0), p(t)) \begin{cases} = 0 & \text{if} \quad p(t) = 0 \\ > 0 & \text{if} \quad p(t) \neq 0 \end{cases}$

(2b) $I[p(0), p(t) + p^*(t)] = I[p(0), p(t)] + I[p(0), p^*(t)]$
for all $p(0), p(t), p^*(t) \in \mathbb{R}^N$ and $p(0) \neq 0$

(2c) $\frac{1}{I[p(0) + p^*(0), p(t)]} = \frac{1}{I[p(0), p(t)]} + \frac{1}{I[p^*(0), p(t)]}$
for all $p(0), p^*(0), p(t) \in \mathbb{R}^N_+$ and $p(0), p^*(0) \neq 0$

(2d) $I[p(0), p(0)] = 1$ for all $p(0) \in \mathbb{R}^N_+$, $p(0) \neq 0$

According to the statements of ACZÉL-EICHHORN [1] and EICHHORN-VOELLER [5] the conditions (2a) to (2d) are necessary and sufficient to define the index I by the following equation

(3) $$I(p(0), p(t)) = \frac{a \cdot p^T(t)}{a \cdot p^T(0)} = \frac{\sum_{\nu=1}^{N} a_\nu p_\nu(t)}{\sum_{\nu=1}^{N} a_\nu p_\nu(0)},$$

where $a \in \mathbb{R}^N_{++}$ and $\mathbb{R}^N_{++} = \{x | x \in \mathbb{R}^N_+ ;\ x_\nu \neq 0;\ \nu = 1, \ldots, N\}$.

<u>Notation:</u> In the following we denote vectors by the cursive letters $(a, b, \ldots)$ and matrices by the cursive capitals $(A, B, \ldots)$. $a \cdot b^T$ and $A \cdot B$ mean the inner product of vectors and the matrix product respectively, where $b = (b_1, \ldots, b_N)$ and $b^T = \begin{pmatrix} b_1 \\ \vdots \\ b_N \end{pmatrix}$. A^T means the transposed matrix of A.

If $q(\tau) \in \mathbb{R}^N_+$ denotes the vector of the quantities of the commodities in period τ $(\tau = 0, t)$ then (3) leads to the

- LASPEYRES index , if $a = q(0)$
- PAASCHE index , if $a = q(t)$.

In case of the index being a CLI, it has to deliver an average statement about M individuals consuming N commodities. But with (3) we only make use of the N commodities and don't pay any attention to the M individuals and for them the

- differences betweeen the quantities consumed and
- differences between the prices paid.

Under these circumstances it seems necessary to expand the given definition of an index.

For these generalizations we have two restrictions concerning prices and quantities:

With respect to empirical applications it seems to be useful to put together quasihomogeneous commodities so that each of the N commodities represents a "class of commodities".
$q_{\nu\mu}(\tau)$ denotes the quantity of the class of commodity ν ($\nu=1,\ldots,N$) which the individual μ ($\mu=1, \ldots, M$) is consuming in τ. τ is a period with a given length (week,month).

$p_{\nu\mu}(\tau)$ denotes the corresponding price, but this price is usually referring to a certain time τ and not to a period with a given length. Thus we have quantities for a period and the corresponding prices for a point of time. In the following we assume, that the price $p_{\nu\mu}(\tau)$ is constant in period τ or the mean price in this period because we don't want to discuss this problem in this work.

Let us assume that all quantities and all prices for all individuals are being written down in appropriate matrices $Q(\tau)$ and $P(\tau)$:

$$(4a) \qquad Q(\tau) = (q_{\nu\mu}(\tau)) = \begin{pmatrix} q_{11}(\tau) & \cdots & q_{1M}(\tau) \\ \vdots & & \vdots \\ q_{N1}(\tau) & \cdots & q_{NM}(\tau) \end{pmatrix}$$

$$(4b) \qquad P(\tau) = (p_{\nu\mu}(\tau)) = \begin{pmatrix} p_{11}(\tau) & \cdots & p_{1M}(\tau) \\ \vdots & & \vdots \\ p_{N1}(\tau) & \cdots & p_{NM}(\tau) \end{pmatrix}$$

We now have two possibilities to compute the index with $Q(\tau)$ and $P(\tau)$:

Case A

We are using the unweighted arithmetic mean of the prices and quantities of the N commodities over all individuals. Thus we get

$$(5) \qquad I = \frac{q(\tau)\cdot p^{T}(t)}{q(\tau)\cdot p^{T}(0)} ,$$

where

$$(6a) \qquad q(\tau) = \frac{1}{M} e_M \cdot Q^{T}(\tau)$$

$$(6b) \qquad p^{T}(\tau) = \frac{1}{M} P(\tau)\cdot e_M^{T}$$

$$e_M = (1,1,\dots,1) \in \mathbb{R}^M, \quad \tau = 0,t$$

(5) and (6) together give:

$$(7) \qquad I = \frac{e_M\cdot Q^{T}(\tau)\cdot P(t)\cdot e_M^{T}}{e_M\cdot Q^{T}(\tau)\cdot P(0)\cdot e_M^{T}}$$

The index defined by (7) is a function

$I(Q(\tau),\, P(0),\, P(t)):\ \mathbb{R}_{+}^{3NM} \longrightarrow \mathbb{R}_{+}^{1}$, $\tau = 0,t$.

Case B

With respect to practical applications it seems to be more convenient to compute $p_\nu(\tau)$ as a weighted mean using the quantities consumed in τ.

$$(8) \qquad p_\nu(\tau) = \frac{\sum_{\mu=1}^{M} q_{\nu\mu}(\tau)p_{\nu\mu}(\tau)}{\sum_{\mu=1}^{M} q_{\nu\mu}(\tau)} = \frac{\sum_{\mu=1}^{M} q_{\nu\mu}(\tau)p_{\nu\mu}(\tau)}{M\, q_\nu(\tau)} \quad ; \quad \nu = 1, \dots, N$$

where $$q_\nu(\tau) = \frac{1}{M}\sum_{\mu=1}^{M} q_{\nu\mu}(\tau).$$

Using (8) and the diagonal-matrix:

$$\text{(9)} \qquad \mathcal{Q}^D(\tau,\tau') = \begin{pmatrix} \frac{q_1(\tau)}{q_1(\tau')} & 0 & 0 & \cdots & 0 & 0 \\ 0 & \ddots & & & & 0 \\ 0 & & \ddots & & & \vdots \\ \vdots & & & \ddots & & 0 \\ 0 & & & & \ddots & 0 \\ 0 & 0 & \cdots & 0 & 0 & \frac{q_N(\tau)}{q_N(\tau')} \end{pmatrix}$$

we get

$$\text{(10)} \qquad I = \frac{Tr\{\mathcal{Q}^D(\tau,t)\cdot\mathcal{Q}(t)\cdot\mathcal{P}^T(t)\}}{Tr\{\mathcal{Q}^D(\tau,0)\cdot\mathcal{Q}(0)\cdot\mathcal{P}^T(0)\}} ,$$

where $Tr\{A\}$ means the trace of the matrix A. The index I now is a function

$$\text{(11)} \qquad I(\mathcal{Q}(0),\mathcal{Q}(t),\mathcal{P}(0),\mathcal{P}(t)): \quad \mathbb{R}_+^{4NM} \to \mathbb{R}_+^1$$

In both cases, A as well as B, we will call the index I a complete index. Note that both, (7) as well as (10), give a formula using the matrices defined by (4a) and (4b) or the elements of the matrices respectively.

Starting with the complete index we get an index as a random variable in two ways which we will analyze in the following sections.

3. A General Stochastic Index

Suppose that the matrix elements $q_{\nu\mu}(\tau)$ and $p_{\nu\mu}(\tau)$ $(\tau=0,t)$ depend on influences of random events. Each $q_{\nu\mu}(\tau)$ and $p_{\nu\mu}(\tau)$ now is considered as a stochastic process. A realization of the stochastic processes is obtained for $\tau = 0$ and $\tau = t$. In other words: each matrix element is a random variable with a probability space

(12a) $(\Omega_{q_{\nu\mu}(\tau)}; \mathcal{B}_{q_{\nu\mu}(\tau)}; P)$ or

(12b) $(\Omega_{p_{\nu\mu}(\tau)}; \mathcal{B}_{p_{\nu\mu}(\tau)}; P)$.

Instead of the (deterministic) matrices $Q(\tau)$ (with $\tau = 0$ we get the LASPEYRES index and with $\tau = t$ we get the PAASCHE index), $P(0)$, $P(t)$ we get random matrices (i.e. 3NM-dimensional random variables)
In the <u>case A</u> we have the probability space:

$$(\Omega', \mathcal{B}', P'),$$

where

(13a) $$\Omega' = \mathop{\times}_{\nu,\mu} \Omega_{q_{\nu\mu}(\tau)} \times \mathop{\times}_{\nu,\mu} \Omega_{p_{\nu\mu}(0)} \times \mathop{\times}_{\nu,\mu} \Omega_{p_{\nu\mu}(t)}$$

(13b) $$\mathcal{B}' = \bigotimes_{\nu,\mu} \mathcal{B}_{q_{\nu\mu}(\tau)} \otimes \bigotimes_{\nu,\mu} \mathcal{B}_{p_{\nu\mu}(0)} \otimes \bigotimes_{\nu,\mu} \mathcal{B}_{p_{\nu\mu}(t)}$$

Here "$\times$" means the cartesian product and "$\bigotimes$" the σ-Algebra generated by the cartesian product. P' is an appropriate product measure.

The function I given by (7) now is a mapping

(14) $$I:(\Omega', \mathcal{B}', P') \to (\mathbb{R}^1_+, \mathcal{B}^1, P_I).$$

In the <u>case B</u> we have the probability space $(\Omega'', \mathcal{B}'', P'')$ where

(15a) $$\Omega'' = \mathop{\times}_{\nu,\mu} \Omega_{q_{\nu\mu}(0)} \times \mathop{\times}_{\nu,\mu} \Omega_{q_{\nu\mu}(t)} \times \mathop{\times}_{\nu,\mu} \Omega_{p_{\nu\mu}(0)} \times \mathop{\times}_{\nu,\mu} \Omega_{p_{\nu\mu}(t)}$$

(15b) $$\mathcal{B}'' = \bigotimes_{\nu,\mu} \mathcal{B}_{q_{\nu\mu}(0)} \otimes \bigotimes_{\nu,\mu} \mathcal{B}_{q_{\nu\mu}(t)} \otimes \bigotimes_{\nu,\mu} \mathcal{B}_{p_{\nu\mu}(0)} \otimes \bigotimes_{\nu,\mu} \mathcal{B}_{p_{\nu\mu}(t)}$$

P'' is an appropriate product measure. With (10) we obtain

(16) $$I: (\Omega'', \mathcal{B}'', P'') \to (\mathbb{R}^1_+, \mathcal{B}^1, P_I).$$

In both cases, I is called a <u>stochastic index</u>.

Defining a stochastic index with the randomness of $q_{\nu\mu}(\tau)$ and $p_{\nu\mu}(\tau)$ (in time) we have to decide what the index formula should represent:

(a) Computing the exact realization of the random variable I. This can be done by using the realizations of the $q_{\nu\mu}(\tau)$ and $p_{\nu\mu}(\tau)$ in (7) or (10).

(b) Computing the trend (meaning the expectation) of the random variable I. If all $q_\nu(\tau)$ and $p_\nu(\tau)$ are stochastically independent by pairs, then E(I) and VAR(I) can be computed using the $E(q_\nu)$, $E(p_\nu)$, $VAR(q_\nu)$ and $VAR(p_\nu)$ in (7) or (10).

4. Sampling Index

Another type of stochastic index is obtained, if we don't compute (7) or (10) using (6), (8) and (9) as a "complete index", but determine $q(t)$ and $p(t)$ by sampling. ($q(0)$ and $p(0)$ from the base period are supposed to be complete furthermore.)

Thus a sample is only taken from the matrices $Q(t)$ and $P(t)$ in time period t. In order to warrant in the sample a unique correspondence of quantities and prices, it is necessary to get the random sample by pairs of numbers (ν,μ). With each chosen pair (ν,μ) we get a pair $(q_{\nu\mu}(t), p_{\nu\mu}(t))$.

Several different possibilities exist to get a random sample from the matrices $Q(t)$ and $P(t)$. The following cases of sampling are of interest:

1) Random sampling in the whole matrices without any restrictions.
   This is hardly possible because some commodities might be excluded by chance. Furthermore this case of sampling seems to be not useful for empirical computations.

2) Random sampling in the rows
   From each class of commodities $\nu(\nu=1, \dots, N)$ we take random pairs $(q_{\nu\mu}(t), p_{\nu\mu}(t))$, $\mu = 1, \dots, m_\nu$.
   To compute the sample index we are considering all commodities (or their classes) but only some individuals (m_ν) consuming the commodities.
   With regard to empirical actualities this method seems to be very complicated.

3) Random sampling of individual vectors

From $P(t)$ and $Q(t)$ we take m column vectors randomly.
As in case 2) we are considering all commodities, but the individuals chosen randomly are the same for all commodities.
We get "sampling-matrices"

$$\hat{P}(t) = (\hat{p}_{\nu\mu}(t))_{Nm}$$
$$\hat{Q}(t) = (\hat{q}_{\nu\mu}(t))_{Nm}$$

with Nm elements. We obtain:

(17) $$\hat{q}(t) = \frac{1}{m} e_m \cdot \hat{Q}^T(t), \quad \hat{p}^T(t) = \frac{1}{m} \hat{P}(t) \cdot e_m^T$$

or using the weighted mean of prices:

(18) $$\hat{p}_\nu(t) = \frac{1}{m} \sum_{\mu=1}^{m} \frac{\hat{q}_{\nu\mu}(t)}{\hat{q}_\nu(t)} \hat{p}_{\nu\mu}(t),$$

where $\hat{q}_\nu(t) = \frac{1}{m} \sum_{\mu=1}^{m} \hat{q}_{\nu\mu}(t)$.

Using (17) we get instead of (7)

(19) $$\hat{I} = \frac{M e_M \cdot Q^T(0) \cdot \hat{P}(t) \cdot e_m^T}{m e_M \cdot Q^T(0) \cdot P(0) \cdot e_M^T}$$

(20) $$\hat{I} = \frac{M e_m \cdot \hat{Q}^T(t) \cdot \hat{P}(t) \cdot e_m^T}{m e_m \cdot \hat{Q}^T(t) \cdot P(0) \cdot e_M^T}$$

for the sample indices of LASPEYRES and PAASCHE.
Instead of (10) we now get

(21) $$\hat{I} = \frac{Tr\{ M \hat{Q}^D(0,t) \cdot \hat{Q}(t) \cdot \hat{P}^T(t) \}}{Tr\{ m Q(0) \cdot P^T(0) \}} \quad \text{(LASPEYRES)}$$

(22) $$\hat{I} = \frac{Tr\{ M \hat{Q}(t) \cdot \hat{P}^T(t) \}}{Tr\{ m \hat{Q}^D(t,0) \cdot Q(0) \cdot P^T(0) \}} \quad \text{(PAASCHE)}$$

for the sample indices of LASPEYRES and PAASCHE in case B. ($\hat{Q}^D$ is a diagonal matrix analogous to (9))

4) Stratified sampling on the individuals

We could also consider the heterogenity of M individuals and divide them into $M^* < M$ stratums of sizes M_j^* $(j=1, \dots, M^*)$. From these M^* stratums we derive samples of sizes m_j. Optimal stratification, for example, has the advantage of diminution of the variances of the estimators $\hat{q}(t)$ and $\hat{p}(t)$.

In all these cases 1) - 4) the randomness of I is caused by sampling. Therefore we want to call this index a sampling index and denote it with $\hat{I}$.

5. Some Stochastic Properties of the Sampling Index $\hat{I}$

With respect to empirical studies we are more interested in the sample index (21), (22) than in the general stochastic index in formula (14) or (16). In this context we are interested in answering the following questions.

1) What is the distribution of $\hat{I}$?
2) What are the properties of $\hat{I}$?
3) Is it possible to form estimators for I?
4) How large must be a change of an index number to be significant?

Of course it is not possible to examine all questions and all cases of sampling methods. In the following we only want to give some examples and initial ideas based on (21) and (22). We are always assuming that we have random samples.

5.1 Laspeyres Index

The estimator $\hat{I}$ in (19) is given by

$$(23) \qquad \hat{I} = \frac{M e_M \cdot Q^T(0) \cdot \hat{P}(t) \cdot e_m^T}{m e_M \cdot Q^T(0) \cdot P(0) \cdot e_M^T} = \sum_{\nu=1}^{N} g_\nu(0) \hat{p}_\nu(t) \quad \text{with } g_\nu(0) = \frac{q_\nu(0)}{q(0) \cdot p^T(0)}$$

Thus $\hat{I}$ is a linear combination of the statistics $\hat{p}_\nu(t)$. If $\hat{p}(t)$ is computed by (17), i.e.

$$\hat{p}_\nu(t) = \frac{1}{m}\sum_{\mu=1}^{m} \hat{p}_{\nu\mu}(t) ,$$

the following equations hold for the estimates:

$$(24) \qquad E\{\hat{p}_\nu(t)\} = \frac{1}{m}\sum_{\mu=1}^{m} E\{\hat{p}_{\nu\mu}(t)\} = \frac{1}{m}\, m\, p_\nu(t) = p_\nu(t)$$

and

$$(25) \qquad E\{\hat{I}\} = \sum_{\nu=1}^{N} g_\nu(0)\, E\{\hat{p}_\nu(t)\} = \sum_{\nu=1}^{N} g_\nu(0)\, p_\nu(t) = I \quad ,$$

i.e. $\hat{I}$ being unbiased.

If the $\hat{p}_{\nu\mu}(t)$ are pairwise stochastically independent we have

$$(26) \qquad \sigma^2_{\hat{p}_\nu}(t) := VAR\{\hat{p}_\nu(t)\} = \frac{1}{m^2}\sum_{\mu=1}^{m} VAR\{\hat{p}_{\nu\mu}(t)\} = \frac{1}{m}\, \sigma^2_{p_\nu}(t) \quad ,$$

where $\sigma^2_{p_\nu}(t)$ is the variance of prices $p_{\nu\mu}(t)$ of the commodity ν for all M individuals. It is necessary to estimate $\sigma^2_{p_\nu}(t)$ by sampling.

$$(27) \qquad \sigma^2_{\hat{I}}(t) := VAR\{\hat{I}\} = \sum_{\nu=1}^{N} (g_\nu(0))^2\, VAR\{\hat{p}_\nu(t)\} = \sum_{\nu=1}^{N} (g_\nu(0))^2\, \sigma^2_{\hat{p}_\nu}(t)$$

Stratified sampling should be an appropriate method to decrease the variance in (27).

In general, one can assume that $m > 30$ and $M \gg m$ and the $\hat{p}_{\nu\mu}(t)$ are stochastically independent. $\hat{p}_\nu(t)$ is asymptotically normally ditributed because of the Central Limit Theorem.

As $\hat{I}$ is a linear combination of asymptotically normally distributed random variables $\hat{p}_\nu(t)$ (see (23)), $\hat{I}$ itself is asymptotically normally distributed if the $\hat{p}_\nu(t)$ are independent.

Thus it is possible to give an interval estimation for I.

We have:

$$Prob\{\ \hat{I} - z(1-\tfrac{\alpha}{2})\sigma_{\hat{I}}(t) \leqq I \leqq \hat{I} + z(1-\tfrac{\alpha}{2})\sigma_{\hat{I}}(t)\ \} = 1 - \alpha$$

$z(1-\frac{\alpha}{2})$ is the value where the distribution function of a standardized Gaussian random variable equals $1-\frac{\alpha}{2}$.

5.2 Paasche Index

In this case the estimator in (20) is given by

$$(28) \qquad \hat{I} = \frac{Me_m \cdot \hat{Q}^T(t) \cdot \hat{P}(t) \cdot e_m^T}{me_M \cdot \hat{Q}^T(t) \cdot P(0) \cdot e_M^T} = \frac{\sum_{\nu=1}^{N} \hat{q}_\nu(t)\hat{p}_\nu(t)}{\sum_{\nu=1}^{N} \hat{q}_\nu(t)p_\nu(0)}$$

Assuming independence for all $\hat{p}_{\nu\mu}(t)$ and $\hat{q}_{\nu\mu}(t)$ we obtain in the denominator an approximately normally distributed sum with

$$(29) \qquad E\{\hat{q}(t)\cdot p(0)\} = q(t)\cdot p(0)$$

$$(30) \qquad \sigma^2_{\hat{q}\cdot p}(t) := VAR\{\hat{q}(t)\cdot p(0)\} = \sum_{\nu=1}^{N} (p_\nu(0))^2\sigma^2_{\hat{q}_\nu}(t) = \frac{1}{m}\sum_{\nu=1}^{N} (p_\nu(0))^2\sigma^2_{q_\nu}(t$$

where $\sigma^2_{q_\nu}(t)$ is defined analogous to (26).

In the numerator we have a sum of products of approximately normally distributec random variables with $E\{\hat{q}_\nu(t)\} = q_\nu(t)$ and $E\{\hat{p}_\nu(t)\} = p_\nu(t)$.
The sum has the expectation

$$(31) \qquad E\{\hat{q}(t)\cdot\hat{p}(t)\} = q(t)\cdot p(t)$$

It is obvious that $\hat{I}$ is unbiased and we get

$$(32) \qquad E\{\hat{I}\} = \frac{q(t)\cdot p(t)}{q(t)\cdot p(0)} = I$$

If we know the variances $VAR\{\hat{q}_\nu(t)\}$ and $VAR\{\hat{p}_\nu(t)\}$ and the expectations $E\{\hat{q}_\nu(t)\}$ and $E\{\hat{p}_\nu(t)\}$ it follows that

$$\sigma^2_{\hat{q}_\nu\hat{p}_\nu}(t) := VAR\{\hat{q}_\nu(t)\,\hat{p}_\nu(t)\} = VAR\{\hat{q}_\nu(t)\}\,VAR\{\hat{p}_\nu(t)\} + E^2\{\hat{q}_\nu(t)\}VAR\{\hat{p}_\nu(t)\} + E^2\{\hat{p}_\nu(t)\}VAR\{\hat{q}_\nu(t)\}$$

and

$$(33) \qquad \sigma^2_{\hat{q}\cdot\hat{p}} := VAR\{\hat{q}(t)\cdot\hat{p}(t)\} = \sum_{\nu=1}^{N} \sigma^2_{\hat{q}_\nu\hat{p}_\nu}$$

Without any supplemental assumption about the distributions of the products $\hat{q}_\nu(t)\hat{p}_\nu(t)$ we can derive the distribution of the numerator as follows: Certainly we have to require that all random variables $\hat{q}_\nu(t)\hat{p}_\nu(t)$ are uniformly bounded,

i.e. Prob $\{\hat{q}_\nu(t)\hat{p}_\nu(t) \le c\} = 1$, $c = \text{const.} > 0$.

A variant of the Central Limit Theorem delivers the asymptotic normality of the numerator for large N. This usual distribution has the expectation given in (31) and the variance given in (33).

Thus the sampling index is a quotient of two asymptotically normally distributed random variables. We are able to compute approximately the variance of $\hat{I}$:

$$\sigma^2_{\hat{I}}(t) := \text{VAR}\{\hat{I}\} = \frac{(\hat{q}(t)\cdot\hat{p}(t))^2}{(\hat{q}(t)\cdot p(0))^2}\left\{\frac{\text{VAR}\{\hat{q}(t)\cdot\hat{p}(t)\}}{(\hat{q}(t)\cdot\hat{p}(t))^2} + \frac{\text{VAR}\{\hat{q}(t)\cdot p(0)\}}{(\hat{q}(t)\cdot p(0))^2}\right\} \tag{34}$$

An interval estimation is possible using , for example, the inequality of BIENAYMÉ-TSCHEBYSCHEFF.

5.3 The Problem of Dependence

Certainly it is possible to examine the other cases of sampling. But in a more important point of view it seems to be necessary to take into consideration some restrictions as to the validity of Central Limit Theorem for each sampling method and the independence which shall be discussed:

While talking about the distribution of a sampling index we assumed that the random variables were independent. But it seems to be plausible that this assumption will not be easy to be verified in each case of sampling. In 5.1 one ought to analyze the dependences between the prices $\hat{p}_\nu(t)$ and $\hat{p}_\rho(t)$ $(\nu \neq \rho)$ and using the PAASCHE index one ought also to analyze the dependences among the prices $\hat{p}_\nu(t)$ and the quantities $\hat{q}_\nu(t)$ in 5.2 . If dependence is involved significantly the Central Limit Theorem cannot be applied without further assumptions.

References

[1] ACZÉL, J.; EICHHORN, W.: Systems of Functional Equations Determining Price and Productivity Indices, in: Utilitas Mathematica, Vol. 5 (1974), p. 213 ff

[2] ANDERSON, O.: Mehr Vorsicht mit Indexzahlen!, in: Allgemeines Statistisches Archiv, Vol. 33 (1949), p. 472 ff

[3] ANDERSON, O.: Und dennoch mehr Vorsicht mit Indexzahlen! Eine Duplik, in: Allgemeines Statistisches Archiv, Vol. 34 (1950), p. 37 ff

[4] BANERJEE, K.S.: Cost of Living Index Numbers, New York 1975

[5] EICHHORN, W.; VOELLER, J.: Theory of the Price Index, Berlin - Heidelberg 1976

[6] HASENKAMP, G.: A Note on the Cost-of-Living Index, research paper, Sonderforschungsbereich 21, Universität Bonn 1976

[7] MENGES, G.; SKALA, H.J.: Grundriß der Statistik, Teil 2: Daten, Opladen 1973

[8] STATISTISCHES BUNDESAMT: Neuberechnung der Preisindices der Lebenshaltung auf Basis 1970, Sonderheft der Fachserie M, Reihe 6, Stuttgart 1974

[9] VOELLER, J.: Theorie des Preis- und Lebenshaltungskostenindex, Doctoral Thesis, Universität Karlsruhe 1975

[10] WALD, A.: Zur Theorie der Preisindexziffern, in: Zeitschrift für Nationalökonomie, Vol. 9 (1937), p. 179 ff

Fisher's Five Tines Fork and other Quantum Theories of Index Numbers

by Yrjö O. Vartia[1)]

1. Introduction

Fisher's (1922) perhaps most interesting contributions concern the biases of index number formulas. Weighted index numbers (omitting modes and medians) seem to cluster into five groups according to the type of the average and the weights used. Fisher explains this using the concepts of 'type bias' and 'weight bias' interacting with each other, see Fisher (1922, p. 83-117, 352-6). His theory is condensed in a graphical representation, called the Five-tined Fork, each tine representing index numbers having the same 'dose of bias', i.e., 2+, 1+, 0, 1- or 2-. For instance the group 2+ consists of weighted index numbers (except modes and medians) having a double upward bias, see Fisher (1922, p. 202-5). Fisher concludes on p. 204-5:

> "Thus, barring 'simples' and 'modes' and their derivates (and possibly medians if we wish to have our results very close), we find that, although we have numerous formulae, they all fall under only five clearly defined heads, namely, those without bias, those with single bias up or down, and those with double bias up or down.
>
> The five tines include all the arithmetic, harmonic, geometric, and aggregative weighted index numbers and their derivates which we have obtained."

1) The Research Institute of the Finnish Economy, Kalevankatu 3 B, 00100 Helsinki 10, Finland
I want to express my sincere gratitude to Prof. Leo Törnqvist for numerous stimulating conversations and to the participants of the symposium for valuable comments. Jaakko Railo, M.A., has checked my English. All remaining errors are mine.

Fisher's 'Five-tined Fork' may be well described as a 'quantum theory' of index numbers to distinguish it from an ordinary view, according to which the results of various index formulas disperse continuously without gaps making a broom-like picture.

Let $a_1,\ldots,a_n$ be n commodities or groups of commodities for which the indices will be defined. Denote the value of a_i by v_i (in money units), its quantity by q_i (in physical units), price by $p_i = v_i/q_i$ and value share by $w_i = v_i/\Sigma v_j$. Periods or places are indicated by superscripts 0, 1 etc. Price and quantity vectors are denoted p and q, $p\cdot q = \Sigma p_i q_i$ is their inner product.

As a summary of Fisher's findings we consider price index number formulas defined as follows

(1) $L = p^1\cdot q^0/p^0\cdot q^0 = \Sigma w_i^0(p_i^1/p_i^0)$, "Laspeyres"

(2) $P = p^1\cdot q^1/p^0\cdot q^0 = 1/\Sigma w_i^1(p_i^0/p_i^1)$, "Paasche"

(3) $F = \sqrt{L\cdot P}$, "Fisher"

(4) $\log \ell = \Sigma w_i^0 \log(p_i^1/p_i^0)$, "Logarithmic Laspeyres"

(5) $\log p = \Sigma w_i^1 \log(p_i^1/p_i^0)$, "Logarithmic Paasche"

(6) $\log t = \frac{1}{2}(\log \ell + \log p)$, "Törnqvist"

(7) $P\ell = \Sigma w_i^1(p_i^1/p_i^0)$, "Palgrave"

(8) $Lh = 1/\Sigma w_i^0(p_i^0/p_i^1)$, "Harmonic Laspeyres"

We have interpreted L and $P\ell$ as arithmetic, P and Lh as harmonic and ℓ, p and t as geometric means of the price relatives.

We need not consider quantity index number formulas separately because everything applies analogically to them after changing p_i:s and q_i:s. These formulas are classified in Fisher's five tines as follows, see Fisher (1922, p. 204).

Table 1. Fisher's Five-tined Fork

Tine	Formula	Fisher's corresponding symbols
Uppermost (2+)	*Pℓ*	9
Mid-upper (1+)	*p*	29
Middle (0)	*P* *F*, *t* *L*	4=5=18=19=54=59 353 , 123 3=6=17=20=53=60
Mid-lower (1-)	*ℓ*	23
Lowermost (2-)	*Lh*	13

The results of Fisher's calculations are presented in the follo-

Table 2. The results of Fisher's calculations

Index number formula	Year					
	1913	1914	1915	1916	1917	1918
Pℓ, 9	100	100.93	102.33	118.29	180.72	187.18
p, 29	100	100.63	101.17	116.26	170.44	182.41
P, 54	100	100.32	100.10	114.35	161.05	177.43
F, 353	100	100.12	99.89	114.21	161.56	177.65
t, 123	100	100.12	99.94	113.83	162.05	177.80
L, 53	100	99.93	99.67	114.08	162.07	177.87
ℓ, 23	100	99.61	98.72	111.45	154.08	173.30
Lh, 13	100	99.26	97.84	111.01	147.19	168.59

Note that Fisher's Ideal Index *F* or 353 may be defined in numerous different ways, which is shown by its other symbols 103, 104, 105, 106, 153, 154, 203, 205, 217, 219, 253, 259, 303 and 305. This means that *F* has many fruitful interpretations; it is not just 'the geometric mean of *L* and *P*', see Fisher (1922, p. 482).

Figure 1: Fisher's Five-tined Fork for 8 Price Indices

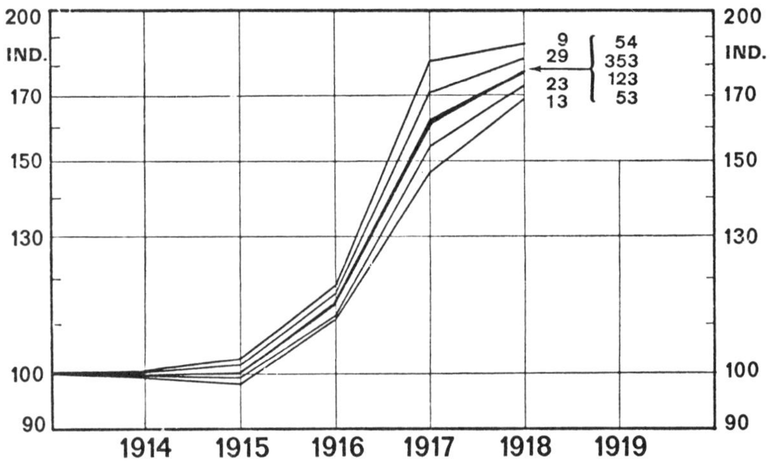

According to his calculations Fisher finds that *L* (=54) and *P* (=53) give approximately the same results and classifies them to the group 0 of unbiased index numbers. On the contrary *p* (=29) and *ℓ* (=23) seem to contain respectively a single upward and downward bias. As Fisher concludes on p. 363:

> "Of the 25 formulae mentioned by previous writers as possibly valuable, we have seen that the following ought never be used because of bias: 1, 2, 9, 11, 23."

And on p. 364 he writes:

> "Thus as to the long controversy over the relative merits of the arithmetic and geometric types, our study shows us that the *simple* geometric, 21, is better than the simple arithmetic, 1, but that, curiously enough, the *weighted* arithmetic, 3, is better than the weighted geometric, 23."

Fisher (see p. 237) did not regard the close agreement of L and P as "an accident merely happening to be true for the 36 commodities selected". He admits on p. 239-240 and 410 that L and P are subject to a "sort of secondary bias", which he regarded, however, as very small. We will show that these conclusions of Fisher are based on an unwarranted belief of the representativeness of his data and are not generally valid. For some other data his inductive reasoning would have given other results.

Our analysis fits in with what has been pointed out by other authors. For instance Samuelson & Swamy (1974, p. 567) comment on Fisher's concept of bias: "Exactly what zero bias meant was never thought through." The well-known inequalities connected with Laspeyres' and Paasche's indices show that these are usually biased respectively upwards and downwards as compared to the 'true indices' in the case of demand theory:

(9) $$P(p^1,p^0;\ q^0) \leq p^1 \cdot q^0 / p^0 \cdot q^0 = L_p \quad ,$$

(10) $$P(p^1,p^0;\ q^1) \geq p^1 \cdot q^1 / p^0 \cdot q^1 = P_p \quad ,$$

(11) $$Q(q^1,q^0;\ p^0) \leq p^0 \cdot q^1 / p^0 \cdot q^0 = L_q \quad ,$$

(12) $$Q(q^1,q^0;\ p^1) \geq p^1 \cdot q^1 / p^1 \cdot q^0 = P_q \quad .$$

Here $P(p^1,p^0;\ q^*)$ is the Economic Price Index and $Q(q^1,q^0;\ p^*)$ is the Economic Quantity Index as defined by Samuelson & Swamy.
In the case of production theory the inequalities are reversed, see Samuelson & Swamy (1974, p. 589) or Fisher & Shell (1972, p. 58).

Only if q^0 and q^1 are indifferent or the indifference surfaces are homothetic are the Economic Price Indices in (9) and (10) equal and we have a double inequality for it. Analogously, only if $p^0 = \lambda p^1$ or under homotheticity have we necessarily $P_q \leq Q(q^1,q^0;\ p^1) = Q(q^1,q^0;\ p^0) \leq L_q$.

It is difficult to understand that these bounds have given rise to so much confusion. Nice examples of the kind of confusion are given e.g. by Leontief (1936, p. 47) and by Frisch (1936, p. 26).

On the other hand it can be shown[1)] that log p and log ℓ are linear approximations to log $P(p^1,p^0;\ q^0)$ and log $P(p^1,p^0;\ q^1)$ in the case of demand theory.

2. EXPLANATION OF FISHER'S FIVE-TINED FORK AND OTHER QUANTUM THEORIES OF INDEX NUMBERS

These facts suggest that the situation is not so simple as Fisher thought. We are not, however, satisfied with these results of the economic approach: they are valid only if our data is generated according to some economic play process, e.g., the demand theory. We want to know how much and why the various price and volume indices differ when prices and quantities 'change freely', i.e., in any way whatsoever. We have calculated relative differences between various indices using a formula given by Törnqvist (1936).

1) Rajaoja (1958) proves only that log $\ell = \log P(p^1,p^0;\ q^0)$ + second order terms in her theorem 8.3. where she makes unrealistic assumptions about observations. The change of real income between observations (p^0,q^0), (p^1,q^1) should be taken into account e.g. in the way Theil (1967, p. 216) does.

Törnqvist considers equally weighted moment means ${}_{\alpha}P_0^1$ and geometric means ${}_0P_0^1$ of price ratios defined by

$$(13) \qquad ({}_{\alpha}P_0^1)^{\alpha} = \Sigma c_i (p_i^1/p_i^0)^{\alpha} = \Sigma c_i \; e^{\alpha \log(p_i^1/p_i^0)} \quad ,$$

$$(14) \quad \log({}_0P_0^1) = \Sigma c_i \log(p_i^1/p_i^0) \quad ,$$

where $c_i \geq 0$ and $\Sigma c_i = 1$. It may be shown that the moment mean ${}_{\alpha}P_0^1$ of positive and nonequal price ratios is a continuously increasing function of α, which approaches $\min(p_i^1/p_i^0)$ when $\alpha \to -\infty$, the geometric mean ${}_0P_0^1$ defined by (14) when $\alpha \to 0$ and $\max(p_i^1/p_i^0)$ when $\alpha \to +\infty$, see Hardy & Littlewood & Polya (1952).
Dividing every term of (13) by $({}_0P_0^1)^{\alpha}$ we get

$$(15) \qquad ({}_{\alpha}P_0^1/{}_0P_0^1)^{\alpha} = \Sigma c_i \; e^{\alpha \log(p_i^1/p_i^0 \, {}_0P_0^1)}$$

$$= \Sigma c_i \; e^{\alpha \dot{p}_i} \; ,$$

where $\dot{p}_i = \log(p_i^1/p_i^0) - \log({}_0P_0^1)$ is the logarithmic deviation[1)] of the price ratio from ${}_0P_0^1$. By expanding (15) to a power series of α we get

$$(16) \qquad ({}_{\alpha}P_0^1/{}_0P_0^1)^{\alpha} = 1 + \frac{\alpha^2}{2!}\Sigma c_i \dot{p}_i^2 + \frac{\alpha^3}{3!}\Sigma c_i \dot{p}_i^3 + \cdots \quad .$$

The expansion converges for all values of $\dot{p}_i$:s and of α.

---

1) Or the arithmetic deviation of the log-change in the price of commodity a_i from the log-change in the price level.

Taking logarithms and expanding we get formally[1)]

$$(17)\qquad \log({}_{\alpha}P_0^1) - \log({}_0P_0^1) = \frac{\alpha}{2} s_p^2 + \frac{\alpha^2}{6}\Sigma c_i \dot{p}_i^3 + \cdots ,$$

where $s_p^2 = \Sigma c_i \dot{p}_i^2$ is the variance of the price log-changes $\log(p_i^1/p_i^0)$ around their mean $\log({}_0P_0^1)$, shortly 'variance of the price changes'. Specifying $\alpha = 1$ and $\alpha = -1$ and neglecting the higher order terms we get:

$$(18)\qquad \log({}_1P_0^1) - \log({}_0P_1^1) \approx + \frac{1}{2} s_p^2 + \frac{1}{6} \Sigma c_i \dot{p}_i^3 ,$$

$$(19)\qquad \log({}_{-1}P_0^1) - \log({}_0P_1^1) \approx - \frac{1}{2} s_p^2 + \frac{1}{6} \Sigma c_i \dot{p}_i^3 .$$

These express that the arithmetic mean ${}_1P_0^1 = \Sigma c_i(p_i^1/p_i^0)$ is greater than the geometric mean ${}_0P_0^1$, which is greater than the harmonic mean ${}_{-1}P_0^1$, ${}_1P_0^1 > {}_0P_0^1 > {}_{-1}P_0^1$, their logarithmic differences being approximately half of the variance of the price changes s_p^2. This is the mathematical basis for a quantitative version of Fisher's qualitative and partly inductive theory about the 'type bias' of index number formulas, cf. Fisher (1922, p. 83-91, 108-111). Although Fisher treated the 'type bias' correctly his inductive reasoning led him to incorrect generalizations in the case of 'weight bias' as we shall demonstrate.

Formulas (13)-(19) are from Törnqvist (1936). Next we apply them to (1)-(8) supposing all the time that the third and higher order terms are small compared to the second order terms.

---

1) The expansion is valid if the right hand side of (16) does not exceed 2. This is certainly true if $|\alpha\dot{p}_i| < \log 2 = 0.693$ for all i. In most practical cases (17) is valid. Note that the first term of the expansion always gives the right sign for the left side difference and they are zero simultaneously.

Using the weights $c_i = w_i^1$ we get the logarithmic differences between (2), (5) and (7):

$$\text{(20)} \quad \log P\ell - \log p \approx \frac{1}{2} s_{1p}^2 + \frac{1}{6}\Sigma w_i^1 \dot{p}_{1i}^3 ,$$

$$\text{(21)} \quad \log P - \log p \approx -\frac{1}{2} s_{1p}^2 + \frac{1}{6}\Sigma w_i^1 \dot{p}_{1i}^3 .$$

These tell us that $\log P\ell$ exceeds $\log p$ by about half of the variance $s_{1p}^2 = \Sigma w_i^1 \dot{p}_{1i}^2$ and $\log p$, again, exceeds $\log P$ by about the same amount. This explains completely why $P\ell$, p and P are found in different tines of Fisher's fork. These three indices differ from each other and $P\ell > p > P$ unless the variance in the price changes is zero when they are equal. In the same way, inserting $c_i = w_i^0$ we get for (1), (4) and (8):

$$\text{(22)} \quad \log L - \log \ell \approx \frac{1}{2} s_{0p}^2 + \frac{1}{6}\Sigma w_i^0 \dot{p}_{0i}^3 ,$$

$$\text{(23)} \quad \log Lh - \log \ell \approx -\frac{1}{2} s_{0p}^2 + \frac{1}{6}\Sigma w_i^0 \dot{p}_{0i}^3 .$$

Thus $L > \ell > Lh$, the relative differences being approximately equal to half of the variance of the price changes $s_{0p}^2 = \Sigma w_i^0 \dot{p}_{0i}^2 \approx s_{1p}^2$. This explains why L, ℓ and Lh are found in different tines of Fisher's fork.

If it so happens - as in the case of Fisher's data - that L and P are approximately equal, then $P\ell > p > P \approx L > \ell > Lh$, and the relative differences between any two consecutive indices are approximately equal to half of the variance in the price changes. Furthermore $F = \sqrt{P \cdot L}$, $t = \sqrt{p \cdot \ell}$ and even[1] $\sqrt{P\ell \cdot Lh}$ being means of indices devia-

---

1) This is Fisher's formula no. 109, which he classifies in the border line of 'good' and 'very good' index number formulas.

ting symmetrically from the middle tine, all belong to the middle tine of unbiased index numbers. This is the essence of Fisher's Five-tined Fork.

Figure 2. Explanation of Fisher's Five-tined Fork

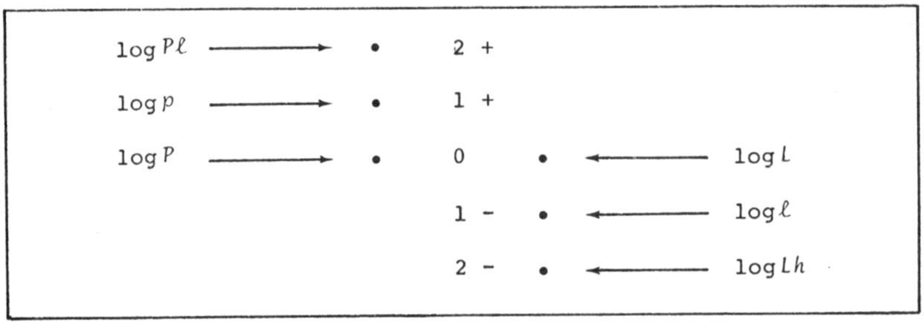

However, Fisher's 'quantum theory' of index numbers is not generally valid because, instead of $P \approx L$, we may have, e.g., $p \approx \ell$. This happens if the value shares remain approximately constant, $w_i^0 \approx w_i^1$, i.e., the commodities are on the average normally elastic. In this case we have a three-tined fork $P\ell \approx L > p \approx \ell > p \approx Lh$:

Figure 3. A three-tined Fork

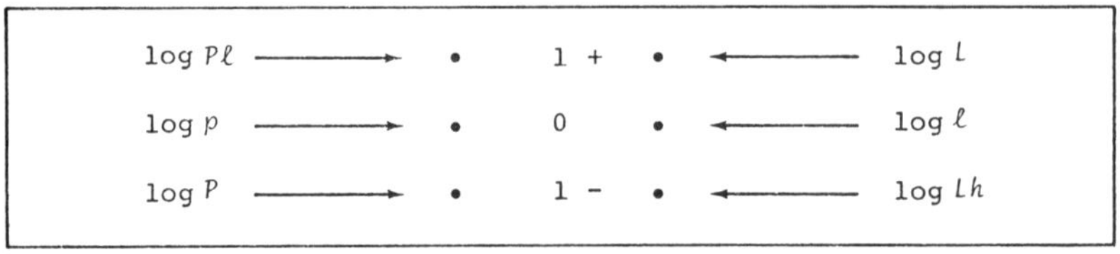

The upper tine (1+) of this three-tined fork contains $P\ell$ and L, while the middle tine now contains p, ℓ and, e.g., F, t and $\sqrt{P\ell \cdot Lh}$ as before, the lower tine containing P and Lh. Now p and ℓ are unbiased index numbers while L and P have respectively one dose of upward and downward bias.

Like Fisher we call an index number *unbiased* in a given situation if it is included in the middle tine of the corresponding fork constructed of the representative two groups of indices of the figures 2 and 3. As is evident from the geometry of the problem the indices of the pairs (*Pℓ*, *Lh*), (*p*, *ℓ*) and (*P*, *L*) are always located symmetrically with respect to the middle tine and thus their symmetric means, e.g. $\sqrt{P\ell \cdot Lh}$, *t* and *F*, are *always unbiased*. Thus an index number formula f is unbiased in a given situation if it is approximately equal to e.g. Fisher's Ideal Index *F*, i.e. log(f/*F*) is only a fraction of variance in the price changes.

Our three tined fork occurs in connection with commodities for which the price and quantity ratios are strongly negatively correlated, so that the value shares remain approximatively constant. This problem was discussed by Fisher (1922) on p. 237-240, 314-317, 410-412 and 428 unsatisfactorily. Fisher tried to show that *ℓ* (=23) is unbiased only if the negative correlation between the price and quantity ratios p_i^1/p_i^0 and q_i^1/q_i^0 is perfect, Fisher (1922, p. 428):

> "If the price and quantity elements are thus correlated to the extreme limit of 100 per cent, the downward bias of 23 will be completely abolished. In the present case, where correlation is -88 per cent, the bias is *nearly* abolished."

This analysis is inadequate.

We derive at the end of the paper and exact formula for the logarithmic difference between *ℓ* and *p* which solves the problem.

These situations are not the most likely to be met in practice. The situation usually encountered in analyzing, e.g., consumption data would be somewhere between them: neither L nor ℓ is unbiased but L has a small upward and ℓ a small downward bias compared to unbiased index numbers such as F or t. If these biases of L and ℓ are equal in size we have $L \approx p$ and $P \approx \ell$, which leads to the following new five-tined fork.

Figure 4. A new five-tined fork

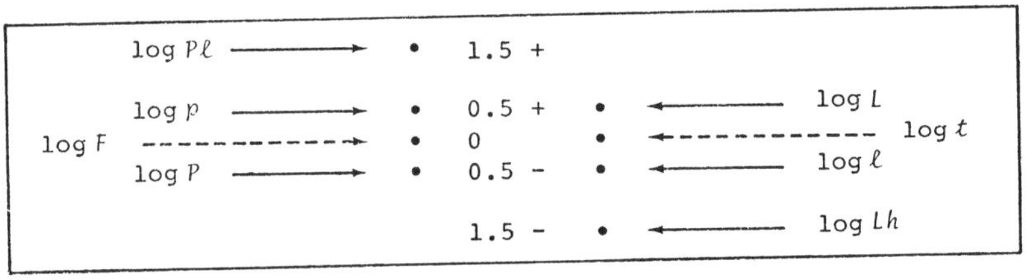

The unbiased index numbers such as $F = \sqrt{P \cdot L}$, $t = \sqrt{p \cdot \ell}$ and $\sqrt{P\ell \cdot Lh}$ shown by dotted arrows are situated half way between $L \approx p$ and $P \approx \ell$ the biases of the latter being now half the former dose of bias, i.e., of the order of $\frac{1}{4}s_p^2$. Thus the three middle tines of this new fork are closer to each other than in Fisher's fork.

Actually we need not have any of the former cases but the two groups of indices $P\ell > p > P$ and $L > \ell > Lh$ may be located quite freely relative to each other. In a situation well explained by the homothetic demand theory we have according to equations (9) and (10) $P_p \leq P(p^1,p^0;\ q^1) = P(p^1,p^0;\ q^0) \leq L_p$ and thus usually $P < L$. We might, e.g., have a seven-tined fork where $\log P\ell > \log p > \log L > \log F \approx \log t > \log P > \log \ell > \log Lh$. Here the five middle tines are quite close to each other and only the uppermost and lowermost tines are clearly separated from all the other ones.

On the other hand, if the data is well explained by the homothetic production theory we have conversely $P_p \geq P(p^1,p^0;\ q^1) = P(p^1;p^0 \cdot q^0) \geq L_p$ and thus usually $P > L$, cf. Allen (1975, p. 64).
Here we have another seven-tined fork, where the indices disperse more widely:

Figure 5. A seven-tined fork

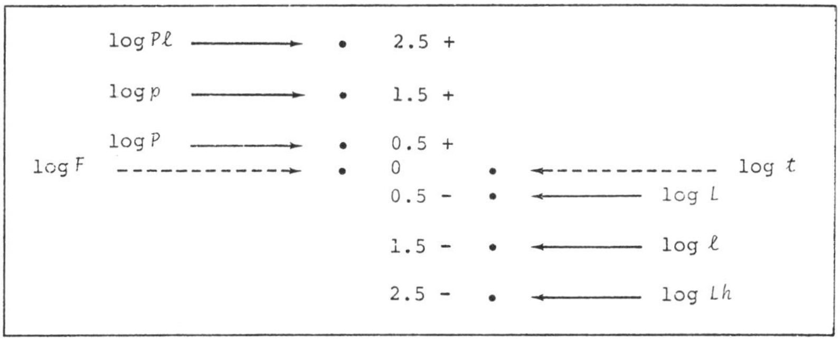

As a summary we have to recognize that, e.g., Fisher's Ideal Index F and the Törnqvist index t always belong to the middle tine of unbiased index numbers while $P\ell$, P, p, L, ℓ and Lh are all biased up or down in some situations.

3. HOW ARE THE TWO GROUPS OF INDICES LOCATED RELATIVE TO EACH OTHER: A THEORY OF THE 'WEIGHT BIAS'

Next we derive an exact and general expression for the logarithmic difference between p and ℓ, which determines the relative position of the two groups of indices $\{P\ell, p, P\}$ and $\{L, \ell, Lh\}$ using respectively new and old value shares as weights. Thus what we are going to give will be essentially a quantitative theory of the 'weight bias'. We have by definition

$$(24) \qquad \log p - \log \ell = \sum (w_i^1 - w_i^0) \log (p_i^1/p_i^0) \ .$$

There are many useful approximations to the change in the value share, $\Delta w_i^1 = w_i^1 - w_i^0 = v_i^1/V^1 - v_i^0/V^0$, e.g. Theil (1967, p. 202) extensively uses

$$(25) \qquad w_i^1 - w_i^0 \approx \tfrac{1}{2}(w_i^1 + w_i^0) \ [\log (v_i^1/v_i^0) - \log (V^1/V^0)]$$

$$= \tfrac{1}{2}(w_i^1 + w_i^0) \ \dot{v}_i \ .$$

The approximation error is of the third degree in the log-changes $\log (v_i^1/v_i^0)$ and $\log (V^1/V^0)$. This leads to

$$(26) \qquad \log p - \log \ell \approx \sum \tfrac{1}{2}(w_i^1 + w_i^0) \log (p_i^1/p_i^0) \ \dot{v}_i$$

$$= \sum \tfrac{1}{2}(w_i^1 + w_i^0) \dot{p}_i \dot{v}_i$$

$$= \operatorname{cov}(\dot{p}, \dot{v}) \quad , \text{ where}$$

$$(27) \qquad \dot{p}_i = \log (p_i^1/p_i^0) - \sum \tfrac{1}{2}(w_i^1 + w_i^0) \log (p_i^1/p_i^0) = \log (p_i^1/p_i^0) - \log t$$

and $\operatorname{cov}(\dot{p}, \dot{v})$ is calculated using the weights $\tfrac{1}{2}(w_i^1 + w_i^0)$. For the ideas behind such covariances, see Theil (1967) or Rajaoja (1958).

We know, however, the exact equation corresponding to (25):

$$(28) \qquad w_i^1 - w_i^0 = L(w_i^1, w_i^0) \log (w_i^1/w_i^0)$$

$$= L(w_i^1, w_i^0) \ [\log (v_i^1/v_i^0) - \log (V^1/V^0)],$$

where the first line is in fact the definition of the *logarithmic mean* $L(w_i^1, w_i^0)$, see Vartia (1976a, b). Thus, identically,

$$(29) \qquad \log p - \log \ell = \sum L(w_i^1, w_i^0) \log(p_i^1/p_i^0)\, \dot{v}_i$$

$$= (\sum L(w_j^1, w_j^0)) \sum \bar{w}_i \dot{p}_i \dot{v}_i$$

$$= (1-\Theta)\, \mathrm{cov}(\dot{p}, \dot{v}) \quad ,$$

where $\bar{w}_i = L(w_i^1, w_i^0)/\Sigma L(w_j^1, w_j^0)$ are the weights of Vartia Index II, see Vartia (1976a, b) and Sato (1976), and now $\dot{p}_i = \log(p_i^1/p_i^0) - \sum \bar{w}_i \log(p_i^1/p_i^0)$. Because $\Theta \geq 0$ is, for small log-changes $\log(w_i^1/w_i^0)$, a very small number

$$(30) \qquad \Theta = 1 - \sum L(w_j^1, w_j^0)$$

$$\approx \frac{1}{12} \sum \frac{1}{2}(w_i^1 + w_i^0)\, [\log(w_i^1/w_i^0)]^2 \quad ,$$

we have apart from terms of the third degree in $\log(w_i^1/w_i^0)$

$$(31) \qquad \log p - \log \ell \approx \mathrm{cov}(\dot{p}, \dot{v}) \quad .$$

This formula determines the relative positions of p and ℓ and therefore of the two groups of indices $\{P\ell,\ p,\ P\}$ and $\{L,\ \ell,\ Lh\}$ using respectively new and old value shares as weights. If $w_i^0 = w_i^1$ for all i we have trivially $p = \ell$. The same happens if the price and value log-changes are uncorrelated or $\mathrm{cov}(\dot{p}, \dot{v}) = 0$. Note that $\log p \gtreqless \log \ell$ if and only if $\mathrm{cov}(\dot{p}, \dot{v}) \gtreqless 0$, so that $\mathrm{cov}(\dot{p}, \dot{v})$ and a variance in the price changes $s_p^2 = \mathrm{cov}(\dot{p}, \dot{p})$ determine the type of our fork. Knowing only the values of three parameters, $a = \log t$, $b = \mathrm{cov}(\dot{p},\dot{v})$ and $c = \frac{1}{2}s_p^2$, we may approximately estimate all the indices considered in our paper.

When $\dot{v}_i = \dot{p}_i + \dot{q}_i$ (i.e., the factor reversal test $P_0^1 Q_0^1 = V^1/V^0$ applies to the index number formula used in the calculation of the logarithmic deviations) we have

$$(32) \qquad \log p - \log \ell \approx \mathrm{cov}(\dot{p},\dot{v}) = s_p^2 + \mathrm{cov}(\dot{p},\dot{q}) \quad ,$$

where $s_p^2 = \mathrm{cov}(\dot{p},\dot{p})$ is the variance of the price changes and

$$(33) \qquad \mathrm{cov}(\dot{p},\dot{q}) = \sum \bar{w}_i \dot{p}_i \dot{q}_i$$

is the covariance of price and quantity log-changes. This is particularly interesting because $\log P - \log L \approx \mathrm{cov}(\dot{p},\dot{q})$ as will be shown later. For instance, the logarithmic quantity deviation

$$(34) \qquad \dot{q}_i = \log(q_i^1/q_i^0) - \log Q_0^1$$

$$= \log(q_i^1/q_i^0) - \sum \bar{w}_i \log(q_i^1/q_i^0)$$

is positive if the relative change in the quantity of a_i consumed, $\log(q_i^1/q_i^0)$, is greater than the relative change in the quantity of total consumption, $\log Q_0^1$. This means that the quantity of a_i has increased more than the average quantity of consumption. The covariance of price and quantity log-changes (33) is negative if positive (negative) price deviations $\dot{p}_i$ are associated with negative (positive) quantity deviations $\dot{q}_i$, see Theil (1967).

This should be the case according to demand theory (if real consumption does not change much or under homotheticity) because, if the price of a_i increases more than the average prices ($\dot{p}_i>0$), the consumer would decrease his consumption of a_i or at least increase it by less than the average volume of consumption ($\dot{q}_i<0$). Only in the nonhomothetic case, when real consumption changes, may positive deviations of price changes $\dot{p}_i>0$ on the average be associated with positive deviations of quantity changes $\dot{q}_i>0$. This may happen if the ceteris paribus effects of price change deviations $\dot{p}_i>0$ are eliminated by positive income effects - e.g., the commodities for which the prices increase more than average prices happen to be luxuries, which react strongly to rising real income, cf. Theil (1967, p. 254). According to equations (9) and (10) we may have $L < P$ only in the nonhomothetic case and, because $\log(P/L) \approx \operatorname{cov}(p,q)$, only then $\operatorname{cov}(\dot{p},\dot{q})$ may be definitely positive.

We can write for $\operatorname{cov}(\dot{p},\dot{q})$, as for any covariance,

(35) $$\operatorname{cov}(\dot{p},\dot{q}) = s_p s_q \, r(\dot{p},\dot{q}) \quad , \text{ where}$$

(36) $$s_p = \sqrt{s_p^2} = (\Sigma \bar{w}_i \dot{p}_i^2)^{1/2} \quad ,$$

(37) $$s_q = \sqrt{s_q^2} = (\Sigma \bar{w}_i \dot{q}_i^2)^{1/2} \quad ,$$

(38) $$r(\dot{p},\dot{q}) = \operatorname{cov}(\dot{p},\dot{q})/s_p s_q \quad \in [-1,1] \quad .$$

Here s_p and s_q are the standard deviations of price and quantity log-changes and $r(\dot{p},\dot{q})$ is the correlation between the price and quantity log-changes.

An exact condition for the equality of ℓ, p and $t = \sqrt{\ell \cdot p}$ according to (29) and (32) may be written

$$\text{(39)} \qquad \operatorname{cov}(\dot{p},\dot{v}) = s_p^2 + \operatorname{cov}(\dot{p},\dot{q}) = 0 \quad ,$$

$$\text{(40)} \qquad r(\dot{p},\dot{q}) = -(s_p/s_q) \; .$$

If the standard deviations in price and quantity log-changes are equal, $s_p = s_q$, then their negative correlation $r(\dot{p},\dot{q})$ should be -100 % (as Fisher demanded) in order that ℓ (or p) could be 'unbiased'. A much lower correlation is sufficient if $s_p < s_q$. Note that log L and log P differ now from log $t \approx$ log F by approximately $\frac{1}{2}s_p^2 = -\frac{1}{2}\operatorname{cov}(\dot{p},\dot{q})$ as is shown in figure 3.

If the standard deviation of the quantity changes s_q happens to be smaller than s_p (as may be the case for necessities with low income and price elasticities) then (40) cannot be satisfied. In this case we have when using weights $\bar{w}_i$ of (29), because $r(\dot{p},\dot{q}) \geq -1$,

$$\text{(41)} \qquad r(\dot{p},\dot{q}) > -(s_p/s_q) \quad ,$$

$$\text{(42)} \qquad \operatorname{cov}(\dot{p},\dot{v}) = s_p^2 + \operatorname{cov}(\dot{p},\dot{q}) > 0 \quad ,$$

$$\text{(43)} \qquad \log p = \log \ell + (1-\Theta)\operatorname{cov}(\dot{p},\dot{v}) > \log \ell \; .$$

It is even possible that log $p <$ log ℓ, which happens if

$$\text{(44)} \qquad r(\dot{p},\dot{q}) < 0 \text{ and } |r(\dot{p},\dot{q})| > s_p/s_q \; .$$

This implies that $s_p < s_q$. The condition (44) is not probable if the periods from which our data (p_i, q_i) comes are long, say one year. In the analysis of, e.g., monthly data it may well be satisfied because of wild fluctuations in the quantity log-changes.

To sum up:

1. If the variance of the price changes s_p^2 is greater than the variance of the quantity changes s_q^2, then $\log p > \log \ell$.
2. If the variance of the price changes s_p^2 is small compared to s_q^2 and the price and quantity changes are negatively correlated, then we may have $\log p < \log \ell$.

The relationship between $\log p$ and $\log \ell$ makes it possible to derive a useful expression for the difference between $\log P$ and $\log L$. Subtracting (22) from (21) and inserting (26) we get

$$(45) \qquad \log P - \log L \approx (\log p - \log \ell) - \tfrac{1}{2}(s_{1p}^2 + s_{0p}^2)$$

$$\approx \operatorname{cov}(\dot{p}, \dot{q}) + s_p^2 - \tfrac{1}{2}(s_{1p}^2 + s_{0p}^2) \; .$$

Consider the variances of the price changes:

$$(46) \qquad \tfrac{1}{2}(s_{1p}^2 + s_{0p}^2) = \sum \tfrac{1}{2}(w_i^1 + w_i^0)\,[\log(p_i^1/p_i^0)]^2 - \tfrac{1}{2}(\log p)^2 - \tfrac{1}{2}(\log \ell)^2$$

$$= \sum \tfrac{1}{2}(w_i^1 + w_i^0)\,[\log(p_i^1/p_i^0) - \log t]^2$$

$$+ (\log t)^2 - \tfrac{1}{2}(\log p)^2 - \tfrac{1}{2}(\log \ell)^2$$

$$= s_p^2 - \tfrac{1}{4}(\log p - \log \ell)^2 \; .$$

Therefore, apart from terms of the third degree in $\dot{p}_i$ and $\dot{q}_i$,

$$(47) \qquad \log P - \log L \approx \mathrm{cov}(\dot{p},\dot{q}) + \tfrac{1}{4}(\mathrm{cov}(\dot{p},\dot{v}))^2$$

$$\approx \mathrm{cov}(\dot{p},\dot{q}) \ .$$

Here the covariance is calculated using the weights $(w_i^1+w_i^0)/2$ and the deviations $\dot{p}_i$ and $\dot{q}_i$ are from the corresponding Törnqvist indices, $\log t_p$ and $\log t_q$.

The covariance $\mathrm{cov}(\dot{p},\dot{q})$ may be calculated using the weights $\bar{w}_i$ of any superlative log-change index number, e.g., the weights of Vartia Index II as in (33), without invalidating (47). Thus the covariance between price and quantity log-changes causes L and P to deviate from each other. This has been qualitatively known see, e.g., Fisher (1922, p. 411) and Samuelson & Swamy (1974, p. 592) but the relationship (47) seems to be new. However, Bortkiewicz (1922, 1924) has derived a very similar and exact relationship for the ratio of P and L, see Allen (1975, p. 63):

$$(48) \qquad P/L = 1 + r\sigma_p\sigma_q/L_pL_q$$

$$= 1 + \mathrm{cov}\,(p_i^1/p_i^0,\ q_i^1/q_i^0)/L_pL_q \quad ,$$

where r is the coefficient of correlation between price and quantity *relatives*, σ_p and σ_q are their standard deviations and $\mathrm{cov}(p_i^1/p_i^0,\ q_i^1/q_i^0) = r\sigma_p\sigma_q$ their covariance, all calculated using w_i^0 as the weights. Our formula (47) seems to be more easily combined with other formulas as will be demonstrated. Some other results together with empirical calculations may be found in Vartia (1976b, p. 142-168, 189-191).

4. COMMENTS ON SOME UNBIASED AND 'SUPERLATIVE' INDEX NUMBERS

Our method applies as well to index numbers belonging always to the middle tine of unbiased index numbers.
Calculate, e.g., the difference between

$$\text{(49)} \qquad \log t = \tfrac{1}{2}(\log p + \log \ell) = \sum \tfrac{1}{2}(w_i^1 + w_i^0) \log(p_i^1/p_i^0)$$

and

$$\text{(50)} \qquad \log F = \tfrac{1}{2}(\log P + \log L) \ .$$

Summing (21) and (22) we get

$$\text{(51)} \qquad \log F - \log t \approx -\tfrac{1}{4}(s_{1p}^2 - s_{0p}^2) + \tfrac{1}{12}(\Sigma w_i^1 \dot{p}_{1i}^3 + \Sigma w_i^0 \dot{p}_{0i}^3) \ .$$

For the difference between the variances we get by direct calculation

$$\text{(52)} \qquad s_{1p}^2 - s_{0p}^2 = \sum (w_i^1 - w_i^0) [\log(p_i^1/p_i^0)]^2 - (\log p)^2 + (\log \ell)^2$$

$$= \sum (w_i^1 - w_i^0) [\log(p_i^1/p_i^0) - \log t]^2 = \sum (w_i^1 - w_i^0) \dot{p}_i^2 \ .$$

Inserting Theil's approximation (25) into (52) leads to

$$\text{(53)} \qquad \log F - \log t \approx -\tfrac{1}{4} \sum \tfrac{1}{2}(w_i^1 + w_i^0) \dot{p}_i^2 \dot{v}_i$$

$$+ \tfrac{1}{6} \sum \tfrac{1}{2}(w_i^1 + w_i^0) \dot{p}_i^3$$

$$\approx -\tfrac{1}{4} \operatorname{cov}(\dot{p}^2, \dot{v}) + \tfrac{1}{6} \operatorname{cov}(\dot{p}^2, \dot{p}) \ .$$

This shows that the logarithmic difference between F and t is of the third degree in the deviations of price and value log-changes or very small indeed. In other words, $\log F$ and $\log t$ are quadratic approximations of each other; quadratic in variables $\dot{p}_i$ and $\dot{v}_i \approx \dot{p}_i + \dot{q}_i$. Note that the variance of the price changes s_p^2 or the covariance $\text{cov}(\dot{p},\dot{q})$ has no effect on their difference $\log F - \log t$, which depends only on the 'skewness' or the other third degree properties of the two dimensional distribution of the pair $(\log(p_i^1/p_i^0), \log(q_i^1,q_i^0))$ with the weights $\frac{1}{2}(w_i^1 + w_i^0)$. The covariances in (53) may be combined in a variety of ways to get other approximations.

We conclude that there is no apparent tendency for F to be greater than t, or vice versa, as could have been expected from all of our forks. It is no accident that Fisher (1922, p. 265) places only 14 formulas ahead of t, or his 123, cf. table 2 and figure 1.

By similar arguments but starting from (20) and (23) we get

$$(54) \qquad \log \sqrt{P\ell \cdot Lh} - \log t \approx \frac{1}{4}\,\text{cov}(\dot{p}^2,\dot{v}) + \frac{1}{6}\,\text{cov}(\dot{p}^2,\dot{p}) \;,$$

which shows that even from usually badly biased index numbers we may get a very good formula.

Finally we will show some connections with the economic theory of index numbers. Our moment means $P(\alpha,c) = [\Sigma c_i (p_i^1/p_i^0)^\alpha]^{1/\alpha}$ using the weights $c_i = w_i^0$ are Economic Price Indices corresponding to the generalized CES utility function given, e.g., by Lloyd (1975), if $\alpha = 1 - \sigma$, where σ is the constant elasticity of substitution.

We have, e.g., $P(1,w^0) = L$, $P(0,w^0) = \ell$ and $P(-1,w^0) = Lh$ for $\sigma = 0$, $\sigma \to 1$ and $\sigma = 2$ respectively, which here are thus 'exact index numbers' corresponding to these special cases of CES specification.

If the data is generated according to the consumer theory and CES utility function we must have $L = P$, $\ell = p$ and $Lh = P\ell$ if $\sigma = 0$, $\sigma \to 1$ and $\sigma = 2$ respectively, because the pairs (L,P), (ℓ,p) and $(Lh,P\ell)$ are time antitheses of each other and the Economic Price Index equals in the homothetic case its time antithesis, i.e., satisfies the time reversal test, see Samuelson & Swamy (1974). Curiously the Vartia Index II, an ideal log-change index $\log P_0^1 = \sum \bar{w}_i \log(p_i^1/p_i^0)$ using weights $\bar{w}_i$ given in (29), is exact here for all values of σ as proved by Sato (1976).

Therefore Fisher's Five-tined Fork corresponds to the case $\sigma = 0$ (zero substitution case, $q^1 = kq^0$), our three-tined fork to the case $\sigma \to 1$ (or Cobb-Douglas case, $w_i^0 = w_i^1$), while $\sigma = 2$ results in a new five-tined fork, where $\log L > \log \ell > \log Lh = \log P\ell > \log p > \log P$. In the third case the substitution effects are unusually strong and L and P have a double bias in respect to the unbiased $Lh = P\ell \approx F \approx t$.

The assumptions leading to these cases are, however, rather special and the formulas $P\ell$, p, P, L, ℓ and Lh give all in turn biased results as our analysis reveals.

Diewert (1976) defines the quadratic mean of order r unit cost function $c_r(p)$ as follows

$$(55) \qquad c_r(p) = \left[\sum_{i=1}^{n} \sum_{i=1}^{n} a_{ij} p_i^{\,r/2} p_j^{\,r/2}\right]^{1/r}, \quad a_{ij} = a_{ji}\,.$$

He shows that the Economic Price Index corresponding to it is the quadratic mean of order r price index P_r:

$$(56) \qquad P_r = [\Sigma w_i^0 (p_i^1/p_i^0)^{r/2} / \Sigma w_i^1 (p_i^1/p_i^0)^{-r/2}]^{1/r} ,$$

which may be written using geometric means of the moment means as follows

$$(57) \qquad P_r = [P(r/2, w^0)\ P(-r/2, w^1)]^{1/2} .$$

We have e.g. $P_2 = F$, $P_0 = t$ and $P_{-2} = \sqrt{P\ell \cdot Lh}$, which all belong to the middle tines in our forks. Just as before we get for the relative difference between P_r and t:

$$(58) \qquad \log P_r - \log t \approx -\frac{r}{8} \operatorname{cov}(\dot{p}^2, \dot{v}) + \frac{r^2}{24} \operatorname{cov}(\dot{p}^2, \dot{p}) .$$

Thus P_r and t are for all r and small price and value deviations $\dot{p}_i$ and $\dot{v}_i$ very accurate approximations of each other and therefore P_r is always unbiased, i.e. P_r is contained for all r in the middle tines of our forks.

Inserting (53) into (58) the relative difference between P_r and F is derived. Diewert (1976) shows, using the demand or production theory, that the P_r:s and t are 'superlative index numbers' in a specified sense and are therefore good approximations of each other. Equation (58) expresses approximately the same thing without any assumptions about, e.g., the maximization behaviour of the economic agents. To derive our equation (58) arithmetic alone was needed.

References

ALLEN, R.G.D., (1975): "*Index numbers in theory and in practice*", The Macmillan Press, Ltd., London.

von BORTKIEWICZ, L., (1922, 1924): "Zweck und Struktur einer Preisindexzahl", *Nordisk Statistisk Tidskrift*, *1* (1922) and *3* (1924).

DIEWERT, W.E., (1976): "Exact and superlative index numbers", *Journal of Econometrics*, *4*, 115-145.

FISHER, F. & SHELL, K., (1972): "*The economic theory of price indices*", Academic Press, New York.

FISHER, I., (1922): "*The making of index numbers*", Houghton Mifflin Company, Boston.

FRISCH, R., (1936): "Annual survey of general economic theory: the problem of index numbers", *Econometrica*, *4*, 1-38.

HARDY, G.H. & LITTLEWOOD, J.E. & POLYA, G., (1962): "*Inequalities*", Cambridge University Press, Cambridge.

LEONTIEF, W., (1936): "Composite commodities and the problem of index numbers", *Econometrica*, *4*, 39-59.

LLOYD, P.J., (1975): "Substitution effects and biases in nontrue price indices", *The American Economic Review*, June 1975.

RAJAOJA, V., (1958): "*A study in the theory of demand functions and price indexes*", Societas Scientiarum Fennica, Helsinki.

SAMUELSON, P.A. & SWAMY, S., (1974): "Invariant economic index numbers and canonical quality: Survey and synthesis", *The American Economic Review*, *64*, 566-593.

SATO, K., (1976): "The ideal log-change index number", *The Review of Economics and Statistics*, *58*, 223-8.

THEIL, H., (1967): "*Economics and information theory*", North Holland Publishing Company, Amsterdam.

TÖRNQVIST, L., (1936): "Levnads kostnadsindexerna i Finland och Sverige, deras tillförlitlighet och jämförbarket", *Ekonomiska Samfundets Tidskrift*, *37*, 1-35.

VARTIA, Y., (1976a): "Ideal log-change index numbers", *Scandinavian Journal of Statistics*, *3*, 121-6.

VARTIA, Y., (1976b): "*Relative changes and index numbers*", Ph.D. Thesis, The Research Institute of the Finnish Economy, Serie A4, Helsinki.

Divisia Indices on Different Paths

by Arthur Vogt[1)]

The index problem in the two-situation-case is presented in the 2n-dimensional quantity-price-space. Certain traditional index numbers can be obtained by evaluating the Divisia line integral on certain paths in this space. Especially the indices coordinated to the most natural path between the two endpoints - the straight line, are given.

1. On the Notations

We conceive the prices p_i and the quantities q_i of each of the n goods as coordinates of the $\mathbb{R}_+^{2n}$. We denote the price vector

$$(p_1, \cdots, p_n) \quad \text{by} \quad \underline{p}$$

and the quantity vector

$$(q_1, \cdots, q_n) \quad \text{by} \quad \underline{q} \; .$$

The <u>statistical index problem in the two-situation-case</u> (Allen 1975, Ruist 1968) can be formulated as follows:

> Two points in $\mathbb{R}_+^{2n}$, i.e. a "base point" $\underline{r}^o = (\underline{p}^o, \underline{q}^o)$ and an "observed point" $\underline{r}^1 = (\underline{p}^1, \underline{q}^1)$ are given. One has to look for a price index P_{01} and a quantity index Q_{01}, so that the value index

---

1) The author is indebted to Professor Dr. W. Eichhorn and Professor Dr. R.W.Shephard for helpful comments; but the author alone is responsible for the remaining errors.

$$(1.1) \qquad W_{o1} = \frac{\underline{p}^1 \; \underline{q}^1}{\underline{p}^o \; \underline{q}^o}$$

is related to P_{o1} and Q_{o1} by

$$(1.2) \qquad W_{o1} = P_{o1} \cdot Q_{o1} \; .$$

We then say that the price index P_{o1} and the quantity index Q_{o1} are consistent.

We now regard the two points $\underline{r}^o$ and $\underline{r}^1$ as connected by a path ($\underline{p}(t)$, $\underline{q}(t)$) parametrised by the "time parameter" $t \in [t_o, t_1]$

Notationally:

$$\underline{p}(t_o) = \underline{p}^o \qquad \underline{q}(t_o) = \underline{q}^o$$

$$\underline{p}(t_1) = \underline{p}^1 \qquad \underline{q}(t_1) = \underline{q}^1 \; .$$

The whole path $\{\underline{p}(t), \underline{q}(t)\}\; t \in [t_o, t_1]$ will be denoted by C . We assume that all components $p_i(t)$ and $q_i(t)$ of $\underline{p}(t)$ and $\underline{q}(t)$ are differentiable with regard to t. We denote these derivatives by $\dot{p}_i$ and $\dot{q}_i$ respectively.

A value $W(t) = \underline{p}(t)\; \underline{q}(t)$

and a value index $W_{ot} = \dfrac{\underline{p}(t)\; \underline{q}(t)}{\underline{p}(t_o)\; \underline{q}(t_o)}$ are defined on C .

2. Derivation of the Divisia Indices

We form the logarithmic derivation, that is to say the development intensity (Kaiser 1974) of W_{ot} which we denote by $\overline{w}(t)$:

$$(2.1) \qquad \overline{w}(t) = \frac{d}{dt} \log W_{ot} = \frac{\dot{W}_{ot}}{W_{ot}} = \frac{\dot{\underline{p}}(t)\ \underline{q}(t) + \underline{p}(t)\ \dot{\underline{q}}(t)}{\underline{p}(t)\ \underline{q}(t)}$$

We now define the value index W_{ot} the other way round. By reversing the processes of logarithm and differentiation we get to a term which Kaiser (1974) describes as index functional:

$$(2.2) \qquad W_{ot} = \exp \int_{t_o}^{t} \overline{w}(\tau)\ d\tau = \exp \int_{t_o}^{t} \frac{\dot{\underline{p}}(\tau)\ \underline{q}(\tau) + \underline{p}(\tau)\ \dot{\underline{q}}(\tau)}{\underline{p}(\tau)\ \underline{q}(\tau)}\ d\tau\ .$$

This integration does not depend on the path but just on its endpoints $\underline{r}^o$ and ($\underline{p}(t)$, $\underline{q}(t)$), because the integrand, being the logarithmic derivation of W_{ot} , is by definition exact. The index problem now consists of an (because of the logarithm) additive decomposition of (2.1). Perhaps the only reasonable decomposition results from the requirement that "quantity changes without price changes should not change the price index and vice versa". This has already been applied by Divisia (1925). This leads to the following development intensities of the price and the quantity index:

$$(2.3) \qquad \overline{p}(t) = \frac{\dot{\underline{p}}(t)\ \underline{q}(t)}{\underline{p}(t)\ \underline{q}(t)}\ ,$$

$$(2.4) \qquad \overline{q}(t) = \frac{\underline{p}(t)\ \dot{\underline{q}}(t)}{\underline{p}(t)\ \underline{q}(t)}\ .$$

To the differentials $\overline{p}(t)\ dt$ and $\overline{q}(t)\ dt$ there exist no integral functions $P(t)$ and $Q(t)$. If they did exist the "index problem" would no longer be a problem. On this Menges (1973) writes:

> One can say about the index problem that it is unsolvable, unsolvable in the sense that the index theory does not provide and can not provide a fitting answer to the question directed at it.

The differentials (2.3) and (2.4) are, in contrast to their sum (2.1), not exact. Thus the Divisia indices

$$(2.5)\qquad P_{01}^{(C)} = \exp \int_{t_0}^{t_1} \frac{\dot{\underline{p}}(\tau)\ \underline{q}(\tau)}{\underline{p}(\tau)\ \underline{q}(\tau)}\, d\tau$$

and

$$(2.6)\qquad Q_{01}^{(C)} = \exp \int_{t_0}^{t_1} \frac{\underline{p}(\tau)\ \dot{\underline{q}}(\tau)}{\underline{p}(\tau)\ \underline{q}(\tau)}\, d\tau$$

are dependent on the path C in $\mathbb{R}_+^{2n}$ which runs from $\underline{r}^0$ to $\underline{r}^1$. Divisia (1925) himself was already aware of this fact (contrary to a remark in Samuelson (1974)) even if he did not yet use the mathematically adequate explanation (exactness of differential forms).

He wrote:

> The current value of the ransom of François I depends on the dominion of Louis XIV, the encyclopaedists and the revolution, the discovery of potatoes and the invention of steam... And so, our monetary index, the line integral, seems to us to merit the name historical index much better...

3. Divisia Indices on Special Paths

One can now conceive some of the traditional indices as Divisia line integrals (2.5) and (2.6) on fictitious paths between the endpoints $\underline{r}^0$ and $\underline{r}^1$ in $\mathbb{R}_+^{2n}$. In Figures 1, some paths are marked each axis symbolically representing an n-dimensional subspace.

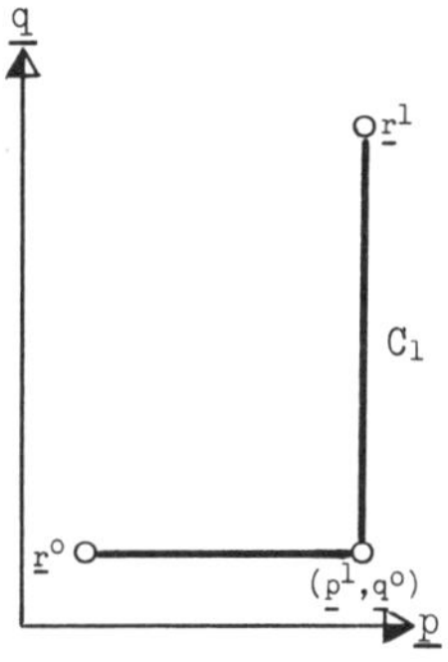

Fig. 1.1

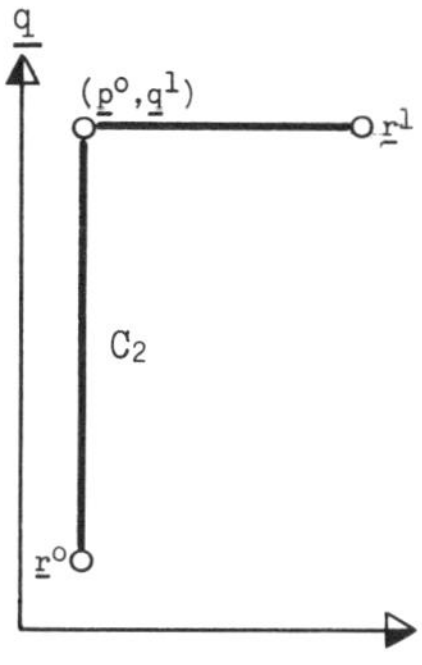

Fig. 1.2

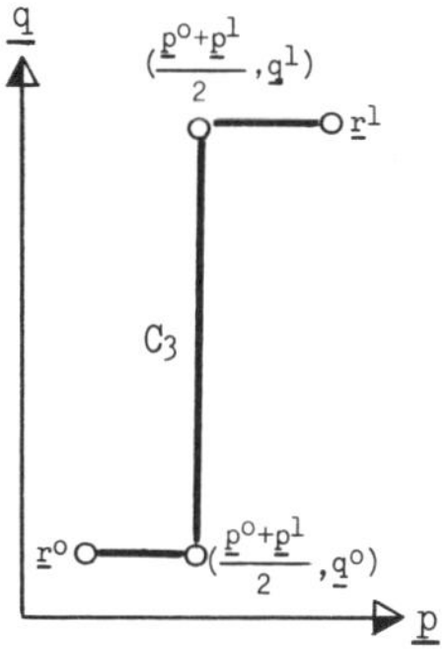

Fig. 1.3

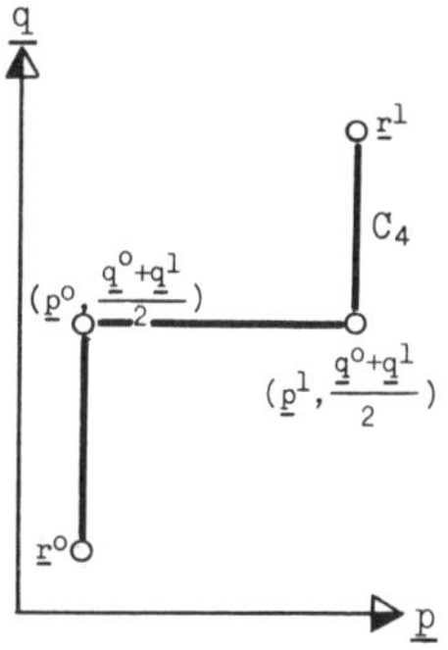

Fig. 1.4

One can show (Vogt 1977) that the corresponding indices are as follows

Path	Price index (2.5)	Quantity index (2.6)
C_1	$\frac{\underline{p}^1 \underline{q}^0}{\underline{p}^0 \underline{q}^0}$ (Laspeyres')	$\frac{\underline{p}^1 \underline{q}^1}{\underline{p}^1 \underline{q}^0}$ (Paasche's)
C_2	$\frac{\underline{p}^1 \underline{q}^1}{\underline{p}^0 \underline{q}^1}$ (Paasche's)	$\frac{\underline{p}^0 \underline{q}^1}{\underline{p}^0 \underline{q}^0}$ (Laspeyres')
C_3	$W_{01}: \frac{(\underline{p}^0 + \underline{p}^1)\, \underline{q}^1}{(\underline{p}^0 + \underline{p}^1)\, \underline{q}^0}$ (Factor antithesis of Marshall - Edgeworth's price index)	$\frac{(\underline{p}^0 + \underline{p}^1)\, \underline{q}^1}{(\underline{p}^0 + \underline{p}^1)\, \underline{q}^0}$ (Marshall - Edgeworth's quantity index)
C_4	$\frac{\underline{p}^1(\underline{q}^0 + \underline{q}^1)}{\underline{p}^0(\underline{q}^0 + \underline{q}^1)}$ (Marshall - Edgeworth's price index)	$W_{01}: \frac{\underline{p}^1(\underline{q}^0 + \underline{q}^1)}{\underline{p}^0(\underline{q}^0 + \underline{q}^1)}$ (Factor antithesis of Marshall - Edgeworth's quantity index)

From the above table one sees that none of the mentioned indices satisfies the factor reversal test. For that the same type of index would have to be on a line in the table (i.e. to belong to the same path). From Figures 1, one can draw the conclusion that of the mentioned indices only Marshall - Edgeworth's and their factor antitheses satisfy the time reversal test.

4. The "Natural" Index

Figures 1 suggest evaluating the integrals (2.5) and (2.6) on the straight line C_8 (Figure 2.4) connecting $\underline{r}^{o}$ and $\underline{r}^{1}$ (Vogt 1977). Numerically the corresponding indices can be approximated by the Divisia indices on the paths displayed in Figures 2.1 - 2.3

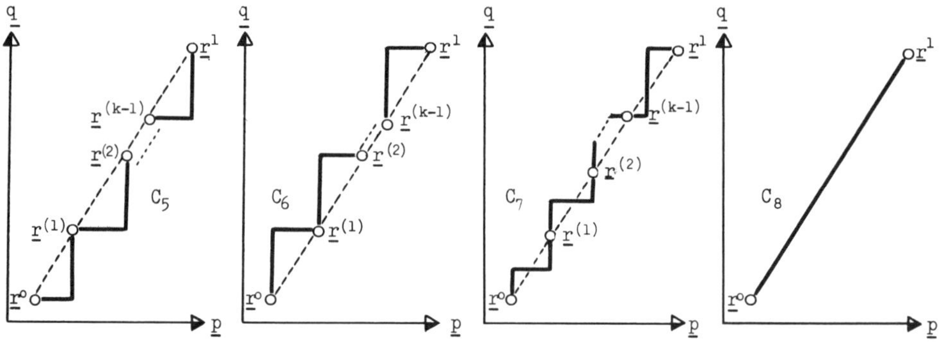

Fig. 2.1 Fig. 2.2 Fig. 2.3 Fig. 2.4

The Divisia indices on path C_5 lead to a product of k Laspeyres price indices or Paasche quantity indices between consecutive intermediate points $\underline{r}^{(i)}$, $\underline{r}^{(i+1)}$, and conversely on path C_6. Analytically the evaluation of the Divisia indices on the straight connection C_8 leads to the following indices, called "natural" indices in Vogt (1977)

$$(4.1)\qquad P_{o1}^{(C_8)} = \begin{cases} \sqrt{\dfrac{v_{11}}{v_{oo}}}\ \left(\dfrac{v_{1o}+v_{o1}+\sqrt{D}}{v_{1o}+v_{o1}-\sqrt{D}}\right)^{\frac{v_{1o}-v_{o1}}{2\sqrt{D}}} & D>0 \\ \sqrt{\dfrac{v_{11}}{v_{oo}}}\ \exp\dfrac{v_{1o}-v_{o1}}{v_{1o}+v_{o1}} & D=0 \\ \sqrt{\dfrac{v_{11}}{v_{oo}}}\ \exp\left(\dfrac{v_{1o}-v_{o1}}{\sqrt{-D}}\ \mathrm{arctg}\dfrac{\sqrt{-D}}{v_{1o}+v_{o1}}\right) & D<0 \end{cases}$$

$$(4.2)\qquad Q_{o1}^{(C_8)} = \begin{cases} \sqrt{\dfrac{v_{11}}{v_{oo}}}\ \left(\dfrac{v_{1o}+v_{o1}+\sqrt{D}}{v_{1o}+v_{o1}-\sqrt{D}}\right)^{\frac{v_{o1}-v_{1o}}{2\sqrt{D}}} & D>0 \\ \sqrt{\dfrac{v_{11}}{v_{oo}}}\ \exp\dfrac{v_{o1}-v_{1o}}{v_{1o}+v_{o1}} & D=0 \\ \sqrt{\dfrac{v_{11}}{v_{oo}}}\ \exp\left(\dfrac{v_{o1}-v_{1o}}{\sqrt{-D}}\ \mathrm{arctg}\dfrac{\sqrt{-D}}{v_{1o}+v_{o1}}\right) & D<0 \end{cases}$$

where the $v_{ij} = \underline{p}^i\ \underline{q}^j$ are elements of the so-called value matrix and

$D = (v_{1o}+v_{o1})^2 - 4\ v_{oo}\ v_{11}$.

It can be shown geometrically that the natural indices satisfy the factor reversal, the time reversal and the identity tests. From the formulas it can be shown that they satisfy many other tests. One test (axiom) they don't satisfy is the <u>linear homogeneity axiom</u> (Eichhorn and Voeller 1976)

$$(4.3)\qquad P(\underline{q}^o, \underline{p}^o, \underline{q}^1, \lambda\ \underline{p}^1) = \lambda\ P(\underline{q}^o, \underline{p}^o, \underline{q}^1, \underline{p}^1)\ .$$

(in the following we only mention the price index, the quantity indices could be treated analogously). The linear homogeneity axiom can be conceived as a special case of the <u>circular test</u>

$$(4.4)\qquad P(\underline{q}^o, \underline{p}^o, \underline{q}^2, \underline{p}^2) = P(\underline{q}^o, \underline{p}^o, \underline{q}^1, \underline{p}^1)\cdot P(\underline{q}^1, \underline{p}^1, \underline{q}^2, \underline{p}^2)\ .$$

The natural index does not satisfy the circular test because $\overline{p}(t)$ is not exact and so on a general triangle T

(4.5) $$\oint_T \overline{p}(t)\, dt \neq 0 \,.$$

Generally integral (4.5) is not zero, either, if the three points are arranged in the more special way of the homogeneity axiom. But if the triangle T is in a subspace parallel to the price space

(4.6) $$\oint_T \overline{p}(t)\, dt = 0$$

is always true. Thus the natural index satisfies the following special case of the homogeneity axiom which we shall call "weak homogeneity axiom"

(4.7) $$P(\underline{q}^o, \underline{p}^o, \underline{q}^o, \lambda\, \underline{p}^1) = \lambda\, P(\underline{q}^o, \underline{p}^o, \underline{q}^o, \underline{p}^1) \,.$$

The natural index also satisfies the proportionality axiom, the special case of the linear homogeneity axiom in which the intermediate point happens to be identical with the base point:

(4.8) $$P(\underline{q}^o, \underline{p}^o, \underline{q}^1, \lambda\, \underline{p}^o) = \lambda \,.$$

The axioms mentioned can be arranged in the following way

Axiom	Base point	Intermediate point	Observed point
Circular	$\underline{q}^o$, $\underline{p}^o$	$\underline{q}^1$, $\underline{p}^1$	$\underline{q}^2$, $\underline{p}^2$
Homogeneity	$\underline{q}^o$, $\underline{p}^o$	$\underline{q}^1$, $\underline{p}^1$	$\underline{q}^1$, $\lambda\, \underline{p}^1$
"Weak homogeneity"	$\underline{q}^o$, $\underline{p}^o$	$\underline{q}^o$, $\underline{p}^1$	$\underline{q}^o$, $\lambda\, \underline{p}^1$
Proportionality	$\underline{q}^o$, $\underline{p}^o$	$\underline{q}^o$, $\underline{p}^o$	$\underline{q}^1$, $\lambda\, \underline{p}^o$

The axiom system of Eichhorn and Voeller (1976) could be made compatible with the natural index in the following manner: The linear homogeneity axiom is replaced by two special cases, proportionality axiom and "weak homogeneity axiom". It remains to be decided whether the resulting new axiom system is suitable.

References

Allen, R.G.D. (1975): Index Numbers in Theory and Practice. Macmillan Press, London.

Divisia, F. (1925): L'indice monétaire et la théorie de la monnaie. Revue d'Economie Politique 39, 980-1008.

Eichhorn, W. and Voeller, J. (1976): Theory of the Price Index, Springer-Verlag, Berlin. Lecture Notes in Economics and Mathematical Systems, Nr. 140.

Kaiser, E. (1974): Die dynamische Relativität: ein Zentralproblem der Sozial- und Wirtschaftsmathematik. Mitteilungen der Vereinigung Schweizerischer Versicherungsmathematiker 74, 29-62.

Menges, G. und Skala, H. (1973): Grundriss der Statistik, Teil 2: Daten. Westdeutscher-Verlag, Opladen.

Ruist, E. (1968): Index Numbers, Theoretical Aspects, International Encyclopaedia of the Social Sciences, Vol. 7, New York.

Samuelson, P.A. and Swamy, S. (1974): Invariant Economic Index Numbers and Canonical Duality: Survey and Synthesis. American Economic Review 64, 566-593.

Vogt, A. (1977): Zum Indexproblem: Geometrische Darstellung sowie eine neue Formel. Schweizerische Zeitschrift für Statistik und Volkswirtschaft, Vol. 113, 1, pp. 73-88.

PART III

Methodological Topics Concerning Economic Indices

Indices of Income Inequality and Societal Income. An Axiomatic Approach*)

by Ralph Bürk and Wilhelm Gehrig

I. Introduction

Although they had for a long period not been in the center of interest of main stream academic economics the questions of how to measure economic inequality and the welfare of a community as a whole are old and perennial ones. The problems we are concerned with in this paper are the measurement of income inequality and of the income of society as a whole. In the literature various forms of alternative indices of income inequality have been proposed. We shall find, however, (in section III) that most of these alternative forms can be traced to a common origin: the family of quasilinear means.

The basic methodological distinction we make and which is introduced in section II is the one between statistical and mechanistic measures of inequality.

A mechanistic index is to measure the actually observed degree of inequality based on a given vector of incomes whereas a statistical index conceives of income as a random process. Hence a statistical index can be thought of as a measure of the degree of inequality that a certain institutional structure of the economy tends to imply by influencing the paramters of the income generating random process.[1)]

---

*) We are indebted to Professors A. Sen and F. Stehling for helpful comments.

1) R. NOZICK [1973] and H. VARIAN [1975] draw a similar distinction between "historical" and "end-state" distributional situations.

Before, in section II, we argue that measures of inequality are, besides in trivial cases, necessarily of a normative nature, no matter whether we choose a conventional index like the standard deviation or employ an "economic" measure based on a Social Welfare Function, like ATKINSON's index. Consequently the normative judgements or postulates which lead to the choice of a particular index or a particular family of indices should be made explicit.
Section V, then, does in fact present a set of postulates that leads, both for our mechanistic and statistical types of indices, to indices of societal income which are themselves composed of two other indices- the pure distributional index and the index of mean income.

II NOTATION AND A SIMPLE CASE

We will find it convenient to think of income as a (discrete) random variable Y with distribution function $F_Y(\cdot)$. Y is assumed to take values in the interval $[0,\bar{y}]$ and only there and we distinguish n possible income levels $y_1,\ldots,y_n$

$$0 = y_1 \leq y_2 \leq \ldots \leq y_n = \bar{y}.$$

Hence, the y_i, $i = 1,\ldots,n$ are assumed with probabilities

$$f_Y(y_i) := F_Y(y_i) - F_Y(y_{i-1})$$

and

$$F_Y(y) \begin{cases} = 0 & y < 0 \\ = 1 & y \geq \bar{y}. \end{cases}$$

Furthermore we consider N income recipients with a corresponding vector of actual incomes $x = (x_1,\ldots,x_N)$, where $x_1,\ldots,x_N$ are realisations of Y.
We shall call an index $d(\cdot)$, say,

<u>statistical</u> and write $d(F_Y)$) if it refers to the <u>random variable Y</u> with distribution function $F_Y(\cdot)$, or

<u>mechanistic</u> and write $d(x)$) if it refers to a particular tupel of realisations $x = (x_1,\ldots,x_N)$[1].

This is an important methodological distinction. Note that, for example, the kind of indices statistical bureaus tend to produce would be called mechanistic in this terminology.

To illustrate the inherent normative character of income inequality measurement we use the well known LORENZ-curve representation.
If we define the function $G_Y: [0,1] \to [0,\bar{y}]$ by [2]

(1) $$G_Y(\alpha) = \inf\{y \mid y \in [0,\bar{y}],\ F_Y(y) \geq \alpha\}$$

then the LORENZ "curve" $L_Y: [0,1] \to [0,1]$ can be written in the form (see e.g. PIESCH [1975, p.23]):

(2) $$L_Y(\alpha) = \frac{1}{\mu_Y} \int_0^{\alpha} G_Y(s)\,ds$$

where μ_Y is the expected value of Y.
For example a uniform density[3] $f_Y(s) = \frac{1}{c}$, $s \in [0,c]$ leads to the LORENZ-curve $L_Y(\alpha) = \alpha^2$, $\alpha \in [0,1]$. The LORENZ-curve L_x for an observed vector of incomes (the mechanistic case) can be computed in much the same way, by taking as $y_1,\ldots,y_n$, $n \leq N$ the different income levels that occur in $x_1,\ldots,x_N$ and define $f_x(y_i)$ as the relative frequencies by which these income levels occur. Then with

(3) $$G_x(\alpha) = \inf\{y_i \mid \sum_{y_j \leq y_i} f_x(y_j) \geq \alpha\}$$

---

1) possibly without even thinking of random variables and all that.

2) G_Y is the so called "inverse distribution function".

3) for continuous Y. A "uniform density" of Y should not be confused with a uniform distribution of incomes, that is a realisation x with $x_1=x_2=\ldots=x_N=\mu$. This in turn would correspond to the distribution function $F_Y(y)=1$, $y \geq \mu$, $F_Y(y)=0$, $y<\mu$.

one obtains from

$$(4) \qquad L_x(\alpha) = \frac{1}{\mu_x} \int_0^{\alpha} G_x(s)ds$$

the LORENZ-curve which is widely used in income distribution theory (e.g. SEN [1973, p. 30]). A simple but illuminating case prevails if, comparing the LORENZ-curves L_x and L_z of two income vectors x and z with the same total income one finds that

$$(5) \qquad L_x(\alpha) \geq L_z(\alpha) \qquad \text{for all } \alpha \in [0,1].$$

In this case one would not hesitate to call the income vector z more or at least as unequal as income vector x. If one asks what properties an equality index $d(\cdot)$ should have in order that in the above case x is always ranked more equal than z, i.e. $d(x) \geq d(z)$, one answer is given by the following theorem.

(6) THEOREM (ROTSCHILD and STIGLITZ [1973, p. 191])
Let $d: \mathbb{R}^n \to \mathbb{R}$ be a quasiconcave and symmetric function. Then

$$d(x) \geq d(z)$$

if and only if

$$L_x(\alpha) \geq L_z(\alpha) \quad \forall \alpha \in [0,1]$$

The Theorem provides a strong motivation to accept quasiconcavity[1)] and symmetry as basic properties of equality indices[2)] because, otherwise, the ranking implied by $d(\cdot)$ could contradict the LORENZ ranking in the " test-case" of nonintersecting L-curves.

But: Why should one want to use an index function if one knew in

---

1) DASGUPTA, SEN, STARRETT [1973] proved a stronger version of this theorem weakening the assumption of "quasiconcavity" to "S-concavity". As "S-concavity" is not a very well known concept we prefer to stick to the original formulation, though.

2) Obviously a corresponding inequality index would be quasiconvex.

the first place that the LORENZ-curves did not intersect? Obviously because one hopes to use this index functions also in cases where the LORENZ-curves do intersect, that is, if

$$L_x(\alpha') > L_z(\alpha')$$

$$L_x(\alpha'') < L_z(\alpha'') \quad \text{for some } \alpha', \alpha'' .$$

In this case, however, it is clear from THEOREM (6) above that there will exist index functions d' and d'' , both quasiconcave and symmetric, such that

$$d'(x) > d'(z)$$

$$\text{and} \quad d''(x) < d''(z) .$$

Here the important point is that because d' and d'' leads to reverse rankings of x and z <u>we have to make our choice</u> which index to use. Whether we make up our own index formula or choose from a set of prefabricated measures, like the coefficient of variation or the Gini-coeffizient, is not the crucial distinction. It is the existence, in principle, of an alternative choice of d - still being quasiconcave and symmetric - that would lead to a reverse ranking of some given pair of income vectors x and y. But that implies, that any index d we use in the case of intersecting L-curves is to be regarded as a <u>normative</u> measure of inequality. Hence, in this general case, the distinction between "positive measures" and "normative measures" made by SEN [1973, p. 24] or the distinction between "equality" and "equity" (i.e. between 'more equal' and 'better' income distributions) made by BONFENBRENNER [1973] loose much of their content. Simply because the concept of a positive measure of equality seems to be restricted to the trivial case of nonintersecting L-curves, and "the concept of distributive equity is largely, if not completely, a subjective matter. This implies the impossibility, in principle, of objectively judging whether something called maldistribution exists in a given society and whether one distribution is better than another", BONFENBRENNER [1973, p. 10].
So even the simple case discussed shows that in income inequality measurement one could say very little without allowing interpersonal (or better inter-income-level) comparisons to be made.

III QUASILINEAR MEANS: AN IMPORTANT FAMILY

In this section we shall examine several index number formulas, some of which have been proposed in the literature as alternative measures of income distribution.

The point we try to make is, that all these alternative measures, though seeming to be of utterly different nature, can be traced to a common origin: the (generalized) quasilinear means[1].

A generalized quasilinear mean (g.q.m), as used here, is of the form

$$(1) \qquad M(x) = u^{-1}\{\sum_{i=1}^{N} w(p(x_i,\mu)) \cdot u(p(x_i,\mu))\}$$

for the mechanistic case, where $\mu := \frac{1}{N}\sum x_i$ and p is a suitable normalization of the vector of incomes $x = (x_1,\ldots,x_N)$. Either

$$p(x_i,\mu) = \frac{x_i}{\mu} \quad \text{or} \quad p(x_i,\mu) = \left|\frac{x_i - \mu}{\mu}\right|$$

will be used.

For the statistical case we have here analogously

$$(2) \qquad M(F_Y) = u^{-1}\{\sum_{i=1}^{n} w(p(y_i,\mu_Y)) \cdot u(p(y_i,\mu_Y))\}^{2)}.$$

The functions $u\colon \mathbb{R}_+ \to \mathbb{R}_+$ and $w\colon \mathbb{R}_+ \to [0,1]$, $\sum_{i=1}^{N} w(p(x_i,\mu)) = 1$ appearing in both (1) and (2) are called valuation function and weighting function respectively[3]. In the statistical case $w(\cdot)$ is always the density $f_Y(\cdot)$. Hence using RIEMANN-STIELTJES notation (2) becomes:

$$(2a) \qquad M(F_Y) = u^{-1}\{\int_{-\infty}^{\infty} u(p(y,\mu_Y))\,dF_Y\}.$$

---

1) for other applications of generalized quasilinear means in economics see STEHLING [1974].

2) M(Y) is a mapping from the space of random variable which possess a density into the reals.

3) The functions u(•) that will be used are continuous and strictly monotonic.

The statistical formulation will not be spelled out for every index dicussed below, because in most cases it is strictly analogous to the mechanistic case.

If we now choose

$$p(x_i,\mu) := x_i/\mu$$

$$w(p) := 1/N$$

$$u(p) := p^{\alpha}$$

we obtain exponential means of order $\alpha \neq 0$

(3) $$l_{\alpha}(x) = \{\sum_{i=1}^{N} \frac{1}{N}(\frac{x_i}{\mu})^{\alpha}\}^{\frac{1}{\alpha}} \quad ; \quad l_{\alpha}(x) \in [1, N^{\frac{\alpha-1}{\alpha}}]$$

If we use the normalization $p = (x_i - \mu)/\mu$ then, for $\alpha = 2$, (3) becomes the standard variation. If for the same p, one chooses $u(p) = |p|$ instead, the relative mean deviation

(4) $$l_1(x) = \frac{1}{N} \sum_{i=1}^{N} \left| \frac{x_i - \mu}{\mu} \right|, \quad l_1(x) \in [0, \frac{N-1}{N}]$$

follows.

To see how the relative range

(5) $$r(x) = \max_i(\frac{x_i}{\mu}) - \min_i(\frac{x_i}{\mu}), \quad r(x) \in [0,N]$$

can be expressed by quasilinear means, define

$$l_{\alpha}^{+}(x) = \{\sum_{i=1}^{N} \frac{1}{N}(\frac{x_i}{\mu})^{\alpha}\}^{\frac{1}{\alpha}} \quad \text{and} \quad l_{\alpha}^{-}(x) = \{\sum_{i=1}^{N} \frac{1}{N}(\frac{x_i}{\mu})^{-\alpha}\}^{-\frac{1}{\alpha}}.$$

Then r can be written as[1)]

(6) $$r(x) = \lim_{\alpha\to\infty}(l_{\alpha}^{+}(x) - l_{\alpha}^{-}(x)).$$

---

1) see HARDY, LITTLEWOOD, PÓLYA [1967, p. 15]

Let us now choose the non-constant weights:

$$w(p) = \frac{p}{N}$$

with

$$p(x_i, \mu) = \frac{x_i}{\mu} .$$

Then for

$$u(p) = p^{\alpha}$$

we obtain the generalized exponential mean of order $\alpha \neq 0$:

$$(7) \qquad l^{*}_{\alpha}(x) = \{ \sum_{i=1}^{N} \frac{x_i}{N\mu} (\frac{x_i}{\mu})^{\alpha} \}^{\frac{1}{\alpha}}, \quad l^{*}_{\alpha} \in [1,N] .$$

With p and w the same but

$$u(p) = \log p$$

we call the resulting index

$$(8) \qquad l^{*}_{o}(x) = \exp\{ \sum_{i=1}^{N} \frac{x_i}{N\mu} \log (\frac{x_i}{\mu}) \}, \quad l^{*}_{o} \in [1,N]$$

the generalized logarithmic mean[1].

Obviously THEIL's measure of inequality

$$(9) \qquad t(x) = \sum_{i=1}^{N} \frac{x_i}{N\mu} \log (\frac{x_i}{\mu})$$

(see THEIL [1967]) is obtained as the logarithm of l^{*}_{o}.

Note that $t(x)$, as well as l^{*}_{α} and l^{*}_{o} are closely related to the entropy measure which plays an important role in information theory and thermodynamics as an indicator for the degree of "structuredness" of probabilistic systems.

---

1) the notation l^{*}_{o} points at the fact that $l^{*}_{o} = \lim_{\alpha \to o} l^{*}_{\alpha}$.

The statistical index corresponding to $l_\alpha(x)$ reads (see (3))

$$(10) \qquad l_\alpha(F_Y) = \{\sum_{i=1}^{n} f_Y(y_i)(\frac{y_i}{\mu_Y})^\alpha\}^{\frac{1}{\alpha}} .$$

We shall return to (10) in section IV in connection with ATKINSON's index concept.

Another index which originally had been used to measure industri concentration is <u>HERFINDAHL's index</u> (see PIESCH [1975, p. 9]), which for our purpose can be written

$$(11) \qquad h(x) = \sum_{i=1}^{N} \frac{1}{N}(\frac{x_i}{\mu})^2, \quad h(x) \in [1,N].$$

It is characterizable by

$$p(x_i,\mu) = x_i/\mu$$

$$w(p) = u(p) = p.$$

HERFINDAHL's proposal is, as it turns out, not as simplistic as it looks at first sight. If we define

$$h_\alpha(x) = \frac{1}{\alpha}\log\{\sum_{i=1}^{N}\frac{p_i}{N}e^{\alpha p_i}\}, \quad h_\alpha(x) \in [1,N]$$

with

$$p_i = x_i/\mu$$

$$w(p) = p/N$$

$$u(p) = e^{\alpha p}$$

then we can also write h(x) as[1)]

$$(12) \qquad h(x) = \lim_{\alpha\to 0} h_\alpha(x).$$

---

1) by using L'HÔPITAL's rule for the evaluation of limits of the form $\frac{0}{0}$; see also BRUCKMANN [1969, p. 196].

But on the other hand

$$h_\alpha(x) = \frac{1}{\alpha}\log\{\sum_{i=1}^{N}\frac{p_i}{N}\sum_{k=0}^{\infty}\frac{(\alpha p_i)^k}{k!}\}$$

$$= \frac{1}{\alpha}\log\{\sum_{k=0}^{\infty}\frac{\alpha^k}{k!}\sum_{i=1}^{N}\frac{1}{N}p_i^{k+1}\}$$

$$= \frac{1}{\alpha}\log\{\sum_{k=2}^{\infty}(\frac{\alpha^{k-1}}{(k-1)!}\mu_p^k) + 1\} .$$

where μ_p^k denotes the k-th moment of the p_i, $i = 1,\dots,N$. Hence, $h_\alpha(x)$ is based on the weighted average of <u>all</u> moments of order greater than 1 of the "sample" $(p(x_1,\mu),\dots,p(x_N,\mu))$ with corresponding weights $\alpha^{k-1}/(k-1)!$. Note the similarity of $h_\alpha(x)$ to the measure l_o^* of the entropy type.

Somewhat less directly one obtains <u>GINI's index g(x)</u>. Define $rk(x_i) = i$ iff x_i is the i-th largest element of the vector x. Then with

$$p(x_i,\mu) = \frac{N+1 - rk(x_i)}{N}$$

$$w(x_i,\mu) = \frac{x_i}{N\mu}$$

$$u(p) = p$$

we have (see (1)):

$$M(x) = \sum_{i=1}^{N}\{\frac{x_i}{N\mu}\left(\frac{N+1 - rk(x_i)}{N}\right) = \left(\frac{N+1}{N} - \sum_{i=1}^{N}\frac{1}{N^2\mu}x_i rk(x_i)\right).$$

On the other hand GINI's index is (see SEN [1973, p. 31])

$$g(x) = 1 + \frac{1}{N} - \frac{2}{N^2\mu}\sum_{i=1}^{N}x_i rk(x_i) ,$$

hence, immediately

$$g(x) = 2M(x) - \frac{N+1}{N}$$

i.e. GINI's index too can be written, for each N, as a 1 - 1

transform of a certain generalized quasilinear mean of the numbers $\frac{1}{N}(1,...,N)$.
We will not at this point indulge into a detailed discussion of the properties of the indices mentioned - for some of them this has been done elsewhere, see SEN [1973, p. 24f.], THEIL [1967]. We note only that all mechanistic index functions considered have the symmetry property, that is they are invariant with respect to permutations of the vector $(x_1,...,x_N)$. Furthermore all are invariant with respect to the scale of income measurement, that is they are homogeneous of zero degree.

IV "ECONOMIC" INDICES AND ATKINSON'S MEASURE

About the crudest categorization one can give for economic activities is into production and consumption. So among the basic questions when we approach the problem of what is an economic index of income inequality are the following:

> What is the effect of a certain degree of income inequality on the production of total income, and vice versa?
> How does the degree of income inequality relate to the "welfare" a society extracts from a certain total income[1]?

Unfortunately contemporary economics, empirical as well as theoretical, seem to have very little to say on these questions. This is so, because modern economics have almost exclusively been dealing with the problem of allocation in terms of microeconomic production-efficiency. To begin with let us aside production[2] - what then about those inequality indices that are based on Social Welfare Functions? Are these indices to be called economic ones?

The idea to base an inequality index on social welfare dates back to 1920, when H. DALTON proposed to use the "ratio of the total economic welfare attainable under an equal distribution to the total economic welfare attained under the given distribution" (p. 349).

---

1) Also more subtle ones: How does the degree of inequality relate to the structural stability of a certain socio-economic system?
2) or, equivalently, assume that macroeconomic production is independent of the degree of inequality.
3) of the BERGSON-SAMUELSON type, because we are comparing welfare levels not welfare functions.

Thus let

(1) $$W: \mathbb{R}^n_+ \to \mathbb{R}$$

be our Social Welfare Function (SWF) then DALTON's index D reads[1)]

(2) $$D(x) = \frac{W(\mu(x),\ldots,\mu(x))}{W(x_1,\ldots,x_N)}$$

where, as always, $\mu(x) := \frac{1}{N}\sum_{i=1}^{N} x_i$.

One obtains weakness of DALTON's measure in that it rigidly chooses the case of complete equality as the reference case - but clearly the <u>fixed</u> reference vector of incomes is something DALTON's index will have in common with any measure that leaves the production side out of the picture[2)].

If one tries to take the stand of an objective economic observer the main drawback, however, of the index D(·) is its blind and complete dependence on an arbitrary Social Welfare Function. But why is this to be a drawback? Undoubtedly many would argue that it is only the comparison of corresponding levels of <u>social welfare</u> which an <u>economic</u> index of inequality should be based on. Fair enough, but we should be careful not to confuse social welfare with the values that a certain function takes, which one happens to call Social Welfare Function and which, of course, one had had to specify in the first place[3)]. As we saw in section II, if LORENZ-curves cross the statement that one distribution of incomes is more equal than another one can only be mode relative

---

1) in the mechanistic formulation, which obviously DALTON had in mind. The statistical case (see section II) would read: $D(F_Y) = W(\mu_Y)/\int_0^{\bar{y}} u(y)\,dF_Y(y)$.

2) Another but related one is the choice of the same total income in the sequence vector, although the same total income might not at all be attainable if a uniform distribution of incomes is enforced.

3) The common assumption that the SWF <u>is given</u> is often no more as an excuse not to enter normative realms.

to our prior choice of the index function. Also in the case of DALTON's measure it is clear that, even by choosing the SWF from the class of quasiconcave and symmetric functions, say, we can make the value of $D(\bar{x})$ equal to any prespecified number (greater than one) given an arbitrary (but fixed) vector of incomes $\bar{x}$. Hence, if we are interested not merely in the definition of an index number as a mathematical object but insist on it being directed towards practical use, then, if we adapt DALTON's approach at all, the choice of the measure of social welfare is the critical step[1).]

Hence, should the choice of the SWF really be the a-priori choice as suggested implicitly by A.B. ATKINSON[2)] - setting the stage, so to speak, for the economic analysis to follow?

We suggest, that economic analysis should step in much earlier and should try to provide precisely quantifiable criteria for the selection of the welfare measure itself. Clearly, such criteria will have to be based on general principles which can be expressed as formal requirements - which we call postulates - on the index number to be constructed. To illustrate this, we mention the following three broad categories of such postulates:

1) technical postulates
   for example the index number should be invariant with respect to changes in the units of income measurement.
2) ethical postulates
   for example the index number of income inequality should not depend on which person is getting a particular income (anonymity).

---

1) We feel that a measure of social welfare should, for example, also depend on such intrinsically public "goods" like the degree of income inequality itself.

2) "In any case it seems more reasonable to approach the question directly by considering the social welfare function, that we should like to employ rather than indirectly through these summary statistical measures", ATKINSON [1970, p. 257].

3) equity postulates
   for example the postulate that inequity increases if there is an income transfer from a poorer person to a richer person.

Surprisingly enough[1] ATKINSON himself provides us with an example of how a measure of social welfare can be constructed from two postulates for the index number we come up with, using DALTON's concept: Consider income as being a random variable which takes values only between 0 and a maximal value $\bar{y}$ (see section II). To determine an index of income inequality which is implied by the distribution function $F_Y(\cdot)$ (that is in our terminology: a statistical index of income inequality) ATKINSON assumes the following:

Postulate 1

The SWF W(Y) is of the form

$$W(Y) = \int_0^{\bar{y}} u(y)\, dF_Y(y) \tag{3}$$

with $u: \mathbb{R}_+ \to \mathbb{R}_+$ being a continuous and strictly monotonic function[2].

Now let y^e be the (unique) number such that

$$u(y^e) = W(Y) \tag{4}$$

and define the index of inequality as[3]

1) Contrast this with the statemant cited from ATKINSON's 1970-paper in footnote 2) of the previous page!

2) Observe that for functions of scalar arguments monotonicity implies quasiconcavity.

3) Note that W(Y) as well as D(Y) are mappings from the space of all random variables into the reals.

(5) $$A(F_Y) = 1 - \frac{y^e}{\mu_Y}$$

where μ_Y is the expected value of Y[1].

Postulate 2

Let Z be the random variable $Z := \lambda Y$, with $\lambda > 0$, then

(6) $$A(F_Z) = A(F_Y)$$

where $F_Z(y) = F_Y(\frac{y}{\lambda})$.

Postulate 2 means that the inequality index $A(\cdot)$ should not depend on the units of income measurement.
From postulates 1 and 2 follows (see also PRATT [1964]) that $u(\cdot)$ has necessarily the form[2]

(7) $$u(y) = \begin{cases} \alpha + \frac{\beta}{\varepsilon} y^{\varepsilon} & \varepsilon \neq 0 \\ \text{or} & \\ \log(y) & \end{cases}.$$

Note that neither postulates 1 nor 2 alone allow to single out a unique index $u(\cdot)$ that is a – up to ε – unique measure of social welfare W(Y). For example under postulate 1 and for fixed Y, A(Y) can be made to take any value by appropiately choosing $u(\cdot)$. Only postulates 1 and 2 uniquely determine the function $u(\cdot)$, the welfare measure $W(\cdot)$ and the inequality index $A(\cdot)$. It follows at once that (for $\varepsilon \neq 1$) the form of ATKINSON's index will be

1) We remark here that CHAMPERNOWNE [1952] defines a similar measure replacing y^e by the median income m($m = G_Y(1/2)$, see II.1), i.e. m is the highest income of the poorest 50%). Accidentally in case of the special PARETO-distribution of income $F(y) = 1 - \frac{a}{y}$, $a > 0$ CHAMPERNOWNE's measure coincides with the value of the LORENZ-curve $L(\alpha)$ at $\alpha = 1/2$.

2) A more precise notation would be $u(\varepsilon,y)$, but as variations of ε are not our main point of interest have, we stick to ATKINSON's original form.

(8) $$A(F_Y) = 1 - \frac{1}{\mu_Y}\left[\int_0^{\bar{y}} y^{\varepsilon} dF_Y(y)\right]^{\frac{1}{\varepsilon}}$$

or equivalently:

(9) $$A(F_Y) = 1 - \left[\sum_{i=1}^{n} \left(\frac{y_i}{\mu_Y}\right)^{\varepsilon} f_Y(y_i)\right]^{\frac{1}{\varepsilon}} .$$

For practical purposes $f_Y(y_i)$ can be interpreted as the percentage of income recipients in the income bracket $\langle y_{i-1}, y_i]$, (see also ATKINSON [1975]).

In fact, assuming postulate 1 and quite independent of postulate 2 ATKINSON's index is nothing but a transformation of DALTON's D. Obviously D can be written $D = u(\mu_Y)/u(y^e)$, that is as the utility of mean income divided by the mean utility of income. But with $A = 1 - y^e/\mu_Y$ we have

$$u(\mu_Y(1-A)) = u(y^e)$$

or, using the monotonicity of $u(\cdot)$

$$\mu_Y(1-A) = u^{-1}\{u(\mu_Y)\frac{1}{D}\}$$

so that

$$A = 1 - u^{-1}\{u(\mu_Y)\frac{1}{D}\}/\mu_Y .$$

It seems that ATKINSON did not fully appreciate this when he suggested that compared to his own "the measure suggested by DALTON is not very useful" (see ATKINSON [1970, p. 250]).

The common interpretation of ATKINSON's index is that y^e represents the "equally distributed equivalent income" that is the income which, if obtained by everybody, produces the same level of expected utility as income Y, distributed with density $f_Y(\cdot)$.

It is well known (see HARDY, LITTLEWOOD, POLYA [1967, Th.23]) that with $u(y) = y^{\varepsilon}$ concave, i.e. $\varepsilon \in [0,1]$, one will always have $y^e \leqq \mu_Y$ implying $A(F_Y) \varepsilon [0,1]$.

A more simple[1] interpretation of ATKINSON's index can be given by writing $\bar{A} := 1 - A$ and (using (9))

$$(10a) \qquad \bar{A} = u^{-1}\{ \sum_{i=1}^{n} u(\frac{y_i}{\mu_Y}) \cdot w(\frac{y_i}{\mu_Y}) \}$$

where $w(\frac{y_i}{\mu_Y}) := f_Y(y_i)$, w being the frequency function of the normalization Y/μ_Y of Y, and

$$(10b) \qquad u(\frac{y_i}{\mu}) = \begin{cases} (\frac{y_i}{\mu})^{\varepsilon} & \text{for } \varepsilon \neq 0 \\ \text{or} & \\ \log(\frac{y_i}{\mu}) & \end{cases} .$$

If we compare (10a) to (10) of section III it becomes immediately clear that ATKINSON's A is a member of the quasilinear-mean-family. Also, in the case $\varepsilon = 0$ it bears a close formal relationship with THEIL's index. If $\varepsilon = 0$ ATKINSON's measure becomes

$$(11) \qquad \bar{A}(F_Y) = \exp\{ \sum_{i=1}^{n} w(\frac{y_i}{\mu_Y}) \log(\frac{y_i}{\mu}) \}$$

or

$$(12) \qquad \log(\bar{A}) = \sum_{i=1}^{n} w(\frac{y_i}{\mu_Y}) \log(\frac{y_i}{\mu}),$$

whereas THEIL's index reads

$$(13) \qquad t(y) = \sum_{i=1}^{N} (\frac{y_i}{N\mu_Y}) \log(\frac{y_i}{\mu}).$$

We see that for $\varepsilon = 0$ ATKINSON's index is, as THEIL's, a member of the "entropy-family", using however as weighting factors not the income share of the i-th recipient but the proportion of income recipients who receive the i-th income level. Note also that in

---

1) in the sense that it does not use the utility function concept.

(13) summation is over individuals whereas in (12) summation is over income levels[1].

Even in the special case that the number of income levels equals the number of individuals, that is $w(\frac{y_i}{\mu_Y}) = \frac{1}{N}$, THEIL's measure would appear to be slightly more revealing because it uses the variable weights $\frac{y_i}{N\mu}$ instead of $\frac{1}{N}$. The real strength of ATKINSON's concept lies in the fact that the parameter ε is not bound to equal zero, which corresponds to the log-case, but can be varied. To arrive at a correct interpretation of the parameter ε let us ask the question:

> What is the (infinitesimal) rate of income transfer[2] from income level i to income level j leaving A invariant?

As the natural ranking of income levels is not perturbed by infinitesimal transfers the number of income recipients receiving the i-th income level is constant, that is $w(\frac{y_i}{\mu_Y})$ is constant. Hence we obtain by total differentation of $\bar{A}$ (see (10a,b))

$$(14) \qquad O = \frac{\partial\{\cdot\}}{\partial y_i} dy_i + \frac{\partial\{\cdot\}}{\partial y_j} dy_j$$

which reduces to[3]

$$(15) \qquad \frac{dy_j}{dy_i} = - \frac{y_i^{\varepsilon-1} w(\frac{y_i}{\mu_Y})}{y_j^{\varepsilon-1} w(\frac{y_j}{\mu_Y})} \quad .$$

As a simple example (see ATKINSON [1975, p. 49]) take a poor man (income $y_j = 1$) and a rich man (income $y_i = 2$) and ask what rate of transformation r, say, of y_i's income into y_j's income would leave $\bar{A}$ invariant. From (15) one obtains

---

1) The reason for these differences lies in the fact that THEIL's index is mechanistic whereas ATKINSON's is statistical (see section II). It is not difficult to write down a statistical version of THEIL's index, it is in fact $e^{\bar{A}}$, but this could no longer be called THEIL's index.

2) Usage of the word "transfer" does not imply constancy of the sum of incomes.

3) The minus sign in (15) has more technical character, expressing the fact that y_i and y_j are inversely related.

$$(16) \qquad r = - \frac{2^{\varepsilon-1}}{1} = - \left(\frac{1}{2}\right)^{1-\varepsilon} .$$

In the more general case covered by (15) the absolute value of the transfer rate r_{ij} from income level i to income level j is

$$(17) \qquad |r_{ij}| = \left(\frac{y_j}{y_i}\right)^{1-\varepsilon} \frac{w\left(\frac{y_i}{\mu_Y}\right)}{w\left(\frac{y_j}{\mu_Y}\right)} \; ; \; i,j \in \{1,\ldots,n\}.$$

Take, without loss of generality, y_j to be the "poor" man and y_i to be the "rich" man, i.e. $y_j \leq y_i$. The second factor then says that the transfer rate, above all, should be proportional to the relative importance income levels in terms of respective numbers of recipients: income taken from $N \cdot w(\frac{y_i}{\mu_Y})$ people and transferred to level j at a certain rate has to be shared out between $N \cdot w(\frac{y_j}{\mu_Y})$ people there.

For an infinitesimal transfer the second term, of (17) involving w, is a constant $c > 0$. Then $|r_{ij}|$ as a function of $(\frac{y_j}{y_i}) \leq 1$ behaves as drawn in the following figure.

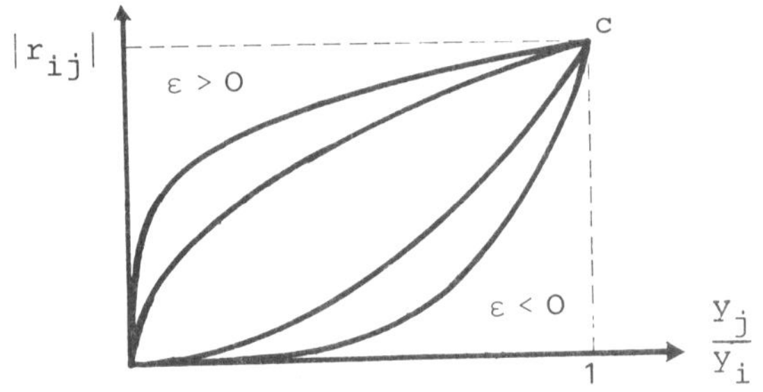

We see that for $0 < \varepsilon < 1$ the transfer rate is sensitive to whether income levels are very different, in the case $\varepsilon < 0$ it tends to be sensitive to whether income level are different at all[1]. In the extreme we have for $\varepsilon = 1$ a transfer rate totally independent of income levels and for $\varepsilon \to -\infty$ the transfer rate is zero if only

---

1) $\varepsilon = 0$, the log-case, corresponds to the transfer rate being linear in y_j/y_i.

the income levels are slightly different. But that says nothing else than that the increase in income at level j necessary to keep A constant, if we decrease income level i, is zero as long as only $y_j \leq y_i$. Hence what is important in the case $\varepsilon \to -\infty$ is the ordinal ranking of income levels[1] and not the cardinal difference[2].

Thus we can think of ε as the degree of cardinality (or ordinality, if you prefer) of our index. Another interpretation of $1-\varepsilon$ as the degree of inequality aversion which is given by ATKINSON himself is justified by the fact that $A(F_Y) = 1 - \bar{A}(F_Y)$ is a strictly increasing function of $(1-\varepsilon)$, $(1-\varepsilon) \in (0,1)$ (see HARDY, LITTLEWOOD, PÓLYA [1967, Th. 23]).

---

1) In fact, it has been shown recently (see HAMMOND [1975]) that a ranking of income vectors $y = (y_1, \ldots, y_N)$ according to an index of the form

$$W(y) = \sum_{j=1}^{N} \frac{1}{1-\varepsilon} y_j^{\,1-\varepsilon}$$

tends for $\varepsilon \to \infty$ to imply a lexicographic ranking of y. Note that (10a,b) is in the language of production theory nothing but a CES-production function. Hence, if we call $\sigma = \frac{1}{\varepsilon}$ the elasticity of substitution between income levels, we see that the RAWLS-SEN case of a lexicographic ranking with $\varepsilon \to \infty$ corresponds to a LEONTIEF production function with $\sigma \to 0$.

2) A very similar phenomenon occurred in III, see (5) (6) where we expressed the relative range as a limit of l_α means for $\alpha \to \infty$. In fact the l_α means are the mechanistic analogue of ATKINSON's statistical index.

V AN AXIOMATIC APPROACH

It was an outcome of the last section (see IV.10) that ATKINSON's measure can be written as a quasilinear mean of the form

$$\bar{A}(Y) = \frac{1}{\mu_Y} u^{-1} \{ \sum_{i=1}^{n} u(y_i) \cdot f_Y(y_i) \} \tag{1a}$$

with

$$u(y_i) = \begin{cases} y_i^{\varepsilon} & \varepsilon \neq 0 \\ \text{or} & \\ \log y_i & \end{cases} \tag{1b}$$

When he discusses ATKINSON's index SEN [1973, p. 70] suggests that (1a) with (1b) "is a highly restrictive form". This section will show, however, that ATKINSON's way of forming the index (1a) and ATKINSON's index with the function u(·) given by (1b) are in fact the most general ones which satisfy certain basic requirements.

Let us make some general remarks on methodology first:

The conventional stages of constructing a measure of social welfare (and an inequality measure corresponding to it) can be labelled by:

individual income
↓
index of individual utility
↓
index of social welfare

whereas we prefer to follow the sequence:

individual income
↓
index of societal income
↓
index of income inequality
↓
index of social welfare .

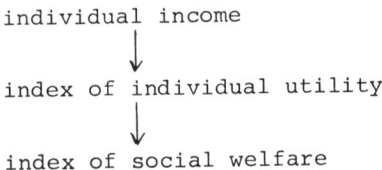

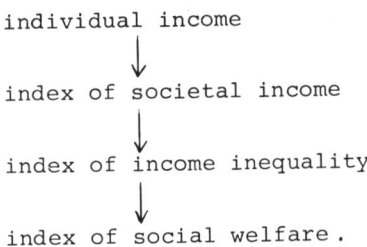

By doing so, we are able eventually to arrive at an index of income inequality without having used the individual-utility-function concept at all[1]. Furthermore, because the concern of this paper is with income alone, and because an index of social welfare should also depend on economic coordinates other than income we stop short of doing the last step of the sequence. So what we are concerned with are indices of societal income and indices of income inequality of the statistical and mechanistic species.

Denote the index of societal income by

$$(2) \qquad s: \begin{cases} D_{[0,\bar{y}]} \to \mathbb{R}_+ \\ F_Y \mapsto s(F_Y) \end{cases}$$

in the statistical case. Here F_Y serves as a representation both of the possible values $0 = y_1, \dots, y_n = \bar{y}$ of the random variable Y as well as the values $F_Y(y)$, $y \in [0,\bar{y}]$ of the distribution function. $D_{[0,\bar{y}]}$ denotes the set of distribution functions on the interval $[0,\bar{y}]$. In the corresponding mechanistic case we write

$$(3) \qquad s: \begin{cases} [0,\bar{y}]^N \to \mathbb{R}_+ \\ x \mapsto s(x). \end{cases}$$

The statistical case will be considered first. We adopt for a statistical index of societal income the following set of postulates.

<u>SP1</u> (identity)

Let $I_\xi : \mathbb{R} \to \mathbb{R}_+$ be defined by[2]

$$I_\xi(y) = \begin{cases} 0 & y < \xi \\ 1 & y \geq \xi \end{cases} \qquad \xi \in \{y_1, \dots, y_n\}$$

---

1) The utility function concept which is very fruitful in connection with existence results for a large <u>class</u> of utility functions becomes rather nasty when it comes down to calculating numbers which depend on the <u>precise form</u> of utility functions.

2) Clearly $I_\xi \in D_{[0,\bar{y}]}$.

then

$$s(I_\xi) = \xi \text{ for all } \xi \in \{y_1,\dots,y_n\}$$

SP2 (homogeneity)

Define the "rescaled" random variable λY, $\lambda > 0$ with income levels $0 = y_o < \lambda y_1 < \dots < \lambda y_n = \lambda \bar{y}$ and with distribution function $F_{\lambda Y}$ given by $F_{\lambda Y}(y) = F_Y(\frac{y}{\lambda})$; $y,\lambda > 0$ and $F_{\lambda Y}(0) = F_Y(0)$, then

$$s(F_{\lambda Y}) = \lambda \cdot s(F_Y) \text{ for all } \lambda > 0.$$

SP3 (sensitivity)

If for $F_Y, G_Y \in D_{[0,\bar{y}]}$

$$F_Y(y) \geq G_Y(y) \text{ for all } y,$$

$$F_Y(y) > G_Y(y) \text{ for some } y,$$

then

$$s(F_Y) < s(G_Y).$$

SP4 (unbiasedness)

If for $\overset{\nu}{F}_Y$, $\overset{\nu}{G}_Y$, $\nu = 1,\dots,k$

$$s(\overset{\nu}{F}_Y) = s(\overset{\nu}{G}_Y)$$

then

$$s(\sum_{\nu=1}^{k} \lambda_\nu \overset{\nu}{F}_Y) = s(\sum_{\nu=1}^{k} \lambda_\nu \overset{\nu}{G}_Y),$$

for all $\lambda_\nu \geq 0$, $\sum \lambda_\nu = 1$.

The meaning of the postulates can be phrased as follows:

SP1 If everybody obtains, with probability 1, an identical income x then the societal income should come out to be x too.

SP2 If the scale of measurement of income is multiplied by $\frac{1}{\lambda} > 0$

then the numerical value of all incomes is multiplied by λ and following SP2, so is the index of societal income[1]. Also, SP2 implies that the units of societal income and individual income can be taken to be the same. Note that somebody who accepts LORENZ-curves would also accept SP2, because LORENZ-curves do have exactly this homogeneity property.

SP3 If the probability of lower incomes is higher then the index of societal income should be lower.

SP4 If two vectors (F_Y^ν), (G_Y^ν) of distribution functions happen to coincide pairwise $\nu = 1,\ldots,k$ in their s-values then any (but the same for both vectors) convex combination of the vectors' elements should produce the same societal income.

As an illustration for SP4 take the case of two countries with social classes $1,\ldots,k$ such that the indices s^ν of income within classes are identical across countries. Assume further that the distribution function of the countries as a whole, say F_Y and G_Y, are obtained by the same convex combination of class specific distributions. In this case SP4 requires that the indices of the countries should be the same. This seems a reasonable postulate to make, because in the case constructed it is hard to think of a relevant distinction between the two countries that would justify a difference in societal income.

(4) THEOREM Any statistical index of societal income (2) satisfying postulates SP1, SP2, SP3, and SP4 can be written as

$$s(F_Y) = \mu_Y \cdot \{\sum_{i=1}^{n} (\frac{y_i}{\mu_Y})^\varepsilon f_Y(y_i)\}^{\frac{1}{\varepsilon}}, \quad \varepsilon > 0, \tag{5}$$

conversely, such an index satisfies postulates SP1 to SP4.

---

1) As opposed to that we shall, in connection with mechanistic indices in postulate MP2, talk about multiplication of incomes by $\lambda \leq 1$ but with the scale of income measurement being kept fixed.

The PROOF is given in the appendix. In fact the theorem is anything but new - it is a reinterpretation of a theorem presented in HARDY, LITTLEWOOD, PÓLYA [1967].
It is natural to interpret the term in parentheses in (5)

(6) $$\bar{A}(F_Y) := \{ \sum_{i=1}^{n} (\frac{y_i}{\mu_Y})^{\varepsilon} f_Y(y_i) \}^{\frac{1}{\varepsilon}} \; ; \; \bar{A}(F_Y) \in [0,1]$$

as a discounting factor applied to mean income[1], and

(7) $$A(F_Y) := 1 - \bar{A}(F_Y)$$

is "the proportion of total income that is absorbed in compensating for the loss of aggregate satisfaction due to inequality", (CHAMPERNOWNE [1952, p. 610]).

We can then think of the index of societal income

(8) $$s(F_Y) = \mu_Y \cdot \bar{A}(F_Y)$$

as the product of two components

a) μ_Y the index of total income,
b) $\bar{A}(F_Y)$ the pure distributional index,

where $\bar{A}(F_Y)$, defined in (9), is the index of income equality implied by and consistent with SP1 to SP4.
The economic significance of the THEOREM lies in the fact that the index formula ATKINSON chose is the only one consistent with postulates SP1 to SP4.
Note that ATKINSON's log-case is not eligible under SP1 to SP4 because $u(y) = \log(y)$ is not continuous for $y = 0$ and thus the

---

1) Note that μ_Y and $A(F_Y)$ are orthogonal to each other in the sense that μ_Y is insensitive to redistributions of a given total income and $A(F_Y)$ is insensitive to variations in total income if the same distribution is maintained.

corresponding index fails to satisfy the sensitivity postulate SP3 for arbitrary F_Y.
Let us now turn to the mechanistic case and see what the postulates SP1 to SP4 translate into, that is which set of postulates corresponds to the indices of the form (5). It should be clear that we cannot expect to carry over the postulates of the statistical case entirely as they stand, simply because SP3, and SP4 in particular, involve statements on distribution functions which have no direct counterpart in the mechanistic case.
We propose the following set of postulates.

MPO (continuity)

$$s^N: [0,\bar{y}]^N \to \mathbb{R}, \; s^N \text{ is continuous.}$$

MP1 (identity)

$$s^N(\xi,\xi,\ldots,\xi) = \xi \text{ for all } \xi \in [0,\bar{y}].$$

MP2 (homogeneity)[1]

$$s^N(\lambda x) = \lambda s^N(x) \quad 0 < x_i \leq \bar{y}, \; \lambda \in (0,1].$$

MP3 (sensitivity)

$$\text{If } x \geqq y, \; x \neq y \Longrightarrow s^N(x) > s^N(y).$$

MP4 (unbiasedness)

a) (symmetry) Let π be a permutation[2] then $s^N(\pi x) = s^N(x)$ for all π.
b) (aggregation) Define $s^k := s^k(x_1,\ldots,x_k)$, $k = 1,2,\ldots$ then $s^N(x_1,\ldots,x_N) = s^N(s^k,s^k,\ldots,s^k, x_{k+1},\ldots,x_N)$, for all $k \leq N$.

---

1) Note that $\lambda \leq 1$ i.e. $\lambda x_i \leq \bar{y}$. Here, as opposed to SP2, the scale of income measurement and $\bar{y}$ are being kept fixed but incomes vary.
2) By a permutation we understand a reordering of the numbers $1,\ldots,N$ and define $\pi x = (x_{\pi(1)},\ldots,x_{\pi(N)})$.

MP1 and MP2 are direct analogues of SP1 and SP2. MP3, the sensitivity postulate, together with MP1 obviously implies "internality" of the index value:

$$\min_i (x_i) \leq s^N(x) \leq \max_i (x_i)$$

A strictly formal analogue of SP4 would be too strong a requirement[1] for the mechanistic index and would in fact exclude every index but the mean income (or total income). Instead the unbiasedness postulate is split into two parts, the symmetry and the aggregation postulate. The former represents a bare ethical minimum. The latter is more disputable. It says that we can, out of a society of N people, replace the incomes of any subgroup of $k \leq N$ people[2] by the societal income of that subgroup without changing the index s for society as a whole. This is a reasonable postulate because indeed the index of societal income is meant to be the representative income a society or group extracts from the individual incomes of its members. Hence allocating just this representative income to its members should not change the overall index.

(13) THEOREM Any mechanistic index of societal income (3) satisfying postulates MPO, MP1, MP2, MP3, and MP4 can be written as

(14) $$s^N(x) = \frac{\sum x_i}{N}\left\{\sum \frac{1}{N}\left[\frac{Nx_i}{\sum x_i}\right]^{\varepsilon}\right\}^{\frac{1}{\varepsilon}}, \quad 0 \leq x_i \leq \bar{y}, \ \varepsilon > 0 .$$

Conversely, such an index satisfies MPO to MP4.

---

1) for example the formulation

(∗) $\quad s(x^{\nu}) = s(y^{\nu}) \Rightarrow s(\sum\lambda^{\nu}x^{\nu}) = s(\sum\lambda^{\nu}y^{\nu})$

leads to a trivial case. Let $y_i^1 = x_i^1$ and $y_i^2 = x_{N-1}^1$, $x_i^2 = x_i^1$ then using the undisputable symmetry postulate we have $s(y^2) = s(x^2)$ and with (∗) $s(\frac{1}{2}y^1 + \frac{1}{2}y^2) = s(x^1)$. But clearly all elements of $\frac{1}{2}y^1 + \frac{1}{2}y^2$ are identical and because x^1 is arbitrary s under postulate (∗) would be totally insensitive to redistributions of income.

2) Note that for k = N we have the identity axiom MP1.

PROOF (see Appendix, p. 33)

It is easy to see (choose $N = 1$) that there is no index satisfying <u>MP0</u>, <u>MP1</u>, <u>MP3</u>, <u>MP4</u> which is homogeneous in x of degree $c \neq 1$. There is, however, an alternative form of the aggregation postulate that leads to the same family of indices (14). Consider now N nations of N people each[1] and suppose we are interested in the societal income of this family of nations as a whole. A natural way to calculate the supra-national index is by using the values of the national indices as if they were individual incomes and then to use the same index formula as on the national level.

Then, we postulate, the supra-national index should be invariant to the exchange of nationalities between any two individuals. More precisely, we have now the following alternative form of the unbiasedness requirement <u>MP4*</u>

a) (symmetry) as in <u>MP4</u>
b) (aggregation) Let x_i^l, $l = 1,\dots,N$; $i = 1,\dots,N$, be the i-th income in the l-th group, then

$$s^N(s^N(x_1^1,\dots,x_N^1),\dots,s^N(x_1^l,\dots,x_i^l,\dots,x_N^l),\dots,s^N(x_1^m,\dots,x_j^m,\dots,x_N^m),\dots,s^N(x_1^N,\dots,x_N^N))$$

$$= s^N(s^N(x_1^1,\dots,x_N^1),\dots,s^N(x_1^l,\dots,x_j^m,\dots,x_N^l),\dots,s^N(x_1^m,\dots,x_i^l,\dots,x_N^m),\dots,s^N(x_1^N,\dots,x_N^N))$$

(15) <u>THEOREM</u> Any mechanistic index of societal income satisfying postulates <u>MP0</u>, <u>MP1</u>, <u>MP2</u>, <u>MP3</u>, and <u>MP4*</u> can be written in the form (14).
Conversely such an index satisfies <u>MP0</u>, <u>MP1</u>, <u>MP2</u>, <u>MP3</u>, and <u>MP4*</u>.

PROOF (see Appendix, p. 33).

Again, in the mechanistic case, defining $\mu(x) = \frac{\sum x_i}{N}$ we can think of the index of societal income

(16) $$s(x) = \mu(x) \cdot \bar{A}(x)$$

---

1) Some nations could be replications of others, of course.

as the product of two components

a) the index of mean income $\mu(x)$,

b) the pure distributional index $\bar{A}(x)$,

where ATKINSON's index $\bar{A}(x)$ is the index consistent with postulates MP0 to MP4 (resp. MP4*). If we write

$$\bar{A}(x) = \frac{s(x)}{\mu(x)}$$

we obtain a form analogous to (IV.5) (with y^e replaced by $s(x)$) and to (IV.2) (with $W(x)$ replaced by $s(x)$); note that $s(\mu,\mu,\ldots,\mu) = \mu$). But now the index does not depend on an arbitrary Social Welfare Function but our judgements are precisely quantified by postulates MP0 to MP4 and our choice of the parameter ε (see section IV.17).

Still, one could feel uneasy about the seemingly arbitrary way the index of societal income is being split up into two multiplicative components, which are then called index of mean income and pure distributional index. To motivate why this makes sense, let us look at the issue the other way round. Assume we were to construct an index of societal income

$$s: \begin{cases} (0,\bar{y}] \times (0,1] \to \mathbb{R}_{++} \\ (\mu,d) \mapsto s(\mu,d) \end{cases} \tag{17}$$

where μ is an index of mean income and d is a pure distributional index[1], not necessarily identical to $\bar{A}$. If we agree that the sensitivity of s to variations of equality should depend on mean income alone (and of course the degree of variation itself (→ (19)) and furthermore that a multiplication of mean income by $\lambda \leqslant 1$ (keeping the distributional index the same) should multiply societal income by λ too (→ (20)), then the following THEOREM shows that the multiplicative form is the only admissible one.

1) with $d = 1$ corresponding to total equality and with inequality increasing with decreasing d.

(18) THEOREM Let the index s given by (17) with $s(\mu,1) = \mu$ be continuous and strictly increasing in the second argument and satisfy

(19) $$s(\mu,\lambda d) = f(\lambda,\mu)\cdot s(\mu,d) \qquad \mu \in (0,\bar{y}];\ \lambda,d \in (0,1]$$

and

(20) $$s(\lambda\mu,d) = \lambda\cdot s(\mu,d) \qquad \mu \in (0,\bar{y}];\ \lambda,d \in (0,1]$$

with f being an arbitrary function[1], then s is necessarily of the form

$$s(\mu,d) = \mu\cdot d^{\varepsilon} \qquad \varepsilon > 0 \text{ const.};\ \mu \in (0,\bar{y}],\ d \in (0,1].$$

PROOF (see Appendix, p. 43)

Obviously for $\varepsilon = 1$, $\mu = \mu_y$ and $d = \bar{A}$ one obtains (8). For $d = 1 - g$, g being the GINI-index and $\mu = \sum x_i$, $\varepsilon = 1$ we obtain the functional form proposed by SHESHINSKI [1972] as another special case. ROSS [1974] postulates "three basic requirements" for a "welfare measure"[2] (here: index of societal income) which in our terminology read as follows:

(1) Given that two distributions have the same mean , the one with the higher pure distributional index is "better".
(2) Given that two distributions have the same distributional index, then the one with the higher mean income is "better".
(3) If one income vector x is PARETO-superior to another income vector y, i.e. $x \geqq y$, $x \neq y$, then x is "better" than y.

If we interpret "better" as "corresponding to a higher index of societal income" then clearly our class of indices satisfies ROSS' basic requirements (1) and (2), as in THEOREM (18) we have $f(\lambda,\mu)$ strictly increasing in λ. Whether requirement (3) is satisfied cannot be decided at this level of generality, i.e. without specifying the indices $\mu(x)$ and $d(x)$. The index given by (14) obviously does satisfy requirement (3).

1) Note that continuity of s implies continuity of f.

2) but he does not ask for the whole class of "welfare measures" that satisfy his requirement.

VI APPENDIX

PROOF OF THEOREM V.5

HARDY, LITTLEWOOD, PÓLYA [1967, Th. 215] prove that an index (V.2) under postulates SP1, SP3, SP4 is of the form

$$(1) \qquad s(F_Y) = \phi^{-1}\{\sum_{i=0}^{n} q_i \phi(y_i)\}$$

with ϕ being a monotonic and continuous function on $[0,\bar{y}]$, where $0 = y_o < y_1 < \dots < y_n = \bar{y}$ and

$$q_o = F_Y(0)$$

$$(2) \qquad q_i = F_Y(y_i) - F_Y(y_{i-1}) \quad \text{for } i = 1,\dots,n.$$

With

$$u(y) = \phi(y) - \phi(0)$$

and using TH. 83 b of HARDY, LITTLEWOOD, PÓLYA [1967] we can write the index (1) as

$$(3) \qquad s(F_Y) = u^{-1}\{\sum_{i=0}^{n} q_i u(y_i)\}.$$

and as $u(0) = 0$ this implies the form

$$(4) \qquad s(F_Y) = u^{-1}\{\sum_{i=1}^{n} q_i u(y_i)\}$$

and u being any monotonic and continuous function on $[0,\bar{y}]$ with $u(0) = 0$.

Hence $s(F_Y)$ is totally independent of the income level $y_o = 0$. Moreover, by the definition of $F_{\lambda Y}$, $\lambda > 0$ given in SP2 we have

$$(5) \qquad u^{-1}\{\sum_{i=1}^{n} q_i u(\lambda y_i)\} = \lambda u^{-1}\{\sum_{i=1}^{n} q_i u(y_i)\}, \ \lambda > 0$$

for strictly positive q_i and y_i.

Again, it has been shown by HARDY, LITTLEWOOD, POLYA [1967, Th. 84 a] that (5) implies either $s(F_Y)$ is of the form

(6) $$s(F_Y) = \{\sum_{i=1}^{n} q_i y_i^{\varepsilon}\}^{\frac{1}{\varepsilon}} \qquad \varepsilon \neq 0$$

or of the form

(7) $$s(F_Y) = \exp\{\sum_{i=1}^{n} q_i \log(y_i)\}.$$

But obviously the log-case (7) violates our supposition that $u(0) = 0$.

Hence we are left with the form (6) which can also be written

$$s(F_Y) = \mu_Y\{\int_0^{\bar{y}} (\frac{y}{\mu_Y})^{\varepsilon} dF_Y(y)\}^{\frac{1}{\varepsilon}}, \qquad \varepsilon \neq 0.$$

Finally, by the condition $u(0) = 0$ ε has to be nonnegative, hence $\varepsilon > 0$. q.e.d.

PROOF OF THEOREM V.13 and THEOREM V.15

NAGUMO [1930, p. 71] proves that under postulates MP0, MP1, MP3 and MP4, and ACZÉL [1948, p. 394] proves that under postulates MP0, MP1, MP3 and MP4* s^N is necessarily of the form

(1) $$s^N(x) = u^{-1}\{\sum_{i=1}^{N} \frac{u(x_i)}{N}\} \qquad 0 \leq x_i \leq \bar{y}$$

where u is a strictly monotonic, continuous function on the interval $[0,\bar{y}]$.

Now we restrict further the class of eligible functions by MP2

(2) $$s^N(\lambda x) = \lambda s^N(x), \quad x_i \in (0,\bar{y}], \quad \lambda \in (0,1].$$

We remark that it would suffice to require homogeneity of the general type

$$s^N(\lambda x) = g(\lambda)\cdot s^N(x) \quad x_i \in (0,\bar{y}], \quad \lambda \in (0,1]$$

and linear homogeneity would follow immediately with MP1.
The proof is carried for u being strictly increasing; the proof for strictly decreasing u runs analogously.

First, we have from (2) and (1)

(3) $$u^{-1}\{\frac{1}{N}\sum_{i=1}^{N} u(\lambda x_i)\} = \lambda u^{-1}\{\frac{1}{N}\sum_{i=1}^{N} u(x_i)\}$$

which implies, because u is strictly monotonic

(4) $$\frac{1}{N}\sum_{i=1}^{N} u(\lambda x_i) = u[\lambda u^{-1}\{\frac{1}{N}\sum_{i=1}^{N} u(x_i)\}]$$

and with

(5) $$g(z) := \frac{1}{N}u(z), \quad z \in (0,\bar{y}]$$

this can be written

(6) $$\sum_{i=1}^{N} g(\lambda x_i) = u[\lambda\cdot u^{-1}\{\sum_{i=1}^{N} g(x_i)\}], \quad x_i \in (0,\bar{y}], \quad \lambda \in (0,1].$$

Write now

(7) $$\begin{cases} \eta_i := g(x_i) \Longleftrightarrow x_i = g^{-1}(\eta_i) \\ g_\lambda^{-1}(\eta_i) := \lambda g^{-1}(\eta_i) = \lambda x_i \\ u_\lambda(y) := u(\lambda y) \end{cases}$$

for $\eta_i \in (\alpha,\beta]$ [1] $\subset \mathbb{R}$, then (6) becomes

1) It is possible, that $\alpha = -\infty$.

(8) $$\sum_{i=1}^{N} g[g_\lambda^{-1}(\eta_i)] = u_\lambda[u^{-1}(\sum_{i=1}^{N}\eta_i)] .$$

Moreover, using the notation

(9) $$\begin{cases} e_\lambda(\eta_i) := g[g_\lambda^{-1}(\eta_i)] \\ d_\lambda(y) := u_\lambda[u^{-1}(y)] \end{cases}$$

we obtain from (8) the form

(10) $$\sum_{i=1}^{N} e_\lambda(\eta_i) = d_\lambda[\sum_{i=1}^{N}\eta_i] \quad \eta_i \in (\alpha,\beta].$$

Define

$$\mathbf{W} := \bigtimes_{i=1}^{N} (\alpha,\beta] \subset \mathbb{R}^N$$

and take an arbitrary inner point

$$(w^o,\dots,w^o) \in W .$$

Then any point $(\eta_1,\dots,\eta_N) \in \mathbf{W}$ can be expressed uniquely in the form

(11) $$(\eta_1,\dots,\eta_N) = (w^o+W_1, w^o+W_2,\dots,w^o+W_N)$$

where $W_i \in (\alpha',\beta']$ with $0 \in (\alpha',\beta']$.

Hence, using (11) we can write (10) as

(12) $$\sum_{i=1}^{N} e_\lambda(w^o+W_i) = d_\lambda[\sum_{i=1}^{N} w^o + \sum_{i=1}^{N} W_i].$$

Put now successively $W_k = 0$, $(k = 1,\dots,i-1,i+1,\dots,N)$ to obtain

(13) $$e_\lambda(w^o+W_i) = d_\lambda[\sum_{i=1}^{N} w^o+W_i] - \underbrace{\sum_{\substack{j\neq i\\ j=1}}^{N} \alpha}_{=(N-1)\alpha}$$

with $\alpha := e_\lambda(w^o)$.

Inserting (13) into (12) we find

$$(14)\quad d_\lambda\left[\sum_{i=1}^{N} w^o + \sum_{i=1}^{N} W_i\right] = d_\lambda\left[\sum_{i=1}^{N} w^o + W_1\right] + \ldots + d_\lambda\left[\sum_{i=1}^{N} w^o + W_N\right] - (N-1)\sum_{i=1}^{N} \alpha .$$

Define now

$$(15)\qquad D_\lambda(y) := d_\lambda\left[\sum_{i=1}^{N} w^o + y\right] - N\alpha, \quad y \in N\cdot(\alpha',\beta'],$$

then (14) becomes

$$(16)\qquad D_\lambda\left(\sum_{i=1}^{N} W_i\right) = \sum_{i=1}^{N} D_\lambda(W_i), \quad W_i \in (\alpha',\beta'].$$

It is well known (see ACZÉL [1966, p. 48]) that all continuous solutions of (16) are given by

$$(17)\qquad D_\lambda(y) = c(\lambda)\cdot y \qquad y \in N\cdot(\alpha',\beta'] .$$

Consequently with (17) we have from (13) and (15)

$$
\begin{aligned}
(18)\qquad e_\lambda(\eta_i) = e_\lambda(w^o + W_i) = D_\lambda(W_i) + \alpha &= c(\lambda)\cdot W_i + \alpha \\
&= c(\lambda)\left[\eta_i - w^o\right] + \alpha \\
&= c(\lambda)\eta_i + b(\lambda)
\end{aligned}
$$

where $b(\lambda) := \alpha - c(\lambda)w^o$.
hence it follows from (9) and (7) that

$$e_\lambda(\eta_i) = g\left[g_\lambda^{-1}(\eta_i)\right] = g(\lambda x_i) = c(\lambda)\cdot g(x_i) + b(\lambda)$$

i.e. we have solved our problem if we have found the general solution of the functional equation

$$(19)\qquad g(\lambda s) = c(\lambda)\cdot g(s) + b(\lambda) \qquad \lambda \in (0,1], \quad s \in (0,\bar{y}] .$$

We show now that all continuous and strictly increasing solutions of (19) are either

$$(20) \qquad g(s) = \gamma \cdot \log s + \delta, \; c(\lambda) \equiv 1, \; b(\lambda) = \gamma \log \lambda$$

$$\gamma > 0, \quad \delta \text{ const.}, \; s \in (0,\bar{y}], \; \lambda \in (0,1]$$

or

$$(21) \qquad g(s) = \varepsilon s^{\alpha} + \rho, \; c(\lambda) = \lambda^{\alpha}, \; b(\lambda) = \rho(1-\lambda^{\alpha})$$

$$\varepsilon \neq 0 \neq \alpha, \; \rho \quad \text{const.}, \; s \in (0,\dot{y}], \; \lambda \in (0,1]$$

$$\text{sign } \alpha = \text{sign } \varepsilon .$$

To see this put first $s = \bar{y}$ to obtain from (19)

$$(22) \qquad g(\lambda\bar{y}) = c(\lambda) \cdot g(\bar{y}) + b(\lambda)$$

and upon subtraction of (22) from (19)

$$(23) \qquad g(\lambda s) - g(\lambda\bar{y}) = c(\lambda)[g(s) - g(\bar{y})].$$

With

$$(24) \qquad G(t) := g(t) - g(\bar{y})$$

this implies

$$(25) \qquad G(\lambda s) = c(\lambda) \cdot G(s) + G(\lambda\bar{y}), \quad \lambda \in (0,1], \quad s \in (0,\bar{y}].$$

Note that G is continuous and strictly increasing.

Write now

$$(26) \qquad y = \frac{1}{\bar{y}} s, \quad s \in (0,\bar{y}], \text{ hence } y \in (0,1],$$

then with (26) we can rewrite (25) as

$$(27) \qquad G(\lambda\bar{y}y) = c(\lambda) \cdot G(\bar{y}y) + G(\bar{y}\lambda); \; \lambda, y \in (0,1],$$

and using the notation

(28) $$G_{\bar{y}}(s) := G(\bar{y}\cdot s) \qquad s \in (0,1]$$

(27) becomes

(29) $$G_{\bar{y}}(\lambda y) = c(\lambda)G_{\bar{y}}(y) + G_{\bar{y}}(\lambda) \qquad \lambda, y \in (0,1].$$

Now we have to distinguish two cases.

Case A $c(\lambda) \equiv 1$

By (29) we have

$$G_{\bar{y}}(\lambda y) = G_{\bar{y}}(y) + G_{\bar{y}}(\lambda) \qquad \lambda, y \in (0,1]$$

and by putting

$$\lambda := e^u \quad y := e^v, \quad u,v \in (-\infty,0]$$

$$\bar{G}_{\bar{y}}(z) := G_{\bar{y}}(e^z) \qquad z \in (-\infty,0]$$

this can be written as

(30) $$\bar{G}_{\bar{y}}(u+v) = \bar{G}_{\bar{y}}(u) + \bar{G}_{\bar{y}}(v), \qquad u,v \in (-\infty,0].$$

All continuous solutions of the functional equation (30) are given by (see ACZÉL [1966, p. 34]) [1)]

(31) $$\bar{G}_{\bar{y}}(z) = \gamma_{\bar{y}}\cdot z \quad \text{with } \gamma_{\bar{y}} > 0, \ z \in (-\infty,0].$$

Hence, working backwards we obtain for $G_{\bar{y}}$

$$G_{\bar{y}}(e^z) = \gamma_{\bar{y}}\cdot z \qquad z \in (-\infty,0]$$

or

[1)] Note that $\bar{G}_{\bar{y}}$ is strictly increasing.

(32) $$G_{\bar{y}}(w) = \gamma_{\bar{y}} \cdot \log w \qquad w \varepsilon (0,1]$$

and the form of G then follows with (28) as

(33) $$G(s) = \gamma_{\bar{y}}(\log s - \log \bar{y}) \qquad s \varepsilon (0,\bar{y}]$$

and finally, using (24)

$$g(s) = G(s) + g(\bar{y}) = \gamma_{\bar{y}} \log s - \gamma_{\bar{y}} \log \bar{y} + g(\bar{y})$$

$$= \gamma_{\bar{y}} \log s + \delta_{\bar{y}}, \qquad \delta_{\bar{y}} := g(\bar{y}) - \gamma_{\bar{y}} \cdot \log \bar{y}$$

and

$$b(\lambda) = g(\lambda s) - g(s) = \gamma_{\bar{y}} \log \lambda .$$

Moreover we see now that any functions g, c, b of the form (20) with arbitrary constants γ, δ solve the functional equation (19) Hence the index "$\bar{y}$" is negligible, and we are finished with case A.

Case B: There exists $\bar{\lambda} \varepsilon (0,1]$ with $c(\bar{\lambda}) \neq 1$.

On interchanging variables in (29) one obtains

(34) $$G_{\bar{y}}(\lambda y) = c(y) \cdot G_{\bar{y}}(\lambda) + G_{\bar{y}}(y); \qquad \lambda, y \varepsilon (0,1]$$

which implies, using (29) again,

(35) $$G_{\bar{y}}(y)\left[c(\lambda) - 1\right] = G_{\bar{y}}(\lambda)\left[c(y) - 1\right] .$$

With $\lambda = \lambda_o \varepsilon (0,1)$ and

$$g_{\bar{y}} := \frac{G_{\bar{y}}(\lambda_o)}{c(\lambda_o) - 1}$$

it follows from (35) that

(36) $$G_{\bar{y}}(y) = g_{\bar{y}} \cdot (c(y) - 1) \qquad y \in (0,1] .$$

Note that $g_{\bar{y}} \neq 0$, because otherwise $G_{\bar{y}}(y) = 0$ for all $y \in (0,1]$ which contradicts the strict monotonicity of $G_{\bar{y}}$.
Now, on the one hand, we have from (34) and (36)

(37) $$G_{\bar{y}}(\lambda y) = c(\lambda) \cdot g_{\bar{y}} \cdot [c(y) - 1] + g_{\bar{y}} \cdot [c(\lambda) - 1]$$
$$= g_{\bar{y}} \cdot c(\lambda) \cdot c(y) - g_{\bar{y}} \text{ for all } \lambda, y \in (0,1]$$

and, on the other hand, from (36)

(38) $$G_{\bar{y}}(\lambda y) = g_{\bar{y}} \cdot c(\lambda y) - g_{\bar{y}} \qquad \lambda, y \in (0,1] .$$

and, immediately, from (37) and (38) the functional equation of the CAUCHY-type

(39) $$c(\lambda y) = c(\lambda) \cdot c(y) \qquad \lambda, y \in (0,1]$$

follows.

As $G_{\bar{y}}$ is strictly monotonic also c is strictly monotonic.
That shows that the trivial solutions of (39)

$$c(z) \equiv 1 \text{ and } c(z) \equiv 0$$

are inadmissable.

Put now

$$\lambda = y = \sqrt{s}, \qquad (\sqrt{s} \in (0,1])$$

to write (39) as

(40) $$c(s) = [c(\sqrt{s})]^2,$$

which shows that all nontrivial solutions of (39) are positive valued.

This permits us to write

(41) $$\log c(\lambda y) = \log c(\lambda) + \log c(y)\,; \quad \lambda, y \in (0,1].$$

We define new variables u and v by

$$u := \log \lambda\,; \quad v := \log y\,; \quad u, v \in (-\infty, 0].$$

With

$$d(z) := \log c(e^z)$$

(41) then becomes

(42) $$d(u+v) = d(u) + d(v)\,; \quad u, v \in (-\infty, 0].$$

The (continuous and strictly monotonic) solution of (42) is

$$d(w) = \alpha w \qquad \alpha \neq 0, \quad w \in (-\infty, 0],$$

hence

(43) $$c(\lambda) = \lambda^{\alpha} \qquad \lambda \in (0,1].$$

Thus we have from (36)

(44) $$G_{\bar{y}}(y) = g_{\bar{y}} \cdot (y^{\alpha} - 1), \qquad y \in (0,1]$$

which, together with (28) implies

(45) $$G(s) = g_{\bar{y}} \cdot \left(\left(\frac{s}{\bar{y}}\right)^{\alpha} - 1 \right) \qquad s \in (0, \bar{y}].$$

By (45) and (24) g has the form

(46) $$g(s) = G(s) + g(\bar{y}) = g_{\bar{y}} \cdot \left[\left(\frac{s}{\bar{y}}\right)^{\alpha} - 1 \right] + g(\bar{y})$$
$$= \varepsilon_{\bar{y}} \cdot s^{\alpha} + \rho_{\bar{y}},$$

with $\varepsilon_{\bar{y}} := g_{\bar{y}} / \bar{y}^{\alpha}$, $\rho_{\bar{y}} := g(\bar{y}) - g_{\bar{y}}$

and, using (19), b is of the form

$$(47)\qquad b(\lambda) = g(\lambda s) - c(\lambda)\cdot g(s) = $$
$$= \varepsilon_{\bar{y}}(\lambda s)^{\alpha} + \rho_{\bar{y}} - \lambda^{\alpha}\cdot[\varepsilon_{\bar{y}}s^{\alpha}+\rho_{\bar{y}}]$$
$$= \rho_{\bar{y}} - \rho_{\bar{y}}\,\lambda^{\alpha} = \rho_{\bar{y}}\cdot[1-\lambda^{\alpha}].$$

Conversely the functions g,c and b given by (21) satisfy (19) and thus we can omit the index "$\bar{y}$". By (20) and (21) we have for u

$$(48)\qquad u(z) = N\cdot[\gamma \log z+\delta] = \mu\cdot\log z+\nu \;;\; \mu:=N\gamma;\nu:=N\delta$$

or

$$(49)\qquad u(z) = N\cdot[\varepsilon z^{\alpha}+\rho] = \xi z^{\alpha}+\zeta \;; \qquad \xi:=N\varepsilon;\zeta:=N\rho \;.$$

From (48) and (49):

$$u^{-1}(y) = e^{\frac{y-\nu}{\mu}} \qquad \text{or} \qquad u^{-1}(y) = ((y-\zeta)/\xi)^{1/\alpha} \text{ resp..}$$

This implies that either (see (1))

$$(50)\qquad s^N(x_1,..,x_N) = u^{-1}\{\sum_{i=1}^{N}\frac{u(x_i)}{N}\} = u^{-1}\{\frac{1}{N}(\sum_{i=1}^{N}(\mu\log x_i+\nu))\}$$

$$= \prod_{i=1}^{N} x_i^{\frac{1}{N}}$$

or

$$s^N(x_1,..,x_N) = u^{-1}\{\sum_{i=1}^{N}\frac{u(x_i)}{N}\} = u^{-1}\{\frac{1}{N}(\sum_{i=1}^{N}(\xi x_i^{\alpha}+\zeta))\}$$

$$= \left[\frac{1}{N}(x_1^{\alpha}+\cdots+x_N^{\alpha})\right]^{\frac{1}{\alpha}} .$$

Moreover the form (50) is not admissable by postulate MP3, because

$$\lim_{x_i \to 0} s^N(x_1,\dots,x_N) = 0 \qquad x_j > 0,\ i \neq j$$

which contradicts the sensitivity postulate requiring strict monotonicity of s^N on the closed interval $[0,\bar{y}]$.

By the same reasoning α is to be restricted to be nonnegative, hence α has to be strictly positive. q.e.d.

PROOF OF THEOREM V.18

In (V.19)

(1) $$s(\mu,\lambda d) = f(\lambda,\mu)\cdot s(\mu,d), \qquad \lambda,d \in (0,1],\ \mu \in (0,\bar{y}]$$

put d = 1 to obtain

(1') $$f(\lambda,\mu) = \frac{s(\mu,\lambda)}{s(\mu,1)} = \frac{1}{\mu}s(\mu,\lambda).$$

Inserting this into (1) we have

(2) $$s(\mu,\lambda d) = \frac{1}{\mu}s(\mu,\lambda)\cdot s(\mu,d).$$

Define

(3) $$F(\mu,x) := \frac{1}{\mu}s(\mu,x) \qquad x \in (0,1],\ \mu \in (0,\bar{y}],$$

then (2) becomes

(4) $$F(\mu,\lambda d) = F(\mu,\lambda)\cdot F(\mu,d).$$

Moreover if we define

$$F_\mu(y) := F(\mu, y) \qquad y \in (0,1]$$

(4) can be written

(5) $$F_\mu(\lambda d) = F_\mu(\lambda) \cdot F_\mu(d) \qquad \lambda, d \in (0,1].$$

The trivial solutions

$$F_\mu(x) \equiv 0, \quad F_\mu(x) \equiv 1$$

are excluded by the strict monotonicity of F_μ.
With

$$\lambda = d = \sqrt{\sigma} \qquad (\sqrt{\sigma} \in (0,1] \Longleftrightarrow \sigma \in (0,1])$$

and, observing that

(6) $$F_\mu(\sigma) = [F_\mu(\sqrt{\sigma})]^2$$

it is clear that every non-trivial solution of (5) is <u>positive</u>.
Hence, we can write (5) in the form

(5') $$\log(F_\mu(\lambda d)) = \log(F_\mu(\lambda)) + \log(F_\mu(d)); \quad \lambda, d \in (0,1].$$

By substituting

(7) $$\lambda = e^u, \quad d = e^v$$

(observe that $u, v \in (-\infty, 0] =: \mathbb{R}_-$) (5') becomes

(5'') $$\log(F_\mu(e^{u+v})) = \log(F_\mu(e^u)) + \log(F_\mu(e^v)).$$

Define now

(8) $$G_\mu(z) := \log[F_\mu(e^z)], \qquad z \in \mathbb{R}_-$$

to obtain from (5'') the functional equation of the CAUCHY-type

(9) $$G_\mu(u+v) = G_\mu(u) + G_\mu(v)$$

with the solution

(10) $$G_\mu(w) = c \cdot w, \qquad c > 0,\ w \in \mathbb{R}_-$$

To see this replace

$$u := -u', \qquad v := -v', \qquad u', v' \in [0,\infty)$$

then (9) becomes

$$G_\mu[-(u'+v')] = G_\mu(-u') + G_\mu(-v')$$

and with $H_\mu(z) := G_\mu(-z)$, $z \in [0,\infty)$

$$H_\mu(u'+v') = H_\mu(u') + H_\mu(v'); \qquad u', v' \in \mathbb{R}_+,$$

with the solution (see ACZÉL [1966, p. 34])

$$H_\mu(t) = -ct, \qquad c > 0, \quad t \in \mathbb{R}_+$$

which implies (10).
Now we are able to compute F_μ from (10) and (8)

$$\log[F_\mu(e^z)] = cz \qquad c > 0, \quad z \in \mathbb{R}_-$$

and with $z = \ln u$, $u \in (0,1]$

(11) $$F_\mu(u) = u^c, \qquad u \in (0,1], \quad c > 0.$$

For F we find

(12) $$F(\mu,y) = y^{c(\mu)} = e^{c(\mu)\cdot\ln y}, \quad \mu \in (0,\bar{y}]$$

(Note that the "constant" c depends on the parameter μ of course.)

hence, with (12) and (3),

(13) $$s(\mu,y) = \mu\cdot e^{c(\mu)\cdot \ln y} \qquad \mu\varepsilon(0,\bar{y}],\ y\ \varepsilon\ (0,1]$$

and, using (1')

(14) $$f(\lambda,\mu) = e^{c(\mu)\cdot \ln \lambda} \qquad \mu\varepsilon(0,\bar{y}],\ \lambda\ \varepsilon\ (0,1].$$

By (V.20)

$$s(\lambda\mu,d) = \lambda\ s(\mu,d) \qquad \mu\varepsilon(0,\bar{y}],\ \lambda,d\ \varepsilon\ (0,1]$$

we obtain from (13)

(15) $$e^{c(\lambda\mu)\cdot \log d} = e^{c(\mu)\cdot \log d},\quad \mu\varepsilon(0,\bar{y}],\ \lambda,d\ \varepsilon\ (0,1]$$

implying (for d < 1)

$$c(\lambda\mu) = c(\mu)$$

i.e.

$$c(\mu) \equiv \text{const.}$$

hence, with (13) we have finally

$$s(\mu,d) = \mu d^{c} \qquad c > 0.$$

q.e.d.

REFERENCES

J. ACZÉL [1948] On Mean Values
Bull.Am.Math.Soc., 54 (1948), p.392-400.

J. ACZÉL [1966] Lectures on Functional Equations and Their Applications
Academic Press, 1966.

A.B. ATKINSON [1970] On the Measurement of Inequality
Journal of Economic Theory, 2 (1970), p. 244 - 263.

A.B. ATKINSON [1975]: The Economics of Inequality.
Clarendon Press, Oxford, 1975.

M. BONFENBRENNER [1973] Equality and Equity
Annals of the American Academy of Political and Social Science, 409 (1973), p. 9 - 23.

G. BRUCKMANN [1969] Einige Bemerkungen zur statistischen Messung der Konzentration
Metrika 14, 1969 S. 183 - 213

D. CHAMPERNOWNE [1952] The Graduation of Income Distribution

H. DALTON [1920] The Measurement of the Inequality of Incomes
Economic Journal, 30 (1920), p. 348-361.

P. DASGUPTA, A. SEN, D. STARRETT [1973] Notes on the Measurement of Inequality
Journal of Economic Theory, 6 (1973), p. 180 - 187.

P.J. HAMMOND [1975] A Note on Extreme Inequality Aversion
Journal of Economic Theory, 11 (1975), p. 465 - 467.

G.H. HARDY, J.E. LITTLEWOOD, G. POLYA [1967] Inequalities
Cambridge U.P., 1967.

M. NAGUMO [1930] Über eine Klasse der Mittelwerte
Jap. J. Math., 7 (1930), p. 71 - 79.

D. NEWBURY [1970] A Theorem on the Measurement of Inequality
Journal of Economic Theory, 2 (1970), p. 264 - 266.

R. NOZICK [1973] Distributive Justice
Philosophy and Public Affairs, 3 (1973 - 1974), p. 45 - 126.

W. PIESCH [1975] Statistische Konzentrationsmaße
J.C.B. Mohr, Tübingen, 1975.

J.W. PRATT [1964] Risk Aversion in the Small and Large
Econometrica, 32 (1964), 1, p..

G. ROSS [1974] Utilities for Distributive Justice Theory and Decision, 4 (1974), p. 239 - 258.

M. ROTHSCHILD [1973] J.E. STIGLITZ Some Further Results on the Measurement of Inequality Journal of Economic Theory, 6 (1973), p. 188 - 204.

A. SEN [1973] On Economic Inequality, Oxford U.P., 1973

E. SHESHINSKI [1972] Relation Between a Social Welfare Function and the Gini Index of Income Inequality Journal of Economic Theory, 4 (1972), p. 98 - 100.

F. STEHLING [1974]: Eine neue Charakterisierung der CD- und ACMS - Produktionsfunktionen. Discussion Paper Nr. 41, 1974, Institut für Wirtschaftstheorie und Operations Research, Universität Karlsruhe.

H. THEIL [1967] Economics and Information Theory North-Holland, 1967.

H. VARIAN [1975] Distributive Justice, Welfare Economics and the Theory of Fairness Philosophy and Public Affairs, 4 (1975)3, p. 223 - 247.

Separability and Index Properties of Ray-Homothetic Dynamic Production Structures

by Rolf Färe

1. Introduction

A dynamic production function is treated here as a correspondence $x \to P(x)$ of input (vector) histories $x \in BM_+^n$ (1) to subsets of output (vector) histories $u \in BM_+^m$ or inversely $u \to L(u) = \{x \in BM_+^n \mid u \in P(x)\}$, with the mutually related (weak) axioms as stated in [7]. $P(x)$ denotes the set of all output histories obtainable from a vector of input histories $x \in BM_+^n$ and $L(u)$ all input histories yielding at least the output histories u. The steady state model of [5] is obtained by merely considering the subspaces of constant input and output histories.

A variety of special structures for production functions has been introduced in steady state, see [2]. Homothetic and ray-homothetic are important cases of such input (output) structures which imply and under quasi-concavity of the input (output) correspondence and free disposability of inputs are implied by (different) separability properties of the cost (return) function [2]. Such separabilities are of great importance for index number theory, see [3].

(1) $BM_+^\alpha = \{f \in BM^\alpha \mid f(t) \geqq 0, t \in [0, +\infty)\}$, $\alpha = m,n$, where $BM^\alpha = \{f = (f_1, f_2, \ldots, f_\alpha) \mid f_i\colon [0, +\infty) \to R$, f_i is bounded and Lebesgue measurable with $\|f_i\| = \sup\{|f_i(t)| \mid t \in [0, +\infty)\}$ and the Euclidian product norm$\}$. BM^α is a Banach space, i.e. complete normed linear, [7].

In this paper, the results on separabilities of cost and return functions for homothetic and ray-homothetic steady state production structures are generalized into the dynamic framework of [7]. For this reason, dualities between the cost functional and the dynamic input correspondence, the return functional and the dynamic output correspondence are first proved. These are then used to show the separabilities of the cost (return) functional related to the homothetic and ray-homothetic dynamic input (output) structures.

Moreover, ray-homothetic dynamic input and output correspondences are characterized by linear structure for expansion paths, and in the final section index numbers for such dynamic correspondences are discussed. See also [6] for a dynamic treatment of index numbers under weaker assumptions on the parent technology.

2. Dualities

Costs and returns may not be finitely evaluated over an infinite planning horizon $t \in [0, +\infty)$. Thus, the input and output spaces BM_+^n and BM_+^m respectively are restricted to closed subspaces $BM_+^n [0,T]$ and $BM_+^m [0,T]$, where $BM_+^\alpha [0,T] = \{f \in BM_+^\alpha \mid f_i(t) = 0$ for $t > T$, $i = 1,2,\ldots,\alpha\}$, $\alpha = m,n$, $T \in (0, +\infty)$.

The dual (conjugate) space of $BM^1 [0,T]$ is given by the space of all bounded finitely additive measures defined on the field of Lebesque measurable subsets of $[0,T]$, see [1, p. 258]. This space will be denoted by ba $[0,T]$, and an output price vector $r = (r_1, r_2,\ldots, r_m)$ is a vector $d\mu = (d\mu_1, d\mu_2,\ldots, d\mu_m)$ of such measures, i.e., $d\mu \in \prod_{i=1}^{m} \text{ba } [0,T]$. A measure $d\nu_i \in \text{ba } [0,T]$ is nonnegative if $(\int_0^T y_i(t)\, d\nu_i) \geqq 0$ for all $y_i \in BM_+^1 [0,T]$, and an input price vector $p = (p_1, p_2,\ldots, p_n)$ is a vector $d\nu = (d\nu_1, d\nu_2,\ldots, d\nu_n)$ of such nonnegative measures, i.e., $d\nu \in \prod_{i=1}^{n} \text{ba}_+ [0,T]$, where the plus sign (+) indicates the nonnegativity.

Costs and returns may now be evaluated as:

Definition 1: For $T \in (0, +\infty)$, $u \in BM_+^m [0,T]$ and an input price vector p of nonnegative measures $d\nu = (d\nu_1, d\nu_2,\ldots, d\nu_n)$ of $\prod_{i=1}^{n} \text{ba}_+ [0,T]$ the (price) minimal cost functional is given by

$$K(u,p,T) = \min \{\int_0^T \sum_{i=1}^{n} x_i(t)\, d\nu_i(t) \mid x \in L_T(u)\},$$

where $L_T(u) = L(u) \cap BM_+^n [0,T]$.

and

Definition 2: For $T \in (0, +\infty)$, $x \in BM_+^n[0,T]$ and an output price vector r of measures $d\mu = (d\mu_1, d\mu_2, \ldots, d\mu_m) \in \prod_{i=1}^{m} ba[0,T]$ the (price) maximal return functional is

$$R(x,r,T) = \max \{\int_0^T \sum_{i=1}^{m} u_i(t)\, d\mu_i(t) \mid u \in P_T(x)\},$$

where $P_T(x) = P(x) \cap BM_+^m[0,T]$.

In [7] the less general formulations of the cost and return functionals are given, with $d\nu = (p_1\, dt, p_2\, dt, \ldots, p_n\, dt)$ and $d\mu = (r_1\, dt, r_2\, dt, \ldots r_m\, dt)$ where $p = (p_1, p_2, \ldots, p_n) \in BM_+^n[0,T]$ $r = (r_1, r_2, \ldots, r_m) \in$ $\in BM^m[0,T]$ and with Lebesque measure dt on $[0,T]$. The axioms of [7] are such that the minimum and maximum of Definitions 1 and 2 exist, respectively.

The distance functionals for the input and output correspondences $L_T(u)$ and $P_T(x)$ are defined by

$$\Psi(u,x,T) = [\min \{\lambda \mid (\lambda\, x) \in L_T(u),\ \lambda \in [0, +\infty)\}]^{-1}$$

and

$$\Omega(x,u,T) = [\max \{\Theta \mid (\Theta\, u) \in P_T(x),\ \Theta \in [0, +\infty)\}]^{-1}.$$

As usual $x \in L_T(u) \Leftrightarrow \Psi(u,x,T) \geqq 1$ and $u \in P_T(x) \Leftrightarrow \Omega(x,u,T) \leqq 1$ with the distance functionals homogenous of degree +1 in their second arguments.

Now, define the price minimal cost functional

$$\Psi^*(u,x,T) = \inf \{\int_0^T \sum_{i=1}^{n} x_i(t)\, d\nu_i(t) \mid K(u,p,T) \geqq 1,\ p = d\nu \in \prod_{i=1}^{n} ba_+[0,T]\}$$

and the price maximal return functional

$$\Omega^*(x,u,T) = \sup \{\int_0^T \sum_{i=1}^m u_i(t)\, d\mu_i(t) \mid R(x,r,T) \leqq 1,\ r = d\mu \in \prod_{i=1}^m ba\,[0,T]\}$$

The proofs of [7] apply to show:

<u>Proposition 1</u>:

$$L_T^*(u) = \{x \in BM_+^n\,[0,T] \mid \Psi^*(u,x,T) \geqq 1\} \supset L_T(u), \quad u \in BM_+^m\,[0,T]$$

and

$$P_T^*(x) = \{u \in BM_+^m\,[0,T] \mid \Omega^*(x,u,T) \leqq 1\} \supset P_T(x), \quad x \in BM_+^n\,[0,T].$$

Moreover the arguments of [7] can be used to prove the following two weak dualities:

<u>First Weak Duality</u>

$$K(u,p,T) = \min \{\int_0^T \sum_{i=1}^n x_i(t)\, d\nu_i(t) \mid \Psi(u,x,T) \geqq 1,\ x \in BM_+^n\,[0,T]\}$$

$$\Psi(u,x,T) \leqq \inf \{\int_0^T \sum_{i=1}^n x_i(t)\, d\nu_i(t) \mid K(u,p,T) \geqq 1,\ p = d\nu \in \prod_{i=1}^n ba_+\,[0,T]\}$$

for $u \in BM_+^m\,[0,T]$ and $T \in (0, +\infty)$.

<u>Second Weak Duality</u>

$$R(x,r,T) = \max \{\int_0^T \sum_{i=1}^m u_i(t)\, d\mu_i(t) \mid \Omega(x,u,T) \leqq 1,\ u \in BM_+^m\,[0,T]\}$$

$$\Omega(x,u,T) \geqq \sup \{\int_0^T \sum_{i=1}^m u_i(t)\, d\mu_i(t) \mid R(x,r,T) \leqq 1,\ r = d\mu \in \prod_{i=1}^m ba\,[0,T]\}$$

for $x \in BM_+^n\,[0,T]$ and $T \in (0, +\infty)$.

Proposition 1 and the two weak dualities do not require assumptions of convexity on $P_T(x)$ or $L_T(u)$, i.e., $P_T(x)$ or $L_T(u)$ are convex for $x \in BM_+^n\,[0,T]$ and $u \in BM_+^m\,[0,T]$ respectively, nor the assumption of strong disposability of inputs, i.e., $x' \geqq x \in L_T(u) \Rightarrow x' \in L_T(u)$. When these additional assumptions are enforced on the production functions $x \to P_T(x)$ and $u \to L_T(u)$ the following strong dualities are obtained.

First Strong Duality

$$K(u,p,T) = \min \{\int_0^T \sum_{i=1}^n x_i(t)\, d\nu_i(t) \,|\, \Psi(u,x,T) \geqq 1, \quad x \in BM_+^n\,[0,T]\}$$

$$\Omega(u,x,T) = \inf \{\int_0^T \sum_{i=1}^n x_i(t)\, d\nu_i(t) \,|\, K(u,p,T) \geqq 1, \; p = d\nu \in \prod_{i=1}^n ba_+\,[0,T]\}$$

for $u \in BM_+^m\,[0,T]$ and $T \in (0, +\infty)$.

Second Strong Duality

$$R(x,r,T) = \max \{\int_0^T \sum_{i=1}^m u_i(t)\, d\mu_i(t) \,|\, \Omega(x,u,T) \leqq 1, \quad u \in BM_+^m\,[0,T]\}$$

$$\Omega(x,u,T) = \sup \{\int_0^T \sum_{i=1}^m u_i(t)\, d\mu_i(t) \,|\, R(x,r,T) \leqq 1, \quad r = d\mu \in \prod_{i=1}^m ba\,[0,T]\}$$

for $x \in BM_+^n\,[0,T]$ and $T \in (0, +\infty)$.

In order to prove the First Strong Duality, it is first shown that $L_T^*(u) \subset L_T(u)$, $u \in BM_+^m\,[0,T]$. Then by Proposition 1, $L_T^*(u) = L_T(u)$ and the equalities of the distance functionals $\Psi^*(u,x,T)$ and $\Psi(u,x,T)$ follows from [4, p. 158]. If $u = 0$ or $\|u\| > 0$ with $L_T(u)$ empty, $L_T^*(u) = L_T(u)$, see [7, p. 38]. Thus assume $\|u\| > 0$ and $L_T(u)$ nonempty and let $x^o \notin L_T(u)$. The assumptions on $L(u)$, i.e., it is a closed, quasi-concave correspondence, imply that $L_T(u)$ is a closed and convex set. Thus by the (strict) separation theorem, [1, p. 417], there is a nonzero element in the dual space of $BM^n [0,T]$ strictly separating x^o and $L_T(u)$, i.e., there is a price vector $p^o = d\nu^o \in \prod_{i=1}^{n} ba [0,T]$ such that $\int_0^T \sum_{i=1}^{n} x_i^o(t)\, d\nu_i^o(t) < K(u,p^o,T)$. Note that $p^o = d\nu^o \in \prod_{i=1}^{n} ba_+[0,T]$, due to strong disposability of inputs. Define $\bar{p}_o = p^o \cdot [K(u,p^o,T)]^{-1}$, i.e., $d\bar{\nu}^o = d\nu^o \cdot [K(u,p^o,T)]^{-1}$, then by the homogeneity of the cost-functional $K(u,p,T)$ in its second argument, $\int_0^T \sum_{i=1}^{n} x_i^o(t)\, d\bar{\nu}_i^o(t) < 1$.

Therefore $\overset{*}{\Psi}(u,x^o,T) < 1$ and $x^o \notin \overset{*}{L}_T(u)$. Thus $\overset{*}{L}_T(u) = L_T(u)$, $u \in BM_+^m [0,T]$, and by similar arguments to those of [4, p. 158], the First Strong Duality follows.

By analogous arguments to those given above one may show the Second Strong Duality.

3. Homothetic and Ray-Homothetic Production Structures

The output correspondence $x \to P(x)$ is called Homothetic if

(1) $P(x) = H(x) \cdot P(1) \qquad x \in BM^n_+$

where $H\colon BM^n_+ \to R_+$ satisfies

$H.1$ $H(0) = \{0\}$, $H(x) > 0$ for some $x \in BM^n_+$,

$H.2$ $H(x)$ is finite for $\|x\| < +\infty$,

$H.3$ $H(\lambda \cdot x) \geqq H(x)$ for $\lambda \geqq 1$,

$H.4$ If $H(\lambda \cdot x) > 0$, $H(\lambda \cdot x) \to +\infty$ as $\lambda \to +\infty$,

$H.5$ $H(x)$ is upper semi-continuous on BM^n_+,

with $P(1)$ being the output set for the unit vector of input histories, i.e., $\{0\} \in P(1)$, $P(1)$ is closed and totally bounded and if $u \in P(1)$, $(\theta \cdot u) \in P(1)$ for $\theta \in [0,1]$.

Let $\lambda \in (0, +\infty)$ and consider $P(\lambda \cdot x) = H(\lambda \cdot x) \cdot P(1)$. For $\lambda = [\|x\|]^{-1}$, $P(x/\|x\|) = H(x/\|x\|) \cdot P(1)$. Thus by (1),

(2) $P(x) = \dfrac{H(x)}{H(x/\|x\|)} \cdot P(x/\|x\|) \quad$ for $\|x\| > 0$.

If the output correspondence $x \to P(x)$ satisfies (2) it is termed Ray-Homothetic. Clearly, a homothetic output correspondence is ray-homothetic. The converse relation is given by:

Proposition 2: A Ray-Homothetic output correspondence is Homothetic if and only if $\Omega(x/\|x\|, u) = \dfrac{\Omega(1,u)}{H(x/\|x\|)}$, where $\Omega(x/\|x\|, u)$ and $\Omega(1,u)$ are the distance functionals of $P(x/\|x\|)$ and $P(1)$, respectively.

Proof: Assume $P(x) = H(x)\cdot P(1)$ and $P(x) = \frac{H(x)}{H(x/\|x\|)}\cdot P(x/\|x\|)$ holds, then $\Omega(x,u) = \frac{\Omega(1,u)}{H(x)} = \frac{H(x/\|x\|)}{H(x)}\cdot\Omega(x/\|x\|,u)$. Thus, $\Omega(x/\|x\|, u) = \frac{\Omega(1,u)}{H(x/\|x\|)}$.

Conversely, if $\Omega(x/\|x\|, u) = \frac{\Omega(1,u)}{H(x/\|x\|)}$, and $P(x) = \frac{H(x)}{H(x/\|x\|)}\cdot P(x/\|x\|)$, i.e., $\Omega(x,u) = \frac{\Omega(x/\|x\|,\ u)}{H(x)}\cdot H(x/\|x\|)$, then

$\Omega(x,u) = \frac{\Omega(1,u)}{H(x)}$ implying that $P(x) = \{u|\Omega(x,u) \leqq 1\} = \{u|\frac{\Omega(1,u)}{H(x)} \leqq 1\}$

$= H(x)\cdot\{u|\Omega(1,u) \leqq 1\} = H(x)\cdot P(1)$.

QED.

For the ray-homothetic output correspondence $x \to P_T(x) = P(x) \cap BM_+^m\,[0,T]$, $x \in BM_+^n\,[0,T]$, i.e., $P_T(x) = \left(\frac{H(x)}{H(x/\|x\|)}\cdot P(x/\|x\|) \cap BM_+^m\,[0,T]\right) = \frac{H(x)}{H(x/\|x\|)}$ $\cdot P_T(x/\|x\|)$, the distance functional is $\Omega(x,u,T) = \frac{H(x/\|x\|)}{H(x)}\cdot\Omega(x/\|x\|, u, T)$.

From the definition of the return functional in terms of the distance functional (see the second weak duality, first part) the following separability properly is clear

(3) $R(x,r,T) = \frac{H(x)}{H(x/\|x\|)}\cdot R(x/\|x\|, r, T)$.

Conversely, if (3) holds and $P_T(x)$ is convex $x \in BM_+^n\,[0,T]$, then by the second strong duality, the distance functional $\Omega(x,u,T)$ is

(4) $\Omega(x,u,T) = \frac{\Omega(x/\|x\|,\ u,T)}{H(x)}\cdot H(x/\|x\|)$.

Thus from the relationship $u \in P_T(x) \Leftrightarrow \Omega(x,u,T) \leqq 1$ one has:

<u>Proposition 3</u>: The output correspondence $x \to P_T(x)$ with $P_T(x)$ convex for $x \in BM_+^n\,[0,T]$, is Ray-Homothetic if and only if $R(x,r,T) = \frac{H(x)}{H(x/\|x\|)}\,R(x/\|x\|, r,T)$, $r = d\mu \in \prod_{i=1}^{m} ba\,[0,T]$, $T \in (0, +\infty)$.

Likewise for the homothetic output structure $P_T(x) = H(x) \cdot P(1)$ one can prove:

Proposition 4: The output correspondence $x \to P_T(x)$, with $P_T(x)$ convex for $x \in BM_+^n [0,T]$, $T \in (0, +\infty)$, is Homothetic if and only if $R(x,r,T) = H(x) \cdot R(1,r,T)$, $r = d\mu \in \prod_{i=1}^{m} ba [0,T]$.

As a result of Propositions 3 and 4 one has

Proposition 5: A Ray-Homothetic output correspondence $x \to P_T(x)$, with $P_T(x)$ convex for $x \in BM_+^n [0,T]$, is Homothetic if and only if $R(x/\|x\|, r,T) = H(x/\|x\|) \cdot R(1,r,T)$, where $R(x/\|x\|, r,T)$ and $R(1,r,T)$ are the return functionals for $P_T(x/\|x\|)$ and $P_T(1)$ respectively.

The input correspondence $u \to L(u)$ is called Homothetic if

(5) $L(u) = F(u) \cdot L(1) \quad u \in BM_+^m$

where $F: BM_+^m \to R_+$ satisfies

$F.1$ $F(u) > 0$ for $\|u\| > 0$,

$F.2$ $F(u)$ is finite for $\|u\| < +\infty$ and $L(u)$ not empty, and $+\infty$ for $L(u)$ empty,

$F.3$ $F(\Theta \cdot u) \geqq F(u)$ for $\Theta \in [1, +\infty)$,

$F.4$ $F(u)$ is lower semi-continuous in u,

$F.5$ If $F(\Theta \cdot u) > 0$, $F(\Theta \cdot u) \to +\infty$ as $\Theta \to +\infty$,

with $L(1)$ being the input set for the unite vector of output histories.

For $\Theta = [\|u\|]^{-1} > 0$, $L(\Theta \cdot u) = F(\Theta \cdot u) \cdot L(1)$, (5) gives:

$$(6) \quad L(u) = \frac{F(u)}{F(u/\|u\|)} \cdot L(u/\|u\|).$$

If the input correspondence $u \to L(u)$ meets (6), it is called <u>Ray-Homothetic</u>. Clearly a homothetic input correspondence is ray-homothetic and the condition for the converse to hold is given by:

<u>Proposition 6</u>: A Ray-Homothetic input correspondence $u \to L(u)$ is Homothetic if and only if $\Psi(u/\|u\|, x) = \frac{\Psi(1,x)}{F(u/\|u\|)}$, where $\Psi(u/\|u\|, x)$ and $\Psi(1,x)$ are the distance functionals of $L(u/\|u\|)$ and $L(1)$, respectively.

The proofs of Proposition 6 and the following two propositions are entirely analogous to the corresponding ones for the output correspondence and hence omitted. For the input correspondence $u \to L_T(u) = L(u) \cap BM_+^n [0,T]$, $u \in BM_+^m [0,T]$, $T \in (0, +\infty)$, one has:

<u>Proposition 7</u>: The input correspondence $u \to L_T(u)$ with $L_T(u)$ convex for $u \in BM_+^m [0,T]$ and strong disposability of inputs holding is Ray-Homothetic if and only if the cost-functional is of form

$$K(u,p,T) = \frac{F(u)}{F(u/\|u\|)} \cdot K(u/\|u\|, p,T), \text{ for}$$

$$p = d\nu \in \prod_{i=1}^{n} ba_+ [0,T].$$

<u>Proposition 8</u>: Under the conditions of Proposition 7, the input correspondence $u \to L_T(u)$ is Homothetic if and only if $K(u,p,T) = F(u) \cdot K(1,p,T)$, for $p = d\nu \in \prod_{i=1}^{n} ba_+ [0,T]$.

From Propositions 7 and 8 follows:

Proposition 9: A Ray-Homothetic input correspondence $u \to L_T(u)$, with $L_T(u)$ convex for $u \in BM_+^m[0,T]$ and strong disposability of inputs holding, is Homothetic if and only if $K(u/\|u\|, p,T) = F(u/\|u\|) \cdot K(1,p,T)$ where $K(u/\|u\|, p,T)$ and $K(1,p,T)$ are the cost functionals for $L(u/\|u\|)$ and $L(1)$ respectively.

4. Linear Structure for Expansion Paths

For the dynamic input correspondence $u \to L_T(u)$ introduce:

Definition 3: For an input price vector $p \neq 0$, $p = d\nu \in \prod_{i=1}^{n} ba_+ [0,T]$, and a vector of output histories $u \in BM_+^m [0,T]$, $T \in (0, +\infty)$ with $L_T(u) \neq \emptyset$, the set of input histories minimizing costs is $E_p(L_T(u)) = \{x \mid x \in L_T(u), \int_0^T \sum_{i=1}^{n} x_i(t)\, d\nu_i(t) = K(u,p,T)\}$.

and

Definition 4: The input correspondence $u \to L_T(u)$ has (global) linear structure for $(u/\|u\|)$ if for each $\Theta \in [0, +\infty)$ there is a scalar $\lambda(\Theta,u) \geqq 0$, independent of prices such that $E_p(L_T(\Theta \cdot u) = \lambda(\Theta,u) \cdot E_p(L_T(u))$ for each input price vector $p \neq 0$.

The relationship between linear structure and cost functional separability is clear from

Proposition 10: The cost functional is of the form

$$K(u,p,T) = \frac{F(u)}{F(u/\|u\|)} \cdot K(u/\|u\|,p,T)$$

if and only if the input correspondence $u \to L_T(u)$ has linear structure for $(u/\|u\|)$.

Proof: Assume the above separability of the cost functional, and let $\Theta \in [0, +\infty)$. Then $K(\Theta \cdot u,p,T) = \dfrac{F(\Theta \cdot u)}{F(u/\|u\|)} \cdot K(u/\|u\|,p,T)$

or $K(\Theta\cdot u,p,T) = \frac{F(\Theta\cdot u)}{F(u)}\cdot K(u,p,T)$. Thus, $E_p(L_T(\Theta\cdot u)) = \frac{F(\Theta\cdot u)}{F(u)}\cdot E_p(L_T(u))$, and $u \to L_T(u)$ has linear structure. In proving the converse, the following lemma is useful:

Lemma: For an input price vector $p \neq 0$, and $u \in BM_+^m[0,T]$, $K(u,p,T) =$

$$\inf\{\int_0^T \sum_{i=1}^n x_i(t)\, d\nu_i(t) \mid x \in E_p(L_T(u))\}.$$

Proof: Define $\tilde{K}(u,p,T) = \inf\{\int_0^T \sum_{i=1}^n x_i(t)\, d\nu_i(t) \mid x \in E_p(L_T(u))\}$.

Then, from the definition of $E_p(L_T(u))$, $\tilde{K}(u,p,T) = K(u,p,T)$.

QED.

To continue the proof of Proposition 10, assume Definition 4 applies. Then for any input price vector $p \neq 0, \Theta \in [0,+\infty)$ using the lemma,

$$K(\Theta\cdot u,p,T) = \inf\{\int_0^T \sum_{i=1}^n x_i(t)\, d\nu_i(t) \mid x \in E_p(L_T(\Theta\cdot u))\}$$

$$= \inf\{\int_0^T \sum_{i=1}^n x_i(t)\, d\nu_i(t) \mid x \in \lambda(\Theta,u)\cdot E_p(L_T(u))\}$$

$$= \lambda(\Theta,u)\cdot \inf\{\int_0^T \sum_{i=1}^n x_i(t)\, d\nu_i(t) \mid x \in E_p(L_T(u))\}$$

$$= \lambda(\Theta,u)\cdot K(u,p,T)$$

Thus, $K(\Theta\cdot u,p,T) = \lambda(\Theta,u)\cdot K(u,p,T)$ and for two positive scalars Θ,Θ', the scaling function $\lambda(\Theta,u)$ must satisfy the functional equation $\lambda(\Theta\cdot\Theta',u) = \lambda(\Theta,\Theta'\cdot u)\cdot\lambda(\Theta',u)$. The solution is here

$\lambda(\Theta,u) = \frac{F(\Theta\cdot u)}{F(u)}$, see [2], and thus by choosing $\Theta = 1/\|u\|$, the proposition is proved. QED.

Under the stronger assumptions on $u \to L_T(u)$, i.e., $L_T(u)$ convex for $u \in BM_+^m[0,T]$ and inputs strongly disposable, Propositions 7 and 10 imply:

Proposition 11: The input correspondence $u \to L_T(u)$ with $L_T(u)$ convex for $u \in BM_+^m[0,T]$ and strong disposability of inputs holding is Ray-Homothetic if and only if it has linear structure for $(u/\|u\|)$.

Turning now to the dynamic output correspondence $x \to P_T(x)$, the following definitions are used.

Definition 5: For an output price vector $r \neq 0$, $r = d\mu \in \prod_{i=1}^{n} ba\,[0,T]$, and a vector of input histories $x \in BM_+^n[0,T]$, $T \in (0, +\infty)$, the set of output histories maximizing return is

$$E_r(P_T(x)) = \{u \mid u \in P_T(x), \int_0^T \sum_{i=1}^{m} u_i(t)\, d\mu_i(t) = R(x,r,T)\}.$$

and

Definition 6: The output correspondence $x \to P_T(t)$ has (global) linear structure for $(x/\|x\|)$ if for each $\lambda \in [0, +\infty)$ there is a scalar $\Theta(\lambda,x) \geqq 0$ independent of prices such that $E_r(P_T(\lambda\cdot x)) = \Theta(\lambda,x)\cdot E_r(P_T(x))$ for each output price vector $r \neq 0$.

The next two propositions clarify the relationships Ray-Homothetic output correspondences and linear structure. The proofs parallel those of Propositions 10 and 11 and are omitted.

Proposition 12: The return functional is

$$R(x,r,T) = \frac{H(x)}{H(x/\|x\|)} \cdot R(x/\|x\|),r,T)$$

if and only if the output correspondence $x \rightarrow P_T(x)$ has linear structure for $(x/\|x\|)$.

Proposition 13: The output correspondence $x \rightarrow P_T(x)$ with $P_T(x)$ convex for $x \in BM_+^n [0,T]$ is Ray-Homothetic if and only if it has linear structure for $(x/\|x\|)$.

Homotheticity, being a special case of ray-homotheticity indicates that such input and output correspondences have linear structure. In particular, $E_p(L_T(\Theta \cdot u)) = F(\Theta \cdot u) \cdot E_p(L_T(1))$ and $E_r(P_T(\lambda \cdot x)) = H(\lambda \cdot x) \cdot E_r(P_T(1))$.

4. Index Numbers for Dynamic Ray-Homothetic Production Structures

Under the stronger axioms for the correspondences $x \to P_T(x)$ and $u \to L_T(u)$ stated above, i.e., $P_T(x)$ and $L_T(u)$ convex for $x \in BM_+^n\ [0,T]$ and $u \in BM_+^m\ [0,T]$ respectively and $x' \geqq x \in L_T(u)$ implying $x' \in L_T(u)$, four indexes are considered, namely

Definition 7: For $p', p^o \in \prod_{i=1}^{n} ba_+\ [0,T]$, $T \in (0, +\infty)$, and $u \in BM_+^m\ [0,T]$ with $L_T(u)$ not empty, the Input Price Index is

$$\Pi_T(p',p^o|u) = \frac{K(u,p',T)}{K(u,p^o,T)}$$

where $K(u,p,T)$ is the (factor) minimal cost functional.

Definition 8: For $r',r^o \in \prod_{i=1}^{m} ba\ [0,T]$, $T \in (0, +\infty)$ and $x \in BM_+^n\ [0,T]$, the Output Price Index is

$$\rho_T(r',r^o|x) = \frac{R(x,r',T)}{R(x,r^o,T)}$$

where $R(x,r,T)$ is the (factor) maximal return functional

Definition 9: For $x',x^o \in BM_+^n\ [0,T]$, $T \in (0, +\infty)$ and $u \in BM_+^m\ [0,T]$ with $L_T(u)$ not empty, the Input Quantity Index is

$$I_T(x',x^o|u) = \frac{\Psi(u,x',T)}{\Psi(u,x^o,T)}$$

where $\Psi(u,x,T)$ is the price minimal cost functional.

and

Definition 10: For $u',u^o \in BM_+^m\ [0,T]$, $T \in (0, +\infty)$, and $x \in BM_+^n\ [0,T]$, the Output Quantity Index is

$$O_T(u',u^o|x) = \frac{\Omega(x,u',T)}{\Omega(x,u^o,T)}$$

where $\Omega(x,u,T)$ is the price maximal return functional.

The distance functionals $\Psi(u,x,T)$ and $\Omega(x,u,T)$ are here treated as the price minimal cost and the price maximal return functionals respectively. So using the strong dualities allow for the above symmetric handling of price and quantity indexes.

Under the assumptions of ray-homothetic input and output structure the four indexes become

$$\Pi_T(p',p^o|u) = \frac{K(u/\|u\|,p',T)}{K(u/\|u\|,p^o,T)} = \Pi_T(p',p^o|u/\|u\|)$$

$$\rho_T(r',r^o|x) = \frac{R(x/\|x\|,r',T)}{R(x/\|x\|,r^o,T)} = \rho_T(r',r^o|x/\|x\|)$$

$$I_T(x',x^o|u) = \frac{\Psi(u/\|u\|,x',T)}{\Psi(u/\|u\|,x^o,T)} = I_T(x',x^o|u/\|u\|)$$

$$O_T(u',u^o|x) = \frac{\Omega(x/\|x\|,u',T)}{\Omega(x/\|x\|,u^o,T)} = O_T(u',u^o|x/\|x\|).$$

Input and output histories $x \in BM_+^n\,[0,T]$ and $u \in BM_+^m\,[0,T]$ can be thought of as determined by their "size", given by $\|x\|$ ($\|u\|$), and their "mix", given by $x/\|x\|$ ($u/\|u\|$). In that terminology, all four indexes are size independent but the input price and quantity indexes are output mix dependent and the output price and quantity indexes are input mix dependent. It is clear from Propositions 6 and 9 that homotheticity of the input correspondences implies that the input price and quantity indexes are both size and mix independent. The analogous properties for the output indexes follow from Propositions 2 and 5.

Five tests are commonly applied for index numbers, namely (see [3]) (1) Homogeneity, (2) Time-reversal, (3) Transitive, (4) Dimensional and (5) Factor-reversal.

The first four tests are here satisfied merely as a consequence of the definitions. For example;

$$\Pi_T(\lambda\cdot p',p^o|u) = \frac{K(u,\lambda\cdot p',T)}{K(u,p^o,T)} = \lambda\Pi_T(p',p^o|u)$$

since $K(u,p,T)$ is homogeneous of degree +1 in its second argument, so homogeneity applies to the input price index.

To satisfy the time-reversal test, $\Pi_T(p',p^o|u)\cdot\Pi_T(p^o,p'|u)$ must equal one, which is clearly the case. The requirement of transitivity for $\Pi_T(p',p^o|u)$ is that, $\Pi_T(p'',p'|u)\cdot\Pi_T(p',p^o|u) = \Pi_T(p'',p^o|u)$. This condition follows from the definition of $\Pi_T(p',p^o|u)$.

Like the case of the input price index, the other three indexes satisfy (1) - (3). Moreover, a dimensional change in the money unit does not affect the two price indexes, nor does a dimensional change in inputs or outputs affect the indexes.

Turning to the factor-reversal test, note first that if x belongs to the isoquant of $L_T(u)$ then $\Psi(u,x,T) = 1$ (see [7]). With this in mind one gets for ray-homotheticity of $u \to L_T(u)$,

$$\frac{K(u',p',T)}{K(u^o,p^o,T)} = \frac{K(u'/\|u'\|,p',T)\cdot F(u')\cdot F(u^o/\|u^o\|)\cdot\Psi(u',x',T)}{K(u^o/\|u^o\|,p^o,T)\cdot F(u^o)\cdot F(u'/\|u'\|)\cdot\Psi(u^o,x^o,T)}$$

$$= \frac{K(u'/\|u'\|,p',T)\cdot\Psi(u'/\|u'\|,x',T)}{K(u^o/\|u^o\|,p^o,T)\cdot\Psi(u^o/\|u^o\|,x^o,T)}$$

Thus for $u' = \lambda\cdot u^o$, $\lambda \in (0, +\infty)$, the factor-reversal test applies. This is clear from

$$\frac{K(\lambda\cdot u^o,p',T)}{K(u^o,p^o,T)} = \frac{K(u^o/\|u^o\|,p',T)}{K(u^o/\|u^o\|,p^o,T} \cdot \frac{\Psi(u^o/\|u^o\|,x',T)}{\Psi(u^o/\|u^o\|,x^o,T)}$$

or

$$\frac{K(\lambda\cdot u^o,p',T)}{K(u^o,p^o,T)} = \Pi_T(p',p^o|u^o/\|u^o\|) \cdot I_T(x',x^o|u^o/\|u^o\|),$$

where the product of the price and quantity indexes equals the ratio of the costs of the two compared situations $(\lambda\cdot u^o,p')$ and (u^o,p^o).

Similar arguments apply to $I_T(x',x^o|u/\|u\|)$ and to show that for a ray-homothetic output correspondence $x \to P_T(x)$, the factor-reversal test for the output price and quantity indexes holds for a fixed input mix.

From earlier discussions of homotheticity clearly, $u \to L_T(u)$ homothetic implies that the factor-reversal test holds for all pairs (u',p') and (u^o,p^o). Likewise $x \to P_T(x)$ homothetic gives similar global application of this test.

The above treatment of input and output indexes for ray-homothetic production structures, showed that such structures are sufficient for "mix" dependent but "size" independent indexes. The necessity for this is next proved.

Consider the input price index $\Pi_T(p',p^o|u) = \Pi_T(p',p^o|u/\|u\|)$, then clearly, for $\Theta = (\|u\|)^{-1}$,

$$\frac{K(\Theta\cdot u,p',T)}{K(\Theta\cdot u,p^o,T)} = \frac{K(u,p',T)}{K(u,p^o,T)}$$

From this expression follows that

$$\frac{K(u,p',T)}{K(u,p',T)} = \Gamma(u/\|u\|,p',p^o,T), \text{ where } \Gamma(u/\|u\|,p',p^o,T) = \frac{K(u/\|u\|,p',T)}{K(u/\|u\|,p^o,T)}$$

Thus,

(7) $K(u,p',T) = \Gamma(u/\|u\|,p',p^o,T) \cdot K(u,p^o,T)$.

Now define

(8) $\Delta(u/\|u\|,p',T) := \Gamma(u/\|u\|,p',\tilde{p}^o,T)$ for $\tilde{p}^o$ constant

and

(9) $F(\theta\cdot u/\|u\|) := K(\theta\cdot u/\|u\|,\tilde{p}^o,T)$ for $\tilde{p}^o$ constant.

Note that in (9), $F(\theta\cdot u/\|u\|)$ is used rather than $F(\theta\cdot u/\|u\|,T)$ since T is treated only as a parameter, and it is clear that $u \in BM_+^m\,[0,T]$. Rewriting (7) as

$$K(\theta\cdot u/\|u\|,p',T) = \Gamma(u/\|u\|,p',p^o,T) \cdot K(\theta\cdot u/\|u\|,p^o,T)$$

and applying (8) and (9) to this expression gives,

(10) $K(\theta\cdot u/\|u\|,p',T) = F(\theta\cdot u/\|u\|)\cdot \Delta(u/\|u\|,p',T)$.

By choosing $\theta = \|u\|$, and $\theta = 1$ in (10) respectively and combining the two expressions one has

(11) $K(u,p',T) = \dfrac{F(u)}{F(u/\|u\|)} \cdot K(u/\|u\|,p',T)$.

This together with Proposition 7 proves the necessity of a ray-homothetic input structure for mix dependent and size independent input price index.

Similar arguments apply to show the analogies for the other three indexes. Thus

Proposition 14: The input price and quantity indexes are output mix dependent, i.e., $\Pi_T(p',p^o|u/\|u\|)$ and $I_T(x',x^o|u/\|u\|)$ respectively, if and only if the input correspondence $u \to L_T(u)$ (under the stronger axioms) is ray-homothetic.

Proposition 15: The output price and quantity indexes are input mix dependent, i.e., $\rho_T(r',r^o|x/\|x\|)$ and $O_T(u',u^o|x/\|x\|)$ respectively, if and only if the output correspondence $x \to P_T(x)$ (under the stronger axioms) is ray-homothetic.

It has been pointed out that homotheticity is sufficient for both size and mix independent indexes. Such structures can, by similar arguments as those given above, be shown to be necessary for such indexes. Thus,

Proposition 16: The input price and quantity indexes are of the forms $\Pi_T(p',p^o)$ and $I_T(x',x^o)$ respectively if and only if the input correspondence $u \to L_T(u)$ (under the stronger axioms) is homothetic.

Proposition 17: The output price and quantity indexes are of the forms $\rho_T(r',r^o)$ and $O_T(u',u^o)$ respectively if and only if the output correspondence $x \to P_T(x)$ (under the stronger axioms) is homothetic.

References

[1] Dunford, N. and J.T. Schwartz: LINEAR OPERATORS, Part I: General Theory, Interscience, New York, (1958)

[2] Färe, R. and R.W. Shephard: "Ray-Homothetic Production Functions", Econometrica forthcoming (1977)

[3] Samuelson, P.A. and S. Swamy: "Invariant Economic Index Numbers and Canonical Duality: Survey and Synthesis", The American Economic Review, vol. 64, No. 4, 1974, 566-593

[4] Shephard, R.W.: THEORY OF COST AND PRODUCTION FUNCTIONS, Princeton University Press, Princeton, (1970)

[5] Shephard, R.W.: INDIRECT PRODUCTION FUNCTIONS, Mathematical Systems in Economics, 10. Verlag Anton Hain, Meisenheim am Glan, (1974)

[6] Shephard, R.W.: "A Dynamic Formulation of Index Functions for the Theory of Cost and Production", in this volume

[7] Shephard, R.W. and R. Färe: "A Dynamic Theory of Production Correspondences", ORC 75-13, Operations Research Center, University of California, (1975)

A System of Indices for the External Analysis of the Earning Capacity Standard and Financial Power of Industrial Joint Stock Companies.[1]

by Rainer Hecker

1. Objectives of Capital Investment and Stockholders' Interest in Information

A financial analysis is aimed at evaluating the earning capacity standard of an enterprise. The earning capacity standard is a company's ability to yield continuous earnings in the future.

This capacity virtually depends, amongst others, on whether the company has sufficient financial power to take advantage of the possibilities for earnings and growth by means of investments and to overcome critical situations.

Yielding future earnings is the typical and dominant objective of stockholders investing their money. For the purpose of being able to decide upon the proper investment of their capital they make certain demands for information towards the reporting of a company.

Stockholders' interest in being well informed - established by empirical methods and deduced from their decisions - is mainly geared at

---

1) Editor's note: This is an outline of R. Hecker's contribution to the seminar. The complete work has been published, under the title "Ein Kennzahlensystem zur externen Analyse der Ertrags- und Finanzkraft von Industrieaktiengesellschaften", by Verlag Harri Deutsch, Frankfurt-Zürich, 1975.

- the development of earnings
- the investments
- longterm planning objectives as to production, financing and marketing.

Indices and systems of indices can help to solve all these problems.

2. Indices and Systems of Indices

The term "index" can cover a broad range. Some authors contend that only ratios can be regarded as indices.
The term in a broader sense, on which this work is based, includes absolute figures as well, if they express economically important facts in a concentrated form.

The individual index cannot immediately answer
- the question of proportion (is the result high or low). Only when compared with the respective indices will they achieve their significance and can be used as a basis of decisions
- the question of causes (why is the result like this instead of being different). Only when dividing the index into two or more ones, can the cause of its extent and changes be demonstrated.

Thanks to consistent analysis we obtain index systems whose individual data are interrelated and show an hierarchy.

3. Catalogue of Requirements Placed upon Index Systems

Before explaining the concept of an index system for the external analysis of industrial joint stock companies a

catalogue of requirements is given.
This list of requirements serves

1) as a basis for evaluating the current application of indices

2) as an objective for the development of a new system of indices.

Asking for the purpose of evaluation:
what purpose are the indices to be applied for -
is the centre of all aspects of development for index systems.

This is the purpose of evaluation to which all further important problems of development of indices have to be geared:

1) who is going to apply the indices ?
(those interested in the use of indices)

2) in what areas are indices to be used ?
(contents of the index system)

3) how are indices to be applied ?
(characteristic features of indices)

4) when should indices be applied ?
(determining the time when indices should be applied).

These requirements derived from the most important aspects of developing systems of indices are included in a list of standards to be met by index systems for the external evaluation of industrial joint stock companies. This catalogue is the base for a stocktaking of the application of indices in financial analysis.
Previous experience in the practice of financial analysis as well as the disussions about new approaches in the literature on securities analysis are to be considered in the concept of the index system in order to achieve comprehensive systematization and uniformity of financial indices.

The concept of an index system for the external evaluation of industrial joint stock companies is aimed at putting indices in such systematic relation that the general significance derived from it is more than the sum total of the value of evidence of the individual indices.

4. Structure and Contents of the Index System

The system of indices suggested consists of

1) the quick analysis by means of unrelated indices
2) the structural analysis by means of arithmetically combined ratios.

The quick analysis is the basis or trigger for a detailed examination of the relative factors within the framework of the arithmetically combined index system.

Based on the list of standards, the most important spheres can be evaluated within the quick analysis by means of unrelated indices.

In the structural analysis, the factual logical interrelations between the relative data (e.g. of input and result) as well as the causes for the level of the ratios are to be analysed.

In order to establish the relativity of indices, ratios have to be formed.

The causes for the level of ratios are determined by further splitting the ratios within the system. Based on the list of standards, a concept is made for arithmetically combined ratios, categorised into spheres of evaluation.

A system of indices for the external analysis of the earning capacity standard and financial power of industrial joint stock companies

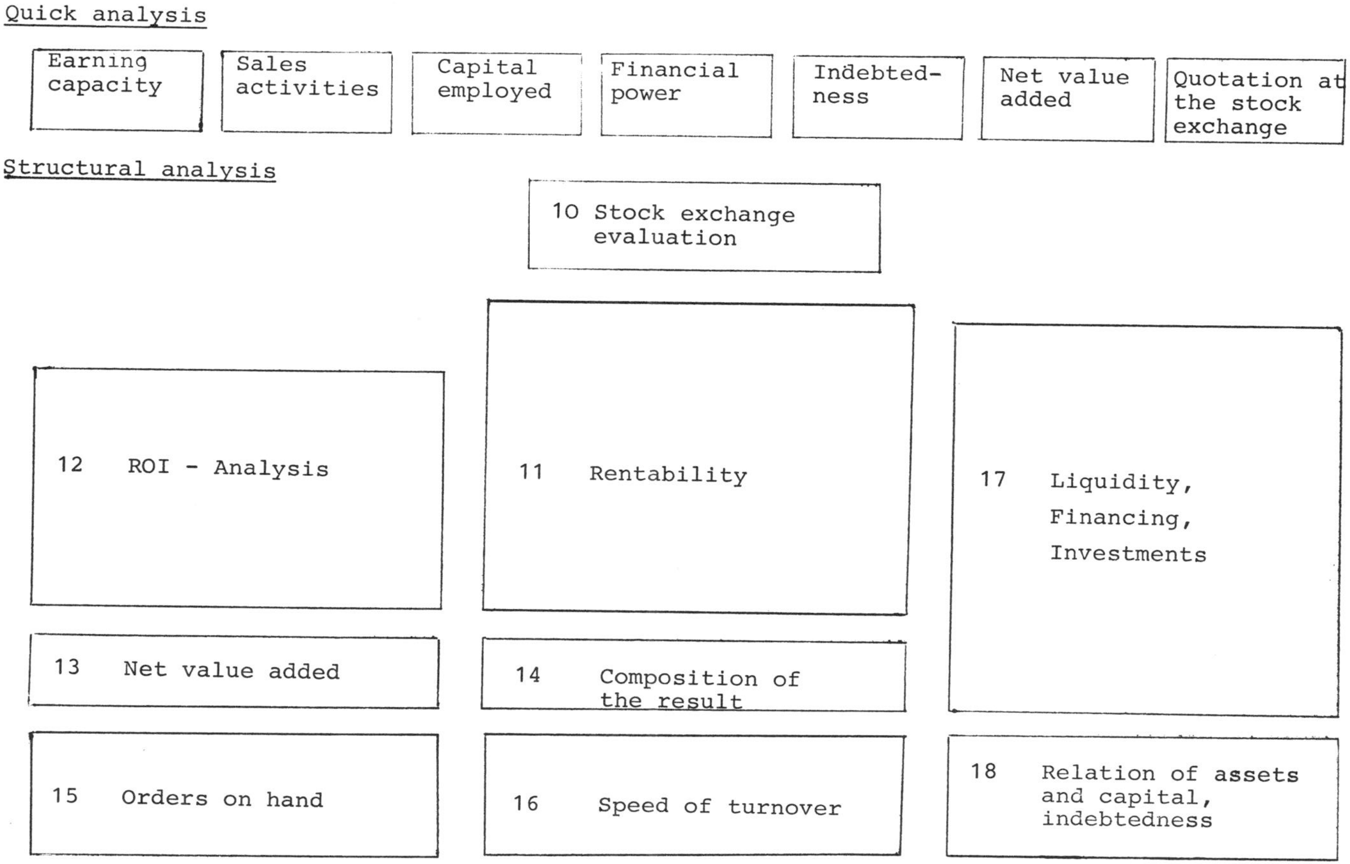

5. Fields of Application of the Index System

For external analysers we can mainly give the following fields of application:

a) Analysis of the enterprise for the purpose of realising

- the relativity of the achieved results and their causes as to time and inter-company relations.
- the consequences of certain measures and influential factors in the individual spheres as well as their effects on other spheres.

b) Estimating the effects of new facts or developments arising as well as measurements announced by the company management within the ratio system:
by means of arithmetic combination it can be determined to what extent the change of one individual ratio will influence the others. Thus the ratio system can be used as a tool of forecasting in so far as - due to the systematic context - conclusions on possible developments in other spheres can be drawn from the forecast on individual spheres.

c) Evaluating the validity or credibility of the explanations and argumentation given by the company management as to
- the past, the present and the future business development.

The ratio system described can be extended in respect of breadth as well as depth as far as its contents of indices are concerned.

The means of extension must be seen under the aspect that the value of an index system is not limited to the information given by the indices but shows the most important points for deeper, possibly very detailed analysis.

Compared with the use of individual indices (set-up, data collection, evaluation), the presented system of indices has the following advantages:

- realising the effective interrelations between individual indices,
- detailed and systematic illustration of this interrelation by means of arithmetical combination,
- extension and deepening when changing the centre of evaluation,
- considering the means of checking of index results under the aspect of super-ordinate views of evaluation.

On the Sensitivity of Key Sector Indices

by Hartmut Kogelschatz and Bernd Goldstein

1. Introduction

"In the recent literature it has been generally asserted that key sectors play an important role in initiating the process of economic development and diversification of the industrial structure of the economy and that a substantial part of investment should be made in the key sectors" (Hazari [1970, p.301]).

The concept of key sector has been developed in the framework of input-output analysis and goes back to Hirschman [1958] and Rasmussen [1956]. In the investigation of technological interrelations between various industries of an economy, sectors are chosen for which a given increase in final demand will induce comparatively large production and employment effects in the whole system. Various methods for identifying key sectors habe been proposed.The procedure associates an index number with each sector for its inter-industry linkages. Some of these methods are based on the nxn input matrix A (Hirschman's approach), some of them start from the Leontief inverse $L(A) := (I-A)^{-1}$ (Rasmussen's approach), the final demand vector being taken into account by a couple of indices.

Recent theoretical and empirical studies mainly refer to Rasmussen's ideas. He suggested several measures for the relative importance of sectors in an interrelated system. The index most frequently used in the literature[1)] is the "power of dispersion" $U_{\cdot j}$ defined by Rasmussen [1956, p.135] as

$$U_{\cdot j} = \frac{L_{\cdot j}}{\frac{1}{n}\sum_{k=1}^{n} L_{\cdot k}} \qquad j = 1,\ldots,n,$$

1) For applications of Rasmussen's index $U_{\cdot j}$ or modifications of it see, for instance, the studies of Hazari[1970], Laumas [1975], Schultz [1976], Yotopoulos and Nugent [1973].

where $$L_{\cdot j} = \sum_{i=1}^{n} \ell_{ij} \quad j = 1,\dots,n$$ [1)]

can be interpreted as the overall output increase of the whole system induced by a unit increase in the final demand for products of industry j. Sine $L_{\cdot j}$ captures the direct as well as the indirect effects which emanate from an increase in final demand for commodity j the indices $L_{\cdot j}$ are called "total linkages" (see Yotopoulos and Nugent [1973,p.161]).[2)] For making inter-industry comparisons it is convenient to relate the column sums of L to their overall average which yields $U_{\cdot j}$. A sector j with a high power of dispersion is in a favourite position to produce strong output stimuli for the economy and may therefore be called a "key sector" at least if the coefficient of variation of the ℓ_{ij} (i=1,...,n) is relatively small (see Rasmussen [1956,p. 140 f.]).

When total final demand $D:= \sum_{i=1}^{n} d_i$ is to be increased by government expenditures of a given amount ΔD that can be distributed over all goods, then the overall output increase will be maximized if ΔD is spent for goods of a single sector, namely that with the highest value of $U_{\cdot j}$ or $L_{\cdot j}$, respectively. For intertemporal or international comparisons the ranking of the indices $U_{\cdot j}$ is of particular interest; obviously it coincides with the ranking of the $L_{\cdot j}$. For the sake of simplicity let us consider the total linkage indices in the following.

As key sector indices are assumed to be able to give hints for efficient public investment decisions, it is worth investigating how these indices are influenced by price changes and by technological change such as process substitution and productivity improvement. These problems are taken up by the following analysis as well as the question how sensitive key sector indices are to aggregation and to errors in the input coefficients. In a sceptical paper Bharadwaj [1966,p.318] sharply pointed out the role of

---

1) ℓ_{ij} denotes the coefficients of the Leontief inverse L(A).

2) A similar index concentrating on the indirect effects was suggested by Lehbert ([1970 ,p.58]) as measure for the drawing effect ("Mitzieh-Effekt") on the system. See also an earlier suggestion of Rasmussen ([1956],p.139).

aggregation for the reliability of key sector indices: "The sensitivity of the linkage effects to the scheme of aggregation would have to be scrutinized before much credence is placed on their estimates based on a particular scheme of aggregation".

As the values of key sector indices obtained from empirical input-output tables lie very close together[1)] for the leading sectors even small changes in some of the values may create a different ranking of sectors.

Throughout the whole paper it will be assumed that the input[2)] matrix A and the changed one denoted by A' are Leontief matrices, i.e. nonnegative square matrices which fulfill the Hawkins-Simon condition. The Leontief inverse of A and A' is in short denoted by L and L', resp., and the set of all Leontief matrices by $\mathcal{L}$.

2. Sensitivity to Changes in Prices

Empirical input-output tables are given in value terms. If there is a change in prices from p_i to

(2.1) $$p_i' := p_i \pi_i \qquad (\pi_i > 0) \quad i = 1,\dots,n,$$

then the input matrix A undergoes a similarity transformation (cf. Chakravarty [1969,p.148]) and becomes

(2.2) $$A' = \Pi A \Pi^{-1},$$

where Π denotes the diagonal matrix of the π_i. It is easily seen that $A \in \mathcal{L}$ implies $A' \in \mathcal{L}$ [3)] and furthermore that the Leontief inverse is subject to the same similarity transformation

(2.3) $$L' := (I-A')^{-1} = \Pi L \Pi^{-1}.$$

---

1) The study of Yotopoulos and Nugent [1973,p.162], for instance, contains a table of total linkages (for developed countries) the first 7 (out of 18) sectors ranging between 2.425 and 2.194. See also section 4.

2) For many problems it is reasonable to work with domestic input coefficients.

3) A similarity transformation of A preserves the eigenvalues.

Hence, the coefficients ℓ'_{ij} of L' are given by

$$\ell'_{ij} = \ell_{ij} \frac{\pi_i}{\pi_j} \qquad i,j = 1,\ldots,n. \tag{2.4}$$

Equation (2.4) shows that the key sector indices $U_{.j}$ are invariant to a change of all prices by the same factor π. Only changes in the price ratios matter.

Let us consider how the indices are influenced by a change of a single price p_k to $p'_k = p_k\pi_k$ with $\pi_k > 1$. In this case [1] the matrix L' differs from L only in row k and column k the elements of which now read

$$\ell'_{ki} = \ell_{ki}\pi_k \text{ and } \ell'_{ik} = \ell_{ik}/\pi_k \quad \text{for all } i \neq k \tag{2.5}$$

the diagonal element remaining unchanged ($\ell'_{kk} = \ell_{kk}$).

For $j \neq k$ it follows with $\pi_k > 1$:

$$L'_{.j} = \sum_i \ell'_{ij} = \sum_{i \neq k} \ell_{ij} + \ell_{kj}\pi_k = L_{.j} + \ell_{kj}(\pi_k - 1) > L_{.j}. \tag{2.6}$$

The total linkages are increasing for these sectors, the change $\Delta L_{.j} := L'_{.j} - L_{.j}$ being proportional to ℓ_{kj}.

For $j = k$ it turns out that $L'_{.k} < L_{.k}$ because of

$$L'_{.k} = \sum_{i \neq k} \ell_{ik}/\pi_k + \ell_{kk} < \sum_{i \neq k} \ell_{ik} + \ell_{kk} = L_{.k}\,. \tag{2.7}$$

Summarizing we can state that an increase in p_k reduces the relative importance of sector k as measured by the above key sector approach and lets the other sectors appear more important.

---

1) It is assumed that the price change does not initiate factor substitutions in the production processes.

3. Sensitivity to Changes in Technology

Two types of technological change will be considered here: substitution of production processes and changes in factor productivity

a) Process Substitution

The production processes are represented by the column vectors of A. If a process k is replaced by a new one then the effect on the key sector indices can be examined if we know how the Leontief inverse is influenced by a change of a column in A. For a matrix M let the k-th column vector be denoted by $m_{.k}$ and the k-th row vector by $m_{k.}$, and let the change in vector $a_{.k}$ be $\Delta a_{.k}$ and the change thereby induced in L be $\Delta L := L'-L$.
Here we make use of a theorem on the inversion of a special sum of matrices (see Bodewig [1959, p. 39]), from which we conclude

(3.1) $$\Delta\ell_{ij} = \frac{1}{1-\ell_{k.}\Delta a_{.k}} \ell_{i.}\Delta a_{.k}\ell_{kj} \qquad i,j = 1,\dots,n.$$

Hence

(3.2) $$\Delta L_{.j} = \frac{1}{1-\ell_{k.}\Delta a_{.k}} (\sum_{i}\sum_{\nu}\ell_{i\nu}\Delta a_{\nu k})\ell_{kj} \qquad j = 1,\dots,n,$$

that is,

(3.3) $$\Delta L_{.j} = \frac{1}{1-\ell_{k.}\Delta a_{.k}} (\sum_{\nu}L_{.\nu}\Delta a_{\nu k})\ell_{kj} \qquad j = 1,\dots,n.$$

Equation (3.3) shows that $\Delta L_{.j}$ is proportional to ℓ_{kj} the proportionality constant being a linear combination of the total linkages $L_{.\nu}$. All indices move in the same direction because the ℓ_{kj} are nonnegative. For input matrices A with all column sums less than one it can be shown (see Kogelschatz [1977]) that L has a weakly dominant diagonal:

(3.4) $$\ell_{kk} > \ell_{kj} \qquad \text{for all} \quad j \neq k.$$

This property is characteristic for empirical input matrices. The maximal change in $L_{.j}$ will occur in sector k where the substitution takes place. In general it can be observed that ℓ_{kk} is much larger than the off-diagonal elements,[1] so that the ranking of key sector indices is likely to be altered. A process substitution is usually accompanied by a factor substitution: the requirement for some factors decreases whereas that for others goes up (see, e.g., Leontief [1953, p. 32]). But here let us consider the special case where process k is replaced by a more efficient process which has lower input requirements for at least one factor and no higher requirement for any other factor ($\Delta a_{.k} \leq 0$). Then all indices tend to decline and that of sector k by the greatest amount. If sector k is a key sector favoured by government investment it may happen that this sector looses this position by working with a more efficient process. Here the following problem comes up: If an industry anticipates that the government will withdraw investment in case of a lower key sector index, then this may hinder technical progress.

b) Changes in Factor Productivity

The productivity of factor k in process j is given by the reciprocal value of the input coefficient a_{kj}. Therefore a change of the productivity of factor k in the various processes is formally represented by a change of the k-th row in A. Applying the above mentioned theorem on the inversion of a sum of matrices we can conclude that a change of $\Delta a_{k.}$ in the row vector $a_{k.}$ implies

$$(3.5) \qquad \Delta \ell_{ij} = \frac{1}{1-\Delta a_{k.} \ell_{.k}} \Delta a_{k.} \ell_{.j} \ell_{ik} \qquad i,j = 1,\ldots,n.$$

Hence

$$(3.6) \qquad \Delta L_{.j} = \frac{1}{1-\Delta a_{k.} \ell_{.k}} L_{.k} \Delta a_{k.} \ell_{.j} \qquad j = 1,\ldots,n.$$

From equation (3.6) it is seen that in case of a productivity change in factor k the resulting change in the indices $L_{.j}$ is

[1] Necessarily $\ell_{kk} \geq 1$ holds while ℓ_{kj} usually is much smaller than 1 for $j \neq k$.

proportional to $\Delta a_{k.} \ell_{.j}$, the proportionality constant being a multiple of $L._k$. In contrast to the results for a process substitution, in this case some indices may increase while others decrease if the components of $\Delta a_{k.}$ have different signs, i.e., if the productivity of factor k is improved in some processes and lowered in others. But all indices must move in the same direction if the productivity change has the same sign for every process; they decrease (increase) for an increasing (decreasing) productivity.

For the special case of a proportional change ($\Delta a_{k.} = \gamma a_{k.}, \gamma > -1$) equation (3.6) is simplified as follows:

$$(3.7) \qquad \Delta L._j = \frac{1}{1-\gamma(\ell_{kk}-1)} L._k \gamma(\ell_{kj}-\delta_{kj}) \qquad i,j = 1,\dots,n^{1)}$$

because of

$$(3.8) \qquad a_{k.} \ell_{.j} = \ell_{kj}-\delta_{kj} \qquad k,j = 1,\dots,n.$$

In case of a productivity improvement ($\gamma<0$) of factor k we obtain

$$(3.9) \qquad |\Delta L._j|<|\gamma| L._k(\ell_{kj}-\delta_{kj}) \qquad j = 1,\dots,n,$$

and in case of a decreasing productivity ($\gamma>0$) (3.7) yields

$$(3.10) \qquad \Delta L._j>\gamma L._k(\ell_{kj}-\delta_{kj}) \qquad j = 1,\dots,n.$$

It should be kept in mind that the analysis of this section has been confined to a substitution of a single process or a productivity change for a single factor; possible trigger effects induced by these types of technological change in other sectors or factors have not been taken into account.

---

1) δ_{kj} denotes the Kronecker symbol.

4. Sensitivity to Errors in Input Coefficients

Empirical input-output tables are affected by measurement errors. The influence of such errors will be considered for the simplest case where only one input coefficient a_{ks} has an error of size Δa_{ks}. Formally, this problem can be treated by the same methods as applied in section 3. An error in a_{ks} has the same effect on the indices $L_{.j}$ as a change of row k in A by $\Delta a_{kj} = \delta_{sj} \cdot \Delta a_{ks}$ $(j=1,\ldots,n)$. Consequently, formula (3.6) yields

$$(4.1) \qquad \Delta L_{.j} = \frac{\Delta a_{ks}}{1-\Delta a_{ks}\ell_{sk}} L_{.k}\ell_{sj} \qquad j = 1,\ldots,n.$$

For every j the induced error in the indices $L_{.j}$ has the same sign as the error Δa_{ks} and is also proportional to ℓ_{sj}. The maximal error in the indices will occur in sector s, the purchasing sector, provided that all column sums of A are less than 1 (cf. relation (3.4)).[1] As for empirical data ℓ_{ss} is usually much larger than ℓ_{sj} for $j \neq s$, it may happen that the ranking of the key sector indices is already disturbed by an error in a single coefficient.
For small errors formula (4.1) yields in the limit

$$(4.2) \qquad \frac{\partial L_{.j}}{\partial a_{ks}} = L_{.k}\,\ell_{sj} \qquad j = 1,\ldots,n$$

and as a first order approximation

$$(4.3) \qquad \Delta L_{.j} \approx L_{.k}\ell_{sj}\Delta a_{ks} \qquad j = 1,\ldots,n.$$

An error of Δa_{ks} in some input coefficient of sector s will yield an error of a somewhat greater amount in $L_{.s}$ because of $L_{.k}, \ell_{ss} > 1$. Let us consider the table of total linkages cited from Yotopoulos and Nugent [1973] in the introduction. If there were an error of, say, 0.1 in one of the input coefficients of sector 7 in the given ranking then this could make this sector hold the first position in the linkage ranking, as formula (4.1) yields for the given values. This example shows that the ranking of key sector indices can be very sensitive to measurement errors in the underlying input-output table.

---

1) To put it in other words, the total linkage index $L_{.j}$ is more sensitive to errors in process j than to errors of the same amount in other processes.

5. Sensitivity to Aggregation

By aggregation of sectors the nxn input matrix A is transformed into a mxm matrix A' with m<n. The aggregated input matrix has the representation

(5.1) $$A' = SAW,$$

where S is a mxn summation matrix and W a nxm weighting matrix whose coefficients are derived from the base period output vector x^0 (see, for instance, Theil [1967, p. 324]).

The effect of a consolidation of sectors on the Leontief inverse will be studied here for elementary aggregations of two sectors, any aggregation being composed of such elementary ones. The results derived here for an aggregation of sector n and (n-1) can be formulated for elementary aggregations of any sectors. Combining the last two sectors the matrices S and W are of the following form

(5.2) $$S = \begin{pmatrix} 1_1 & & 0 \\ & \ddots & \\ 0 & & 11 \end{pmatrix} \qquad W = \begin{pmatrix} 1 & & 0 \\ & \ddots & \\ & & 1 \; w_{n-1} \\ 0 & & w_n \end{pmatrix}.$$

The weights w_n and w_{n-1} can be derived from the definition of the input coefficients as

(5.3) $$w_n = x_n^0/(x_{n-1}^0 + x_n^0), \quad w_{n-1} = x_{n-1}^0/(x_{n-1}^0 + x_n^0).$$

Instead of w_n we just write w; then $w_{n-1} = 1-w$ because of (5.3).

The interconnection between the Leontief inverses L and L' was investigated by Kogelschatz [1977]. The matrix L' can be directly computed from L as the following proposition shows:

Proposition 1:

In an input matrix $A \varepsilon \mathcal{L}$ let two sectors, e.g. sectors n and (n-1), be aggregated. Then, provided that $A' \varepsilon \mathcal{L}$, the following connection between the corresponding Leontief inverses L and L' holds:

(5.4) $$\ell'_{ij} = \bar{\ell}_{ij} + c(\bar{\ell}_{in}-\bar{\ell}_{i,n-1})(w\ell_{n-1,j}-(1-w)\ell_{nj}) \qquad i,j=1,\ldots n-1,$$

where

(5.5) $$\bar{L} := SL, \quad c := 1/((1-w)(\ell_{nn}-\ell_{n,n-1})-w(\ell_{n-1,n}-\ell_{n-1,n-1})).$$

For an input matrix A with all column sums less than 1 it can be shown that $A' \varepsilon \mathcal{L}$ holds, and, moreover, that c is a positive constant.

By means of proposition 1 we are able to answer the question how key sector indices are influenced by elementary aggregations. For the aggregation under consideration it follows:

(5.6) $$\begin{aligned} L'_{\cdot j} &= \sum_{i=1}^{n-1} \ell'_{ij} \qquad j = 1,\ldots,n-1 \\ &= \sum_{i=1}^{n-1} (\bar{\ell}_{ij} + c(\bar{\ell}_{in}-\bar{\ell}_{i,n-1})(w\ell_{n-1,j}-(1-w)\ell_{nj}) \\ &= \sum_{i=1}^{n-1} \bar{\ell}_{ij} + c(w\ell_{n-1,j}-(1-w)\ell_{nj})(\sum_{i=1}^{n-1}\bar{\ell}_{in}-\sum_{i=1}^{n-1}\bar{\ell}_{i,n-1}) \end{aligned}$$

Hence

(5.7) $$L'_{\cdot j} = L_{\cdot j} + c(w\ell_{n-1,j}-(1-w)\ell_{nj})(L_{\cdot n}-L_{\cdot n-1}) \qquad j=1,\ldots,n-1.$$

This equation gives the connection between the indices $L_{\cdot j}$ and $L'_{\cdot j}$. Whenever $L_{\cdot n}$ and $L_{\cdot n-1}$ happen to be equal the indices $L_{\cdot j}$ are not affected by the aggregation procedure. For $L_{\cdot n}>L_{\cdot n-1}$ formula (5.7) yields

(5.8) $$L'_{\cdot j} \gtreqless L_{\cdot j} \text{ for } w\ell_{n-1,j} \gtreqless (1-w)\ell_{nj} \qquad j=1,\ldots,n-1$$

or in view of the definition of w (provided $\ell_{nj} \neq 0$):

(5.9) $$L'_{.j} \lesseqgtr L_{.j} \quad \text{for} \quad \frac{\ell_{n-1,j}}{\ell_{nj}} \gtreqless \frac{x^0_{n-1}}{x^0_n} \qquad j = 1,\dots,n-1.$$

In case of $L_{.n} < L_{.n-1}$, just change the inequality signs in (5.8) and (5.9), respectively. As L is a nonsingular matrix it is ruled out that $\ell_{n-1,j}/\ell_{nj} = x^0_{n-1}/x^0_n$ for all j. Taking into account

(5.10) $$\sum_{j=1}^{n} \ell_{n-1,j} d^0_j = x^0_{n-1} \quad \text{and} \quad \sum_{j=1}^{n} \ell_{nj} d^0_j = x^0_n$$

it follows that there exists at least one sector j_1 with $\ell_{n-1,j_1}/\ell_{nj_1} > x^0_{n-1}/x^0_n$ and another sector j_2 with $\ell_{n-1,j_2}/\ell_{nj_2} < x^0_{n-1}/x^0_n$. Consequently, for $L_{.n} \neq L_{.n-1}$ some indices increase by the aggregation procedure, while others decline. The ranking of key sector indices may well be affected by aggregation. For instance, for the original input matrix A let sector 1 and 2 hold position 1 and 2, respectively, in the ranking of key sector indices. Then, by an aggregation of other industries of the economy, it may turn out that sector 1 - in comparison to sector 2 - shows a relatively lower importance as measured by the key sector indices for the aggregated system. The ranking of total linkages depending on the scheme of aggregation justifies Bharadwaj's scepticism mentioned above.

References

BHARADWAJ, K.R.: A Note on Structural Interdependence and the Concept of 'Key' Sector. Kyklos 19 (1966), p.315 - 319.

BODEWIG, E.: Matrix Calculus. Amsterdam 1959.

CHAKRAVARTY, S.: Capital and Development Planning. Cambridge (Mass.) London 1969.

GOLDSTEIN, B.H.: Potentialtheorie Markoffscher Ketten. Operations Research-Verfahren IV, p.270 - 594, Meisenheim 1967.

HAZARI, B.R.: Empirical Identification of Key Sectors in the Indian Economy. The Review of Economics and Statistics 52, 1970, p.301-305.

HIRSCHMAN, A.O.: The Strategy of Economic Development. New Haven 1958.

KOGELSCHATZ,H.: Zur Bestimmung des aggregationsbedingten Prognosefehlers in Input-Output-Modellen. Forthcoming in: Quantitative Wirtschaftsforschung (Festschrift für W.Krelle). (Ed. by H. Albach, E. Helmstädter, R. Henn), Tübingen 1977.

LAUMAS, P.S.: Key Sectors in Some Underdeveloped Countries. Kyklos 28 (1975), p.62-79.

LAUMAS, P.S.: The Weighting Problem in Testing the Linkage Hypothesis. The Quarterly Journal of Economics 90 (1976), p. 308-312.

LEHBERT, B.: Bedeutung und Auswertung regionaler Input-Output-Tabellen. Kieler Studien Bd. 105. Tübingen 1970.

LEONTIEF, W. (ed.): Studies in the Structure of the American Economy. New York 1953.

RASMUSSEN, P.N.: Studies in Inter-Sectoral Relations. Kopenhagen-Amsterdam 1956.

SCHULTZ, S.: Intersectoral Comparison as an Approach to the Identification of Key Sectors. In: Advances in Input-Output Analysis. (Ed.by K.R.Polenske and J.V.Skolka). Proceedings of the Sixth International Conference on Input-Output Techniques, Vienna 1974. Cambridge, Mass. 1976, p. 137-159.

STRASSERT, G.: Zur Bestimmung strategischer Sektoren mit Hilfe von Input-Output-Modellen. Jahrbücher für Nationalökonomie und Statistik 182 (1968/69), p. 211-215.

THEIL,H.: Economics and Information Theory. Amsterdam 1967.

YOTOPOULOS, P.A. and J.B. NUGENT: A Balanced-Growth Version of the Linkage-Hypothesis. A Test. The Quarterly Journal of Economics 87, 1973, p. 157-171.

A Taste-Dependent True Wage Index

by Louis Phlips*

1. Introduction

This paper presents the results of an exercise aimed at measuring the evolution over time of real hourly wages with reference to a "true" or functional wage index, defined in a way analogous to the well-known constant-utility index of the cost of living. The paper elaborates on an idea put forward by Pencavel (1977), who suggests to solve the true index problem, not for the "income" that leaves the consumer indifferent w.r.t. base period utility, but directly for the constant-utility wage rate.

In standard practice, movements in real wages are measured by comparing changes in nominal earnings with changes in a price index. Attempts to construct a constant-utility price index are meant, in fact, to provide the correct price index to use in this context, or at least to provide a better index than the currently used empirical Laspeyres-type consumer price index.

---

* Professor of Economics, C.O.R.E. I am grateful to P. Pieraerts and D.Van Grunderbeeck for research and computational assistance, and to R. Anderson, J. Drèze, J. Pencavel and the participants at the seminar for helpful discussions of an earlier draft.

It should be clear, however, that the constant-utility price index, as defined in the framework of standard demand analysis, presents a number of deficiencies when used to measure changes in real earnings. First of all, it is based on a model in which the length of work time (or leisure time) is ignored, although the consumer is probably not indifferent between an increase in earnings through a wage increase, with constant (or reduced) work time, and the same increase obtained after a longer working day, with a constant hourly wage rate.

Secondly, the true index problem ignores current income : only base year income (together with base year and current prices) appears in the analysis as it is usually set up, although the consumer's present situation obviously depends not only on today's prices but also on today's income. This deficiency is inevitable as long as "income" is defined as the sum of total expenditures on consumption goods.

We are thus led to a third criticism : to talk about "income" when what is meant is "total consumption expenditures" is a source of confusion. There is a real need for a theory of demand in which the word "income" designates what it suggests, i.e. the sum of labour and non-labour income, and in which labour income depends both on the wage rate and on the number of hours worked (or not worked). If such a theory can be used to define a true index, it provides a natural way of introducing the length of work time into the measurement of real wages, as requested above.

Pencavel (1977) has successfully remedied each of these deficiencies, by defining the true wage index in the framework of a model of the allocation of time and implementing it within the (enlarged) linear expenditure system, as worked out by Abbott and Ashenfelter (1976). Further improvements are possible, though.

Indeed, given the static character of the approach, savings(out of labour and non-labour income) are simply supposed to be zero, while earnings foregone by holding cash balances are ignored. There is thus a need for enlarging the budget constraint (recoined the "full income" constraint to allow for the allocation of time between work and leisure) even further and embedding it in a wealth constraint defining savings. Simultaneously, one may want to allow tastes to change over time, especially since this may destroy the familiar inequalities between the true index and empirical indexes (in particular the Laspeyres and the Paasche index), as emphasized by Fisher and Shell (1969). It may indeed reveal losses in welfare which outweigh the gains resulting from the celebrated substitution effect which true indexes try to capture.

The enlargement of the budget constraint, coupled with the "dynamization" of the utility function, is what characterizes the approaches presented here.

2. Taste-Dependent True Wage Indexes

The taste-dependent true wage index may be defined as follows. Suppose the average consumer maximizes the "dynamized" instantaneous utility function

$$(1) \qquad u = u(x, \ell, m; R),$$

where x is an n-vector of commodity purchases, ℓ represents hours of leisure and m represents real cash balances held for transactions purposes. R designates the preference ordering represented by u, and is a function of the current values of n + 2 state variables whose movements determine taste changes, i.e.

$$(2) \qquad R = R(s, s_\ell, w)$$

where s is an n-vector of state variables, each associated with a corresponding quantity purchased, s_ℓ is the state variable associated with leisure, and w is real non-human wealth. These n + 2 states are defined as the solutions of

$$(3a) \qquad \dot{s}_i = x_i - \delta_i s_i$$

$$(3b) \qquad \dot{s}_\ell = \ell - \delta_\ell s_\ell$$

$$(3c) \qquad \dot{W} = r(W - p_m m) + p_\ell(T - \ell) - \sum_i p_i x_i \qquad (i = 1, \ldots, n)$$

respectively, with $W = p_m w$ (for simplicity). p_m is the price of money in terms of all consumption goods, p_ℓ is the wage rate, r is the rate of interest, and T is the maximum number of hours available (so that $T - \ell$ represents the number of hours worked).

The utility function (1) is maximized subject to the enlarged "full income" constraint

$$(4) \qquad y = \sum_i p_i x_i + p_\ell \ell + r p_m m$$

which is part of the wealth constraint (3c). The latter can be rewritten as

$$(5) \qquad \dot{W} = rW + p_\ell T - y.$$

All variables in (5), including full income y, are given to the consumer. Savings ($\dot{W}$), although present in the model, are unexplained, i.e. exogenous.

Insertion of the demand equations

$$(6) \qquad \begin{aligned} x &= x(p, p_\ell, rp_m, y; R) \\ \ell &= \ell(p, p_\ell, rp_m, y; R) \\ m &= m(p, p_\ell, rp_m, y; R) \end{aligned}$$

into the utility function gives the indirect utility function

$$u^* = u^*(p, p_\ell, rp_m, y; R).$$

The true or constant-utility wage rate $p_{\ell t}^{*}$ is then the solution of

$$u^{*}(p_o, p_{\ell o}, r_o p_{mo}, y_o; R_o) = u^{*}(p_t, p_{\ell t}^{*}, r_t p_{mt}, y_t; R_t) \tag{7}$$

and the <u>true wage index</u> is $p_{\ell t}^{*}/p_{\ell o}$, where the subscript o designates the base year, while what we shall call the <u>real wage index</u> is $p_{\ell t}/p_{\ell t}^{*}$, i.e. the ratio of the current wage over the true wage, and measures the change in real wages between period t and the base year. When the real wage index is larger than one, the consumer is better off than in the base year.

The numbers derived by solving (7) will henceforth be called "cardinal" - to be consistent with the terminology used in Phlips (1974, Chapter 9) and Phlips and Sanz-Ferrer (1975) - because a comparison of utility levels over time is involved. Alternatively, one can define the true wage rate $p_{\ell t}^{**}$ as a solution of

$$u^{*}(p_o, p_{\ell o}, r_o p_{mo}, y_o; R_t) = u^{*}(p_t, p_{\ell t}^{**}, r_t p_{mt}, y_t; R_t), \tag{8}$$

i.e. with reference to the <u>current</u> preference ordering only, to follow the recommendations made by Fisher and Shell (F-S). The corresponding indexes may then be called F-S true and real wage indexes.

Once so far, there seems to be no reason not to redefine the true index of the cost of living, in the framework of the model sketched above, as the ratio of the true full income to base year full income. The "cardinal" true full income is then the value y^* that minimizes (4) subject to the condition $u_t = u_o$. The corresponding F-S constant-utility full income is the value y_t^{**} that minimizes (4) subject to $u_t = \hat{u}_t$, where $\hat{u}$ is the maximum current (direct) utility obtainable under the base year constraint. These indexes do take past and current wage rates, leisure time, rates of interest and cash holdings into account.

3. Specification of the Model

For empirical purposes we specify (1) as a generalized Stone-Geary utility function

(9) $$u = \sum_i \beta_i \log(x_i - \gamma_i) + \beta_\ell \log(\ell - \gamma_\ell) + \beta_m \log(m - \gamma_m)$$

and dynamize it by supposing that the minimum required quantities change over time according to

(10) $$\gamma_i = \theta_i + \alpha_i s_i$$

$$\gamma_\ell = \theta_\ell + \alpha_\ell s_\ell$$

$$\gamma_m = \theta_m + \alpha_m w$$

Specifications (10) illustrate what Beckmann (1977) calls Harrod-neutral taste changes. When α is positive, the taste change is "quantity diminishing" : there is habit formation. When α is negative, the taste change is "quantity augmenting" as can be seen from equation (9) : this is typical for durable goods (in the absence of habit formation). The properties of the system of demand equations resulting from the maximization of (9) subject to (10) and the constraints (3) and (4) are discussed in Phlips (1977), which the reader is referred to for further details.

We proceed immediately with the derivation of the cardinal constant-utility wage rate $p^*_{\ell t}$. It turns out simply to be the solution of

$$(11) \qquad 1 = \frac{\tilde{y}_o + p_{\ell o}\gamma_{ho} - \sum_i p_{io}\gamma_{io} - r_o p_{mo}\gamma_{mo}}{\tilde{y}_t + p^*_{\ell t}\gamma_{ht} - \sum_i p_{it}\gamma_{it} - r_t p_{mt}\gamma_{mt}} \prod_{i=1}^{n} \left(\frac{p_{it}}{p_{io}}\right)^{\beta_i} \left(\frac{p^*_{\ell t}}{p_{\ell o}}\right)^{\beta_\ell} \left(\frac{r_t p_{mt}}{r_o p_{mo}}\right)^{\beta_m}$$

for each t. This solution can easily be computed by the Gauss-Seidel method, once estimates of γ_{it}, γ_{ht} and γ_{mt} are available. γ_h is defined as $T - \gamma_\ell$, and $\tilde{y} = \sum_i p_i x_i + p_\ell(-h) + rp_m m$. h measures the number of hours worked.

To compute the Fisher-Shell constant-utility wage rate $p^{**}_{\ell t}$, one simply replaces γ_{ho}, γ_{io} and γ_{mo} by γ_{ht}, γ_{it} and γ_{mt} respectively in (11). Both the cardinal and the F-S results are invariant under monotonic transformations of the utility function.

4. Empirical Results for the U.S. (1939-1967)

The empirical results presented here are based on the data used and the estimates obtained in Phlips (1977). The data include the eleven (n = 11) U.S. consumption series in nominal terms (expressed per person engaged in production) published in the *Survey of Current Business* for the period 1938-67. The rate of interest r_t is measured using the Aaa series (corporate bonds), while the implicit price deflator for total consumption expenditures measures p_{mt}. The stock of money (currency plus demand deposits) of American households at the end of the year t is taken from the flow of funds data of the Federal Reserve, and also expressed per person engaged in production. Given that T is unknown - and cannot be estimated in the present state of the art - observations on $\ell = T - h$ (where h is the number of hours worked per person engaged in production) cannot be constructed in a sensible way. To circumvent this difficulty, the estimating equations were redefined so as to make it possible to use $-h_t$ (instead of ℓ_t) as observations in the leisure equation. (This is why γ_h and $\tilde{y}$ appear in (11) rather than γ_ℓ and y!) As an estimate of h, and of the price $p_{\ell t}$, we use Abbott and Ashenfelter's series, which end in 1967. Wages ($p_{\ell t}$) are after taxes.

Table 1 reproduces the estimates of some key structural coefficients in the model, and of the short-run uncompensated wage and own price elasticities. Leisure appears to be habit-forming ($\alpha_\ell > 0$), while the supply of labour is slightly backward bending (its uncompensated wage elasticity is -0.09). Table 2 gives observed wage rates and true wage rates for selected years. (The complete series are given in Appendix A). The year 1939 was chosen as the base year, so that the results can be compared directly with Pencavel's.

Table 1. Structural Coefficients

Commodity	β	θ	α	Wage elasticity	Price elasticity
(1) Automobiles and parts	0.068	-23.8	2.504	1.85	-0.53
(2) Furniture and household equipment	0.073	10.9	0.858	0.95	-0.38
(3) Other durable goods	0.022	-6.0	0.246	0.89	-0.34
(4) Food and beverage	0.271	641.9	0.080	0.74	-0.47
(5) Clothing and shoes	0.080	10.8	0.187	0.60	-0.29
(6) Gasoline and oil	0.035	-3.9	0.842	0.95	-0.34
(7) Other nondurable goods	0.053	26.0	0.344	0.40	-0.19
(8) Housing	0.078	-0.6	0.523	0.46	-0.23
(9) Household operation	0.031	-1.0	0.848	0.42	-0.18
(10) Transportation	0.029	67.2	0.123	0.67	-0.27
(11) Other services	0.124	-184.9	0.210	0.63	-0.33
(12) Leisure (ℓ) or supply of labour (h)	0.130(β_ℓ)	629.2(θ_h)	0.582(α_ℓ)	-0.09(h)	-0.09(h)
(13) Money	0.006	816.3	-0.007	0.54	-0.08

Looking at the cardinal constant-utility wages first, we see that they are slightly below the observed wages, except for the war years, during which the war effort led to working hours that came very close to the maximum number of hours the average worker was ready to work, and to constraints on wage rates. Otherwise, real wages, as measured by the real wage index $p_{\ell t}/p^*_{\ell t}$ (see Table 3), increased slightly. In 1967, the improvement was about 16 % only. This is much below the improvement of about 148 % reported by Pencavel on the basis of the static linear expenditure system. The only possible explanation seems to be that taste changes have had a systematic influence. Taste changes due to habit formation seem to have been dominating, so that the consumer needs systematically "more" to obtain the same utility. This phenomenon is reflected in the positive α-coefficients, and especially in the positive α_ℓ for the demand for leisure. With an ever increasing minimum amount of leisure, the wage rate that keeps utility constant is continuously increased with the result that the gain in real wages is reduced.

Our estimated rise in real wages is even lower than the one recorded by the *Bureau of Labor Statistics* on the basis of measurements which tend to ignore not only substitution effects but also changes in tastes. While the inclusion of the former tend to indicate greater gains, (as illustrated in Pencavel's approach based on static utility theory), the latter bring us below the descriptive BLS measurements. All in all then, the neglect of dynamic phenomena may bias measurements of real wages as much - and probably more, in fact - as the neglect of substitution phenomena.

Table 2. Wage Rates after Taxes (U.S. dollars per hour)

	Observed $p_{\ell t}$	Cardinal $p^*_{\ell t}$	F-S $p^{**}_{\ell t}$
1939	0.370	0.370	0.370
1943	0.570	0.791	0.780
1946	0.700	0.676	0.630
1950	0.970	0.958	0.690
1955	1.280	1.229	0.720
1960	1.600	1.466	0.570
1965	1.980	1.705	0.500
1967	2.180	1.876	0.430

Table 3. Wage Index Numbers (1939 = 100)

	Cardinal $p^*_{\ell t} / p_{\ell o}$	F-S $p^{**}_{\ell t} / p_{\ell o}$		Cardinal $p_{\ell t} / p^*_{\ell t}$	F-S $p_{\ell t} / p^{**}_{\ell t}$
1939	100	100		100	100
1943	187	211		72	73
1946	160	170		104	111
1950	227	186		101	141
1955	291	195		104	178
1960	347	154		109	281
1965	403	135		117	396
1967	444	116		116	507

The Fisher-Shell cost-of-living index is known to reduce the impact of habit formation in comparison with the cardinal cost-of-living index. One expects therefore the F-S constant-utility wage rate to be below the cardinal $p^*_{\ell t}$, and therefore to indicate a greater rise in real wages when compared to the observed wage rate. This is exactly what happens in Tables 2 and 3. Rather surprisingly, the F-S constant-utility wage rate $p^{**}_{\ell t}$ even starts to decline in the sixties.

At this point, a word of warning is in order : to the extent that the estimates of the α-coefficients may be biased upwards (which may be the case for a number of items in the system, and is certainly true for the α-coefficient of the item "automobiles and parts"), the evolutions of both $p^{*}_{\ell t}$ and $p^{**}_{\ell t}$ may be exaggerated, especially in the sixties. Nevertheless, the numbers reported convey three messages which are very clear : a) a static utility maximization approach exaggerates the gain in real wages; b) the same is even more true in a dynamic approach, when the Fisher-Shell index, focusing on current tastes, is used; c) to the extent that habit formation is properly taken into account, the gain in real wages appears as small, and smaller than indicated by the Laspeyres-type index numbers used by the *Bureau of Labor Statistics*.

To conclude, our numerical exercises tend to corroborate the general feeling that the increases in nominal wages, however impressive, do not more than catch up with our ever increasing needs. In other words, to end in a philosophical mood : while our incomes are higher than those of our parents, this does not imply that we enjoy life more.

REFERENCES

ABBOTT, M. and O. ASHENFELTER (1976), Labor Supply, Commodity Demand and the Allocation of Time, *Review of Economic Studies 43,* 389-411.

BECKMANN, M.J. (1977), Neutral Changes in Tastes and Utility, *this volume.*

DE SOUZA, E. (1974), Taste Change in the True Cost-of-Living Index, *Recherches Economiques de Louvain 40,* 55-68.

FISHER, F.M. and K. SHELL (1969), Taste and Quality Change in the Pure Theory of the True Cost-of-Living Index, in WOLFE, J. (ed.), *Value, Capital and Growth, Essays in Honour of J.R. Hicks,* Oxford.

PENCAVEL, J.H. (1977), Constant-Utility Index Numbers of Real Wages, *American Economic Review 67,* 91-100.

PHLIPS, L. (1974), *Applied Consumption Analysis,* Advanced Textbooks in Economics, Vol.5, North-Holland Publ. Co., Amsterdam.

PHLIPS, L. (1977), The demand for Leisure and Money, C.O.R.E. Discussion Paper N° 7715, forthcoming in *Econometrica.*

PHLIPS, L. and R. SANZ-FERRER (1975), A Taste-Dependent True Index of the Cost-of-Living, *Review of Economics and Statistics 57,* 495-501.

	Observed $p_{\ell t}$	Cardinal $p^{*}_{\ell t}$	Cardinal true index $p^{*}_{\ell t} / p_{\ell o}$	Cardinal real index $p_{\ell t} / p^{*}_{\ell t}$	F-S $p^{**}_{\ell t}$	F-S true index $p^{**}_{\ell t} / p_{\ell o}$	F-S real index $p_{\ell t} / p^{**}_{\ell t}$
1939	0.370	0.370	1.000	1.000	0.370	1.000	1.000
1940	0.390	0.482	1.139	0.809	0.450	1.220	0.870
1941	0.450	0.574	1.357	0.784	0.530	1.430	0.850
1942	0.530	0.722	1.707	0.734	0.680	1.840	0.780
1943	0.570	0.791	1.870	0.721	0.780	2.110	0.730
1944	0.610	0.823	1.946	0.741	0.830	2.240	0.730
1945	0.630	0.770	1.820	0.818	0.780	2.110	0.810
1946	0.700	0.676	1.598	1.036	0.630	1.700	1.110
1947	0.790	0.803	1.898	0.984	0.660	1.780	1.200
1948	0.880	0.932	2.203	0.944	0.720	1.950	1.220
1949	0.900	0.919	2.173	0.979	0.690	1.860	1.300
1950	0.970	0.958	2.265	1.013	0.690	1.860	1.410
1951	1.040	1.112	2.629	0.935	0.790	2.140	1.320
1952	1.090	1.178	2.785	0.925	0.830	2.240	1.310
1953	1.180	1.175	2.778	1.004	0.790	2.140	1.490
1954	1.230	1.205	2.849	1.021	0.800	2.160	1.540
1955	1.280	1.229	2.905	1.041	0.720	1.950	1.780
1956	1.360	1.345	3.180	1.011	0.750	2.030	1.810
1957	1.440	1.448	3.423	0.994	0.740	2.000	1.950
1958	1.500	1.444	3.414	1.039	0.690	1.860	2.170
1959	1.560	1.456	3.442	1.071	0.580	1.570	2.690
1960	1.600	1.466	3.466	1.091	0.570	1.540	2.810
1961	1.660	1.486	3.513	1.117	0.550	1.490	3.020
1962	1.720	1.536	3.631	1.120	0.540	1.460	3.190
1963	1.790	1.539	3.638	1.163	0.500	1.350	3.580
1964	1.910	1.636	3.868	1.167	0.510	1.380	3.750
1965	1.980	1.705	4.031	1.161	0.500	1.350	3.960
1966	2.090	1.739	4.111	1.202	0.430	1.160	4.860
1967	2.180	1.876	4.435	1.162	0.430	1.160	5.070

A Dynamic Formulation of Index Functions for the Theory of Cost and Production

by R.W. Shephard

1. Introduction

Index numbers are introduced usually in the context of static (steady state) models, yet they are intended clearly to relate to dynamic situations. In a paper of Samuelson and Swamy [1] an account is given in such static terms for definition of price and quantity index for a bundle of consumption goods by minimal cost ratios to attain a level of living as measured by a cardinal utility function. For index numbers of "production possibilities", a scalar function of output vectors, called "aggregate size"!, is used as a reference for maximal value ratios to define a price index for outputs, while the quantity index is merely a ratio of "aggregate sizes". It would have been less arbitrary, perhaps, if the "aggregate size" scalar function had been developed on some production theoretic basis. Throughout, the role of homothetic structure of cardinal utility is emphasized for invariance of cost of living price and quantity indexes with respect to "level of living".

For the theory of cost and production it is useful to formulate index functions for prices and quantities for both outputs and the factors of production in such a fashion that they may relate for an aggregate expression of the theory. Also the use of value ratios to define index numbers is of long tradition in economics and there is some purpose to take this approach, but in a proper dynamic context.

This paper is written to serve both of these two purposes. The dynamic model of production used is that of Shephard and Färe [2], in which vectors of time histories of inputs are mapped into sets of vectors of output time histories.

Without assumptions as to special structure for production, index functions for both price and quantity are defined for inputs and outputs in terms of value ratios expressed by minimal cost and maximal return functionals. Homotheticity of structure is defined, both when input and output structure are independently homothetic and when they are inversely related homothetic. Under these special structures, particularly the latter, the index functions are independent of the reference vectors taken for their definition, satisfy the usual properties for indices and provide compact aggregate expressions for the theory of cost and production.

Saving the existence of a duality gap, which may be avoided by additional restrictive assumptions on the dynamic structure of production beyond homotheticity, such as convexity of map sets $\mathbb{P}(x)$ and $\mathbb{L}(u)$ and free disposability of inputs, the quantity index functions for outputs and inputs may be defined alternatively by ratios of values for cost and return which are dual to those previously used for price indices. In the inversely related homothetic case, the two quantity index functions take the same form under no duality gap as those previously obtained without the use of duality.

2. The Dynamic Model of Production Correspondences

Let BM_+^α denote the nonnegative domain of the space of bounded Lebesgue measurable functions defined on $[0,+\infty)$ with sup norm for the components of a point of BM^α, and for any two points $k = (f_1\ f_2,\ldots,f_\alpha)$, $\ell = (g_1,g_2,\ldots,g_\alpha)$ of BM^α an ordering is given by

$$k \geqq \ell \quad \text{iff} \quad f_i \geqq g_i \quad \text{for} \quad i \in \{1,2,\ldots,\alpha\}$$

$$k \geq \ell \quad \text{iff} \quad f_i \geq g_i \quad \text{for} \quad i \in \{1,2,\ldots,\alpha\} \quad , k \neq \ell$$

$$k > \ell \quad \text{iff} \quad f_i \geq g_i \quad \text{for} \quad i \in \{1,2,\ldots,\alpha\}$$

where $f_i \geq g_i$ iff $f_i(t) \geqq g_i(t)$ for all $t \in [0,+\infty)$ but $f_i(t) \neq g_i(t)$ for some subset $S \subset [0,+\infty)$ of positive Lebesgue measure. The norm of $k \in BM^{\alpha}$ ist taken as the Euclidian norm of the norms of the components of k. With such specifications, BM^{α} is a complete, normed, linear space, i.e. a Banach space. For some purposes equivalence classes of the functions f_i may be used as primal elements.

Denote the inputs by a vector of functions $x = (x_1,x_2,\ldots,x_n)$, with $x_i(t)$ representing at time t the amount of the i-th exogenous input applied per unit time in production. The related net outputs are denoted by $u = (u_1,u_2,\ldots,u_m)$, with $u_i(t)$ representing at the time t the amount per unit time of the i-th net output.

The dynamic production correspondence is a mapping $\mathbb{P} : x \in BM_+^n \to \mathbb{P}(x) \in 2^{BM_+^m}$, in which $\mathbb{P}(x)$ denotes the set of all output function vectors $u \in BM_+^m$ obtainable from $x \in BM_+^n$.

Axioms for this mapping to define a production correspondence are:

$\mathbb{P}.1$ $\mathbb{P}(0) = \{0\}$

$\mathbb{P}.2$ $\mathbb{P}(x)$ is totally bounded for $\| x \| < +\infty$

$\mathbb{P}.3$ $\mathbb{P}(\lambda x) \supseteq \mathbb{P}(x)$ for $\lambda \in [1,+\infty)$

$\mathbb{P}.4$ If $\|x\| > 0$, either $\mathbb{P}(x) = \{0\}$ or there exists $\bar{u} \varepsilon BM_+^m$ with $\|\bar{u}\| > 0$ such that $u \varepsilon \mathbb{P}(\bar{\lambda}x)$ for some $\bar{\lambda} \varepsilon (0,+\infty)$. In the second case, there exists for each scalar $\theta \varepsilon (0,+\infty)$ a scalar $\lambda_\theta \varepsilon (0,+\infty)$ such that $(\theta\bar{u}) \varepsilon \mathbb{P}(\lambda_\theta \cdot x)$. For each $i \varepsilon \{1,2,\ldots.m\}$ there exists $y \varepsilon BM_+^n$, $\|y\| > 0$, such that $\mathbb{P}(y)$ contains $u \varepsilon BM_+^m$ with $\|u_i\| > 0$.

$\mathbb{P}.5$ The correspondence $x \rightarrow \mathbb{P}(x)$ is closed, i.e. $[\{x_\alpha\} \rightarrow x_o$, $\{u_\alpha\} \rightarrow u_o$, $u_\alpha \varepsilon \mathbb{P}(x_\alpha)\ \forall\alpha] \Rightarrow u_o \varepsilon \mathbb{P}(x_o)$.

$\mathbb{P}.6$ If $u \varepsilon \mathbb{P}(x)$, $(\theta u) \varepsilon \mathbb{P}(x)$ for $\theta \varepsilon [0,1]$.

Axioms $\mathbb{P}.3$ and $\mathbb{P}.6$ are weak disposal properties, and $\mathbb{P}.2$ is an extension of boundedness in the steady state case.

The steady state model is merely a subcase of this dynamic model, obtained by considering BM_+^n[constant] and BM_+^m[constant] as Banach subspaces where all functions are constant so that the inputs are (in time) fixed amounts per unit time. Then the dynamic correspondence reduces to $P : x \varepsilon R_+^n \rightarrow P(x) \varepsilon 2^{R_+^m}$ with properties which are exactly those postulated in [3], [4] for the steady state case, except for clarification of $\mathbb{P}.4$.

The inverse dynamic correspondence is a mapping $u \varepsilon BM_+^m \rightarrow \mathbb{L}(u) \varepsilon 2^{BM_+^n}$ in which $\mathbb{L}(u) = \left\{x \varepsilon BM_+^n \mid u \varepsilon \mathbb{P}(x)\right\}$ is the set of all input function vectors $x \varepsilon BM_+^n$ yielding at least $u \varepsilon BM_+^m$. The properties of the correspondence $u \rightarrow \mathbb{L}(u)$ follow from those taken for $x \rightarrow \mathbb{P}(x)$. See Shephard and Färe [2] for details. In addition, as an asymmetric axiom, the efficient subset of $\mathbb{L}(u)$ is taken totally bounded for all $u \varepsilon BM_+^m$.

3. Globally Homothetic Correspondences

Definition:

$x \to \mathbb{P}(x)$ ist globally homothetic iff $\mathbb{P}(x) = F(\mathbb{H}(x)) \cdot \mathbb{P}_{ff}(1)$ for $x \in BM_+^n$, where: (1) $\mathbb{P}_{ff}(1) \subset BM_+^m$ is a closed and totally bounded set with $0 \in \mathbb{P}_{ff}(1)$ and $(\theta \cdot u) \in \mathbb{P}_{ff}(1)$ for $\theta \in [0,1]$ when $u \in \mathbb{P}_{ff}(1)$; (2) $F(\cdot)$ is a nonnegative, nondecreasing scalar valued function mapping $R_+ \to R_+$, and upper semi-continuous with $F(0) = 0$ and $F(v) \to +\infty$ as $v \to +\infty$; (3) $\mathbb{H}(x)$ ist a functional $\mathbb{H} : BM_+^n \to R_+$ satisfying

$\mathbb{H}$.1 $\mathbb{H}(0) = 0$, $\mathbb{H}(x) > 0$ for some $x \in BM_+^n$

$\mathbb{H}$.2 $\mathbb{H}(x)$ is finite for $\|x\| < +\infty$

$\mathbb{H}$.3 $\mathbb{H}(\lambda x) \geqq \mathbb{H}(x)$ for $\lambda \in [1,+\infty)$

$\mathbb{H}$.4 If $\mathbb{H}(\lambda x) > 0$, $\mathbb{H}(\lambda x) \to +\infty$ as $\lambda \to +\infty$

$\mathbb{H}$.5 $\mathbb{H}(x)$ is upper semi-continuous on BM_+^n .[1)]

The distance functional of $\mathbb{P}_{ff}(1)$ is given by

$$ff(u) = [\text{Max}\{\theta \mid (\theta u) \in \mathbb{P}_{ff}(1) , \theta \in [0,+\infty)\}]^{-1} , \quad u \in BM_+^m$$

and

$$(1) \quad \mathbb{P}(x) = \left\{u \mid ff(u) \leq F(\mathbb{H}(x)) , u \in BM_+^m\right\} , \; x \in BM_+^n$$

may be taken as a representation for the globally homothetic dynamic output correspondence. See [2], §6.

---

1) $\mathbb{H}(x)$ is u.s.c. on BM_+^n iff $\{x \mid x \in BM_+^n , \mathbb{H}(x) \geqq \alpha\}$ is closed for all $\alpha \in R$.

Definition:

$u \to \mathbb{L}(u)$ is globally homothetic iff $\mathbb{L}(u) = G(\mathbb{J}(u)) \cdot \mathbb{L}_{\phi\phi}(1)$ for $u \in BM_+^m$, where: (1) $\mathbb{L}_{\phi\phi}(1) \subset BM_+^n$ is a closed set with totally bounded efficient subset Eff $\mathbb{L}_{\phi\phi}(1)$, and $(\lambda x) \in \mathbb{L}_{\phi\phi}(1)$ for $\lambda \in [1,+\infty)$ when $x \in \mathbb{L}_{\phi\phi}(1)$; (2) $G(\cdot)$ is a positive, nondecreasing scalar valued function mapping $R_{++} \to R_{++}$ [2), and lower semi-continuous with $G(w) \to +\infty$ for $w \to +\infty$; (3) $\mathbb{J}(u)$ is a functional $\mathbb{J} : \left(BM_+^m - \{0\}\right) \to R_+$ satisfying

$\mathbb{J}$.1 $\mathbb{J}(u) > 0$ for $u \in \left(BM_+^m - \{0\}\right)$

$\mathbb{J}$.2 $\mathbb{J}(u)$ is finite for $\|u\| < +\infty$ and $\mathbb{L}(u)$ not empty, and is $+\infty$ for $\mathbb{L}(u)$ empty.

$\mathbb{J}$.3 $\mathbb{J}(\theta u) \geqq \mathbb{J}(u)$ for $\theta \in [1,+\infty)$

$\mathbb{J}$.4 If $\mathbb{J}(\theta u) > 0$, $\mathbb{J}(\theta u) \to +\infty$ as $\theta \to +\infty$

$\mathbb{J}$.5 $\mathbb{J}(u)$ is lower semi-continuous on $\left(BM_+^m - \{0\}\right)$. [3)

The distance functional of $\mathbb{L}_{\phi\phi}(1)$ is given by

$$\phi\phi(x) = [\text{Min}\,\{\lambda \mid (\lambda x) \in \mathbb{L}_{\phi\phi}(1)\,,\ \lambda \in [0,+\infty)\}]^{-1}\,,\quad x \in BM_+^n$$

and

$$(2)\quad \mathbb{L}(u) = \left\{x \mid \phi\phi(x) \geqq G(\mathbb{J}(u))\,,\ x \in BM_+^n\right\}\,,\quad u \in \left(BM_+^m - \{0\}\right)$$

may be taken as a representation for the globally homothetic dynamic input correspondence.

---

2) $R_{++} = \{\alpha \in R \mid \alpha > 0\}$

3) $\mathbb{J}(u)$ is l.s.c. on $\left(BM_+^m - \{0\}\right)$ iff for any $\{u^\nu\} \subset \left(BM_+^m - \{0\}\right)$ with $\{u^\nu\} \to u^0 \in \left(BM_+^m - \{0\}\right)$, $\liminf_{\nu \to +\infty} \mathbb{J}(u^\nu) \geqq \mathbb{J}(u^0)$.

Suppose the functional $\mathbb{H}(x)$ is taken to be homogeneous of degree + 1, e.g. $\mathbb{H}(x) = \phi\phi(x)$ with $\phi\phi(\lambda x) = \lambda\phi\phi(x)$. Then global homotheticity for $x \to \mathbb{P}(x)$ implies

$$\mathbb{L}(u) = \left\{x \mid u \in \mathbb{P}(x) \ , \ x \in BM_+^n\right\}$$
$$= \left\{x \mid \phi\phi(x) \geqq F^{-1}(ff(u)) \ , \ x \in BM_+^n\right\} , \ u \in \left(BM_+^m - \{0\}\right)$$

where the inverse function $F^{-1}(\cdot)$ is defined by

$$F^{-1}(w) = \text{Min}\ \{v \in R_+ \mid F(v) \geqq w\} \ , \ w \in R_+ \ .$$

Note then, that

$$\mathbb{L}(u) = F^{-1}(ff(u)) \left\{x \mid \phi\phi(x) \geqq 1 \ , \quad x \in BM_+^n\right\}$$

and $\phi\phi(x)$ is a distance functional for a fixed set

$$\mathbb{L}_{\phi\phi}(1) = \left\{x \mid \phi\phi(x) \geqq 1 \quad , \ x \in BM_+^n\right\} .$$

Hence, when $\mathbb{H}(x)$ is a homogeneous functional $\phi\phi(x)$ of degree one, global homotheticity for $x \to \mathbb{P}(x)$ implies that $u \to \mathbb{L}(u)$ is globally homothetic. Conversely, when $u \to \mathbb{L}(u)$ is globally homothetic with $\mathbb{J}(u)$ taken as a homogeneous functional $ff(u)$ of degree one, the correspondence $x \to P(x)$ becomes globally homothetic with

$$\mathbb{P}(x) = G^{-1}(\phi\phi(x)) \left\{u \mid ff(u) \leqq 1 \ , \ u \in BM_+^m \right\} , \ x \in BM_+^n$$

where $ff(u)$ is a distance functional for the fixed set

$$\mathbb{P}_{ff}(1) = \left\{ u \mid ff(u) \leqq 1 \ , \ u \in BM_+^n \right\} .$$

Thus a special and interesting case for later use is one where

$$(3)\quad \begin{aligned}\mathbb{P}(x) &= F(\phi\phi(x)) \cdot \mathbb{P}_f(1)\\ &= F(\phi\phi(x)) \cdot \left\{u \mid ff(u) \leqq 1 \ , \ u \in BM_+^m\right\}, \quad x \in BM_+^n \ ,\end{aligned}$$

$$(4)\quad \begin{aligned}\mathbb{L}(u) &= F^{-1}(ff(u)) \cdot \mathbb{L}_{\phi\phi}(1)\\ &= F^{-1}(ff(u)) \cdot \left\{x \mid \phi\phi(x) \geqq 1 \ , \ x \in BM_+^n\right\}, \quad u \in \left(BM_+^m - \{0\}\right)\end{aligned}$$

in which the functionals $ff(u)$ and $\phi\phi(x)$ are distance functionals with the properties stated above for $\mathbb{J}(u)$ and $\mathbb{H}(x)$ respectively, and $F(\cdot)$ has the properties stated.

4. Price and Quantity Index Functions

As notation we take

$$BM_+^\alpha \cdot [0,T] = \left\{f \in BM_+^\alpha \mid f(t) \ \text{taken zero for } t > T\right\}$$

$$BM_{++}^\alpha = \left\{f \in BM_+^\alpha \mid f \neq 0\right\}$$

$$f \cdot [0,T] = f(t) \text{ for } t \in [0,T] \text{ and zero for } t > T$$

$$\mathbb{K}(u,p,T) = \underset{x}{\text{Min}}\left\{\int_0^T \left(\sum_{i=1}^n p_i(\tau)x_i(\tau)\right) d\tau \mid x \in \mathbb{L}(u) \cap BM_+^n \cdot [0,T]\right\}, \quad \begin{array}{l} p \in BM_+^n \cdot [0,T] \\ u \in BM_+^m \cdot [0,T]\end{array}$$

$$\mathbb{R}(x,r,T) = \underset{u}{\text{Max}}\left\{\int_0^T \left(\sum_{i=1}^m r_i(\tau)u_i(\tau)\right) d\tau \mid u \in \mathbb{P}(x) \cap BM_+^m \cdot [0,T]\right\}, \quad \begin{array}{l} r \in BM^m \cdot [0,T] \\ x \in BM_+^n \cdot [0,T]\end{array}$$

The following definitions of index functions are used for the theory of cost and production:

Definition: PRICE INDEX FUNCTION FOR INPUTS

For two vectors of price functions $p^1 \varepsilon BM_{+}^{n}$, $p^0 \varepsilon BM_{++}^{n}$ for inputs, the index function at any time $T \varepsilon (0,+\infty)$ comparing p^1 to p^0 equals the ratio of the minimal total cost over $[0,T]$ under $p^1[0,T]$ of obtaining a reference vector of output functions $u \varepsilon \tilde{BM}_{++}^{m}$ 4) $\cdot$ $[0,T]$, $\mathbb{L}(u)$ not empty, to the minimal cost over $[0,T]$ under $p^0 \cdot [0,T]$.

Definition: QUANTITY INDEX FUNCTION FOR OUTPUTS

For two vectors of output functions $u^1 \varepsilon BM_{+}^{m}$, $u^0 \varepsilon BM_{++}^{m}$, $\mathbb{L}(u^1)$ not empty, $\mathbb{L}(u^0)$ not empty, and reference price vector $p \varepsilon \hat{BM}_{++}^{n}$ 5) for inputs, the index function at any time $T \varepsilon (0,+\infty)$ comparing u^1 to u^0 equals the ratio of an arbitrarily chosen nonnegative, nondecreasing transformation of "standardized minimal cost" 6) over $[0,T]$ of obtaining $u^1 \cdot [0,T]$ under prices $p \varepsilon [0,T]$ for inputs to the same transformation of standardized minimal cost of obtaining $u^0 \cdot [0,T]$ under prices $p \cdot [0,T]$ for inputs.

Definition: PRICE INDEX FUNCTION FOR OUTPUTS

For two vectors of price functions $r^1 \varepsilon BM^m$, $r^0 \varepsilon BM^m$, $r^0 \nleqq 0$, for outputs, the index function at any time $T \varepsilon (0,+\infty)$ comparing r^1 to r^0 equals the ratio of the maximal total value over $[0,T]$ under $r^1 \cdot [0,T]$ obtainable from a reference input vector $x \cdot [0,T] \varepsilon \check{BM}_{++}^{n} \cdot [0,T]$ 7) to the maximal total value obtainable over $[0,T]$ under prices $r^0 \cdot [0,T]$.

---

4) $\tilde{BM}_{++}^{m} = \left\{ f \varepsilon BM_{++}^{m} \mid \mathbb{K}(f,p,T) > 0,\ p \varepsilon \{p^1,p^0\},\ T \varepsilon (0,+\infty) \right\}$.

5) $\hat{BM}_{++}^{n} = \left\{ f \varepsilon BM_{++}^{n} \mid \mathbb{K}(u,f,T) > 0,\ u \varepsilon \{u^1,u^0\},\ T \varepsilon (0,+\infty) \right\}$.

6) "Standardized minimal cost" over $[0,T]$ is monetary cost deflated by total cost over $[0,T]$ of some standard input set A restricted to $A \cdot [0,T]$.

7) $\check{BM}_{++}^{n} = \left\{ f \varepsilon BM_{++}^{n} \mid \mathbb{R}(f,r,T) > 0,\ r \varepsilon \{r^1,r^0\},\ T \varepsilon (0,+\infty) \right\}$.

Definition: QUANTITY INDEX FUNCTION FOR INPUTS

For two vectors of input functions $x^1 \in BM^n_+$, $x^0 \in BM^n_{++}$, $\mathbb{P}(x^0) \neq \{0\}$, and reference price vetor $r \in \overline{BM}^m$ 8), the index function at any time $T \in (0,+\infty)$ comparing x^1 to x^0 equals the ratio of an arbitrarily chosen nonnegative, nondecreasing transformation of "standardized maximal return" 9) over [0,T] obtainable from $x^1[0,T]$ under prices $r \cdot [0,T]$ for outputs to the same transformation of "standardized maximal return" obtainable from $x^0[0,T]$ under prices $r[0,T]$ for outputs.

Minimal costs over an interval [0,T] for given vector u of output functions and vector p of price functions for inputs depend upon both u and p. However, if the vector u is held fixed for comparison with respect to two vectors p^1 and p^0 , the corresponding minimal costs vary only due to price changes and the ratio of minimal cost with p^1 to minimal cost with p^0 is a scalar for the period [0,T] which reflects only price function changes. If all components of p^1 are a multiple (say 2) for those of p^0 , the ratio will be 2. The homogeneity of minimal costs with respect to vector p of price functions for given vector u of output functions provides an essential property for the index function at the time T. Generally the comparison will not be invariant (independent of) for vectors u of output functions. As will be seen later, homotheticity of the input structure of production will yield this independence.

---

8) $\overline{BM}^m = \{f \in BM^m \mid \mathbb{R}(x,f,T) > 0,\ x \in \{x^1,x^0\}\ ,\ T \in (0,+\infty)\}$.

9) "Standardized maximal return" over [0,T] is monetary return deflated by total maximal return over [0,T] of some standardized output set B restricted to $B \cdot [0,T]$.

Since the vector r of output price functions serves to value output, two vectors r^1 and r^0 may be compared in terms of the maximal return over [0,T] obtainable from a given vector x of input functions, and the definition of an index function for vectors of output price functions is parallel in these terms to that for vectors of input price functions.

Comparison of two vectors u^1 and u^0 of output functions over an interval [0,T] can be made in monetary terms by the ratio of "real" minimal costs to achieve them for given vector p of input price functions, i.e. by "standardized minimal costs", and any nonnegative nondecreasing transformation of these "real" minimal costs may be used for calculating the ratio, since there is no absolute unit for the ratio. However, one may seek a transformation which yields for any interval [0,T] the result that the ratio of maximal returns obtainable from x^1 and x^0 under r^1 and r^0 respectively equals the product of the price index for outputs comparing r^1 to r^0 and the quantity index for outputs comparing u^1 to u^0 when the latter are taken as the vectors maximizing the returns obtainable from $x^1[0,T]$ and $x^0[0,T]$ respectively. In this way a natural unit may be obtained for the index function comparing real minimal costs of getting two vectors of output functions for given vector p of input price functions.

Similarly, two vectors of x^1 and x^0 of input functions may be compared over an interval [0,T] in terms of the "real" maximal returns obtainable from them for a vector r of price functions for outputs, transformed so that the ratio of minimal costs of obtaining vectors u^1 and u^0 over [0,T] under vectors p^1 and p^0 of price functions for inputs equals the product of the price index for inputs comparing p^1 to p^0 and the quantity index for inputs comparing x^1 to x^0 when the latter are taken as the vectors minimizing the costs of obtaining u^1 [0,T] and $u^0[0,T]$ respectively.

For precision of statement, the index functions defined above are here stated in mathematical form:

PRICE INDEX FUNCTION FOR INPUTS: $\pi(p^1, p^O/u)$

$$\pi : (p^1, p^O/u) \in BM_+^n \times BM_{++}^n \times \widetilde{BM}_{++}^m \rightarrow \pi(p^1, p^O/u) \in BM_+(O, +\infty)$$

$$\pi(p^1, p^O/u) : \pi_T(p^1, p^O/u) = \frac{\mathbb{K}(u, p^1, T)}{\mathbb{K}(u, p^O, T)} \quad , \quad T \in (O, +\infty)$$

QUANTITY INDEX FUNCTION FOR OUTPUTS: $O(u^1, u^O/p)$

$$O : (u^1, u^O, p) \in BM_+^m \times BM_{++}^m \times \hat{BM}_{++}^n \rightarrow O(u^1, u^O/p) \in BM_+(O, +\infty)$$

$$O(u^1, u^O/p) : O_T(u^1, u^O/p) = \frac{F(\hat{\mathbb{K}}(u^1, p, T))}{F(\hat{\mathbb{K}}(u^O, p, T))} \quad , \quad T \in (O, +\infty)$$

$\hat{\mathbb{K}}$ is standardized minimal cost, $\mathbb{L}(u^1) \neq \emptyset$, $\mathbb{L}(u^O) \neq \emptyset$, $F(\cdot)$ is upper semi-continuous, nonnegative, nondecreasing with $F(O) = O$, $F(v) > O$ for $v \in (O, +\infty)$, with $F(v) \rightarrow +\infty$ as $v \rightarrow +\infty$.

PRICE INDEX FUNCTION FOR OUTPUTS: $\rho(r^1, r^O/x)$

$$\rho : (r^1, r^O, x) \in BM^m \times BM^m(r \nleq O) \times \check{BM}_{++}^n \rightarrow \rho(r^1, r^O/x) \in BM_+(O, +\infty) ,$$

$$\rho(r^1, r^O/x) : \rho_T(r^1, r^O/x) = \frac{\mathbb{R}(x, r^1, T)}{\mathbb{R}(x, r^O, T)} \quad , \quad T \rightarrow (O, +\infty)$$

QUANTITY INDEX FUNCTION FOR INPUTS: $I(x^1,x^0/r)$

$$I : (x^1,x^0,r) \in BM_{+}^{n} \times BM_{++}^{n} \times \overline{BM}^{m} \rightarrow I(x^1,x^0/r) \in BM_{+} \cdot (0,+\infty)$$

$$I(x^1,x^0/r) : I_T(x^1,x^0/r) = \frac{G(\hat{\mathbb{R}}(x^1,r,T))}{G(\hat{\mathbb{R}}(x^0,r,T))} , \quad T \in (0,+\infty)$$

$\hat{\mathbb{R}}$ is standardized maximal return, $\mathbb{P}(x^0) \neq \{0\}$, $G(\cdot)$ is lower semi-continuous, nonnegative, nondecreasing with $G(0) = 0$, $G(v) > 0$ for $v \in (0,+\infty)$, with $G(v) \rightarrow +\infty$ as $v \rightarrow +\infty$.

For a steady state model of production one need only restrict consideration to the nonnegative domains of the subspaces of constant functions, i.e. $x \in R_{+}^{n}$, $u \in R_{+}^{m}$, $p \in R_{+}^{n}$, $r \in R^{m}$, taking x,u,p and r as vectors of real numbers with the components of x and u being constant time rates. Then minimal total costs $\mathbb{K}$ and maximal returns $\mathbb{R}$ over an interval [0,T] reduce to

$$\mathbb{K}(u,p,T) = T \cdot Q(u,p)$$

$$\mathbb{R}(x,r,T) = T \cdot R(x,r)$$

$$\hat{\mathbb{K}}(u,p,T) = \hat{Q}(u,p), \text{ i.e. real cost}$$

$$\hat{\mathbb{R}}(x,r,T) = \hat{R}(x,r), \text{ i.e. real return}$$

where

$$Q(u,p) = \underset{x}{\text{Min}} \{p \cdot x \mid x \in R_{+}^{n} , x \in L(u)\}$$

$$R(x,r) = \underset{u}{\text{Max}} \{r \cdot u \mid u \in R_{+}^{m} , u \in P(x)\}$$

and the model of production is given by correspondences

$$P : x \in R_+^n \to P(x) \in 2^{R_+^m}$$

$$L : u \in R_+^m \to L(u) \in 2^{R_+^n} \quad .$$

Then the index functions reduce to index numbers, independent of time, given by

PRICE INDEX FUNCTION FOR INPUT:

$$\pi(p^1,p^0 \mid u) = \frac{Q(u,p^1)}{Q(u,p^0)}$$

PRICE INDEX FUNCTION FOR OUTPUTS:

$$\rho(r^1,r^0 \mid x) = \frac{R(x,r^1)}{R(x,r^0)}$$

QUANTITY INDEX FUNCTION FOR OUTPUTS:

$$O(u^1,u^0 \mid p) = \frac{F(\hat{Q}(u^1,p))}{F(\hat{Q}(u^0,p))}$$

where $\hat{Q}$ is "real costs".

QUANTITY INDEX FUNCTION FOR INPUTS:

$$I(x^1,x^0 \mid r) = \frac{G(\hat{R}(x^1,r))}{G(\hat{R}(x^0,r))}$$

where $\hat{R}$ is "real" return.

5. Index Functions for Homothetic Production Structure

Consider the case of inversely related homothetic dynamic structure where

$$\mathbb{P}(x) = F(\phi\phi(x)) \cdot \mathbb{P}_f(1)$$

$$= F(\phi\phi(x)) \cdot \left\{u \mid ff(u) \leqq 1 \ , \ u \in BM_+^m\right\}, \quad x \in BM_+^n$$

$$\mathbb{L}(u) = F^{-1}(ff(u)) \cdot \mathbb{L}_{\phi\phi}(1)$$

$$= F^{-1}(ff(u)) \cdot \left\{x \mid \phi\phi(x) \geqq 1 \ , \ x \in BM_+^n\right\}, \ u \in \left(BM_+^m - \{0\}\right),$$

in which $\phi\phi(x)$ and $ff(u)$ are homogeneous distance functionals and $F(\cdot)$ is a nonnegative, nondecreasing scalar valued function with $F(0) = 0$ and $F(v) \to +\infty$ for $v \to +\infty$, and upper semi-continuous. The cost and return functions over an interval $[0,T]$ take the forms

$$\mathbb{K}(u,p,T) = F^{-1}(ff_T(u)) \cdot M_T(p)$$

$$\mathbb{R}(x,r,T) = F(\phi\phi_T(x)) \cdot N_T(r)$$

where $ff_T(u) = ff(u)$, $u \in BM_+^m[0,T]$, $\phi\phi_T(x) = \phi\phi(x)$, $x \in BM_+^n[0,T]$, and

$$M_T(p) = \underset{p}{\text{Min}} \left\{\langle p \cdot x\rangle_T \mid x \in BM_+^n[0,T], \ \phi\phi(x) \geqq 1\right\}$$

$$N_T(r) = \underset{u}{\text{Max}} \left\{\langle r \cdot u\rangle_T \mid u \in BM_+^n[0,T], \ ff(u) \leqq 1\right\}$$

are minimal total costs and maximal total returns respectively over $[0,T]$ of vectors of input functions and vectors of output functions restricted respectively to "standard" sets.

$\langle s \cdot z \rangle_T$ denotes

$$\int_0^T \left(\sum_{i=1}^{n} s_i(\tau) \; z_i(\tau) \right) d\tau \; .$$

$$\mathbb{L}^T_{\Phi\Phi}(1) = \left\{ x \; \varepsilon \; BM^n_+ \mid \Phi\Phi(x) \geqq 1 \right\} \cap BM^n_+[0,T]$$

$$\mathbb{P}^T_{ff}(1) = \left\{ u \; \varepsilon \; BM^m_+ \mid ff(u) \leqq 1 \right\} \cap BM^m \cdot [0,T] \; .$$

The minimal costs and maximal returns $\mathbb{K}(u,p,T)$ and $\mathbb{R}(x,r,T)$ occur for vectors $x^* \cdot [0,T]$ of input functions and $u^* \cdot [0,T]$ of output functions satisfying

$$\Phi\Phi_T(x^*) = F^{-1}(ff_T(u))$$

$$ff_T(u^*) = F(\Phi\Phi_T(x))$$

due to the homogeneity of $\Phi\Phi_T(x)$ and $ff_T(u)$, $T \; \varepsilon \; (0,+\infty)$.

The index function for comparing vectors p^1 and p^0 of price functions for inputs then takes the form

$$\pi_T(p^1,p^0) = \frac{M_T(p^1)}{M_T(p^0)} \; , \quad T \; \varepsilon \; (0,+\infty)$$

independent (invariant) of the output vector $u \; \varepsilon \; \widetilde{BM}^m_{++}$, and the index function for comparing output vectors u^1 and u^0 becomes

$$O_T(u^1,u^0) = \frac{F\left(\dfrac{\mathbb{K}(u^1,p,T)}{M_T(p)}\right)}{F\left(\dfrac{\mathbb{K}(u^0,p,T)}{M_T(p)}\right)} \; , \quad T \; \varepsilon \; (0,+\infty) \; ,$$

$$= \frac{ff_T(u^1)}{ff_T(u^0)} \; , \quad T \; \varepsilon \; (0,+\infty)$$

independent (invariant) of the price vector $p \in \hat{BM}^n_{++}$. The function $M_T(p)$ is taken as a price deflator for real costs.

Further, the index function for comparing vectors r^1 and r^0 of output price functions takes the similar form in maximal returns

$$\rho_T(r^1,r^0) = \frac{N_T(r^1)}{N_T(r^0)} , \quad T \in (0,+\infty)$$

independent (invariant) of the input vector $x \in \check{BM}^n_{++}$, and the index function comparing input vectors x^1 and x^0 becomes

$$I_T(x^1,x^0) = \frac{F^{-1}\left(\frac{\mathbb{R}(x^1,r,T)}{N_T(r)}\right)}{F^{-1}\left(\frac{\mathbb{R}(x^0,r,T)}{N_T(r)}\right)} , \quad T \in (0,+\infty)$$

$$= \frac{\Phi_T(x^1)}{\Phi_T(x^0)} , \quad T \in (0,+\infty) .$$

where $N_T(r)$ is a price deflator for real returns.

For the steady state model of production these index functions are independent of time and they become

$$\pi(p^1,p^0) = \frac{M(p^1)}{M(p^0)}$$

$$O(u^1,u^0) = \frac{f(u^1)}{f(u^0)}$$

$$\rho(r^1,r^0) = \frac{N(r^1)}{N(r^0)}$$

$$I(x^1,x^0) = \frac{\rho(x^1)}{\rho(x^0)}$$

where the production correspondences take the forms

$$x \varepsilon R^n_+ \to P(x) = F(\phi(x)) \cdot \left\{u \mid f(u) \leqq 1 , u \varepsilon R^m_+\right\} \varepsilon 2^{R^m_+}$$

$$u \varepsilon R^m_+ \to L(u) = F^{-1}(f(u)) \cdot \left\{x \mid \rho(x) \geqq 1 , x \varepsilon R^n_+\right\} \varepsilon 2^{R^n_+} ,$$

in which

$$\phi : x \varepsilon R^n_+ \to \phi(x) \varepsilon R_+$$

$$f : u \varepsilon R^m_+ \to f(u) \varepsilon R_+$$

and

$$M(p) = \underset{x}{\text{Min}} \left\{p \cdot x \mid \phi(x) \geqq 1 , x \varepsilon R^n_+\right\}, p \varepsilon R^n_+$$

$$N(r) = \underset{u}{\text{Max}} \left\{r \cdot u \mid f(u) \leqq 1 , u \varepsilon R^m_+\right\}, r \varepsilon R^m .$$

It remains to consider whether the index functions (in the dynamic and static cases) satisfy the usual tests. The first of these, *as stated here*, 1o) requires

$$\frac{\mathbb{K}(u^1,p^1,T)}{\mathbb{K}(u^O,p^O,T)} = \frac{M_T(p^1)}{M_T(p^O)} \cdot \frac{\phi\!\!\phi_T(x^{*1})}{\phi\!\!\phi_T(x^{*O})}$$

where x^{*1} and x^{*O} are vectors of input functions yielding $\mathbb{K}(u^1,p^1,T)$ and $\mathbb{K}(u^O,p^O,T)$ respectively. By direct calculation

$$\frac{\mathbb{K}(u^1,p^1,T)}{\mathbb{K}(u^O,p^O,T)} = \frac{F^{-1}(ff(u^1))}{F^{-1}(ff(u^O))} \cdot \frac{M_T(p^1)}{M_T(p^O)} .$$

1o) Samuelson and Swamy [1] refer to this when it must hold for any x^1 and x^O as the "weak factor-reversal" test. As applied here it would then be superweak.

But, due to the homogeneity of $\Phi(x)$,

$$\Phi_T(x^{*1}) = F^{-1}(ff(u^1))$$

$$\Phi_T(x^{*0}) = F^{-1}(ff(u^0))$$

and

$$\frac{\mathbb{K}(u^1,p^1,T)}{\mathbb{K}(u^0,p^0,T)} = \frac{M_T(p^1)}{M_T(p^0)} \cdot \frac{\Phi_T(x^{*1})}{\Phi_T(x^{*0})}, \quad T \varepsilon (0,+\infty)$$

$$= \pi_T(p^1,p^0) \cdot I_T(x^{*1}, x^{*0}), \quad T \varepsilon (0,+\infty)$$

Thus, assuming that production is carried out for known vectors of price functions for inputs by minimizing costs over an interval [0,T] to attain vectors of output functions over [0,T], the so "Revealed Factor Demand Histories" for inputs will be such that the price index function and quantity index function at any time T will multiply to yield the corresponding ratio of minimal costs over the period [0,T].

By similar argument it may be shown that

$$\frac{\mathbb{R}(x^1,r^1,T)}{\mathbb{R}(x^0,r^0,T)} = \rho_T(r^1,r^0) \cdot O_T(u^{*1}, u^{*0}), \quad T \varepsilon (0,+\infty)$$

where u^{*1} and u^{*0} are vectors of output functions yielding $\mathbb{R}(x^1,r^1,T)$ and $\mathbb{R}(x^0,r^0,T)$ respectively, and the test is satisfied by "Revealed Output Offer Histories".

Other tests commonly applied for index functions are: (1) Homogeneity, (2) Time-reversal, (3) Transitive, (4) Dimensional.

The index functions for the homothetic structure considered here are clearly homogeneous. For example

$$\pi_T(\lambda p^1,p^0) = \frac{M_T(\lambda p^1)}{M_T(p^0)} = \lambda \frac{M_T(p^1)}{M_T(p^0)} = \lambda\pi_T(p^1,p^0)$$

since $M_T(p)$ is homogeneous in p. Similarly $\rho_T(r^1,r^0)$ is homogeneous in r^1 , and the functions $\phi\phi_T(x)$, $ff_T(u)$ are also homogeneous.

To satisfy the time reversal test in the case of $\pi(p^1,p^0)$, one needs to show that $\pi_T(p^1,p^0) \cdot \pi_T(p^0,p^1) = 1$ for $T \varepsilon (0,+\infty)$. Clearly this equality is satisfied and similar equalities hold for the other index functions.

In order to be transitive the index function $\pi(p^1,p^0)$ must satisfy $\pi_T(p^2,p^1) \cdot \pi_T(p^1,p^0) = \pi_T(p^2,p^0)$ for all $T \varepsilon (0,+\infty)$, which is clearly satisfied and likewise for the other index functions.

A dimensional change in the unit of money value clearly does not affect the two price index functions $\pi(p^1,p^0)$ and $\rho(r^1,r^0)$, when likewise changes in the dimensions of the components of x and u lead to multiplication of $\phi\phi_T(x)$ and $ff_T(u)$ by a constant which cancels out for the index functions $O(u^1,u^0)$ and $I(x^1,x^0)$. Thus the index functions are invariant of the monetary and physical units used. Hence all of Fisher's tests are satisfied.

At this point we may relax the specialization of homothetic structure used above, and consider the general case where

$$\begin{aligned}\mathbb{P}(x) &= F(\mathbb{H}(x)) \cdot \mathbb{P}_f(1)\\ &= F(\mathbb{H}(x)) \cdot \left\{u \mid ff(u) \leqq 1 \ , \ u \,\varepsilon\, BM^m_+\right\} , \ x \,\varepsilon\, BM^n_+\end{aligned}$$

$$\begin{aligned}\mathbb{L}(u) &= G(\mathbb{J}\mathbb{J}(u)) \cdot \mathbb{L}_{\phi\phi}(1)\\ &= G(\mathbb{J}\mathbb{J}(u)) \cdot \left\{x \mid \phi\phi(x) \geqq 1 \ , \ x \,\varepsilon\, BM^n_+\right\} , \ u \,\varepsilon\, BM^m_+ \ ,\end{aligned}$$

where $F(\cdot)$, $G(\cdot)$, $\mathbb{H}(x)$ and $\mathbb{J}(u)$ satisfy the general properties stated in Section 3 above, and $\phi\phi(x)$ and $ff(u)$ are distance functions for $\mathbb{L}_{\phi\phi}(1)$ and $\mathbb{P}_{ff}(1)$ as defined above. Then

$$\mathbb{K}(u,p,T) = G(\mathbb{J}_T(u)) \cdot M_T(p)$$

$$\mathbb{R}(x,r,T) = F(\mathbb{H}_T(x)) \cdot N_T(r)$$

with

$$\phi\phi_T(x^*) = G(\mathbb{J}(u))$$

$$ff_T(u^*) = F(\mathbb{H}_T(x)) \quad ,$$

where $x^*[0,T]$, $u^*[0,T]$ yield $\mathbb{K}(u,p,T)$ and $\mathbb{R}(x,r,T)$ respectively.

As defined above the index functions become

$$\pi_T(p^1,p^0) = \frac{M_T(p^1)}{M_T(p^0)} \quad , \quad T \in (0,+\infty)$$

$$\rho_T(r^1,r^0) = \frac{N_T(r^1)}{N_T(r^0)} \quad , \quad T \in (0,+\infty)$$

$$O_T(u^1,u^0) = \frac{\mathbb{J}_T(u^1)}{\mathbb{J}_T(u^0)} \quad , \quad T \in (0,+\infty)$$

$$I_T(x^1,x^0) = \frac{\mathbb{H}_T(x^1)}{\mathbb{H}_T(x^0)} \quad , \quad T \in (0,+\infty)$$

Since $\mathbb{J}_T(u)$ and $\mathbb{H}_T(x)$ are functionals, not necessarily homogeneous, the index function forms for $O_T(u^1,u^0)$ and $I_T(x^1,x^0)$ are not entirely convenient. However, note that when $ff_T(u^1)/ff_T(u^0)$ is used for $O_T(u^1,u^0)$ instead, and $\phi\phi_T(x^1)/\phi\phi_T(x^0)$ is used for $I_T(x^1,x^0)$, the so-called "weak factor reversal test", or value ratio consistency test, is satisfied, since

$$\frac{\phi\phi_T(x^{*1})}{\phi\phi_T(x^{*0})} = \frac{G(\mathbb{J}(u^1))}{G(\mathbb{J}(u^0))}, \quad \frac{ff_T(u^{*1})}{ff_T(u^{*0})} = \frac{F(\mathbb{H}(x^1))}{F(\mathbb{H}(x^0))} .$$

and

$$\frac{\mathbb{K}(u^1,p^1,T)}{\mathbb{K}(u^0,p^0,T)} = \frac{\phi\phi_T(x^{*1})}{\phi\phi_T(x^{*0})} \cdot \frac{M_T(p^1)}{M_T(p^0)}$$

$$\frac{\mathbb{R}(x^1,r^1,T)}{\mathbb{R}(x^0,r^0,T)} = \frac{ff_T(u^{*1})}{ff_T(u^{*0})} \cdot \frac{N_T(r^1)}{N_T(r^0)}$$

where x^{*1}, x^{*0} yield $\mathbb{K}(u^1,p^1,T)$, $\mathbb{K}(u^0,p^0,T)$ respectively and u^{*1}, u^{*0} yield $\mathbb{R}(x^1,r^1,T)$, $\mathbb{R}(x^0,r^0,T)$ respectively.

Thus, one may define

$$O_T(u^1,u^0) = \frac{ff_T(u^1)}{ff_T(u^0)}, \quad T \in (0,+\infty)$$

$$I_T(x^1,x^0) = \frac{\phi\phi_T(x^1)}{\phi\phi_T(x^0)}, \quad T \in (0,+\infty)$$

as index functions for vectors of output and input functions, with "Revealed Output Offer Histories" and "Revealed Input Demand Histories" showing satisfaction of the "weak factor-reversal" test. However in this case we will have departed from the transformed real value ratios given above for definition of the quantiy index functions. Nevertheless, for the homothetic production structures it is natural to define the quantity index functions in this way, because

$$\mathbb{P}_T(x) = \left\{ u \mid ff_T(u) \leqq F(\mathbb{H}_T(x)) \right\}, \quad x \in BM^n_+[0,T]$$

$$\mathbb{L}_T(u) = \left\{ x \mid \phi\phi_T(x) \leqq G(\mathbb{J}_T(u)) \right\}, \quad u \in BM^m_+[0,T]$$

and the two functions $ff_T(u)$ and $\phi\phi_T(x)$ play the role of scalar measures of input and output vectors for their qualification for inclusion in $\mathbb{P}_T(x)$ and $\mathbb{L}_T(u)$ respectively.

One thing to notice is that with these definitions price and quantity index are not independent of each other. The price index functions are defined by minimum and maximum problems in terms of the two distance functions $\phi\phi_T(x)$ and $ff_T(u)$ defining the quantity index functions. The function $M_T(p)$ is the minimal cost over [O,T] of a standard set of vectors of input functions which can be scaled to yield any set $\mathbb{L}_T(u)$ of vectors of input functions, and, except for a scale factor $F^{-1}(ff_T(u))$ (or $G(\mathbb{J}_T(u))$) depending upon the vector $u \in BM^m_+[0,T]$, it represents minimal cost over [O,T] . Thus $M_T(p)$ is a standard cost over [O,T] of inputs, and the variation of this cost defines the price index function for $p \in BM^n_+$. Similarly $N_T(r)$ is a standard return function over [O,T] which can be scaled by $F(\mathbb{H}_T(x))$ for any vector x of input functions.

6. Alternative Definition of Quantity Index Number Functions for Inputs and Outputs

In the previous section comparison of two output vectors u^1, u^0 (or input vectors x^1, x^0) is made in monetary terms by the ratio of "real" minimal costs ("real" maximal returns) to achieve them (obtainable from them), transformed to "standardized" terms since there is no absolute unit for comparing such real values.

With more symmetry of definitions one may use the following alternative definitions: In the dynamic model of production the minimal cost function $\mathbb{K}(u,p,T)$ is dual to the distance functional (see [2])

$$\bar{\Psi}(u,x,T) = [\operatorname{Min}\{\lambda \mid (\lambda x) \in \mathbb{L}_T(u),\quad \lambda \in [0,+\infty)\}]^{-1}$$

for the input correspondence $u \rightarrow \mathbb{L}_T(u)$, by

$$\mathbb{K}(u,p,T) = \operatorname*{Min}_{x} \left\{\langle p \cdot x\rangle_T \mid \bar{\Psi}(u,x,T) \geqq 1\right\}$$

$$\bar{\Psi}(u,x,T) \leqq \operatorname*{Inf}_{p} \left\{\langle p \cdot x\rangle_T \mid \mathbb{K}(u,p,T) \geqq 1\right\} .$$

The inequality for the second relationship indicates the possible existence of a duality gap. For convenience of discussion we shall consider first

$$\bar{\Psi}^{*}(u,x,T) = \operatorname*{Inf}_{p} \left\{\langle p \cdot x\rangle_T \mid \mathbb{K}(u,p,T) \geqq 1\right\} .$$

The functional $\bar{\Psi}^{*}(u,x,T)$ is a dual analogue of the cost functional $\mathbb{K}(u,p,T)$, giving the infimal value of $\langle p \cdot x\rangle_T$ with respect to the vector p of price functions (dual variables to x) constrained by the minmal cost over [0,T] with respect to x being at least unity.

Analogous to the definition given for the index function comparing two price vectors p^1 , p^0 for inputs, the dual definition of the index function comparing two vectors x^1 , x^0 of input functions is:

ALTERNATIVE DEFINITION OF QUANTITY INDEX FUNCTION FOR INPUTS:

$$I(x^1,x^0/u)$$

$$I\ :\ (x^1,x^0,u)\ \varepsilon\ BM_+^n \times BM_{++}^n \times \overline{BM}_+^m(*) \rightarrow I(x^1,x^0/u)\ \varepsilon\ BM_+ \cdot (0,+\infty)\ ,$$ [11)]

$$I(x^1,x^0/u)\ :\ I_T(x^1,x^0/u) = \frac{\bar{\Psi}^*(u,x^1,T)}{\bar{\Psi}^*(u,x^0,T)}\ ,\quad T\ \varepsilon\ (0,+\infty)\ .$$

Similarly, one may define more symmetrically a quantity index function for two output vectors by use of the duality relationship:

$$\mathbb{R}(x,r,T) = \underset{u}{\text{Max}} \left\{ \langle r \cdot u \rangle_T \mid \bar{\Omega}(x,u,T) \leqq 1 \right\}$$

$$\bar{\Omega}(x,u,T) \geqq \underset{r}{\text{Sup}} \left\{ \langle r \cdot u \rangle_T \mid \mathbb{R}(x,r,T) \leqq 1 \right\}$$

where $\bar{\Omega}(x,u,T)$ is the distance functional for the output correspondence $x \rightarrow \mathbb{P}_T(x)$, defined by

$$\bar{\Omega}(x,u,T) = [\text{Max}\ \{\theta \mid (\theta u)\ \varepsilon\, \mathbb{P}_T(x),\ \theta\ \varepsilon\ [0,+\infty)\}]^{-1}\ .$$

Again, because of the possible duality gap indicated in the second statement, we shall consider

$$\bar{\Omega}^*(x,u,T) = \underset{r}{\text{Sup}} \left\{ \langle r \cdot u \rangle_T \mid \mathbb{R}(x,r,T) \leqq 1 \right\}\ .$$

Then by analogy with the definition given for the index function comparing two vectors r^1 , r^0 of price functions for outputs, we may similarly compare the values of outputs obtainable from a reference vector x for input functions by:

---

11) $\overline{BM}_+^m(*) = \left\{ f\ \varepsilon\ BM_+^m \mid \bar{\Psi}^*(f,x,T) > 0,\ x\ \varepsilon\ \{x^1,x^0\},\ T\ \varepsilon\ (0,+\infty) \right\}.$

ALTERNATIVE DEFINITION OF QUANTITY INDEX FUNCTION FOR OUTPUTS:

$O(u^1,u^O/x)$

$$O : (u^1,u^O,x) \in BM_+^m \times BM_{++}^m \times \hat{BM}_+^n(*) \overset{12)}{\rightarrow} O(u^1,u^O/x) \in BM_+ \cdot (O,+\infty)$$

$$O(u^1,u^O/x) : O_T(u^1,u^O/x) = \frac{\bar{\Omega}^*(x,u^1,T)}{\bar{\Omega}^*(x,u^O,T)}, \quad T \in (O,+\infty) .$$

Observe that quantity and price index function are in each case defined with respect to the same reference vector. For example $\pi(p^1,p^O/u)$ and $I(x^1,x^O/u)$, referring to price and quantity for inputs can be referenced to a common output vector. Also they are defined by a common ratio of values, inputs in one case and outputs in the other case. Thus the definitions used are symmetric in these respects.

When the dynamic correspondences $x \rightarrow \mathbb{P}(x)$, $u \rightarrow \mathbb{L}(u)$ are inversely related homothetic, the two distance functionals become

$$\bar{\Psi}^*(u,x,T) = \frac{\Phi\Phi_T^*(x)}{F^{-1}(ff_T(u))}$$

$$\bar{\Omega}^*(x,u,T) = \frac{ff_T^*(u)}{F(\Phi\Phi_T(x))}$$

where

$$\Phi\Phi_T^*(x) = \operatorname*{Inf}_p \left\{ \langle p \cdot x \rangle_T \mid M_T(p) \geqq 1 \right\}, \quad x \in BM_+^n[O,T]$$

$$ff_T^*(u) = \operatorname*{Sup}_r \left\{ \langle r \cdot u \rangle_T \mid N_T(r) \leqq 1 \right\}, \quad u \in BM_+^m[O,T] .$$

It may be noted here that, subject to a possible duality gap, $\Phi\Phi_T(x)$, $M_T(p)$ and $ff_T(u)$, $N_T(r)$ are two pairs of dual functionals.

---

12) $\hat{BM}_+^n(*) = \left\{ f \in BM_+^n \mid \bar{\Omega}^*(f,u,T) > O , \ u \in \{u^1,u^O\}, \ T \in (O,+\infty) \right\}$.

With these special forms of $\bar{\Psi}^*(u,x,T)$ and $\bar{\Omega}^*(x,u,T)$, the quantity index functions for inputs and outputs become respectively

$$I : I_T(x^1,x^0/u) = \frac{\phi\phi^*_T(x^1)}{\phi\phi^*_T(x^0)} , \quad T \in (0,+\infty)$$

$$O : O_T(u^1,u^0/x) = \frac{ff^*_T(u^1)}{ff^*_T(u^0)} , \quad T \in (0,+\infty) ,$$

which are index functions independent of reference vector and similar to those obtained before by more indirect definition with less restriction on the parent correspondences. If the parent correspondences are defined for equivalence classes and satisfy certain additional restrictions to those taken generally for the correspondences $x \to \mathbb{P}(x)$ and $u \to \mathbb{L}(u)$, such as convexity and strong disposability of input histories, and weak star topologies are used for relative compactness of map sets, the duality gaps may be null, in which case

$$\phi\phi^*_T(x) = \phi\phi_T(x) , \quad T \in (0,+\infty) , \quad x \in BM^n_+ \cdot [0,T] ,$$

$$ff^*_T(u) = ff_T(u) , \quad T \in (0,+\infty) , \quad u \in BM^m_+ \cdot [0,T]$$

and the alternative definitions for quantity index functions for inputs and outputs yield the same results as before, *without the restriction however* that the expressions hold only for optimal vectors of the arguments of the functions involved.[13)]

If the duality gap exists,

$$\phi\phi_T(x) \leqq \phi\phi^*_T(x) , \quad T \in (0,+\infty) , \quad x \in BM^n_+ [0,T]$$

$$ff_T(u) \geqq ff^*_T(u) , \quad T \in (0,+\infty) , \quad u \in BM^m_+ [0,T] ,$$

---

13) Since this manuscript was prepared, R. Färe has shown that dualities hold with equal sign for realized optimal values - giving same result by earlier treatment. See paper this volume: "Production Theory Dualities for Optimally Realized Values".

the "weak factor reversal tests", i.e.

$$\frac{\mathbb{K}(u,p^1,T)}{\mathbb{K}(u,p^0,T)} = \pi_T(p^1,p^0/u) \cdot I_T(x^{*1},x^{*0}/u)$$

$$\frac{\mathbb{R}(x,r^1,T)}{\mathbb{R}(x,r^0,T)} = \rho_T(r^1,r^0/x) \cdot O_T(u^{*1},u^{*0}/x)$$

is not enforced where (*) indicates that the related vector is optimal for the value comparisons made. [13)]

In the steady state model case, the quantity indexes of inputs and outputs become:

$$I(x^1,x^0) = \frac{\phi^*(x^1)}{\phi^*(x^0)} \quad , \; x^1 \in R_+^n \; , \; x^0 \in R_+^n$$

$$O(u^1,u^0) = \frac{f^*(u^1)}{f^*(u^0)} \quad , \; u^1 \in R_+^m \; , \; u^0 \in R_+^m$$

Here, if the map sets $P(x)$ and $L(u)$ are convex with strong disposal of inputs and outputs,

$$\phi^*(x) = \phi(x) \; , \; x \in R_+^n$$

$$f^*(u) = f(u) \; , \; u \in R_+^m \; , \; ^{13)}$$

and, for any pairs x^1 , x^0 and u^1 , u^0 of R_+^n and R_+^m respectively,

$$I(x^1,x^0) = \frac{\phi(x^1)}{\phi(x^0)}$$

$$O(u^1,u^0) = \frac{f(u^1)}{f(u^0)} \; .$$

For the general case of independently homothetic input and output structure, these quantity index functions for vectors of input and output functions are not changed structurally. One merely has

$$\bar{\Psi}^*(u,x,T) = \frac{\Phi\!\!\Phi_T^*(x)}{G(\mathbb{J}(u))}$$

$$\bar{\Omega}^*(x,u,T) = \frac{ff_T^*(u)}{F(\mathbb{H}_T(x))} .$$

7. Aggregate Relationships for Cost and Production

When $x \to \mathbb{P}(x)$ and $u \to \mathbb{L}(u)$ are inversely related homothetic, the cost and return functionals take the forms

$$\mathbb{K}_T : (u,p) \in [BM_+^m[0,T] \times BM_+^n \cdot [0,T]] \to F^{-1}(ff_T(u)) \cdot M_T(p) \in R_+$$

$$\mathbb{R}_T : (x,r) \in [BM_+^n[0,T] \times BM^m \cdot [0,T]] \to F(\Phi\!\!\Phi(x)) \cdot N_T(r) \in R_+$$

As aggregate variables, let

$$ff_T : u \in BM_+^m[0,T] \to ff_T(u) \in R_+ , \quad T \in (0,+\infty)$$

$$N_T : r \in BM^m[0,T] \to N_T(r) \in R_+ , \quad T \in (0,+\infty)$$

$$\Phi\!\!\Phi_T : x \in BM_+^n[0,T] \to \Phi\!\!\Phi_T(x) \in R_+ , \quad T \in (0,+\infty)$$

$$M_T : p \in BM_+^n[0,T] \to M_T(p) \in R_+ , \quad T \in (0,+\infty)$$

denote scalar index functions on $(0,+\infty)$ of physical quantity and price of output and input respectively. In such aggregate terms, the total minimal cost over [0,T] of attaining $u \varepsilon BM_+^m[0,T]$ at prices $p \varepsilon BM_+^n[0,T]$ is

$$\mathbb{K}(u,p,T) = \phi\phi_T(x^*) \cdot M_T(p)$$

where x^* denotes the vector of input functions $x \varepsilon BM_+^n[0,T]$ yielding $\mathbb{K}(u,p,T)$. Similarly in aggregate terms, the total maximal return over [0,T] obtainable from $x \varepsilon BM_+^n[0,T]$ at prices $r \varepsilon BM^m[0,T]$ is

$$\mathbb{R}(x,r,T) = ff_T(u^*) \cdot N_T(r)$$

ehere u^* denotes the vector of output functions $u \varepsilon BM_+^m[0,T]$ yielding $\mathbb{R}(x,r,T)$. These expressions result from the fact that x^* and u^* satisfy

$$\left.\begin{aligned} \phi\phi_T(x^*) &= F^{-1}(ff_T(u)) \\ ff_T(u^*) &= F(\phi\phi_T(x)) \end{aligned}\right\} \quad T \varepsilon (0,+\infty)$$

respectively. If the production system operates so that minimal cost and maximal return are obtained, i.e. for given resource vector a maximal return vector is produced, and to obtain a given output vector a minimal cost resource vector is used, the realized values of outputs and inputs satisfy

$$\left.\begin{aligned} ff_T &= F(\phi\phi_T) \\ \phi\phi_T &= F^{-1}(ff_T) \end{aligned}\right\} \quad T \varepsilon (0,+\infty)$$

as aggregate production (and inverse production) functions.

Aggregate indirect production functions are likewise obtained as

$$ff_T = F\left(\frac{\mathbb{K}_T}{M_T}\right) \qquad T \in (0,+\infty)$$

$$\phi\phi_T = F^{-1}\left(\frac{\mathbb{R}_T}{N_T}\right)$$

expressing that aggregate output obtainable from a total cost $\mathbb{K}_T$ over [0,T] is a function of real cost $(\mathbb{K}_T/M_T)$, and that aggregate input needed to sustain a return $\mathbb{R}_T$ over [0,T] is the inverse function of real return $(\mathbb{R}_T/N_T)$.

By combining these two types of aggregate production functions one obtains the aggregate relationship

$$\frac{\mathbb{R}_T}{N_T} = F\left(\frac{\mathbb{K}_T}{M_T}\right) \qquad T \in (0,+\infty)$$

that real aggregate return is a function F of real aggregate cost.

Thus $F(\cdot)$ signifies returns to scale in both physical and monetary terms.

References

[1] P.A. Samuelson & S. Swamy: "Invariant Economic Index Numbers and Canonical Duality: Survey and Synthesis", American Econ. Review, vol 64, No. 4, 1974 pp 566-593

[2] R.W. Shephard & R. Färe: "A Dynamic Theory of Production Correspondences", Operations Research Center Report 75-13, Univ. California Berkeley, Sept. 1975

[3] R.W. Shephard: "Semi-Homogenous Production Functions and Scaling of Production", Vol 99 Lecture Notes in Economics and Mathematical Systems, Production Theory, Springer Verlag, 1974

[4] R.W. Shephard: "Indirect Production Functions, Verlag Anton Hain, Meisenheim am Glan, 1974, 99 pp

On Household Production Theory

by Ronald W. Shephard

1. Introduction

In a paper by Muellbauer [3] on the subject of this paper, a joint production function is used to relate consumption goods vectors to vectors of intrinsic qualities derived from the consumables, upon which household preference is expressed. This model of consumer behavior was first introduced by Lancaster [2] in terms of a simple linear activity analysis correspondence between commodity vectors and vectors of intrinsic qualities. The aim of Muellbauer's paper is to formulate a theoretically constant utility price index when quality changes are taken into account, and in so doing to divulge the restrictive conditions under which the "hedonic technique" may be used to correct prices for quality change.

The joint production function is a tricky concept, seemingly simple but not shown to exist except under very restrictive conditions. In [4] it has been shown by counter example that the existence of the function could not be assured if outputs were not freely disposable, which in the case of the correspondence for intrinsic qualities would mean that intrinsic qualities are freely disposable. One would not wish to impose this property for intrinsic qualities, implying for example in the case of bread that vitamins and nutrients could be enjoyed without the calories.

Bol and Moeschlin [1] have established the existence of the joint production function under continuity of the correspondence and its inverse, and free disposability of inputs and outputs, if all inputs (consumers goods) are each essential by themselves, i.e. if any single commodity input is zero the vector of outputs (intrinsic qualities) is the null output vector. One would not want to make such structural assumptions concerning the correspondence for intrinsic qualities. Hence there is no guarantee under existing propositions for the joint production function that it exists for meaningful use in developing a household production theory of the Lancaster type.

Partly for these reasons the author of this paper has endeavored to develop a household production theory in his own terms, using a general model for the correspondence of intrinsic qualities. In this development an ordinal "household production function" is defined, and cardinalized under the usual assumptions of homogeneity for the correspondence of intrinsic qualities and homotheticity of utility (preference ordering) function. The typical argument against homotheticity of utility function is disputed, and under such circumstances a constant utility index of prices of consumption goods may be formed, which is independent of the utility level with changes in taste and quality accommodated therein.

In this development it is necessary to consider the utility (preference ordering) function in some detail, because not all intrinsic qualities need be wanted nor disposable. Because it is not easy to accept the assumptions ordinarily made for nonsatiation in the preference ordering, household size is introduced as an input component along with the commodity vector and the analysis is revised to include this variable in a meaningful way. Then the previous simplifications of cardinalization of the household production function and utility-level-free-price index may no longer hold, showing the strength of the non-satiation assumptions for consumption theory.

Some thought is given to the computational problems, by linear approximation of the isoquants of the utility function and a linear model for the correspondence of intrinsic qualities.

Although the discussion throughout is expressed for a household it may just as well apply to a "publichold." Nothing in the assumptions made is peculiar to a household unit as opposed to a public unit, the latter being merely a nonsanguinary extension with common purposes as in latter day communes.

2. The Household Production Model

Let x denote a vector of n goods and services used per unit time in consumption. We restrict

$$x \in R_+^n = \{x = (x_1, x_2, \ldots, x_n) \mid x_i \in R, x_i \geqq 0, i = 1, \ldots, n\} .$$

A consumption bundle x is regarded as yielding one or other of a collection of vectors z of m intrinsic qualities per unit time. The vectors z are restricted by

$$z \in R_+^m = \{z = (z_1, \ldots, z_m) \mid z_i \in R, z_i \geqq 0, i = 1, 2, \ldots, m\} .$$

Hedonistically, the correspondence

$$x \in R_+^n \rightarrow P(x) = \{z \mid z \text{ is obtainable from } x\} \in 2^{R_+^n}$$

is a mapping of commodity bundles into subsets $P(x)$ of vectors z of intrinsic qualities which belong to the set of all subsets of R^n_+. It defines the output of consumption for a household, in terms of which choice is made for consumption, i.e. the household expresses a preference ordering for the vectors z and not directly for the vectors x.

The properties taken for the correspondence $x \to P(x)$ are essentially the weak axioms of production theory, see [5], i.e.

P.1 $P(0) = \{0\}$.

P.2 $P(x)$ is bounded for x bounded.

P.3 $P(\lambda x) \supset P(x)$ for $\lambda \in [1,+\infty)$.

P.4 If $x \geq 0$,[(1)] either $P(x) = \{0\}$, or there exists a vector $\bar{z} \geq 0$ with $\bar{z} \in P(\bar{\lambda} x)$ for some scalar $\bar{\lambda} > 0$. In the latter case, there exists for any scalar $\theta > 0$ a scalar $\lambda_\theta > 0$ such that $(\theta \bar{z}) \in P(\lambda_\theta \cdot x)$. For each intrinsic quality there exists a commodity vector x yielding a positive value for that quality.

P.5 $x \to P(x)$ is closed.

P.6 If $z \in P(x)$, $(\theta z) \in P(x)$ for $\theta \in [0,1]$.

Properties P.1 and P.2 are self evident. Property P.3 expresses weak disposability of inputs, stating that if a commodity vector is scaled upward at least what was obtained before can still be obtained. Property P.4 merely defines attainability in the correspondence, and nothing about efficiency is presumed. Property P.5 guarantees that the sets $P(x)$ of inherent qualities are closed, and similarly for the inverse correspondence.

(1) $x \geq 0$ means $x_i \geqq 0$ for $i = 1,2, \ldots, n$, but $x \neq 0$.

Property P.6 expresses weak disposability of outputs. Not all components of an output vector z need be wanted. Moreover they cannot be disposed freely, but may be decreased proportionately.

Nothing about convexity of the output sets $P(x)$ is assumed. Typically an output set $P(x)$ of vectors of intrinsic qualities obtained from a commodity bundle x might appear (in the two-quality case) as:

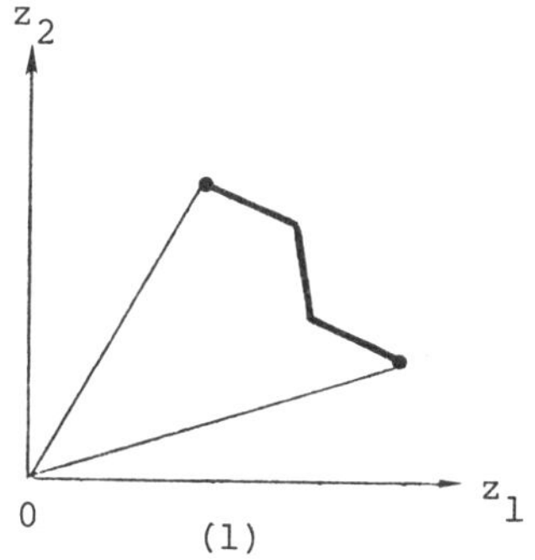

(1)

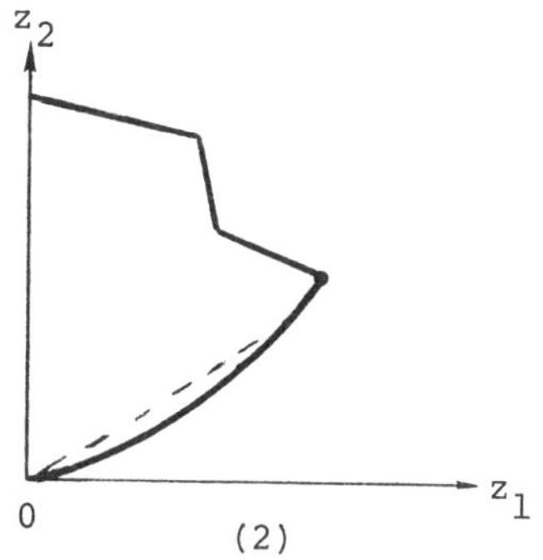

(2)

In Example (1) neither intrinsic quality can be positive when the other is zero, while in Example (2) the second quality can be positive when the first is zero. The assumptions of the model even permit a situation like Example (3) below, where only a discrete set of intrinsic quality mixes are possible, which is what one might expect to occur in the practical case.

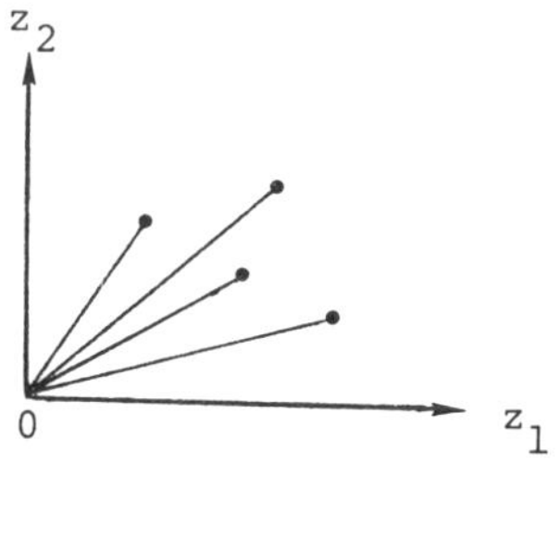

Thus one can see the generality of the assumptions made for the output correspondence $x \rightarrow P(x)$ between commodity vectors x and vectors z of intrinsic qualities. The "frontier" of the output set $P(x)$ need not bound a convex region, nor even be a connected surface of vectors z, let alone being defined by a twice differentiable function.

Inverse to the output correspondence $x \rightarrow P(x)$ there is a correspondence $z \rightarrow L(z)$, relating to each vector z of intrinsic qualities the subset of commodity vectors x which yield at least the vector z by the output correspondence, i.e.

$$z \in R_+^m \rightarrow L(z) \in 2^{R_+^n}$$

where $L(z) = \{x \mid z \in P(x)\}$. The properties of the inverse correspondence $z \rightarrow L(z)$ follow (except for one) from those taken for the direct correspondence $x \rightarrow P(x)$. They are:

L.1 $L(0) = R_+^n$, $0 \notin L(z)$ for $z \geq 0$.

L.2 $\bigcap_{\nu=1}^{\infty} L(z^\nu)$ is empty for $\{||z^\nu||\} \rightarrow +\infty$.

L.3 If $x \in L(z)$, $(\lambda x) \in L(z)$ for $\lambda \in [1,+\infty)$.

L.4 If $x \geq 0$ and $(\bar{\lambda} x) \in L(\bar{z})$ for some $\bar{z} \geq 0$ and $\bar{\lambda} > 0$, the ray $\{\lambda x \mid \lambda \geqq 0\}$ intersects all commodity subsets $L(\theta \bar{z})$ for $\theta \geqq 0$.

L.5 $z \rightarrow L(z)$ is closed.

L.6 $L(\theta z) \subset L(z)$ for $\theta \geqq 1$.

Property L.3 states weak disposability of inputs (following from P.3) and L.6 is the analogue of P.3 for the correspondence $z \rightarrow L(z)$.

Typically a subset $L(z)$ of commodity vectors can appear (2-dimensionally) as

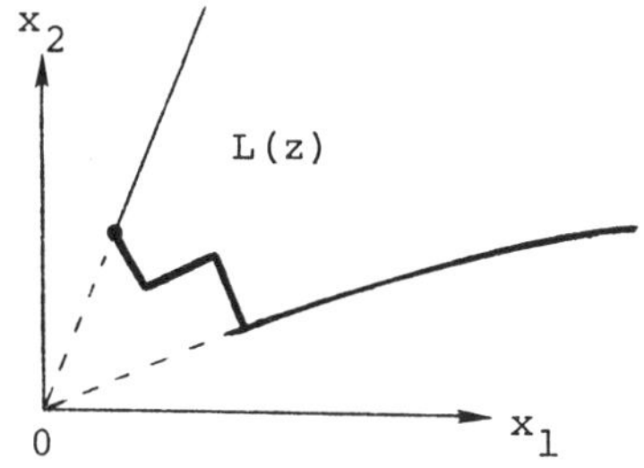

(1)

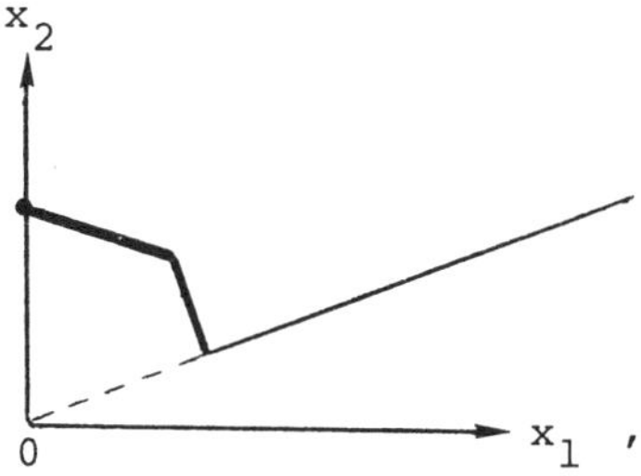

(2)

with or without any commodity being essential for positive intrinsic qualities, and even allowing only discrete commodity vector mixes to obtain a given vector z of inherent qualities, as illustrated below

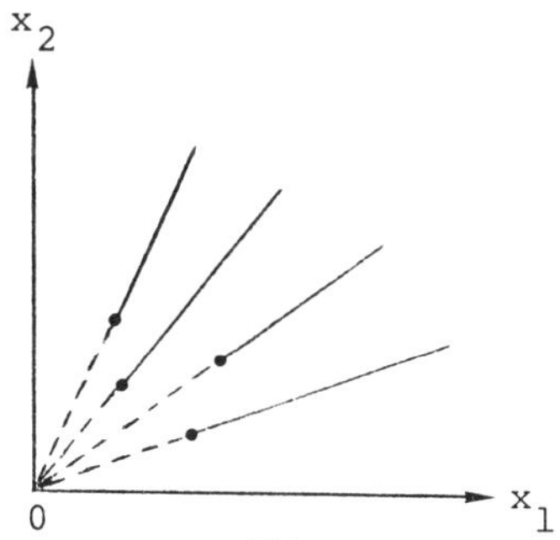

(3)

To the foregoing properties for the inverse correspondence $z \to L(z)$ we add asymmetrically:

L.0 The efficient subset of $L(z)$, i.e.
$\text{Eff } L(z) = \{x \mid x \in L(z) , y \notin L(z) \text{ for } y \leq x\}$,
is bounded for each $z \geq 0$, $\text{Eff } L(0) = 0$.

This property states that one commodity cannot be substituted efficiently for another in indefinitely large amounts to attain a given vector z of intrinsic qualities.

The foregoing properties (axioms) for the correspondence $x \to P(x)$ and $z \to L(z)$ are very weak as compared to the usual properties taken for such structures. But they are all we need for a household production theory concerning the output and input correspondences of intrinsic qualities of commodity vectors.

The household is taken to express a preference ordering for vectors of intrinsic qualities in terms of an ordinal utility function $u : z \in R_+^m \to u(z) \in R$, such that

$$z \succsim z' \text{ iff } u(z) \geqq u(z')$$

$$z \succ z' \text{ iff } u(z) > u(z')$$

with

$$z \sim z' \text{ iff } z \succsim z' \text{ and } z' \succsim z .$$

This relation is a partial ordering which is reflexive, transitive and complete.

Since some components of z may be unwanted it is possible that some vectors $z \geq 0$ are less preferred than the null vector, i.e. there exists $z \geq 0$ such that $u(0) > u(z)$. For this reason the ordinal values of $u(z)$ are not restricted to nonnegative real numbers.

The following properties are taken for the ordinal utility function $u(z)$:

u.1 $u(0) = 0$.

u.2 $u(z)$ is bounded for z bounded.

u.3 If $z = (w,\bar{w})$ is a separation into wanted and unwanted subvectors of intrinsic qualities, $u(z') \geqq u(z)$ for $z' = (w,\bar{w}')$, $z = (w,\bar{w})$, with $\bar{w}' \leqq \bar{w}$.

u.4 $u(\lambda z) \geqq u(z)$ for $u(z) > 0$, $\lambda \in [1,+\infty)$.
$u(\lambda z) \leqq u(z)$ for $u(z) < 0$, $\lambda \in [1,+\infty)$.

u.5 If $u(z) > 0$, $u(\lambda z) \to +\infty$ as $\lambda \to +\infty$.
If $u(z) < 0$, $u(\lambda z) \to -\infty$ as $\lambda \to +\infty$.

u.6 $u(z)$ is upper semi-continuous on $\{z \mid u(z) \geqq 0\}$, i.e. $\{z \mid u(z) \geqq E\}$ is closed for $E \geqq 0$.
$u(z)$ is lower semi-continuous on $\{z \mid u(z) < 0\}$, i.e. $\{z \mid u(z) \leqq E\}$ is closed for $E < 0$.

The ordinal utility function is defined up to a real monotone homogeneous transformation, but one can choose the origin of the scale so that $u(0) = 0$ without loss of generality. Thus u.1 is taken by choice and u.2 is essential for our purposes. Property u.3 expresses that wanted qualities are preferred to unwanted intrinsic qualities. Property u.4 states that if the utility of a vector z is positive, then any upward scaling of z is at least as preferred as the vector scaled, and contrarywise when $u(z)$ is negative. Property u.5 is an assumption of nonsatiation (no upper bound on $u(z)$) for vectors with positive utility and no lower bound for vectors with negative utility. Property u.6 is taken merely to close certain level sets of $u(z)$.

It is useful for our purposes to consider the following two families of level sets for the ordinal utility function $u(z)$

$$V(E) = \{z \mid u(z) \geqq E\} , \; E \in [0,+\infty)$$

$$W(E) = \{z \mid u(z) \leqq E\} , \; E \in (0,+\infty) ,$$

defining subsets of "at least as preferred" vectors z and "at most as preferred" vectors z corresponding to nonnegative and negative levels of utility.

In a two dimensional case the level sets might appear as

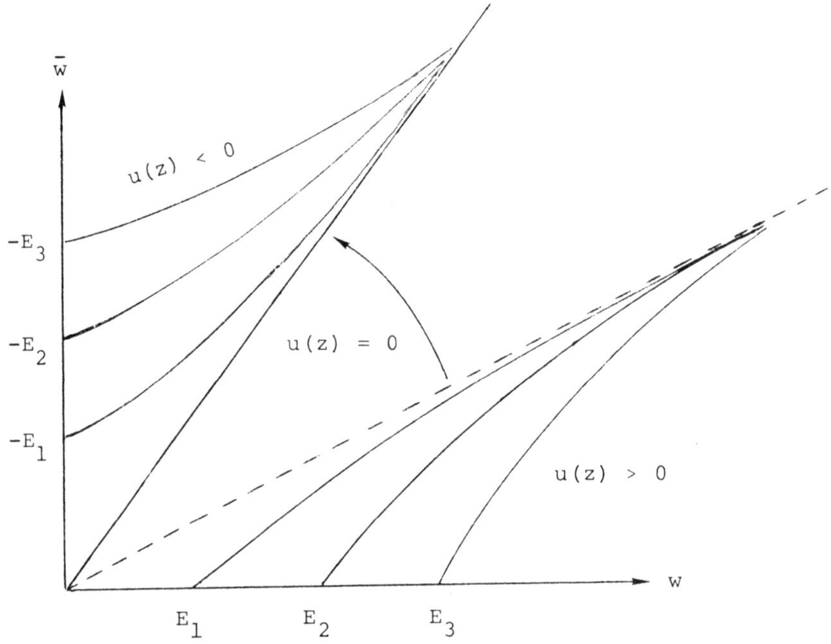

$$E_3 > E_2 > E_1 > -E_1 > -E_2 > -E_3$$

Convexity of the level sets is illustrated, but this need not apply. Vectors indifferent to the null vector need not be only the boundary of V(0) , as shown.

Since we shall be using these level sets it is convenient to list their properties implied by those of the utility function $u(z)$.

V.1 $V(0)$ is a proper subset of R_+^m , if z contains unwanted intrinsic qualities.

V.2 $\bigcap_{\sigma=1}^{\infty} V(E_\sigma)$ is empty for $E_\sigma > 0 \ \forall\sigma$ and $\{E_\sigma\} \to +\infty$.

$\bigcap_{\sigma=1}^{-\infty} W(E_\sigma)$ is empty for $E_\sigma < 0 \ \forall\sigma$ and $\{E_\sigma\} \to + - \infty$.

V.3 If $z \in V(E)$, $E \geqq 0$, then $(\lambda z) \in V(E)$ for $\lambda \in [1,+\infty)$.

If $z \in W(E)$, $E < 0$, then $(\lambda z) \in W(E)$ for $\lambda \in [1,+\infty)$.

V.4 If $\bar{z} \geq 0$ and $(\bar{\lambda}\bar{z}) \in V(\bar{E})$ for $\bar{\lambda} > 0$, $\bar{E} > 0$, the ray $\{\lambda\bar{z} \mid \lambda \geqq 0\}$ intersects all sets $V(E)$ for $E \geqq 0$. When $\bar{E} < 0$ and $(\bar{\lambda}\bar{z}) \in W(\bar{E})$, the ray intersects all sets $W(E)$ for $E < 0$.

V.5 $V(E)$ is closed for $E \geqq 0$.

$W(E)$ is closed for $E < 0$.

V.6 $V(E_2) \subset V(E_1)$ for $E_2 \geqq E_1 \geqq 0$.

$W(E_2) \subset W(E_1)$ for $E_2 \leqq E_1 < 0$.

The inclusion of unwanted intrinsic qualities (components of z) requires certain special treatment for the definition of a homothetic utility function. If $g(z)$ is taken as a real valued function defining a preference ordering, and $g(\lambda z) = \lambda g(z)$ for $\lambda \in [0,+\infty)$, then $F(g(z))$ is an ordinal utility function when $F : v \in R \to F(v) \in R$ is nondecreasing in positive v , nonincreasing in negative v , finite for $|g| < +\infty$, upper semi-continuous for $g \in [0,+\infty)$, lower semi-continuous for $g \in (-\infty,0)$, with $F(0) = 0$, $F(g) \geqq 0$ for $g \geqq 0$, $F(g) < 0$ for $g < 0$,

$F(g) \to +\infty$ for $g \to +\infty$, $F(g) \to -\infty$ for $g \to -\infty$, and otherwise arbitrary. Moreover,

$$V(E) = \{z \mid F(g(z)) \geqq E\} = \{z \mid g(z) \geqq F^{-1}(E)\}$$
$$= F^{-1}(E) \cdot \{z \mid g(Z) \geqq 1\} \ , \ E > 0$$

and $F(g(z))$ is homothetic for vectors z at least as preferred as the null vector of intrinsic qualities. On the other hand, when $E < 0$

$$W(E) = \{z \mid g(z) \leqq F^{-1}(E)\} \ ,$$

and, since $F^{-1}(E) < 0$, it does not make sense to express $W(E)$ as $F^{-1}(E)\ \{z \mid g(z) \leqq 1\}$. Thus we shall take $u(z)$ to be *positive homothetic* if it is representable by $F(g(z))$ where $F(\cdot)$ has the properties stated above and $g(z)$ is a homogeneous real function expressing a preference ordering for vectors $z \in R^m_+$ with the properties u.1, ..., u.6.

3. The Household Production Function

We turn now to certain correspondences which support the definition of a household production function. Consider the correspondence (mapping)

$$\sum : E \in R \to \sum(E) = \{x \mid x \in L(z)\ ,\ u(z) \geqq E\} \in 2^{R^n_+} \ ,$$

relating to each real number ordinal value E of utility the subset of commodity vectors x yielding consumption satisfying inherent quality vectors z which provide an ordinal level of utility at least as large as E , i.e. vectors z which are at least as preferred as those of the indifference class defined by E . The properties of this correspondence follow closely those of the parent correspondence $z \to L(z)$. They are

$\Sigma.1$ $\Sigma(E) = R^n_+$ for $E \leqq 0$.

$\Sigma.2$ $\bigcap_{\nu=1}^{\infty} \Sigma(E_\nu)$ is empty for $\{E_\nu\} \to +\infty$.

$\Sigma.3$ If $x \in \Sigma(E)$, $(\lambda x) \in \Sigma(E)$ for $\lambda \in [1,+\infty)$.

$\Sigma.4$ If $x \geq 0$ and $(\bar{\lambda} \cdot x) \in \Sigma(\bar{E})$ for $\bar{\lambda} > 0$ and some $\bar{E} > 0$, the ray $\{\lambda x \mid \lambda \in [0,+\infty)\}$ intersects all sets $\Sigma(E)$ for $E > 0$.

$\Sigma.5$ $\Sigma(E_2) \subset \Sigma(E_1)$ for $E_2 \geqq E_1$.

Property $\Sigma.1$ holds, since $0 \in L(0)$ by L.1 and $u(0) \geqq E$ for $E \leqq 0$. The remaining properties follow by similar simple arguments, using the properties of the correspondence $z \to L(z)$.

Note that closure of $\Sigma(E)$ has not been listed as a property, the reason for which is evident when one takes the equivalent form

$$\Sigma(E) = \bigcup_{u(z) \geqq E} L(z)$$

of the map set.

The inverse correspondence of $E \to \Sigma(E)$ is

$$\Sigma^{-1} : x \in R^n_+ \to \Sigma^{-1}(x) = \{E \mid x \in \Sigma(E)\}$$
$$= \{E \mid E \leqq u(z) \ , \ z \in P(x)\} \in 2^R .$$

The map set $\sum^{-1}(E)$ of $E \rightarrow \sum^{-1}(E)$ is an interval $(-\infty, H(x)]$ where

$$H(x) = \text{Max}\ \{E \mid E \leqq u(z)\ ,\ z \in P(x)\}\ .$$

That $H(x)$ is so defined is easily seen from the equivalent definition

$$H(x) = \text{Max}\ \{u(z) \mid z \in P(x)\}\ .$$

The function

$$H : x \in R^n_+ \longrightarrow H(x) \in R_+$$

is an ordinal valued "Household Production Function."

The properties of $H(x)$ are:

H.1 $H(0) = 0\ ,\ H(x) \geqq 0$ for all $x \in R^n_+$.
H.2 $H(x)$ is bounded for x bounded.
H.3 $H(\lambda x) \geqq H(x)$ for $\lambda \in [1,+\infty)$.
H.4 If $H(x) > 0\ ,\ H(\lambda x) \rightarrow +\infty$ for $\lambda \rightarrow +\infty$.

For $x = 0\ ,\ z = 0$ is only possible and one seeks max E such that $E \leqq u(0) = 0$. Hence $H(0) = 0$. Further since $0 \in P(x)$ for all $x \in R^n_+$, $H(x) \geqq 0$ for all $x \in R^n_+$, and thus Property H.1 holds. Property H.2 holds since x bounded implies $z \in P(x)$ bounded, implying $u(z)$ bounded. For Property H.3, note that $P(\lambda x) \supset P(x)$ for $\lambda \in [1,+\infty)$, by Property P.3 of the correspondence $x \rightarrow P(x)$ (weak disposability of inputs), and $\text{Max}\ \{u(z) \mid z \in P(\lambda x) \supset P(x)\} \geqq H(x)$. Hence $H(\lambda x) \geqq H(x)$ for $\lambda \in [1,+\infty)$. Finally, if $H(x) > 0$ there exists $z^o \in P(x)$ $(x \in L(z^o))$ such that $u(z^o) > 0$. Then by Property

L.4, there exists for any scalar θ a scalar λ_θ such that $(\lambda_\theta \cdot x) \in L(\theta z^o)$. But by Property u.5 (nonsatiation) $u(\theta z^o) \to +\infty$ as $\theta \to +\infty$. Hence $H(\lambda x) \to +\infty$ as $\lambda \to +\infty$. Property H.4 is a direct consequence of the nonsatiation assumption u.5 for the ordinal utility function $u(z)$.

The household production function is an analogue of the technical production function, giving the maximal ordinal utility attainable from a commodity vector x . The level sets

$$\{x \mid H(x) \geqq E\} \text{ , } E \in (-\infty, +\infty)$$

of the household production function $H(x)$ are the same as the map sets $\sum(E)$ of the correspondence $E \to \sum(E)$ inverse to $x \to \sum^{-1}(x)$ defining $H(x)$, i.e.

$$\sum(E) = \{x \mid H(x) \geqq E\} \text{ , } E \in (-\infty, +\infty) \text{ .}$$

To see this: (a) Suppose $x \in \{x \mid H(x) \geqq E\}$, implying that there exists a vector $z^* \in P(x)$ with $u(z^*) \geqq E$, or $x \in L(z^*)$ with $u(z^*) \geqq E$ and $x \in \sum(E)$. Thus $\{x \mid H(x) \geqq E\} \subset \sum(E)$ for $E \in (-\infty, +\infty)$. (b) Suppose $x \in \sum(E)$, implying that there exists a vector z^o such that $x \in L(z^o)$ with $u(z^o) \geqq E$, or $z^o \in P(x)$ with $u(z^o) \geqq E$, implying $H(x) \geqq E$ and $x \in \{x \mid H(x) \geqq E\}$, whence $\sum(E) \subset \{x \mid H(x) \geqq E\}$. Thus equality holds.

When the correspondence $x \to P(x)$ $(z \to L(z))$ is homogeneous of degree $+1$ and the utility function is positively homothetic, the level sets $\sum(E)$ take a particularly simple form, and likewise for the household production function $H(x)$, because

$$\textstyle\sum (E) = \{x \mid x \varepsilon L(z) , g(z) \geqq F^{-1}(E)\} , E > 0$$

$$= F^{-1}(E) \cdot \textstyle\sum (1) , E > 0 ,$$

where

$$\textstyle\sum (1) = \{x \mid x \varepsilon L(z) , g(z) \geqq 1\}$$

is a fixed set independent of the positive utility level E .

The distance function for the level sets $\sum (E)$ of $H(x)$ is given by

$$\Psi(E,x) = \left[\text{Inf}\left\{\theta \mid (\theta x) \varepsilon \textstyle\sum (E) , \theta \varepsilon [0,+\infty)\right\}\right]^{-1}$$

$$= \left[\text{Inf}\left\{\theta \mid (\theta x) \varepsilon F^{-1}(E) \cdot \textstyle\sum (1)\right\}\right]^{-1}$$

$$= \frac{1}{F^{-1}(E)} \left[\text{Inf}\left\{\theta \mid (\theta x) \varepsilon \textstyle\sum (1)\right\}\right]^{-1}$$

$$= \frac{h(x)}{F^{-1}(E)} , E > 0$$

where

$$h(x) = \left[\text{Inf}\left\{\theta \mid (\theta x) \varepsilon \textstyle\sum (1)\right\}\right]^{-1}$$

is homogeneous of degree $+1$ and clearly satisfies the Properties H.1, ..., H.4 .

In these terms the map sets $\sum (E)$ are expressed for $E > 0$ by

$$\textstyle\sum (E) = \left\{x \mid \frac{h(x)}{F^{-1}(E)} \geqq 1\right\} = \{x \mid F(h(x)) \geqq E\} , E > 0$$

and

$$\sum^{-1}(E) = (-\infty, F(h(x))] \ .$$

Thus the household production function takes the homothetic form

$$H(x) = F(h(x)) \ , \ x \in R^n_+ \ ,$$

because when

$$\sum(E) = \{x \mid x \in L(z) \quad \text{for} \quad g(z) \geqq F^{-1}(E) \geqq 0\} \ , \ E \leqq 0$$

$x \in \sum(E)$ implies $H(x) = 0$, and also $\sum(1) \subset \{x \mid x \in L(z) \ , \ g(z) \geqq 0\}$ implying $h(x) = 0$ and $F(h(x)) = 0$ by the assumptions for $F(\cdot)$.

The level sets of $H(x) = F(h(x))$ are

$$\begin{aligned} \sum(E) &= \{x \mid F(h(x)) \geqq E\} \\ &= F^{-1}(E) \cdot \{x \mid h(x) \geqq 1\} = F^{-1}(E) \sum(1) \end{aligned}$$

for $E > 0$, and $F(h(x))$ is homothetic for $E > 0$.

4. The Household Cost Function

The minimal cost of attaining a given level of satisfaction (ordinal utility) is defined by

$$\chi(E,p) = \underset{x}{\text{Inf}} \left\{(p \cdot x) \mid x \in \sum(E)\right\} \ , \ E \in (-\infty, +\infty)$$

for price vector $p \in R^n_+$ of a commodity vector x, or equivalently by

$$\chi(E,p) = \underset{x}{\text{Inf}} \{(p \cdot x) \mid H(x) \geqq E\},$$

and the cost function $\chi(E,p)$ is an analogue of the cost function

$$Q(u,p) = \underset{x}{\text{Inf}} \{(p \cdot x) \mid \rho(x) \geqq u\}$$

for a scalar valued production function $\rho(x)$ with values $u \in [0,+\infty)$.

The properties of the cost function $\chi(E,p)$ are similar to those of the cost function $Q(u,p)$ and are here stated without proof:

χ.1 $\chi(E,p) = 0$ for $E \leqq 0$, $p \in R^n_+$ and $p = 0$, $E \in (-\infty, +\infty)$.

χ.2 $\chi(E,p) \geqq 0$, $E \in (-\infty, +\infty)$, $p \in R^n_+$ and $\chi(E,p) > 0$ for $E > 0$, $p > 0$.

χ.3 $\chi(E,\lambda p) = \lambda\chi(E,p)$, $\lambda \in [0,+\infty)$, $p \in R^n_+$.

χ.4 $\chi(E,p+q) \geqq \chi(E,p) + \chi(E,q)$, $p \in R^n_+$, $q \in R^n_+$, $E \in (-\infty, +\infty)$.

χ.5 $\chi(E,p)$ is a concave function of $p \in R^n_+$, $E \in (-\infty, +\infty)$.

χ.6 $\chi(E,p)$ is continuous in $p \in R^n_+$, $E \in (-\infty, +\infty)$.

χ.7 $\chi(E,p') \geqq \chi(E,p)$ for $p' \geqq p \in R^n_+$, $E \in (-\infty,+\infty)$.

χ.8 $\chi(E',p) \geqq \chi(E,p)$ for $E' \geqq E \in (-\infty, +\infty)$, $p \in R^n_+$.

In case the correspondence $x \to P(x)$ $(z \to L(z))$ for intrinsic qualities is homogeneous degree $+1$ and the utility function is positively homothetic,

$$\chi(E,p) = \operatorname*{Inf}_{x} \{(p \cdot x) \mid F(h(x)) \geqq E\}$$

and

$$\chi(E,p) = \begin{cases} F^{-1}(E) \cdot \Gamma(p) & \text{for } E > 0 \\ 0 & \text{for } E \leqq 0 \end{cases}$$

where

$$\Gamma(p) = \operatorname*{Inf}_{x} \{(p \cdot x) \mid h(x) \geqq 1\}$$

$$= \operatorname*{Inf}_{x} \{(p \cdot x) \mid x \in \textstyle\sum(1)\} .$$

The cost function $\chi(E,p)$ and the distance function $\Psi(E,x)$ for the level sets of the household production function are duals, expressed by

$$\chi(E,p) = \operatorname*{Inf}_{x} \{p \cdot x \mid \Psi(E,x) \geqq 1\}$$

$$\Psi(E,x) = \operatorname*{Inf}_{p} \{p \cdot x \mid \chi(E,p) \geqq 1\} ,$$

with equality sign holding globally in the second statement when: (a) the components of x are freely disposable visa vis $H(x)$, i.e. $H(x') \geqq H(x)$ for $x' \geqq x$, (b) the level sets $\sum(E)$ of $H(x)$ are convex, but otherwise holding for "realizable" vectors x for any $p \in R^n_+$ in the cost minimization, i.e. $\{x \mid p \cdot x = \chi(E,p)$, $x \in \sum(E)\}$ (see [6]). Under the same conditions the functions $h(x)$ and $\Gamma(p)$ are duals, i.e.

$$\Gamma(p) = \operatorname*{Inf}_{x} \{p \cdot x \mid h(x) \geqq 1\}$$

$$h(x) = \operatorname*{Inf}_{p} \{p \cdot x \mid \Gamma(p) \geqq 1\} .$$

5. Cardinalizing H(x) and Index Functions

The minimal cost of realizing any value $H(x)$ of the household production function is $\chi(H(x),p)$. Given any price vector $p \in R^n_+$ for inputs, one may assign the values $\chi(H(x),p)$ as a cardinal measure (in resource cost terms) of household output $H(x)$. This assignment is feasible, because $\chi(H(x),p)$ is a monotone nondecreasing function of the values $H(x)$. In such terms, for fixed price vector p for commodity vectors, the household production function becomes

$$H : x \in R^n_+ \longrightarrow \chi(H(x),p) \in R_+ .$$

The dependence upon the price vector p is an inconvenience. However, under somewhat less generality, i.e. $x \to P(x)$ $(z \to L(z))$ being homogeneous degree $+1$, and $u(z) = F(g(z))$ being positively homothetic, a price free relationship may be obtained. One obtains

$$\begin{aligned} \chi(H(x),p) &= F^{-1}(F(h(x)) \cdot \Gamma(p) \\ &= h(x) \cdot \Gamma(p) , \quad h(x) > 0 , \end{aligned}$$

a product of two homogeneous scalar valued functions, one on the input vector x and the other on the related price vector p, so that $\Gamma(p)$ is a price deflator, and

$$\frac{\chi(H(x),p)}{\Gamma(p)} = h(x) ,$$

i.e. the "real value" of the cost $\chi(H(x),p)$ equals $h(x)$. Accordingly, one may use the positive homogeneous function $h(x)$ as a cardinal measure of the ordinal utility $H(x) = F(h(x))$. The factor price free cardinalization in resource terms of the household production function $H(x)$ is the value of the kernal function $h(x)$.

Under the same specializations the constant utility index of price vectors p is given by

$$I(p^1,p^0) = \frac{F^{-1}(E) \cdot \Gamma(p^1)}{F^{-1}(E) \cdot \Gamma(p^0)} = \frac{\Gamma(p^1)}{\Gamma(p^0)} ,$$

independent of the reference utility level E . For this index the price function $\Gamma(p)$ is defined by

$$\Gamma(p) = \underset{x}{\text{Inf}} \{p \cdot x \mid h(x) \geqq 1\} ,$$

which is a dual of the cardinalized household production function $h(x)$.

Homotheticity of utility function is not as artificial an assumption as usually considered, upon the grounds that the Engel curves are straight lines emanating from the origin of the commodity space. In the case at hand an Engel curve consists of the solution points in the commodity space of the minimum problem

$$\chi(E,p) = \underset{x}{\text{Min}} \{p \cdot x \mid F(h(x)) \geqq E\}$$

for given price vector p and E ranging over $[0,+\infty)$, with $F(h(x))$ being homothetic for positive E . The level sets of $F(h(x))$ will exhibit homothetic structure for positive E , but this does not imply that an Engel curve is necessarily positive. Only if the level sets $\{x \mid F(h(x)) \geqq E\}$ are strictly convex will the Engel curve have to be a straight line, and this condition need not apply at all, and the level sets of the homothetic utility function need not be strictly convex. For a given price vector p as illustrated below the vectors x^* solving the minimal problem satisfy

$$p \cdot x^* = \chi(E,p) \ , \ x^* \in \sum(E) \ , \ E \in (0,+\infty) \ ,$$

and instead of a line one gets the cone as illustrated below. The observed Engel curve may take any path in this cone. See the illustration below.

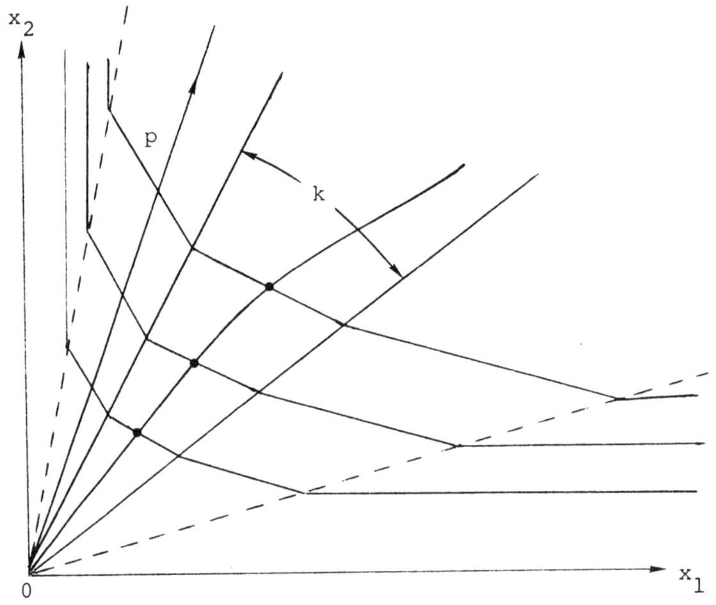

The imposition of strict convexity may be convenient for defining the derivatives used in elasticities, but this is not sufficient reason for rejecting homotheticity of utility function.

6. Quality and Taste Changes

In the foregoing model of intrinsic qualities arising from commodities (Section 2) and the utility (preference) function on these qualities, quality and taste changes are easily identified. Quality change is reflected in a change of the correspondence $x \to P(x)$ $(z \to L(z))$. Taste changes lead to alterations of the utility function $u(z)$ or the real kernel function $g(z)$ in case $u(z)$ is positively homothetic.

Let $x \to P_1(x)$ $(z \to L_1(z))$ and $x \to P_0(x)$ $(z \to L_0(z))$ refer to two situations with quality change, and $g_1(z)$, $g_0(z)$ reflect to taste changes for the same two periods being compared. Then the constant utility price index for commodities is

$$I(p^1,p^0) = \frac{F^{-1}(E) \cdot \Gamma_1(p^1)}{F^{-1}(E) \cdot \Gamma_0(p^0)} = \frac{\Gamma_1(p^1)}{\Gamma_0(p^0)} ,$$

independent of utility level, where

$$\Gamma_1(p^1) = \operatorname*{Inf}_x \left\{ p^1 \cdot x \mid x \in \bigcup_{g_1(z) \geqq 1} L_1(z) \right\}$$

$$\Gamma_0(p^0) = \operatorname*{Inf}_x \left\{ p^0 \cdot x \mid x \in \bigcup_{g_0(z) \geqq 1} L_0(z) \right\} .$$

The functions $\Gamma_1(\cdot)$ and $\Gamma_0(\cdot)$ depend upon both the form of the correspondence $z \to L(z)$ and the real function $g(z)$ at each of the two periods, since both quality and taste were taken to change.

7. Linear Structure for the Inherent Quality Correspondence

Similar to the treatment of Lancaster, consider the vector $x = (x_1, x_2, \ldots, x_n)$ of commodities consumed per unit time by the household to be inputs into consumption activities $A_1, A_2, \ldots, A_n$, with intensities of the latter denoted by a vector $\xi = (\xi_1, \xi_2, \ldots, \xi_n)$. Let A be the unit diagonal matrix of n rows and n columns. Take

$$B = \begin{vmatrix} b_{11} & \cdots & b_{1m} \\ b_{21} & \cdots & b_{2m} \\ \vdots & & \vdots \\ b_{n1} & \cdots & b_{nm} \end{vmatrix} , \quad b_{ij} \geqq 0$$

to be a matrix of output coefficients for inherent qualities, with at least one positive element in each row and column. Specifically

b_{ij} = output of the jth inherent quality per unit time per unit intensity of the ith activity.

Then, assuming weak disposability of outputs and inputs:

$$P(x) = \left\{ z \mid \xi A = \frac{x}{\lambda}, \ \lambda \in [1,+\infty) , \ \xi \geqq 0 , \ z = \frac{\xi B}{\theta} , \ \theta \in [1,+\infty) \right\}$$

$$L(z) = \{ x \mid \xi B = \theta z , \ \theta \in [1,+\infty) , \ x = \lambda \xi A , \ \lambda \in [1,+\infty) \}$$

This linear structure is homogeneous but not all vectors $z \in R^m_+$ need be feasible, i.e. $L(z)$ may be empty for some $z \geq 0$. By thinking of $\lambda = +\infty$ one obtains $P(0) = \{0\}$ and $0 \in P(x)$ for all $x \in R^n_+$.

For the positively homothetic utility function $F(g(z))$ one may compute the kernal function of the ordinal household production function $F(h(x))$ by (taking $\lambda = 1$, $\theta = 1$)

$$h(x) = [\text{Inf}\,\{\sigma \mid \sigma x = \xi\ ,\ \xi B = z\ ,\ g(z) \geqq 1\}]^{-1}$$

$$= [\text{Inf}\,\{\sigma \mid \sigma xB = \xi B = z\ ,\ g(z) \geqq 1\}]^{-1}$$

$$= [\text{Inf}\,\{\sigma \mid g(\sigma xB) \geqq 1\}]^{-1} = g(xB)\ .$$

The ordinal household production function is then

$$F(g(xB))$$

with the cardinalized form $g(xB)$.

To go one step further for detailed computations, a specific form for the homogeneous function needs to be taken together with definition of the subset of R_+^m on which $g(z)$ applies, i.e. for which $u(z) > 0$. One possible form is the modified Cobb-Douglas function

$$g(z) = g_0 \prod_{\nu=1}^{N} z_\nu^{\alpha_\nu} \prod_{\nu=N+1}^{m} \left(\sum_{j=1}^{N} a_{\nu_j} z_j - z_\nu \right)^{\alpha_\nu} ,$$

where $z_{N+1}, z_{N+2}, \ldots, z_m$ $(1 < N < m)$ denote amounts per unit time of unwanted inherent qualities, and $g(z)$ is so defined for

$$\left\{ z \mid z_\nu < \sum_{j=1}^{N} a_{\nu_j} z_j\ ;\ \nu = N+1, N+2, \ldots, m \right\} ,$$

with parameters satisfying $g_0 > 0$, $\alpha_\nu > 0$ for $\nu = 1,2, \ldots, m$, $\sum_{\nu=1}^{m} \alpha_\nu = 1$, and $||a_{\nu_j}||$ has at least one nonzero element in each row. For $N = 1$, $m = 2$, one obtains the illustration of Section 2 above. The calculation of the function

$$\Gamma(p) = \operatorname*{Inf}_{x} \left\{ \sum_{1}^{n} p_i x_i \mid g(xB) \geqq 1 \right\}$$

cannot be made in any closed form because of non-linearities. The difficulties of such a calculation are well known.

If one uses, however, a linear homogeneous function for $g(z)$, the demands x yielding $\Gamma(p)$ can be found by linear program for any price vector p. For example one might take

$$g(z) = \sum_{\nu=1}^{N} \alpha_\nu z_\nu + \sum_{\nu=N+1}^{m} \left(\sum_{j=1}^{N} \alpha_{\nu_j} z_j - z_\nu \right),$$

for

$$z \in R_+^m , \left(\sum_{j=1}^{N} a_{\nu_j} z_j - z_\nu \right) \geqq 0 , \quad \nu = N+1, N+2, \dots, m ,$$

the linear program is:

$$\Gamma(p) = \operatorname{Min} \left\{ \sum_{1}^{n} p_i x_i \right\} \quad \text{subject to}$$

$$x \geqq 0 , \quad \sum_{\sigma=1}^{n} \left\{ \sum_{j=1}^{N} a_{\nu_j} b_{\sigma_j} - b_{\sigma_\nu} \right\} x_\sigma \geqq 0 \quad (\nu = N+1, \dots, m)$$

$$\sum_{j=1}^{n} \left\{ \sum_{\nu=1}^{N} \left(a_\nu + \sum_{\sigma=N+1}^{m} a_{\sigma_\nu} \right) b_{j_\nu} - \sum_{\nu=N+1}^{m} b_{j_\nu} \right\} x_j \geqq 1 .$$

Then the constant utility price index can be computed in these terms as given in Section 5 above. The solutions for the components of x obtained from this linear program provide unit output demand functions depending upon the price vector p, which may be scaled to any level of utility E by multiplication by a scalar $F^{-1}(E)$.

8. Introduction of Household Size*

Assumption u.4 and particularly u.5 for the utility function are difficult to accept. The ordinal value of $u(z)$ pertains to the household as a given unit which is assumed to be nonsatiable by u.5. This property is taken as a convenience, although experience would show that a fixed household would regard increases (λz) for $u(z) > 0$ to be indifferent after some large positive value of λ, i.e. $u(\lambda z)$ would be bounded for $\lambda \to +\infty$.

If household size is introduced as a component of the argument of $u(\cdot)$, say $u(z,y)$, where $y \in R_+$ denotes household size, Properties u.4 and u.5 can be accepted when $u(z,y)$ pertains to total utility of a household of size y, since $u(\lambda z, \lambda y)$ for $u(z,y) > 0$ can sensibly be assumed nondecreasing in λ tending to $+\infty$ for $\lambda \to +\infty$ as a nonsatiation property. Interpreted as a preference relationship, $\lambda(z,y) \succsim (z,y)$ for $\lambda \in [1,+\infty)$ and no bounded vector (z,y) is at least as preferred as all possible vectors $(z,y) \in R_+^{m+1}$. The Properties u.1, ..., u.6 for $u(z,y)$ are taken as:

u.1' $u(0,y) = u(z,0) = u(0,0) = 0$.

u.2' $u(z,y)$ is bounded for (z,y) bounded.

u.3' If $z = (w,\bar{w})$, $u(z',y) \geqq u(z,y)$ for $z' = (w,\bar{w}')$, $\bar{w}' \leqq \bar{w}$.

---
*This approach was suggested by Leif Jansson, IUI, Stockholm.

u.4' $u(\lambda z,\lambda y) \geqq u(z,y)$ for $u(z,y) \geqq 0$, $\lambda \in [1,+\infty)$, and
$u(\lambda z,\lambda y) \leqq u(z,y)$ for $u(z,y) < 0$, $\lambda \in [1,+\infty)$.

u.5' If $u(z,y) > 0$, $u(\lambda z,\lambda y) \to +\infty$ as $\lambda \to +\infty$, and if
$u(z,y) < 0$, $u(\lambda z,\lambda y) \to -\infty$ as $\lambda \to +\infty$, $y \geq 0$.

u.6' $u(z,y)$ is upper semi-continuous on
$\{(z,y) \mid u(z,y) \geqq 0\}$, and lower semi-continuous
on $\{(z,y) \mid u(z,y) < 0\}$.

The properties of the level sets of $u(z,y)$ are similarly modified forms of V.1, ..., V.2 .

Household size y may be introduced into the correspondence between commodity vectors and inherent qualities, in the following way: In place of x use a vector (x,y) . Take the output vectors of $P(x,y)$ to be of the form (z,y) with $z \in P(x)$, as illustrated below

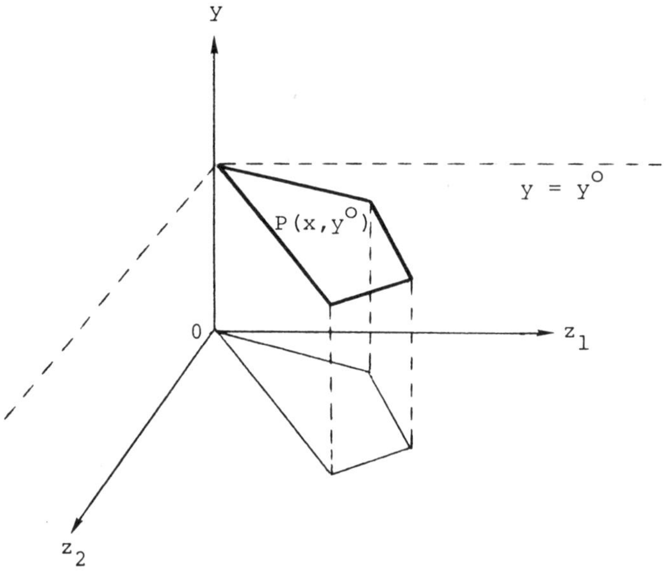

Then Properties P.1 and P.2 are carried over in terms of the vector (x,y) . Properties P.3 and P.4 are changed to

P.3' $P(\lambda x,y) \supset P(x,y)$ for $\lambda \in [1,+\infty)$, $y \in R_+$.

P.4' If $\bar{x} \geq 0$ and there exists $\bar{z} \geq 0$ such that $(\bar{z},y) \in P(\lambda\bar{x},y)$ for $y \in R_+$ and some $\bar{\lambda} > 0$, then for any $\theta \in (0,+\infty)$ there exists $\lambda_\theta > 0$ such that $(\theta\bar{z},y) \in P(\lambda_\theta\bar{x},y)$.

Properties P.5 and P.6 are altered to

P.5' $(x,y) \rightarrow P(x,y)$ is a closed correspondence for each $y \in R_+$.

P.6' If $(z,y) \in P(x,y)$, $(\theta z,y) \in P(x,y)$ for $\theta \in [0,1]$.

The properties of the inverse correspondence are similarly modified.

With these changes the analysis of household production includes family size in a meaningful way, and substantial alterations of the first treatment are involved. The map sets of the correspondence $E \rightarrow \sum(E)$ are given by

$$\sum(E) = \{(x,y) \mid (x,y) \in L(z,y) \ , \ u(z,y) \geqq E\} \ ,$$

with the inverse correspondence $(x,y) \rightarrow \sum^{-1}(x,y)$ defined by

$$\sum^{-1}(x,y) = \{E \mid E \leqq u(z,y) \ , \ (z,y) \in P(x,y)\} \ ,$$

and the household production function takes the form

$$H(x,y) = \text{Max}\ \{E \mid E \leqq u(z,y)\ ,\ (z,y) \in P(x,y)\}\ .$$

Here household size y is an explicit variable in the argument of the household production function. Moreover, *household size* is an *essential* factor, since $y = 0$ implies $E \leqq u(z,0) = 0$ because vectors of $P(x,0)$ are of the form $(z,0)$ and u.1' enforces $u(z,0) = 0$. Accordingly $H(x,0) = 0$ for all $x \in R^n_+$. If the level sets of $H(x,y)$ have bounded efficient subsets, it is known that there exists a bound y^o on household size such that $H(x,y)$ is bounded for $y \leqq y^o$, $x \in R^n_+$ (see [7]) and under some additional mathematical conditions, $H(x,y)$ is bounded for any bound y^o on y while x is unrestricted in R^n_+ (see [8]). Thus a household of finite size may be satiated as the commodity vector x is increased without limitation, as one would expect.

A word or two about the level sets $\sum(E)$ of $H(x,y)$. They are directly defined by

$$\sum(E) = \{(x,y) \mid H(x,y) \geqq E\}\ ,$$

or the equivalent form

$$\sum(E) = \{(x,y) \mid (x,y) \in L(z,y)\ ,\ u(z,y) \geqq E\}\ .$$

From the latter one may deduce that Properties $\sum$.1 and $\sum$.2 hold as stated earlier. Properties $\sum$.3 is modified to:

$\sum$.3' If $(x,y) \in \sum(E)$, $(\lambda x,y) \in \sum(E)$ for $\lambda \in [1,+\infty)$,

Property $\sum$.4 has no counterpart when household size y is introduced, and Property $\sum$.5 holds as previously stated.

The properties of the household production function $H(x,y)$ are:

H.1' $H(0,y) = H(x,0) = H(0,0) = 0$.
H.2' $H(x,y)$ is bounded for (x,y) bounded.
H.3' $H(\lambda x,y) \geqq H(x,y)$ for $\lambda \in [1,+\infty)$.

Property H.4 cannot be extended. Property H.3' clearly holds because

$$\{E \mid E \leqq u(z,y) \;,\; (z,y) \in P(x,y)\} \subset$$
$$\{E \mid E \leqq u(z,y) \;,\; (z,y) \in P(\lambda x,y)\}$$

for $\lambda \in [1,+\infty)$, by virtue of Property P.3'. Note that H.3' does not preclude household size y being an essential factor which is limitational for output when the commodity vector is unrestricted. See Appendix 1 for mathematical assumptions sufficient to guarantee that y is a limitational factor for the household production function $H(x,y)$.

Under the assumption of positively homothetic utility function, expressed by $F(g(z,y))$ where $g(\theta z,\theta y) = \theta g(z,y)$, $\theta \in (0,+\infty)$ for (E,y) more preferred than $(0,0)$, and the assumption of homogeneity of the correspondence $(x,y) \rightarrow P(x,y)$ expressed by $P(\lambda x,y) = \lambda P(x,y)$ for $y \in R_+$, the level sets $\sum(E)$ of $H(x,y)$ take the form

$$\sum(E) = F^{-1}(E) \cdot \sum(1) \;,\; E > 0$$

where now

$$\sum(1) = \{(x,y) \mid (x,y) \in L(z,y) \;,\; g(z,y) \geqq 1\} .$$

Then the ordinal household production function becomes

$$F(h(x,y)) \; ; \; h(x,y) = \left[\text{Inf} \left\{ \theta \mid \theta(x,y) \in \textstyle\sum(1) \, , \, \theta \geqq 0 \right\} \right]^{-1} .$$

Again the household production function is positively homothetic since

$$\begin{aligned} \textstyle\sum(E) &= F^{-1}(E) \cdot \textstyle\sum(1) \qquad && E > 0 \\ &= R_+^{n+1} && E \leqq 0 \end{aligned}$$

and the real valued kernel function is homogeneous in (x,y) , as well as satisfying Properties H.1', H.2', H.3'.

Note that an extension of Property H.4 is implied for $H(x,y) = F(h(x,y))$ as well as an extension of Property $\sum$.4 for the level sets of $H(x,y)$. Still the household size variable y plays a meaningful role. For fixed y , $h(x,y)$ may be bounded for $x \in R_+^n$ with $F(h(x,y))$ likewise bounded - implying satiation, provided more detailed assumptions are made about the correspondence $(z,y) \to L(z,y)$ and the sets $V(E)$. See Appendix 1.

For the household cost function one would not ordinarily think of including a price vector for household size y , nor consider minimizing cost by varying household size. Accordingly the cost function will depend upon household size in the following way:

$$\chi(E,p,y) = \underset{x}{\text{Inf}} \{ p \cdot x \mid h(x,y) \geqq F^{-1}(E) \}$$

without factoring ordinal utility level as before. However, if the household is regarded as controlling size as well as commodities used to achieve a given level of ordinal utility, the cost function takes the form: $(E > 0)$

$$\begin{aligned}\chi(E,p) &= \operatorname*{Inf}_{(x,y)} \{p \cdot x \mid h(x,y) \geqq F^{-1}(E)\} \\ &= F^{-1}(E) \cdot \operatorname*{Inf}_{(x,y)} \{p \cdot x \mid h(x,y) \geqq 1\} \\ &= F^{-1}(E) \cdot \tilde{\Gamma}(p)\end{aligned}$$

where the price function $\tilde{\Gamma}(p)$ has more general definition than that of $\Gamma(p)$ when household size was not explicitly introduced. In this case a constant utility commodity price index exists just as before with $\Gamma(p)$ replaced by $\tilde{\Gamma}(p)$, and quality and taste changes are accommodated as previously done. A cardinalization of the ordinal household production function with variable household size can be made, as before, to yield $h(x,y)$ as the cardinal valued household output for commodity bundle x and household size y.

For the linear activity analysis model of the intrinsic qualities correspondence $(x,y) \to P(x,y)$ one may proceed as follows: Augment the matrices B and A to

$$B^+ = \left|\begin{array}{cccc|c} b_{11} & b_{12} & \cdots & b_{1m} & 0 \\ b_{21} & b_{22} & \cdots & b_{2m} & 0 \\ & & & & \vdots \\ b_{n1} & b_{n2} & \cdots & b_{nm} & 0 \\ \hline 0 & 0 & \cdots & 0 & 1 \end{array}\right| , \quad A^+ = \left|\begin{array}{cccc|c} 1 & 0 & \cdots & 0 & 0 \\ 0 & 1 & \cdots & 0 & 0 \\ \vdots & & \ddots & & \\ 0 & 0 & \cdots & 1 & 0 \\ \hline 0 & 0 & \cdots & 0 & 1 \end{array}\right|$$

with $(n + 1)$ rows and columns for A^+. External the intensity vector $\xi^+ = (\xi_1, \xi_2, \ldots, \xi_n, \eta)$. Then

$$P(x,y) = \Big\{(z,y) \mid \xi^+A^+ = \frac{1}{\lambda}(x,y) , \lambda \in [1,+\infty) ,$$
$$(z,y) = \frac{1}{\theta}\xi^+B^+ , \xi^+ \geqq 0 , \theta \in [1,+\infty)\Big\}$$

$$L(z,y) = \Big\{(z,y) \mid \xi^+B^+ = \theta(x,y) , \theta \in [1,+\infty) ,$$
$$(x,y) = \lambda\xi^+A^+ , \xi^+ \geqq 0 , \lambda \in [1,+\infty\Big\} .$$

On this basis the kernel function $h(x,y)$ is computed by

$$h(x,y) = [\operatorname{Inf}\{\sigma \mid \sigma(x,y) = \xi^+ , (z,y) = \xi^+B^+ , g(z,y) \geqq 1\}]^{-1}$$
$$= [\operatorname{Inf}\{\sigma \mid (z,y) = \xi^+B^+ = \sigma \cdot (x,y)B^+ , g(z,y) \geqq 1\}]^{-1}$$
$$= g(x,y) \cdot B^+) = g(xB,y)$$

where $z = xB$, i.e. $z_j = \sum_{i=1}^{n} b_{ij}x_i$, $j = 1,2, \ldots, n$.

References

[1] G. Bol and O. Moeschlin: "Isoquants of Continuous Production Correspondences," Naval Logistics Research Quarterly, June 1975, Vol. 22, No. 2, pp. 391-398.

[2] K. J. Lancaster: "A New Approach to Consumer Theory," Journal of Political Economy, April 1966, Vol. 74, pp. 132-157.

[3] John Muellbauer: "Household Production Theory, Quality and the Hedonic Technique," American Economic Review, December 1974, Vol. 64, No. 6.

[4] R. W. Shephard: Theory of Cost and Production Functions, Princeton University Press, 1970.

[5] R. W. Shephard: Indirect Production Functions, No. 10 of Mathematical Systems in Economics, Verlag Anton Hain, Meisenheim am Glan, 1974.

[6] R. Färe: "Production Theory Dualities for Optimally Realized Values," see this volume.

[7] R. W. Shephard: "Proof of the Law of Diminishing Returns," Zeitschrift für Nationalökonomie, 1970, No. 1-2, Springer Verlag.

[8] R. Färe: "Strong Limitationality of Essential Proper Subsets of Factors of Production," Zeitschrift für Nationalökonomie, 1972, Vol. 32, pp. 417-424.

Appendix 1
Strong Limitationality of Household Size

Consider the efficient subset $\text{Eff} \sum (E)$ defined by

$$\text{Eff} \sum (E) = \left\{ (x,y) \mid (x,y) \in \sum (E) \, , \, (x',y') \notin \sum (E) \text{ for } (x',y') \leqq (x,y) \right\} .$$

Clearly

$$\text{Eff} \sum (E) \subset \bigcup_{(z,y) \in \text{ISOQ } V(E)} \text{Eff } L(z,y) .$$

By assumption on $(z,y) \to L(z,y)$, $\text{Eff } L(z,y)$ is relatively compact for $(z,y) \in R_+^{m+1}$. Assume further that $\text{ISOQ } V(E)$ is relatively compact. Also, assume further that the correspondence

$$(z,y) \twoheadrightarrow \text{Eff } L(z,y)$$

is upper semi-continuous, i.e. for any $(\bar{z},\bar{y}) \in R_+^{m+1}$ there exists for every open set N containing $\text{Eff } L(\bar{z},\bar{y})$ an open set T of R_+^{m+1} containing $(\bar{z},\bar{y})$ such that $\text{Eff } L(z,y) \cdot N$ for $(z,y) \in T$. Then

$$\bigcup_{(z,y) \in \text{ISOQ } V(E)} \text{Eff } L(z,y)$$

is relatively compact and likewise for $\text{Eff} \sum (E)$.

The foregoing assumptions imply together with the properties of $\sum (E)$ that y is a limitational factor for $H(x,y)$. See [7]. In order that y be strong limitational, it is sufficient that the closed cone

$$\text{Closure} \bigcup_{E \varepsilon (0,+\infty)} \Big\{ (x,y) \mid (x,y) = \lambda(\xi,\eta) \ , \ (\xi,\eta) \ \varepsilon \ \text{Eff} \sum (E) \ , \ \lambda \ \varepsilon \ [0,+\infty) \Big\}$$

does not contain points of the form (x,0) . See [8]. This restriction is primarily a mathematical property visa vis large values of E .

The Degree of Monopoly and Multivariable Sales Policies

by Klaus Spremann

SUMMARY: The degree of monopoly for multivariable sales policies and multi-part tariffs, where these output decisions may be corner solutions of the admissible set, and where there may be kinks in the demand or cost functions is analyzed within a general model. A monopoly is understood as a *situation* where an agent (the firm) affects the aggregate welfare of the economy by his output decisions via *external effects*. These external effects and the marginal loss of welfare due to the selfishness of the agent can be measured by two real numbers ω^+, ω^-, which have the meaning of indices of *aggression* against and *consideration* of the society's objective. Hence the degree of monopoly is defined as a function, which assigns to every situation a pair (ω^+,ω^-). The determination of this pair (ω^+,ω^-) for a given situation requires a special linearization technique for sets and functionals which is termed *homogeneous approximation* of the situation under consideration. The main result states the failure of efficiency of situations, which reveal $\omega^+ > \omega^-$; and examples illustrate that almost all situations with *multivariable* sales policies are non-efficient in the following sense : There is a slight modification of the agent's policy which is admissible and increases both his own utility (profit) and the society's welfare. Conditions for such a "non-tangency" of iso-profit and iso-welfare loci are derived in real Banach spaces and expressed in terms of (the value of) the degree of monopoly (ω^+,ω^-) .

ACKNOWLEDGMENT: I am indebted to Ralph Bürk and Wolfgang Eichhorn for numerous contributions and for their critical and constructive reviews of a draft. I have benefited as well from suggestions of Axel Sell, Kiel, concerning paragraph 7. Of course, the usual responsibility remains with the author alone.

CONTENTS :

I. Motivation

1. The degree of monopoly is an economic index number which is relevant to models of price setting firms, the analysis of imperfect industrial market structures, and to statistical measurements of welfare losses. Whereas the monopoly power in the *economic* sense refers to the power relationship between producer and (the group of) consumers, the *legal* concept of monopoly power is primarily concerned with the power relationship between different firms in an oligopoly. According to these different aspects of imperfect competition and the various effects of a monopolistic market structure on the distribution of income and benefits, on the quality and durability of the product offered, on the exploitation of exhaustible resources, various different degrees of monopoly have been suggested.

2. Some features in models of price setting firms, however, have not yet been discussed with respect to the degree of monopoly, namely

- multivariable sales policies
- multipart tariffs
- output decisions which are corner solutions on the admissible set
- kinks in the demand and cost functions .

Entrepreneurs, who are acting in a market of limited competition, cannot properly be described by models of a firm which sets one price for the one (or for each, resp.) commodity produced. One important feature of monopolies can be seen in the possibility and in the profitability of actions like price discrimination, price differentiation over time, two-part tariffs, imposing licence fees, granting quantity discounts and subscription offers, advertising, door prizes, services free of charge (i.e., non-price competition), control and shifts of the quality and durability of the product or the services. Even in the one-product case, the exclusive control is a *multivariable* policy which describes prices, dues, discounts, levels of advertising, expenditures for distribution, qualitative supply and customers' services. Some of these controls may lie on the boundary of the admissible set (e.g. dues may be zero because the decision maker did not have the idea to claim an entrance fee). The demand and cost functions may show kinks. The *degree of monopoly for multivariable sales policies, corner solutions, and kinks* is the topic of this paper.

3. How can we measure the degree of monopoly for multivariable sales policies ? Aside from the degrees of monopoly, which are based on supernormal profits, on the number of firms in an industry, on statistical measures of concentration, the degrees of monopoly proposed in the literature on economic theory are valid for the one-commodity-one-price case only. (A brief presentation of these indices is given in section II). The measure of the degree of monopoly suggested here is derived from the following conception : *every monopolistic market structure corresponds to the existence of* relevant marginal *external effects* [4] *on the (aggregate) welfare of the economy*, caused by the firm's (in most cases empirically) chosen sales policy. We show in the sections III, IV, V, how the policy realized in a monopoly (a policy which not necessarily maximizes total

profits ignoring all consumer's desires) reveals the extension to which the firm's decision maker has taken into account his influence and power on the welfare of the economy. These marginal external effects and the marginal loss of aggregate welfare due to the selfishness of the agent depend on both the model data (market structure, demand, production possibilities, costs, legal injunctions, regulatory constraints) and the actually chosen sales policy, i.e., they depend on what we call the *situation*.

4. Taking corners, kinks, and the multivariability of decisions into account, the marginal external effects revealed in a given situation, can be characterized by *two* real numbers ω^+, ω^-, which can be interpreted as *indices of aggression and consideration*. Roughly speaking, it is assumed, that the firm's utility (profit) and the consumers' utility (surplus) can be measured in some money metric, at least locally. Then we ask for the lowest loss in the firm's profits caused by an admissible change of action which generates an additional benefit of one dollar for consumers. This loss defines the degree of aggression ω^+. Then we ask for the greatest gain in profit which could be achieved by an admissible change of the action that causes only a one dollar loss in the benefits to consumers. This gain defines the degree of consideration ω^-. In the one-commodity-one-price case (without corners or kinks), these indices coincide, $\omega^+ = \omega^-$, and differ from Lerner's degree of monopoly power only by the elasticity of demand as a factor. If there are corner solutions or kinks, $\omega^+ < \omega^-$ may be possible. For multivariable sales policies, $\omega^+ > \omega^-$ holds except for mere accidents. A situation with $\omega^+ > \omega^-$, however, fails to satisfy an efficiency condition, i.e., there is a slight modification of the sales policy which is admissible and leads to increases of both the profit and the welfare of society. Note, that this concept of efficiency differs from the common use of language in price theory, where every situation is termed to be non-efficient if it does not correspond to a maximum of welfare. Similar to bargaining problems (think of an Edgeworth-Bowley diagram with iso-profit and iso-welfare loci which are non tangent almost everywhere, namely everywhere except on the contract curve), the set of *multivariable* efficient sales policies is 'thin' and consequently *almost all empirically chosen multivariable sales policies could be modified such that both the firm's profit and the society's welfare could be increased.*

II. Measures of the Degree of Market Imperfections

5. The most popular degree of monopoly has been suggested by A. P. Lerner. He stressed the fact "that the mark of the absence of monopoly is the equality of price or *average* receipts to *marginal* costs, and the mark of the absence of monopsony is the equality of *average* costs to *marginal* receipts" [13, p.161] . Consequently, Lerner measures the monopoly power by the (relative) difference of price p and marginal costs mc,

5.1 $$\omega_{LERNER} = \frac{p - mc}{p} .$$

J. R. Hicks did not actually suggest an index, but he characterized the *welfare loss* as the proper problem of monopoly. This loss (on the summ of producer's and consumers' surplus) can be approximated by the half of the reduction Δq of the actual output q below the "optimal" output $q + \Delta q$, times the difference $p - mc$ between price p and marginal costs mc [10], [22] . According to Hicks, this social loss depends "partly upon the gap between price and marginal cost, partly upon the effect of that gap upon upon output" [10,p.114] . A large value of ω_{LERNER} would not be important unless the difference between p and mc affects the output seriously. Hence, we are tempted to write

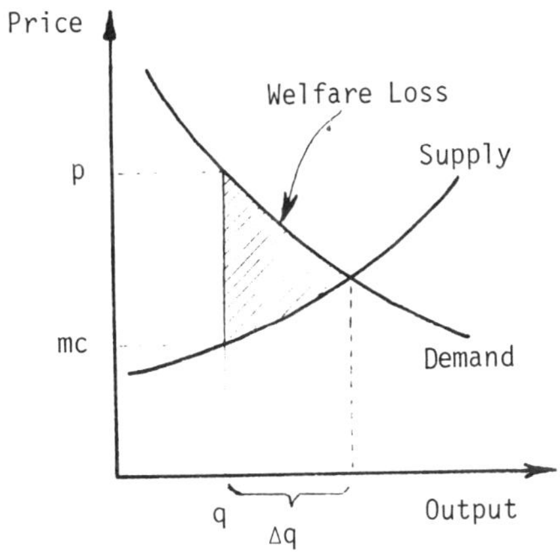

5.2 Marshall's diagram

5.3 $$\omega_{HICKS} \simeq \frac{1}{2} (p - mc) \Delta q .$$

Example 13 below will show that, while ω_{HICKS} has in view the *absolute* value of the welfare loss, ω_{LERNER} tends to the *marginal* welfare loss at the price p actually claimed. The concept, that the degree of monopoly should characterize the marginal welfare loss due to the selfishness of a greedy decision maker, is also the basis of our subsequent analysis.

6. The impacts of the output decisions of a monopoly on the distribution of benefits between producer and consumers and between different (kinds of) consumers is not considered unless they are related to some shifts in the amount of aggregate welfare. The rationale for such an approach can be seen in the Kaldor-Hicks test. If two output decisions x and y are under consideration and y leads to a higher level of aggregate welfare than x , switching from policy x to y will *theoretically* enable the winners to compensate the losers. However, we have also to ask : is there *in practice* a way to compensate the losers ? Is there some feasible form of taxation and subsidy which could achieve the redistribution ? Note, that these questions are independent of a requirement that compensation must *actually* be paid. And even if there exists a suitable mechanism of taxation and subsidy for the compensation, it may be very *costly, wasteful, and inefficient*. Such costs for a transfer of benefits must be reflected in the welfare function. For illustration, consider the following numerical example. Assume that a firm has the exclusive right to choose between two policies x and y ; the outcomes are given in the table 6.1 :

6.1

Policy	Profit	Benefits to consumers	
x	100	200	(dollars)
y	80	250	(dollars)

Assume, that all members of the economy admit that the firm can decide without any restrictions, and that there is no regulation. If the firm chooses the policy x, the firm will be called with the name 'monopoly' since there will be a welfare loss of 30 dollars. If, however, the redistribution of 50 dollars from consumers to the firm could only be achieved by a waste of more than 30 dollars, the policy y cannot be preferred to x from the view of the whole economy, because the winners (consumers) would not be able to compensate the loser (firm). Consequently, the firm cannot be termed to be a monopoly under such a costly transfer, even if policy x is applied. Transfer costs, of course, are opportunity costs, and the necessity of an approach of general equilibrium becomes apparent.

7. Some other indices proposed in the literature are mentioned in the appendix. See page 38.

III. Situations with External Effects

8. Consider an agent (a firm) whose actions (production decisions, sales policies, prices, tariffs) can be characterized by vectors of a real linear space X. Assume that this agent actually realizes the policy $x \in X$, and that he has the exclusive right, the legal and technical possibility to switch from x to any action in a set $A \subset X$ of admissible actions (or to keep up x - we assume $x \in A$ for simplicity). The transition from x to an action $y \in A$ influences the individual utility of the agent (profit of the firm) and the social utility (aggregate welfare of the economy). At least locally, for all decisions y in a neighborhood U of x in X, the change of the levels of profit and aggregate welfare due to a switch from x to y are known to the firm. Hence we presuppose the existence and the knowledge of both an

8.1 individual utility function $R : X \to \mathbb{R}$,
(profit function of the firm)

and a

8.2 social utility function $W : X \to \mathbb{R}$,
(aggregate welfare function for the economy)

which are defined at least on $X \cap U$, where the neighborhood U of x in X describes the scope of information. These functions R and W should express utility in some money metric, at least in U, see also paragraph 11. We will see below, that the determination of the degree of monopoly requires only the existence and knowledge of directional derivatives of R and W at x. The set of admissible actions $A \subset X$ as well as the functions R and W may depend on the action x actually realized. Such a dependency is required for kinked demand and cost functions (where the kink is always at the actually realized sales policy) but is not separately symbolized here for notational convenience. We say, that $x \in A \subset X$ and $R, W : X \to \mathbb{R}$ specify a *situation*. This view of an individual's (the firm's) situation shows the *presence of an externality* in the sense of Buchanan and Stubblebine.

The only difference to [4] may be seen in the fact, that here the externally effected party is not a second individual, but the whole economy. One problem concerns the dimension of the action space X . Consider a monopolistic public enterprise setting price $p \in \mathbb{R}$ per unit of the commodity produced (e.g., electric energy), and which did not recognize that it is possible to switch over to a uniform two-part tariff (l,p) with non zero licence fee l . Is the action space $X = \mathbb{R}^1$ or $X = \mathbb{R}^2$? We will say that the action space in this case is $X = \mathbb{R}^2$ and that, by now, the action realized is $(0,p) \in \mathbb{R}^2$. For what follows, the space of actions X is assumed to be normed and to be complete with respect to this norm .

9. Definition. Every 5-tuple $\mathcal{S}$;

9.1 $$\mathcal{S} = (X,A,x,R,W)$$

is called *situation*, iff: X is a real Banach space, $A \subset X$ a subset, $x \in A$, and $R,W : X \to \mathbb{R}$ functionals, and $x \in A \subset X$, R , W have the economic meaning discussed in paragraph 8.

9.2 A situation $(X,A,x,R,W,)$ is called *homogeneous*, iff: $x = o$, the set A of admissible actions is a cone in X with vertex o , and the functionals R, W are linear homogeneous.

9.3 A situation $\mathcal{S}$ is said to reveal *aggression* of the individual against society, iff: there exists an admissible action $y \in A$ with greater social utility, $W(y) > W(x)$.

9.4 A situation $\mathcal{S}$ is said to reveal *consideration* of the individual for the social utility, iff: there exists an admissible action $z \in A$ with greater individual utility, $R(z) > R(x)$.

9.5 A situation $\mathcal{S}$ is called *utopic* and it is said that the *external effects* in $\mathcal{S}$ *are irrelevant*, iff: there is neither aggression nor consideration in $\mathcal{S}$, i.e., $J(x) = \max\{J(y) \mid y \in A\}$ for $J \in \{R,W\}$.

9.6 A situation $\mathfrak{X}$ is said to reveal *local aggression (local consideration)* or to be *local utopic*, resp., iff: for all neighborhoods U of x in X, the situation $(X, A \cap U, x, R, W)$ reveals aggression (consideration) or is utopic, resp.

10. Remark. Utopic situations are often considered to happen in complete competition : the selfishness of each individual household leads under certain circumstances to an economic state, which is denoted as a "maximum of welfare" or as a "social optimum". Utopic situations are here of no further interest. A situation, which reveals aggression but no consideration, is the traditional case of profit maximizing monopoly. We define the degree of monopoly for this case to be equal to one. Note that with this terminology, also a regulated industry which works with modest profits but *exhausts all legal possibilities*, is characterized by a degree of monopoly equal to one - if the regulation mechanism is reflected in the set A of admissible actions. A situation which reveals consideration but no aggression would be the ideal mode of operation for a public enterprise and we assign to these situations the degree of monopoly zero. Note that with this terminology, also the budget constraint maximization of welfare is characterized by a degree of monopoly equal to zero. Consequently, a decentralized public utility which receives no subsidy by the government, is no "monopoly" in our sense. Obviously, situations which reveal *both aggression and consideration*, are of special interest. Such situations characterize decision makers, who beyond the firm's goal to maximize profits, take into account the benefits of society, at least to some "extent". To measure this "extent", is what we attempt here.

11. It has been supposed in 8 that the functionals R, W measure the profit $R(y)$ and the aggregate welfare $W(y)$ of an action $y \in A$ in some *numeraire* or *money metric*, at least locally in some neighborhood U of x. Hence, $R(y)$ and $W(y)$ can be compared and the difference

11.1 $\quad S(y) := W(y) - R(y) \quad$ is called consumers' surplus .

Sometimes we use the function $S : X \to \mathbb{R}$ defined in 11.1 as a shorthand expression. From the discussion of transfer costs in 6 follows, that if a surplus function S and R are given, the aggregate welfare can only be defined via $W = S + R$ if S determines a *net* surplus which considers opportunity costs for a transfer of additional benefits. These problems, however, are not involved in the subsequent analysis.

12. Definition. For a situation $\mathcal{X} = (X,A,x,R,W)$ consider the convex combinations

12.1 $$J_\omega := \omega R + (1-\omega)W \quad , \qquad \omega \in \mathbb{R}$$

of the individualistic utility function R and the social utility function W. If there is a set $\Omega = [\omega^+,\omega^-] \subset [0,1]$ such that the inequality

12.2 $$J_\omega(y) \leq J_\omega(x) \qquad \text{for all } y \in A$$

holds for all $\omega \in \Omega$, then the pair (ω^+,ω^-) is called *degree of monopoly* in the situation $\mathcal{X}$.

12.3 Parametric Representation of the Set $\{(R(y),S(y)) \in \mathbb{R}^2 \mid y \in A\}$.
Note, that $J_\omega = R + (1-\omega) S$.

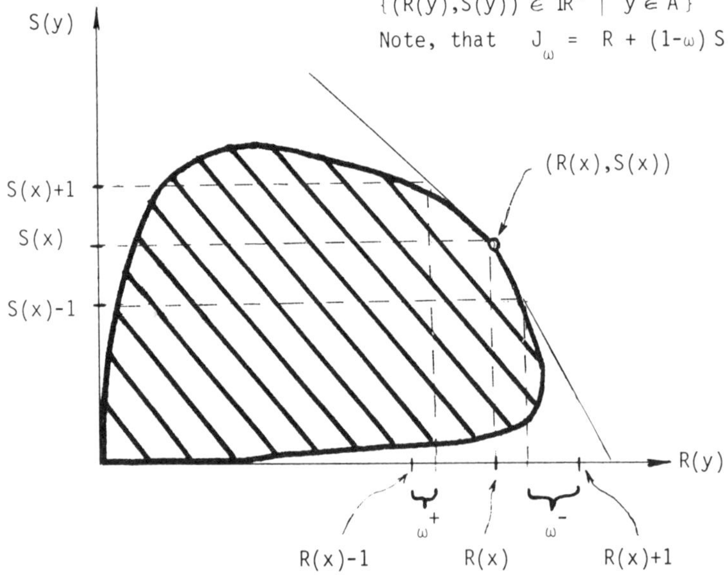

13. Example. A first interpretation of such an index (ω^+,ω^-) can be given by means of the situation

13.1 $$\mathcal{T} = (\mathbb{R}, \mathbb{R}_{++}, p, R, W)$$

of a one-commodity-one-price firm, where

13.2 $$\begin{cases} \mathbb{R}_{++} := \{\alpha \in \mathbb{R} \mid \alpha > 0\} , \\ R(p) = pf(p) - c(f(p)) , \\ p \text{ the price actually claimed,} \\ f \text{ the demand function,} \\ c \text{ the cost function ,} \\ W := R + S \quad \text{where the surplus is defined by} \\ S(p) = \int_p^\infty f(\pi)d\pi \quad \text{, existence of the integral assumed .} \end{cases}$$

Because of $p \in \text{int}(\mathbb{R}_{++}) = \mathbb{R}_{++}$, the inequality 12.2 leads with differentiability of f and c to :

13.3 $$\begin{cases} \text{If } \omega \in [0,1] \text{ satisfies 12.2, then } J'_\omega(p) = 0 \text{ , where} \\ J'_\omega(p) = \omega R'(p) + (1-\omega)W'(p) = R'(p) + (1-\omega)S'(p) = \\ \qquad = (p-mc)f'(p) + \omega f(p) \quad , \quad mc := c'(f(p)) \ ; \end{cases}$$

that is the usual marginal revenue equals marginal cost' formula

13.4 $$p(1 - \frac{\omega}{\eta}) = mc \quad \text{or} \quad \frac{p - mc}{p} = \frac{\omega}{-\eta} \quad , \quad \eta = f'(p) \frac{p}{f(p)} \quad ,$$

with inflated elasticity. With 5.1 one has

13.5 $$\omega = |\eta| \cdot \omega_{LERNER} \quad .$$

Because of $J_\omega = \omega R + (1-\omega)W = R + (1-\omega)S$, in this example

13.6 $$J'_\omega(p) = 0 \quad \text{means} \quad R'(p) = (1-\omega)(-S'(p)) \quad .$$

The last equation in 13.6 allows the following interpretation : *The marginal rate of substitution between profit and consumers' surplus is equal* $1-\omega$. The price p claimed in $\mathcal{V}$ reveals, that the entrepreneur gives to one dollar of consumer's surplus the value $1-\omega$ in terms of dollars of his own profit. The degree of monopoly is determined by the difference between the value of benefits for the externally effected party (which is here the group of consumers) and the value which gives the individual (the firm) to these benefits; ω is a *devaluation numeral*, a *value slack*.

13.7 In order to deduce from 13.6 the inequality 12.2, additional convexity assumptions are required. With some conditions of that kind, we have in the above case

13.8 $$\omega^{+} = \omega^{-} = \omega = \frac{p - mc}{p} \cdot |\eta| \quad \text{and} \quad \Omega = \{\omega\} \quad .$$

13.8 Now assume, that the firm is confronted with a cost function which reflects a capacity constraint in such a way, that there is a jump in marginal costs from mc^{-} to mc^{+} at a certain production rate. Further, the firm had reduced the price as far, such that the output increased up to this jump where the peak load costs begin. Then, the set Ω is given by $\Omega = [\omega^{+},\omega^{-}]$, where

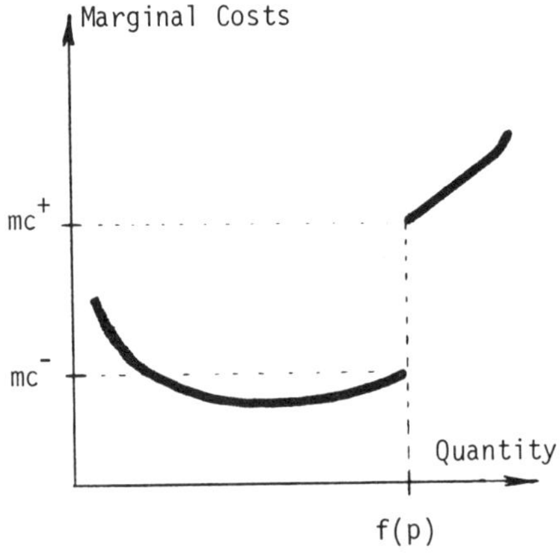

$$\omega^{+} = \frac{p - mc^{+}}{p} \cdot |\eta| \quad ,$$

$$\omega^{-} = \frac{p - mc^{-}}{p} \cdot |\eta| \quad ,$$

if $p < mc^{+}$; and $\Omega = [0,\omega^{-}]$, if $p > mc^{+}$. It seems, that the estimation of the "degree of monopoly" requires only *one* number, namely $\inf \Omega$. This is not true as the following example shows.

13.9 If the firm in an oligopolistic industry is confronted to a kink in the perceived demand function, such that a price cut would attract a large number of buyers, it would still be possible to determine numbers

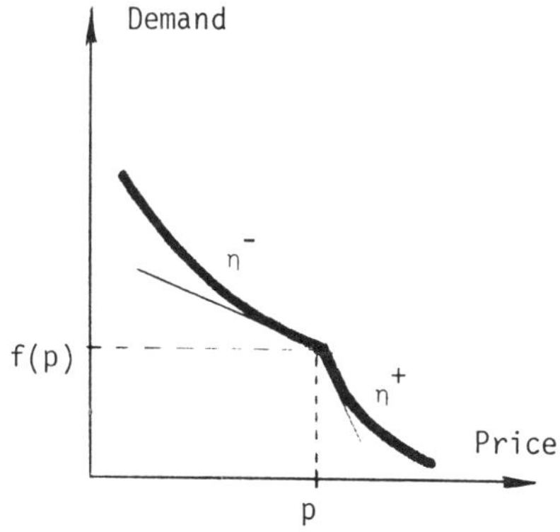

$$\omega^+ = \frac{p - mc}{p} \cdot |\eta^-| \quad ,$$

$$\omega^- = \frac{p - mc}{p} \cdot |\eta^+| \quad .$$

These numbers ω^+, ω^-, however, are now in the ordinal relation $\omega^+ > \omega^-$ and the set Ω of all $\omega \in \mathbb{R}$ with 12.2 is empty, $\inf \Omega = +\infty$.

14. The first approach given in 12 and illustrated in 13 presents the degree of monopoly as *a mapping which asigns to situations pairs* (ω^+, ω^-) *of real numbers*. However, the degree of monopoly is defined only on a subclass of situations, as is indicated by example 13.9. And apart from the differentiability assumptions, this subclass is very "small" . As we shall see in section VI, in most situations there does not exist a number ω with 12.2. To overcome this difficulty, we first weaken the definition 12 in the sense, that we replace the *global* inequality 12.2 by a *local, first order* inequality of the form

14.1 $$\nabla J_\omega(x,h) \leqq 0 \qquad \text{for all} \qquad h \in LC(A,x)$$

where $\nabla J_\omega(x,h)$ is the Gateau-derivative of J_ω at x in direction h , and $LC(A,x)$ is the local closed cone of A at x . These concepts of linearization are introduced in the next section IV. We second do not ask for a given situation $\mathfrak{T}$, if there is a set $\Omega \subset [0,1]$ such that 14.1 holds for all $\omega \in \Omega$ and define then $\omega^- = \inf \Omega$, $\omega^+ = \sup \Omega$ (if Ω is closed and connected), since Ω may be empty. In lieu of this, we define two sets

14.2 $$\Omega^{+} \subset [0,\infty] \qquad \text{and} \qquad \Omega^{-} \subset [-\infty,1]$$

and define

14.3 $$\omega^{+} := \sup \Omega^{+} \quad , \qquad \omega^{-} := \inf \Omega^{-}$$

such that ω^{+}, ω^{-} can be interpreted as degrees of aggression and consideration, resp., and such that

14.4 $$\Omega = [0,1] \setminus (\Omega^{+} \cup \Omega^{-})$$

holds, i.e.,

14.5 $$\Omega = [\omega^{+},\omega^{-}] \quad , \text{ if } \quad \omega^{+} \leq \omega^{-} \quad ,$$

and that also in the case $\Omega = \emptyset$ (there exists no $\omega \in [0,1]$ with 14.1, i.e. $\omega^{+} > \omega^{-}$) these indices ω^{+}, ω^{-} keep up their economic meaning. This economic meaning is discussed in detail in paragraph 32 ; for a simple case this meaning is shown in figure 12.3 and dashed off in paragraph 4 .

15. Then we shall see, that in the case $\Omega = \emptyset$, i.e. $\omega^{+} > \omega^{-}$, the situation *fails to be efficient* in the following sense :

15.1 Definition. A situation $\mathcal{T} = (X,A,x,R,W)$ is called *non-efficient*, iff: there is some $y \in A$ with $R(y) > R(x)$ and $W(y) > W(x)$, both the individual utility level and the social welfare could be improved. $\mathcal{T}$ is said to be *local non-efficient*, iff: for all neighborhoods U of x in X the situation $(X, A \cap U, x, R, W)$ is non-efficient.

15.2 Of course, every non-efficient situation reveals both aggression and consideration and consequently cannot correspond to any of the cases discussed in the remark 10. In the language of the theory of vector maximization, the efficiency concept used in 15.1 is called *weak Pareto* or *Slater efficiency*. The efficiency discussed in micro-economic theory has the meaning of a social optimum and is equivalent to the absence of aggression. Consequently, every non-efficient situation (in the sense of 15.1) does not represent a social optimum. The converse, however, is not true.

IV. Homogeneous Approximation of Situations

16. Definition. Let X be a real Banach space, $J : X \to \mathbb{R}$ a continuous functional and $x \in X$. If, for some $h \in X$, the limit

16.1 $$\nabla J(x,h) := \lim_{\substack{\tau \to 0 \\ \tau > 0}} \frac{1}{\tau} (J(x+\tau h) - J(x))$$

exists, it is termed *Gateau-derivative* and J is said to be *Gateau-differentiable* at x *in direction* h ; [15], [19], [28]. J is called *Gateau-differentiable at* x, iff: there is a function $\nabla J(x,.) : X \to \mathbb{R}$ with 16.1 for all $h \in X$, i.e., if J is Gateau-differentiable at x in all directions $h \in X$.

17. If $J : X \to \mathbb{R}$ is Gateau-differentiable at $x \in X$, then the functional $\nabla J(x,.) : X \to \mathbb{R}$ is *homogeneous* of degree 1, i.e.,

17.1 $$\nabla J(x,\lambda h) = \lambda \cdot \nabla J(x,h) \quad \text{for all } h \in X \text{ and all } \lambda \geqq 0 ,$$

but not necessarily *additive*. Every functional J which is differentiable (in the sense of Frechet [5], [19], [28]) at $x \in X$, is Gateau-differentiable at x. If $DJ(x) \in X^*$ denotes the derivative of J at x, then

17.2 $$\nabla J(x,h) = DJ(x)(h) \quad \text{for all } h \in X .$$

Especially let $X = \mathbb{R}^n$ and $(\partial J/\partial x_i)_{i=1,\ldots,n}$ the gradient, one has :

17.3 $$\nabla J(x,h) = \sum_{i=1}^{n} \frac{\partial J(x_1,\ldots,x_n)}{\partial x_i} h_i .$$

For the case of kinks in the demand or cost functions (which cause kinks in R and W), the following result [6,p.50] is of importance :

If $J_1, J_2, \ldots, J_m : X \to \mathbb{R}$ are functionals which are Gateau-differentiable at $x \in X$ in direction $h \in X$, then the maximum J,

17.4 $$J(z) := \max\{J_1(z), J_2(z), \ldots, J_m(z)\}, \qquad z \in X$$

is Gateau-differentiable in direction of h and

17.5 $$\nabla J(x,h) = \max\{\nabla J_i(x,h) \mid J_i(x) = J(x)\}$$

holds.

18. Definition. Let X be a real Banach space, $A \subset X$ a non-empty subset, and $x \in X$. The *local closed cone of* A *at* x is the set of *directional convergent sequences* [8] in A, i.e. the set

18.1 $$LC(A,x) = \left\{ h \in X \;\middle|\; \begin{array}{l} \text{there are sequences } \{x_\nu\}_{\nu \in \mathbb{N}},\ x_\nu \in A, \\ \text{and } \{r_\nu\}_{\nu \in \mathbb{N}},\ r_\nu \in \mathbb{R}_+, \\ \text{with } \{x_\nu\} \to x \text{ and } \{r_\nu(x_\nu - x)\} \to h \end{array} \right\}.$$

19. Remark. See appendix, page 39.

20. Examples.

20.1 $LC(A,x) \supset \{o\}$ iff: $x \in cl(A)$.

20.2 If $x \in int(A)$, then $LC(A,x) = X$.

20.3 If $A = \{a\}$, then $LC(A,a) = \{o\}$.

20.4 If $X = \mathbb{R}$, $A = [a,b]$ with $a < b$, then
$LC(A,a) = \mathbb{R}_+$ and
$LC(A,b) = \mathbb{R}_-$.

20.5 If : X_1, X_2 are real Banach spaces, $A_i \subset X_i$ and $x_i \in X_i$ for $i=1,2$

then : for $X = X_1 \times X_2$, $A = A_1 \times A_2$, and $x = (x_1, x_2)$ holds

$$LC(A,x) = LC(A_1,x_1) \times LC(A_2,x_2) .$$

Consequently : $LC(\mathop{\times}\limits_{i=1}^{m} A_i, (x_1,x_2,\ldots,x_m)) = \mathop{\times}\limits_{i=1}^{m} LC(A_i,x_i)$.

20.6 If : A is convex and $x \in cl(A)$

then : $LC(A,x)$ is convex and

$$LC(A,x) = cl(\{h \in X \mid h = \lambda(y-x) , \lambda > 0 , y \in cl(A)\})$$.

20.7

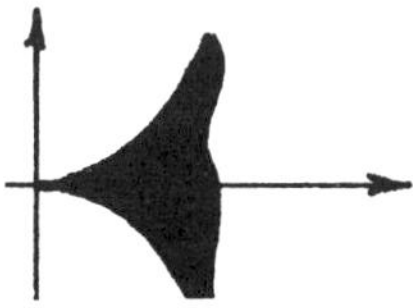

If : $X = \mathbb{R}^2$ and

$A = \{(y_1,y_2) \in \mathbb{R}^2 \mid y_1 \geqq 0 , |y_2| \leqq y_1^2 \}$

then : $LC(A,o) = \{(h_1,h_2) \mid h_1 \geq 0 , h_2 = 0 \}$.

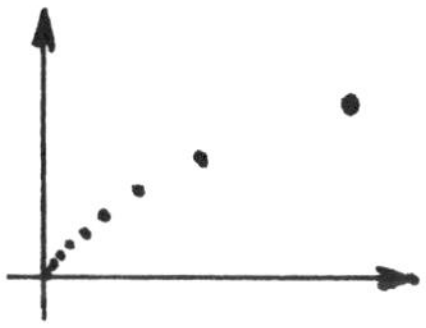

If : $X = \mathbb{R}^2$ and

$A = \{(\frac{1}{n}, \frac{1}{n+1}) \in \mathbb{R}^2 \mid n \in \mathbb{N}\}$

then : $LC(A,o) = \{(h_1,h_2) \mid h_1 = h_2 \geq 0\}$.

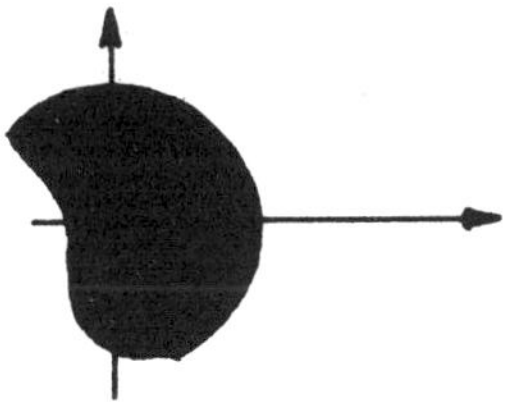

If : $X = \mathbb{R}^2$ and

$A = \{(y_1,y_2) \in \mathbb{R}^2 \mid y_1^2 + y_2^2 < 1\}$

then : $LC(A, (1,0)) =$

$= \{(h_1,h_2) \mid h_1 \leqq 0 , h_2 \in \mathbb{R}\}$.

20.8 If : X , Y are real Banach spaces, $F : X \to Y$ a mapping which is continuously differentiable [5] at some $x \in A$, where $A = \{y \in X \mid F(y) = o \in Y\}$, and the derivative $DF(x) : X \to Y$ is surjective,

then : $LC(A,x) = Kern(DF(x)) = \{h \in X \mid DF(x)(h) = o \in Y\}$.

20.9 If : X, Y are real Banach spaces, $B \subset Y$ a nonempty subset of Y,
$F : X \to Y$ a mapping which is continuously differenatiable
at some $x \in A := \{y \in X \mid F(y) \in B \subset Y\}$, and the derivative
$DF(x) : X \to Y$ is surjective,
then : $LC(A,x) = \{h \in X \mid DF(x)(h) \in LC(B,F(x))\}$.
If, in addition, B is convex, then $LC(A,x)$ is convex.

The proofs of the statements 20.2, 20.3, 20.4, 20.5 are straightforward and direct conclusions of the definition 18 ; the examples 20.1, 20.6, 20.7 are taken from [12,pp. 7 ff] ; the theorems 20.8 and 20.9 are proved in detail in [26,pp-289-291] .

21. Definition. A homogeneous situation $\mathcal{G}$ (see 9.2)

21.1 $$\mathcal{G} = (X,C,o,R',W'),$$

is said to be a *homogeneous approximation of* a *situation* γ,

21.2 $$\gamma = (X,A,x,R,W),$$

iff : C is the local closed cone of A at x and R', W' are Gateau-derivatives of R, W at x ; i.e. (X,C,o,R',W') *approximates* (X,A,x,R,W) *homogeneously*, iff:

21.3 $$C = LC(A,x),$$
$$R' = \nabla R(x,.), \quad \text{and} \quad W' = \nabla W(x,.).$$

22. Denote by $\P$ the class of all situations, by $\P_O$ the subset of all situations to which there is a homogeneous approximation, and by $\P_H$ the set of all homogeneous situations. Then we have the inclusions

22.1 $$\P \supset \P_O \supset \P_H,$$

since every homogeneous situation $\mathcal{G} \in \P_H$ posseses $\mathcal{G}$ itself as a homogeneous approximation. Note, that the homogeneous approximation of a situation is *unique*, if $\mathcal{G}_{\gamma_1}, \mathcal{G}_{\gamma_2} \in \P_H$ are two homogeneous approximations of the same situation γ $\P_O$, then $\mathcal{G}_{\gamma_1} = \mathcal{G}_{\gamma_2}$. Consequently, the homogeneous approximation of situations is a *mapping*

22.2 $$\mathfrak{A} : \P_O \to \P_H$$

of $\P_O$ onto $\P_H$. Since $\mathfrak{A}$ restricted to $\P_H$ is the identity, this mapping $\mathfrak{A}$ is *idempotent*, $\mathfrak{A} \circ \mathfrak{A} = \mathfrak{A}$. The equivalence relation $\div$ defined on $\P_O$ by

22.3 $$\gamma_1 \div \gamma_2 \qquad \text{iff:} \qquad \mathfrak{A}(\gamma_1) = \mathfrak{A}(\gamma_2) \quad ,$$

could be called *local first order identity*. In every equivalence class, there is exactly one element of $\P_H$, and in what follows, we define the degree of monopoly on the set of these equivalence classes, i.e. we define first a mapping ν on the set $\P_H$ of homogeneous situations, such that the degree of monopoly is the mapping $\nu \circ \mathfrak{A}$ which is defined on $\P_O$. Any two situations in $\P_O$, which are local first order identical, have then the same (value of the) degree of monopoly. The definition of the mapping ν on $\P_H$ is the topic of the next section V . Previously, we elaborate the common properties of situations in $\P_O$ which are local first order identical. Therefore we state some results concearning the three properties *existence of aggression, existence of consideration, non-efficiency* of situations $\gamma \in \P_O$ and their homogeneous approximations $\mathfrak{A}(\gamma) \in \P_H$.

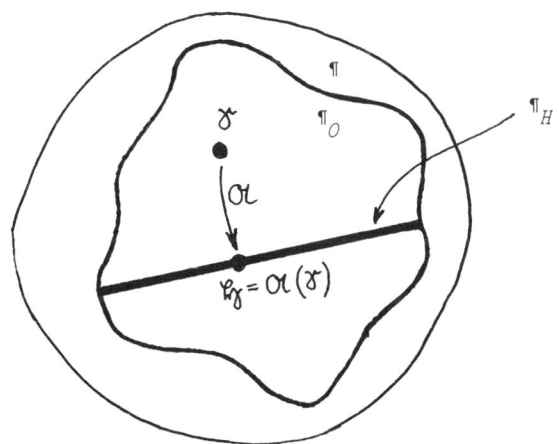

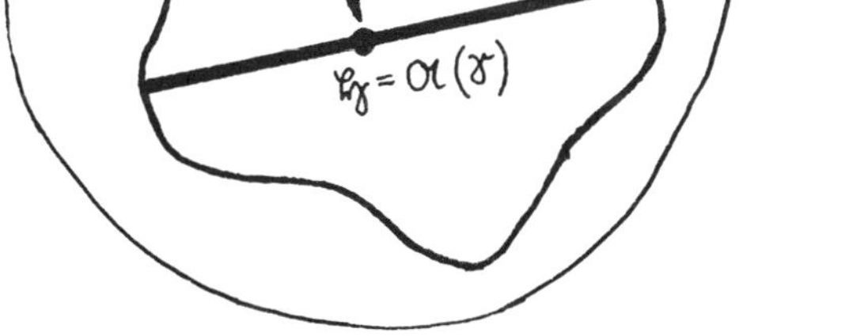

23. Theorem. Let $\mathcal{S} = (X,A,x,R,W)$ a situation in $\P_0$, where R and W satisfy a *local Lipschitz condition* at x, namely for $J_1 = R$, $J_2 = W$:

23.1 for J_i there are numbers $\beta_i > 0$, $\varepsilon_i > 0$ such that for all $y,z \in X$ with $\|y-x\| < \varepsilon_i$, $\|z-x\| < \varepsilon_i$ holds : $\|J_i(y)-J_i(z)\| \leq \beta_i \|y-z\|$.

Denote by $\mathcal{G}$ the homogeneous approximation of $\mathcal{S} \in \P_0$; then

23.2 if there is aggression in $\mathcal{G}$, then there is (local) aggression in $\mathcal{S}$.

23.3 if there is consideration in $\mathcal{G}$, then there is (local) consideration in $\mathcal{S}$,

23.4 if $\mathcal{G}$ is non-efficient, then also $\mathcal{S}$ is (local) non-efficient.

The proof of theorem 23 requires a lemma.

24. Lemma. Let X be a real Banach space, $A \subset X$ a subset, $x \in A$, and $J_i : X \to \mathbb{R}$, $i=1,2$ functionals which are Gateau-differentiable at x and which satisfy the local Lipschitz condition 23.1. Denote $C:=LC(A,x)$ and $J_i' := \nabla J_i(x,.)$, $i=1,2$. If there is some $k \in C$ with $J_i'(k) > 0$ for $i=1,2$, then

24.1 $\left\{ \begin{array}{l} \text{there exists a sequence } \{x_\nu\},\ \nu = n,n+1,n+2,\ldots \text{ with} \\ x_\nu \in A,\ \{x_\nu\} \to x \text{ and } J_i(x_\nu) > J_i(x) \text{ for all } \nu \geqq n \\ \text{and } i=1,2 . \end{array} \right.$

25. Proof of lemma 24. See appendix, page 39.

26. Proof of theorem 23 with the aid of lemma 24.
Ad 23.2 : The presence of aggression in $\mathcal{G}$ means the existence of a vector $k \in C$ with $W'(k) > 0$, see 9.3 . We apply lemma 24 for $J_1 = J_2 = W$ and get

the existence of a sequence $\{x_\nu\}$, $\nu \geqq n$, with $x_\nu \in A$, $\{x_\nu\} \to x$ and $W(x_\nu) > W(x)$, see 24.1, i.e. we get the presence of local aggression in $\mathfrak{F}$. Local aggression in $\mathfrak{F}$, of course, implies the presence of aggression in $\mathfrak{F}$.

Ad 23.3 : Apply lemma 24 for $J_1 = J_2 = R$.

Ad 25.4 : Apply lemma 24 for $J_1 = R$, $J_2 = W$.

27. What can be said about the converse of the statement of theorem 23 ? To shorten this discussion, we use the symbol "pp" for any of the properties *existence of aggression, existence of consideration, non-efficiency* in this paragraph 27. Now let $\mathfrak{H} = \mathfrak{A}(\mathfrak{F})$ be the homogeneous approximation of a situation $\mathfrak{F} \in ¶_O$. Then, in $\mathfrak{F}$ there may exist pp but not in $\mathfrak{H}$. This is obvious for a case, where $\mathfrak{F}$ reveals pp but is not local pp. However, even when $\mathfrak{F}$ reveals local pp, it may happen, that there is no pp in $\mathfrak{H}$. In accordance to [4] , one could term a local property pp in $\mathfrak{F}$ to be *inframarginal*, if $\mathfrak{H}$ does not reveal pp. Local pp in $\mathfrak{F}$, which leads to the existence of pp in $\mathfrak{H}$, is called *marginal*. Consequently,

27.1
- there is no pp in $\mathfrak{H} = \mathfrak{A}(\mathfrak{F})$ iff:
- either there is no pp in $\mathfrak{F}$,
- or there is pp in $\mathfrak{F}$ but no local pp ,
- or there is local pp in $\mathfrak{F}$ which is (only) inframarginal.

27.2 For homogeneous situations, the properties *pp, local pp, and marginal pp* are equivalent.

27.3 To sum up, denote by $¶_1$ the set of all situations $(X,A,x,R,W) \in ¶_O$, where the functionals $J_1 = R$ and $J_2 = W$ satisfy the local Lipschitz condition 23.1 . Clearly one has with 22.1

$$¶ \supset ¶_O \supset ¶_1 \supset ¶_H ,$$

since every homogeneous functional satisfies the Lipschitz condition.

Further let $\mathcal{S} \in \P_1$ and $\mathcal{G} = \mathfrak{A}(\mathcal{S})$. Then,

27.4
$$\begin{cases} \mathcal{G} \text{ reveals pp, iff :} \\ \mathcal{G} \text{ reveals local pp, iff :} \\ \mathcal{G} \text{ reveals marginal pp, iff :} \\ \mathcal{S} \text{ reveals marginal pp ;} \\ \text{then : } \mathcal{S} \text{ reveals local pp,} \\ \text{then : } \mathcal{S} \text{ reveals pp .} \end{cases}$$

Remembering the equivalence relation $\div$ of *local first order identity*, which is defined on $\P_0 \supset \P_1$, this result can also be stated in the following form. The properties *existence of marginal aggression, existence of marginal consideration, marginal non-efficiency* are *properties of equivalence classes of situations* : if $\mathcal{S}' \div \mathcal{S}''$, $\mathcal{S}'; \mathcal{S}'' \in \P_1$, then *either both* $\mathcal{S}'$ *and* $\mathcal{S}''$ *or none of them* show presence of marginal aggression, presence of marginal consideration, or marginal non-efficiency . *Inframarginal* aggression, consideration, and non-efficiency, is not measured by our degree for obvious reasons.

V. Aggression, Consideration and Non-Efficiency

28. Definition. Let $\mathcal{G} = (X,C,o,R',W') \in \P_H$. Then the number ω^+ , $\omega^+ \in \mathbb{R} \cup \{-\infty\}$, defined by

28.1
$$\omega^+ := \sup \Omega^+ \text{ , where}$$
$$\Omega^+ := \{\omega \in [0,\infty[\;\mid\; \text{there exists some } k \in C \text{ with } W'(k) > 0 \text{ and } J'_\omega(k) \geqq 0 \}$$

where

28.2
$$J'_\omega = \omega R' + (1-\omega)W' = R' + (1-\omega)S' \qquad \text{for} \quad \omega \in \mathbb{R} ,$$

is called *degree of aggression in* $\mathcal{G}$. And the number $\omega^- \in \mathbb{R} \cup \{+\infty\}$, defined by

$$\omega^- := \inf \Omega^- \text{, where}$$

28.3 $$\Omega^- := \{\omega \in]-\infty, 1] \mid \text{there exists some } h \in C \text{ with } R'(h) > 0 \text{ and } J'_\omega(h) \geqq 0\}$$

is called *degree of consideration in* $\mathcal{G}$. The pair (ω^+, ω^-) of the degrees of aggression and consideration is called *degree of monopoly of the homogeneous situation* $\mathcal{G}$ and denoted by: $\vartheta(\mathcal{G}) = (\omega^+, \omega^-)$. Let $\gamma \in \P_0$, then $\vartheta(\mathfrak{A}(\gamma))$ is called the *degree of monopoly of the situation* $\gamma \in \P_0$. The mapping $\vartheta \circ \mathfrak{A}$,

28.4 $$\vartheta \circ \mathfrak{A}: \P_0 \to (\mathbb{R} \cup \{-\infty\}) \times (\mathbb{R} \cup \{+\infty\}) \text{ ,}$$

is called *degree of monopoly*.

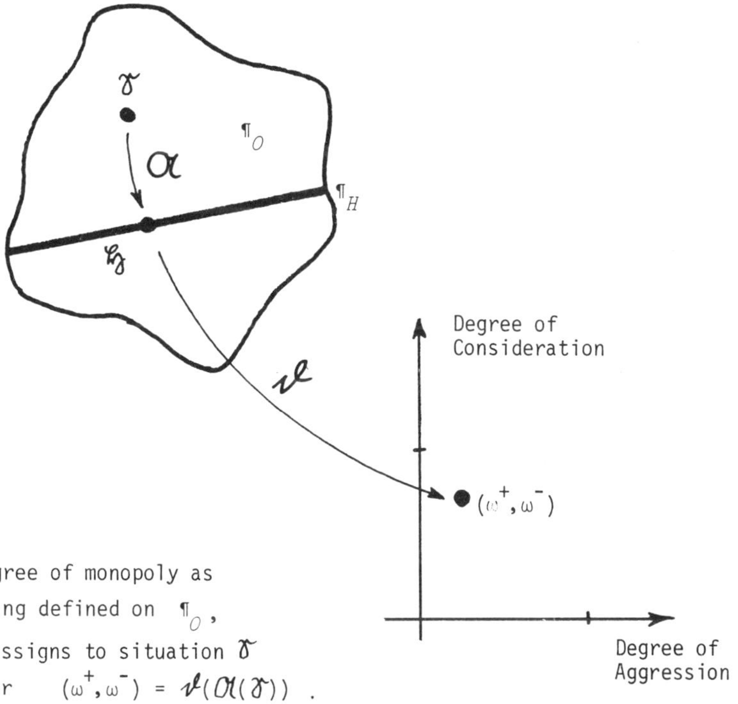

28.9 The degree of monopoly as a mapping defined on $\P_0$, which assigns to situation γ the pair $(\omega^+, \omega^-) = \vartheta(\mathfrak{A}(\gamma))$.

29. Lemma. The sets Ω^+ and Ω^- which are defined in 28.2 and 28.3 have the following properties :

29.1 $\left\{ \begin{array}{l} \Omega^+ \neq \emptyset \text{, iff:} \\ 0 \in \Omega^+ \text{, iff:} \\ \text{there is aggression in } \mathcal{G}; \end{array} \right.$

29.2 $[0,\omega^+[\subset \Omega^+ \subset \mathrm{cl}([0,\omega^+[)$, (if $\mathcal{G}$ reveals aggression);

29.3 if $\omega^+ > 1$, then $\mathcal{G}$ is non-efficient .

29.4 $\left\{ \begin{array}{l} \Omega^- \neq \emptyset \text{, iff:} \\ 1 \in \Omega^- \text{, , iff:} \\ \text{there is consideration in } \mathcal{G}; \end{array} \right.$

29.5 $]\omega^-,1] \subset \Omega^- \subset \mathrm{cl}(]\omega^-,1])$, (if $\mathcal{G}$ reveals consideration);

29.6 if $\omega^- < 0$, then $\mathcal{G}$ is non-efficient .

The set of possible (ω^+,ω^-) values is shown below :

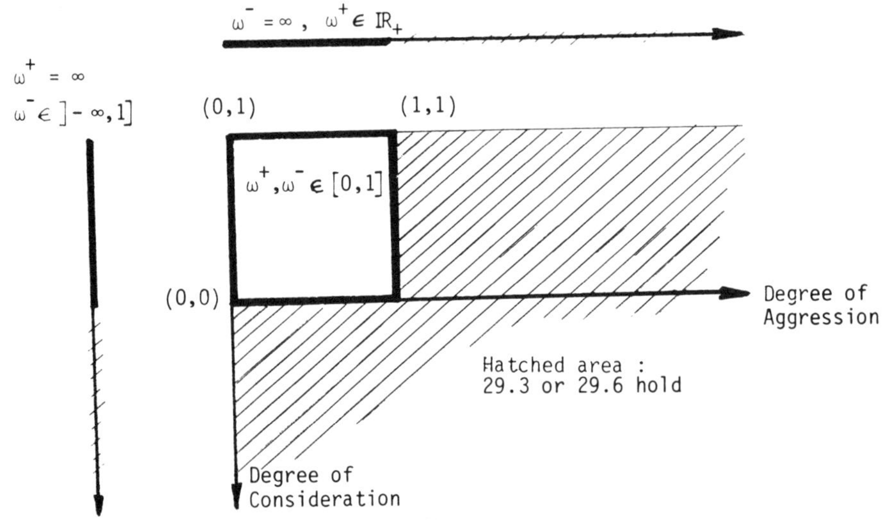

30. Proof. See appendix, page 41.

31. Note, that the condition $\omega^+ \leqq 1$ *and* $\omega^- \geqq 0$ does not imply the efficiency of the situation $\mathfrak{g}$. The cases 29.3 or 29.6 rather refer to a *very simple type of non-efficiency*, which is comparable with the situation of a firm who fixes such a high price, that a price cut would increase both the firm's profits and the benefits to consumers.

32. From the definition 28 follow directly the following economic interpretation of the indices ω^+, ω^- of aggression and consideration, resp.; see also example 13 . $S' = W' - R'$ denotes the consumers' surplus in $\mathfrak{g}$, and hence, approximates the change of consumers' surplus in every situation $\gamma \in \Pi_0$ with $\mathfrak{A}(\gamma) = \mathfrak{g}$. First we ask for the *lowest loss in the firm's profits caused by an admissible action (change) which generates an additional benefit of at least one dollar for consumers* and we have

32.1 $$\omega^+ = 1 + \inf\{-R'(h) \mid h \in C , S'(h) \geqq 1\} .$$

The degree of aggression ω^+ *is the greatest value slack (devaluation numeral) which corresponds to those admissible modifications of the policy applied hitherto that would increase the society's welfare.* Consequently, the firm's decision maker can argue, that one more dollar benefits to consumers is valued internally by him at a $1 - \omega^+$ dollar loss in profits, and if his aggression against society had been greater than ω^+ , he would have changed his policy. Then we ask for the *greatest gain in profit which could be achieved by an admissible (change of the) action that caused at most a one dollar loss to consumers* :

32.2 $$\omega^- = 1 - \sup\{R'(k) \mid k \in C , S'(k) \geqq -1\} .$$

The degree of consideration is the smallest value slack (devaluation numeral) which corresponds to those admissible modifications of the policy applied hitherto that allow to increase the firm's profit. Hence, the decision maker can argue, that a one dollar loss of benfits to consumers is internally valued by the firm equally to a $1 - \omega^-$ dollar's increase of profits, and that, if his consideration of the consumers' benefits would be smaller than indicated by ω^- he could have changed his policy. Note, that "small" values of the index ω^- indicate a deep feeling of the firm for the consumers' desires, whereas a value of ω^- near by 1 reveals negligible consideration and testifies selfishness.

33. For the non-efficiency theorem 34 below, we need a *regularity condition* for homogeneous situations $\mathcal{G} = (X,C,o,R',W') \in \P_H$. Certain kinds of regularities are sufficient for what follows, and we choose here for simplicity the subsequent condition.

33.1 $\left\{\begin{array}{l} \text{Assume that the cone } C \text{ is } \textit{convex}, \\ \text{and that for } J_1' = R', \ J_2' = W' \text{ the} \\ \textit{superadditivity} \quad J_i'(y+z) \geqq J_i'(y) + J_i'(z) \\ \text{hold for all } y,z \in C \text{ and for } i=1,2 . \end{array}\right.$

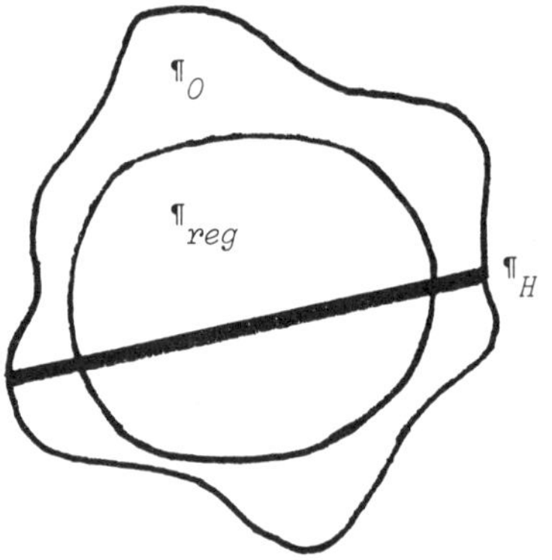

Further denote by $\P_{reg}$ the set of all situations $\mathfrak{S} \in \P_O$ with the property, that their homogeneous approximation $\mathfrak{A}(\mathfrak{S}) \in \P_H$ satisfies the regularity condition 33.1. For all situations $\mathfrak{S}$ in this set $\P_{reg}$, the relation $\omega^+ > \omega^-$ implies the non-efficiency.

34. Theorem. Let $\mathfrak{S} \in \P_O$ be a situation and $(\omega^+,\omega^-) = \mathfrak{v}(\mathfrak{A}(\mathfrak{S}))$ the degree of monopoly of $\mathfrak{S}$. If the indices of aggression ω^+ and consideration ω^- satisfy (at least) one of the following ordinal relations, then the homogeneous approximation $\mathcal{G} = \mathfrak{A}(\mathfrak{S}) \in \P_H$ of $\mathfrak{S}$ is non-efficient :

34.1 $\omega^+ > 1$,

34.2 $\omega^- < 0$,

34.3 $\omega^+ > \omega^-$ and $\mathfrak{T} \in \P_{reg}$ (i.e., $\mathfrak{A}(\mathfrak{T})$ satisfies 33.1) .

If in addition $\mathfrak{T} \in \P_1$ holds, i.e., $\mathfrak{T}$ satisfies the Lipschitz condition 23.1 (see also 27.3), then also the situation $\mathfrak{T}$ itself is non-efficient.

35. Proof. See appendix, page 42 .

36. Remark. The non-efficiency caused by 34.1 is of the following special kind, see also the statements 29.3 and 29.6 of lemma 29 and the remark 31 :

36.1 $0 < W'(l) \leqq R'(l)$ for some $l \in C$.

On the other hand, 36.1 implies $\Omega^+ = [0,\infty[$. From 36.1 follows $S'(l) = W'(l) - R'(l) < 0$ and hence $J'_\omega(l) = \omega R'(l) + (1-\omega)W'(l) =$ $= R'(l) + S'(l) - \omega S'(l) \geq 0$ for all $\omega \geqq 1$, i.e., it follows with 29.2 $\Omega^+ = [0,\infty[$. The non-efficiency caused by 34.2 is of the following special type :

36.2 $0 < R'(k) \leqq W'(k)$ for some $k \in C$.

Conversely, 36.2 implies $\Omega^- =]-\infty,1]$. Since the non-efficiency caused by 37.3 must be of the type 36.1 or of the type 36.2 , we have the following result : If a situation $\mathfrak{T} \in \P_{reg}$ reveals $\omega^+ > \omega^-$, i.e. the non-efficiency via 34.3; then the statement 36.3 holds,

36.3
$$\begin{cases} \text{either } \omega^- \in [0,1] \text{ and } \omega^+ = \infty \text{ and } 36.1 \\ \text{or } \omega^- = -\infty \text{ and } \omega^+ \in [0,1] \text{ and } 36.2 \\ \text{or } \omega^- = -\infty \text{ and } \omega^+ = \infty \text{ and } \\ \qquad 0 < R'(l) = W'(l) \text{ for some } l \in C \end{cases}$$.

It follows, that *the only situations* $\mathfrak{S} \in \P_O$ *, which have a chance to be efficient, are described by* $\omega^+, \omega^- \in [0,1]$ *and*

36.4 *either :* $\mathfrak{S} \in \P_O \setminus \P_{reg}$, i.e., $\mathfrak{A}(\mathfrak{S}) \in \P_H$ does not satisfy the regularity condition 33.1,

or : it holds $\omega^+ < \omega^-$, the degree of aggression is smaller than the degree of consideration .

36.5 Homogeneous situations, which satisfy the regularity condition 33.1, are non-efficient, if $\omega^+ > \omega^-$. The following examples ($X = \mathbb{R}^n$, C is a rectangle and hence convex, R' , W' are gradients and hence additive) give straightforward conditions which are sufficient for $\omega^+ > \omega^-$, i.e., which imply the non-efficiency of the situation $\mathfrak{H} \in \P_H$ with $(\omega^+,\omega^-) = \mathcal{V}(\mathfrak{H})$, or the non-efficiency of a situation $\mathfrak{S} \in \P_{reg}$ with $(\omega^+,\omega^-) = \mathcal{V}(\mathfrak{A}(\mathfrak{S}))$.

37. For this purpose, we now "calculate" the indices ω^+ , ω^- for the simple case, where

37.1
$$\begin{cases} X = \mathbb{R}^n , \\ A = [a,b] \subset \mathbb{R}^n \text{ is a rectangle, } a \leqq b , \\ R , W : \mathbb{R}^n \to \mathbb{R} \text{ are differentiable at } x \in A . \end{cases}$$

Let $\mathfrak{S} = (X,A,x,R,W)$ be a situation with 37.1 ; then $\mathfrak{S} \in \P_O$ and $\mathfrak{H}$, $\mathfrak{H} = (\mathbb{R}^n, C, o, R', W')$ is the homogeneous approximation of $\mathfrak{S}$, where

37.2
$$\begin{cases} C = \{ h \in \mathbb{R}^n \mid h_i \in C_i \} \text{ with} \\ C_i = \begin{cases} \mathbb{R}_+ , & \text{if } a_i = x_i < b_i , \\ \mathbb{R}_- , & \text{if } a_i < x_i = b_i , \\ \mathbb{R} , & \text{if } a_i < x_i < b_i , \\ \{0\} , & \text{if } a_i = x_i = b_i ; \end{cases} \end{cases}$$

see 20.5 , 20.4 , 20.2 , 20.3 ; and where $R' = (\partial R/\partial x_i)$, $W' = (\partial W/\partial x_i)$

are the gradients, see 17, of R and W at x. It is easy to see that $\mathcal{G}$ satisfies the regularity condition 33.1 and $\mathcal{T}$ satisfies the local Lipschitz condition 23.1, i.e., one has $\mathcal{G}, \mathcal{T} \in \P_1 \cap \P_{reg}$ in this case.

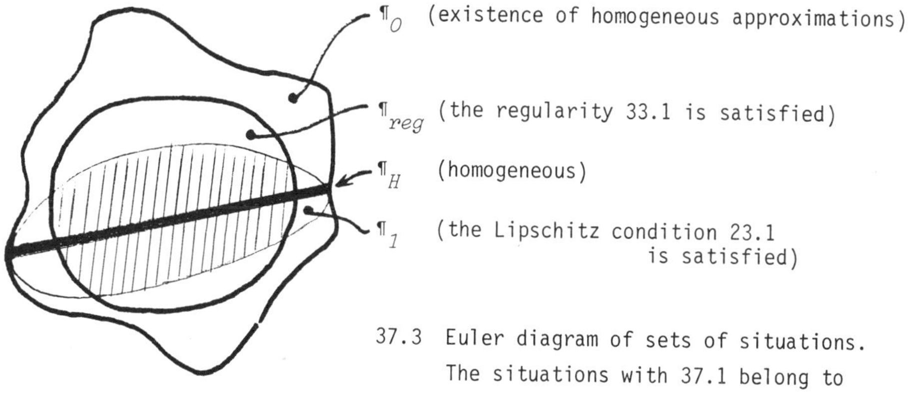

37.3 Euler diagram of sets of situations. The situations with 37.1 belong to the hatched area $\P_1 \cap \P_{reg}$.

We now can assume for simplicity, that there is no admissible *single* action (which concearns only one coordinate of the policy $x \in \mathbb{R}^n$) that would allow to increase profits without any influence on the consumers' surplus $S' = W' - R'$, i.e.,

37.4
$$\begin{cases} \text{assume that } \dfrac{\partial R}{\partial x_i} = \dfrac{\partial W}{\partial x_i} \text{ implies} \\ \text{either } \partial R/\partial x_i > 0 \text{ and } C_i \subset \mathbb{R}_- , \\ \quad \text{or } \partial R/\partial x_i = 0 , \\ \quad \text{or } \partial R/\partial x_i < 0 \text{ and } C_i \subset \mathbb{R}_+ . \end{cases}$$

If 37.4 is not satisfied, then the situations $\mathcal{G}$ and $\mathcal{T}$ are non-efficient.

38. Theorem. Let $\mathfrak{S} = (X,A,x,R,W)$ be a situation of the form 37.1, which satisfies the condition 37.4. Abbreviate $\frac{\partial S}{\partial x_i} = \frac{\partial W}{\partial x_i} - \frac{\partial R}{\partial x_i}$ for $i=1,2,\ldots,n$ and define finite sets Λ^+, Λ^- by

38.1 $$\Lambda^+ := \left\{ \frac{\frac{\partial W}{\partial x_i}}{\frac{\partial S}{\partial x_i}} \;\middle|\; \begin{array}{l} \frac{\partial W}{\partial x_i} > 0 \text{ and } x_i < b_i \text{ or} \\ \frac{\partial W}{\partial x_i} < 0 \text{ and } a_i < x_i \end{array} \right\}$$

and

38.2 $$\Lambda^- := \left\{ \frac{\frac{\partial W}{\partial x_i}}{\frac{\partial S}{\partial x_i}} \;\middle|\; \begin{array}{l} \frac{\partial R}{\partial x_i} > 0 \text{ and } x_i < b_i \text{ or} \\ \frac{\partial R}{\partial x_i} < 0 \text{ and } a_i < x_i \end{array} \right\}$$

Then :

38.3 $\Lambda^+ \neq \emptyset$, iff : there is marginal aggression in $\mathfrak{S}$,

38.4 $\Lambda^- \neq \emptyset$, iff : there is marginal consideration in $\mathfrak{S}$,

38.5 $\omega^+ \geqq \max \Lambda^+$ (if $\Lambda^+ \neq \emptyset$, and where $(\omega^+,\omega^-) = \mathscr{V}(\mathfrak{A}(\mathfrak{S}))$);

38.6 $\omega^- \leqq \min \Lambda^-$ (if $\Lambda^- \neq \emptyset$);

38.7 If both Λ^+ and Λ^- are not empty (there is marginal aggression and marginal consideration present in $\mathfrak{S}$), and $\min \Lambda^- < \max \Lambda^+$, then $\mathfrak{S}$ is non-efficient.

39. Proof. See appendix, page 44.

40. Corollary. If $\mathcal{T} = (X,A,x,R,W)$ is a situation of the form 37.1 which satisfies

40.1 $$a < x < b \quad \text{, i.e.,} \quad a_i < x_i < b_i \quad \text{for all} \quad i=1,2,\dots,n \; .$$

Then $\mathcal{T}$ is non-efficient if

40.2 either : 37.4 does not hold ,

or : $\max \Lambda > \min \Lambda$ where $\Lambda := \left\{ \dfrac{\frac{\partial W}{\partial x_i}}{\frac{\partial S}{\partial x_i}} \;\middle|\; i=1,2,\dots,n \right\}$

41. The proof of 40 requires only to consider $\Lambda = \Lambda^+ = \Lambda^-$ in 38.7 .

42. Corollary. If $\mathcal{T} = (X,A,x,R,W)$ is a situation of the form 37.1. Then $\mathcal{T}$ is non-efficient, if there exist two coordinates $i,j \in \{1,2,\dots,n\}$ such that

42.1 $$\begin{cases} a_i < x_i < b_i \quad \text{and} \quad a_j < x_j < b_j \; , \\ \dfrac{\partial W}{\partial x_i} \cdot \dfrac{\partial S}{\partial x_j} \neq \dfrac{\partial W}{\partial x_j} \cdot \dfrac{\partial S}{\partial x_i} \end{cases}$$

holds.

43. Proof. The above condition 42.1 implies either the failure of 37.4 or that $\max \Lambda > \min \Lambda$ holds for the set Λ defined in 40.2 .

44. Remark. Our assertion, that almost all situations with multivariable sales policies reveal non-efficiency, is based on the corollary 42. Note also, that 42.1 is the classical condition for non-efficiency which is derived in production theory.

VI. Price Discrimination, Two-part Tariffs, Advertising and Services Expenditures

Three simple models with multivariable sales policies are discussed here to illustrate some applications of our results. The first model is one of price discrimination, and it shows, that "in general", *the absence of price discrimination is non-efficient.* Hence, (a special type of) price discrimination will lead to an increase of both the firm's profit and the *aggregate* welfare, which is a bit antagonistic to the common believe, that price differentiation is an advantage for the greedy monopolist but a burden to society. The second example is a model of two-part tariffs, where it can be the case that *it is non-efficient to fix the licence fee or the dues equal to zero* . The third model treats an advertising and service expenditure sales policy, and it illustrates, that *the common policy to invest in each branch so much that one additional dollar investment yields in all branches to the same return is non-efficient in almost all cases where external effects are present.* Needless to say, that aim and purpose of our analysis in the sections IV and V are not the corollaries 40 , 42 and these simple examples. The generality of our analysis allows to approach more complicated situations (e.g., price differentiation over time, where the time is a continuous parameter), which are not discussed here since they are too extensive.

45. Price discrimination. A commodity is sold at price p_i per unit to the consumers' group i , $i=1,2,\ldots,n$, which demands the quantity $q_i = Q_i(p_i)$. The firm's policy $x = (p_1,p_2,\ldots,p_n)$ is a vector of prices and we have

45.1
$$\begin{cases} X = \mathbb{R}^n \ , \quad A = \mathbb{R}^n_{++} \ , \quad x = (p_1,p_2,\ldots,p_n) \ , \\ R(x) = \sum_{i=1}^{n} p_i Q_i(p_i) - c\left(\sum_{i=1}^{n} Q_i(p_i)\right) \quad \text{where} \\ c \text{ is a cost function .} \end{cases}$$

We assume differentiability of the functions $Q_1,Q_2,\ldots,Q_n$, c and get

45.2
$$\begin{cases} \dfrac{\partial R}{\partial p_i} = (p_i - mc)\dfrac{Q_i}{p_i} - Q_i(p_i) \\ \text{where } mc \text{ denote the marginal costs,} \\ mc := c'\left(\sum_{i=1}^{n} Q_i(p_i)\right) \end{cases} .$$

In order to define a welfare function, we make the usual assumption

45.3
$$\frac{\partial S}{\partial p_i} = - Q_i(p_i)$$

for the consumer's surplus, which follows from the rationality of the consumer and the separability of his utility function. Then, the set Λ defined in 40.2 is given by

45.4
$$\Lambda = \left\{ \frac{p_i - mc}{p_i} \cdot |\eta_i| - 1 \;\middle|\; i=1,2,\ldots,n \right\} ,$$

where η_i denotes the elasticity of the demand of the i'th consumer group with respect to the price,

45.5
$$\eta_i = Q'(p_i) \cdot \frac{p_i}{Q_i(p_i)} .$$

Assume now, that the actually chosen sales policy is one of non-discrimination, i.e., $x = (p,p,\ldots,p)$ with some $p \in \mathbb{R}$. Consequently, one has $\omega^+ \leqq \omega^-$ if and only if all elasticities η_i, $i=1,2,\ldots,n$ are identical. In general, of course, this will not be the case. Hence, except for the special case, where

45.6
$$\eta_1 = \eta_2 = \ldots = \eta_n$$

we have

45.7
$$\omega^+ \geqq \max \Lambda > \min \Lambda \geqq \omega^- ,$$

for the situation (X,A,x,R,W) with $x = (p,p,\ldots,p)$. *The absence of price discrimination is non-efficient*, if the consumers' benefits are aggregated .

If there are no interrelationships between different consumer groups, a sales policy $x = (p_1, p_2, \ldots, p_n)$ can only be efficient, if

45.8
$$mc = c'\left(\sum_{i=1}^{n} Q_i(p_i)\right) = p_1\left(1 - \frac{\omega}{\eta_1}\right) = p_2\left(1 - \frac{\omega}{\eta_2}\right) = \ldots = p_n\left(1 - \frac{\omega}{\eta_n}\right) .$$

holds for some $\omega \in [0,1]$. This condition means, that all prices have to satisfy the usual "marginal cost equals marginal revenue" formula (here in elasticity form, see also [3] and [23]), where all elasticities are inflated by a *common* scalar. In the situation with a sales policy given by 45.8, the degree of monopoly is (ω, ω), the degrees of aggression and consideration coincide with this scalar which inflates the elasticities.

46. Two-part Tariffs [3] , [9] , [14] , [17] , [20] , [26] . In order to analyze two-part tariffs, we assume that a monopolist offers two goods. To all consumers in the market he offers a member's ticket at a price $l \geq 0$ which allows entry into his club (and in our model of *first-fee pricing*, which is discussed here, makes complete information about the club's services available to members - customers have only a vague expectation on the benefits which result from beeing a member before they pay the licence fee l).
To the members, the monopolist offers the essential commodity at a price $p \geq 0$ per unit. It is clear, that each prospective customer buys either none or one ticket, and if he has bought one, he purchases a real quantity (greater or equal zero) of the proper commodity. Assume, that the membership gives benefits over and above the right to buy the commodity, and that only members are completely informed on the service and usefullness of the club. Every customer has *first* to pay the dues l (or not) and is only then able to determine the quantity he likes to purchase. Examples and more details are discussed in [26] . To make our argumentation clearer we suppose, that the demand for the membership card depends only on the subscription l and not on p. Thus we put

46.1
$$\begin{cases} m = M(l) & \text{membership} \\ q = Q(m,p) & \text{quantity of the proper product or service} \\ C(m,q) & \text{production and metering costs} \end{cases}$$

In what follows, treat the membership m as a real number, assume differentiability of M, Q, C and suppose the usual monotonicity for the demand functions. For the profit function R,

46.2
$$R(l,p) = lm + pq - C(m,q) = l\cdot M(l) + p\cdot Q(M(l),p) - C(M(l), Q(M(l),p))$$

holds then at the sales policy $x = (l,p)$:

46.3
$$\frac{\partial R}{\partial l} = M(l) + \left((p - mc_2)\frac{\partial Q}{\partial m} - mc_1\right)\cdot M'(l) ,$$
$$\frac{\partial R}{\partial p} = Q(m,p) + (p - mc_2)\cdot \frac{\partial Q}{\partial p} ,$$

where mc_1 and mc_2 denote the marginal costs,

$$mc_1 = \frac{\partial C}{\partial m}(m,q) \quad \text{and} \quad mc_2 = \frac{\partial C}{\partial q}(m,q) .$$

In order to define the welfare function W, we assume that the consumers' surplus $S = W - R$ satisfies

46.4
$$S(l,p) = s_1(l) + s_2(m,p) \quad \text{with}$$
$$\frac{ds_1}{dl} = -m \quad \text{and} \quad \frac{\partial s_2}{\partial p} = -q .$$

Consequently, at the sales policy $x = (l,p)$ holds

46.5
$$\frac{\partial S}{\partial l} = -m + \beta\cdot M'(l) \quad \text{where} \quad \beta := \frac{\partial s_1}{\partial m} ,$$
$$\frac{\partial S}{\partial p} = -q .$$

We now analyse the situation, where the sales policy $x = (0,p)$ opens the market by means of zero dues $l = 0$. To simplify the notation, norm the units for the membership and the money such that at the sales policy (0,p) actually realized

46.6 $$M(0) = 1 \quad \text{and} \quad M'(0) = -1$$

hold. Further, denote the *dynamic marginal costs* in 46.3 by

46.7 $$dmc_1 := mc_1 - (p - mc_2)\frac{\partial Q}{\partial m} .$$

Then one has :

46.8 $$\left\{ \begin{array}{l} \dfrac{\frac{\partial R}{\partial T}}{\frac{\partial S}{\partial T}} = \dfrac{1 - dmc_1}{1 + \beta} \quad \text{and} \quad \dfrac{\frac{\partial R}{\partial p}}{\frac{\partial S}{\partial p}} = \dfrac{p - mc_2}{p} \cdot |\eta_2| - 1 \\ \qquad\qquad\qquad\qquad\qquad \text{where} \quad \eta_2 = \dfrac{\partial Q}{\partial p} \cdot \dfrac{p}{q} \end{array} \right.$$

Assume now, that it is profitable for the firm to introduce positive dues, i.e., assume $dmc_1 > 1$. (In difference to models of *two-part tariffs*, in models of *first-fee pricing* the greedy monopolist may be forced to set zero dues). Then the sets Λ^+, Λ^- defined in 38.1 and 38.2 are here

46.9 $$\Lambda^+ = \{ \frac{p - mc_2}{p} |\eta_2| - 1 \} ,$$
$$\Lambda^- = \{ \frac{p - mc_2}{p} |\eta_2| - 1 , \frac{1 - dmc_1}{1 + \beta} \} ,$$

If then

46.10 $$\frac{1 - dmc_1}{1 + \beta} < \frac{p - mc_2}{p} |\eta_2| - 1$$

holds, one has $\min \Lambda^- < \max \Lambda^+$ and via 38.7 the non-efficiency of the policy $x = (0,p)$ with zero dues.

47. Advertising and Services Expenditures. Assume that a firm offers a consumer durable at a constant price $p > 0$ (there is regulation), but varies the *total advertising expenditure* $\alpha \in \mathbb{R}_+$ and the additional *services expenditure* $\beta \in \mathbb{R}_+$ *per unit*. Consequently, $x = (\alpha, \beta) \in \mathbb{R}_+^2$ is the sales policy and R,

47.1 $$R(\alpha,\beta) = pq - C(q) - \alpha - \beta q$$

the profit function, where C is a production cost function and q denotes the quantity of the product brought into the market with the policy $x = (\alpha,\beta)$. Suppose, that there are two groups of consumers : the first type of buyers respond to the advertising level α and the second is influenced by the service flow β,

47.2 $$q = Q_1(\alpha) + Q_2(\beta) .$$

Under differentiability of the functions Q_1, Q_2, C follows from 47.1 and 47.2 that :

47.3 $$\begin{aligned} \frac{\partial R}{\partial \alpha} &= (p - mc - \beta)\, Q_1'(\alpha) - 1 , \\ \frac{\partial R}{\partial \beta} &= (p - mc - \beta)\, Q_2'(\beta) - (Q_1(\alpha) + Q_2(\beta)) . \end{aligned}$$

According to a common rule of thumb, the decision maker had adjusted his sales policy such that

47.4 $$\frac{\partial R}{\partial \alpha} = \frac{1}{q} \cdot \frac{\partial R}{\partial \beta} \quad ; \text{ i.e.,} \quad Q_1'(\alpha) = \frac{1}{q} \cdot Q_2'(\beta)$$

holds at $x = (\alpha,\beta)$. The surplus function S may be differentiable and we denote $s_\alpha := \partial S/\partial \alpha$, $s_\beta := \partial S/\partial \beta$. Then, if $\alpha, \beta > 0$, the set defined in corollary 40 is here given by

47.5 $$\Lambda = \left\{ \frac{\frac{\partial R}{\partial \alpha}}{s_\alpha} , \frac{\frac{1}{q}\frac{\partial R}{\partial \beta}}{s_\beta} \right\} .$$

Consequently, $qs_\beta \neq s_\alpha$ implies $\min \Lambda < \max \Lambda$, hence $\omega^- < \omega^+$, and the non-efficiency of the policy $x = (\alpha,\beta)$.

VII. Appendix

7. (From section II on page 6). Visualizing increasing returns to scale industries operating with losses, J.S. Bain's measure [1] of *supernormal profits* becomes understandable. This index is based on the discrepancy between price and average cost ac,

7.1 $$\omega_{BAIN} = \omega(p,ac) \ .$$

Such a discrepancy, according to Bain, "is significant because of its influence directly on the functional distribution of income and indirectly on the propensity to consume, the level of employment, etc." [2] . K.W. Rotschild based his measure on the *reactions of all other competitors* in an industry on price changes of the firm under consideration. He took the firm's "species" demand function (i.e., the sales curve confronting the firm on the assumption that all other prices remain unchanged) and their "genus" demand function (i.e., the sales curve confronting the firm on the assumption, that the competitors in the industry react on the firm's price changes), assumed differentiability and defined his index as the ratio of the slope of the species demand curve to the slope of the genus demand curve [24] . As has been pointed out by A. G. Papandreou [21] , the measure of Rothschild emphasizes the position of a firm opposite to its competitors in the market, and therefore comes closer to the *legal* concept of monopoly. A more elaborate analysis of these power relations between different firms and for different types of market structures (such as atomistic and circular [29] homeopoly and heteropoly as for the pure monopoly) is presented in [21] . Classifications of market structures (and hence criteria for imperfections), which are based on the *number of firms* that form an industry, or which are based on a "state of mind and a type of behaviour which is usually associated with large numbers of sellers in a market" [16], have been proposed by F. Machlup. T. Morgan defined a coefficient of *insulation of the firm from competition*. His index is a function of several values; increasing in the firm's size relative to the industry, decreasing in the substituability of the products of its competitors for the firm's product [18] . Finally, we refer to the *concentration measures*, which are based on the Lorenz curve, the Gini coefficient and the Herfindale index; see [25,p.51] , [9] and the paper by R. Bürk and W. Gehrig in this volume.

19. (From section IV on page 16). The local closed cone LC(A,x) of A at $x \in X$ can also be defined for general linear topological spaces X . Let X be such a topological linear space, $A \subset X$ a non-empty subset and $x \in X$. The intersection of all closed cones in X which contain the set $A - x$, $A - x = \{y \in X \mid y+x \in A\}$, is called the *closed cone of* A *at* x and denoted by C(A,x) . The *local closed cone of* A *at* x is the cone

19.1 $$LC(A,x) := \bigcap_{U \in \mathfrak{U}} C(A \cap U, x)$$

where $\mathfrak{U}$ is the set of neighborhoods of x in X [30] . In normed spaces, the definitions 18.1 and 19.1 coincide. According to [12] , it is possible to characterize LC(A,x) by "déplacements adhérents pour A à partir de x ",

19.2 $$LC(A,x) = \{ h \in X \mid \text{for all } \varepsilon > 0 \text{ there is some } k \in X \text{ with } \|k-h\| < \varepsilon \text{ and there is some } \varepsilon_h \in]0,\varepsilon] \text{ such that } x + \eta k \in A \text{ for all } \eta \in]0,\varepsilon_h] \} .$$

25. (From section IV on page 20). Let $k \in C$ such that

25.1 $$J_i'(k) =: \rho_i > 0 \qquad \text{for } i=1,2 .$$

From $k \in C$, $C = LC(A,x)$ and 18.1 follow the

25.2 $$\begin{cases} \text{existence of sequences } \{x_\nu\}, \{\xi_\nu\}, \ \nu \in \mathbb{N} \\ \text{with } x_\nu \in A , \ \xi_\nu \in \mathbb{R}_+ , \text{ and} \\ \{x_\nu\} \to x , \ \{\xi_\nu(x_\nu - x)\} \to k . \end{cases}$$

$J_i'(k) > 0$ implies $k \neq o$ because of the homogeneity of J_i' , and hence 25.2 implies that $\xi_\nu > 0$ for all $\nu \in \mathbb{N}$ greater than some number m .

Define

25.3 $$k_\nu \quad := \quad \frac{1}{\xi_\nu}\, k \qquad \text{for all} \quad \nu > m \; .$$

Then 25.1 means by 16.1 that

25.4 $$\lim_{\substack{\nu \to \infty \\ \nu > m}} \; \xi_\nu \,(J_i(x + k_\nu) - J_i(x)) \quad = \quad \rho_i$$

From 25.4 follows the existence of some number $n(\rho_i) > m$ such that

25.5 $$J_i(x + k_\nu) - J_i(x) \quad > \quad \frac{\rho_i}{2\xi_\nu} \qquad \text{holds for all} \quad \nu > n(\rho_i) \; .$$

Now, the local Lipschitz condition 23.1 means, that

25.6 $$\| J_i(x + k_\nu) - J_i(x_\nu) \| \quad \leqq \quad \beta_i \; \| x + k_\nu - x_\nu \|$$

holds as long as for some $\varepsilon_i > 0$,

25.7 $$\| k_\nu \| \quad = \quad \frac{1}{\xi_\nu} \| k \| \quad < \quad \varepsilon_i \qquad \text{and} \qquad \| x_\nu - x \| \quad < \quad \varepsilon_i$$

are satisfied. Because of 25.2 , this condition 25.7 is satisfied for all $\nu \in \mathbb{N}$ which are greater than some number n_i . Put 25.5 and 25.6 together, it results in

25.8 $$\left\{ \begin{array}{llll} J_i(x_\nu) > J_i(x) & , \text{ if} & \nu > \max\{ n(\rho_i) , n_i \} & \text{and} \\ \beta_i \; \| x + k_\nu - x_\nu \| & < \; \rho_i/2\xi_\nu & , \text{ i.e.,} & \\ \xi_\nu \; \| x + k_\nu - x_\nu \| & < \; \rho_i/2\beta_i & , \text{ i.e.,} & \\ \| k + \xi_\nu (x_\nu - x) \| & < \; \rho_i/2\beta_i & . & \end{array} \right.$$

Remember the directional convergence 25.2 which means that

25.9 $$\begin{array}{l} \text{for} \quad \varepsilon_i = \rho_i/2\beta_i \quad \text{there is a number} \quad \bar{m}_i \quad \text{such that} \\ \| k + \xi_\nu (x_\nu - x) \| \; < \; \rho_i/2\beta_i \quad \text{for all} \quad \nu > \bar{m}_i \quad . \end{array}$$

Consequently, from 25.7 follows the assertion 24.1 with

25.10 $$n := \max\{n(\rho_1), n_1, n(\rho_2), n_2, \bar{m}_1, \bar{m}_2\} .$$

30. (From section V on page 25). Proof of lemma 29.
Ad 29.1 : $\Omega^+ \neq \emptyset$ implies the existence of some $k \in C$ with $W'(k) > 0$, i.e., the presence of aggression in $\mathcal{G}$. For $\omega = 0$, $J'_\omega(k) = W'(k) > 0$, hence $0 \in \Omega^+$. If there is aggression in $\mathcal{G}$, there is a vector $k \in C$ with $W'(k) > 0$. This implies $J'_0(k) \geqq 0$ and consequently $0 \in \Omega^+$, especially one has then $\Omega^+ \neq \emptyset$.
Ad 29.2 : Assume $\omega \in \Omega^+$ for some $\omega > 0$, i.e., there exists some $k \in C$ with $W'(k) > 0$ and $J'_\omega(k) \geqq 0$. On the other hand, $J'_\omega(k) = \omega R'(k) + W'(k) - \omega W'(k) \geqq 0$, iff : $W'(k) \geqq \omega(W'(k) - R'(k))$. Because both ω and $W'(k)$ are positive, this inequality is equivalent to

30.1 $$\frac{1}{\omega} \geqq \frac{W'(k) - R'(k)}{W'(k)} .$$

From 30.1 follows

30.2 $$\frac{1}{\zeta} \geqq \frac{1}{\omega} \geqq \frac{W'(k) - R'(k)}{W'(k)}$$

for all $\zeta \in]0,\omega]$ and hence one has $]0,\omega] \in \Omega^+$. With 29.1 follows then the assertion 29.2 .
Ad 29.3 : With 28.1 follows from $\omega^+ > 1$ that $1+\varepsilon \in \Omega^+$ for some $\varepsilon > 0$. Consequently, there is a vector $k \in C$ with $W'(k) > 0$ and $J'_{1+\varepsilon}(k) = (1+\varepsilon)R'(k) - \varepsilon W'(k) \geqq 0$, i.e., $R'(k) > 0$; $\mathcal{G}$ is non-efficient.
The proofs of the dual statements 29.4 , 29.5 , 29.6 are similar to those of 29.1 , 29.2 , 29.3 and are therefore omitted.

35. (From section V on page 27). Proof of theorem 34.
That the conditions 34.1, 34.2 imply the non-efficiency of $\mathcal{G} = \mathfrak{A}(\mathfrak{T})$ are the statements 29.3, 29.6 of lemma 29 and is proved in 30. Consequently, also the situation $\mathfrak{T} \in \P_1$ is then non-efficient according to the statement 23.4 of theorem 23; remember the definition of $\P_1$ in paragraph 27.3.
Ad 34.3: Assume $\omega^+, \omega^- \in [0,1]$, $\omega^+ > \omega^-$ (and the regularity 33.1). From 28.1, 28.3 follow the existence of two numbers λ^+, λ^- with $\lambda^+ > \lambda^-$ and $\lambda^+ \in \Omega^+$, $\lambda^- \in \Omega^-$. From $\lambda^+ \in \Omega^+$ follows the existence of some vector $k \in C$ with

35.1 $$\lambda^+ \cdot R'(k) + (1-\lambda^+)W'(k) \geqq 0 \quad \text{and} \quad W'(k) > 0 .$$

From $\lambda^- \in \Omega^-$ follows the existence of some vector $h \in C$ with

35.2 $$\lambda^- \cdot R'(h) + (1-\lambda^-)W'(h) \geqq 0 \quad \text{and} \quad R'(h) > 0 .$$

Now we deduce the non-efficiency of $\mathcal{G} = \mathfrak{A}(\mathfrak{T})$ for all of the following three cases 35.3, 35.4, 35.5. According to the statement 23.4 of theorem 23 the non-efficiency of $\mathcal{G} = \mathfrak{A}(\mathfrak{T})$ implies the non-efficiency of $\mathfrak{T}$, if $\mathfrak{T} \in \P_1$, which then completes the proof of 34.3. The three cases are:

35.3 $$R'(k) \geqq 0 \quad \text{and} \quad W'(h) \geqq 0 ,$$

35.4 $$R'(k) < 0 ,$$

35.5 $$W'(h) < 0 .$$

From 35.3 follows with the regularity 33.1 for the vector sum $l := h + k$

35.6 $$\begin{cases} l \in C , & \text{since } C \text{ is convex ;} \\ R'(l) \geqq R'(h) + R'(k) \geqq R'(h) > 0 ; \\ W'(l) \geqq W'(h) + W'(k) \geqq W'(k) > 0 ; \end{cases}$$

i.e., it follows the non-efficiency of $\mathcal{G}$. From 35.4 and the homogeneity (of degree one) of R' follows for the vector $\tilde{k}$ defined by

35.7 $$\tilde{k} \quad := \quad \frac{1}{-R'(k)} \cdot k$$

that 35.1 can be written in the form

35.8 $$-\lambda^{+} + (1-\lambda^{+})W'(\tilde{k}) \geqq 0 \quad \text{and} \quad W'(\tilde{k}) > 0 \ .$$

Likewise, 35.2 implies for the vector $\tilde{h}$ defined by

35.9 $$\tilde{h} \quad := \quad \frac{1}{R'(h)} \cdot h$$

that

35.10 $$\lambda^{-} + (1-\lambda^{-})W'(\tilde{h}) \geqq 0 \quad \text{and} \quad R'(\tilde{h}) > 0$$

hold. The sum of both sides of the inequalities 35.8 and 35.10 yields to

35.11 $$\left\{ \begin{array}{l} -\lambda^{+} + \lambda^{-} + (1-\lambda^{+})W'(\tilde{k}) + (1-\lambda^{-})W'(\tilde{h}) \geqq 0 \ , \\ \text{i.e., for the vector } \quad \ell := (1-\lambda^{+})\tilde{k} + (1-\lambda^{-})\tilde{h} \in C : \\ W'(\ell) \geqq \lambda^{+} - \lambda^{-} > 0 \ . \end{array} \right.$$

Clearly, 35.7 , 35.9 imply

35.12 $$\left\{ \begin{array}{rcl} R'(\ell) & \geqq & R'((1-\lambda^{+})k) + R'((1-\lambda^{-})h) = \\ & = & (1-\lambda^{+})R'(k) + (1-\lambda^{-})R'(h) = \\ & = & (1-\lambda^{+})(-1) + (1-\lambda^{-})(+1) = \lambda^{+} - \lambda^{-} > 0 \ . \end{array} \right.$$

These formulas 35.11 , 35.12 state $\ell \in C$, $W'(\ell) > 0$, $R'(\ell) > 0$, i.e., the non-efficiency of $\mathscr{C}_{\gamma}$. The remaining case 35.5 is treated quite analogously to the above analysis of case 35.4 and is therefore omitted .

39. (From section V on page 30). Proof of theorem 38.
First note, that in the definitions 38.1 and 38.2 the case $\partial S/\partial x_i = 0$ is excluded because of 37.4. At first, we show 38.5 and afterwards 38.3. The proofs of 38.6 and 38.4 are quite similar and therefore omitted. The last statement 38.7 is a simple consequence of 38.5, 38.6 and theorem 34.
Ad 38.5 : Let $\lambda \in \Lambda^+$, i.e.,

39.1 $$\lambda \frac{\partial S}{\partial x_i} = \frac{\partial W}{\partial x_i} \quad \text{or} \quad \lambda \frac{\partial R}{\partial x_i} + (1-\lambda) \frac{\partial W}{\partial x_i} = 0$$

and

39.2 $$\frac{\partial W}{\partial x_i} k_i > 0 \quad \text{for some} \quad k_i \in C_i \quad .$$

Now define the vector $k \in \mathbb{R}^n$ by

39.3 $$k_\sigma = \begin{cases} 0 \ , & \text{if} \quad \sigma \neq i \ , \\ k_i \ , & \text{if} \quad \sigma = i \ , \end{cases}$$

from which follow

39.4 $$k \in C \ ,$$

39.5 $$W'(k) = \sum_{\sigma=1}^{n} \frac{\partial W}{\partial x_\sigma} \cdot k_\sigma = \frac{\partial W}{\partial x_i} \cdot k_i > 0 \ ,$$

and

39.6 $$J'_\lambda(k) = \lambda \sum_{\sigma=1}^{n} \frac{\partial R}{\partial x_\sigma} \cdot k_\sigma + (1-\lambda) \sum_{\sigma=1}^{n} \frac{\partial W}{\partial x_\sigma} \cdot k_\sigma =$$
$$= (\lambda \frac{\partial R}{\partial x_i} + (1-\lambda) \frac{\partial W}{\partial x_i}) k_i = 0 \cdot k_i = 0 \geqq 0 \ .$$

The statements 39.4, 39.5, 39.6 mean $\lambda \in \Omega^+$, and consequently, we have : $\sup \Omega^+ \geqq \max \Lambda^+$, and 38.5 is proved.
Ad 38.3 : $\Lambda^+ \neq \emptyset$ implies $\Omega^+ \neq \emptyset$, see the above proof of 38.5, which means the existence of aggression in $\mathcal{G} = \mathfrak{A}(\mathcal{T})$, and since situations of the form 37.1 belong to the set $\P_1$ (see 37.3), there is also aggression in $\mathcal{T}$ because of theorem 23. On the other hand, assume the presence of

marginal aggression in $\mathfrak{T}$, i.e., the presence of aggression in $\mathcal{G}$ by 27 . Then 29.1 says $0 \in \Omega^+$, i.e., the existence of some $k \in C$ with

39.7 $$J_0'(k) = W'(k) = \sum_{\sigma=1}^{n} \frac{\partial W}{\partial x_\sigma} k_\sigma > 0 .$$

This ineaquality 39.7 implies

39.8 $$\frac{\partial W}{\partial x_j} \cdot k_j > 0 \qquad \text{for some} \quad j \in \{1,2,\ldots,n\}$$

and $k \in C$ implies $k_j \in C_j$; hence, $\Lambda^+ \neq \emptyset$.

VIII. References

1. J.S. BAIN : *The Profit Rate as a Measure of Monopoly Power* , Quarterly Journal of Economics, Vol. LV(1941), 271-293.

2. J.S. BAIN : *Measurements of the Degree of Monopoly : a Note* , Economica, Vol. 10(1943), 66 .

3. W.J. BAUMOL and D. BRADFORD : *Optimal Departures From Marginal Cost Pricing,* American Economic Review, Vol. 60(1970), 265-283.

4. J.M. BUCHANAN and W.C. STUBBLEBINE : *Externality*, Economica, Vol. 29(1962), 371-384.

5. J. DIEUDONNÉ : *Foundations of Modern Analysis,* Vol. 10-I in Pure and Applied Mathematics, Academic Press, New York 1969, ch. VIII.

6. I.V. GIRSANOV : *Lectures on Mathematical Theory of Extremum Problems,* Lecture Notes in Economics and Mathematical Systems, Vol. 67, Springer-Verlag, Berlin 1972, p.50 f.

7. O.C. HERFINDAHL : *Concentration in the Steel Industry,* doctoral dissertation, Columbia University, New York, 1950.

8. M.R. HESTENES : *Calculus of Variations and Optimal Control Theory,* Applied Mathematics Series, Wiley, New York, 1966.

9. Y.-K. NG and M. WEISSER : *Optimal Pricing with a Budget Constraint - The Case of the Two-part Tariff,* Review of Economic Studies, Vol. 41 (July 1974)137, 337-345.

10. J.R. HICKS : *The rehabilitation of Consumers' Surplus*, The Review of Economic Studies, Vol. 9(1941), 108-116.

11. R.W. KILPATRICK : *The Choice Among Alternative Measures of Industrial Concentration*, Review of Economics and Statistics, (May 1967), 258-260.

12. P.J. LAURENT : *Approximation et optimisation*, Collection Einseignement des sciences, Vol. 13, Hermann, Paris, 1972.

13. A.P. LERNER : *The Concept of Monopoly and the Measurement of Monopoly Power*, The Review of Economic Studies, Vol. 1(1934), 157-175.

14. S.C. LITTLECHILD : *Two-part Tariffs and Consumption Externalities*, Bell Journal of Economics and Management Science, Autumn 1975, 661-670.

15. L.A. LJUSTERNIK and W.I. SOBOLEW : *Elemente der Funktionalanalysis*, Mathematische Lehrbücher Band VIII, Akademie-Verlag, Berlin, 1968.

16. F. MACHLUP : *Monopoly and Competition : A Classification of Market Positions*, American Economic Review, Vol. XXVII(1937), 445-451.

17. R.A. MEYER : *Monopoly Pricing Structures with Imperfect Discrimination*, Bell Journal of Economics and Management Science, Autumn 1976,

18. T. MORGAN : *A Measure of Monopoly in Selling*, Quarterly Journal of Economics, Vol. LX(1946), 461-463.

19. M.Z. NASHED : *Differentiability and Related Properties of Nonlinear Operators : Some Aspects of the Role of Differentials in Nonlinear Functional Analysis*, in : L.B. BELL (ed.) : *Nonlinear Functional Analysis*, Publication No. 26 of the Mathematics Research Center of the University of Wisconsin, Academic Press, New York, 1971, 103-309.

20. W. OI : *A Disneyland Dilemma : Two Part Tariffs for a Mickey Mouse Monopoly*, Quarterly Journal of Economics, Vol. 85(1971), 77-96.

21. A.G. PAPANDREOU : *Market Structure and Monopoly Power*, American Economic Review, Vol. XXXIX(1949), 883-897.

22. T. RADER : *Equivalence of Consumer Surplus, the Divisia Index of Output, and Eisenberg's Addilog Social Utility*, Journal of Economic Theory, Vol. 13(1976), 58-66.

23. F. RAMSEY : *A Contribution to the Theory of Taxation*, Economic Journal, Vol. 37(March 1927), 47-61.

24. K.W. ROTHSCHILD : *The Degree of Monopoly*, Economica, Vol. 9(1942), 21-39.

25. F.M. SCHERER : *Industrial Market Structure and Economic Performance*, Rand Mc Nally, Chicago, 1970, 50-71.

26. K. SPREMANN : *Über Vektormaximierung und Analyse der Gewichtung von Subzielen,* in : W. OETTLI and K. RITTER (eds.) : *Optimization and Operations Research,* Lecture Notes in Economics and Mathematical Systems, Vol. 117, Springer-Verlag, Berlin, 1976, 283-296.

27. K. SPREMANN : *On Welfare Implications and Efficiency of First Fee Pricing,* Discussion Paper des Instituts für Wirtschaftstheorie und Operations Research der Universität Karlsruhe, No. 78, (Feb. 1977).

28. R.A. TAPIA : *The Differentiation and Integration of Nonlinear Operators,* in : L.B. BELL (ed.) : *Nonlinear Functional Analysis,* Publication No. 26 of the Mathematics Research Center of the University of Wisconsin, Academic Press, New York, 1971, 45-102.

29. R. TRIFFIN : *Monopolistic Competition and General Equilibrium Theory,* Cambridge, 1940.

30. P.P. VARAIYA : *Nonlinear Programming in Banach Space,* SIAM Journal on Applied Mathematics, Vol. 15(1967)2, 284-293.

31. R.D. WILLIG : *Consumer's Surplus Without Apology,* American Economic Review, Vol. 66(Sept. 1976), 589-597.

Indices of Preference Inequality and the Construction of Social Preference Relations

by Frank Stehling

0. Introduction

Indices of inequality of preference relations are not very popular in economic theory. Nevertheless, the question of constructing such indices which should measure how strongly any two given preference relations (PRs) differ, arises when PRs of several persons or groups of persons must be compared, for example, in order to find a social PR, i.e., a single PR which should represent in a certain sense the individual PRs of the persons or the groups.

Several methods of constructing social PRs have been analysed in the economic literature, for example the majority rule or the method of ranking the alternatives or the dictatorship rule. The most important result in this direction may be the famous dictatorship theorem of J.K. Arrow [1963]. This theorem says, roughly speaking, that whenever there are at least 3 different (but a finite number m of) alternatives and a finite number n of persons i, each of them having a PR R_i on the set $\mathcal{A}$ of alternatives and whenever the social decision rule f assigns to every n-tuple of PRs on $\mathcal{A}$ a PR on $\mathcal{A}$, the so-called social PR, and satisfies the Pareto-principle and the independence of irrelevant alternatives then there must be a dictator, i.e. there exists a person $j \in \{1,\ldots,n\}$ such that

$$f(R_1,\ldots,R_j,\ldots,R_n) = R_j \quad \text{for all PRs } R_i (i=1,\ldots,n) \text{ on } \mathcal{A}.$$

That means: the social PR copies the PR of person j.

Many efforts have been made to escape from the dilemma of the dictatorship theorem. They can be divided into two groups, one of which consists of attempts to weaken the assumptions of Arrow about the properties of the social decision function. The other group consists of attempts to characterize more democratic decision functions like the majority rule by properties which are similarly intuitive as Arrow's (Sen [1970], pp. 71 ff.). In the following, we will give a completely different approach to the problem of finding a social decision function. The approach is based on the definition of indices of inequality of preference relations (section 1). If it is possible to define such an index it suggests itself to define a social PR as such a PR R* which minimizes the (square-) sum of the values of the index for all pairs (R,R_i), where R runs through all PRs on $\mathcal{A}$ and R_i is the PR of person i (section 2). In section 3 we discuss some properties of the social decision functions which are implicitely defined by the minimization procedure. Furthermore, it can be shown that the ranking method - an often applied procedure to find a social PR - is generated by such an optimization process, in the sense that a PR is a social PR with respect to the ranking method if and only if it is a social PR with respect to a certain index of inequality of PRs (section 4). Further applications to cases where individual preferences are not complete and/or not transitive are given in section 5.

1. Indices of inequality of preference relations

We will not give here an axiomatic characterization of indices of inequality of PRs though that would be of great interest and was done with great success for other indices, e.g. for indices of income inequality or for price indices (see S.-Ch. Kolm [1976], R. Bürk and W. Gehrig [this volume], I. Fisher [1967], W.Eichhorn and J. Voeller [1976]). The aim of this section is to define special indices and to discuss some of their properties.

Let $\mathcal{A}$ be a set of a finite number of distinct abstract alternatives:

$$\mathcal{A} = \{A_1, A_2, \ldots, A_m\} \qquad (m \geqq 3).$$

Let R be a PR on $\mathcal{A}$, i.e. a reflexive, transitive and complete ordering on $\mathcal{A}$. Then, $x R y$ means that x is (not necessarily strictly) preferred to y. Denote by P the corresponding strict PR, such that $x P y$ means that x is strictly preferred to y. In the following we work only with strict PRs.

Every strict PR P on $\mathcal{A}$ can be uniquely represented by an ordered m - tuple the components of which are a permutation (denoted by π) of the elements of $\mathcal{A}$. Hence we can write

(1.1) $$R := (A_{\pi(1)}, A_{\pi(2)}, \ldots, A_{\pi(m)})$$

which means that $A_{\pi(m)}$ is the most preferred alternative, $A_{\pi(m-1)}$ the second most preferred alternative,..., and $A_{\pi(1)}$ is the least preferred alternative; the usual notation for this is

(1.1') $$A_{\pi(1)} \prec A_{\pi(2)} \prec \cdots \prec A_{\pi(m)}.$$

In order to construct an index of the inequality of a pair of PRs we assign to each alternative an integer according to its place in the vector P:

(1.2) $$v(A_\ell) = \pi^{-1}(\ell) \qquad (\ell = 1, \ldots m),$$

where π^{-1} is the permutation inverse to π. Hence, for example, the best alternative (with respect to R) gets the value m and the worst alternative gets the value 1. We call v the value function belonging to R (resp. π). This procedure is well-known from the ranking method (see U. Krause [1973]). An index of inequality can now be defined as the sum of the absolute values of the differences between the numbers which are assigned to each alternative by two PRs, i.e.

(1.3') $$I_1(P,P') := \sum_{\ell=1}^{m} |v(A_\ell)-v'(A_\ell)| .$$

In view of (1.2), I_1 can be written as

(1.3') $$I_1(P,P') = \sum_{\ell=1}^{m} |\pi^{-1}(\ell) - \pi'^{-1}(\ell)|,$$

where v and v' are the value functions of P and P', respectively, and π and π' are the corresponding permutations with their inverses π^{-1} and π'^{-1}.

Of course, another index can be defined by

(1.4) $$I^s(P,P') := \sum_{\ell=1}^{m} (\pi^{-1}(\ell) - \pi'^{-1}(\ell))^2$$

or by

(1.5) $$I_r(P,P') := \left(\sum_{\ell=1}^{m} | \pi^{-1}(\ell) - \pi'^{-1}(\ell)|^r\right)^{1/r}$$

for any $r \in \mathbb{N}$, the set of all positive integers.
It is easy to prove that I_r (and I^s) has the properties of a metric, i.e. for all strict PRs P,P', and P'' on $\mathcal{A}$ we have:

(1.6i) $I_r(P,P') \geqq 0$ and $I_r(P,P') = 0$ if and only if $P = P'$;

(1.6ii) $I_r(P,P') = I_r(P',P)$;

(1.6iii) $I_r(P,P') \leqq I_r(P,P'') + I_r(P'',P')$.

Additionally,

(1.6iv) I_r is independent of the numbering of the alternatives[1].
Now, the following definition suggests itself:

Def. 1.7: Let $\mathfrak{P}(\mathcal{A})$ be the set of all strict PRs on $\mathcal{A}$. Every function

$$I : \mathfrak{P}(\mathcal{A}) \times \mathfrak{P}(\mathcal{A}) \to \mathbb{R}_+$$

satisfying the properties (1.6i), (1.6ii), (1.6iii), and (1.6.iv) is called an index of inequality of PRs on $\mathcal{A}$.

Obviously, the identification of a strict PR P on $\mathcal{A}$ with a permutation π of the first m positive integers is an arbitrary one; nevertheless it is an often used procedure. It implies that the distance of two successive alternatives $A_{\pi(i)}$ and $A_{\pi(i+1)}$ is measured by 1, independently from i. That may be unsatisfactory in situations when it is necessary to distinguish between the distance of two successive alternatives which seem to be almost indifferent (with respect to a certain PR P) and the distance of two other successive alternatives the one of which is very strongly preferred to the other. There exist concepts to take into account such differences; but these concepts have other disadvantages so that we restrict ourselves to the indices defined above.

2. Social preference relations

We return to the question of defining a social PR by means of individual strict PRs $P_1,\ldots,P_n$ of n persons or groups of persons. For that purpose one has to define a social decision f (or more general: a social decision correspondence c) which

---

[1] A proof of that property is given at the end of section 3.

maps the set of all n-tupels $(P_1,\dots,P_n)$ of strict PRs on $\mathcal{A}$ into the set $\mathcal{P}(\mathcal{A})$ of all strict PRs on $\mathcal{A}$ (or more general: into the set of all subsets of strict PRs on $\mathcal{A}$):

$$f\colon (P_1,\dots,P_n) \to f(P_1,\dots,P_n) = P \in \mathcal{P}(\mathcal{A})$$

or

$$c\colon (P_1,\dots,P_n) \to c(P_1,\dots,P_n) \subseteq \mathcal{P}(\mathcal{A}).$$

Our method of defining such a social decision correspondence is an implicit one and is - as was mentioned above - related to our definitions of an index of inequality of PRs.

<u>Def. 2.1:</u> Let I be an index of inequality of PRs on $\mathcal{A}$. The strict PR $P^* \in \mathcal{P}(\mathcal{A})$ is called a <u>social PR of the individual PRs $P_1,\dots,P_n$ on $\mathcal{A}$ with respect to I</u> if

$$\sum_{i=1}^{n} I(P^*,P_i) \leqq \sum_{i=1}^{n} I(P,P_i) \qquad \text{for all PRs } P \in \mathcal{P}(\mathcal{A}).$$

In other words: a social PR P^* minimizes the sum of the indices of inqualities of all individual PRs with respect to a single PR on $\mathcal{A}$. Of course, there are other possibilities to define a social PR; for example it seems to be reasonable to call $\bar{P} \in \mathcal{P}(\mathcal{A})$ a social PR of the individual PRs $P_1,\dots,P_n$ on $\mathcal{A}$ with respect to I if

$$g(I(\bar{P},P_1),\dots,I(\bar{P},P_n)) \leqq g(I(P,P_1),\dots,I(P,P_n))$$
$$\text{for all strict PRs } P \in \mathcal{P}(\mathcal{A}),$$

with any function g having some suitable properties as monotonicity and symmetry. But in the following we restrict ourselves to social PRs in the sense of def. 2.1.
It is clear that there may be more than one social PR for a given n-tupel of PRs which implies that the social decision

correspondence defined implicitly in def. 2.1 is indeed a correspondence. For example, if there are three persons and three alternatives A,B, and C and

$$P_1 = (C,B,A), \quad P_2 = (B,C,A), \quad P_3 = (A,C,B)$$

it can easily be shown that

$$P^* = (C,B,A) = P_1 \text{ and } P^{**} = (B,C,A) = P_2$$

are both social PRs of P_1, P_2, and P_3 with respect to the index I_1.

It is not surprising that different indices of inequality lead, in general, to different social PRs. Thus, we have in the example above that P_2 is not a social PR with respect to I^s; P_1 is the single social PR with respect to I^s. There are examples that the social PRs with respect to I_1 and I^s differ completely:
If there are 7 persons with the individual PRs

$$P_1 = (C,B,A) = P_2, \; P_3 = (A,C,B), \; P_4 = (B,C,A), \; P_5 = (A,B,C)$$

$$P_6 = P_5, \; P_7 = (B,A,C),$$

then P_5 is the only social PR with respect to I_1 and P_7 is the only social PR with respect to I^s. This shows that relationships between the social decision correspondences generated by two different indices of inequality of PRs cannot be expected. Nevertheless, there are relationships between such decision correspondences and decision correspondences generated by the well-known ranking method which will be discussed in section 4.

3. Properties of the social PRs generated by indices of preference inequality

In view of Arrow's dictatorship theorem, it may be of interest to analyse which of Arrow's conditions are satisfied by the social decision correspondences defined implicitly in section 2. Arrow's conditions are (see A. Sen [1970], p. 41-42):[1)]

(i) Unrestricted domain: The domain of the social decision function (or correspondence) consists of the n-tuples of all logically possible individual PRs.

(ii) Pareto principle: If all individuals strictly prefer the alternative A_k to the alternative A_j then, A_k is strictly preferred to A_j with respect to any social PR P of the individual PRs $P_1,\ldots,P_n$; formally

$$A_k \; P_i \; A_j \quad \text{for } i = 1,\ldots,n \text{ implies } A_k \; P \; A_j.$$

(iii) Independence of irrelevant alternatives: Let $(P_1,\ldots,P_n)$ and $(P'_1,\ldots,P'_n)$ be two n-tupels of individual strict PRs, and let P and P' be two corresponding social PRs. Then, for all pairs A_k, A_j of alternatives

$$\{A_k \; P_i \; A_j \iff A_k \; P'_i \; A_j \text{ for all } i\} \text{ implies } \{A_k \; P \; A_j \iff A_k P' A_j\}.$$

(iv) Nondictatorship: There is no individual i_o, such that for all pairs A_k, A_j of alternatives

$$A_k \; P_{i_o} \; A_j \quad \text{implies} \quad A_k \; P \; A_j \; ,$$

regardless of the strict PRs P_ℓ ($\ell \neq i_o$) of the other individuals.

1) In the following the properties are formulated for strict PRs which differ from Sen's formulation.

Now let P_i be the strict PR of person i represented by the permutation π_i (i=1,...,n). Let the index of inequality of PRs be given by (1.5) or (1.4), i.e.

$$(3.1) \qquad I_r(P,P') = \left(\sum_{\ell=1}^{m} |\pi^{-1}(\ell)-\pi'^{-1}(\ell)|^r\right)^{1/r} \qquad (r \in \mathbb{N})$$

or

$$(3.2) \qquad I^s(P,P') = \sum_{\ell=1}^{m} (\pi^{-1}(\ell)-\pi'^{-1}(\ell))^2 ,$$

where π and π' are the permutations corresponding to P and P' (with their inverses π^{-1} and π'^{-1}).
Since there is only a finite number of different (strict) PRs on the finite set $\mathcal{A}$ of alternatives the problem

$$(3.3) \qquad \sum_{i=1}^{n} I(P,P_i) \to \min. \qquad (P \in \mathcal{P}(\mathcal{A}))$$

has at least one solution P(I) on $\mathcal{P}(\mathcal{A})$ for any n-tuple $(P_1,...,P_n)$ of individual PRs and for any index $I = I_r$ $(r \in \mathbb{N})$ or $I = I^s$. Hence property (i) is satisfied for social decision correspondences generated by such indices.
Next, let us consider the validity of the Pareto-principle. We show

<u>Theorem 3.4:</u> Let P(I) be any solution of (3.3).

(*) If $I = I_1$, then $P(I_1)$ does not satisfy, in general, the Pareto-principle (ii).

(**) If $I = I_r$ $(r \in \mathbb{N},\ r \geqq 2)$ or $I = I^s$, then P(I) satisfies the Pareto-principle (ii).

<u>Proof:</u> <u>ad(*):</u> Consider two persons with the stricht PRs

$$P_1 = (A,B,C,D) \quad \text{and} \quad P_2 = (C,D,A,B).$$

Then, for $I = I_1$ the problem (3.3) has 8 solutions one of which being

$$P(I_1) = (C,B,A,D).$$

Here A is strictly preferred to B whereas in both individual PRs B is strictly preferred to A which contradicts (ii).

<u>ad (**):</u> Assume that the proposition is not true, i.e. for $I = I_r (r \in \mathbb{N}, r \geqq 2)$ or $I = I^s$ there is a solution $P(I)$ of (3.3) which does not satisfy the Pareto-principle. Hence, there exist $k, \ell \in \{1,\dots,m\}$ such that

$$\pi_i^{-1}(k) < \pi_i^{-1}(\ell) \qquad (i = 1,\dots,n) \tag{3.5}$$

which means that each person strictly prefers A_ℓ to A_k, but

$$\pi^{-1}(k) > \pi^{-1}(\ell), \tag{3.6}$$

where π is the permutation corresponding to $P(I)$, so that the group prefers A_k to A_ℓ.
We define a strict PR $\hat{P}$ by the permutation $\hat{\pi}$:

$$\hat{\pi}(j) := \begin{cases} \pi(j) & \text{for } j \neq k,\ j \neq \ell, \\ \pi(\ell) & \text{for } j = k, \\ \pi(k) & \text{for } j = \ell. \end{cases} \tag{3.7}$$

We will show that for $I = I_r (r \in \mathbb{N}, r \geqq 2)$ or $I = I^s$

$$\sum_{i=1}^{n} I(P(I),P_i) > \sum_{i=1}^{n} I(\hat{P},P_i) \tag{3.8}$$

which would contradict the minimality of $P(I)$.

By definition (3.7) of $\hat{P}$ and (3.1) of I_r we have for $i = 1,\dots,n$

$$[I_r(P(I),P_i)]^r - [I_r(\hat{P},P_i)]^r = \sum_{j=1}^{m} |\pi^{-1}(j) - \pi_i^{-1}(j)|^r -$$

$$-\sum_{j=1}^{m} |\hat{\pi}^{-1}(j) - \pi_i^{-1}(j)|^r = |\pi^{-1}(k) - \pi_i^{-1}(k)|^r + |\pi^{-1}(\ell) - \pi_i^{-1}(\ell)|^r$$

$$-|\pi^{-1}(\ell) - \pi_i^{-1}(k)|^r - |\pi^{-1}(k) - \pi_i^{-1}(\ell)|^r.$$

But for arbitrary real numbers a,b,c,d with $a > b$, $c < d$ and $r \in \mathbb{N}$, $r > 1$ the following inequality holds

$$(3.10) \qquad |a - c|^r + |b - d|^r > |a - d|^r + |b - c|^r.$$

To prove (3.10) six cases have to be distinguished. For example, if $c < d \leqq b < a$ we have

$$|a-c|^r + |b-d|^r = ((a-d) + (d-c))^r + (b-d)^r =$$

$$= (a-d)^r + \sum_{\nu=1}^{r-1} \binom{r}{\nu} (a-d)^{r-\nu}(d-c)^\nu + (d-c)^r + (b-d)^r$$

$$> (a-d)^r + \sum_{\nu=1}^{r-1} \binom{r}{\nu} (b-d)^{r-\nu}(d-c)^\nu + (d-c)^r + (b-d)^r$$

$$= (a-d)^r + ((b-d) + (d-c))^r = |a-d|^r + |b-c|^r$$

The proofs of the other cases are similar.
If we apply (3.10) to (3.9) with $a = \pi^{-1}(k)$, $b = \pi^{-1}(\ell)$, $c = \pi_i^{-1}(k)$, and $d = \pi_i^{-1}(\ell)$ we get

(3.11) $$[I_r(P(I),\ P_i)]^r > [I_r(\hat{P},P_i)]^r \qquad (i = 1,\ldots,n),$$

and hence

$$I_r(P(I),P_i) > I_r(\hat{P},P_i)$$

and a forteriori

$$\sum_{i=1}^{n} I_r(P(I),P_i) > \sum_{i=1}^{n} I_r(\hat{P},P_i)$$

which contradicts the minimality of P(I) in the case of $I = I_r$ for $r \in \mathbb{N}$, $r > 1$. In the case of $I = I^S$ we get directly from (3.11) for r = 2

$$I^S(P(I),P_i) > I^S(\hat{P},P_i) \qquad (i= 1,\ldots,n),$$

which implies

$$\sum_{i=1}^{n} I^S(P(I),P_i) > \sum_{i=1}^{n} I^S(\hat{P},P_i),$$

again a contradiction. Therefore, the assumptions (3.5) and (3.6) cannot be satisfied simultaneously, which means that the Pareto-principle holds.

As the next point we want to clarify whether the minimization procedure described above leads to the independence of irrelevant alternatives or not.

Theorem 3.12: Let $(P_1,\ldots,P_n)$ and $(P_1',\ldots,P_n')$ be two n-tuples of individual PRS and P(I) and P'(I) any corresponding social PRs with respect to I. Then, in general,

$$\{A_k P_i A_j \Leftrightarrow A_k P_i' A_j \text{ for all } i\}$$

does not imply

$$\{A_k P(I) A_j \Leftrightarrow A_k P'(I) A_j\},$$

for

$$I = I_r \ (r \in \mathbb{N}) \text{ or } I = I^S.$$

Proof: The theorem can be proved by suitably chosen examples. In each example take $n = 6$ (number of persons), $m = 3$ (number of different alternatives) and

$P_1 = (A,B,C)$, $P_2 = (B,A,C)$, $P_3 = (A,C,B)$, $P_4 = (B,C,A)$,

$P_5 = P_6 = (C,A,B)$.

a) For $I = I^S$, we have $P(I^S) = (A,C,B)$ (the only social PR with respect to I^S). Let

$P_1' = P_2' = (B,A,C)$, $P_3' = (A,C,B)$, $P_4' = P_5' = P_6' = (C,B,A)$.

Then, $A P_i C$ if and only if $A P_i' C$. But $P'(I^S) = (B,C,A)$ and $P'(I^S) = (C,B,A)$ are the only solutions of (3.3), which shows that $C P(I^S) A$ and $A P'(I^S) C$.

b) For $I = I_1$, $P(I_1) = (A,C,B)$ and $P(I_1) = (C,A,B)$ are the only solutions of (3.3). Let

$P_1' = P_2' = P_4' = (B,A,C)$, $P_3' = (A,C,B)$, $P_6' = P_5' = (C,B,A)$.

Then, $B P_i C$ if and only if $B P_i' C$. But here $P'(I_1) = (B,A,C)$, such that $C P'(I_1) B$ and $B P(I_1) C$.

c) For $I = I_2$, $P(I_2) = (C,A,B)$ is the only PR with respect to I_2. Let

$$P'_1 = P'_2 = P'_3 = (A,B,C),\ P'_4 = (B,C,A),\ P'_5 = P'_6 = (C,A,B).$$

Then, $C\,P_i\,A$ if and only if $C\,P'_i\,A$. But $P'(I_2) = (A,B,C)$, such that $C\,P'(I_2)\,A$ but $A\,P(I_2)\,C$.

d) For $I = I_r$ with $r \in \mathbb{N}$, $r > 2$, we have $P(I_r) = (A,C,B)$. Let

$$P'_1 = P'_2 = (B,A,C),\ P'_3 = (A,C,B),\ P'_4 = P'_5 = P'_6 = (C,B,A).$$

Then, $A\,P_i\,C$ if and only if $A\,P'_i\,C$. In this case, $P'(I_r) = (C,B,A)$, which shows that $A\,P'(I_r)\,C$ but $C\,P\,(I_r)\,A$, q.e.d..

Theorem 3.12 shows that the social decision procedure generated by minimization process (3.3) does not satisfy the independence of irrelevant alternatives.

Finally, it is trivial to prove that the nondictatorship (iv) is quaranted by the minimization process (3.3) in which the criterion function is symmetric with respect to the individual PRs.

In the next chapter we will make use of an additional property of social PRs constructed by the indices I_r and I^s:

(v) Independence of the numbering of the alternatives: Let P^* be any social PR of $P_1,\dots,P_n$ with respect to an index I of the form (1.4) or (1.5). Let $\bar{P}^*$, $\bar{P}_1,\dots,\bar{P}_n$ be the same PRs according to another numbering of the alternatives. Then, $\bar{P}^*$ is a social PR of $\bar{P}_1,\dots,\bar{P}_n$ with respect to the same index I.

(v) can be shown as follows: The new numbering of the alternatives $A_1,\dots,A_m$ is generated by a permutation $\bar{\pi}$ of the numbers $1,2,\dots,m$.

If $P(P')$ is represented by the permutation π (π') before the renumbering, then, the corresponding PR $\bar{P}(\bar{P}')$ after the renumbering is represented by $\bar{\pi}\cdot\pi$ $(\bar{\pi}\cdot\pi')$. Since $(\bar{\pi}\;\pi)^{-1} = \pi^{-1}\bar{\pi}^{-1}$ we have for $I = I_r$

$$I_r(P,P') = \left(\sum_{\ell=1}^{m} |\pi^{-1}(\ell)-\pi'^{-1}(\ell)|^r\right)^{1/r} =$$

$$= \left(\sum_{\ell=1}^{m} |\pi^{-1}(\bar{\pi}^{-1}(\ell)) - \pi'^{-1}(\bar{\pi}^{-1}(\ell))|^r\right)^{1/r} =$$

$$= \left(\sum_{\ell=1}^{m} |(\bar{\pi}\;\pi)^{-1}(\ell)-(\bar{\pi}\;\pi')^{-1}(\ell)|^r\right)^{1/r} = I_r(\bar{P},\bar{P}').$$

Hence we get, in view of the minimality of P^*

$$\sum_{i=1}^{n} I_r(\bar{P}^*,P_i) = \sum_{i=1}^{n} I_r(P^*, P_i) \leq \sum_{i=1}^{n} I_r(P,P_i) =$$

$$= \sum_{i=1}^{n} I_r(\bar{P},\bar{P}_i)$$

for all $P,\bar{P}\in\mathfrak{P}(\mathcal{A})$, which shows the minimality of $\bar{P}^*$.

4. A characterization of the ranking method

So long, nothing has been said about methods for computing the social PRs with respect to a certain index I, i.e. for solving the problem

$$(4.1) \qquad \sum_{i=1}^{n} I\;(P,P_i) \rightarrow \text{min.} \qquad P\in\mathfrak{P}(\mathcal{A}),$$

where $P_1,\ldots,P_n$ are arbitrary individual strict PRs. Actually, at this stage of research, we cannot give efficient algorithms for an arbitrary index of the form $I = I_r$. But surprisingly, it is extremely easy to determine solution of (4.1) in the case of

$$(4.2) \qquad I(P,P') = I^{S}(P,P') = \sum_{\ell=1}^{m} (\pi^{-1}(\ell) - \pi'^{-1}(\ell))^2 .$$

The reason is that there is a strong relationship between the solution of (4.1) for $I = I^S$ and the determination of social PRs by the well-known ranking method.

Def. 4.3:[1] Let the strict P_i of person i ($i = 1,\ldots,n$) be represented by π_i. The PR $\hat{P} \in \mathcal{P}(\mathcal{A})$ is called a social PR of $P_1,\ldots,P_n$ with respect to ranking the alternatives if for all pairs $j,k, \in \{1,\ldots,m\}$ with $\sum_{i=1}^{n} \pi_i^{-1}(j) \neq \sum_{i=1}^{n} \pi_i^{-1}(k)$

$$A_j \hat{P} A_k \quad \text{if and only if} \quad \sum_{i=1}^{n} \pi_i^{-1}(j) > \sum_{i=1}^{n} \pi_i^{-1}(k).$$ [2]

If we have, for example, three persons with three alternatives A,B, and C, where $P_1 = (C,B,A)$, $P_2 = (B,C,A)$, $P_3 = (A,C,B)$, it follows that

$\sum_{i=1}^{3} \pi_i^{-1}(A) = 7$, $\sum_{i=1}^{3} \pi_i^{-1}(B) = 6$, $\sum_{i=1}^{3} \pi_i^{-1}(C) = 5$, which implies that

$$\hat{P} = (C,B,A)$$

is the only social PR of P_1,P_2,P_3 with respect to the ranking method.

---

[1] For a definition of the ranking method in the case of not necessary strict PRs see U. Krause [1973].

[2] The definition implies that $\hat{P}$ is not in any case uniquely determined.

The important relationship can now be formulated:

<u>Theorem 4.4 :</u> If $\hat{P}$ is a social PR of $P_1,\ldots,P_n \in \mathcal{P}(\mathcal{A})$ with respect to the ranking method then, $\hat{P}$ is also a social PR of $P_1,\ldots,P_n$ with respect to the index I^s.

Before proving the theorem we want to give two of it's most important implications. At first, the theorem shows that the ranking method of constructing a social PR by means of individual PRs which has been, up to this date, a "good" method only in an intuitive sense has a very rational foundation: it is not only a good but also an <u>optimal</u> method with respect to a criterion-function which is now well-known, namely the function $\sum_{i=1}^{n} I^s(.,P_i)$. Secondly, the theorem shows that social PRs with respect to the index I^s can be found without any optimization procedure, namely with the ranking method which gives the social PR by an extremely simple procedure.

<u>Proof of theorem 4.4</u>

Let the PR P_i of person i be represented by the permutation π_i. Because of property (v) of section 3 we may assume, without loss of generality, that the ranking method leads to the social PR

$$\hat{P} = (A_1,A_2,\ldots,A_m) \tag{4.5'}$$

such that it is represented by the permutation $\hat{\pi}$ defined by

$$\hat{\pi}(\ell) = \ell \; . \tag{4.5}$$

Thus, $\hat{\pi}$ is the identity permutation which implies

$$\hat{\pi}(\ell) = \hat{\pi}^{-1}(\ell) . \tag{4.5"}$$

---

1) Another proof of this theorem has been given by N. Senghas [1976].

In view of def. 4.3 the fact that $\hat{P}$ in (4.5') is a social PR with respect to ranking the alternatives means that

$$(4.6) \qquad \sum_{i=1}^{n} \pi_i^{-1}(j) \leqq \sum_{i=1}^{n} \pi_i^{-1}(k) \qquad \text{for } j \leqq k.$$

Now, let P be any PR on $\mathcal{A}$ represented by the permutation π. We will show that

$$(4.7) \qquad \sum_{i=1}^{n} I^S(P,P_i) \geqq \sum_{i=1}^{n} I^S(\hat{P},P_i)$$

from which the theorem will follow.
By definition of I^S,

$$\sum_{i=1}^{n} I^S(P,P_i) = \sum_{i=1}^{n} \sum_{\ell=1}^{m} (\pi^{-1}(\ell)-\pi_i^{-1}(\ell))^2 =$$

$$= \sum_{\ell=1}^{m} \sum_{i=1}^{n} ([\pi^{-1}(\ell)]^2-2\pi^{-1}(\ell)\cdot\pi_i^{-1}(\ell)+[\pi_i^{-1}(\ell)]^2) =$$

$$= n\cdot \sum_{\ell=1}^{m} (\pi^{-1}(\ell))^2-2\sum_{\ell=1}^{m} \pi^{-1}(\ell)\cdot \sum_{i=1}^{n} \pi_i^{-1}(\ell)+\sum_{\ell=1}^{m} \sum_{i=1}^{n} (\pi_i^{-1}(\ell))^2$$

and similarly, in view of (4.5) and (4.5"),

$$\sum_{i=1}^{n} I^S(\hat{P},P_i) = n\sum_{\ell=1}^{m} \ell^2-2\sum_{\ell=1}^{m} \ell\cdot \sum_{i=1}^{n} \pi_i^{-1}(\ell) + \sum_{\ell=1}^{m} \sum_{i=1}^{n} (\pi_i^{-1}(\ell))^2 .$$

Since

$$\{\pi^{-1}(\ell) \mid \ell \in \{1,\ldots,m\}\} = \{1,2,\ldots,m\}$$

one has

$$\sum_{\ell=1}^{m} \left[\pi^{-1}(\ell)\right]^2 = \sum_{\ell=1}^{m} \ell^2$$

which implies

$$\sum_{i=1}^{n} I^S(P,P_i) - \sum_{i=1}^{n} I^S(\hat{P},P_i) = 2 \sum_{\ell=1}^{m} \Big(\ell \cdot \sum_{i=1}^{n} \pi_i^{-1}(\ell)\Big) - 2 \sum_{\ell=1}^{m} \Big(\pi^{-1}(\ell) \cdot \sum_{i=1}^{n} \pi_i^{-1}($$

This shows that (4.7) is valid if and only if

$$(4.8) \qquad \sum_{\ell=1}^{m} \Big(\ell \cdot \sum_{i=1}^{n} \pi_i^{-1}(\ell)\Big) \geqq \sum_{\ell=1}^{m} \Big(\pi^{-1}(\ell) \cdot \sum_{i=1}^{n} \pi_i^{-1}(\ell)\Big)$$

That this is true under the conditions (4.6) follows from

<u>Lemma 4.9:</u> Let m be any integer greater than 1 and let $s_1,\dots,s_m$ be positive real numbers satisfying

$$(4.10) \qquad s_j \leqq s_k \qquad \text{for } j<k;\ j,k \in \{1,\dots,m\}\ .$$

If π is any permutation of $1,2,\dots,m$, then,

$$(4.11) \qquad \sum_{\ell=1}^{m} \pi(\ell) s_\ell \leqq \sum_{\ell=1}^{m} \ell \cdot s_\ell\ .$$

<u>Proof</u> (by induction on m):
For $m = 2$ the only non-trivial case is $\pi(1) = 2$ and $\pi(2) = 1$. By assumption (4.10),

$$2s_1 + s_2 \leqq 2s_1 + s_2 + (s_2-s_1) = s_1 + 2s_2\ ,$$

which proves (4.11) for this case.

Assume that the lemma is valid for m - 1. Let $t \in \{1,2,\dots,m\}$ be defined by

$$\pi(t) = m.$$

Then,

$$\sum_{\ell=1}^{m} \pi(\ell)s_\ell = \sum_{\ell \neq t} \pi(\ell)s_\ell + m \cdot s_t . \tag{4.12}$$

Here, the m - 1 integers $\pi(1),\dots, \pi(t-1), \pi(t+1),\dots, \pi(m)$ constitute a permutation σ of $1,2,\dots,m - 1$:

$$\sigma(\ell) = \begin{cases} \pi(\ell), & \ell = 1,\dots,t - 1 \\ \pi(\ell+1), & \ell = t,\dots,m - 1. \end{cases}$$

Setting

$$s_i' = \begin{cases} s_i, & i = 1,\dots,t - 1 \\ s_{i+1}, & i = t,\dots,m - 1 \end{cases},$$

we have

$$s_j' \leqq s_k' \qquad \text{for } j \leqq k \leqq m - 1.$$

Hence we can apply the induction hypothesis to the permutation σ and the positive real numbers s_i' $(i=1,\dots,m-1)$ in order to get

$$\sum_{\ell=1}^{m-1} \sigma(\ell)s_\ell' \leqq \sum_{\ell=1}^{m-1} \ell \cdot s_\ell'$$

which means nothingelse than

$$\sum_{\ell \neq t} \pi(\ell)s_\ell \leqq \sum_{\ell=1}^{t-1} \ell \cdot s_\ell + \sum_{\ell=t+1}^{m} (\ell-1)s_\ell .$$

By equation (4.12), it follows that

$$\sum_{\ell=1}^{m} \pi(\ell) s_\ell \leqq \sum_{\ell=1}^{t-1} \ell s_\ell + \sum_{\ell=t+1}^{m} (\ell-1) s_\ell + m \cdot s_t \leqq$$

$$\leqq \sum_{\ell=1}^{t-1} \ell s_\ell + \sum_{\ell=t+1}^{m} (\ell-1) s_\ell + m s_t + (s_m - s_t) + (s_{m-1} - s_t) + \ldots + (s_{t+1} - s_t)$$

$$= \sum_{\ell=1}^{t-1} \ell s_\ell + \sum_{\ell=t+1}^{m} \ell s_\ell + (m-(m-t)) s_t = \sum_{\ell=1}^{m} \ell s_\ell ,$$

which proves the lemma.

If we now apply the lemma to $s_\ell = \sum_{i=1}^{n} \pi_i^{-1}(\ell)$ and to the permutation π^{-1} (instead of π), we have (4.10) by (4.6) and obtain by (4.11) exactly the inequality (4.8) which has been shown to be equivalent to (4.7). This completes the proof of the theorem.

The characterization of the ranking method by the index I^S can be completed by showing that the converse statement of theorem 4.4 is true:

<u>Theorem 4.13:</u> If $\bar{P}$ is a social PR of $P_1, \ldots, P_n \in \mathcal{P}(\mathcal{A})$ with respect to the index I^S then, $\bar{P}$ is also a social PR of $P_1, \ldots, P_n$ with respect to the ranking method.

<u>Proof:</u> Without loss of generality let $\hat{P}$ be a social PR with respect to the ranking method represented by $\hat{\pi}$ where

$$(4.14) \qquad \hat{\pi}(\ell) = \ell = \hat{\pi}^{-1}(\ell) \qquad \text{for } \ell \in \{1, \ldots, m\} .$$

If $\bar{P} = \hat{P}$ nothing has to be shown. Let $\bar{\pi}$ be the permutation representing $\bar{P}$. Since, by theorem 4.4, $\hat{P}$ is, as well, a social PR with respect to I^s, we have

$$(4.15) \qquad \sum_{i=1}^{n} I^s(\hat{P},P_i) = \sum_{i=1} I^s(\bar{P},P_i)$$

From that we obtain analogously to (4.7) and (4.8)

$$(4.16) \qquad \sum_{\ell=1}^{m}\Big(\ell \cdot \sum_{i=1}^{n} \pi_i^{-1}(\ell)\Big) = \sum_{\ell=1}^{m}\Big(\bar{\pi}^{-1}(\ell) \cdot \sum_{i=1}^{n} \pi_i^{-1}(\ell)\Big) \quad ,$$

where

$$(4.17) \qquad \sum_{i=1}^{n} \pi_i^{-1}(j) \leqq \sum_{i=1}^{n} \pi_i^{-1}(k) \qquad \text{for } j < k.$$

since $\hat{P}$ is a social PR with respect to the ranking method represented by $\hat{\pi}$ given by (4.14).

We continue the proof of the theorem similarly to the proof of theorem 4.4 by showing the following

<u>Lemma 4.18:</u> Let m be any integer greater than 1 and let $s_1,\ldots,s_m$ be positive real numbers satisfying

$$(4.19) \qquad s_j \leqq s_k \qquad \text{for } j < k;\ j,k \in \{1,\ldots,m\}.$$

Let $\tilde{\pi}$ be any permutation of $1,2,\ldots,m$. If there exist $r,t \in \{1,\ldots,m\}$ such that

$$(4.20) \qquad r < t\ ,\quad \tilde{\pi}(r) > \tilde{\pi}(t),\ \text{and}\quad s_r < s_t\ ,$$

then

$$(4.21) \qquad \sum_{\ell=1}^{m} \ell \cdot s_\ell > \sum_{\ell=1}^{m} \tilde{\pi}(\ell) \cdot s_\ell\ .$$

<u>Proof:</u> From lemma 4.9 we know that

$$(4.11) \qquad \sum_{\ell=1}^{m} \ell s_\ell \geqq \sum_{\ell=1}^{m} \pi(\ell) s_\ell$$

for an <u>arbitrary</u> permutation π of $1,2,\dots,m$. Using $\tilde{\pi}$ we define a new permutation $\tilde{\sigma}$ by

$$\sigma(\ell) = \begin{cases} \tilde{\pi}(\ell)' & \text{for } \ell \neq r,\ \ell \neq t, \\ \tilde{\pi}(r) & \text{for } \ell = t, \\ \tilde{\pi}(t) & \text{for } \ell = r. \end{cases}$$

That implies, in view of (4.20),

$$\sum_{\ell=1}^{m} \tilde{\pi}(\ell) s_\ell - \sum_{\ell=1}^{m} \tilde{\sigma}(\ell) s_\ell = \tilde{\pi}(r) s_r + \tilde{\pi}(t) s_t - \tilde{\pi}(t) s_r - \tilde{\pi}(r) s_t =$$

$$= \left(\tilde{\pi}(r) - \tilde{\pi}(t)\right)(s_r - s_t) < 0.$$

Now, if we would have equality in (4.11) for $\pi = \tilde{\pi}$, it would follow by the last inequality that

$$\sum_{\ell=1}^{m} \ell s_\ell = \sum_{\ell=1}^{m} \tilde{\pi}(\ell) s_\ell < \sum_{\ell=1}^{m} \tilde{\sigma}(\ell) s_\ell$$

a contradiction to (4.11). Hence the lemma is proved.

If we now apply the lemma to $s_\ell = \sum_{\ell=1}^{m} \pi_i^{-1}(\ell)$ and to the permutation $\bar{\pi}^{-1}$ (instead of $\tilde{\pi}$), we have (4.19) by (4.17) and are able to conclude:

If $\sum_{i=1}^{n} \pi_i^{-1}(j) \neq \sum_{i=1}^{n} \pi_i^{-1}(k)$, then, $j < k$ if and only if $\sum_{i=1}^{n} \pi_i^{-1}(j) < \sum_{i=1}^{n} \pi_i^{-1}(k)$ by the assumption that the identity permutation $\hat{\pi}$

represents the social PR $\hat{R}$ with respect to the ranking method. But by lemma 4.18 and equation (4.16), we have for all

$j,k \in \{1,\dots,m\}$ with $\sum_{i=1}^{n} \pi_i^{-1}(j) \neq \sum_{i=1}^{n} \pi_i^{-1}(k)$ that $j < k$ if and only if $\bar{\pi}^{-1}(j) < \bar{\pi}^{-1}(k)$; hence for those j, k,

$$\sum_{i=1}^{n} \pi_i^{-1}(j) < \sum_{i=1}^{n} \pi_i^{-1}(k) \text{ if and only if } \bar{\pi}^{-1}(j) < \bar{\pi}^{-1}(k)$$

which shows that $\bar{R}$, represented by $\bar{\pi}$, is a social PR of $P_1,\dots,P_n$ with respect to the ranking method, too, and the theorem is proved.

5. Open problems and further applications

The concepts developped in the foregoing chapters and the rather surprising results of theorem 4.4 and theorem 4.13 lead to some questions which are still open:

1. Is it possible to generate other methods of voting than the ranking method by a minimization procedure with a suitably chosen index of inequality of PRs and criterion function ?

2. What properties will have the social decision correspondence if instead of $\sum_{i=1}^{n} I(.,P_i)$ a more general criterion function $g(I(.,P_1),\dots,I(.,P_n))$ is used, where g has some reasonable properties ?

3. What properties will have the social decision correspondence if other indices of inequality than I^S and I_r are used ?

4. Are there efficient algorithms to compute social PRs with respect to other indices than I^S ?

5. Is it possible to use the (suitably modified) concept of a social PR as a minimizor of a certain criterion function in the case of an infinite number of alternatives ?

Concerning the first question, it is clear that the majority rule cannot be generated by such a procedure, because it leads for certain combinations of individual PRs to intransitive orderings of the alternatives, whereas the minimization process leads, by construction, to one or several strict PRs on $\mathcal{A}$, i.e. to transitive and complete orderings on $\mathcal{A}$. Of course, the dictatorship rule can easily be generated by a minimization process if instead of $\sum_{i=1}^{n} I(.,P_i)$ the (unsymmetric) criterion function $I(.,P_{i_o})$ is chosen which, clearly, makes person i_o a dictator for every index I.

Finally, let us give an application of the described procedure to the case where the individual preferences are neither necessarily transitive nor complete. That case applies if the number of alternatives is great such that the individuals are not able to bring these alternatives in a linear order; i.e. they are not able to construct an individual PR. But in many cases they are able to decide which of two certain alternatives they strictly prefer to the other.
Then, one can represent their preferences P_i (which may be neither transitive nor complete) by an oriented graph or by a matrix $\mathfrak{A}^i=(a^i_{jk})$ where (for example)

(5.1) $$a^i_{jk}=\begin{cases}1 \text{ if } A_j\ P_i\ A_k \\ 0 \text{ otherwise}\end{cases}$$

for i = 1,...,n; j,k = 1,...,m. Now, let $\mathcal{P}(\mathcal{A})$ again be the set of all strict PRs on $\mathcal{A}$ (corresponding to the set of all PRs, i.e. all reflexive, transitive, and complete orderings on $\mathcal{A}$) and let $\mathfrak{A}(P)$ be the 0-1-matrix which represents $P\in\mathcal{P}(\mathcal{A})$ in the sense of (5.1). Then, one can define a measure I_r of inequality between any 0-1-matrix $\mathfrak{A} = (a_{jk})$ and such a matrix $\mathfrak{A}(P) = (a_{jk}(P))$ by

(5.2) $$I_r(\mathfrak{A}(P), \mathfrak{A}) = \left(\sum_{j,k} |a_{jk}(P) - a_{jk}|^r\right)^{1/r}.$$

It seems reasonable to define a social PR of any given n-tupel $(P_1, \ldots, P_n)$ of preferences as a $P^* \varepsilon\, \mathfrak{P}(\mathcal{A})$ such that

(5.3) $$\sum_{i=1}^{n} I_r(\mathfrak{A}(P^*), \mathfrak{A}^i) \leqq \sum_{i=1}^{n} I_r(\mathfrak{A}(P), \mathfrak{A}^i) \quad \text{for all } P \varepsilon\, \mathfrak{P}(\mathcal{A}).$$

Even in the case n = 1 the minimization procedure for the determination of such a P^* seems to be non-trivial. It may be that the problem can be solved by graph-theoretical methods or by integer programming.

A practical application of that concept with, indeed, intransitive preferences is the problem of ranking the football teams T_ℓ ($\ell = 1, \ldots, m$) of a certain division. Here we have n = 1 (or n = 2 if the whole season consisting of two periods is considered) and we can define

$$a^i_{jk} = \begin{cases} 1 \text{ if } T_j \text{ has beaten } T_k \text{ (in period i)}, \\ -1 \text{ if } T_k \text{ has beaten } T_j \text{ (in period i)}, \\ 0 \text{ otherwise.} \end{cases}$$

The usual method of ranking the teams (in a single period i) is to define in the case of $\sum_{\ell=1}^{m} a_{j\ell} \neq \sum_{\ell=1}^{m} a_{k\ell}$

$$T_j \, P \, T_k \text{ if and only if } \sum_{\ell=1}^{m} a_{j\ell} > \sum_{\ell=1}^{m} a_{k\ell}\,.^{1)}$$

---

1) In the case $\sum_{\ell=1}^{m} a_{j\ell} = \sum_{\ell=1}^{m} a_{k\ell}$ additional criterions are used.

It is an open question in which other sense than an intuitive one that method of ordering is a good or an optimal one. Perhaps it is possible to answer this question with the aid of the concepts developped above.

References

Arrow, K.J.: Social Choice and Individual Values. New York, 1963.

Bürk, R. and Gehrig, W.: Indices of Income Inequality and Societal Income. This volume.

Eichhorn, W. and Voeller, J.: Theory of the Price Index. Berlin, Heidelberg, New York, 1976.

Fisher, I.: The Making of Index Numbers. New York, 1967.

Kolm, S.-Ch.: Unequal Inequalities. Journal of Economic Theory 12, 1976, pp. 416 - 442.

Krause, U.: Analyse und Synthese von Präferenzen. Operations Research-Verfahren XV, 1973, ed. by R. Henn et. al., pp. 108 - 116.

Sen, A.K.: Collective Choice and Social Welfare. San Francisco, 1970.

Senghas, N.: Aggregation individueller Präferenzordnungen. Karlsruhe, 1976 (unpublished).

PART IV

Methodological Topics Concerning Economic Indices

Some Recent Applications of Functional Equations to Combinatorics, Probability Distributions, Information Measures and to the Theory of Index Numbers in Mathematical Economics

Dedicated, with friendship and admiration,
to G. Aumann on his 70th and to O. Haupt
on his 90th birthday

by J. Aczél

1. D.A. Sprott (personal communication) has asked the following question in connection with placing m objects into n cells so that no cell remain empty. If the number of possibilities is denoted by $A(m,n)$ then, evidently, the recursive equation

$$A(m,n+1) = \sum_{k=1}^{m} \binom{m}{k} A(m-k,n) \tag{1}$$

holds.

[If we know already in how many ways fewer objects can be placed into n cells, then distribute m objects into n cells, take away k objects from these cells and put them into the (n + 1)st cell; $k = 1,2,\ldots,m$]. The summation in (1) is from 1 to m, but really the last n members are 0, because, by the restriction of no empty cells,

$$A(j,n) = 0 \quad \text{if} \quad j < n. \tag{2}$$

As one can see immediately, (2) follows already from (1), if only

$$A(0,n) = 0 \quad \text{for } n = 1,2,\ldots, \quad A(0,0) = 1 \tag{3}$$

is supposed.

Let us form the generating functions of $A(m,n)$, first

$$F_m(t) = \sum_{n=0}^{\infty} A(m,n)t^n \quad (m = 0,1,\ldots). \tag{4}$$

By (3),

(5) $$F_o(t) = 1$$

and, by (1),

(6) $$F_m(t) = t\sum_{k=1}^{m}\binom{m}{k}F_{m-k}(t).$$

Finally, we define

$$G(s,t) = \sum_{m=0}^{\infty} F_m(t)s^{m+1} = \sum_{m=0}^{\infty}\sum_{n=0}^{\infty} A(m,n)s^{m+1}t^n .$$

(The resulting equation will be somewhat nicer with s^{m+1} rather than with s^m). By (5) and (6),

$$G(s,t) - s = \sum_{m=1}^{\infty} F_m(t)s^{m+1} = st\sum_{m=1}^{\infty}\sum_{k=1}^{m}\binom{m}{m-k}F_{m-k}(t)s^m =$$

$$= st\sum_{j=0}^{\infty}\sum_{m=j+1}^{\infty}\binom{m}{j}F_j(t)s^m = t\sum_{j=0}^{\infty}F_j(t)s^{j+1}\left(\frac{1}{(1-s)^{j+1}} - 1\right) =$$

$$= tG\left(\frac{s}{1-s},t\right) - tG(s,t) \qquad (j = m-k)$$

or

(7) $$(1+t)G(s,t) - s = tG\left(\frac{s}{1-s},t\right) \qquad (s \neq 1,\ t \neq -1).$$

D.A. Sprott has asked about the general solution of this functional equation.

Substituting $s = -\frac{1}{u}$ and introducing a new function f by

(8) $$f(u,t) = \left(1+\frac{1}{t}\right)^{-u}G\left(-\frac{1}{u},t\right)$$

we get

(9) $$f(u+1,t) - f(u,t) = \frac{1}{tu}\left(1+\frac{1}{t}\right)^{-u-1} \quad (u,t\in\mathbb{R}^2,\ u\neq 0,-1;\ t\neq 0,-1).$$

This is an inhomogeneous linear difference equation in u, with t as parameter (really a simple summation problem). As usual, it is enough to know one solution f_o of the inhomogeneous equation (9) and add the general solution p of the corresponding homogeneous equation

(10) $$p(u+1,t) - p(u,t) = 0$$

in order to get the general solution of the inhomogeneous equation (9). But (10) simply means that p is periodic with period 1 in u:

$$p(u+1,t) = p(u,t).$$

So the general solution of (9) is given by

$$f(u,t) = f_o(u,t) + p(u,t)$$

and, from (8), we have the general solution of (7) given by

$$G(s,t) = \left(1+\frac{1}{t}\right)^{-1/s}\left[f_o\left(-\frac{1}{s},t\right) + p\left(-\frac{1}{s},t\right)\right] \quad (0,1\neq s\in\mathbb{R};\ 0,-1\neq t\in\mathbb{R}),$$

where f_o is a particular solution of (9) and p is an arbitrary function, periodic in its first variable (with period 1).

Particular solutions of (9) can be found, e.g. in Maier-Kiesewetter (1971) and Meschkowski (1959), after appropiate changes are made. Dr. P. Schroth (Braunschweig, FRG) has, in correspondence, suggested the solution

$$f_o(u,t) = \int_0^{\log t - \log(t+1)} \left(e^{uz}/e^z - 1) - 1/z\right) dz + \psi(u) \quad (u\neq 0,-1,-2,\ldots),$$

where $\psi = \Gamma'/\Gamma$ is Euler's psi function.

2. It has been noticed by Rota and Mullin (1969) that many polynomials, which play important roles in combinatorics, are of the "binomial type", that is, they satisfy

(11) $$P_k(t+u) = \sum_{j=0}^{k} \binom{k}{j} P_j(t) P_{k-j}(u)$$ for all real t,u and for all nonnegative integers k.

The name comes, of course, from the "binomial law" satisfied by $P_k(t) = t^k$ $(k = 0,1,2,\ldots)$. In (11) each P_k was supposed to be a polynomial of exactly k-th degree. More generally, Aczél and Vranceanu (1972) have determined all sequences of functions $\{P_k\}$ satisfying (1).

This is related to the definition of "composed (or compound) Poisson distributions". (Jánossy-Rényi-Aczél 1950). The probability $p_k(t)$ of an event happening k times during a time interval of length t satisfies, under homogeneity and Markov suppositions, the following equations and inequalities

(12) $$\sum_{k=0}^{\infty} p_k(t) = 1,$$

(13) $$0 \leq p_k(t) \leq 1,$$

and

(14) $$p_k(t+u) = \sum_{j=0}^{k} p_j(t) p_{k-j}(u) \qquad (k = 0,1,2,\ldots).$$

Actually, in [(12), (13) and] (14), the time variables t,u go only through the positive reals, but it is easy to extend the solutions so that (14) should hold for all real t,u [we will not need (12), (13) for nonpositive t]. Obviously, the equations (11) imply (14) for the functions

(15) $$p_k = \frac{P_k}{k!} \qquad (k = 0,1,2,\ldots)$$

and vice versa.

The domain is different in the functional equations satisfied by the so called Bell polynomials (1934 , cf. Riordan 1958) which are also essential in combinatorics. These are polynomials of k-th degree which depend on k variables and satisfy a.o.

(16) $$B_o = 1$$

and

(17) $$B_k(t_1+u_1,t_2+u_2,\ldots,t_k+u_k) = B_k(t_1,t_2,\ldots,t_k)+B_k(u_1,u_2,\ldots,u_k)+ \\ + \sum_{j=1}^{k-1}\binom{k}{j}B_j(t_1,t_2,\ldots,t_k)B_{k-j}(u_1,u_2,\ldots,u_{k-j}) \left(t_i,u_i \varepsilon \mathbb{R}; \begin{matrix} i=1,2,\ldots \\ k=1,2,\ldots \end{matrix}\right)$$

If we introduce the (dummy) variable t_o, we get the simpler and slightly more general system

(18) $$B_k(t_o+u_o,t_1+u_1,\ldots,t_k+u_k) = \sum_{j=o}^{k}\binom{k}{j}B_j(t_o,t_1,\ldots,t_j)B_{k-j}(u_o,u_1,\ldots,u_{k-j}) \\ \left[(t_o,t_1,\ldots,t_j),(u_o,u_1,\ldots,u_j)\varepsilon \mathbb{R}^{j+1};\ j = 0,1,\ldots;\ k = 0,1,\ldots\right].$$

Obviously, (18) is a generalization of (11). Again, we determined not only all polynomials, but all functions satisfying (17) or (18) (Aczél-Vranceanu 1972).

As a matter of fact, now we can determine to such functional equations the general solutions which map an arbitrary group (G,+) into a commutative divisible field (F,t,•). We call F a divisible <u>field</u>, if every equation of the form nx = a, where a ε F and nx = x+x+...+x (n members) has a unique solution x ε F, which is denoted by $\frac{a}{n}$. In particular, divisible fields are of characteristic 0.–Indeed, let h_k: G → F (k = 0,1,2,...) satisfy

(19) $$h_k(x+y) = \sum_{j=0}^{k} h_j(x)h_{k-j}(y) \qquad (x,y \in G;\ k = 0,1,2,\ldots).$$

Let us write first (19) for $k = 0$. We get

(20) $$h_o(x+y) = h_o(x)h_o(y)$$

which, of course, simply means that h_o <u>is a homomorphism of</u> $(G,+)$ <u>into</u> $(F,\cdot)$, the multiplicative structure of F. It is immediate that either

(21) $$h_o(x) = 0 \quad \text{for all } x \in G$$

or

(22) $$h_o(x) \neq 0 \quad \text{for all } x \in G,$$

because, if $h_o(x_o) = 0$, then $h_o(x) = h_o[(x-x_o)+x_o] = h_o(x-x_o)h_o(x_o) = 0$

We write now (19) for $k = 1$:

(23) $$h_1(x+y) = h_o(x)h_1(y) + h_1(x)h_o(y) \qquad (x,y \in G).$$

In the case (21) we have $h_1(x) = 0$ $(x \in G)$ and, from (19) by induction,

(24) $$h_k(x) = 0 \text{ for all } x \in G \text{ and all nonnegative integer } k.$$

So we can restrict ourselves now to the case (22). In this case, divide (23) by (20) and get, for

(25) $$f_1 := \frac{h_1}{h_o}$$

the equation

(26) $$f_1(x+y) = f_1(x) + f_1(y) \qquad (x,y \in G),$$

that is, f_1 <u>is a homomorphism of</u> (G,+) <u>into</u> (F,+), the additive structure of F. From (25), we get

$$h_1(x) = h_o(x) f_1(x) \quad \text{for all } x \in G. \tag{27}$$

Next, for k = 2, (19) reads, taking (27) into consideration,

$$h_2(x+y) = h_o(x)h_2(y) + h_o(x)f_1(x)h_o(y)f_1(y) + h_2(x)h_o(y). \tag{28}$$

We divide again by (20) and introduce a new function by

$$f_2(x) = \frac{h_2(x)}{h_o(x)} - \frac{1}{2}f_1(x)^2 \qquad (x \in G). \tag{29}$$

In view of (28), (26), and (29), we get

$$f_2(x+y) = f_2(x) + f_2(y)$$

[again a homomorphism of (G,+) into (F,+)] and

$$h_2(x) = h_o(x)\left[f_2(x) + \frac{1}{2}f_1(x)^2\right].$$

(division by integers is possible in F).

By induction (see, e.g., Aczél-Vranceanu 1972), one can prove

$$h_k(x) = h_o(x) \sum_{r_1+2r_2+\ldots+kr_k=k} \prod_{j=1}^{k} \frac{1}{r_j!} f_j(x)^{r_j} \quad (x\in G; k=1,2,\ldots), \tag{30}$$

where the f_j's are homomorphisms of (G,+) into (F,+). Conversely, the mappings given by (30) always satisfy (19), with arbitrary homomorphisms h_o: (G,+) → (F,·) and f_j: (G,+) → (F,+). Also (24) is contained in (30). So we have the following.

<u>Theorem 1.</u> <u>The general solutions</u> h_k: G → F (k = 0,1,2,...,) <u>of</u> <u>(19), where G is a group and F a commutative divisible field, are given by (30), where</u> h_o <u>and</u> f_j (j = 1,2,...) <u>are arbitrary homomor-</u>

phisms of (G,+) into (F,·) or (F,+), respectively. The general solutions H_k: G → F (k = 0,1,2,...) of

$$(31) \qquad H_k(x+y) = \sum_{j=0}^{k} \binom{k}{j} H_j(x) H_{k-j}(y) \qquad (x,y \in G;\ k = 0,1,2,\ldots)$$

are given by $H_k = k!h_k$, where h_k (k = 0,1,2,...) are arbitrary solutions of (19).

Under the conditions (13) each real function p_k will be bounded on any subinterval of the positive reals. Since the mappings f_j (j = 1,2,...) were expressed with aid of h_k (now p_k), so they are bounded too, and since they were homomorphisms, i.e., now the Cauchy equation

$$f_j(x+y) = f_j(x) + f_j(y) \qquad (j = 1,2,\ldots)$$

holds for all real (or positive) x,y, therefore (cf. Aczél 1966), there exist constants c_j such that

$$(32) \qquad f_j(x) = c_j x \qquad (j = 1,2,\ldots).$$

As to the equation (20), for similar reasons, either $h_o(x) \equiv 0$ and then, by (24),

$$(33) \qquad h_k(x) \equiv 0 \qquad (k = 0,1,2,\ldots)$$

or there exists a c such that

$$(34) \qquad h_o(x) = e^{cx} .$$

Here $c \leq 0$ because of $p_o(x) \leq 1$. It is also easy to show (Jánossy-Rényi-Aczél 1950), that $c_j \geq 0$, and equation (12) implies that (33) is impossible and that, in (34),

$$c = - \sum_{j=1}^{\infty} c_j$$

(including the convergence of the series on the right). So, the general solution of the system (12), (13), (14) is given by

$$p_k(t) = e^{-\sum_{j=1}^{\infty} c_j t} \sum_{r_1+2r_2+\ldots+kr_k=k} \prod_{j=1}^{k} \frac{(c_j t)^{r_j}}{r_j!} \qquad (k=0,1,2,\ldots)$$

where the c_j are arbitrary nonnegative constants for which $\sum c_k$ converges. This describes a compound Poisson distribution.

Similarly, for equation (11), if the functions $P_k: \mathbb{R} \to \mathbb{R}$ $(k = 0,1,2,\ldots)$ are supposed to be bounded on a set of positive measure, then we get again (32) and either (33) or (34). So, the general solutions of (11), bounded on a set of positive measure, are given by either $P_k(t) = 0$ $(k = 0,1,2,\ldots)$, or

$$(35) \qquad P_k(t) = e^{ct} k! \sum_{r_1+2r_2+\ldots+kr_k=k} \prod_{j=1}^{k} \frac{(c_j t)^{r_j}}{r_j!}, \quad (t \in \mathbb{R}; k=0,1,2,\ldots$$

where $c, c_1, c_2, \ldots$ are arbitrary constants. Notice that, in (35), the expressions after e^{ct} are polynomials. These are the most general polynomials of the binomial type. The most general functions of binomial type, bounded on a set of positive measure, differ from them only in a common exponential factor.

We can get to [(17) and] (18) by choosing $G = \mathbb{R}^{\infty}$ with the usual addition

$$(x_0,x_1,x_2,\ldots,) + (y_0,y_1,y_2,\ldots) = (x_0+y_0,x_1+y_1,x_2+y_2,\ldots)$$

(this is different from Aczél-Vranceanu 1972).

We can apply Theorem 1, taking into consideration that each h_k (here $B_k/k!$) depends only upon the first k+1 components of x $(k = 0,1,2,\ldots)$. Therefore, by (25), (29) and the similar equations defining f_j, also each f_j depends only upon the first j+1 components of x. Since the general solution of

$$f_j(x_o+y_o, x_1+y_1,\ldots,x_j+y_j) = f_j(x_o,x_1,\ldots,x_j)+f_j(y_o,y_1,\ldots,y_j)$$
$$(x_i,y_i \in \mathbb{R}; \; i= 0,1,\ldots,j)$$

is given (see, e.g., Aczél 1966) by

$$f_j(x_o,x_1,\ldots,x_j) = f_{jo}(x_o)+f_{j1}(x_1)+\ldots+f_{jj}(x_j),$$

where f_{ji} satisfies

$$(36) \qquad f_{ji}(t+u) = f_{ji}(t) + f_{ji}(u) \qquad (t,u \in \mathbb{R}; \; i=0,1,\ldots,j),$$

we have the following.

Corollary. The general solutions $B_k: \mathbb{R}^{k+1} \to \mathbb{R}$ $(k=0,1,2,\ldots,)$ of (18) are given by

$$(37) \qquad B_k(t_o,t_1,\ldots,t_k) = k!h_o(t_o) \sum_{r_1+2r_2+\ldots+kr_k=k} \prod_{j=1}^{k} \frac{[f_{jo}(t_o)+f_{j1}(t_1)+\ldots+f_{jj}(t_j)]^{r_j}}{r_j!}$$
$$(k = 0,1,\ldots).$$

where h_o and f_{ji} $(i=0,1,\ldots,j;\; j=1,2,\ldots,)$ satisfy (20) or (36), respectively. If, in particular, the B_k are supposed to be bounded on a set of positive measure, then the general solutions are given by $B_k = 0$ and by

$$B_k(t_o,t_1,\dots,t_k) =$$

(38)

$$= k!e^{ct_o} \sum_{r_1+2r_2+\dots+kr_k=k} \prod_{j=1}^{k} \frac{(c_{jo}t_o+c_{j1}t_1+\dots+c_{jj}t_j)^{r_j}}{r_j!}$$

where c, c_{ji} are arbitrary constants. We obtain the general solutions of (17) by choosing in (37) ($h_o=0$ or) $h_o=1$ and $f_{jo} \equiv 0$ $(j=1,2,\dots)$ and the general bounded solutions by choosing, in (38), $c=c_{jo}=0$ (in addition to $B_k=0$).

Another way of determining these functions is by using, similarly as in section 1, (4), generating functions (Jánossy-Rényi-Aczél 1950, Redheffer 1953, Schmidt 1974).

For instance, in the case of equation (11), if we denote

(39) $$F(t,x) = \sum_{k=0}^{\infty} \frac{1}{k!} P_k(t)x^k,$$

then F satisfies

(40) $$F(t+u,x) = F(t,x)F(u,x)$$

which is easy to solve (cf. section 7), but one has to worry about the convergence in (39), or develop a calculus of formal power series, appropriate for this purpose.

3. A controversy (Patil-Seshadri 1964, Menon 1966) on the determination of the independent random variables X,Y from the conditional distribution of X, given X + Y has led to the question for the general solution of the equation

(41) $$f(x+y) = f(x)f(y)$$

[cf. (20)] on a (complex) lattice, that is, for

(42) $$x, y \varepsilon S = \{a, a+d, \ldots, a+nd\}.$$

By using, among others, arguments somewhat similar to those of Daróczy and Losonczi (1967), I have proved (Aczél 1974) without any regularity suppositions that <u>the general solutions of (41) on (42) are given by</u>

$$f(x) = \begin{cases} \alpha e^{\gamma x} & (x \varepsilon S) \\ \alpha^2 e^{\gamma x} & (x \varepsilon S+S) \end{cases},$$

(43) $$f(x) = \begin{cases} \beta & (x = a) \\ \beta^2 & (x = 2a) \\ 0 & \text{else} \end{cases},$$

<u>and</u>

(44) $$f(x) = \begin{cases} \beta & (x = a+nd) \\ \beta^2 & (x = 2a+2nd) \\ 0 & \text{else} \end{cases}$$

<u>where</u> $S + S = \{2a, 2a+d, \ldots, 2a+2nd\}$ <u>and</u> α, β, γ <u>are arbitrary constants if</u> $S \cap (S+S) = \emptyset$, <u>else only</u> $\alpha = 0$ <u>or</u> 1 <u>and</u> $\beta = 0$ <u>are admissible, except in the cases</u> $a = 0$ <u>and</u> $a+nd = 0$, <u>when</u> $\beta = 1$ <u>is also admissible, in (43) or (44), respectively</u> <u>(γ is still arbitrary).</u>

It is easy to extend this result to <u>infinite</u> lattices.

<u>4.</u> In connection with the determination of the mixing distributions, given the mixture (binomial, Neyman type A), Sh. Talwalker has asked me at the International Conference on Characterizations of Statistical Distributions in Calgary, August 1974, about the solutions of the functional equation

(45) $$g(st) - g(s) = e^{c(1-s)} g(1-s+st) \qquad (s \in]0,1[, t \in [-1,1]),$$

where c is a positive constant. I presented there the following argument, which determines the general solution without any regularity suppositions (unpublished).

Write in (45)

$$x = st, \; y = 1 - s.$$

Then

(46) $$x \in]-1,1[, \quad y \in]0,1[, \quad x + y \leq 1, \text{ and } x - y \geq -1$$

(the last two from $t = x/(1-y) \in [-1,1]$) and (45) goes over into

(47) $$g(x+y) = [g(x) - g(1-y)]e^{-cy}$$

on the domain (46). Let us substitute here $x = 0$ and get, with $g(0) = \alpha$,

$$g(1-y) = \alpha - g(y)e^{cy} \qquad (y \in]0,1[).$$

Putting this back into (47), we get

$$g(x+y) = [g(x) - \alpha]e^{-cy} + g(y)$$

on (46). By symmetry we have also

$$g(x+y) = [g(y) - \alpha]e^{-cx} + g(x),$$

but on the domain obtained from (46) by interchanging x and y. Comparing the last two equations, we get

$$(48)\qquad [g(x)-\alpha]e^{-cy} + g(y) = [g(y)-\alpha]e^{-cx} + g(x),$$

but only for

$$(49)\qquad x\in\,]0,1[,\quad y\in\,]0,1[,\quad x+y\le 1$$

$[x-y \ge -1,\ y-x \ge -1$ are now consequences of (49)$]$. Substitute into (48) $x=\varepsilon$ (a small positive number) and get

$$(50)\qquad g(y) = \frac{g(\varepsilon)-\alpha e^{-c\varepsilon} + [\alpha - g(\varepsilon)]e^{-cy}}{1+e^{-c\varepsilon}} = \beta + \gamma e^{-cy} \text{ for all } y\in\,]0,1-\varepsilon[.$$

If we put this back into (47), we get

$$\beta + \gamma e^{-c(x+y)} = [\beta + \gamma e^{-cx} - \beta - \gamma e^{-c(1-y)}]e^{-cy}\ .$$

All restrictions on x,y are satisfied if, for instance, $x\in\,]0,\frac{1}{2}-\varepsilon[$, $y\ \varepsilon\ [\varepsilon,\frac{1}{2}[$, so we have to have

$$\beta = -\gamma e^{-c},\ \text{i.e.,}\ \gamma = -\beta e^{c}\ .$$

So (50) goes over into

$$(51)\qquad g(z) = \beta\left(1-e^{-c(z-1)}\right)$$

for all $z\in\,]0,1-\varepsilon[$ and, since we can choose ε arbitrarily small, also for all

$$z\in\,]0,1[\ .$$

(The constant β has to be the same on all intervals $]0,1-\varepsilon_n[$, since they are overlapping, $\varepsilon_n \to 0$).

We want to extend (51) for the interval $]-1,1]$. First put into (47) $x = 1-y$ and get $g(1) = 0$, that is, <u>(51) remains true on</u> $]0,1]$. Suppose that I $(\supseteq]0,1])$ would be the largest interval on which (51) holds. We show that $I =]-1,1]$. Indeed, else there would exist a $z_o \in]-1,0]$ not in I and a $\delta \in]0, z_o+1[$ so that (51) would hold for $z_o + \delta$ $(\in I)$, but not for z_o. Put into (47) $x = z_o$, $y = \delta$ $(x+y = z_o+\delta < 1,\ x-y = z_o - \delta > -1)$ and get

$$\beta(1 - e^{-c(z_o + \delta - 1)}) = [g(z_o) - \beta(1 - e^{c\delta})]e^{-c\delta}$$

or

$$g(z_o) = \beta\left(1 - e^{-c(z_o - 1)}\right),$$

that is, (51) is true for z_o too, in contradiction to the supposition.

Thus we have proved the following.

<u>Theorem 2.</u> <u>The general solution of (45) is given without any regularity suppositions by</u>

$$g(z) = \beta\left(1 - e^{-c(z-1)}\right) \quad \text{for all } z \in]-1,1]. \tag{52}$$

[Direct substitution shows that (52) does indeed satisfy (45).]

We may wonder, why (52) is not proved for $z = -1$. This value of the argument does not really enter into (45) because $s \in]0,1[$, $st \in]-1,1[$, and $1 - s + st \in]-1,1]$.

<u>5</u>. Srivastava and Srivastava (1970) have pronounced the following conjecture. Let X and Y be nonnegative discrete random variables and U, V (damaging) random variables so that the conditional

probabilities are of the binomial type:

$$P(U=r,V=s \mid X=m,Y=n) = \binom{m}{r} p^r (1-p)^{m-r} \binom{n}{s} q^s (1-q)^{n-s}$$

$$\left(m,n,r,s \text{ positive integers, } p,q \in \left]0,1\right[\right)$$

whenever $P(X=m,Y=n) > 0$ and so that

$$(53) \qquad P(U=r,V=s) = P(U=r,V=s \mid X > U, Y > V) = P(U=r,V=s \mid X=U, Y=V)$$

Their conjecture was that then $\{P(U=r,V=s)\}$ is the joint distribution of two independent random variables obeying the Poisson law.

They have noticed that the conjecture says that

$$G(x,y) = e^{\lambda(1-x)+\mu(1-y)}$$

is the general solution of the functional equation

$$(54) \qquad G(px,qy) = G(p,q)G(px+1-p,qy+1-q)$$

among functions which can be generating functions of bivariate probability distributions. In the case where, in (54), in addition to x,y ($\in \mathbb{R}$) also p,q ($\in \left]0,1\right[$) are variables, this conjecture has been proved by Aczél (1972; cf. also van der Vaart 1972) under weaker regularity suppositions (continuity at a point, say, and $G \not\equiv 0$). On the other hand, Shanbhag (1974) has given a counter example which shows that the conjecture is not true if, in (54), p and q are fixed constants.

He proved also (cf. Talwalker 1970) that the above result is true again if p and q are fixed constants but, in addition to (53), also

(55) $$P(U=r,V=s) = P(U=r,V=s \mid X=U, Y>V)$$

is supposed, that is, G satisfies, in addition to (54),

(56) $$G(px,qy) = \frac{G(p,q)}{G(1,y)} G(px+1-p,qy).$$

His conditions were that the functions G_i $(i = 1,2,3)$, defined by

$$G_1(t) = G(t,0),\ G_2(t) = G(0,t),\ G_3(t) = G(x+t, y+\frac{q}{p}t)\ (t \in \mathbb{R}),$$

have the following properties.

(57) G_i is analytic, $G_i(t) > 0$, and $\frac{d}{dt}\frac{G_i'(t)}{G_i(t)} \geq 0$ $(i = 1,2,3; t \in \mathbb{R})$

and

(58) $$G(1,1) = 1.$$

He has derived them from the fact that G is the generating function of a probability distribution.

Aczél (1976) has proved the same result under the only condition that G_i is log-convex $(i = 1,2,3)$. Notice that (57) implies the log-convexity of G_i and that (58) is not supposed here. He has also determined without any regularity suppositions the general solutions of (54) both with variable and with fixed p,q, the general solution of the latter equation alone under the above log-convexity conditions and the general solutions of the pair (54) and (56) $(G(1,1)>0)$ with and without the log-convexity conditions $(x,y \in \mathbb{R}$ all over).

The observation, essential for the proofs, is that (54) and (56) go over, with the notations $u = p(1-x)$, $v = q(1-y)$, $F(u,v) = G(1-u,1-v)$ into

$$F(u+1-p, v+1-q) = F(1-p, 1-q)F(u,v)$$

or into

$$F(u+1-p, v+1-q) = \frac{F(1-p, 1-q)}{F(0, 1-q)} F(u, v+1-q)$$

$(u,v \in \mathbb{R})$, respectively.

6. Kamiński and Mikusiński (1974) have found, with aid of distributions (in the sense of L. Schwartz) that

$$(59) \quad H(x,y,z) = cx\log x + cy\log y + cz\log z - c(x+y+z)\log(x+y+z),$$

$$(x \geq 0, y \geq 0, z \geq 0, x+y+z > 0)$$

(that is, x,y,z are nonnegative but at least one of them is positive, $0 \log 0 := 0$), with an arbitrary constant c, is the general continuous, symmetric and homogeneous (positively, of degree 1) solution of what they call the "<u>entropy equation</u>", i.e., of

$$(60) \quad H(x,y,z) = H(x+y,0,z) + H(x,y,0) \quad (x \geq 0, y \geq 0, z \geq 0, xy+yz+zx > 0)$$

(at least two of x,y,z are positive).

Aczél (1977), noticed that, whenever H satisfies (60), then the function f defined by

$$(61) \quad f(x) = H(1-x,x,0) \qquad (x \in [0,1])$$

is an <u>information function</u>, that is, it satisfies

$$f(x) + (1-x)f\left(\frac{y}{1-x}\right) = f(y) + (1-y)f\left(\frac{x}{1-y}\right),$$

whenever

$$0 \le x < 1, \ 0 \le y < 1, \ x + y \le 1$$

and

$$f(0) = f(1).$$

Concerning such information functions, it is known (see, e.g., Aczél-Daróczy 1975, Diderrich 1977; actually the functions which we have defined above are constant multiples of the information functions there), that their general form is given by

$$f(x) = cx \log x + c(1-x)\log(1-x), \quad \left(x \in [0,1], \ 0 \log 0 := 0\right)$$

if f is supposed to be continuous at a point or bounded on an interval or measurable on $]0,1[$. Also the most general form of information functions is known (Aczél-Daróczy 1975), without any regularity suppositions, to be given by

$$f(x) = x\ell(x) + (1-x)\ell(1-x) \qquad \left(x \in [0,1], \ 0\ell(0) := 0\right)$$

where ℓ is an arbitrary solution of

$$(62) \qquad \ell(xy) = \ell(x) + \ell(y) \qquad \left(x,y \in]0,1]\right).$$

So the general symmetric and homogeneous solution of (60), for which f, defined by (61), is continuous at a point or bounded on an interval or measurable on $]0,1[$, is given by (59), while the general symmetric and homogeneous solutions of (60), without any regularity conditions, are given by

$$H(x,y,z) = x\ell(x) + y\ell(y) + z\ell(z) - (x+y+z)\ell(x+y+z)$$

$$(x,y,z \ge 0, \ x+y+z > 0, \ 0\ell(0) := 0),$$

<u>where ℓ is an arbitrary solution of (62).</u>

Of course, the general solution of (62) is given (see, e.g., Aczél 1966) by

$$\ell(x) = f_1(-\log x) \quad (x \in]0,1]),$$

where f_1 is an arbitrary solution of Cauchy's equation [cf. (36)]

$$f_1(u+v) = f_1(u) + f_1(v) \quad (u,v \geq 0).$$

7. Aczél and Eichhorn (1974) have given two proofs of the theorem that the traditional price (or productivity) index

$$F(\underline{v},\underline{x}) = \frac{\underline{a} \cdot \underline{x}}{\underline{b} \cdot \underline{v}} \quad (\underline{x} \in \bar{\mathbb{R}}_+^n,\ \underline{v} \in \bar{\mathbb{R}}_+^m \setminus \{(0,\ldots,0)\};\ \bar{\mathbb{R}}_+ := \{t \mid t \geq 0\})$$

[$\underline{v} = (v_1, v_2, \ldots, v_m)$ are the base year prices, $\underline{x} = (x_1, x_2, \ldots, x_n)$ the present prices, $\underline{a}$ and $\underline{b}$ are constant vectors, "$\cdot$" the scalar multiplication] is the general solution of the system

$$F(\underline{v},\underline{x}) > 0 \quad (\underline{x} \in \bar{\mathbb{R}}_+^n \setminus \{(0,\ldots,0)\},\ \underline{v} \in \bar{\mathbb{R}}_+^m \setminus \{(0,\ldots,0)\})$$

(63) $$F(\underline{v},\underline{x}_1+\underline{x}_2) = F(\underline{v},\underline{x}_1) + F(\underline{v},\underline{x}_2)$$

$(\underline{x}_1, \underline{x}_2 \in \bar{\mathbb{R}}_+^n,\ \underline{v} \in \bar{\mathbb{R}}_+^m \setminus \{(0,\ldots,0)\})$ and

(64) $$\frac{1}{F(\underline{v}_1+\underline{v}_2,\underline{x})} = \frac{1}{F(\underline{v}_1,\underline{x})} + \frac{1}{F(\underline{v}_2,\underline{x})}$$

$(\underline{x} \in \bar{\mathbb{R}}_+^n \setminus \{(0,\ldots,0)\},\ \underline{v}_1, \underline{v}_2 \in \bar{\mathbb{R}}_+^m \setminus \{(0,\ldots,0)\}$.

Aczél (1975) has given <u>the most general solutions of (63)</u> $(\underline{v} \in S,\ \underline{x}_1 \in \underline{T},\ \underline{x}_2 \in \underline{T})$, <u>and (64)</u> $(\underline{v},\underline{w} \in S,\ \underline{x} \in {}^{O}\underline{T})$ <u>in the case where</u>

F: $\underline{S} \times \underline{T} \to \underline{F}$, $\underline{S}$ and $\underline{T}$ being groupoids, $\underline{F}$ a commutative field and $F(\underline{v},\underline{x}) \neq 0$ for $\underline{v} \in \underline{S}$, $\underline{x} \in {}^{0}\underline{T}$ (if $\underline{T}$ has a unit $\underline{0}$, then we denote ${}^{0}\underline{T} = \underline{T} \setminus \{\underline{0}\}$, else ${}^{0}\underline{T} = \underline{T}$) as

$$F(\underline{v},\underline{x}) = \frac{f(\underline{x})}{g(\underline{v})} \qquad (\underline{v} \in S,\ \underline{x} \in T).$$

If $\underline{S}$ and $\underline{T}$ are cartesian products of abelian semigroups, $\underline{S} = \underline{S}_1 \times \underline{S}_2 \times \ldots \times \underline{S}_n$, $\underline{T} = \underline{T}_1 \times \underline{T}_2 \times \ldots \times \underline{T}_m$, then the most general solutions are given by

$$F(\underline{v},\underline{x}) = \sum_{k=1}^{n} f_k(x_k) \Big/ \sum_{j=1}^{m} g_j(v_j) \quad (v_j \in \underline{S}_j, x_k \in \underline{T}_k; j=1,2,\ldots,m;\ k=1,2,\ldots,n),$$

where [cf. (26) and (36)] $f(x) \neq 0$ $(x \in {}^{0}\underline{T})$, $g(\underline{v}) \neq 0$ $(v \in \underline{S})$,

$$f(\underline{x}+\underline{y}) = f(\underline{x}) + f(\underline{y}) \quad (\underline{x},\underline{y} \in \underline{T}), \qquad g(\underline{v}+\underline{w}) = g(\underline{v})+g(\underline{w}) \quad (\underline{v},\underline{w} \in \underline{S}),$$

$$f_k(x_k+y_k) = f_k(x_k)+f_k(y_k) \quad (x_k,y_k \in \underline{T}_k), \qquad g_j(v_j+w_j)=g_j(v_j)+g_j(w_j) \quad (v_j,w_j \in \underline{S}_j),$$

and, from this, three further proofs for the original theorem were obtained.

8. Eichhorn (1974) calls "technical effectiveness of a production process" a real valued, not identically zero function G of the time t, the cost u, and of the output vector $\underline{v}$ of this process, if it satisfies (among others) the following conditions, which are partial generalizations of the homogeneity (cf. section 6)

(65) $$G(st,su,\underline{v}) = h_o(s)G(t,u,\underline{v})$$

(66) $$G(t,su,s\underline{v}) = h_1(s)G(t,u,\underline{v})$$

(67) $$G(st,u,s\underline{v}) = h_2(s)G(t,u,\underline{v})$$

and

(68) $$G(t,u,s\underline{v}) = h_3(s)G(t,u,\underline{v})$$

($s\in\mathbb{R}_+$, $t,u\in\bar{\mathbb{R}}_+$, $\underline{v}\in\bar{\mathbb{R}}_+^n$), where $h_j: \mathbb{R}_+ \to \mathbb{R}$ ($j=0,1,2,3$) satisfy

(69) $$h_j(rs) = h_j(r)h_j(s) \quad (r,s \in \mathbb{R}_+ := \{t \mid t > 0\})$$

and

(70) the h_j are strictly monotonic ($j=0,1,2,3$), h_o decreasing, h_j ($j=1,2,3$) increasing.

He proves, among others, that (65), (66), (67) and (69), (70) for $j=0,1,2$ imply (68) and (69), (70) for $j=3$. I give here a shorter (unpublished) proof of a theorem which is, in a sense, stronger: We first derive (68) from (65), (66), (67) alone, then prove (69) for $j = 0,1,2,3$, and finally we prove that (70) holds for $j=3$, if it is true for $j=0,1,2$.

Theorem 3. If the real valued, not indentically zero function G satisfies the equations (65), (66), (67) for all $s\in\mathbb{R}_+$, $t,u \in\bar{\mathbb{R}}_+$, and $\underline{v} \in \bar{\mathbb{R}}_+^n$, then (68) holds too for the same $s,t,u,\underline{v}$ and (69) holds for $j=0,1,2,3$. If, further, (70) is true for $j=0,1,2$, then also for $j=3$.

Proof. From (67), (66) and (65) (in this order) we have

$$G(t,u,s^2\underline{v}) = h_2(s)G(\tfrac{t}{s},u,s\underline{v}) = h_2(s)h_1(s)G(\tfrac{t}{s},\tfrac{u}{s},\underline{v}) =$$

$$= h_2(s)h_1(s)h_o(\tfrac{1}{s})G(t,u,\underline{v})$$

for all $s \in \mathbb{R}_+$, $t,u \in \bar{\mathbb{R}}_+$, $\underline{v} \in \bar{\mathbb{R}}_+^n$. Thus, with $s' = s^2$,

(71) $$G(t,u,s'\underline{v}) = h_3(s')G(t,u,v)$$

for all $s' \in \mathbb{R}_+$, $t,u \in \bar{\mathbb{R}}_+$, $\underline{v} \in \bar{\mathbb{R}}_+^n$, if we define

(72) $$h_3(s') := h_o(\tfrac{1}{\sqrt{s'}})h_1(\sqrt{s'})h_2(\sqrt{s'}).$$

This proves (68).

Since G is not identically zero, (69) follows from (65), (66), (67), (68). For instance, from (68), cf. (71), we have

$$h_3(rs)G(t,u,\underline{v}) = G(t,u,rs\underline{v}) = h_3(r)G(t,u,s\underline{v}) = h_3(r)h_3(s)G(t,u,\underline{v})$$

and thus, with t_o, u_o, $\underline{v}_o$ such that $G(t_o,u_o,\underline{v}_o) \neq 0$, we get (69) for j=3 and, similarly, for j=0,1,2. The validity of (69) for j=3 follows also from its validity for j=0,1,2 and from (72). Similarly, (70) holds for j=3, if it is supposed to be true for j=0,1,2, because of (72). This concludes the proof.

This research has been supported in part by the National Research Council of Canada Grant nr. A - 2972.

References

J. Aczél (1966) Lectures on Functional Equations and Their Applications. Academic Press, New York - London.

(1972) On a Characterization of Poisson Distributions. J. Appl. Probability 9, 852-856.

(1974) General Solution of a Functional Equation Connected with a Characterization of Statistical Distributions. In: Statistical Distributions in Scientific Work, Proc. NATO Adv. Study Inst. Calgary, 1974, D. Reidel, Dordrecht-Boston, 1975, Vol. 3, pp. 47-55.

(1975) On a System of Functional Equations Determining Price and Productivity Indices. Utilitas Math. 7, 345 - 362.

(1976) On Two Characterizations of Poisson Distributions. Abh. Math. Sem. Hamburg 44, 91 - 100.

(1977) Results on the Entropy Equation. Bull. Acad. Polon. Sci. Ser. Sci. Math. Phys. Astronom. 35, 13-17.

J. Aczél - Z. Daróczy (1975) On Measures of Information and Their Characterizations. Academic Press. New York-London-San Francisco.

J. Aczél - W. Eichhorn (1974) Systems of Functional Equations Determining Price and Productivity Indices. Utilitas Math. 5, 213-226.

J. Aczél - G. Vranceanu (1972) Equations fonctionelles aux groupes linéaires commutatifs. Colloquium Math. 26, 371-383.

E.T. Bell (1934) Exponential Polynomials. Ann. Math. 35, 258-277.

Z. Daróczy- (1967) Über die Erweiterung der auf einer Punkt-
L.Losonczi menge additiven Funktionen. Publ. Math. Debrecen 14, 239-245.

G.T. Diderrich (1977) Local Boundedness and the Shannon Entropy. Information and Control.

W. Eichhorn (1974) Systems of Functional Equations Determining the Effectiveness of a Production Process. In: Mathematical Methods in Economics. North Holland, Amsterdam-London, 1974, pp. 433-439.

L. Jánossy-
A. Rényi- (1950) On Composed Poisson Distributions, I. Acta
J. Aczél Math. Acad. Sci. Hungar. 1, 209-224.

A. Kamiński-(1974) On the Entropy Equation. Bull. Acad. Polon.
J. Mikusiński Sci.Sér.Sci. Math. Astronom. Phys. 22, 319-323.

W. Maier - (1971) Funktionalgleichungen mit analytischen Lösungen.
H. Kiesewetter DVW Berlin, Vandenhoeck & Ruprecht, Göttingen-Zürich.

M.V. Menon (1966) Characterization Theorems for Some Univariate Probability Distributions. J.Roy. Statist.Soc. Ser. B 28, 143-145.

H. Meschkowski (1959) Differenzengleichungen. Vandenhoeck % Ruprecht, Göttingen.

G.P. Patil- (1964) Characterization Theorems for Some Univariate
V. Seshadri Probability Distributions. J. Roy. Statist. Soc. Ser. B 26, 286-292.

R.M. Redheffer (1953) A Note on the Poisson Law. Math. Mag. 26, 183-186.

J. Riordan (1958) An Introduction to Combinatorial Analysis. Wiley, New York; Chapman & Hall, London.

G.C. Rota- R. Mullin (1969) On the Foundations of Combinatorial Theory III. Theory of Binomial Enumeration. In: Graph Theory and its Applications, Proc. Advanced Seminar Math. Research Center, Madison, Wis. 1969, Academic Press, New York, 1970, 167-213.

Herm. Schmidt (1974) Über das Additionstheorem der Binomialkoeffizienten. Reports of Meetings. Aequationes Math. 10, 302-306.

D.N. Shanbhag (1974) An Elementary Proof of the Rao-Rubin Characterization of the Poisson Distribution. J. Appl. Probability 11, 211-215.

R.C. Srivastava- A.B.L. Srivastava (1970) On a Characterization of Poisson Distribution. J. Appl. Probability 7, 497-501.

Sh. Talwalker (1970) A Characterization of the Double Poisson Distribution. Sankhyā Ser.A 32 , 265-270.

H.R. van der Vaart (1972) A Note on a Functional Equation for the Generating Function of a Poisson Distribution. Sankhyā Ser. A 34, 191-193.

Neutral Changes in Tastes and Utility

by Martin J. Beckmann *

In the analysis of consumer behavior and of welfare over time, particularly in connection with the problem of the pure cost of living index (Fisher and Shell [1968]), it is of interest to distinguish special types of change in the utility functions, in particular

(i) utility shifts or Hicks neutral changes which leave the indifference surfaces unchanged but vary only the utility index associated with these indifference surfaces and

(ii) quality and/or taste changes which act as if the quantity of a commodity would be augmented, "Harrod neutral" changes, say.

The question is whether these types of utility changes may be associated with certain invariant properties of those variables derived from utility functions which are amenable to observation and testing. In this note it is shown that Hicks and Harrod neutrality as defined above are, in fact, the only type of change that may occur in time when loosely speaking <u>expenditure depends only on the elasticity of substitution.</u>

More precisely we shall show the following. Suppose that relative expenditure on commodities varies over time but remains unchanged whenever the direct elasticities of substitution are unchanged. Then, the utility function is homothetic and is Hicks and Harrod neutral in the sense that

$$(1) \qquad u = M\left(x_i\, H\left(A_1(t)\frac{x_1}{x_i}, \ldots, A_n(t)\frac{x_n}{x_i}\right), t\right) .$$

*I wish to thank Ryuzo Sato for many useful comments. The work is supported by NSF Grant 4567-4, (GS-2325).

Here x_i denotes consumption of the ith good. This relationship may also be stated in reverse form: In order that the elasticity of substitution should depend only on relative expenditures the utility function must have the form (1).

Notation: Let $R_{ij} = \frac{u_j}{u_i}$ denote the marginal rate of substitution of commodity i for commodity j. The hypothesis is that

$$\frac{x_j\, u_j}{x_i\, u_i} = G_j\left(\frac{\partial \log R_{ij}}{\partial \log \frac{x_j}{x_i}}, \ldots \frac{\partial \log R_{ik}}{\partial \log \frac{x_k}{x_i}}, \ldots\right), \tag{2}$$

i fixed; $j = 1,\ldots,n$; $j \neq i$; $k = 1,\ldots,n$; $k \neq i,j$.

Let the equations (2) represent an independent system so that the determination is nonzero and the equation system may be inverted

$$\frac{\partial \log \frac{u_j}{u_i}}{\partial \log \frac{x_j}{x_i}} = g_j\left(\frac{x_1 u_1}{x_i u_i}, \ldots, \frac{x_n u_n}{x_i u_i}\right), \quad j \neq i;\ j = 1,\ldots,n.$$

Write $v_j = \log \frac{x_j\, u_j}{x_i\, u_i}$, $\xi_j = \log \frac{x_j}{x_i}$, then

$$\frac{\partial v_j}{\partial \xi_j} = 1 + h_j\,(v_1,\ldots,v_n) \quad \text{where } h_j(y) = g_j(\log y)\,.$$

Separating variables we obtain

$$\int \frac{dv_j}{1 + h_j(v_1,\ldots,v_n)} = \int d\xi_j + \log A_j(t)$$

or

$$\log \phi_j(v_1,\ldots,v_n) = \log \frac{x_j}{x_i} + \log A_j \quad \text{(say)}.$$

Thus,

$$\phi_j\left[\frac{x_1 u_1}{x_i u_i}, \ldots, \frac{x_j u_j}{x_i u_i}, \ldots, \frac{x_n u_n}{x_i u_i}\right] = A_j \frac{x_j}{x_i}\,. \tag{3}$$

Write $u(x_1,\ldots,x_i,\ldots,x_j,\ldots,x_n) =$

$$w(A_1x_1,\ldots,x_i,\ldots,A_jx_j,\ldots,A_nx_n) = w(z_1,\ldots,z_n)$$

where $z_k = A_kx_k$, $z_i = x_i$ for $k \neq i$.

Note that

$$\frac{\partial u}{\partial x_k} = w_k A_k, \frac{\partial u}{\partial x_i} = w_i \quad .$$

Substituting in (3) we obtain

$$\phi_j \left[\frac{x_kA_kw_k}{x_iw_i} ,\ldots,\right] \equiv \phi_j \left[\ldots \frac{z_kw_k}{z_iw_i} ,\ldots,\right] = \frac{z_j}{z_i} \quad .$$

The system may be transformed to:

$$(4) \qquad \frac{z_j}{z_i}\frac{w_j}{w_i} = \psi_j\left[\frac{z_1}{z_i},\ldots,\frac{z_n}{z_i}\right]$$

or

$$(5) \qquad \frac{\partial w}{\partial z_j} + H_j\left(\frac{z_1}{z_i},\ldots,\frac{z_n}{z_i}\right)\frac{\partial w}{\partial z_i} = 0 \quad \text{where } H_j = -\frac{z_i}{z_j}\psi_j \quad .$$

We now make use of the following.

<u>Lemma:</u> The general solution of a system of partial differential equations

$$(6) \qquad \frac{\partial w}{\partial z_j} = a_{ij}\left(\frac{z_1}{z_i},\ldots,\frac{z_n}{z_i}\right)\frac{\partial w}{\partial z_i} , \quad i,j = 1,\ldots,n \ ; \ j \neq i$$

is a (monotone) tranform of

$$(7) \qquad w = z_i\phi\left(\frac{z_1}{z_i} , \frac{z_2}{z_i} ,\ldots, \frac{z_n}{z_i}\right) .$$

Proof of the lemma. Consider a particular equation of this system of linear homogeneous partial differential equations. We first show that a particular solution of the form (7) exists.

Substituting (7) in (6) we have

$$z_i \frac{\partial \phi}{\partial y_j} \cdot \frac{1}{z_i} =$$

$$a\left[\phi + z_i \sum_{\substack{i=1\\ j\neq i}}^{n} \frac{\partial \phi}{\partial y_j}\left(-\frac{z_j}{z_i^2}\right)\right] \qquad \text{for } i \neq j$$

where we have written $y_j = \frac{z_j}{z_i}$. Using the y notation throughout

$$\frac{\partial \phi(y_1,\ldots,y_n)}{\partial y_j} = a(y_1,\ldots,y_n)\left[\phi(y_1,\ldots,y_n) - \sum_j y_j \frac{\partial \phi(y_1,\ldots,y_n)}{\partial y_j}\right].$$

This is a first order linear partial differential equation in $\phi(y_1,\ldots,y_n)$ which has a solution under the usual conditions producing a particular solution of the form (7) to the differential equation (6). The general solution of a partial differential equation (6) in terms of z_i and z_j is then

$$W = M\left(z_i\,\phi\left(\frac{z_1}{z_i},\ldots,\frac{z_n}{z_i}\right), t,\ z_1,\ldots,z_k,\ldots,z_n\right),\quad k \neq i,j$$

where M is monoton in the first variable. Since i and j were arbitrary it follows that none of the variables z_k may occur in the right-hand expression so that

$$z = M\left(z_i\phi\left(\frac{z_1}{z_i},\ldots,\frac{z_n}{z_i}\right), t\right)$$

is the general solution.

Q.E.D.

Applying the lemma, the general solution of (5) is found to be

$$w(z_1,\ldots,z_n) = M\left(z_i\phi\left(\frac{z_1}{z_i},\ldots,\frac{z_n}{z_i}\right), t\right)$$

where M denotes a function monotone in the first variable (Kamke [1952, p. 301]).

Substituting for z and w we have

$$u(x_1,\ldots x_n) = M\left(x_i\ \phi\left(A_1(t)\frac{x_1}{x_i},\ldots,A_j(t)\frac{x_j}{x_i},\ldots\right),t\right)$$

proving equation (1). Note that the utility function is homothetic, i.e., that the indifference curves depend only on the ratios $\frac{x_j}{x_i}$ of commodity quantities. This corresponds to homogeneous production functions in production theory. The result is an extension of results on homogeneous production functions (Sato and Beckmann [1968, p. 63]).

The multipliers $A_j(t)$ of the commodity quantities express a "quantity augmenting" type of quality improvement through technical change or a quantity augmenting change of tastes analogous to Harrod neutral technical change in production. The monotone tranformation M(.,t) may be interpreted as a "Hicks neutral" change of tastes leading to no change in behavior since the marginal rates of substitution are unaffected. In fact, we have the following:

Theorem: Suppose that the marginal rates of substitution as functions of the commodity quantities are invariant with respect to time. Then any changes in the utility function must be Hicks neutral.

Proof: The hypothesis states that:

$$\frac{u_i}{u_j} = R_{ji}(x_1,\ldots,x_n) \quad , \qquad i,j = 1,\ldots,n.$$

Consider a particular equation

$$\frac{\partial u}{\partial x_i} - R_{ji}\ (x_1,\ldots,x_n)\ \frac{\partial u}{\partial x_j} = 0.$$

The equations of the characteristics are

$$\frac{dx_i}{ds} = 1 \frac{dx_j}{ds} = - R_{ji} (x_1,\dots,x_n)$$

or

$$\frac{dx_j}{dx_i} = - R_{ji} (x_1,\dots,x_n) \; . \tag{8}$$

To obtain a particular solution introduce an integrating factor, if (8) has a unique solution then there exists an infinity of integrating factors (Ince [1956, p. 27]).

Let $I(x_1,\dots,x_n)$ be such an integrating factor. It follows that

$$I(x_1,\dots,x_n)\, dx_i + IR(x_1,\dots,x_n)\, dx_j = 0$$

is exact so that an integral

$$\phi(x_1,\dots,x_n) = \text{constant} = c(u,\dots,x_k,\dots,) \text{ exists} (k \neq i,j).$$

Solving for u we obtain a particular solution

$$u = \psi(x_1,\dots,x_n).$$

The general solution is a (monotone) transform (Kamke [1952, p. 301]).

$$u = M(\psi(x_1,\dots,x_n),t).$$

Q.E.D.

This theorem may be extended to the case where the marginal rates of substitution are given functions of certain commodity quantities x_i and of the utility level u. It is also straightforward to show that when the marginal rate of substitution is homogeneous of degree zero in commodity quantities, then the utility function is homothetic.

References

FISHER, Franklin, M. and K. SHELL: "Quantity and Quality Change and the Pure Theory of the True Cost of Living Index". Value Capital and Growth, Essays in Honor of Sir Hicks, University of Edingurgh Press, 1968.

INCE, E.L.: Ordinary Differential Equations. Dover, 1956, p. 27.

SATO, R. and M. BECKMANN: "Neutral Inventions and Production Functions". Review of Economic Studies, Vol. 35, No. 1, January, 1968, pp. 57-66.

KAMKE, E.: Differentialgleichungen reeller Funktionen. Leipzig, 1952.

Some Considerations on Related Discrete and Continuous Dynamic Economic Models

by Karl-Heinz Bertsch

1. Introduction

Dynamic models are widely used in economic theory, a fact for which we easily can give some reasons:

First of all the behavior of economic agents depends on information, which they can get only with some delay, and so their decisions of today depend on yesterday-values of economic variables; furthermore they are influenced by experience from the past, by plans and expectations for the future. For these reasons the equations of economic models link variables at different points of time (or changes of these variables).

Furthermore static models are necessarily equilibrium models. Markets must be cleared at every moment, it is not possible to take any excess-demand or -supply from or to any other moment. If we want to take into consideration distortions of such market equilibrium, we are forced to install dynamic moments in our models.

Finally the study of static models in comparative statics may lead to the introduction of dynamics. As Hicks already pointed out in his "Value and Capital" [6, Chapter V], the results of comparative statics have no meaning unless the regarded economic system is dynamically stable. (We must be sure, that the disturbed system approaches its new equilibrium value.) This dynamic stability of the real world (Negishi,[8, p. 639] : "It is known empirically, that the economy is in fact fairly shock-proof") is tacitly assumed when doing comparative statics. But the stability of the dynamic model has then an additional importance: often when assuming this stability we can get further results in comparative statics, a fact which was called "Correspondence Principle" by Samuelson [11, p. 257 ff]. 1)

When constructing a dynamic model it is necessary to decide how time should be considered, as a continuous or as a discrete variable. Discrete time often leads to difference equations, while dynamic models with continuous time often can be formulated in terms of differential equations. Both aspects appear in economic theory, in macroeconomics as well as in microeconomics. Most authors give no reasons why deciding for a certain aspect, and the question could arise, how the choice between discrete or continuous time could influence the results.

Allen in his "Macroeconomic Theory" [1, p. 5 f.] is one of the few authors, who notice and discuss the two possibilities. In his opinion the question, which choice should be made, "is quite largely a matter of taste, with an eye on economic and mathematical convenience." [1, p. 5].

As far as mathematical convenience is concerned, he tells us that
1. often there is little difference between the two approaches
2. otherwise the continuous approach is to be handled more quickly and has simpler solutions.

From these reasons Allen concludes, that "the mathematician's preference is to use continuous analysis". [1, p. 6]

But one should be cautious with this result: the first point is vague (the ways to treat difference- or differential-equations are often similar, but the results may differ essentially), the second - as to the simplicity of the solution - is seen by Allen as an argument for the continuous version, (see also [1, p. 85]) but Samuelson [11, p. 265 and p. 304 f.] takes this greater range of solutions of the difference equation as an argument to try the discrete approach. In the context of mathematical convenience we further mention:

1) The use of this principle is not without problems: the assumption of the stability of the dynamic model - because of the stability of the real world - is not conclusive. This was pointed out by Newman [9]. It is not within the scope of this paper to discuss this principle, as for further limits see also Rader [10].

3. From the natural sciences the mathematician is more familiar with the techniques of differential equations, here he has a large theory which he can overtake, especially when qualitative properties of the solutions are asked.
4. If if is possible to transform the discrete model into the form

$$y(t+n) = F(y(t),y(t+1), \ldots ,y(t+n-1),t)$$

where y also may be a vector, we need not worry about the existence and uniqueness of the solution for $t>t_o$, when initial values $y(t_o),\ldots, y(t_o+n-1)$ are given. And when only certain values of this solution are sought (and not the explicit form of this solution), simple calculation by iteration can give the desired results. For these questions the discrete model is surely the simpler one.

As far as economic convenience is concerned, Allen [1, p. 6] quotes the following points of view:

1. Economic agents think and plan in period terms; for that reason at least microeconomic models should be formulated in discrete time. To this one could say, that some structures which lead to such microeconomic decisions, such as tastes e. g., may change in a continuous way.
2. Real life data come in period form. To this Allen mentions, that this may be only an artificial summing up of a continuous flow of economic variables in order to present statistical tables.
3. If we aggregate a mass of economic agents (as we do in macro-economics) who don't have one and the same period in their plans, a continuous approach might be more appropriate than a discrete one.

When there is no stringent argument for the discrete or for the continuous approach, we could ask how the results may be influenced by the choice of one of them. In this article we investigate some influences of this choice on the stability properties of the equilibrium solution. For this question reasons are given by the above reflections on dynamic models, and it is just the analogous question which is asked and answered by Garcia in his contribution [4] to the controversy between the liquidity preference- and the loanable funds theory of interest. He literally argues [4, p. 542]:

"If the theories are indeed equivalent, then not only should they give the same equilibrium solution, but also they should be stable to the same degree." Here we will compare the stability behavior of simple continuous or discrete dynamic models which can be related in some formal sense.

2. Notation and Definitions

Let f be a real-valued function of time, $f = f(t)$. We then use the following operator-notation (for some $h > 0$):[1)]

I = Identity operator, defined by $If(t) = f(t)$

$E_{+,h}$ = forward-shift operator : $E_{+,h}f(t) = f(t+h)$

$E_{-,h}$ = backward-shift operator: $E_{-,h}f(t) = f(t-h)$

Δ_h = forward-difference operator: $\Delta_h f(t) = f(t+h) - f(t)$

∇_h = backward-difference operator: $\nabla_h f(t) = f(t) - f(t-h)$

D = differentialoperator with respect to time: $Df(t) = \frac{df(t)}{dt}$

Defining as usually the sum of two operators A and B by $(A+B)f = Af + Bf$, the multiplication with a number a by $(aA)f = a(Af)$, and the product of A and B as their composition $(AB)f = A(B(f))$, the following relations between this operators hold:

(1) $$\Delta_h = E_{+,h} - I \quad ; \quad \nabla_h = I - E_{-,h} \quad ; \quad (E_{+,h})^{-1} = E_{-,h}$$

(2) $$D^k = \lim_{h\to 0} \left(\frac{1}{h}\cdot\Delta_h\right)^k = \lim_{h\to 0} \left(\frac{1}{h}\cdot\nabla_h\right)^k \qquad (k \in \mathbb{N})$$

Equation (2) should be applied only on sufficiently often differentiable functions, the convergence of a sequence of operators A_n being taken as: $A_n \to A \overset{}{\underset{\text{Def}}{\Longleftrightarrow}} A_n f(t) \to Af(t)$ for any $f(t)$ (pointwise convergence).

As for our operators the formation of the product is commutative, we further have for $k = o, 1, 2, \ldots$:

1) We don't worry about the domain of these operators: they should be applied only on functions for which they are defined, all relations between operators should be understood in this sense.

$$(3)\quad \begin{aligned} \Delta_h^k &= \sum_{i=0}^{k} \binom{k}{i} (-1)^{k-i} E_{+,h}^i \;; & E_{+,h}^k &= \sum_{i=0}^{k} \binom{k}{i} \Delta_h^i \\ \nabla_h^k &= \sum_{i=0}^{k} \binom{k}{i} (-1)^i E_{-,h}^i \;; & E_{-,h}^k &= \sum_{i=0}^{k} \binom{k}{i} (-1)^i \nabla_h^i \end{aligned}$$

In most cases of models with discrete time it is possible to take h as time unit: h = 1. If nothing other is said, we will use h=1 and omit the subscript h.

A relation of the form

$$(4)\qquad F(t,f(t),Af(t),A^2f(t),\dots,A^nf(t)) = 0$$

is a differential equation of finite order, if A = D, and a difference equation of finite order, if $A \in \{E_+,E_-,\Delta,\nabla\}$.

By means of equations (1) and (3) and with appropriate dating before (application of E_+ to (4)) or back (application of E_- to (4)) a difference equation can always be written in any one of the operators E_+, E_-, Δ, or ∇. The order of a differential equation is given by the exponent of the highest power of the D-operator occuring in it. The order of a difference equation is given by the number of discrete time steps lying between the earliest and the latest date occuring in the equation (see e. g. [5, p. 253]). For this purpose a notation with the shift operators is more convenient than with difference operators: the highest occuring power of the difference operator does not necessarily give the order of the equation. This order can be less than the highest exponent of Δ, as the following proposition - in some extremal case - shows (for a less extremal example see [5, p. 253]):

Proposition 1: If for any $k \geq 1$ we take in the equation

$$\sum_{i=0}^{k} a_i \Delta^i f(t) = 0$$

the coefficients $a_i = \binom{k}{i}$, this equation becomes

$$E_+^k f(t) = f(t+k) = 0,$$

i. e. we have no difference equation of positive order.

<u>Proof:</u> By equation (3) we immediately have

$$\sum_{i=0}^{k} \binom{k}{i} \Delta^i = (\Delta + I)^k = E_+^k .$$

Remark: An analogous proposition can be given for the ∇-operator. The coefficients then must be taken as $a_i = (-1)^i \binom{k}{i}$ to give $E_-^k f(t) = 0$.

Here we will confine our considerations to linear difference- or differential equations. Equation (4) then becomes

$$(5) \qquad \left(\sum_{i=0}^{n} a_i(t) A^i \right) f(t) = b(t)$$

where $A = D$ or - without loss of generality - $A = E_+$.

Further we take the coefficients $a_i(t)$ as constant over time; in Samuelson's classification ([11, p. 315 ff]) this means that we regard only nonhistorical systems. If we take $b(t) = 0$ in (5), we have the corresponding homogeneous equation.

Now we must clarify on which stability concept we shall base our considerations: in the mathematical theory of motions - as well as in economic theory - there are several concepts. Here we shall adopt the most frequently used concept of asymptotic stability: a solution of (5) with given initial conditions is called asymptotically stable, if its difference to any solution with other initial conditions tends to zero for $t \to \infty$. (Limiting ourselves to linear models we need not distinguish between local or global stability.)

The difference of two solutions of the linear model (5) is a solution of the corresponding homogeneous model; therefor stability can generally be investigated by the stability behavior of the trivial solution $f(t) = 0$ of the homogeneous model. This behavior can be studied with the roots of the characteristic polynomial

$$(6) \qquad \sum_{i=0}^{n} a_i x^i = 0 \qquad :$$

- If $A = D$, then a solution of (5) is asymptotically stable if and only if (= iff) the real part of each root of (6) is less than zero;

- if $A = E_+$, then a solution of (5) is asymptotically stable, iff each root of (6) is less than one in absolute value;
- if $A = E_-$, then a solution of (5) is asymptotically stable, iff each root of (6) is greater than one in absolute value, or - using the above mentioned transcription into E_+-notation - iff each root of

(7) $$\sum_{i=0}^{n} a_{n-i}x^i = 0$$

  is less than one in absolute value;
- if $A = \Delta$, then a solution of (5) is asymptotically stable iff each root λ of (6) satisfies the inequality $|1+\lambda| < 1$, that is (6) has only roots in the interior of the circle with centre $\lambda_o = -1$ and radius 1 (in the complex plane) (see also [3, p. 581]);
- if $A = \nabla$, then a solution of (5) is asymptotically stable, iff each root λ of (6) satisfies the inequality $|\lambda-1| > 1$, that is (6) has only roots in the exterior of the circle with centre $\lambda_o = 1$ and radius 1 (in the complex plane) (see also [3, p. 581]).

By means of the Routh-Hurwicz-criterium (see e. g. [2, p. 303][1), 11, p. 430 ff]) we can see, whether or not all roots of a polynomial have real parts less than zero, the Schur-Cohn-conditions [2, p. 247 f] can help to decide, whether or not all roots of a polynomial are less than one in absolute value.

3. "Related" discrete and continuous models

Now we must clarify the question, when we should call a discrete and a continuous model "related". This question can't be answered unambiguously:

A) When coming from a discrete model we could try to construct a

---

1) In Baumol's representation of the Routh-Hurwicz-criterium the general assumption $a_o>0$ is not mentioned (multiplying all coeficients with -1 would leave the roots invariant, but change the signs of some of the determinants), although it is tacitly made by Baumol.

sequence of models with time steps h_j converging to zero. Using the mean value theorem (as is done by Vogt in [14]) or substituting Δ/h_j (resp. ∇/h_j) in the limit-model by the D-operator (see [3, p. 575 f]) then would give a continuous model.

The results to which Vogt [14] comes in the case of the Samuelson-Hicks-model are not very satisfying: the resulting model is not unambiguous (Vogt offers two different continuous models) and has in both cases solutions with typical behavior differing from the discrete model. As we shall see later, they have not even similar stability behavior. (As Vogt mentions in [14, p. 419], in his limit models the behavior of the economic agents has changed essentially, delay structures have got lost.) We don't want to follow this way here.

B) In a second way we could substitute the difference operators (in the discrete model) by the D-operator and vice versa.

This proceeding can be motivated as an approximation of the first derivative Df by the quotient $\frac{f(t+\tau)-f(t)}{\tau}$ for $\tau=1$ (forward difference operator) resp. $\tau=-1$ (backward difference operator). It is used in numerical analysis and we can find also examples in the economic literature: in [7, p. 286 ff] Metzler regards a continuous and a "related" discrete system, where the discrete system is got from the continuous one by substituting the D-operator by Δ.

For the transition from a discrete to a continuous model by means of this method we have the following propositions:

<u>Proposition 2:</u> Let the discrete model $(\sum_{i=0}^{n} a_i E_+^i) f(t) = 0$ lead to the continuous model (C1), when substituting Δ by D. Let for some $0<m<n$ be $a_0 = a_1 = \ldots = a_{m-1} = 0$. (C2) may be the continuous model which we get when substituting Δ by D in the discrete model $(\sum_{i=m}^{n} a_i E_+^{i-m}) f(t) = \sum_{j=0}^{n-m} a_{j+m} E_+^j) f(t) = 0$.

Then (C1) is stable iff (C2) is stable.

Proof: As $E_+ = I+\Delta$, the characteristic polynomial of (C1) is

8) $$0 = \sum_{i=0}^{n} a_i (1+x)^i = \sum_{i=m}^{n} a_i (1+x)^i = (1+x)^m \cdot \sum_{i=m}^{n} a_i (1+x)^{i-m}$$

the characteristic polynomial of (C2) is

9) $$0 = \sum_{i=m}^{n} a_i (1+x)^{i-m}.$$

The roots of (8) are just the roots of (9) plus m-times the root -1, the real part of which is negative. Therefor (C1) is stable if and only if (C2) is stable.

Corollary: Dating before a discrete model has no influence on the stability properties of the continuous model which we get from the discrete model by substituting Δ by D.

Proposition 3: Let the discrete model $(\sum_{i=0}^{n} a_i E_-^i) f(t) = 0$ lead to the continuous model (C) when substituting ∇ by D. Then (C) is stable only if $a_0 \neq 0$.

Proof: Let be $a_0=0$. With $E_- = I-\nabla$ (C) then has the characteristic polynomial

$$0 = \sum_{i=0}^{n} a_i (1-x)^i = (1-x) \cdot \sum_{i=1}^{n} a_i (1-x)^{i-1}$$

having the root $x = 1 > 0$. Thus (C) is unstable.

Here we have:

Corollary: If we date back the discrete model $(\sum_{i=0}^{n} a_i E_-^i) f(t)=0$ and then substitute ∇ by D, the resulting continuous model is unstable.

This influence of a dating back on the stability properties of the related continuous model is surely an unsatisfactory result for method B, when working with the backward difference operator.

C) A third way to come from a discrete to a continuous model is given by the theory of continuous and discrete lags, described e. g. by Allen [1, p. 86 ff][1]. Allen takes the one-period backward lag

(10) $$Y_t = Z_{t-1}$$

as a special case of a geometrically distributed discrete lag; as corresponding to this discrete lag he regards the simple exponential lag (see [1, p. 88]) which is given by

$$Y(t) = \lambda\int_0^\infty e^{-\lambda\tau} Z(t-\tau)d\tau \qquad (\lambda>0),$$

we can transform this equation into

(11) $$DY = \lambda(Z - Y)\ .$$

(see [1, p. 89]; λ = speed of response, $T = \lambda^{-1}$ = time constant of the lag)

If we write (10) as

(12) $$(\Delta + I)Y_t = Z_t$$

and (11) as

(13) $$\frac{1}{\lambda}(D + \lambda I)Y(t) = Z(t)\quad ,$$

we see that this use of lags also justifies the above given method B (as a special case with $\lambda=1$) for the forward difference operator.

For method B with backward difference operator we can also give a formal generalization with continuous lags: we must only take our lags on forthcoming values. The one-period forward lag

(14) $$Y_t = Z_{t+1}$$

can be regarded as a special case of a forward geometrically distributed lag, which has its continuous correspondence in a forward exponentially distributed lag

---

1) Allen is not correct when saying [1, p. 88], that a T-period delay $Y(t)=Z(t-T)$ can be given as a continuously distributed lag with weighting function $w(t) = \begin{cases} 0 & \text{for } t\neq T \\ 1 & \text{for } t=T \end{cases}$; in order to write this delay with help of a weighting "function", this should be Dirac's δ-distribution which is no longer a function.

(15) $$Y(t) = \lambda\int_0^\infty e^{-\lambda\tau} Z(t+\tau)\,d\tau = \lambda e^{\lambda t}\int_t^\infty e^{-\lambda\nu} Z(\nu)\,d\nu$$

From this we get

(16) $$DY = \lambda\left(e^{\lambda t}\cdot\lambda\cdot\int_t^\infty e^{-\lambda\nu} Z(\nu)\,d\nu - (e^{\lambda t}\cdot e^{-\lambda t} Z(t))\right) = \lambda(Y(t) - Z(t))$$

If we write (14) as

(17) $$Z_t = E_- Y_t = (I - \nabla)Y_t$$

and (16) as

(18) $$Z(t) = \frac{1}{\lambda}(\lambda I - D)Y(t)$$

we can see the analogy of method B with backward differences and this method for forward lags with $\lambda=1$.

D) A fourth formal method of relating discrete and continuous models, which is also used in numerical analysis and the idea of which can be found also in Samuelson's Foundations ([11, p. 383, Exercise 7]) can be described in the following way: Expanding f(t+1) in a Taylor series [1)] we get

(19) $$E_+ f(t) = \left(\sum_{k=0}^{\infty} \frac{D^k}{k!}\right) f(t) = e^D f(t)$$

the last equation being understood as a formal exponential function of the operator D defined by the power series.

If we write our discrete equation in the operator E_+ and then substitute this operator by the above power series, we get a differential equation of infinite order, and thus a continuous model, the solutions of which are also solutions of the initial discrete model.[2)3)] We therefor can ask, if the sequence of

1) Here we must assume that the solution of the discrete model, which initially need only be defined as a sequence, must now be an infinitely often differentiable function which satisfies the difference equation in each point.

2) In numerical analysis the reverse way is gone from a continuous model to discrete models by means of the power series for D: $D=\frac{1}{h}\cdot\ln(1+\Delta_h) = \frac{1}{h}\cdot\sum_{k=1}^{\infty} (-1)^{k+1}\cdot\frac{\Delta^k}{K}$

3) A theorem of Shidkov, which can be found without proof in [12, p. 135], says that under certeain strong assumptions for a discrete model of order n there exists a continuous model of order (2n+1), the solutions of which are also solutions of the discrete model. We therefor can hope that in some cases there...

continuous models, which we get by cutting this series after a finite number of terms, will have stability properties which approximate the properties of the initial discrete model the better the greater n.

4. The stability of related models - models of first order

Let us begin with the simplest case of linear models of first order. The discrete model can be written as

(20) $$(E_+ + aI)y_t = y_{t+1} + ay_t = 0 \qquad (a \neq 0)$$

or

$$\Delta y_t + (1+a)y_t = 0$$

resp.

$$(I + aE_-)y_t = ((1+a)I - a\nabla)y_t = 0.$$

Hence by method B we get the related models

(21) $$Dy + (1+a)y = 0$$ (forward difference operator)

(22) $$Dy - (1+a^{-1})y = 0$$ (backward difference operator).

Here we see immediately that

(20) is stable iff $-1 < a < 1$

(21) is stable iff $-1 < a$

(22) is stable iff $1 + \frac{1}{a} < 0$ which is equivalent with $-1 < a < 0$.

Therefor our simple result is:
if the two models are related in the sense of method B by means of the forward difference operator, then stability of the discrete model implies stability of the continuous model, but not vice versa; if they are related by means of the backward difference operator, then stability of the continuous model implies stability of the discrete model, but not vice versa.

As we have seen above, method B can formally be conceived as a special case (for $\lambda=1$) of method C, which gives a transition from

---

... exists a differential equation of finite order having in the discrete points $t=0,1,2,\ldots$ the same solutions as the difference equation.

discrete to continuous models by means of simple exponential lag. Now we may ask, how the last considerations are affected by generalization to method C.

Comparing (12) and (13) or (17) and (18) we see, that formally the transition can be done by substituting the difference operators by $\frac{1}{\lambda}D$. In the most frequently used case of a backward simple exponential lag formally the forward difference operator must be replaced by $\frac{1}{\lambda}D$. Thus we get from (20)

(23) $$Dy + \lambda(1+a)y = 0 \quad .$$

In the case of a simple exponential lag which is directed on future values we formally must replace ∇ by $\frac{1}{\lambda}D$, and then we get from (20)

(24) $$Dy - \lambda(1+\frac{1}{a})y = 0 \; .$$

In both cases we see that the stability behavior is the same for all positive λ, the choice of some specific $\lambda > 0$ can't give or destruct stability. Thus method C leads to the same results as method B.

Until now we have seen, that the transition from a discrete to a continuous model by means of method B with forward difference operator - or method C with backward simple exponential lag - enlarges the domain of parameters, for which the models are stable. We now can ask, if it is possible to exclude from economic considerations that part, for which an originally unstable model becomes a stable one. In this context we quote the following examples:

a) In [1, p. 5] Allen gives the discrete model

(25) $$Y_t - (1-s)Y_{t-1} = A$$

and

(26) $$DY + \lambda sY = \lambda A$$

as related continuous model. (25) being stable iff $0<s<2$ and (26) being stable iff $0<s$, the enlargement of the stability domain ($s\geq 2$) is economically irrelevant: s is from economic reasons always restricted by $0<s<1$. Thus in this case Allen can say, that there is no difference between the discrete and the continuous model.

b) But in the context of the cobweb-theorem Allen [1, p. 81 ff,

p. 100, Exercise 5.4] gives the discrete model

(27) $$P_t + \frac{b}{a}P_{t-1} = \frac{\alpha - \beta}{a} \qquad (a,\ b > 0)$$

and the continuous form

(28) $$-a\cdot DP + \lambda(\alpha - aP - \beta - bP) = 0$$

which can be written as

(29) $$DP + \lambda(1 + \frac{b}{a})P = \frac{\lambda}{a}(\alpha - \beta)$$

(in analogy to our equation (21). Here the discrete model is stable iff $b < a$, whilst the continuous model is always stable and there is no economic reasoning to exclude this enlargement of the stability domain in the parameter space.

After having found this different stability behavior of discrete and related continuous models we now ask, if our method D could give a sequence of continuous models which approximate the stability properties of the discrete model. But already in the case of a discrete linear model of first order the answer is disappointing: (20), which is stable iff $|a| < 1$, would now give with $E_+ = e^D$:

$$(\sum_{i=0}^{\infty} a_i D^i)y(t) = 0 \qquad \text{with } a_i = \begin{cases} 1+a & \text{for } i=0 \\ \frac{1}{i!} & \text{for } i>1 \end{cases}$$

Method D then gives the sequence of models

(30;1) $$Dy + (1+a)y = 0$$

(30;2) $$D^2y + 2!\cdot Dy + 2!(1+a)y = 0$$

(30;3) $$D^3y + 3D^2y + 3\cdot 2\cdot Dy + 3!(1+a)y = 0$$

$\vdots$

(30;m) $$\sum_{i=1}^{m} b_i D^i y + m!(1+a)y = 0 \qquad \text{with } b_i = \frac{m!}{i!}$$

$\vdots$

The stability behavior of these models is given by the following

Proposition 4: For the continuous models (30;i), i=1,2,3,... we have:

(30;1) is stable iff $-1 < a$

(30;2) is stable iff $-1 < a$

(30;3) is stable iff $-1 < a < 2$

(30;4) is stable iff $-1 < a < \frac{1}{2}$
(30;m) is unstable for all $m > 4$.

Proof: (30;1) is the same as (21).

(30;2) is stable iff $2! > 0$ and $(1+a) > 0$ (see [11, p. 431]) that is we have here the same necessary and sufficient condition as in (30;1).

(30;3) is stable iff $3 > 0$; $3\cdot 2 > 0$; $3!(1+a) > 0$; $(3\cdot 6 - 3!(1+a)) > 0$ (see [11, p. 432]) these conditions being equivalent with $-1 < a < 2$.

(30;4) is stable iff

a) $4 > 0$

b) $\begin{vmatrix} 4 & 4\cdot 3\cdot 2 \\ 1 & 4\cdot 3 \end{vmatrix} = 24 > 0$

c) $\begin{vmatrix} 4 & 4\cdot 3\cdot 2 & 0 \\ 1 & 4\cdot 3 & 4!(1+a) \\ 0 & 4 & 4! \end{vmatrix} = 4\cdot 4!(2-4a) > 0$ that is $a < \frac{1}{2}$.

d) $\begin{vmatrix} 4 & 4\cdot 3\cdot 2 & 0 & 0 \\ 1 & 4\cdot 3 & 4!(1+a) & 0 \\ 0 & 4 & 4! & 0 \\ 0 & 1 & 4\cdot 3 & 4!(1+a) \end{vmatrix} > 0$, which with validity of c) gives $a > -1$.

(30;5) can only be stable if

$$\begin{vmatrix} 5 & 5\cdot 4\cdot 3 & 5!(1+a) & 0 \\ 1 & 5\cdot 4 & 5! & 0 \\ 0 & 5 & 5\cdot 4\cdot 3 & 5!(1+a) \\ 0 & 1 & 5\cdot 4 & 5! \end{vmatrix} = 5!\cdot 5\cdot 4\cdot 2\cdot(-8 + 4a - 3a^2) > 0$$

As $h(a) = -8 + 4a - 3a^2$ has its maximum at $a = \frac{2}{3}$ with $h(\frac{2}{3}) = -6\frac{2}{3} < 0$, this necessary condition can't be fulfilled $\Longrightarrow$ (30;5) must be unstable.

(30;m) with $m > 5$ can only be stable if

$$\begin{vmatrix} m & m(m-1)(m-2) & m(m-1)(m-2)(m-3)(m-4) \\ 1 & m(m-1) & m(m-1)(m-2)(m-3) \\ 0 & m & m(m-1)(m-2) \end{vmatrix} =$$

$$= 2m^2(m-1)(m-2)(5-m) > 0,$$

which can't be fulfilled for $m > 5$.

$\Longrightarrow$ (30;m) is unstable for $m > 5$. q. e. d.

5. The stability of related models - models of higher order

We now ask, which of the above results also hold for models of higher order. One of these models - the growth model of Samuelson-Hicks (without autonomous investment) - is considered by Vogt in [14], we therefor sometimes take this model as an example.

The results of Vogt should be taken as an example for method A: The discrete Samuelson-Hicks model can be written as (see [14, p. 411])

(31) $$Y_{t+2} - (c+d)Y_{t+1} + dY_t = 0 \qquad (0<c<1;\ d>0)$$

Vogt offers the two models

(32) $$Dy - \frac{1-c}{d}y = 0 \qquad \text{or}$$

(33) $$D^2y - \frac{1-c}{d}y = 0$$

as possible continuous analogues for (31).

Let us first clarify the stability properties of these models:
Proposition 5: (31) is stable iff $0 < c < 1$; $0 < d < 1$.

Proof: Using Baumol's result ([2, p. 247 f (example)]) we have: (31) is stable iff $(c+d)^2 < (1+d)^2$ and $d^2 < 1$. Both c and d being positive this is equivalent with $0 < c+d < 1+d$ and $d < 1$, that is with $c<1$ and $d<1$.

For the two other models we see immediately: (32) is stable iff $(1-c)/d < 0$ which is not possible for $0<c<1$, $d>0$; (33) is not stable. Thus both models which are proposed by Vogt have no satisfactory stability properties compared with the discrete model. Which results would we get when applying the other methods?

Writing (31) as

$$((I+\Delta)^2 - (c+d)(I+\Delta) + dI)Y_t = 0$$

or as

$$Y_t - (c+d)Y_{t-1} + dY_{t-2} = (I - (c+d)(I-\nabla) + d(I-\nabla)^2)Y_t = 0$$

would by means of method B lead to the two continuous models

(34) $[D^2 + (2 - (c+d))D + (1-c)I]Y(t) = 0$ or

(35) $[dD^2 + (c-d)D + (1-c)I]Y(t) = 0$.

The stability properties of these models can be seen immediately:

Proposition 6: (34) is stable iff $0 < c < 1$ and $d < 2-c$; (35) is stable for $d > 0$ iff $d < c < 1$.

Proof: Use [2, p. 304]: $D^2y + aDy + by = 0$ is stable iff $a > 0$ and $b > 0$.

Our result is therefor similar with that in the case of a first order model: (35) is stable $\Rightarrow$ (31) is stable $\Rightarrow$ (34) is stable; and here there are no economic arguments to exclude those possibilities for c and d, which prevent a conclusion in the other direction.

This result is a special case of the following two propositions:

Proposition 7: Let (D) be the discrete model

$$(\sum_{i=0}^{n} a_i E_+^i) f(t) = 0 \quad .$$

Let (C1) be the continuous model which we get by substituting Δ by D. Then the stability of (D) implies the stability of (C1), but not vice versa.

Proof: (D) can be written as

$$0 = (\sum_{i=0}^{n} a_i (I+\Delta)^i) f(t) = (\sum_{i=0}^{n} b_i \Delta^i) f(t) \ .$$

As noted above (in section 2) (D) is stable iff

(36) $$\sum_{i=0}^{n} b_i x^i = 0$$

has only roots in the interior of the circle with centre -1 and radius 1. By definition of (C1) (36) is also the characteristic polynomial of (C1), and as each point inside that circle has real part less than zero, the stability of (D) implies the stability of (C1).

Proposition 8: Let (D) be the discrete model

$$(\sum_{i=0}^{n} a_i E_-^i) f(t) = 0 \qquad (a_0 \neq 0) \ ;$$

let (C2) be the continuous model which we get by substituting ∇ by D. Then (C2) is stable only if (D) is stable (but not vice versa).

Proof: (D) can be written as

$$0 = (\sum_{i=0}^{n} a_i (I-\nabla)^i) f(t) = (\sum_{i=0}^{n} b_i \nabla^i) f(t) \ .$$

As noted in section 2, (D) is stable iff all roots of

$$(37) \qquad \sum_{i=0}^{n} b_i x^i = 0$$

ly outside the circle with centre 1 and radius 1. As (37) is also the characteristic polynomial of (C2), and as all points with negative real part ly outside that circle, the stability of (C2) implies the stability of (D).

Turning to method C we see in the following proposition (as in the case of a linear model of first order), that the stability properties of the continuous model do not depend on the choice of a special $\lambda > 0$. Therefor the results of method B, which is formally a special case of method C with $\lambda = 1$, remain valid also for method C. We have

Proposition 9: When we construct a continuous model from a discrete one with method C by means of a backward lag with speed of response $\lambda > 0$, then the stability properties of the resulting model are the same for all $\lambda > 0$ (they depend only on the original discrete model).

Proof: The discrete model may be written in the form

$$(\sum_{i=0}^{n} a_i \Delta^i) f(t) = 0$$

then the characteristic polynomial of the continuous model can be written as

(38) $$0 = \sum_{i=0}^{n} a_i \cdot (\frac{1}{\lambda})^i x^i = \sum_{i=0}^{n} a_i (\frac{x}{\lambda})^i .$$

The complex number ξ is a root of this characteristic polynomial iff ξ/λ is a root of

(39) $$\sum_{i=0}^{n} a_i x^i = 0.$$

λ being positive thus we have, that all roots of (38) have negative real parts iff all roots of (39) have negative real parts, where the last equation is independent of λ. Thus the stability properties of the continuous model do not depend on the choice of a special $\lambda > 0$.

In the case of method C with forward lag the corresponding proposition can be proved in the same way.

Method D had brought unsatisfactory results in the case of first-order models. Although we must not exclude that in some special cases of higher order models the results may perhaps be better, we don't trace this method further.

6. The stability of related models - systems of equations

Often economic models link several endogenous variables, and then we get a system of simultaneous equations. Therefor in this section we want to consider briefly the n-dimensional linear model with constant coefficients, which for questions of stability can assumed to be homogeneous. We therefor can write our model in the form

(40) $A\underline{y}(t) = \underline{M}\underline{y}(t)$ where

- $\underline{y}(t)$ is a (n,1)-vector of endogeneous variables
- $A \in \{D, \Delta, E_+, \nabla, E_-\}$, where A should be understood to operate on each component of $\underline{y}$
- $\underline{M}$ is a (n,n)-matrix with constant components.

The results of this section are the same as in the previous one. This does not surprise, because we can write a higher order model

$$(\sum_{i=0}^{n} a_i A^i) f(t) = 0 \qquad (a_n \neq 0)$$

also as the system

$$A\underline{y}(t) = \underline{M}\underline{y}(t)$$

with

$$y(t) = (f(t), Af(t), A^2 f(t), \ldots, A^{n-1} f(t))'$$

and

$$\underline{M} = \begin{pmatrix} 0 & 1 & 0 & \ldots & & 0 \\ 0 & 0 & 1 & 0 & \ldots & 0 \\ & & & 1 & & \\ & & & & \ddots & \\ & & & & & 1 \\ -\frac{a_0}{a_n} & -\frac{a_1}{a_n} & & \ldots\ldots & & -\frac{a_{n-1}}{a_n} \end{pmatrix}$$

The trivial solution $\underline{y}(t) \equiv \underline{0}$ of (40) is asymptotically stable, if any other solution of (40) (with initial condition $\underline{y}(t_0) \neq 0$) tends to zero in each of its components for $t \to \infty$. Necessary and sufficient conditions can be given by means of the eigenvalues of $\underline{M}$:

- If $A = D$, then $\underline{y}(t) = 0$ is asymptotically stable iff each eigenvalue of $\underline{M}$ has negative real part;
- if $A = E_+$, then $\underline{y}(t) = 0$ is asymptotically stable iff each eigenvalue of $\underline{M}$ is less than one in absolute value.

Without loss of generality we take a discrete model written by means of the forward shift operator E_+:

(41) $$E_+\underline{y}(t) = \underline{M}\underline{y}(t) .$$

As we want to apply method B, we must write (41) with difference operators. (41) becomes

(42) $$\Delta\underline{y}(t) = (\underline{M} - \underline{I}_n)\underline{y}(t) \quad ,$$

where $\underline{I}_n$ denotes the (n,n)-unit matrix.

If we want to write (41) with the ∇-operator, we must assume that $\underline{M}$ has an inverse $\underline{M}^{-1}$; then we get

(43) $$\nabla\underline{y}(t) = \underline{y}(t) - \underline{M}^{-1}\underline{y}(t) = (\underline{I}_n - \underline{M}^{-1})\underline{y}(t) .$$

Thus method B leads to the two continuous models

(44) $$D\underline{y}(t) = (\underline{M} - \underline{I}_n)\underline{y}(t)$$

or

(45) $$D\underline{y}(t) = (\underline{I}_n - \underline{M}^{-1})\underline{y}(t) \quad .$$

The stability properties of these models - compared with those of (41) - are given by the following

Proposition 10: If (41) is stable then (44) is stable; and (45) is stable only if (41) is stable. In both cases the reverse does not hold.

Proof: As each vector of $\mathbb{R}^n$ is eigenvector of $\underline{I}_n$ for the eigenvalue 1, we have:

λ is eigenvalue of $\underline{M} \Longleftrightarrow \lambda-1$ is eigenvalue of $\underline{M} - \underline{I}_n$

λ is eigenvalue of $\underline{M} \Longleftrightarrow 1-\lambda^{-1}$ is eigenvalue of $\underline{I}_n - \underline{M}^{-1}$

(provided M^{-1} exists).

Therefor:

(41) is stable iff $|\lambda| < 1$ for each eigenvalue λ of $\underline{M}$

(44) is stable iff $\text{Re}(\lambda-1) = \text{Re}\lambda - 1 < 0$ for each eigenvalue λ of $\underline{M}$

(45) is stable iff $\text{Re}(1-\frac{1}{\lambda}) = 1 - \frac{1}{|\lambda|^2}\text{Re}\lambda < 0$, that is iff

$$\text{Re}\lambda > |\lambda|^2 \text{ for each eigenvalue } \lambda \text{ of } \underline{M}.$$

As we have $\text{Re}\lambda > |\lambda|^2 \Longleftrightarrow (\text{Re}\lambda - \frac{1}{2})^2 + (\text{Im}\lambda)^2 < \frac{1}{4}$, that is λ belongs to the interior of the circle with centre $\frac{1}{2}$ and radius $\frac{1}{2}$, we also have

$$\text{Re}\lambda > |\lambda|^2 \Longrightarrow |\lambda| < 1 \Longrightarrow \text{Re}\lambda < 1 \text{ , that is:}$$

If (45) is stable then (41) is stable, and if (41) is stable then (44) is stable; and the proof has also shown that the reverse does not hold generally.

Thus also in this case we have got the result, that by a transition from a discrete to a related continuous model (or vice versa) we generally can win or loose stability according as this transition is done. Only in special cases - with additional assumptions based on economic reasons - it is possible to get an equivalent stability behavior. One example in this sense can be found in Metzler's article [7, p. 286]: he considers the stability of a continuous system by means of a discrete system, both being related as our models (41) and (44). Without any additional assumption then we only can state, that the stability of (41) implies the stability of (44), and it is an important part of Metzler's article, that for his model of multiple markets the reverse can be shown in those special cases, where all goods are gross substitutes.

Finally let us remark, that for systems of equations method C may give results different from those of method B, if we take lags with different time constants in different equations.

7. Final remarks

We have seen discrete and "related" continuous dynamic models which do not have equivalent stability behavior; we may win or loose stability according as the transition is done. If one seeks arguments for the exchangeability of the discrete and the continuous approach, this result is surely not satisfactory (and an improvement by means of a cut power series for $E_+ = e^D$ seems not to be possible). Only in special cases - with additional assumptions on the parameters - we may get such an equivalence, but there are also cases - e. g. the cobweb-model - where no economic reasons could lead to such additional assumptions.

On the other hand the results could show ways to make an instable model stable. In [13] Tokoyama and Murakami proceed in a way which can be brought in line with this idea:
They take the dynamic Leontief System

$$\underline{B}^{-1}(\underline{I}_n - \underline{A})\underline{X}(t) = \Delta\underline{X}(t) \quad ,$$

which for empirical data turns out to be instable. With some economic arguments they vary this model, formally this change is done by a substitution of Δ by ∇. The new model then has a larger stability zone. Although the authors use a different stability concept (the concept of relative stability), we can find a connection between their article and our results.

References:

[1] Allen, R. G. D.: Macroeconomic Theory
London 1967

[2] Baumol, W. J.: Economic Dynamics. An Introduction
3 rd edition, New York 1970

[3] Folsom, R. N., Boger, D. C., and Mullikin, H. C.: Stability Conditions for Linear Constant Coefficient Difference Equations in Generalized Differenced Form
Econometrica 44, 1976, 575 - 591

[4] Garcia, G.: Olech's Theorem and the Dynamic Stability of Theories of the Rate of Interest
Journal of Economic Theory 4, 1972, 541 - 544

[5] Gelfond, A. O.: Differenzenrechnung
Hochschulbücher für Mathematik Bd. 41
Berlin 1958

[6] Hicks, J. R.: Value and Capital
London 1939

[7] Metzler, L. A.: Stability of Multiple Markets; the Hicks Conditions
Econometrica 13, 1945, 277 - 292

[8] Negishi, T.: The Stability of a Competitive Economy: A Survey Article
Econometrica 30, 1962, 635 - 669

[9] Newman, P. K.: Some Notes on Stability Conditions
Review of Economic Studies 72, 1959, 1 - 9

[10] Rader, T.: Impossibility of Qualitative Economics: Excessively Strong Correspondence Principles in Production-Exchange Economics Zeitschrift für Nationalökonomie 32, 1972, 397 - 416

[11] Samuelson, P. A.: Foundations of Economic Analysis New York 1971

[12] Sibirsky, K. S.: Introduction to Topological Dynamics Leyden 1975

[13] Tokoyama, K. and Murakami, Y.: Relative Stability in Two Types of Dynamic Leontief Models International Economic Review 13, 1972, 408 - 415

[14] Vogt, H.: Grenzübergänge von einem diskreten Wachstumsmodell zu mehreren stetigen Modellen Jahrbücher für Nationalökonomie und Statistik Bd. 189, 1975, 411 - 422

Dynamic Utility and Aggregator Functions for the Allocation of Private Consumption in Input-Output Models; An Econometric Analysis

by Klaus Conrad

1. Introduction

For projections of the levels of output in the sectors of an economy, an econometric analysis of the input structure of the sectors has to be carried out first. For the same reason an econometric analysis of the structural composition of the components of final demand in yearly input-output tables has to precede a projection of the magnitude of these components. Especially the allocation of private consumption as the quantitatively most important part of final demand is of interest. The purpose of the paper is an application of indices for the analysis of the structure of consumer expenditure.

The commonly used procedure in input-output analysis for predicting consumer demand for products of different sectors is to employ consumption functions with disposable income or total consumption expenditure as the only explaining variable. The structure of consumer demand for products of the sectors changes over time; some sectors become more important as supplier of consumption goods (chemistry, services) whereas other sectors become nearly insignificant (coal). Higher income, changes in relative prices and factors like taste and habit are some of the reasons for a changed structural composition of private consumption. For a serious analysis of consumer behavior the price of the sector has to be included in the demand function as well as the prices of substitutable and complementary goods. As private consumption consists of a relatively large number of goods with their corresponding prices, aggregation is necessary in order to reduce the number of parameters to be estimated in an econometric model of consumer behavior. The analysis based on such a model has to start therefore with aggregates and price indices for these aggregates. When the overall model has been developed and demand functions for the aggregates have been estimated, the next step is to formulate submodels for the allocation of the aggregates by using utility functions as an index. However, such an approach has to be carried out in a theoretically consistent framework with a utility function in the aggregates and with sub-utility functions as indices in order to derive demand functions for the components of the aggregates.

The next problem is to set up demand functions for this kind of analysis. First of all, there are countless possibilities of specifying a functional form of these demand functions. Usually a trial and error process starts with estimating a number of possible combinations of specifications and ends with a specification with a satisfactory goodness of fit, usually measured by the highest R^2. Second, we cannot neglect the simultaneous structure of the system of demand functions as otherwise the consumer demand for sectoral products will not add up to private consumption (the "adding up" problem). Furthermore, in ignoring a theoretical deduction of the demand system from the hypothesis of utility maximization there will be no linkage between the system of demand functions and the corresponding preference structure. Therefore additivity, homotheticity and changes of preferences over time can hardly be analysed and statistically tested. Finally, demand functions for the components also have to be based on maximizing behavior which implies special functional forms of the sub-utility functions as indices.

Our investigation of the problem of allocation of private consumption in input-output models is based on the methodology used by Christensen and Jorgenson[1] and Jorgenson and Lau[2]. The characteristic feature of this approach is that at the first stage a system of equilibrium prices of minimal unit-costs is determined. For this purpose Jorgenson et.al. (1973) carry out an econometric analysis of the structure of production in each sector and derive cost-minimizing demand functions for intermediate and

[1]See chapter 4 in Jorgenson et al.(1973).

[2]This methodology has been developed by Jorgenson and Lau and is described in Jorgenson and Lau (1975a, 1975c).

primary inputs. In estimating the cost-minimizing input coefficients as functions of the prices of the sectors, estimated parameters of the unit-cost function can be obtained. The output price of each sector is a function of all input prices and by predicting the prices of primary inputs the solution of the simultaneous system of n equations in n sectoral prices results in a price system for the year under consideration. This system of cost-minimizing prices can be employed at the second stage of the analysis for the allocation of private consumption by means of a system of price-dependent demand functions derived from utility functions as indices.

The model by Christensen and Jorgenson (1973) is based on the characterization of the preferences by an indirect utility function in the prices as arguments. Due to Roy's identity this approach permits to derive immediately the utility maximizing quantities as functions of the prices and total expenditure. The functional form of these demand functions depend on the spezification of the indirect utility function.

The Christensen-Jorgenson model is based, however, on a static system of demand functions consistent with utility maximization of a static utility function. For periods of high price increase and for "habit forming" goods dynamic demand systems replace the static approach. Individual's current preferences depend on their past consumption pattern so that lagged variables will influence current demand. Due to the "remanence" of the consumer's behavior relative price changes will lead to "hysteresis"-like demand functions, that is the demand for a good is not an unique function of its price. The same relative price observed in two different time periods usually implies two different levels of demand for that good. This problem of irreversible demand functions is caused by habit persistence and the influence of lagged values of some of the variables involved[1]. Nowadays using lagged variables in demand functions is a standard routine whereas the problem of consistency of the dynamic demand functions with utility maximization is often ignored by econometricians.

---

1 See Brown (1952) on habit persistence and Farell (1952) on irreversible demand functions.

As the reaction of the consumer on changes in prices and income does not occur immediately but instead will influence the preference structure of the consumer gradually, dynamic utility functions and dynamic demand systems derived from utility maximization have been considered. Different aspects of this problem have been analysed theoretically by Gorman (1967), von Weizsäcker (1971) and Lluch (1974). Approaches to habit formation which are of theoretical and empirical interest are characterized however by an explicit specification of a dynamic utility function and a dynamic demand system derived from the corresponding utility function. Two approaches can be chosen- a dynamic direct utility function in the quantities as arguments and a dynamic indirect utility function in the prices as arguments. As functional forms of a dynamic direct utility function a Cobb-Douglas utility function (Peston (1967)) has been used, the Klein-Rubin utility function in several versions (Pollak and Wales (1969), Pollak (1970), Phlips (1972) and Krelle (1975)) and a quadratic utility function in the quantities of the current and the previous period (Krelle (1972)). As a functional form of a dynamic indirect utility function the "translog" representation[1] in the logarithms of prices and lagged quantities will be employed here[2]. Using "Roy's identity" we will obtain a system of dynamic demand functions giving the quantities consumed as functions of the prices, total expenditure and lagged variables.

After the derivation and estimation of the demand functions for the aggregates the allocation of the expenditures on the aggregates have to be carried out. This is done by employing sub-utility functions as price indices. In estimating the corresponding demand functions we will obtain price indices of the aggregates for the overall model of consumer behavior.

---

1 The translog representation of an utility function has been introduced by Christensen, Jorgenson and Lau (1975).

2 See also Conrad (1976).

2. Dynamic Direct and Indirect Utility Functions

To take into consideration the fact that choices depend on tastes and tastes on past behavior we consider a consumer whose direct utility function,

(1) $U = U(x; s,t) = U(x_1,\ldots,x_n; s_1,\ldots,s_n t).$

depends on the commodities x_j $(j=1,\ldots,n)$ consumed and a set of state variables s_j $(j=1,\ldots,n)$ representing stocks of habits of the corresponding goods x_j. The variable t is time and is a catch-all for changes in the distribution of income, the introduction of new products and changes of preferences over time. We assume that the utility function is twice differentiable in (x,s,t) and increasing and quasiconcave in x, in a domain X x S x T in the (x,s,t) space. At each time, given the state of habits, the consumer maximizes utility, subject to the budget constraint,

$$\sum_j p_j x_j = M \tag{2}$$

where p_j $(j=1,\ldots,n)$ are the prices of the goods, M is the value of total expenditure and $P/_M = (p_{1/M},\ldots,p_{n/M})$ is the vector of "real" prices. Nesessary conditions for an optimum consist of (2) and:

$$\frac{\partial U}{\partial x_j} - \lambda(p_{j/M}) = 0 \qquad j = 1,\ldots,n \tag{3}$$

where λ is the Lagrange multiplier. The system (2) and (3) may be solved to give the dynamic demand functions:

$$x_j = f_j\,(P/_M;s,t)\ , \quad j = 1,\ldots,n\ . \tag{4}$$

By direct substitution of (4) into the utility function (1) we obtain the dynamic indirect utility function:

(5) $V\,(P/_M;s,t) = V(p_{1/M},\ldots,p_{n/M};\ s_1,\ldots,s_n,t).$

$V(P/_M;s,t)$ is strictly decreasing and convex in $P/_M$ and gives the value of the maximized utility for specified values of the real prices, given the state of habit and the validity of the budget constraint. Finally, it can be shown that:

$$(6)\quad \min_{P/M,\ \lambda} [V(P/M;\ s,\ t) - \lambda(\ \Sigma\ P_j/M\ x_j - 1)] = U(x;\ s,\ t),$$

that is, the dual to the dual is the primal[1]. The state variables and time play a passive role in the dual transformation relations and do not influence the theorems on duality.

Instead of solving (2) and (3), if possible, to obtain the quantities demanded as function of the prices, state variables and time, we employ Roy's Identity. With the state variables and time as passive variables Roy's Identity is as follows[2]:

$$(7)\quad x_j = \frac{\dfrac{\partial V(P/M;\ s,\ t)}{\partial P_j/M}}{\sum_{i=1}^{n} P_j/M\ \dfrac{\partial V(P/M;\ s,\ t)}{\partial P_i/M}}\quad ,\ j = 1,\ 2,\ \ldots,\ n\ .$$

Given the state of habit, the two approaches , that is the dynamic direct utility approach in the commodity space and the dynamic indirect utility approach in the price space, are dual characterizations of the same preference structure.

We next turn to a specific form of the habit formation variables s_j and assume:

$$(8)\quad s_{jt} = \sum_{\tau=0}^{\infty} (1 - \delta)^{\tau}\ x_{j,t-\tau-1} \qquad (0<\delta\leq 1).$$

with a geometric decline of "memory"[3]. For econometric implementa-

---

1 For a discussion of duality see Roy (1942), Lau (1969), Diewert (1974a, 1974b) and Jorgenson and Lau (1975b).

2 See Lau (1969) for Roy's Identity in real prices.

3 See Pollak (1970)and Krelle (1975).

tion we have to assume a rate of memory loss of $\delta = 1$ for each good:

(9) $$s_{jt} = x_{j,t-1} \qquad (j=1,\ldots,n) \quad .$$

The stock of habits for each good is given by the consumption of this good in the previous period but consumption in the more distant past does not influence current preferences and demand.

3. Dynamic Indirect Translog Utility Functions

For the empirical analysis of the structure of consumer expenditures in input-output tables we begin with a direct utility function in thirteen commodity groups delivered by the sectors to private consumption:

(10) $$U = U(x_1,x_2,\ldots,x_{13};\ s_1,s_2,\ldots,s_{13},\ t) \quad .$$

We employ the classification in the yearly input-output tables compiled by the DIW[1] ; the sectors are:

1 - coal
2 - electric utilities
3 - gas utilities
4 - petroleum refining
5 - chemicals
6 - iron and steel
7 - maschinery
8 - electrical maschinery
9 - traffic
10- agriculture
11- food
12- woods products
13- trade and services[2] .

To reduce the number of variables, we first construct sub-utility functions, category functions or group indices. In the framework of a concept developed by Strotz (1957) in terms of an utility tree we assume that the utility function in (10) is weakly separable in the following category functions:

---

1 See Krengel et. al. (1972).

2 We are grateful to Mr. G.Friede for providing us with data of the disaggregated energy sector.

$$(11)\quad U = U(U_1(x_1,\ldots,x_4),\ U_2(x_5,\ldots,x_9),\ U_3(x_{10},\ldots,x_{13}),\ s_E,s_A,s_B,t)$$

Utility therefore depends on the sub-utilities as branches of the utility tree. The state variables s_E, s_A, s_B refer to the habits concerning the categories which do not incude state variables or time. The commodities of U_1 consist of the four types of energy, the commodities of U_2 consist of products of the sectors chemicals (no.5),iron and steel (no.6),maschinery (no.7) etc., or short "consumer durables", and the commodities of U_3 of non-durable goods like agriculture (no.10), food (no.11) and so on. This assumption implies that the consumer first allocates his income to budget groups like energy, durables and non-durables and in a second stage he carries out an optimal allocation within the category budget without taking into consideration goods of other categories. The state variables s_E, s_A, s_B refer to the three aggregates and we do not claim them to be aggregator functions of the corresponding s_j $(j=1,\ldots,13)$.

For deriving utility-maximizing demand functions we prefer the corresponding indirect utility function:

$$(12)\quad V=V(V_1(p_1/M,\ldots,p_4/M),V_2(p_5/M,\ldots,p_9/M),V_3(p_{10}/M,\ldots,p_{13}/M),\ s_E,s_A,s_B,t)$$

where the sub-utility functions V_i $(i=1,2,3)$ are price indices. In general, however, the weak separability in the direct form does not imply the weak separability in the indirect form. But if we postulate that the weakly separable direct utility function has homothetic category functions, then the indirect form (12) is also weakly separable in the same partitioning[1]. If, on the other hand, the direct and indirect utility functions are weakly separable then each category function has to be homothetic. An indirect utility function is aggregate-wise weakly separable,

---

[1] For a proof see Lau (1969), p. 385.

if the ratio of the budget shares of any two commodities within the aggregate is independent of the prices outside the aggregate[1]. A sub-utility function or category function is homothetic if the budget shares of commodities within the group are independent of total expenditure on the group depending only on the prices of commodities that make up the group. For instance, the four types of energy make up a separable and homothetic aggregate if the ratio of the budget shares of any two types of energy depends only on the prices of energy and not on the prices of non-energy commodities. Second, the allocation of expenditure on energy among individual types of energy depends on the prices of all four types of energy, but is independent of total expenditure on energy; all commodities have constant energy outlay elasticities of one. If we therefore want to employ theoretically consistent price aggregator functions $V_i (i=1,2,3)$ for the allocation of private consumption we have to put up with homothetic sub-utility functions (of course, the utility functions U or V must not be homothetic. Therefore, the price for an empirical analysis on a theoretically well-founded base is high and might be too high for some economists. We will come later to the aggregator functions and define for the time being:

$$
\begin{aligned}
P_{E/M} &= V_1(p_{1/M},\ldots,p_{4/M}) \\
P_{A/M} &= V_2(p_{5/M},\ldots,p_{9/M}) \qquad (13)\\
P_{B/M} &= V_3(p_{10/M},\ldots,p_{13/M})
\end{aligned}
$$

For the study of the effect of changes in real prices, consumption expenditure and changes in preferences over time on the allocation of private consumption we begin the first stage of our analysis with the overall model:

$$(14) \quad V = V(P_{E/M}, P_{A/M}, P_{B/M}, s_E, s_A, s_B, t).$$

subject to the budget constraint:

$$P_{E/M} \cdot X_E + P_{A/M} \cdot X_A + P_{B/M} \cdot X_B = 1$$

---

[1] For further definitions and for tests of separability see Jorgenson and Lau (1975a).

where X_E is the energy aggregate, X_A is the consumers durables aggregate and X_B is the non-durables aggregate. Given the state of habits we obtain from Roy's Identity the utility maximizing demand functions. We next transform the indirect utility function (14) logarithmically and consider the following dynamic indirect utility function:

$$(15) \quad \ln V = \ln V\,({}^{P_E}/_M,\ {}^{P_A}/_M,\ {}^{P_B}/_M,\ s_E,\ s_A,\ s_B,\ t)\ .$$

The equivalent version of Roy's Identity is as follows:

$$(16) \quad x_j = \frac{\dfrac{\partial}{\partial \ln P_j/_M} \ln V\,({}^{P_E}/_M, \ldots, s_B, t)}{P_{j/M} \sum\limits_i^3 \dfrac{\partial}{\partial \ln P_i/_M} \ln V\,({}^{P_E}/_M, \ldots, s_B, t)}$$

$j = E,A,B.$

We choose as a special functional form for the dynamic indirect utility function the translog representation introduced by Christensen, Jorgenson and Lau (1975) which provides a local second-order Taylor approximation to any twice differentiable dynamic indirect utility function[1]. This function is here quadratic in the logarithms of the real prices, the state variables and of time t:

$$(17) \quad \begin{aligned} \ln V &= \alpha_o + a^T \ln {}^P/M + a_S^T \ln s + \alpha_t \cdot t \\ &+ \frac{1}{2} (\ln {}^P/M,\ \ln s, t)^T \begin{pmatrix} B & C & b \\ C^T & B^S & c \\ b^T & c^T & \beta_{tt} \end{pmatrix} \begin{pmatrix} \ln {}^P/M \\ \ln s \\ t \end{pmatrix}, \end{aligned}$$

[1] See Diewert (1974a) for further examples of indirect utility functions.

where the unknown parameters of the matrices B, C and B^s, of the vectors α, α_s, b, c, and the parameters α_t and β_{tt} can be identified with the values of the partial derivatives of the first and second order of the dynamic indirect utility function (15) at the point of approximation $(P/_M{}^T, s^T, t) = (u^T, u^T, o)$ where $u^T = (1,1,1)$. Employing the utility function (17) we obtain the system of dynamic translog demand functions in terms of the budget shares:

$$(18)\quad \frac{P_j X_j}{M} = \frac{\alpha_j + \sum_i \beta_{ji} \ln {}^{P_i}/_M + \sum_i \gamma_{ji} \ln s_i + \beta_{jt} \cdot t}{\alpha_M + \sum_i \beta_{Mi} \ln {}^{P_i}/_M + \sum_i \gamma_{Mi} \ln s_i + \beta_{Mt} \cdot t}$$

$$j = E, A, B.$$

with the simplified notation

$$(19)\quad \begin{aligned} \alpha_M &= \sum_{k=1}^{3} \alpha_k \;, & \beta_{Mi} &= \sum_k \beta_{ki} \\ \gamma_{Mi} &= \sum_k \gamma_{ki} \;, & \beta_{Mt} &= \sum_k \beta_{kt} \;. \end{aligned}$$

As we can make a normalisation on the parameters without affecting the budget shares we choose

$$(20)\quad \sum_K \alpha_K = \alpha_M = -1.$$

For econometric implementation the specification of the state variables s_i is as mentioned above: $s_i = X_i\,(-1)$, $i = E, A, B$.

We estimate this system of demand functions. To ensure consistency of this system with maximization of utility we have to impose a set of parameter restrictions[1]. First, there is the adding-up condition; that is, the sum of the budget shares is equal to

[1] See Jorgenson and Lau (1975b).

unity. As the estimated parameters in the fitted equations for the budget shares will not in general satisfy the parameter relations of the theoretical model, we have to postulate that the parameters in the denominator β_{Mi}, γ_{Mi}, β_{Mt} are the same for all equations. If this is the case, the parameter relations in (19) are necessary and sufficient conditions for the adding-up property. Furthermore we have to observe integrability conditions to ensure consistency of our system of demand functions with utility maximization. For the translog demand system symmetry of the matrix B, $\beta_{ij} = \beta_{ji}$, ensures this consistency. These conditions result from the symmetry of the matrix of compensated own-and cross-price substitution effects and provide a link between the equations for the budget shares and the utility function. We observe that the paraments in B^s, c and the parameter α_t and β_{tt} have no effect on the budget shares and cannot be identified by econometric estimation.

We assume that the deviation of the budget shares from their functional forms in (18) results from disturbances on the utility maximizing behavior and impose the following parameter restrictions:

the parameters in the denominator of each equation in (18),

(21) $\{\beta_{M1}, \beta_{M2}, \beta_{M3}, \gamma_{M1}, \gamma_{M2}, \gamma_{M3}, \beta_{Mt}\}$, are the same.

(22) $\beta_{ij} = \beta_{ji}$ (i,j = 1,2,3) .

To reduce the number of parameters in (18) we assume the indirect utility function V to be group-wise homogeneous of degree r in the state variables s_j (j = 1,2,3). This implies:

$$\sum_K \frac{\partial \ln V}{\partial \ln s_K} = r$$

and by differentiating partially with respect to the logarithms of the real prices we obtain:

$$\sum_k \frac{\partial^2 \ln V}{\partial \ln p_{i/M}\,\partial \ln s_k} = 0 \quad \text{or} \quad \sum_k \frac{\partial^2 \ln V}{\partial \ln s_k\,\partial \ln p_{i/M}} = 0 \qquad i = 1,2,3.$$

Is ln V the translog utility function given in (17), these sums of partial derivatives imply the following parameter restrictions:

$$(23) \quad \beta_{jM} = 0 \qquad \beta^{j}_{MM} = 0, \qquad j = 1,2,\ldots,n.$$

Under these parameter restrictions the translog system in (18) is homogeneous of degree zero in the state variables.

For econometric estimation we add to each of the three equations an error term. As the budget shares sum to unity, these error terms are not distributed independently but sum to zero in each year. This implies that the variance-covariance matrix is singular. We therefore drop the last equation and compute the parameters of this equation from the parameter restrictions (19) to (23). With the parameter restrictions given in (20) to (23) and the assumption (9) on the state variable we obtain the following system of dynamic demand functions:

$$(24) \quad \frac{P_E X_E}{M} = [\alpha_E + \beta_{EE} \ln P_{E/M} + \beta_{EA} \ln P_{A/M} + \beta_{EB} \ln P_{B/M} + \gamma_{EE} \ln X_E(-1) + \gamma_{EA} \ln X_A(-1) + \gamma_{EB} \ln X_B(-1) + \beta_{Bt}\cdot t] / (-1 + \beta_{ME} \ln P_{E/M} + \beta_{MA} \ln P_{A/M} + \beta_{MB} \ln P_{B/M} + \beta_{Mt}\cdot t)$$

$$(25) \quad \frac{P_A X_A}{M} = [\alpha_A + \beta_{EA} \ln P_{E/M} + \beta_{AA} \ln P_{A/M} + \beta_{AB} \ln P_{B/M} + \gamma_{AE} \ln X_E(-1) + \gamma_{AA} \ln X_A(-1) + \gamma_{AB} \ln X_B(-1) + \beta_{At}\cdot t] / (-1 + \beta_{ME} \ln P_{E/M} + \beta_{MA} \ln P_{A/M} + \beta_{MB} \ln P_{B/M} + \beta_{Mt}\cdot t)$$

For the estimation we use annual time series data for private consumption expenditures on the three aggregates E, A and B in per capita terms and price indices $P_{E/M}$, $P_{A/M}$, and $P_{B/M}$, computed from the yearly input-output tables in current and constant prices.

This terminates the first stage in our model for the allocation of private consumption. We next turn to the sub-models for the aggregates.

4. Models of Aggregations and Sub-Utility Functions

For the construction of sub-models for the allocation of the category expenditures we have to derive demand functions for the components of the aggregates from the price aggregator functions. We consider three approaches:

1. a model with a static formula for the price indices P_E, P_A, P_B ,[1]
2. a model with expenditures minimizing price indices P_E, P_A, P_B ,
3. a model with a dynamic formula for the price indices P_E, P_A, P_B .[2]

We start with the derivation of explicit formulas for the static price index function by defining for each price aggregate an indirect utility function in the ratios of prices of the goods of the aggregate to the expenditure for the aggregate. For this purpose we first consider the homothetic direct utility function in the quantities, say, of the energy aggregate:

$$X_E = U_1(E_1,\dots,E_4) = F(U_1^*(E_1,\dots,E_4)) \quad (26)$$

where $U_1^* = F^{-1}(X_E)$ is homogeneous of degree one. For homothetic utility functions the demand functions can be

[1] See Jorgenson et al. (1973), chapter 4.

[2] See Jorgenson and Lau (1975a,c).

written as:[1]

(27) $E_i = M_E \cdot f_i(p_1,\ldots,p_4) = M_E \cdot f_i(p)$,

where M_E is expenditure on all forms of energy and f_i is homogeneous of degree -1. Substituting (27) into (26) we obtain because of U_1^* linear homogeneous:

(28) $F^{-1}(X_E) = M_E \cdot U_1^*(f_i(p),\ldots,f_4(p)) = M_E \cdot W_1^*(p)$

where $W_1^*(P)$ is the corresponding indirect utility function which is homogeneous of degree -1.[2] Finally,

(29) $F^{-1}\ (\frac{1}{P_E}) = W_1^*(p)$

because of $F^{-1}(X_E)$ homogeneous of degree 1 and $M_E = X_E \cdot P_E\ (p_1,\ldots,p_4)$ where P_E is the price index for energy.

We first show that the reciprocal indirect utility function[3] of $W_1^*(p/M)$ is the homothetic aggregator function introduced in (13)[4]. We multiply both sides of (29) by M and obtain because of the homogeneity of degree one for F^{-1} and degree minus one for W_1^* :

(30)
$$F^{-1}\ (M/_{P_E}) = W_1^*\ (p/_M) \quad \text{or}$$
$$M/_{P_E} = F(W_1^*(p/_M)) = W_1(p_{/M})$$

and finally :

(31) $P_{E/_M} = W_1(p/_M)^{-1} = V_1(p_{1/_M},\ldots,p_{4/_M})$,

which is the homothetic sub-utility function introduced in (13).

---

[1] See Lau (1969), p.394.

[2] See Lau (1969), p. 376.

[3] See Diewert (1974a), p.126 for the concept of an reciprocal indirect utility function

[4] $p/_M = (p_{1/_M},\ldots,p_{4/_M})$.

Whereas in the overall model preferences have been characterized by an indirect utility function, the sub-utility functions turn out to be reciprocal indirect utility functions.

For a model of allocating energy expenditures among different forms of energy, we multiply (29) by M_E and obtain the indirect utility function for the energy aggregate W_1 in the real energy prices:

$$\frac{M_E}{P_E} = F(W_1^*(p_{1/M_E},\ldots,p_{4/M_E})) = W_1(p/_{M_E}) .$$

The indirect utility function W_1 in $p/_{M_E}$ gives the maximum of utility by deflating energy expenditures by the energy price. The reciprocal indirect utility function is:

$$(32) \quad \frac{P_E}{M_E} = W_1(p/_{M_E})^{-1} = V_1(p/_{M_E}) = V_1(p_{1/M_E},\ldots,p_{4/M_E}) .$$

We note that V_1 is positive homothetic as W_1 is negative homothetic. By using the definition

$$W_1(^{p/}M_E) := \underset{E_1,\ldots,E_4}{\mathrm{Max}} \{U_1(E_1,\ldots,E_4) \mid \sum_i \frac{p_i}{M_E} E_i = 1\} ,$$

$V_1(P/_{M_E})$ can be derived from U_1:

$$(33) \quad V_1(p/_{M_E}) := 1/ [\underset{E_1,\ldots,E_4}{\mathrm{Max}} \{U_1(E_1,\ldots,E_4) \mid \Sigma \frac{p_i}{M_E} E_i = 1\}]$$

$$= \underset{E_1,\ldots,E_4}{\min} \{\frac{1}{U_1(E_1,\ldots,E_4)} \mid \Sigma \frac{p_i}{M_E} E_i = 1\} .$$

Conversely, one can derive the direct utility function U_1 from V_1 by using the definition:[1]

$$(34) \quad U_1(E_1,\ldots,E_4) := \underset{p/_{M_E}}{\min} \{W_1(^{p}/M_E) \mid \Sigma \frac{p_i}{M_E} E_i = 1\}$$

$$= \underset{p/_{M_E}}{\min} \{\frac{1}{V_1(p/_{M_E})} \mid \Sigma \frac{p_i}{M_E} E_i = 1\}.$$

[1]See Diewert (1974a), p. 126 for the symmetry of U_1 and V_1 in (33) and (34).

To derive utility maximizing demand functions for the energy products we employ the modified version of Roy's Identity for the reciprocal indirect utility function $V_1 = W_1^{-1}$:[1]

$$(35)\quad \frac{p_j E_j}{M_E} = \frac{\frac{\partial}{\partial \ln p_j/M_E} \ln V_1(p/_{M_E})}{\sum_i \frac{\partial}{\partial \ln p_i/M_E} \ln V_1\ (p/_{M_E})} \qquad j = 1,\dots,4.$$

As the preferences are homothetic, we can write the reciprocal indirect utility function as

$$(36)\quad \ln V_1 = F\ (\ln V_1^*\ (p/_{M_E}))$$

where V_1^* is homogeneous of degree one in the real prices. By differentiating (36) partially with respect to the logarithm of the real price:

$$\frac{\partial \ln V_1}{\partial \ln \frac{p_j}{M_E}} = \frac{dF}{d\ln V_1^*} \frac{\partial \ln V_1^*}{\partial \ln \frac{p_j}{M_E}}, \qquad j = 1,\dots,4.$$

and by summing over j we obtain due to the linear homogeneity of V_1^*:

$$\sum_j \frac{\partial \ln V_1}{\partial \ln \frac{p_j}{M_E}} = \frac{dF}{d\ln V_1^*} .$$

Therefore Roy's Identity (35) in terms of the budget shares becomes:

$$(37)\quad \frac{p_j E_j}{M_E} = \frac{\partial \ln V_1^*(p/_{M_E})}{\partial \ln p_j/_{M_E}} = g_j\ (p_1,\dots,p_4)$$

that is the equations for the budget shares are independent of energy expenditures. As V_1 is homothetic, the demand functions are homogeneous of degree minus one in the real prices and

[1] See Diewert (1974a), p. 126.

therefore the budget shares are homogeneous of degree zero.

We choose again a translog approximation to the function of the aggregate energy price $P_{E/M_E} = V_1(p/_{M_E})$. Under homothetic preferences the reciprocal indirect translog utility function as an index is:

$$(38) \qquad \ln V_1^* = \alpha_o + \sum_j \alpha_j \ln \frac{p_j}{M_E} + \frac{1}{2} \sum_{i,j} \beta_{ij} \ln \frac{p_i}{M_E} \ln \frac{p_j}{M_E} \ .$$

As V_1^* is linear homogeneous, we obtain:

$$(39) \quad \sum_j \frac{\partial \ln V_1^*}{\partial \ln p_{j/M_E}} = 1, \qquad (40) \quad \sum_j \frac{\partial^2 \ln V_1^*}{\partial \ln p_{i/M_E} \, \partial \ln p_{j/M_E}} = 0$$

implying the parameter restrictions:

$$(41) \quad \begin{array}{l} \sum_j \alpha_j = 1 \\ \sum_j \beta_{ij} = 0 \end{array} \quad , \ i = 1,\ldots,4.$$

Furthermore, as we can change the order of differentiation in (40), that is, due to the symmetry $\beta_{ij} = \beta_{ji}$, we obtain:

$$(42) \quad \sum_j \beta_{ji} = \beta_{Mi} = 0 \ , \quad i = 1,\ldots,4.$$

Under the parameter restrictions (41) and (42) the utility function (38) can be written as:

$$(43) \quad \ln V_1^* = \alpha_o + \sum_j \alpha_j \ln p_j + \frac{1}{2} \sum_{i,j} \beta_{ij} \ln p_i \ln p_j - \ln M_E,$$

which results because of $\ln P_{E/M_E} = \ln V_1^*$ in the aggregator function for the energy price:

$$(44) \quad \ln P_E = \alpha_o + \Sigma \alpha_j \ln p_j + \frac{1}{2} \sum_{i,j} \beta_{ij} \ln p_i \ln p_j .$$

From (37) we obtain the equations for the budget shares:

$$(45) \quad \frac{p_j E_j}{M_E} = \alpha_j + \sum_i \beta_{ji} \ln p_i \ , \qquad j = 1,\ldots,4.$$

By estimating the parameters of the budget shares we end up with an estimated price function as well. We take the base period for the energy price index P_E and the prices of individual types of energy to be the same ($p_{1962} = 1$) so that the parameter α_o is equal to zero. Similar formulas can be derived for price indices P_A for durables and P_B for non-durables as functions of the prices of commodities in each group.

This approach by Christensen and Jorgenson[1] to employ the trans-log utility function as an index of the energy price is based on a static approach. The reason for that is that in implementing the overall model in the aggregate prices they employ Divisia index numbers and consider their translog representation to be an approximation to a Divisia index. This type of index number implies that aggregator functions are independent of time. By differentiating $\ln P_{E/M_E} = \ln P^*(p_{1/M_E}, \ldots, p_{4/M_E}, t)$, P^* linear homogeneous, totally with respect to time we obtain:

$$\frac{d\ln P_{E/M_E}}{dt} = \sum_{j=1}^{4} \frac{\partial \ln P^*}{\partial \ln p_j/M_E} \frac{d \ln p_j/M_E}{dt} + \frac{\partial \ln P^*}{\partial t},$$

or because of (37),

$$\frac{\dot{P}_{E/M_E}}{P_{E/M_E}} - \sum_{j=1}^{4} \frac{p_j E_j}{M_E} \frac{\dot{p}_j/M_E}{p_j/M_E} = \frac{\partial \ln P^*}{\partial t}.$$

implying $\frac{\partial \ln P}{\partial} = o$ for a Divisia index.

A second and equivalent approach to the aggregation problem consists in formulating an aggregate expenditure or cost minimizing problem and making use of the duality in the theory of cost and production. Under homotheticity Roy's Identity in (37) and Shephard's Lemma[2] coincide. With the linear homogeneous and concave aggregator function U_1^* the problem is as follows:

---

[1] See Jorgenson et al. (1973), chapter 4.

[2] See Shephard (1953, 1970).

$$\underset{E_1,\ldots,E_4}{\mathrm{Min}} \{\sum_i \frac{p_i}{M_E} E_i \mid X_E = U_1^* (E_1,\ldots,E_4)\}$$

The corresponding cost (or expenditure) function $C_1(X_E; p_1/M_E,\ldots, p_4/M)$ gives the minimal costs for the composition of X_E. Due to the linear homogeneity of U_1^* we can factor[1]:

$$C_1(X_E; p_{1/M_E},\ldots,p_{4/M_E}) = X_E \cdot V_1^* (p_{1/M_E},\ldots,p_{4/M_E})$$

where V_1^* is a linear homogeneous unit cost function. From Shephard's Lemma we obtain the expenditures minimizing demand functions:

$$E_j = X_E \frac{\partial V_1^*}{\partial p_{j/M_E}} \qquad \text{or, equivalent,}$$

(46) $$\frac{p_j E_j}{M_E} = X_E \cdot V_1^* \cdot \frac{\partial \ln V_1^*}{\partial \ln p_{j/M_E}} = \frac{\partial \ln V_1^*}{\partial \ln p_{j/M_E}}, \quad j = 1,\ldots,4$$

because of $X_E \cdot V_1^* (p_{1/M_E},\ldots,p_{4/M_E}) = 1$ by summing (46) over j. Therefore, the price aggregator function is:

(47) $$P_{E/M_E} = V_1^* (p_{1/M_E},\ldots,p_{4/M_E}).$$

The translog representation of V_1^* is:

(48) $$\ln \frac{P_E}{M_E} = \alpha_o + \sum_i \alpha_i \ln \frac{p_i}{M_E} + \frac{1}{2} \sum_{i,j} \beta_{ij} \ln \frac{p_i}{M_E} \ln \frac{p_j}{M_E}$$

subject to

(49) $$\Sigma\alpha_i = 1, \ \beta_{ij} = \beta_{ji}, \text{ und } \sum_j \beta_{ij} = 0 \text{ für } i = 1,\ldots,4.$$

In this case we obtain the unknown parameters of the aggregator function by estimating the cost-minimizing aggregate shares (46):

(50) $$\frac{p_j E_j}{M_E} = \alpha_j + \sum_i \beta_{ji} \ln \frac{p_i}{M_E} = \alpha_j + \sum_i \beta_{ji} \ln p_i, \quad j = 1,\ldots,4.$$

---

[1] See Diewert (1974b), p. 111.

A translog approximation to the unit cost or expenditure function results in the same system of equations to be estimated and in the same aggregator function for P_E as derived above from the homothetic reciprocal indirect utility approach.

We finally turn to the dynamic approach of an aggregator function. In this alternative approach the aggregates are given as explicit functions of their components rather than index numbers and time t will be an additional variable. In calculating an aggregate price index we take into consideration the effect of changing preferences for the commodities of the aggregate and use a model with a dynamic price aggregator function. To design such a model we measure the prices of the types of energy in utility- effective units by multiplying the real prices with price-augmenting or diminishing factors $a_i(t)$, which are functions of time[1]. Under this characterization of preferences in the sense of a changing price experience due to changes in taste we can write the reciprocal indirect utility function as follows:

$$(51)\quad P_{E/M_E} = V_1(a_1(t) \cdot p_{1/M_E},\ldots,a_4(t) \cdot p_{4/M_E})$$

where the product of price times augmentation factor determines the utility or aggregate response to price effects.

If we start with the direct utility approach with quantity augmenting taste factors, $b_i(t)$, we can write:

$$X_E = U_1(b_1(t) \cdot E_1,\ldots,b_4(t) \cdot E_4) \quad .$$

The corresponding indirect utility function is[2]:

$$M_E/P_E = W_1(b_1^{-1}(t) \cdot p_{1/M_E} \quad \ldots,b_4^{-1}(t) \cdot p_{4/M_E}).$$

This can be shown by means of the definition of the indirect utility function:

---

[1] See Jorgenson and Lau (1975a,c) and Muellbauer (1975).

[2] See Muellbauer (1975), p. 271.

$$W_1(p_1^*/M_E,\dots,p_4^*/M_E) = \max_{E_1^*,\dots,E_4^*} \{U_1(E_1^*,\dots,E_4^*) \Big| \frac{p_i^*}{M_E} E_i^* = 1\}$$

and, by substituting $p_i^* = b_i^{-1}(t)\cdot p_i$ and $E_i^* = b_i(t)\cdot E_i$:

$$W_1(b_1^{-1}(t)\frac{p_1}{M_E},\dots,b_4^{-1}(t)\frac{p_4}{M_E}) = \max_{b_i(t)\cdot E_i} \{U_1(b_1(t)E_1,\dots,b_4(t)E_4) \Big| \Sigma \frac{p_i}{M_E} E_i = 1\}$$

Therefore our price augmenting factors $a_i(t) = b_i^{-1}(t)$ in the reciprocal indirect utility function $V_1 = U_1^{-1}(t)$ in (51) are augmenting if the factor is quantity diminishing.

We first choose a translog representation of

$\ln P_E/M_E = \ln V_1^*(p_{1/M_E},\dots,p_{4/M_E},t)$ in the real prices and time t:

$$(52)\quad \ln V_1^* = \alpha_o + \Sigma\, \alpha_i \ln\frac{p_i}{M_E} + \alpha_t\cdot t + \frac{1}{2}\sum_{i,j} \beta_{ij} \ln\frac{p_i}{M_E}\ln\frac{p_j}{M_E} + \sum_j \beta_{jt}\cdot t\cdot\ln\frac{p_j}{M_E} + \frac{1}{2}\beta_{tt}\cdot t^2$$

where

$$(53)\quad \Sigma\,\alpha_i = 1,\ \beta_{ij} = \beta_{ji},\ \sum_i \beta_{it} = 0 \text{ and } \sum_i \beta_{ij} = 0 \quad (j = 1,\dots,4),$$

because of the linear homogeneity of V_1^* in the real prices. Under these parameter restrictions we obtain a dynamic functional form for the price index P_E:

$$(54)\quad \ln P_E = \alpha_o + \Sigma\,\alpha_j \ln p_j + \alpha_t\cdot t + \frac{1}{2}\sum_{i,j}\beta_{ij}\ln p_i \ln p_j + \sum_j \beta_{jt}\cdot t\cdot\ln p_j + \frac{1}{2}\beta_{tt}\cdot t^2 .$$

The utility maximizing or expenditure minimizing budget shares can be derived from (37) or (46):

$$(55)\quad \frac{p_j E_j}{M_E} = \alpha_j + \sum_i \beta_{ji} \ln p_i + \beta_{jt} \cdot t \qquad j = 1,\dots,4.$$

The estimation of this system results in the econometric determination of the parameters of the demand functions for the components of the energy budget as well as in the determination of the unknown parameters in the price function (54). As the parameters α_t and β_{tt} do not appear in the system (55), they can not be identified by econometric estimation of this system. They can be determined, however, by setting up a relationship between the parameters α_i, β_{jt} and β_{tt} and the price-augmenting factors. We therefore differentiate (51) with respect to time[1]:

$$(56)\quad \frac{\partial \ln V_1^*}{\partial t} = \sum_i \frac{\partial \ln V_1^*}{\partial \ln p_{i/M_E}} \frac{d \ln a_i(t)}{dt} \quad .$$

For the translog representation of $\ln V_1^*$ we obtain at the point of approximation the following parameter restrictions:

$$(57)\quad \frac{\partial \ln V_1^*}{\partial t} = \sum_i \alpha_i \frac{d \ln a_i(t)}{dt} = \alpha_t \ .$$

Under the assumption of a constant rate of growth of the augmentation factors,

$$(58)\quad a_i(t) = e^{\lambda_i t} \qquad i = 1,\dots,4,$$

these parameter restrictions are:

$$\Sigma\, \alpha_i \cdot \lambda_i = \alpha_t \ .$$

Similarly, the differentiation of (56) with respect to a price:

$$\frac{\partial^2 \ln V_1^*}{\partial \ln p_j/M_E \cdot \partial t} = \sum_i \frac{\partial^2 \ln V_1^*}{\partial \ln p_i/M_E \cdot \partial \ln p_j/M_E} \frac{d \ln a_i(t)}{dt}$$

and with respect to time results in the additional parameter restrictions:

[1] See Jorgenson and Lau (1975a), p. 68.

(59) $$\beta_{jt} = \sum_i \beta_{ij} \lambda_i \qquad j = 1,\ldots,4$$

and

$$\beta_{tt} = \sum_i \beta_{it} \lambda_i = \sum_{i,j} \beta_{ij} \lambda_i \lambda_j \quad .$$

We note that we can rewrite the parameters α_t, β_{tt} and β_{jt} in terms of the remaining translog parameters and the rates of augmentation. We replace the parameters β_{jt} in (55) by the expressions in (59) and obtain estimates for the λ_i's which enable us to determine, together with the parameters β_{ij}, the parameters α_t and β_{tt} in the price function (54)[1]. To provide an interpretation of the parameters β_{jt}, one can consider the bias of the change in preferences defined as the change of the aggregate shares with respect to a change in t:

(60) $$\sum_i \lambda_i = 0$$

If this bias of the preferences, β_{jt}, is positive, the share increases over time, if it is negative, the share decreases and if it is zero, the share is independent of time. Similar models can be employed for the allocation of the components $A_i (i=1,..,5)$ of the aggregate X_A and the components $B_i (i=1,\ldots,4)$ of the aggregate X_B.

For analysing the structure of consumer expenditure we can either employ this dynamic approach or the static one outlined before. For allocating total private consumption we multiply the budget shares of the overall model with the budget shares of the aggregation sub-models. For instance, the budget share for electricity (E_2) can be derived by multiplying the budget share for energy in the overall model ((18),j=1) with the budget share for electricity in the energy sub-model ((45),j=2):

$$\frac{P_E \cdot X_E}{M} \cdot \frac{p_{E_2} \cdot E_2}{M_E} = \frac{p_{E_2} \cdot E_2}{M} \quad \text{because of } P_E \cdot X_E = M_E \,.$$

[1] As $\sum_j \beta_{jt} = o$ because of V_1^* linear homogeneous, there are only three independent equations in the four unknown λ_i's in (59) so that we add a normalisation $\sum_i \lambda_i = o$ to get four equations for the four λ_i.

5. Estimation and Data

For the analysis of the structure of consumer expenditures we estimate the utility maximizing budget shares of the overall model in the aggregates E, A, B and the state variables s_j (j=E,A,B), and the cost-minimizing shares within the aggregates E, A and B. We first add additive error terms to the equations for the budget and aggregate shares. Due to the budget constraint in the overall model and in the aggregate sub-models the corresponding stochastic terms for the shares add to zero so that only m-1 of the m equations are required for analysing consumer behavior. We therefore estimate the first m-1 equations and compute the parameters of the m-th equation from the parameter restrictions. We have fitted the two equations (24) for energy E and (25) for aggregate A subject to the parameter restrictions (20) to (23). This reduces the number of parameters in the simultaneous system to seventeen. To estimate the parameters of the aggregate sub-models we have employed the static approach. Under the parameter restrictions of symmetry and linear homogeneity (41) the number of parameters to be estimated are reduced to nine in the case of energy and aggregate B (for instance (45)), and to fourteen in the case of aggregate A[1].

Our empirical results are based on time series on private consumption and its sectoral components computed by the "Deutsches Institut für Wirtschaftsforschung" in current and constant prices over the period 1954-1967[2]. With static aggregator functions the prices in the overall model are Divisia indices. We have first estimated the system (45) for the energy aggregate; the estimated parameters under the parameter restritions (41) and $\beta_{ij} = \beta_{ji}$ are given in the first column of Table 1. In the second and third columns we present the estimated parameters of the aggregator models A and B in five and four components, respectively. The subcripts indicate the order of the sectors given in section 3. The parameter β_{35} of the aggregate A model

[1] Our estimator of the unknown parameters is based on the maximum likelihood estimator, discussed, for example, by Malinvaud (1970), pp. 338-341.

[2] See Krengel et. al. (1972).

represents the response of the share "maschinery and vehicle construction" in the consumers durable aggregate to a change of the price for goods of the sector "traffic". In column four we present the parameters of the dynamic overall model. Whereas the interpretation of the parameters in these budget shares makes some difficulties, this is not the case for the parameters of the aggregate shares.

Table 1: Estimated parameters of the translog price aggregator functions and the overall consumer model

Parameter	PE	PA	PB	Param.	Dyn.Model
α_1	0,219	0,156	0,044	α_E	-0,042
α_2	0,333	0,022	0,264	α_A	-0,158
α_3	0,116	0,296	0,181	α_B	-0,800
α_4	0,332	0,304	0,511	β_{EE}	0,020
α_5	-	0,222	-	β_{EA}	0,038
β_{11}	-0,579	0,224	-0,015*	β_{EB}	- 0,039
β_{12}	-0,309	0,011*	0,113	γ_{EE}	-0,003
β_{13}	-0,242	-0,331	0,040	γ_{EA}	0,004
β_{14}	1.130	-0,136*	-0,138	γ_{EB}	-0,001
β_{15}	-	0,232	-	β_{Et}	-0,002
β_{22}	0,585	0,022*	0,413	β_{ME}	0,019
β_{23}	-0,374	-0,030	-0,105	β_{MA}	0,109
β_{24}	0,098	0,009*	-0,421	β_{MB}	0,296
β_{25}	-	-0,012	-	β_{Mt}	-0,014
β_{33}	-0,156	1,230	0,270	β_{AA}	0,430
β_{34}	0,772	-0,530	-0,205	β_{AB}	-0,359
β_{35}	-	-0,339	-	γ_{AE}	0,006
β_{44}	-2,000	0,751	0,764	γ_{AA}	-0,030
β_{45}	-	-0,093	-	γ_{AB}	0,024
β_{55}	-	0,212	-	β_{At}	-0,0035
R_1^2	0,80	0,93	0,98	β_{BB}	0,695
R_2^2	0,92	0,83	0,99	γ_{BE}	-0,003
R_3^2	0,81	0,96	0,83	γ_{BA}	0,026
R_4^2	-	0,87	-	γ_{BB}	-0,023
				β_{Bt}	-0,0085

*) Parameters not significantly different from zero at a level of significance of 5%.

For their interpretation Jorgenson and Lau (1975d) have introduced share elasticities which indicate the change in the budget shares with respect to a proportional change in the prices for the components of the aggregate. For the translog budget-or cost shares this share eleasticity is a constant defined as the partial derivative of the share with respect to the logarithm of the prices; for the E-model, for instance:

$$\frac{\partial}{\partial \ln p_k}\left(\frac{p_i E_i}{M_E}\right) = \beta_{ik} \qquad (i,k=1,\ldots,4).$$

If the share elasticity with respect to a price is positive, the share increases with an increase in the corresponding price, if it is negative, the share decreases and if it is zero, the share is independent of the corresponding price. With the aid of the estimated parameters in Table 1 the influence of prices on the allocation of the aggregate expenditure can be analysed.

For a further evaluation of the empirical results we can compute yearly direct and cross-price elasticities and income elasticities. For deriving the formalas we denote the nominator by Z and the denominator by N:

$$\frac{p_j x_j}{M} = \frac{Z_j}{N_j} \quad \text{or} \ln x_j = \ln Z_j - \ln N_j + \ln M - \ln p_j .$$

By differentiating partially with respect to the logarithm of the variables we obtain the direct price elasticity:

$$\varepsilon_{jj} = \frac{\partial \ln x_j}{\partial \ln p_j} = \frac{\beta_{jj}}{Z_j} - \frac{\beta_{Mj}}{N_j} - 1 \quad ;$$

the cross-price elasticity:

$$\varepsilon_{ji} = \frac{\partial \ln x_j}{\partial \ln p_i} = \frac{\beta_{ji}}{Z_j} - \frac{\beta_{Mi}}{N_j} \quad ,$$

and the income elasticity:

$$\varepsilon_{jM} = \frac{\partial \ln x_j}{\partial \ln M} = -\frac{\beta_{Mj}}{Z_j} + \frac{\Sigma\beta_{Mj}}{N_j} + 1$$

If the β's are different from zero the budget shares are not constant and the elasticities vary over time. For the aggregate models the formulas for the elasticities can be simplified as all β_{Mj} are zero because of homogeneity.

To get an idea of the size of the elasticities we have computed them in the base year 1962. For the overall model in the aggregates we obtain:

$$(62)\quad \varepsilon_{ji} = \frac{\beta_{ji}}{\alpha_j} + \beta_{Mj} - \delta_{ji} \qquad (j,i=E,A,B;\ \delta_{ji}=1 \text{ for } i = j \text{ and zero otherwise})$$

$$(63)\quad \varepsilon_{jM} = -\frac{\beta_{Mj}}{\alpha_j} - \beta'_{Mj} + 1 .$$

With the parameters given in the last column of Table 1 the elasticities are:

$$\begin{pmatrix} \varepsilon_{EE} & \varepsilon_{EA} & \varepsilon_{EB} & \varepsilon_{EM} \\ \varepsilon_{AE} & \varepsilon_{AA} & \varepsilon_{AB} & \varepsilon_{AM} \\ \varepsilon_{BE} & \varepsilon_{BA} & \varepsilon_{BB} & \varepsilon_{BM} \end{pmatrix} = \begin{pmatrix} -1{,}47 & -0{,}80 & 1{,}24 & 1{,}03 \\ -0{,}22 & -3{,}61 & 2{,}56 & 1{,}27 \\ 0{,}07 & 0{,}56 & -1{,}57 & 0{,}94 \end{pmatrix} .$$

These results are economically reasonable because the direct price elasticities are negative and the income elasticities for energy and consumers durables are greater than one and for non-durables smaller than one. Furthermore, $\varepsilon_{EA} < o$ and $\varepsilon_{AE} < o$ indicate that energy and consumers durables are complementary goods, and $\varepsilon_{AB} > o$, $\varepsilon_{BA} > o$ indicate that consumers durables and non-durables are substitute goods.

For the study of influences of habit formation and changes of preferences on the budget shares we carry out a partial analysis in the point of approximation. We first set prices $p/_M$ equal to one and time t equal to zero. From (24) we obtain:

$$\frac{P_E \cdot X_E}{M} = 0{,}042 + 0{,}003 \ln X_E(-1) - 0{,}004 \ln X_A(-1) + 0{,}001 \ln X_B(-1)$$

and from (25):

$$\frac{P_A \cdot X_A}{M} = 0{,}158 - 0{,}006 \ln X_E(-1) + 0{,}030 \ln X_A(-1) - 0{,}024 \ln X_B(-1);$$

The third equation becomes:

$$\frac{P_B \cdot X_B}{M} = 0{,}8 + 0{,}003 \ln X_E(-1) - 0{,}026 \ln X_A(-1) + 0{,}023 \ln X_B(-1)$$

Thus, all goods consumed in the previous period have a positive influence on the present budget shares. For analysing the change of the structure of preferences we keep all prices and the normalized lagged variables constant to one. From (24), (25), and the parameter values in Table 1 follows:

$$\frac{P_E \cdot X_E}{M} = \frac{0{,}042 + 0{,}002 \cdot t}{1 + 0{,}014 \cdot t}, \text{ or } \frac{\partial}{\partial t}\left(\frac{P_E \cdot X_E}{M}\right) > o ,$$

showing a change of preferences towards energy consumption;

$$\frac{P_A \cdot X_A}{M} = \frac{0{,}158 + 0{,}0035 \cdot t}{1 + 0{,}014 \cdot t}, \text{ or } \frac{\partial}{\partial t}\left(\frac{P_A \cdot X_A}{M}\right) > o,$$

showing a change of preferences towards consumer durables; and finally:

$$\frac{P_B \cdot X_B}{M} = \frac{0{,}8 + 0{,}0085 \cdot t}{1 + 0{,}014 \cdot t}, \text{ or } \frac{\partial}{\partial t}\left(\frac{P_B \cdot X_B}{M}\right) < o,$$

showing a change of preferences away from non-durables.

For an interpretation of the parameters of the aggregate models a matrix of price elasticities can also be calculated. We choose again the base year and obtain from (62) because of $\beta_{Mj} = o$ the reduced formula:

$$\varepsilon_{ji} = \frac{\beta_{ji}}{\alpha_j} - \delta_{ji} .$$

While a matrix of elasticities for the components of the aggregates A and B is of minor interest due to the heterogeneous commodities within these aggregates, this is not the case for the components of the energy aggregate. We therefore have calculated price elasticities for the various types of energy (ε_{ij}), $i,j = 1,\dots,4$:

$$(\varepsilon_{ij}) = \begin{pmatrix} -3,64 & -1,42 & -1,10 & 5,16 \\ -0,93 & 0,76 & -1,12 & 0,29 \\ -2,08 & -3,22 & -2,35 & 6,65 \\ 3,40 & 0,29 & 2,33 & -7,02 \end{pmatrix}.$$

The signs of ε_{14}, ε_{41} and ε_{34}, ε_{43} indicate that coal and gas are substitutes for mineral oil. All direct price elasticities are negative except for electricity, and the high absolute values for some of the elasticities reveal their long-term character due to the static approach to the price index numbers.

References

Blackorby, C., Primont, D. und R.R. Russell (1975), "Budgeting , Decentralization, and Aggregation", Annals of Economic and Social Measurement, 4, 23-44.

Brown, T.M. (1952), "Habit Persistence and Lags in Consumer Behaviour", Econometrica, 20; 355-371.

Christensen, L.R. und D.W. Jorgenson (1973), "Demand Analysis", chapter 4 in Jorgenson et.al.(1973), U.S. Energy Resources and Economic Growth, Final Report to the Energy Policy Project, Washington.

Christensen, L.R., D.W. Jorgenson und L.J.Lau (1975), "Transcendental Logarithmic Utility Functions", American Economic Review, 65; 367-383.

Conrad, K. (1976), "Gewohnheitsbildung und dynamische Nutzen- und Nachfragefunktionen", Jahrbücher für Nationalökonomie und Statistik, forthcoming.

Diewert, W.E. (1974a), "Applications of Duality Theory", in: Frontiers of Quantitative Economics, M. Intrilligator and D. Kendrick (Hrsg.), Amsterdam: North-Holland, Vol. 2.

Diewert, W.E. (1974b), "Intertemporal Consumer Theory and the Demand for Durables", Econometrica, 42; 497-516.

Farell, M.J. (1952), "Irreversible Demand Functions", Econometrica, 20: 171-186.

Gorman, W.M. (1967), "Tastes, Habits and Choices", International Economic Review, 218-222.

Hudson, E.A. und D.W. Jorgenson (1974), "U.S. Energy Policy and Economic Growth, 1975-2000", Bell Journal of Economics and Management Science, 5: 261-314.

Jorgenson, D.W. (1975, Hrsg.), Econometric Studies of U.S.Energy Policy, Amsterdam, North-Holland.

Jorgenson, D.W. et.al. (1973), U.S. Energy Resources and Economic Growth, Final Report to the Energy Policy Project, Washington.

Jorgenson, D.W. und L.J. Lau (1975a), "The Structure of Consumer Preferences", Annals of Social and Economic Measurement, 4: 49-101.

Jorgenson, D.W. und L.J. Lau (1975b), "The Integrability of Consumer Demand Functions", Harvard Institute of Economic Research, Discussion Paper No. 425.

Jorgenson, D.W. und L.J. Lau (1975c), "Consumer Demand in the Interindustry Model", Memorandum, Harvard University, Cambridge, Mass.

Jorgenson, D.W. und L.J. Lau (1975d), Duality and Technology, Contributions to Economic Analysis, Amsterdam: North-Holland, forthcoming.

Krelle, W. (1972), "Dynamisierung der Nutzenfunktion", Zeitschrift für Nationalökonomie, 32: 59-70.

Krelle, W. (1975), "Factor Shortages and Disequilibrium Prices in Econometric Forecasting Models", Institut für Gesellschafts- und Wirtschaftswissenschaften der Universität Bonn, Discussion Paper No. 69.

Krengel, R. et.al. (1972), "Input-Output and Import Relationships at Current and Constant Prices for the FRG, 1954-1967", Deutsches Institut für Wirtschaftsforschung, Berlin.

Lau, L.J. (1969), "Duality and the Structure of Utility Functions", Journal of Economic Theory, 1 : 374-396.

Lluch, C. (1974), "Expenditure, Savings and Habit-Formation", International Economic Review, 15: 786-797.

Malinvaud, E. (1970), Statistical Methods of Econometrics, Amsterdam: North-Holland.

Muellbauer, J. (1975), "The Cost of Living and Taste and Quality Change", Journal of Economic Theory, 10: 269-283.

Peston, M.H. (1967), "Changing Utility Functions", in: M. Shubik, ed., Essays in Mathematical Economics, Princeton, N.Y.: 233-236.

Phlips, L.(1972), "A Dynamic Version of the Linear Expenditure Model", Review of Economics and Statistics, 54: 450-458.

Pollak, R.A. (1970),"Habit Formation and Dynamic Demand Functions", Journal of Political Economy, 78: 745-763.

Pollak, R.A. und T.J. Wales (1969), "Estimation of the Linear Expenditure System", Econometrica, 37: 611-628.

Roy, R. (1942),De L'Utilité, Paris: Hermann.

Roy, R. (1949), "La Distribution du Revenu entre les Diverses Biens", Econometrica,15: 205-225.

Shephard, R.W. (1953), Cost and Production Functions, Princeton.

Shephard, R.W. (1970), Theory of Cost and Production Functions, Princeton University Press.

Strotz, H. (1957), "The Empirical Implications of a Utility Tree", Econometrica, 25: 269-280.

von Weizsäcker, C.C. (1971), "Notes on Endogeneous Changes in Tastes", Journal of Economic Theory, 3: 345-372.

Production Theory Dualities for Optimally Realized Values

by Rolf Färe

Introduction

Duality theorems are useful tools in the theory of cost and production (see [2,5,9]) as well as in the related theory of economic index numbers (see [4]). Traditionally, such theorems are proved on a global basis, i.e., they hold for each entire input or output set or for the whole technology. Global requirements of that kind imply the need of convexity assumptions as well as that of cost, revenue or profit evaluations are made for all prices belonging to the duals of the input and output or both spaces, respectively.

Convexity is often a too rigid assumption in the theory of production, e.g., it excludes important classes of technologies (see [3,6]). Prices picked from the duals of the input or output spaces are uncontroversial in steady state models treated in Euclidian real number spaces. On the other hand when economic models are discussed in more general locally convex linear spaces, the price space becomes an issue (see [1,8]).

A possibility to have duality theorems, in the theory of cost and production, without invoking convexity or without enforcing pricing by all vectors of the duals of the input or output spaces is not to insist on a global validity of the theorems. Rather the theorems should hold for a subset of the input or output vectors determining the technology.

In this paper duality theorems for cost and revenue are proved for subsets of the input and output sets, respectively. These subsets are shown to be closely related to realized vectors under assumptions of cost minimization and revenue maximization.

The framework for the dualities is the dynamic input and output correspondences developed in [8]. There a dynamic input correspondence is a mapping $u \rightarrow L(u)$ from vectors $u \in BM_+^m$ (1) of output histories to subsets $L(u)$ of input histories, where $L(u)$ contains all input histories yielding at least the output histories u. The output correspondence $x \rightarrow P(x) = \{u \in BM_+^m | x \in L(u)\}$ denotes the set of all output histories obtainable from a vector of input histories $x \in BM_+^n$. The axioms taken for $L(u)$ and $P(x)$ are the weak set given [8], in particular $L(u)$ and $P(x)$ are not assumed convex nor are strong disposability of inputs or outputs enforced.

(1) $BM_+^\alpha = \{f = (f_1, f_2, \ldots, f_\alpha) \in BM^\alpha | f_i(t) \geqq 0, \; t \in [0, +\infty)\}$, $\alpha = m$ or n, where $BM^\alpha = \{f = (f_1, f_2, \ldots, f_\alpha) | f_i : [0, +\infty) \rightarrow R_+$, f_i is bounded and Lebesque measurable with $\|f_i\| = \sup \{|f_i(t)| \,|\, t \in [0, +\infty)\}$ and the Euclidian product norm$\}$. BM^α is a Banach space (see [8]).

Dualities

For a finite planing horizon $t \in [0,T]$, $T \in (0, +\infty)$ define the input correspondence $x \to L_T(u) = L(u) \cap BM_+^n [0,T]^{(2)}$, and the output correspondence $u \to P_T(x) = P(x) \cap BM_+^m [0,T]$. The distance functionals for these correspondences are (see [8])

$$\Psi(u,x,T) = [\min \{\lambda | (\lambda \cdot x) \in L_T(u), \lambda \in [0, +\infty)\}]^{-1}$$

and

$$\Omega(x,u,T) = [\max \{\Theta | (\Theta \cdot u) \in P_T(x), \Theta \in [0, +\infty)\}]^{-1}$$

respectively.

As usual, $x \in L_T(u) \leftrightarrow \Psi(u,x,T) \geqq 1$ and $u \in P_T(x) \leftrightarrow \Omega(u,x,T) \leqq 1$ with the distance functionals homogeneous of degree +1 in their second arguments.

For an input price vector $p \in BM_+^n [0,T]$, denote the "inner product" by $\langle p,x \rangle_T = \int_0^T (\sum_{i=1}^n p_i(t)\, x_i(t))dt$ and define the cost functional by

$$K(u,p,T) = \min_x \{\langle p,x \rangle_T \mid x \in L_T(u)\}.$$

Likewise for an output price vector $r \in BM^m [0,T]$ define the revenue functional by

$$R(x,r,T) = \max_x \{\langle r,u \rangle_T | u \in P_T(x)\},$$

where $\langle r,u \rangle_T = \int_0^T \sum_{i=1}^m (r_i(t)u_i(t))dt$. The axioms of [8] are such that the above minimum and maximum exists. Also in [8] the following two dualities are proved.

---

(2) $BM_+^\alpha [0,T] = \{f \in BM_+^\alpha | f(t) = 0 \quad t > T\}, \alpha = m$ or n.

First Weak Duality

$$K(u,p,T) = \min_x \{<p,x>_T | \Psi(u,x,T) \geqq 1, x \in BM_+^n [0,T]\}$$

$$\Psi(u,x,T) \leqq \inf_p \{<p,x>_T | K(u,p,T) \geqq 1, p \in BM_+^n [0,T]\}$$

for $u \in BM_+^n [0,T]$ and $T \in (0, +\infty)$.

Second Weak Duality

$$R(x,r,T) = \max_u \{<r,u>_T | \Omega(x,u,T) \leqq 1, u \in BM_+^m [0,T]\}$$

$$\Omega(x,u,T) \geqq \sup_r \{<r,u>_T | R(x,r,T) \leqq 1, r \in BM^m [0,T]\}$$

for $x \in BM_+^n [0,T]$ and $T \in (0, +\infty)$.

The main topic of this paper is to characterize the subsets of $L_T(u)$ and $P_T(x)$ for which the second parts of the two weak dualities are given by equalities. For this reason introduce:

Definition 1: The cost minimizing input vectors for $u \in BM_+^m [0,T]$, $p \in BM_+^n [0,T]$, $T \in (0, +\infty)$ are $C(u,p,T) = \{x | x \in L_T(u), <p,x>_T = K(u,p,T)\}$.

Under the behaviour assumption of costminimization, $C(u,p,T)$ are the realized input vectors. Of importance is also,

Definition 2: The aureoled closure of $C(u,p,T)$ is $\hat{C}(u,p,T) = \{x | x = \lambda \cdot y, y \in C(u,p,T), \lambda \geqq 1\}$.

From the assumption of weak disposability of input histories, i.e., $x \in L_T(u) \Rightarrow (\lambda \cdot x) \in L_T(u)$ for $\lambda \geqq 1$, follows that $\hat{C}(u,p,T) \subset L_T(u)$.

The distance functional for $\hat{C}(u,p,T)$ is

$$\Psi(u,x,p,T) = [\inf \{\lambda | (\lambda \cdot x) \in \hat{C}(u,p,T)\}]^{-1}$$

and clearly $\hat{C}(u,p,T) = \{x | x \in L_T(u),\ \Psi(u,x,p,T) \geqq 1\}$. Also ISOQ $\hat{C}(u,p,T) =$ $= \{x | x \in L_T(u),\ \Psi(u,x,p,T) = 1\} = C(u,p,T)$. The relationship between $\Psi(u,x,p,T)$ and $\Psi(u,x,T)$ is clear from:

Proposition 1: For $u \in BM_+^m [0,T]$, $p \in BM_+^m [0,T]$, $T \in (0, +\infty)$,

$$x \in \hat{C}(u,p,T) \Leftrightarrow \Psi(u,x,T) = \Psi(u,x,p,T) \geqq 1.$$

Proof: Assume $\Psi(u,x,T) = \Psi(u,x,p,T) \geqq 1$, then clearly $x \in \hat{C}(u,p,T)$. Conversely, let $x \in \hat{C}(u,p,T)$. Then $x = \lambda \cdot y$, $y \in C(u,p,T)$, $\lambda \geqq 1$ by Definition 2. $y \in C(u,p,T)$ implies $y \in$ ISOQ $\hat{C}(u,p,T) \subset$ ISOQ $L_T(u)$ thus $\Psi(u,y,T) = \Psi(u,y,p,T) = 1$. Since the distance functionals $\Psi(u,y,T)$ and $\Psi(u,y,p,T)$ are homogeneous of degree +1 in their second arguments, $\Psi(u,x,T) = \Psi(u,\lambda \cdot y,T) = \lambda \cdot \Psi(u,y,T)$ and $\Psi(u,x,p,T) = \Psi(u,\lambda \cdot y,p,T) =$ $= \lambda \cdot \Psi(u,y,T)$ implying that $\Psi(u,x,T) = \Psi(u,x,p,T) \geqq 1$.

QED.

It is next shown that equality of the second part of the first weak duality holds for $x \in \hat{C}(u,p,T)$. For this reason consider $x \in \hat{C}(u,p,T)$. Then by Proposition 1,

$$\Psi(u,x,p,T) = \Psi(u,x,T) \leqq \inf_p \{\langle p,x\rangle_T | K(u,p,T) \geqq 1,\ p \in BM_+^n [0,T]\}.$$

Clearly,

$$\inf_p \{\langle p,x\rangle_T | K(u,p,T) \geqq 1,\ p \in BM_+^n [0,T]\} \leqq \inf_\lambda \{\langle \lambda \cdot p,x\rangle_T |$$

$$K(u,\lambda \cdot p,T) \geqq 1,\ (\lambda \cdot p) \in BM_+^n [0,T]\} = \langle p,x\rangle_T \cdot [K(u,p,T)]^{-1}$$

Thus

$$\Psi(u,x,p,T) \leqq \langle p,x\rangle_T\ [K(u,p,T)]^{-1}$$

Also from Definition 2, $x = \lambda \cdot y$, $\lambda \geqq 1$, and $y \in C(u,p,T)$.

From the latter and Definition 1,

$$\Psi(u,x,p,T) = \lambda \cdot \Psi(u,y,p,T) \leqq \lambda.$$

Thus $\Psi(u,y,p,T) = 1$ since $y \in \hat{C}(u,p,T)$. Furthermore, $\Psi(u,x,p,T) =$ $= \lambda = \lambda \cdot \langle p,y\rangle_T\ [K(u,p,T)]^{-1} = \langle p,x\rangle_T\ [K(u,p,T)]^{-1}$ proving:

<u>Proposition 2</u>: For $x \in \hat{C}(u,p,T)$, $u \in BM_+^m\ [0,T]$, $T \in (0, +\infty)$ and $p \in BM_+^n\ [0,T]$, $\Psi(u,x,p,T) = \inf_\lambda \{\langle \lambda \cdot p,x\rangle_T \mid K(u,\lambda . p,T) \geqq 1,$ $(\lambda \cdot p) \in BM_+^n\ [0,T]\}$.

A direct consequence of Propositions 1 and 2 is the following duality theorem:

<u>First Partial Duality</u>

For $x \in \hat{C}(u,p,T)$, $u \in BM_+^m\ [0,T]$, $p \in BM_+^n\ [0,T]$ and $T \in (0, +\infty)$,

$$K(u,p,T) = \min_x \{\langle p,x\rangle_T \mid \Psi(u,x,T) \geqq 1,\ x \in BM_+^n\ [0,T]\}$$

$$\Psi(u,x,T) = \inf_\lambda \{\langle \lambda \cdot p,x\rangle_T \mid K(u,\lambda \cdot p,T) \geqq 1,\ (\lambda \cdot p) \in BM_+^n\ [0,T]\}.$$

The next step is to show that for $x \in L_T(u)$, if equality in the second part of the first weak duality holds, then $x \in \hat{C}(u,p,T)$. For this reason define

$$\Psi^*(u,x,p,T) = \inf_\lambda \{\langle \lambda \cdot p,x\rangle_T \mid K(u,\lambda \cdot p,T) \geqq 1,\ (\lambda \cdot p) \in BM_+^n\ [0,T]\},$$

and

$$\hat{C}^*(u,p,T) = \{x \mid x \in L_T(u),\ \Psi^*(u,x,p,T) \geqq 1\}.$$

The following lemma is of use,

Lemma: $\hat{C}^*(u,p,T) = \hat{C}(u,p,T)$ for $\hat{C}^*(u,p,T)$ and $\hat{C}(u,p,T)$ not empty and $u \in BM_+^n[0,T]$, $p \in BM_+^n[0,T]$, $T \in (0, +\infty)$.

Proof: Let $x^o \in \hat{C}(u,p,T)$. From the definition of $K(u,p,T)$, $<\lambda \cdot p, x^o>_T \geqq K(u,\lambda \cdot p,T)$ for $(\lambda \cdot p) \in BM_+^n[0,T]$, and in particular if $(\lambda \cdot p) \in \{\lambda \cdot p | K(u,\lambda \cdot p,T) \geqq 1\}$, $<\lambda \cdot p,x^o>_T \geqq K(u,\lambda \cdot p,T) \geqq 1$. From the definition of $\Psi^*(u,x,p,T)$ it follows that for any $\varepsilon > 0$ there is a $(\lambda_\varepsilon \cdot p) \in \{\lambda \cdot p | K(u,\lambda \cdot p,T) \geqq 1\}$ such that $\Psi^*(u,x^o,p,T) + \varepsilon > <\lambda_\varepsilon \cdot p, x^o>_T \geqq 1$. Thus $x^o \in \hat{C}^*(u,p,T)$ and $\hat{C}(u,p,T) \subset \hat{C}^*(u,p,T)$.

Conversely, assume $x^o \notin \hat{C}(u,p,T)$. If $(\lambda \cdot x^o) \notin \hat{C}(u,p,T)$ for any $\lambda \in [0, +\infty)$, then $\Psi(u,x^o,p,T) = 0$ and $K(u,p,T) = +\infty$. Thus $\Psi^*(u,x^o,p,T) = 0$ and $x^o \notin \hat{C}^*(u,p,T)$. If on the other hand $(\lambda \cdot x^o) \in \hat{C}(u,p,T)$ for some $\lambda \in [0, +\infty)$, then $\lambda > 1$ and also $<p,x^o>_T < K(u,p,T)$. Now define $\tilde{p} = p \cdot [K(u,p,T)]^{-1}$, then $<\tilde{p},x^o>_T < 1$ and $\Psi^*(u,x^o,\tilde{p},T) \leqq <\tilde{p},x^o>_T$ and hence $x^o \notin \hat{C}^*(u,p,T)$. Thus $\hat{C}^*(u,p,T) \subset \hat{C}(u,p,T)$.

QED.

Using the lemma, it follows from [5, p. 158] that $\Psi^*(u,x,p,T) = \Psi(u,x,p,T)$ and consequently the following proposition may be proved,

Proposition 3: For $u \in BM_+^m[0,T]$, $p \in BM_+^n[0,T]$ and $T \in (0, +\infty)$, if $x \in L_T(u)$ and $\Psi(u,x,T) = \Psi^*(u,x,p,T)$, then $x \in \hat{C}(u,p,T)$.

Proof: Let $x \in L_T(u)$ with $\Psi(u,x,T) = \Psi^*(u,x,p,T)$. Then by the above, $1 \leqq \Psi(u,x,T) = \Psi(u,x,p,T)$ and by Proposition 1, $x \in \hat{C}(u,p,T)$.

QED.

To summarize, Proposition 3 shows that for $x \in L_T(u)$ with

$\Psi(u,x,T) = \inf_\lambda\{<\lambda\cdot p,x>_T | K(u,\lambda\cdot p,T) \geqq 1,\ (\lambda\cdot p) \in BM_+^n\ [0,T]\}$,

then x belongs to the aureoled closure of the realized input vectors. Conversely, the first partial duality shows that such input vectors imply that there is no duality gap in the first weak duality.

To determine the subset of output vectors $u \in P_T(x)$ for which there is no duality gap in the second weak duality, introduce:

Definition 3: The revenue maximizing output vectors for $x \in BM_+^n\ [0,T]$, $r \in BM^m\ [0,T]$, $T \in (0, +\infty)$ are $B(x,r,T) = \{u | u \in P_T(x), <r,u>_T = R(x,r,T)\}$, and $\hat{B}(x,r,T) = \{u | u = \Theta\cdot\omega, \omega \in B(x,r,T), \Theta \in [0,1]\}$ is the starred closure of $B(x,r,T)$.

Clearly, if revenue maximizing is assumed, B(x,r,T) are the realized output vectors. Also, due to weak disposability of outputs (see [8]), i.e., $u \in P_T(x) \Rightarrow (\Theta\cdot u) \in P_T(u)$ for $\Theta \in [0,1]$, $\hat{B}(x,r,T)$ is a subset of $P_T(x)$.

By arguments parallelling those for the first partial duality, the following is valid:

Second Partial Duality

For $u \in \hat{B}(x,r,T)$, $x \in BM_+^n\ [0,T]$, $r \in BM^m\ [0,T]$ and $T \in (0, +\infty)$,

$$R(x,r,T) = \max_u \{<r,u>_T | \Omega(x,u,T) \leqq 1,\ u \in BM_+^m\ [0,T]\}$$

$$\Omega(x,u,T) = \sup_\Theta \{<\Theta\cdot r,u>_T | R(x,\Theta\cdot r,T) \leqq 1,\ (\Theta\cdot r) \in BM^m\ [0,T]\}.$$

Also from the arguments parallelling those leading to Proposition 3, it can be shown that:

<u>Proposition 4:</u> For $x \in BM_+^n[0,T]$, $r \in BM^m[0,T]$, $T \in (0, +\infty)$

if $u \in P_T(x)$ and $\Omega(x,u,T) = \Omega^*(x,u,r,T) =$

$= \inf_{\Theta} \{<\Theta \cdot r, u>_T \mid R(x,\Theta \cdot r,T) \leqq 1,\ (\Theta \cdot r) \in BM^m[0,T]\}$,

then $u \in \hat{B}(x,r,T)$.

Thus, the second partial duality and Proposition 4 characterize those $u \in P_T(x)$ for which there is no duality gap in the second weak duality.

References

[1] Bewley, T.: "Existence of Equilibria in Economics with Infinitely Many Commodities", Journal of Economic Theory, (1972), 514-540.

[2] Diewert, W.E.: "Applications of Duality Theory", in Frontiers of Quantitative Economics, vol. II, ed. Intriligator, M.D. and D.A. Kendrick, North-Holland Publishing Company, (1974).

[3] Färe, R.: "A Note on Ray-Homogeneous and Ray-Homothetic Production Functions", The Swedish Journal of Economics, (1975), 366-372.

[4] Färe, R.: "Separability and Index Properties of Ray-Homothetic Dynamic Production Structures", in this volume.

[5] Shephard, R.W.: Theory of Cost and Production Functions, Princeton University Press, (1970).

[6] Shephard, R.W.: "Semi-Homogeneous Production Functions and Scaling of Production", Lecture Notes in Economics and Mathematical Systems, vol. 99, entitled: Production Theory, Springer-Verlag, (1974).

[7] Shephard, R.W.: "A Dynamic Formulation of Index Functions for the Theory of Cost and Production", in this volume.

[8] Shephard, R.W. and R. Färe: "A Dynamic Theory of Production Correspondences", ORC 75-13, Operations Research Center, University of California, (1975).

[9] Uzawa, H.: "Duality Principles in the Theory of Cost and Production", International Economic Review, (1964), 216-220.

Linear Models with Variable Coefficients

by Erich Härtter

1. Introduction

Here I will consider some aspects for generalizations of economic models.

The recursive market model (let be p_t the price in the period t ($t \in \mathbb{N}_0$ [1])), $x_{N,t}$ the demand in the period t and $x_{A,t}$ the supply in the period t)

$$
(1)\quad \begin{cases} \text{demand function:} & x_{N,t} = \alpha^* - \alpha\, p_t \quad (0 \leq p_t \leq \frac{\alpha^*}{\alpha}) \\ \text{supply function:} & x_{A,t} = -\beta^* + \beta p_{t-1} \quad (p_{t-1} \geq \frac{\beta^*}{\beta}) \\ \text{condition for equilibrium:} & x_{N,t} = x_{A,t} \end{cases}
$$

with the constant coefficients (parameters) α^*, α, β^*, β ($\alpha^*, \alpha, \beta^*, \beta \in \mathbb{R}_+$) leads to the linear difference equation

$$
(2)\qquad p_t = -\frac{\beta}{\alpha}\, p_{t-1} + \frac{\alpha^* + \beta^*}{\alpha} \qquad (t = 1,2,3,\ldots)
$$

with constant coefficients. [2]

---

1) $\mathbb{N}_0$ is the set $\{0,1,2,\ldots\}$; $\mathbb{R}$ is the set of the reals; $\mathbb{R}_c = \{x \in \mathbb{R} \mid x \geq c\}$; $\mathbb{R}_+ = \{x \in \mathbb{R} \mid x > 0\}$.

2) See, for instance, Ott [5], Allen [1].

Now we allow, that the coefficients α^*, α, β^*, β also depend from the time t, that is we consider instead of (1) the model

$$(3) \quad \begin{cases} x_{N,t} = \alpha_t^* - \alpha_t\, p_t \\ x_{A,t} = -\beta_t^* + \beta_t\, p_{t-1} \\ x_{N,t} = x_{A,t}; \end{cases}$$

there are $\alpha_t^*, \alpha_t, \beta_t^*, \beta_t \in \mathbb{R}_+$ for all $t \in \mathbb{N}_0$, $\alpha_t^*, \alpha_t, \beta_t^*, \beta_t$ exogenous. Now we obtain the linear difference equation

$$(4) \qquad p_t = -\frac{\beta_t}{\alpha_t}\, p_{t-1} + \frac{\alpha_t^* + \beta_t^*}{\alpha_t} \qquad (t = 1,2,3,\dots)$$

with coefficients dependent on t.

In(3) the demand function and the supply function geometrically imply groups of straight lines with the group parameter t (fig.1).

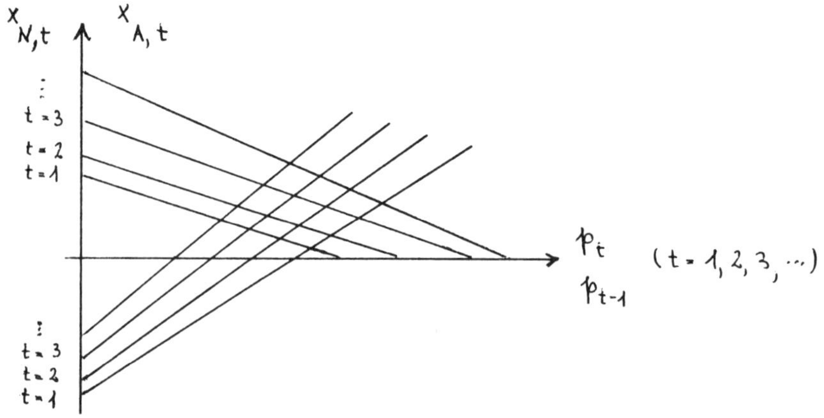

Fig. 1.

2. Solution and Discussion of the Difference Equation

In general the linear difference equation of first order

$$y_{t+1} = A_t\, y_t + B_t \qquad (t = 0,1,2,\dots)$$

has the solution (see, for instance, Gelfond [2], p. 257)

$$y_t = \{\prod_{j=0}^{t-1} A_j\}\{C + \sum_{\nu=0}^{t-1} B_\nu \prod_{j=0}^{\nu} A_j^{-1}\} \quad (A_t \neq 0 \text{ for all } t \in \mathbb{N}_0);$$

here empty products are to set = 1 and empty sums = 0. Further is the any constant $C = y_0$.

For the difference equation (4) we thus get

$$(5) \qquad p_t = \{\prod_{j=0}^{t-1} (-\frac{\beta_j}{\alpha_j})\}\{C + \sum_{\nu=0}^{t-1} \frac{\alpha_\nu^* + \beta_\nu^*}{\alpha_\nu} \prod_{j=0}^{\nu} (-\frac{\beta_j}{\alpha_j})^{-1}\};$$

here is certainly $-\frac{\beta_t}{\alpha_t} \neq 0$ for all $t \in \mathbb{N}_0$. From (5) follows immediately

$$(6) \qquad p_t = C \prod_{j=0}^{t-1} (-\frac{\beta_j}{\alpha_j}) + \sum_{\nu=0}^{t-1} \frac{\alpha_\nu^* + \beta_\nu^*}{\alpha_\nu} \prod_{j=\nu+1}^{t-1} (-\frac{\beta_j}{\alpha_j}).$$

We prove the following

theorem 1: If p_t in (6) is convergent for $t \to \infty$ to an equilibrium for any $C = p_0 \neq 0$ then

$\beta_j < \alpha_j$ for infinite many j

or there exists to every $\varepsilon > 0$ an index j_ε, so that

$\beta_j < (1 + \varepsilon)\alpha_j$ for all $j \geq j_\varepsilon$.

Remark: The last condition can be written as

$\beta_j < \alpha_j + \varepsilon_1$ for all $j \geq j_{\varepsilon_1}$

if $0 < \gamma < \alpha_j$ is bounded.

Proof: That $\lim_{t\to\infty} p_t$ exists for any C necessary must be

$$\prod_{j=0}^{\infty} (- \frac{\beta_j}{\alpha_j})$$

convergent or divergent to 0. By the necessary convergence condition for infinite products (see, for instance, Knopp[3], p.224) we obtain

$\frac{\beta_j}{\alpha_j} \to 1$ for $j \to \infty$

or

$|\frac{\beta_j}{\alpha_j}| < 1$ for infinite many j.

Since $\alpha_j, \beta_j > 0$ we can do without absolute value; therefore

$\beta_j < (1 + \varepsilon)\alpha_j$ $(\varepsilon > 0)$ for all $j \geq j_\varepsilon$

or

$\beta_j < \alpha_j$ for infinite many j.

Thus the theorem is proved.

Now we consider the special case where $\alpha_t^* = \alpha^*$, $\alpha_t = \alpha$, $\beta_t^* = \beta^*$ are constants. That is, only supply is changed in every period. Figur 1 becoms now to figur 2.

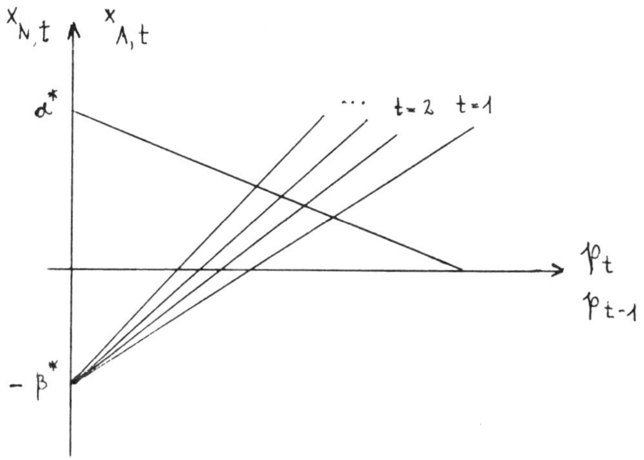

Fig. 2.

Then (6) becomes to

$$(7) \quad p_t = C\,\alpha^{-t} \prod_{j=0}^{t-1} (-\beta_j) + (\alpha^* + \beta^*) \sum_{\nu=0}^{t-1} \alpha^{\nu-t} \prod_{j=\nu+1}^{t-1} (-\beta_j).$$

The corresponding cobweb diagramm gives figur 3.

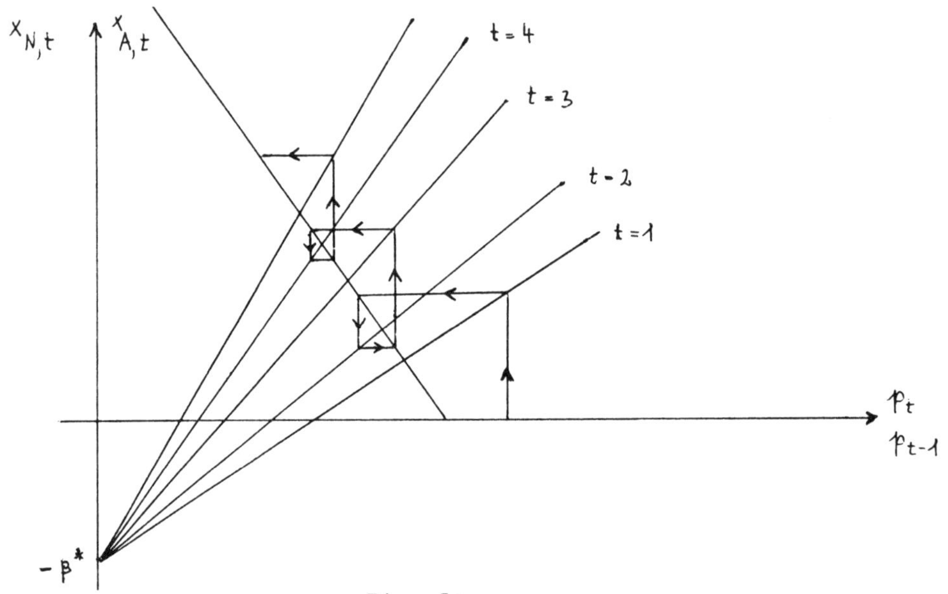

Fig. 3a.

Here is $\alpha^* = 9$; $\beta^* = 2,5$; $\alpha = 1,38$; $\beta_1 = 0,65$; $\beta_2 = 0,81$; $\beta_3 = 1,11$; $\beta_4 = 1,43$; $\beta_5 = 1,73$.

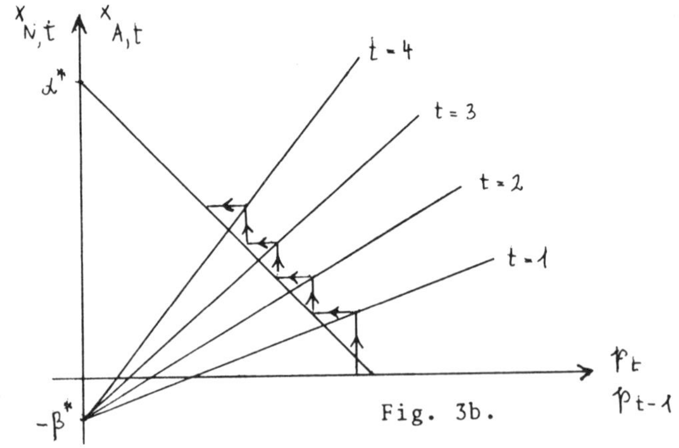

Fig. 3b.

$\alpha^* = 5$; $\beta^* = 0,75$; $\alpha = 0,5$; $\beta_1 = 0,36$; $\beta_2 = 0,60$; $\beta_3 = 0,90$; $\beta_4 = 1,23$.

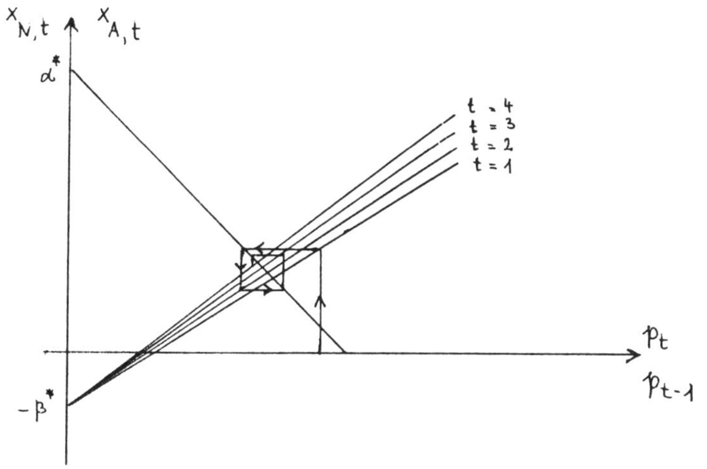

Fig. 3c.

$\alpha^* = 5;\ \beta^* = 1;\ \alpha = 0{,}5;\ \beta_1 = 0{,}6;\ \beta_2 = 0{,}7;\ \beta_3 = 0{,}75;\ \beta_4 = 0{,}80.$

For $\beta_j = \beta$ constant in (7) one obtains the former known result: From (7) we have

$$p_t = C(-\frac{\beta}{\alpha})^t + \frac{\alpha^* + \beta^*}{\alpha} \sum_{\nu=0}^{t-1} (-\frac{\beta}{\alpha})^{t-\nu-1}$$

and, putting $-\frac{\beta}{\alpha} = A;\ \frac{\alpha^* + \beta^*}{\alpha} = B$, follows

$$p_t = C\,A^t + B \sum_{\nu=0}^{t-1} A^{t-\nu-1} =$$

$$= A^t\{C + B \sum_{\nu=0}^{t-1} (\frac{1}{A})^{\nu+1}\} =$$

(using the formula for the sum of geometric series)

$$= A^t\,C + B\,\frac{1-A^t}{1-A} =$$

$$= A^t(C - \frac{B}{1-A}) + \frac{B}{1-A} \quad \text{for } A \neq 1.$$

If $\beta < \alpha \implies |A| < 1 \implies \lim_{t\to\infty} A^t = 0$

$$\implies \lim_{t\to\infty} p_t = \frac{B}{1-A} = \frac{\alpha^* + \beta^*}{\alpha} \frac{1}{1 + \frac{\beta}{\alpha}} = \frac{\alpha^* + \beta^*}{\alpha + \beta} .$$

With this we have the know result (see, for instance, Stöwe - Härtter [6], p. 305).

3. Some Remarks to Difference Equations of second Order

We consider the difference equation of second order

$$(8) \qquad y_{t+2} + a_t y_{t+1} + b_t y_t = 0 \qquad (t = 0,1,2,\dots)$$

In the case where a_t and b_t are constants, we can find a fundamental system for the general solution (i. e. a system of basis vectors for the vector space of solutions) by the statement $y_t = \lambda^t$ ($0 \neq \lambda$ constant) (see, for instance, Stöwe - Härtter [6], p. 288).

For example the difference equation

$$y_{t+2} + t y_{t+1} + (t-1) y_t = 0$$

has the solution $y_t = (-1)^t$. We will show, that equation (8) with a_t or b_t not constant has at most one solution of the form $y_t = \lambda^t$ ($\lambda \neq 0$).

Proof: Suppose there are solutions $y_t = \lambda^t$ of (8) (a_t and b_t not both constant; $\lambda \neq 0$);

$$\implies \lambda^{t+2} + a_t \lambda^{t+1} + b_t \lambda^t = 0;$$

$$\lambda^t (\lambda^2 + a_t \lambda + b_t) = 0;$$

because $\lambda^t \neq 0 \implies \lambda^2 + a_t\lambda + b_t = 0;$

$$\lambda_{1,2} = -\frac{a_t}{2} \pm \sqrt{\frac{a_t^2}{4} - b_t}.$$

On the right we can't have in both cases a constant.

For the difference equation (8)

$$y_{t+2} + a_t\, y_{t+1} + b_t\, y_t = 0$$

now we suppose that the limites

$$\lim_{t\to\infty} a_t = a \quad \text{and} \quad \lim_{t\to\infty} b_t = b$$

exist. The equation

(9) $$\lambda^2 + a\lambda + b = 0$$

is the "generalised characteristic equation" of (8); the roots of (9) are λ_1 and λ_2. For these roots we make the assumption $|\lambda_1| \neq |\lambda_2|$ (consequently are $\lambda_i \in \mathbb{R}$ $(i = 1,2)$). Then we have the

theorem of Poincaré (see Gelfond [2], p. 287 or Meschowski [4], p. 104):

$$\lim_{t\to\infty} \frac{y_{t+1}}{y_t} = \lambda_1 \text{ or } = \lambda_2.$$ 1)

From this theorem we draw a

conclusion: If $|\lambda_i| < 1$ $(i = 1,2)$ $\implies$ $\lim_{t\to\infty} y_t = 0.$

1)This theorem and the next conclusions are also valid for difference equations of order > 2.

<u>Proof:</u> From $|\lambda_i| < 1$ it follows that

$$\left|\frac{y_{t+1}}{y_t}\right| < \mu < 1 \quad \text{for all } t \geq t_o;$$

$$\rightarrow |y_t| = \left|\frac{y_t}{y_{t-1}}\right| \left|\frac{y_{t-1}}{y_{t-2}}\right| \cdots \left|\frac{y_{t_o+1}}{y_{t_o}}\right| |y_{t_o}| <$$

$$< |y_{t_o}| \mu^{t-t_o}.$$

From $0 < \mu < 1$ we get $\lim\limits_{t\to\infty} y_t = 0$.

Now we consider conditions that $|\lambda_i| < 1$.

<u>Theorem 2</u>: A necessary and sufficient condition for $|\lambda_i| < 1$ is

$$(10) \qquad \begin{cases} |b_t| < b^* < 1 \quad \text{and} \\ |a_t| < a^* < a^{**} < 1 + b_t \text{ for all } t_o \leq t \in \mathbb{N}. \end{cases}$$

<u>Proof:</u> I. Suppose $|\lambda_1| < 1$ and $|\lambda_2| < 1$. By Vieta's root theorem we get

$$|\lambda_1\lambda_2| = |b| < 1;$$

$$\Longrightarrow \qquad |b_t| < b^* < 1 \quad \text{for all } t_1 \leq t \in \mathbb{N}.$$

Moreover also by Vieta's root theorem

$$(11) \qquad \begin{cases} 0 < (1+\lambda_1)(1+\lambda_2) = 1 + \lambda_1 + \lambda_2 + \lambda_1\lambda_2 = 1 - a + b \quad \text{and} \\ 0 < (1-\lambda_1)(1-\lambda_2) = 1 - \lambda_1 - \lambda_2 + \lambda_1\lambda_2 = 1 + a + b; \end{cases}$$

$$\rightarrow \begin{cases} a < 1 + b \\ -a < 1 + b; \end{cases} \qquad \rightarrow |a| < 1 + b;$$

$\Longrightarrow$ there are numbers a^*, a^{**} with

$$|a_t| < a^* < a^{**} < 1 + b_t \text{ for all } t_2 \leq t \in \mathbb{N}.$$

Setting $t_o = \max(t_1, t_2)$ we have the statement (10).

II. Now suppose (10). Then $|b| < 1$ and $|a| < 1 + b$ and from (11) $\Longrightarrow$

$$0 < 1 - a + b = (1+\lambda_1)(1+\lambda_2) \quad \text{and}$$

$$0 < 1 + a + b = (1-\lambda_1)(1-\lambda_2).$$

By multiplication we have

$$0 < (1-\lambda_1^2)(1-\lambda_2^2).$$

Therefore $(1-\lambda_1^2)$ and $(1-\lambda_2^2)$ both > 0 or both < 0.

If $(1-\lambda_1^2) < 0$ and $(1-\lambda_2^2) < 0 \Longrightarrow \lambda_1^2 > 1$ and $\lambda_2^2 > 1$;

$\Longrightarrow |\lambda_1| > 1$ and $|\lambda_2| > 1$; $\Longrightarrow |\lambda_1||\lambda_2| = |\lambda_1\lambda_2| > 1$;

that is a contradiction to $|b| = |\lambda_1\lambda_2| < 1$.

Thus $(1-\lambda_1^2) > 0$ and $(1-\lambda_2^2) > 0$; $\Longrightarrow \lambda_1^2 < 1$ and $\lambda_2^2 < 1$;

$\Longrightarrow |\lambda_1| < 1$ and $|\lambda_2| < 1$.

So the theorem is proved.

The theorem of Poincaré holds first only for linear homogeneous difference equations. Now we will consider linear inhomogeneous difference equations

$$(12) \qquad y_{t+2} + a_t y_{t+1} + b_t y_t = c_t .$$ [1]

The general solution y_t^* of (12) is representable as sum of the general solution y_t of the analogous homogeneous equation and a special solution $y_t^{(0)}$ of (12); that is

$$y_t^* = y_t + y_t^{(0)} .$$

Then we have as a correspondence to Poincaré's theorem the <u>theorem 3</u>: If

$$(13) \qquad \lim_{t\to\infty} \frac{y_t^{(0)}}{y_t} = k \neq -1,$$

then also

$$\lim_{t\to\infty} \frac{y_{t+1}^*}{y_t^*} = \lambda_i .$$

<u>Proof</u>: $$\frac{y_{t+1}^*}{y_t^*} = \frac{y_{t+1} + y_{t+1}^{(0)}}{y_t + y_t^{(0)}} = \frac{y_{t+1}}{y_t} \, \frac{1 + \dfrac{y_{t+1}^{(0)}}{y_{t+1}}}{1 + \dfrac{y_t^{(0)}}{y_t}};$$

using (13) we have

$$\lim_{t\to\infty} \frac{y_{t+1}^*}{y_t^*} = \lim_{t\to\infty} \frac{y_{t+1}}{y_t} = \lambda_i .$$

4. Some Aspects for nonlinear Models

If we dismiss the linearity in the models [2] the considerations become complicated. Instead of the model (3) we have more general

---

1) The next conclusions are also valid for difference equations of order > 2.

2) For some hints see, for instance, Allen [1], p. 4, 51; Samuelson [7], p. 48

$$(14)\quad \begin{cases} \text{demand function:} & x_{N,t} = f_t(p_t) \\ \text{supply function:} & x_{A,t} = g_t(p_{t-1}) \\ \text{condition for equilibrium:} & x_{N,t} = x_{A,t} \end{cases}$$

with functions f_t and g_t defined on $\mathbb{R}_o$ [1] $(t = 0,1,2,3,\ldots)$. Further we suppose

$f_t(\xi) > 0$ and strictly monotone decreasing for all $\xi \in \mathbb{R}_o$;

$g_t(\xi) > 0$ for all $\xi \in \mathbb{R}_c$ and strictly monotone increasing for all $\xi \in \mathbb{R}_o$.

That is we have sets of demand functions and supply functions (fig. 4).

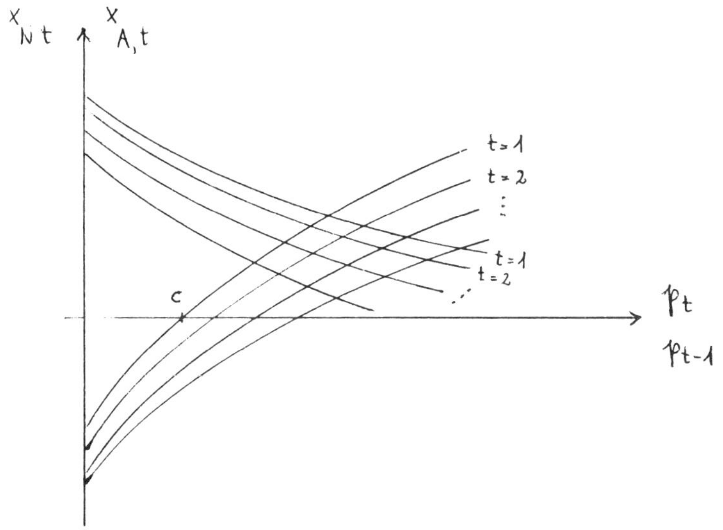

Fig. 4.

1) For g_t is sufficient the definition on $\mathbb{R}_c$.

From (14) we obtain the difference equation

(15) $$f_t(p_t) = g_t(p_{t-1}) \qquad (t = 1,2,3,\dots).$$

This is not necessary linear. Because f_t is strictly monotone decreasing on $\mathbb{R}_0$ exists the inverse f_t^{-1}; consequently

(16) $$p_t = f_t^{-1}(g_t(p_{t-1}))$$

is the explicit form of the difference equation (15). Results for the solution of (16) depend on the special form of f_t and g_t.

5. Some Remarks for stochastic Models

So far in the models we used only deterministic quantities, in particular all parameters were well defined functions of the time t. For the investigation of linear models where the parameters are random variables changing from one time period to the next period we give here only some hints. The parameters are in this case to conceive as states of a stochastic process which satisfy the Markov condition. The solution therefore depends on the elements of the corresponding transition matrices.

References

[1] ALLEN, R.G.D.: Mathematische Wirtschaftstheorie
Berlin 1971

[2] GELFOND, A.O.: Differenzenrechnung
Berlin 1958; p.253

[3] KNOPP, K.: Theorie und Anwendung der unendlichen Reihen
Berlin 1964

[4] MESCHKOWSKI, H.: Differenzengleichungen
Göttingen 1959

[5] OTT, A.E.: Einführung in die dynamische Wirtschaftstheorie
Göttingen 1970

[6] STÖWE, H., and E. HÄRTTER: Lehrbuch der Mathematik für Volks- und Betriebswirte
Göttingen 1972

[7] SAMUELSON, P.A.: Volkswirtschaftslehre, II
Köln 1972

Aggregation of Substitutional Production Functions by Functional Equation Methods

by Fritz Pokropp

1. Introduction

The problem of aggregation is closely related to the problem of constructing index-numbers. In this note I shall consider index-numbers as measurements of aggregates. The construction of aggregates resp. index-numbers can be attacked from two sides: (1) the semantic approach, (2) the relation approach (more commonly known as KLEIN-NATAF approach).

The semantic approach has been successful in large parts of index-number theory and of aggregation analysis. However, against the semantic approach it has been argued that it does not secure the existence of macroeconomic relations between aggregates. This in contrast is done by the relation approach. Both methods will be briefly illustrated (in section 2) in particular in the context of production theory although other applications are possible.

Formally, the relation approach considers the functional equation

$$(1.1)\quad y(f^1(x_{11},\dots,x_{1m}),\dots\dots,f^n(x_{n1},\dots,x_{nm})) = F(g^1(x_{11},\dots,x_{n1}),\dots\dots,g^m(x_{1m},\dots,x_{nm})).$$

That problem originally has been suggested by L.R.KLEIN [1946a], [1946b] and solved by A.NATAF [1948] under the assumption that all functions in (1.1) have positive partial derivatives. (See also the monograph H.A.J.GREEN [1964].) Continuous solutions of (1.1) can be found in W.M.GORMAN [1968].

In this note I shall show how the relation approach can work if "analytic" properties (differentiability, continuity) are replaced by "functional" properties. For that purpose the concept of "positive substitution" (for production functions) will be introduced (in section 3). In section 4 main results on general solutions of (1.1) - called aggregate solutions - are collected (from F.POKROPP [1972a] , [1972b]). In particular we shall see that (1.1) can be reduced to a functional equation for two functions only:

(1.2) $$y_o(F_o(a_{11},\dots,a_{1m}),\dots\dots,F_o(a_{n1},\dots,a_{nm})) = F_o(y_o(a_{11},\dots,a_{n1}),\dots\dots,y_o(a_{1m},\dots,a_{nm})).$$

For the treatment of (1.2) the notion of "elementary production functions (and/or index functions)" will be helpful. Such functions are generated by functions of two variables only (see section 5). We then shall find (in section 6) that "positively substitutional aggregate solutions" consist of elementary functions. Their functional behaviour is described in terms of "semigroups". Similar to J.ACZEL [1966] where algebraic methods are used when analytic tools are not at hand we reduce the structure of (certain) aggregate solutions to the structure of ordered semigroups. (For the algebraic terminology we refer to L.FUCHS [1963].)

Under the assumption that production functions (and/or index functions) are "unbounded" in the sense that any possible output quantity can be produced by sufficient high multiples of a fixed factor combination -- under that assumption all functions in (1.1) turn out to be "generalized quasilinear":

(1.3) $$f(x_1,\dots,x_k) = h(\textstyle\sum_i h^i(x_i)).$$

Note that functions of the form (1.3) occur in many functional equations in economics; see W.EICHHORN [forthcoming].

It is known (see e.g. H.A.J.GREEN [1964] , W.M.GORMAN [1968]) that differentiable solutions as well as continuous solutions of (1.1) also have the structure (1.3). We thus see that in solving (1.1) functional equation methods can lead to results similar to those obtained by analytic methods.

2. Semantic Approach Versus Relation Approach

Semantic approach. Consider an economy with n firms. The i-th firm produces good number i using m(i) production factors according to the i-th production function:

$$w_i = f^i(x_{i1},\ldots,x_{im(i)})$$

is the output quantity produced with input quantities $x_{i1},\ldots,x_{im(i)}$.
There are m(1) + ... + m(n) microeconomic production factors. We now look at the "economic character" (semantic characteristics) of those factors. Suppose that we find m different "types" -- e.g. type 1: labour of type 1, type 2: labour of type 2, type 3: capital of type 1, etc... For simplicity we rewrite f^i in such a way that type j occurs as the j-th variable in f^i. Note that this is not too strong an assumption if the f^i need not be strictly increasing!

Let from now on be

x_{ij} = quantity of the j-th factor type in the i-th firm.

We now look for index functions

$y(w_1,\ldots\ldots,w_n)$ = index for total output,

$g^j(x_{1j},\ldots,x_{nj}) = z_j$ = index for total quantity of factor j.

To determine y, $g^1,\ldots, g^m$ we impose (certain) requirements

on them according to their economic character. For instance, if g^1 represents "labour" it has often been considered natural (with the help of the deus ex machina "homogeneity") to take g^1 as a weighted sum of its variables. An analogous statement can be made about y. For a capital index g^2 (say) famous controversies have been carried out why or why not g^2 must or must not have a certain structure. (See e.g. G.C.HARCOURT [1969].)
Anyhow: ultimately we make up our mind about (at least some of) the index functions. What remains to do is to investigate how it is possible to find (the remaining index functions and) a macroeconomic production function , i.e. a function $F = F(z_1,\dots,z_m)$ such that (1.1) holds.

Very often, (1.1) will be possible merely for some but not all factor combinations. Specification of y and some (or all) g^j and some (or all) f^i and perhaps F does not leave too many "degrees of freedom" for the variables. Economically speaking: in the semantic approach the distribution of factors among firms will play a decisive part in the construction of a macroeconomic production function. The extreme case is given with a fixed distribution which admits to write $x_{ij} = x_{ij}(z_j)$ for all i,j.
We then trivially obtain a macroeconomic production function F:

$$F(z_1,\dots,z_m) = y(f^1(x_{11}(z_1),\dots,x_{1m}(z_m)),f^2(x_{21}(z_1),\dots\dots)).$$

<u>Relation approach</u>. If we want (1.1) to be a macroeconomic relation

$$y(w_1,\dots\dots,w_n) = F(z_1,\dots\dots,z_m)$$

we must require (1.1) to hold for all x_{ij}. The relation approach starts with that very point as the only requirement for index functions and production functions. We are (at this stage) not at all interested in the "economic character" of g^1, g^2, etc..., but we want functions y, $f^1,\dots,F$, $g^1,\dots$ which satisfy (1.1) for all x_{ij}.

To make that point clear, suppose that again we are given n production functions $f^1,\ldots,f^n$ where each f^i is written as a function of m variables, $x_{i1},\ldots,x_{im}$, say. The labelling of the variables is arbitrary but fixed. Nontheless the labelling is important since it decides what factors are to be aggregated together. After we have found (and not before!) functions y, $g^1,\ldots,g^m$, F such that (1.1) holds for all x_{ij} we are justified to talk about m "different types of production factors" and to call

y = index for total output,
g^j = index for the total j-th factor,
F = macroeconomic production function.

Clearly, in the relation approach the index functions might become "unusual" (e.g. not weighted sums). (There was a vehement controversy on that point between S.S.PU [1946] and K.MAY [1946], [1947] on one side and L.R.KLEIN [1946a], [1946b] on the other.) I myself do not consider unusual index functions to be a serious argument against the relation approach. All we have to do is to get used to such functions and to suggest their use in national statistical bureaus. The reward will be "distributionfree" macroeconomic relations. (Note: Physicists had to get used to an "index" for "total velocity" which is not the sum of the single velocities but is given according to the Lorentz Transformation!)

3. Positive Substitution

From an economist's view-point continuity and/or differentiability might be considered unsatisfactory properties of production functions (and/or index functions) because they need production factors which can be devided arbitrarily often into "infinitely small" parts. To avoid that shortcoming I shall merely assume that production functions and indexes are monotonically increasing in each variable. Under that assumption we must redefine what "substitution" can mean. The concept of substitution as given by R.FRISCH [1965] will be formulated without analytic tools.

Let the set

$$X_{ij} \subset R_+ \quad \text{for} \quad i=1,\dots,n;\ j=1,\dots,m$$

represent all possible input quantities of the j-th factor in the i-th firm. For abbreviation we write for cartesian products

$$X_{i\cdot} = \times_j X_{ij}\ , \quad X_{\cdot j} = \times_i X_{ij}$$

with elements

$$x_{i\cdot} = (x_{i1},\dots,x_{im}),\ x_{\cdot j} = (x_{1j},\dots,x_{nj}).$$

We use the following notation throughout this paper: a function of several variables is called a

↑-function (resp. ⇑-function)

if it is monotonically (resp. strictly monotonically) increasing in each variable.

Suppose that the i-th production function is

(3.1) $f^i: X_{i\cdot} \longrightarrow \mathbb{R}_+$, a ↑-function.

$X_{i\cdot}$ represents all possible factor combinations in the i-th firm. Note that for instance limitational factors are not excluded so far since f^i is a ↑-function but not necessarily a ⇑-function. Clearly, (3.1) is in accordance with the axioms for production functions given by R.W.SHEPHARD [1970].

In order to give a formal definition of substitution we go back to R.FRISCH [1965,p.55]: "If, taking as our starting point a definite factor combination, we can alternatively increase the product quantity, either by increasing the quantity of a given factor (e.g.No.h) and keeping the quantities of all other factors constant, or by increasing the quantity of another given factor (e.g.No.k) and keeping the quantities of all the other factors (now including No.h) constant, then we say that the two factors (No.h and No.k) are in a substitution relationship to one another in the factor combination concerned."

To formalize that verbal definition we have to consider factor increases. Let

(3.2) $[x_{ij}] = \{x'_{ij}: x'_{ij} \in X_{ij}, x'_{ij} \geq x_{ij}\}$.

(3.3) Definition:
f^i is positively (j,s)-substitutional in $x^o_{i.}$ ($x^o_{i.} \in X_{i.}$) if

(3.4) $$f^i(x^o_{i1},\ldots,[x^o_{ij}],\ldots,x^o_{is},\ldots,x^o_{im}) = f^i(x^o_{i1},\ldots,x^o_{ij},\ldots,[x^o_{is}],\ldots,x^o_{im}),$$

where in an obvious notation the left hand side of (3.4)(e.g.) equals the set $\{f^i(x^o_{i1},\ldots,x_{ij},\ldots,x^o_{is},\ldots,x^o_{im}): x_{ij} \geq x^o_{ij}\}$.

As concernes index functions we assume that for the j-th factor we have

(3.5) $g^j: X_{.j} \longrightarrow \mathbb{R}_+$, a $\uparrow$-function.

Clearly, (3.5) is a very mild axiom for an index function. In particular, $\uparrow$-property rather than $\Uparrow$-property admits the possibility of "inefficient" increases of j-th input quantities in firms. The concept of substitution for an index function will now have to refer to firms. We start with a given distribution $x^o_{.j} \in X_{.j}$ of the j-th factor among the n firms. We then consider alternatively an increase of the j-th factor in the i-th firm or in the t-th firm:

(3.6) Definition:
g^j is called positively (i,t)-substitutional in $x^o_{.j}$ if

(3.7) $$g^j(x^o_{1j},\ldots,[x^o_{ij}],\ldots,x^o_{tj},\ldots,x^o_{nj}) = g^j(x^o_{1j},\ldots,x^o_{ij},\ldots,[x^o_{tj}],\ldots,x^o_{nj}).$$

It will turn out that positive substitution will help us to find definite solutions of (1.1) resp. (1.2) (in a similar way as did "full substitution" in F.POKROPP [1972b]). In that sense it is a good substitute for positive partial derivatives. Conditions (3.4) and (3.7) are statements about the range of certain functions. We might consider them to be of a "functional equation character".

4. Aggregate Solutions

By an aggregate solution we mean a set of functions satisfying (1.1). We do however assume that the index for total output and the macroeconomic production function are $\uparrow$-functions. (Possible "inefficiencies" have been taken care of in the $\uparrow$-property of the f^i and the g^j.) In this section we collect main results on aggregate solutions. (For detailled proofs see F.POKROPP [1972a], [1972b].)

(4.1) Definition:

Let be given

production functions f^i from (3.1),

index functions g^j from (3.5).

Let $W_i = f^i(X_{i\cdot})$, $Z_j = g^j(X_{\cdot j})$ and let be

(4.2) $y: \times_i W_i \longrightarrow \mathbb{R}_+$, a $\uparrow$-function,

(4.3) $F: \times_j Z_j \longrightarrow \mathbb{R}_+$, a $\uparrow$-function.

Let equation (1.1) hold, i.e.

(4.4) $y(f^1(x_{1\cdot}),\dots,f^n(x_{n\cdot})) = F(g^1(x_{\cdot 1}),\dots,g^m(x_{\cdot m}))$ for all x_{ij}.

Then $\{y;\ f^1,\dots,f^n/\ F;\ g^1,\dots,g^m\}$ is called an aggregate solution for (G,G^*) where the $\uparrow$-functions G and G^* are defined by

(4.5) $G(x_{1\cdot},\dots,x_{n\cdot}) = y(f^1(x_{1\cdot}),\dots,f^n(x_{n\cdot}))$,

(4.6) $G^*(x_{\cdot 1},\dots,x_{\cdot m}) = F(g^1(x_{\cdot 1}),\dots,g^m(x_{\cdot m}))$.

y is called index for total output, F is called macroeconomic production function.

All aggregate solutions for (G,G^*) can be generated from one solution for (G,G^*) by means of monotonic transformations.

(4.7) Theorem:

Let $\{y; f^1,..,f^n/ F; g^1,..,g^m\}$ and $\{y_o;f_o^1,..,f_o^n/F_o;g_o^1,..,g_o^m\}$ be aggregate solutions for (G,G^*). Then there exist $\uparrow$-functions α^i, β^j $(i=1,...,n;\ j=1,...,m)$ such that

(4.8) $f^i = \alpha^i f_o^i, \quad g^j = \beta^j g_o^j$

and hence

(4.9) $y_o(u_1,...,u_n) = y(\alpha^1(u_1),...,\alpha^n(u_n)),$

$$F_o(v_1,...,v_m) = F(\beta^1(v_1),...,\beta^m(v_m)).$$

Proof:

Let $u_i = f_o^i(x_{i.})$. Then define

(4.10) $\alpha^i(u_i) = f^i(x_{i.})$.

Show: α^i is welldefined, i.e. it does not depend on the chosen representatives $x_{i.}$ for u_i. Show: if $f_o^i(x_{i.}) = f_o^i(x'_{i.})$ then $f^i(x_{i.}) = f^i(x'_{i.})$. According to (4.5) both statements ("if" and "then") are equivalent with

$$G(x_{1.}^o,..,x_{i.},..,x_{n.}^o) = G(x_{1.}^o,..,x'_{i.},..,x_{n.}^o)$$

where $x_{1.}^o,...,x_{n.}^o$ is an arbitrary point. In a similar way α^i is shown to be a $\uparrow$-function. The second part follows analogously by means of (4.6).

From now on we can concentrate on special solutions. Their construction is given in

(4.11) Theorem:

Suppose that there exists an aggregate solution for (G,G^*).

Then the following construction leads to an aggregate solution $\{y_o;f_o^1,..,f_o^n/F_o;g_o^1,..,g_o^m\}$ for (G,G^*): take an arbitrary but fixed point $x^o = (x_{11}^o,...,x_{1m}^o,x_{21}^o,.....,x_{nm}^o)$ and define

(4.12) $f_o^i(x_{i.}) = G(x_{1.}^o,...,x_{i.},...,x_{n.}^o)$,

(4.13) $g^j(x_{.j}) = G^*(x_{.1}^o,...,x_{.j},...,x_{.m}^o)$,

(4.14) $y_o(u_1,..,u_n)=G(x_{1.},..,x_{n.})$ with $x_{i.}$ such that $f_o^i(x_{i.})=u_i$,

(4.15) $F_o(v_1,..,v_m)=G^*(x_{.1},..,x_{.m})$ with $x_{.j}$ such that $g_o^j(x_{.j})=v_j$.

Proof:

The main point is to show that y_o and F_o are welldefined and $\uparrow$-functions. To show y_o (e.g.) to be welldefined show: $f_o^i(x_{i.}) = f_o^i(x_{i.}')$ for all i implies $G(x_{1.},..,x_{n.})=G(x_{1.}',..,x_{n.}')$. As in the proof of (4.7), $f_o^i(x_{i.}) = f_o^i(x_{i.}')$ implies $f^i(x_{i.}) = f^i(x_{i.}')$ (say) where $\{y;f^1,..,f^n/F;g^1,..,g^m\}$is an arbitrary aggregate solution for (G,G^*). Use now (4.5) to conclude $G(x_{1.},...,x_{n.}) = G(x_{1.}',...,x_{n.}')$. In a similar way y_o is shown to be a $\uparrow$-function.

(4.16) Definition:

$\{y_o;\ f_o^1,...,f_o^n/\ F_o;\ g_o^1,...,g_o^m\}$ as defined in (4.11) is called the by x^o normed aggregate solution for (G,G^*).

By means of normed solutions we reduce the functional equation (4.4) to a functional equation for y_o and F_o only. Define $\uparrow$-functions $k_o^{ij}: X_{ij} \longrightarrow \mathbb{R}_+$ by

(4.17) $k_o^{ij}(x_{ij}) = G(x_{1.}^o,...,x_{i1}^o,..,x_{ij},..,x_{im}^o,...,x_{n.}^o)$.

We then apparently have

(4.18) $f_o^i(x_{i1}^o,..,x_{ij},..,x_{im}^o)=k_o^{ij}(x_{ij})=g_o^j(x_{1j}^o,..,x_{ij},..,x_{nj}^o)$,

and for $x_{ij} = x_{ij}^o$ we obtain

(4.19) $k_o^{ij}(x_{ij}^o)=f_o^i(x_{i.}^o)=g_o^j(x_{.j}^o)=e;\ y_o(e,..,e)=e=F_o(e,..,e)$.

We now observe (4.12), (4.14) and (4.13), (4.15) to conclude:

(4.20) $y_o(e,...,u_i,...,e) = u_i;\ F_o(e,...,v_j,...,e) = v_j$.

The most interesting fact about normed solutions is stated in

(4.21) <u>Theorem</u>:

(4.22) $f_o^i(x_{i.}) = F_o(a_{i.})$ where $a_{ij} = k_o^{ij}(x_{ij})$,

(4.23) $g_o^j(x_{.j}) = y_o(a_{.j})$,

(4.24) $y_o(F_o(a_{1.}),...,F_o(a_{n.})) = F_o(y_o(a_{.1}),...,y_o(a_{.m}))$.

<u>Proof</u>:

It is sufficient to prove (4.22). According to (4.4), (4.5), (4.6) we have

(4.25) $G(x_{1.}^o,..,x_{i.},..,x_{n.}^o) =$

$$G^*(x_{11}^o..x_{i1}..x_{n1}^o,...,x_{1j}^o..x_{ij}..x_{nj}^o,...,x_{1m}^o..x_{im}..x_{nm}^o).$$

The left hand side of (4.25) is $f_o^i(x_{i.})$ according to (4.12), according to (4.15) and (4.18) the right hand side of (4.25) equals $F_o(k_o^{i1}(x_{i1}),..,k_o^{ij}(x_{ij}),..,k_o^{im}(x_{im}))$.

Theorem (4.21) deserves our attention for two reasons. <u>First</u>: All production functions in an aggregate solution must be "of the same kind" in the sense of (4.8) and (4.22). To put it different if we measure factor quantities in a suitable way -- in "units" of $k_o^{ij}(x_{ij})$ rather than in "units" of x_{ij} -- then all production functions are identical up to $\ddagger$-transformations. <u>Second</u>: We have to solve a functional equation for two functions only -- (4.24) resp. (1.2) -- rather than equation (4.4) resp. (1.1) for $n + m + 2$ functions. We shall continue with (4.24) in section 6.

5. Elementary Processes

It will turn out that aggregate solutions which are positively substitutional (see (6.1)) are constructed in a simple way. All production functions and indexes are generated by functions of two variables only.

(5.1) Definition:
Let $f = f(x_1,\dots,x_k)$ be a $\uparrow$-function (e.g. a production function, an index function). f is called elementary in $x^* = (x_1^*,\dots,x_k^*)$ if there exists a $\updownarrow$-function δ such that for all $r=1,..,k-1$ we have

(5.2) $f(x_1,\dots,x_k) = \delta(f(x_1..x_r,x_{r+1}^*..x_k^*),f(x_1^*..x_r^*,x_{r+1}..x_k))$.

δ is called the x^* -elementary process of f.

(5.3) Lemma:
If f is elementary in x^*, then any $\updownarrow$-transformation αf is also elementary in x^*.
Proof:
$\alpha f = \alpha\delta(\alpha^{-1}\alpha f(x_1..x_r,x_{r+1}^*..x_k^*),\alpha^{-1}\alpha f(x_1^*..x_r^*,x_{r+1}..x_k))$ or
$\alpha f = \delta'(\alpha f(x_1..x_r,x_{r+1}^*..x_k^*),\alpha f(x_1^*..x_r^*,x_{r+1}..x_k))$ with
$\delta'(x,y) = \alpha\delta(\alpha^{-1}(x),\alpha^{-1}(y))$. Clearly, δ' is a $\updownarrow$-function.

Consider now an aggregate solution $\{y;f^1,..,f^n/F;g^1,..,g^m\}$ for (G,G^*). Let

(5.4) f^i: elementary in $x_{i.}^o$; g^j: elementary in $x_{.j}^o$.

For the by x^o normed solution $\{y_o;f_o^1,..,f_o^n/F_o;g_o^1,..,g_o^m\}$ we obtain from (5.4) by means of (5.3) that

f_o^i is elementary in $x_{i.}^o$, g_o^j is elementary in $x_{.j}^o$.

Let be

(5.5) H^i: $x_{i.}^o$-elementary process of f_o^i,

K^j: $x_{.j}^o$-elementary process of g_o^j.

(5.6) Definition:

$(H^1,\ldots,H^n/K^1,\ldots,K^m)$ (with H^i and K^j from (5.5)) is called the elementary process set for (G,G^*) normed by x^o.

(5.7) Definition:

(G,G^*) is said to have a x^o-elementary process H if in the by x^o normed elementary process set for (G,G^*) all elementary processes are equal to H. We then have

(5.8) $H^i = H = K^j$ for all i,j.

Let (G,G^*) have an x^o-elementary process H. (5.2), (5.5), (5.8) then yield:

(5.9) $f_o^i(x_{i.}) = H(f_o^i(x_{i1}..x_{ij},x_{ij+1}^o..x_{im}^o),f_o^i(x_{i1}^o..x_{ij}^o,x_{ij+1}..x_{im}))$,

(5.10) $g_o^j(x_{.j}) = H(g_o^j(x_{1j}..x_{ij},x_{i+1j}^o..x_{nj}^o),g_o^j(x_{1j}^o..x_{ij}^o,x_{i+1j}..x_{nj}))$.

Consider now theorem (4.21). (5.9) with (4.22), (4.19) and (5.10) with (4.23), (4.19) show

(5.11) $F_o(a_{i.}) = H(F_o(a_{i1}\ldots a_{ij},e\ldots e),F_o(e\ldots e,a_{ij+1}\ldots a_{im}))$,

(5.12) $y_o(a_{.j}) = H(y_o(a_{1j}\ldots a_{ij},e\ldots e),y_o(e\ldots e,a_{i+1j}\ldots a_{nj}))$.

The following statement is trivial:

(5.13) Lemma:

(G,G^*) has an x^o-elementary process H if and only if (5.11) and (5.12) hold.

6. Positively Substitutional Aggregate Solutions

(6.1) Definition:
An aggregate solution $\{y;f^1,..,f^n/F;g^1,..,g^m\}$ for (G,G^*) is called positively substitutional in x^o if

f^i is positively (j,s)-substitutional in $x^o_{i.}$

g^j is positively (i,t)-substitutional in $x^o_{.j}$

for all $i,t=1,...,n$ and $j,s=1,...,m$.

Let $\{y;f^1,..,f^n/F;g^1,..,g^m\}$ be an in x^o positively substitutional aggregate solution for (G,G^*). The by x^o normed solution $\{y_o;f^1_o,..,f^n_o/F_o;g^1_o,..,g^m_o\}$ will then also be positively substitutional in x^o (as is seen from (3.3), (3.6) and (4.7)). From (3.4), (3.7) and (4.18) we conclude (for notation: see (3.2)) that the following set is independent of i,j:

(6.2) $k^{ij}_o([x^o_{ij}]) = A = [e]$.

We now make the following restriction:

(6.3) $X_{ij} = [x^o_{ij}]$ (and hence $A = k^{ij}_o(X_{ij})$).

Remark: We need (6.3) for convenience only. If (6.3) does not hold statements "for all $x_{ij} \in X_{ij}$" will be valid for all $x_{ij} \in [x^o_{ij}]$.

(6.4) Theorem:
Let (G,G^*) have aggregate solutions which are positively substitutional in x^o. Then (G,G^*) has an x^o-elementary process H with the following properties:

(6.5) H is a $\updownarrow$-function,

(6.6) $H(a,e) = a = H(e,a)$ for all $a \in A$,

(6.7) $H(H(a,b),c) = H(a,H(b,c))$ for all $a,b,c \in A$,

(6.8) $H(a,b) = H(b,a)$ for all $a,b \in A$.

Proof:

Define H in the following way:

$$(6.9)\quad H(p,q) = \begin{cases} F_o(p,q,e,\dots,e) & \text{for } m \leq n \\ y_o(p,q,e,\dots,e) & \text{for } m > n. \end{cases}$$

We first show that (5.11) and (5.12) hold. Let $m \leq n$ without loss of generality. According to (6.2), (6.3) we have in (4.20) $u_i \in F_o(A^m)$, $v_j \in y_o(A^n)$ (see (4.22), (4.23)), and it does not matter at all at what places the variables in (4.20) stand! Write $F_o(a_{i.})$ in the following form:

$$(6.10)\quad F_o(a_{i.}) = F_o(y_o(\dots e,a_{i1},e\dots),\dots,y_o(\dots e,a_{im},e\dots)).$$

If in (6.10) we put a_{ij} at place j in y_o ($j \leq m \leq n$) we obtain after application of (4.24) and (4.20)

$$(6.11)\quad F_o(a_{i1},\dots,a_{im}) = y_o(a_{i1},\dots,a_{im},e,\dots,e) \quad (\text{for } m \leq n).$$

If in (6.10) $a_{i1},\dots,a_{ij}$ are placed as first variables of y_o, $a_{ij+1},\dots,a_{im}$ are placed as second variables of y_o we obtain after application of (4.24), (4.20)

$$(6.12)\quad F_o(a_{i.}) = y_o(F_o(a_{i1}..a_{1j},e..e),F_o(e..e,a_{ij+1}..a_{im}),e,\dots,$$

Since the procedure for (6.12) as well as (6.10) did not use $m \leq n$ we analogously to (6.12) have

$$(6.13)\quad y_o(a_{.j}) = F_o(y_o(a_{1j}..a_{ij},e..e),y_o(e..e,a_{i+1j}..a_{nj}),e,\dots,$$

Now (6.13) and (6.9) yield (5.12) and (6.11) yields (5.11). According to (5.13), H from (6.9) is the x^o-elementary process of (G,G^*).

(6.5) follows from (6.9) since F_o and y_o are ↟-functions.

(6.6) follows from (4.20). (6.7) follows from (4.24) and (6.6). To show (6.8) we show: y_o and F_o are symmetric functions. Because of (4.24) it is sufficient to show: F_o is symmetric on A^m, y_o is symmetric on A^n. (!!) Analogous to (6.12) we can obtain

$$F_o(a_1,\dots,a_m) = y_o(F_o(..e..a_j..a_s..e..),F_o(a_1..\underset{j}{e}..\underset{s}{e}..a_m),e...e).$$

Thus F_o will be symmetric on A^m if

$$F_o(e,..,e,a_j,..,a_s,e,..,e) = F_o(e,..,e,a_s,..,a_j,e,..,e)$$

for all j,s. Analogous to (6.12) both expressions are equal to $y_o(a_j,a_s,e,\dots,e)$ (say).

The elementary process generates the f^i and g^j but not necessarily y and F. According to (5.11), (5.12) F_o is generated on A^m and y_o is generated on A^n (but not necessarily on $(y_o(A^n))^m$ resp. $(F_o(A^m))^n$). To generate y_o and F_o everywhere according to (5.11) and (5.12) we consider the case $H(A,A) \subset A$.

(6.14) Definition:
The x^o-elementary process H of (G,G^*) is closed if $H(A,A) \subset A$.

(6.15) Theorem:
Let (G,G^*) have an aggregate solution $\{y;f^1,..,f^n/F;g^1,..,g^m\}$ which is positively substitutional in x^o. Let further exist subscripts i, j, s such that

(6.16) f^i is positively (j,s)-substitutional in
$(x^o_{i1},\dots,x_{ij},\dots,x^o_{im})$ for each $x_{ij} \in X_{ij}$.

On A (see (6.2), (6.3)) define a binary operation by means of the x^o-elementary process H of (G,G^*) in the following way:

(6.17) $a \,\square\, b = H(a,b)$ for $a, b \in A$.

Then $A(\square)$ is a naturally ordered cancellative abelian semigroup. (see L.FUCHS [1963] p.153f.)

Proof:
Consider f^i_o in the by x^o normed aggregate solution for (G,G^*). f^i_o also satisfies (6.16) as is seen from (4.8). Use (4.22)

to obtain: $F_o(e,..,\underset{j}{a},..,\underset{s}{[e]},..,e) = F_o(e,..,\underset{j}{[a]},..,\underset{s}{e},..,e)$.

This according to (6.9) means:

(6.18) $H(a,A) = [a]$.

In particular we have (by (6.2), (6.3)): H is closed. From theorem (6.4) we then conclude: $A(\square)$ is a (fully) ordered cancellative abelian semigroup. Since all elements in A are "positive" ($a \square b \geq a$, $a \square b \geq b$ for all $a, b \in A = [e]$) and since according to (6.18) to any $a, b \in A$ with $a < b$ there exists an element $c \in A$ such that $a \square c = b$, $A(\square)$ is naturally ordered.

(6.19) Corollary

Under the assumptions of (6.15) we have

$$G(x_{1.},\dots,x_{n.}) = k_o^{11}(x_{11}) \square k_o^{12}(x_{12}) \square \dots\dots \square k_o^{nm}(x_{nm}),$$

where $\square$ defines a naturally ordered cancellative abelian semigroup .

Proof:

(4.11), (4.21), (5.11), (5.12), (6.15).

Thus far we have reduced the structure of aggregate solutions to the structure of certain semigroups. For further determination of that structure we need further assumptions. If H in (6.17) is continuous then "generalized quasilinearity" of G (see (6.25)) can be proved (see J.ACZEL [1966],p.255ff). Since we do not want to use continuity we have to look for other powerful properties of H in (6.17).

Consider the quantity $a \in A$, $a > e$. We define recursively

(6.20) $H^o(a)=e$, $H^r(a)=H(H^{r-1}(a),a)$ for $r=1,2,\dots$

We apparently have: $H^r(a) > H^{r-1}(a)$ for all r. What happens for $r \longrightarrow \infty$?

(6.21) Definition:
Let H be the x^o-elementary process of (G,G^*). Let H be closed. H is called archimedean if for any a, b $\in$ A, a > e there exists a natural number r such that

(6.22) $H^r(a) > b$.

What is the economic meaning of (6.22)? Since H by assumption is closed the set A represents all possibles output quantities of the production function F_o as well as all input quantities for F_o $(A = H(e,A) \subset H(A,A) \subset A$ and hence $H(A,A) = A)$. Consider b in (6.22) as a given outputquantity, a as a given fixed input quantity. If the elementary process H is repeated sufficiently often where at the i-th repetition the input quantities "a" and "product quantity of the (i-1)-th repetition" are used (see (6.20)) then ultimately b will be exceeded. If we aggree to say:

$H^r(a) \in A$ represents the quantity "r times a"

(or $H^r(a)$ is the product quantity if a is given r times into the elementary process H according to (6.20)) we then can read (6.22) as follows: a sufficient high "multiple" of a will exceed b.

In the analysis of R.W.SHEPHARD [1970,p.22] the following "unboundedness" for a production function Φ occurs: to any point $(x_1,\ldots,x_k)$ (with $x_j > 0$ for some j) and any constant c there exists a natural number r such that

(6.23) $\Phi(r\cdot x_1,\ldots,r\cdot x_k) > c$.

In my opinion there is a close semantic relationship between (6.23) and (6.22). Consequently, I take (6.23) to justify (6.22) as possible and worth while to be discussed.

(6.24) Theorem:
If under the conditions of (6.15) the x^o-elementary process H of (G,G^*) is archimedean then there exist a $\updownarrow$-function h and $\uparrow$-functions k^{ij} such that

(6.25) $G(x_{1\cdot},\ldots,x_{n\cdot}) = h\left(\sum_i\sum_j k^{ij}(x_{ij}) \right) = G^*(x_{\cdot 1},\ldots,x_{\cdot m})$.

Proof:
Under (6.22), A(□) in (6.14) is archimedean(see L.FUCHS [1963,p.162]). According to a theorem by HÖLDER and CLIFFORD (see L.FUCHS [1963,p.165]), A(□) is then order isomorphic to a subsemigroup of the additive semigroup of $\mathbb{R}_+$. Thus there exists a ↑-function h^- such that

(6.26) $h^-(a \,\square\, b) = h^-(a) + h^-(b).$

Let h be the inverse function of h^-. Apply h to (6.26) to obtain

$$a \,\square\, b = h\,(\,h^-(a) + h^-(b)\,).$$

The rest follows from (6.19).

References

J.ACZEL [1966]: Lectures on Functional Equations and their Applications. New York, London.
W.EICHHORN [forthcoming]: Functional Equations in Economics.
R.FRISCH [1965]: Theory of Production. Dordrecht, Holland.
L.FUCHS [1963]: Partially Ordered Algebraic Systems. Oxford et al.
W.M.GORMAN [1968]: The Structure of Utility Functions. Review of Economic Studies Vol.35, p.367-390.
H.A.J.GREEN [1964]: Aggregation in Economic Analysis. Princeton.
G.C.HARCOURT [1969]: Some Cambridge Controversies in the Theory of Capital. Journal of Economic Literature Vol.7, p.369-405.
L.R.KLEIN [1946a]: Remarks on the Theory of Aggregation. Econometrica Vol.14, p.303-312.
L.R.KLEIN [1946b]: Macroeconomics and the Theory of Rational Behavior. Econometrica Vol.14, p.93-108.
K.MAY [1946]: The Aggregation Problem for a One-Industry Model. Econometrica Vol.14, p.285-297.
K.MAY [1947]: Technological Change and Aggregation. Econometrica Vol.15, p.51-63.

A.NATAF [1948]: Sur la Possibilité de Construction de Certain Macromodèles. Econometrica Vol.16, p.232-244.

F.POKROPP [1972a]: A Note on the Problem of Aggregation. Review of Economic Studies Vol.39, p.221-230.

F.POKROPP [1972b]: Aggregation von Produktionsfunktionen. Berlin, Heidelberg, New York.

S.S.PU [1946]: A Note on Macroeconomics. Econometrica Vol.14, p.299-302.

R.W.SHEPHARD [1970]: Theory of Cost and Production Functions. Princeton.

On the Problem of Using Aggregate Predictions

by Klaus Reeh

0. Introduction

Econometricians working on predictions for economic variables are often confronted with different predictions for the same economic variable differing only with respect to the economic units the variables refer to. Consider, for example, the problem of predicting prices for a subset of all goods under consideration when there is available a prediction for the price index for the entire set of goods. Another problem encoutered is one of predicting the regional distribution of demand for a consumer good when predictions are available of the demand for the same good according to some social attributes of consumers, like occupation, age or family-size. These problems arise because of different levels of aggregation and different classifications of observed economic units by various social characteristics.

The questions to be answered by the econometrican in this context are as follows: Is it possible to make use of these predictions. If it is possible, how should they be used, and what can be said about the success of using them? Our answers depend on the basic prediction model, the definition of the respective economic units as well as the aggregated or pooled variables, and the assumptions we can make concerning the stochastic and deterministic properties of the additional predictions. Here we confine ourselves to a simple model for combining time-series of cross-sections. Primarily we will treat the case of different levels of aggregation, leading to what can be described briefly as the external case. The case of different classifications of data by social characteristics, leading to what can be named the internal case, will only be briefly outlined by considering two specific but rather instructive cases.

1. The basic predictions

There are N economic units. For each unit $i=1,2,\dots,N$ in periods $t=1,2,\dots,T,T+1$ we can observe an endogenous economic variable $y_{i,t}$ as well as a set of n exogenous economic or non-economic variables $x_{i,1,t},\dots,x_{i,n,t}$. At the end of period T we have to predict the endogenous variable for all N economic units in period T+1 by using an econometric prediction model. Therefore we arrange the N variables $y_{i,t}$ to Nx1 vector variables $y_{N,t}$. Likewise we arrange the N sets of exogeneous variables $x_{i,1,t},\dots,x_{i,n,t}$ for all periods to Nxn matrix variables $X_{N,t}$. Thereupon we specify the basic N-prediction model introducing latent variables $u_{i,t}$ for all economic units and periods suitably arranged to Nx1 vector variables $u_{N,t}$.+)

(N-1) $y_{N,t} = X_{N,t}\beta + u_{N,t}$

(N-2.1) $E(u_{N,t}|X_{N,1},\dots,X_{N,T+1}) = 0$

(N-2.2) $E(u_{N,t}u'_{N,t'}|X_{N,1},\dots,X_{N,T+1}) = \begin{cases}\sigma^2 I_N & t=t' \\ 0 & t\neq t'\end{cases}$

(N-3.1) $\beta\in R^n$

(N-3.2) $0 < \sigma^2 < \infty$ $\qquad t,t'=1,2,\dots,T,T+1$

Accordingly β is the nx1 parameter vector of the regression coefficients and σ^2 the scalar parameter of the variance.

We estimate the regression coefficients having arranged the time-series of matrix and vector variables suitably by the OLS-estimator

+) The label N indicates only the order of the vectors and matrices and must not be mixed up with the notation for the N'th unit which will not be used in the sequel.

(1) $\hat{\beta} = (\underline{X}_N'\underline{X}_N)^{-1}\underline{X}_N'\underline{y}_N$; $\underline{X}_N' = (X_{N,1}', \ldots, X_{N,T}')$, $\underline{y}_N' = (y_{N,1}', \ldots, y_{N,T}')$

and use these estimates to predict the endogenous variable for all economic units by

(2) $\hat{y}_{N,T+1} = X_{N,T+1}\hat{\beta}$

As we know we cannot avoid prediction errors

(3) $y_{N,T+1} - \hat{y}_{N,T+1} = u_{N,T+1} - X_{N,T+1}(\hat{\beta} - \beta)$.

For these errors we have zero conditional expectations and conditional variances and covariances

$$V(y_{N,T+1} - \hat{y}_{N,T+1} | X_{N,1}, \ldots, X_{N,T+1}) = \sigma^2 (I_N + X_{N,T+1}(\underline{X}_N'\underline{X}_N)^{-1} X_{N,T+1}').$$

These predictions and especially their characteristics are our guideline when we propose procedures using predictions for the same endogenous variable but with respect to different economic units.

2. The use of an aggregate prediction, external specification

An aggregate variable can be obtained by summing up the N basic variables; if we consider extensive variables like stocks and flows we use a simple sum, if we consider intensive variables like prices and rations we use a weighted sum. We obtain a prediction for such an aggregate variable by summing up the predictions for the N basic variables respectively. To consider only the simple extensive case we predict the aggregate variable

(4) $y_{1,T+1} = \iota_N' y_{N,T+1}$; $\iota_N' = (1,1,\ldots,1)$

by

(5) $\hat{y}_{1,T+1} = \iota_N' \hat{y}_{N,T+1} = \iota_N' X_{N,T+1}\hat{\beta} = X_{1,T+1}\hat{\beta}$.

Suppose now that we are confronted with an aggregate prediction $\tilde{y}_{1,T+1}$ for $y_{1,T+1}$ which is based neither on the basic N-prediction model nor a simplified version of it. In order to be able to use this prediction it is necessary to make reasonable assumptions connecting this prediction to the deterministic as well as stochastic part of the basic N-prediction model.

2.1. The external specification

Knowing that the additional aggregate prediction is affected by a prediction error

$$(6)\quad y_{1,T+1} - \tilde{y}_{1,T+1} = \iota_N' u_{N,T+1} - (\tilde{y}_{1,T+1} - \iota_N' X_{N,T+1}\,\beta)$$

$$(6')\quad = u_{1,T+1} - (\tilde{y}_{1,T+1} - X_{1,T+1}\,\beta)$$

we suppose

$$(A-1)\quad E(y_{1,T+1} - \tilde{y}_{1,T+1} \mid X_{N,1},\ldots,X_{N,T+1}) = 0$$

Here it matters only whether the conditional unbiasedness of the aggregate prediction with respect to the explaining and conditioning variables within the basic N-prediction model is assured. It is of no interest, however, wether the aggregate prediction is conditionally unbiased with respect to other variables Z_t not included in the basic N-prediction model but included in an aggregate 1-prediction model.

Next we assume that the conditional prediction error variance of the aggregate prediction is proportional to the number N of the basic economic units, i.e.

$$(A-2)\quad V(y_{1,T+1} - \tilde{y}_{1,T+1} \mid X_{N,1},\ldots,X_{N,T+1}) = \omega^2 N$$

As we consider only a constant number of basic units we do nothing but to normalize by this assumption. Furthermore we assume that the aggregate prediction is uncorrelated with the latent variables of the reference periods, i.e.

$$(A-3)\quad E(\tilde{y}_{1,T+1} u_{N,t}' \mid X_{N,1},\ldots,X_{N,T+1}) = 0 \qquad \Big| \; t=1,2,\ldots,T$$

It is this assumption that constitutes the external character of the aggregate prediction. Note that the corresponding correlation of the aggregate prediction obtained by summing up the N basic predictions is not zero; in fact

$$E(\hat{y}_{1,T+1}u'_{N,t} \mid X_{N,1},\ldots,X_{N,T+1}) = \sigma^2 \iota'_N X_{N,T+1}(X'_N X_N)^{-1} X'_{N,t} \quad \Big| \; t=1,\ldots,T$$

Finally we assume that we have the same correlation between the aggregate prediction and all N latent variables of the prediction period, i.e.

$$\text{(A-4)} \quad E(\tilde{y}_{1,T+1}u'_{N,T+1} \mid X_{N,1},\ldots,X_{N,T+1}) = \rho\iota'_N$$

It is obvious that our assumptions are rather specific. But before justifying and discussing the assumptions we want to demonstrate the way to use the aggregate prediction under this specification.

2.2. The improved predictions

According to our assumptions we can define a latent variable corresponding to the external aggregate prediction by

$$\text{(7)} \quad \tilde{u}_{1,T+1} = \tilde{y}_{1,T+1} - \iota'_N X_{N,T+1}\beta$$

$$\text{(7')} \quad \phantom{\tilde{u}_{1,T+1}} = u_{1,T+1} - (\tilde{y}_{1,T+1} - y_{1,T+1}),$$

the stochastic properties of which are

$$\text{(A-1')} \quad E(\tilde{u}_{1,T+1} \mid X_{N,1},\ldots,X_{N,T+1}) = 0$$

$$\text{(A-2')} \quad E(\tilde{u}^2_{1,T+1} \mid X_{N,1},\ldots,X_{N,T+1}) = N(\omega^2-\sigma^2+2\rho)$$

$$\text{(A-3')} \quad E(\tilde{u}_{1,T+1}u'_{N,t} \mid X_{N,1},\ldots,X_{N,T+1}) = 0 \quad \Big| \; t=1,2,\ldots,T$$

$$\text{(A-4')} \quad E(\tilde{u}_{1,T+1}u'_{N,T+1} \mid X_{N,1},\ldots,X_{N,T+1}) = \rho\iota'_N$$

But we have to realize that the two parameters ω^2 and ρ together with the parameter σ^2 have to fulfill the inequality

$$\text{(A-5)} \quad \omega^2/\sigma^2 \geq (\rho/\sigma^2 - 1)^2$$

in order that the joint conditional covariance matrix of the basic and the additional latent variables is positive semi-definite.

Now we can treat the aggregate prediction like an additional observation and therefore replace the basic OLS-estimator by the GLS-estimator

$$(8)\quad \check{\beta}=\Big(\underline{X}_N'\underline{X}_N+\frac{\sigma^2}{\omega^2-\sigma^2+2\rho}X_{N,T+1}'\,\bar{P}_N X_{N,T+1}\Big)^{-1}\Big(\underline{X}_N'\underline{y}_N+\frac{\sigma^2}{\omega^2-\sigma^2+2\rho}\,\frac{1}{N}\,X_{1,T+1}\tilde{y}_{1,T+1}\Big)$$

$$\bar{P}_N=\frac{1}{N}\,\iota_N\iota_N'$$

leading to the GLS-predictions

$$(9)\quad \check{y}_{N,T+1}=X_{N,T+1}\check{\beta}+\frac{\rho}{\omega^2-\sigma^2+2\rho}\,\frac{1}{N}\iota_N\Big(\tilde{y}_{1,T+1}-\frac{1}{N}X_{1,T+1}\check{\beta}\Big).$$

Obviously these GLS-predictions can be calculated also by working with the OLS-predictions and the difference between the external aggregate and the OLS-aggregate prediction.

$$(9')\quad \check{y}_{N,T+1}=\hat{y}_{N,T+1}+\frac{1}{N(\omega^2-\sigma^2+2\rho)+D\sigma^2}\Big(\rho I_N+\sigma^2 X_{N,T+1}(\underline{X}_N'\underline{X}_N)^{-1}X_{N,T+1}'\Big)\iota_N(\tilde{y}_{1,T+1}-\hat{y}_{1,T+1})$$

$$D=X_{1,T+1}(\underline{X}_N'\underline{X}_N)^{-1}X_{1,T+1}'$$

It is immediately clear that these predictions have prediction errors with conditional expectations zero and conditional variances and covariances

$$V(y_{N,T+1}-\check{y}_{N,T+1}\mid X_{N,1},\dots,X_{N,T+1})=V(y_{N,T+1}-\hat{y}_{N,T+1}\mid X_{N,1},\dots,X_{N,T+1})$$
$$-\frac{1}{N(\omega^2-\sigma^2+2\rho)+D\sigma^2}\Big(\rho I_N+\sigma^2X_{N,T+1}(\underline{X}_N'\underline{X}_N)^{-1}X_{N,T+1}'\Big)\iota_N\iota_N'\Big(\rho I_N+\sigma^2X_{N,T+1}(\underline{X}_N'\underline{X}_N)^{-1}X_{N,T+1}'\Big)$$

It is also obvious that we prefer the GLS- to the OLS-predictions because of the difference of the conditional covariance matrices being positive semi-definite. Moreover we can obtain aggregate predictions

$$(10)\quad \check{y}_{1,T+1}=X_{1,T+1}\check{\beta}+\frac{\rho}{\omega^2-\sigma^2+2\rho}\big(\tilde{y}_{1,T+1}-X_{1,T+1}\check{\beta}\big)$$

$$(10')\quad =\frac{N\rho+D\sigma^2}{N(\omega^2-\sigma^2+2\rho)+D\sigma^2}\,\tilde{y}_{1,T+1}+\frac{N(\omega^2-\sigma^2+\rho)}{N(\omega^2-\sigma^2+2\rho)+D\sigma^2}\,\hat{y}_{1,T+1}$$

preferable not only to the OLS-aggregate but also to the external aggregate prediction because of

$$V(y_{1,T+1}-\hat{y}_{1,T+1}\mid X_{N,1},\dots,X_{N,T+1})-V(y_{1,T+1}-\check{y}_{1,T+1}\mid X_{N,1},\dots,X_{N,T+1})$$
$$=\frac{(N\rho+D\sigma^2)^2}{N(\omega^2-\sigma^2+2\rho)+D\sigma^2}\geq 0$$

and

$$V(y_{1,T+1}-\tilde{y}_{1,T+1}|X_{N,1},\dots,X_{N,T+1})-V(y_{1.T+1}-\check{y}_{1,T+1}|X_{N,1},\dots,X_{N,T+1})$$
$$= \frac{N(\omega^2-\sigma^2+\rho)^2}{N(\omega^2-\sigma^2+2\rho\ )+D\sigma^2} \geqq 0$$

With the GLS-estimator and the GLS-predictions we have a usefull instrument we can apply to many cases. To see this we have to bear in mind that we have restricted the two parameters ω^2 and ρ together with the parameter σ^2 only by the inequality (A-5); thus a multitude of different parameter combinations is admissible, to all of which the GLS-procedures apply. Obviously the procedures are determined by the ratios ω^2/σ^2 and ρ/σ^2, so that we can represent the set of admissable parameter combinations as a set of points above the parabola as shown in the figure.

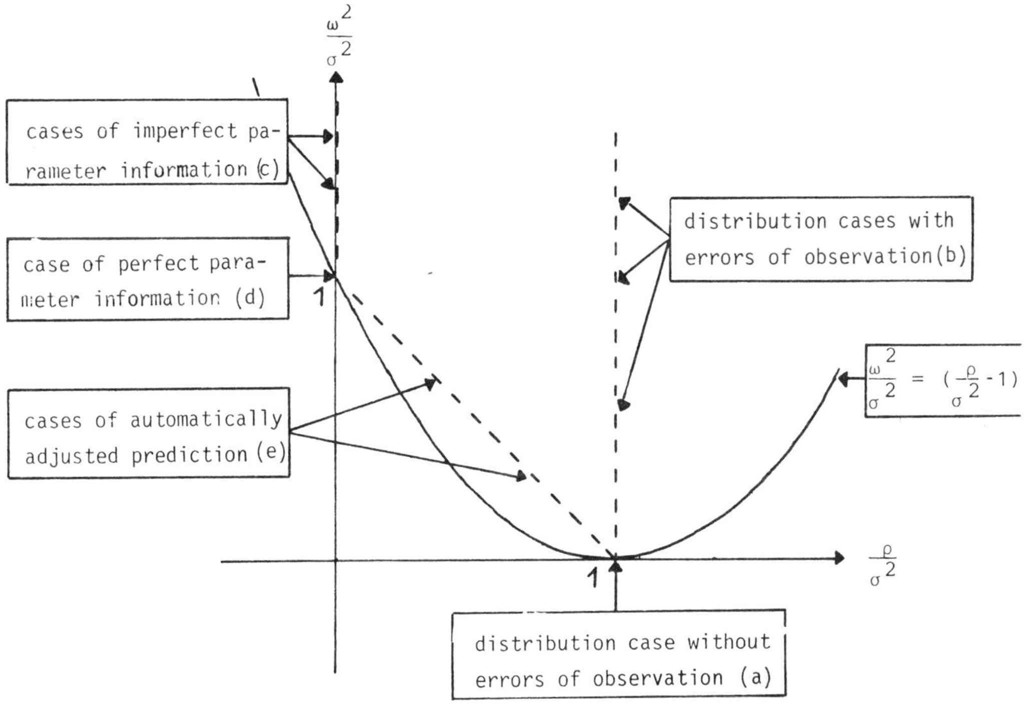

Now we want to discuss briefly some specific parameter combinations plotted in the figure.

2.3. Some special cases

(a) If we know by means of $\tilde{y}_{1,T+1}$ the realization of the aggregate variable for the prediction period exactly, we come to $\omega^2 = 0$ and therefore $\rho=\sigma^2$. Thus we have to do no more but to estimate the unknown realizations of the basic variable, i.e. to distribute the aggregate realisation. We then estimate by

$$(11)\quad \check{y}_{N,T+1} = X_{N,T+1}\check{\beta} + \frac{1}{N}\iota_N(\tilde{y}_{1,T+1} - X_{1,T+1}\check{\beta})$$

It is not surprising, that we come to

$$(12)\quad \check{y}_{1,T+1} = \tilde{y}_{1,T+1}.$$

(b) If we suppose that $\tilde{y}_{1,T+1}$ is an observation of the realization of the aggregate variable probably effected by errors, and that the observation errors are uncorrelated with all latent variables, we get

$$E(\tilde{y}_{1,T+1}u'_{N,T+1}\,|X_{N,1},\ldots,X_{N,T+1}) = \sigma^2\iota'_N,$$

too. Therefore we estimate the realizations of the basic variables by

$$(13)\quad \check{y}_{N,T+1} = X_{N,T+1}\check{\beta} + \frac{\sigma^2}{\omega^2+\sigma^2}\,\frac{1}{N}\,\iota_N(\tilde{y}_{1,T+1} - X_{1,T+1}\check{\beta})$$

$$(13')\quad = \hat{y}_{N,T+1} + \frac{\sigma^2}{N\omega^2+(N+D)\sigma^2}\,(I_N + X_{N,T+1}(\underline{X}'_N\underline{X}_N)^{-1}X'_{N,T+1})\iota_N(\tilde{y}_{1,T+1}-\hat{y}_{1,T+1}).$$

Using

$$a = V(y_{1,T+1}-\tilde{y}_{1,T+1}|X_{N,1},\ldots,X_{N,T+1})/V(y_{1,T+1}-\hat{y}_{1,T+1}|X_{N,1},\ldots,X_{N,T+1}) = \frac{N\,\omega^2}{(N+D)\sigma^2},$$

the ratio of the respective conditional variances, we estimate the aggregate variable by

$$(14)\quad \check{y}_{1,T+1} = \frac{1}{a+1}\,\tilde{y}_{1,T+1} + \frac{a}{a+1}\,\hat{y}_{1,T+1}.$$

This means that the smaller the variance of the observation error is in comparison with the variance of the prediction error of the basic OLS-aggregate predictions, the more the improved aggregate prediction approaches the error effected observation.

(c) If we suppose that we cannot get any information about the realization of the latent variables of the prediction period from the aggregate prediction, we have to assume $\rho = 0$ and necessarily $\omega^2 \geqq \sigma^2$. Now we can utilize the aggregate prediction only for improving the estimation of the regression coefficients. Using the improved estimator

$$(15)\quad \check{\beta} = \hat{\beta} + \frac{\sigma^2}{N(\omega^2-\sigma^2)+D\sigma^2} (\underline{X}_N'\underline{X}_N)^{-1} X_{1,T+1}' (\tilde{y}_{1,T+1} - \hat{y}_{1,T+1})$$

we predict the basic variables by

$$(16)\quad \check{y}_{N,T+1} = X_{N,T+1}\check{\beta}.$$

The corresponding aggregate prediction can be reduced to a weighted sum of the additional and basic OLS-aggregate prediction by

$$(17)\quad \check{y}_{1,T+1} = \frac{D}{N(a-1)+D(a+1)} \tilde{y}_{1,T+1} + \frac{N(a-1)+Da}{N(a-1)+D(a+1)} \hat{y}_{1,T+1}.$$

(d) The aggregate prediction is of a greater importance if we assume that we know by $(\tilde{y}_{1,T+1}, X_{1,T+1})$ a point on the regression plane, which means that we assume $\omega^2 = \sigma^2$ and $\rho = 0$. Then we have to consider $\tilde{y}_{1,T+1} = X_{1,T+1}\beta$ as a restriction conditionally valid with probability one and estimate the regression coefficients by

$$(18)\quad \check{\beta} = \hat{\beta} + \frac{1}{D}(\underline{X}_N'\underline{X}_N)^{-1} X_{1,T+1}' (\tilde{y}_{1,T+1} - \hat{y}_{1,T+1})$$

leading to the improved predictions

$$(19)\quad \check{y}_{N,T+1} = \hat{y}_{N,T+1} + \frac{1}{D} X_{N,T+1} (\underline{X}_N'\underline{X}_N)^{-1} X_{1,T+1} (\tilde{y}_{1,T+1} - \hat{y}_{1,T+1})$$

It is clear that we use the additional aggregate prediction for making the aggregate prediction, since this prediction is the best we can obtain because of our complete ignorance of the latent variables in period T+1. Nevertheless this aggregate prediction is, of course, affected by a prediction error.

(e) Often we cannot predict the basic variables by the GLS-predictions, because we are forced, no matter what, to look for adjusted predictions, i.e. for predictions of the micro-variables that sum up to the externally given prediction of the aggregate variable. Neither the basic nor the improved prediction are automatically adjusted to the additional aggregate prediction. But there is an exception. If $\omega^2/\sigma^2 = 1-\rho/\sigma^2$ all improved predictions are adjusted, too.

Motivated by the special cases we finally want to point out an interesting interpretation of $\phi=\sigma^2/(\omega^2-\sigma^2+2\rho)$. ϕ is the weight attached to the additional prediction and prediction conditions when estimating the regression coefficients by (8). We have $\phi=1$, the standard treatment of an additional observation, for the distribution case without errors of observation, while the distribution case with errors of observation leads to $\phi<1$ treating the additional prediction more cautiously. We have also $\phi=1$ if we treat the additional prediction as an independent observation, independent in every respect ($\omega^2 = 2\sigma^2$ and $\rho = 0$) and come to $\phi \to \infty$ for the restriction case putting greatest faith possible in the aggregate prediction. Therefore choosing an element of the set of admissible parameters (ω^2,ρ) means to judge the additional aggregate prediction with respect not only to its use for prediction but also to its use for estimation.

2.4. Justification and discussion

We intend to take a more general position in order to discuss our assumptions and procedures. On the one hand, as we have seen, there is always something to gain if we utilize the aggregate prediction , because there is a broader empirical basis for our predictions. Moreover we have to bear in mind that we do not necessarily lose if we utilize the aggregate predictions with parameters possibly chosen wrongly. But on the other hand there is always something to pay for, because we run the risk of misspecification. Worse, we sometimes know that misspecification is inevitable. But from our point of view misspecification is not as disastrous as it is seen normally. We have always to decide between misspecification on the one hand and simplification and a broader empirical basis on the other hand.

Exposing some well known prediction problems as special problems to be treated with our procedures as well as the simplicity of the proposed procedures are remarkable facts justifying our assumptions. But we should not deceive ourselves, we have to pay a high price for not looking for a comprehensive prediction model covering both the basic N-prediction model and a 1-prediction model the aggregate prediction refers to. Not only the separation of the aggregate prediction from the reference period, constituting the external character, but especially the conditioning of all assumptions by the exogenous variables of the basic N-prediction model are crucial and weak points of our specification.

3. The use of aggregate predictions, internal specification

Suppose now that the aggregate prediction is based on a prediction model, too. If it is the 1-prediction model implied by the basic N-prediction model there is nothing to gain by the aggregate prediction not even a confirmation for the basic prediction, because of the smaller empirical basis of the aggregate prediction. But suppose that there are R economic units derived from the basic N units by a grouping procedure and we have to predict the corresponding R grouped variables only. If we are able to use the basic N-prediction model we can obtain the predictions for the grouped variables by simply summing up the basic predictions respectively. But suppose that there are only grouped R-data instead of ungrouped N-data available, then we have to predict by using a R-prediction model implied by the N-prediction model. And if we are now confronted with S predictions for the same economic variable which refer to S economic units obtained by another grouping of the N basic units and which are based on an implied S-prediction model, we have to look for a way using these predictions. And even if we can only use the aggregate prediction based on the S-predictions it is worth while looking for such a way.

3.1. The internal specification

We only want to discuss a special case demonstrating the problems we run into. Therefore we consider only a simple grouping procedure using grouping matrices G_R and G_S.

$$G_R=(g_{ir})\quad \begin{array}{l} i=1,\ldots,N \\ r=1,\ldots,R \end{array} \quad \text{and } g_{ir}=\begin{cases} 1,\text{if the } i^{th} \text{ N-unit is an element of the } r^{th} \text{ R-unit} \\ 0,\text{otherwise} \end{cases}$$

and G_S constructed in strict analogy, both being suitable for extensive variables. Moreover we partition the exogenous variables into dummy variables and proper exogenous variables by

$$X_{N,t} = (G_R, G_S, Z_{N,t}) \quad \Big| \quad t=1,2,\ldots,T,T+1$$

and the regression coefficients accordingly by

$$\beta' = (\alpha_R', \alpha_S', \gamma').$$

Such a partition with an introduction of dummy variables as well as R- and S-specific level parameters is reasonable because we have to bear in mind that in most cases the data are grouped with respect to qualitative or quantitative attributes that are also important for explaining and predicting the variable under consideration. Using

$$y_{R,t} = G_R'y_{N,t},\ Z_{R,t} = G_R'Z_{N,t},\ H_R = G_R'G_R,$$

we can specifiy the R-prediction model (and analogously the S-prediction model) by

$$\left.\begin{array}{ll}
\text{(R-1)} & y_{R,t} = H_R\alpha_R^* + Z_{R,t}\gamma + u_{R,t} \\
\text{(R-2.1)} & E(u_{R,t}|Z_{N,1},\ldots,Z_{N,T+1}) = 0 \\
\text{(R-2.2)} & E(u_{R,t}u_{R,t'}'|Z_{N,1},\ldots,Z_{N,T+1}) = \begin{cases} \sigma^2 G_R'G_R & t=t' \\ 0 & t\neq t' \end{cases} \\
\text{(R-3.1)} & \gamma\in R^m,\ \alpha_R^*\in R^R\ ;\ \ (\alpha_R^*=\alpha_R+H_R^{-1}G_R'G_S\alpha_S) \\
\text{(R-3.2)} & 0 < \sigma^2 < \infty
\end{array}\right| \quad t,t'=1,2,\ldots,T,T+1$$

leading to the R-predictions

$$(20)\quad \hat{y}_{R,T+1|R} = H_R\hat{\alpha}_{R|R}^* + Z_{R,T+1}\hat{\gamma}_{.|R}$$

with

$$(21)\quad \hat{\gamma}_{.|R} = \{\underline{Z}_R'((I_T - \tfrac{1}{T}\iota_T\iota_T')\otimes H_R^{-1})\underline{Z}_R\}^{-1}\ \underline{Z}_R'((I_T - \tfrac{1}{T}\iota_T\iota_T')\otimes H_R^{-1})\underline{y}_R$$

and

$$(22)\quad \hat{\alpha}_{R|R}^* = (\tfrac{1}{T}\iota_T'\otimes H_R^{-1})(\underline{y}_R - \underline{Z}_R\,\hat{\gamma}_{.|R}).$$

3.2. The improved predictions

We now intend to improve the R-predictions obtained above by using the corresponding S-predictions $y_{S,T+1|S}$ or the derived aggregated 1-predictions $y_{1,T+1|S}$. First of all we have to pay attention to an identification problem concerning the R- and S-specific level parameters. Because of

$$G_R'(G_R\alpha_R+G_S\alpha_S) = G_R'G_R(\alpha_R+(G_R'G_R)^{-1}G_R'G_S\alpha_S)= H_R\alpha_R^*$$

it becomes immediately clear that we cannot identify the R- and S-structural regression coefficients within the R- as well as S-prediction model. Nevertheless there are no immediate prediction problems caused by the identification problem because of

$$E\,\{y_{R,T+1} - \hat{y}_{R,T+1|R}\,|Z_{N,1},\ldots,Z_{N,T+1}\} = 0.$$

But this identification problem is responsible for the limited use of the S-predictions or the S-based 1-prediction for the improvement of the R-predictions. For if we try to combine the initial R-predictions with the additional available S-predictions linearly so that the predictions so obtained are conditionally unbiased, we discover very restrictive conditions. Considering the linear combination

$$(23)\quad \check{y}_{R,T+1} = A\,\hat{y}_{R,T+1|R} + B\,\hat{y}_{S,T+1|S}$$

we get the prediction errors

$$(24)\quad y_{R,T+1}-\check{y}_{R,T+1}= A(y_{R,T+1}-\hat{y}_{R,T+1|R}) + B(y_{S,T+1}-\hat{y}_{S,T+1|S})$$
$$+(I-A)y_{R,T+1}- By_{S,T+1}\;.$$

And because of

$$E(y_{R,T+1}-\check{y}_{R,T+1}|Z_{N,1},\ldots,Z_{N,T+1})=\{(I-A)G_R'-BG_S'\}E(y_{N,T+1}|Z_{N,1},\ldots,Z_{N,T+1}) = 0,$$

considering the desired unbiasedness, we need

$$\{(I-A)G_R' - BG_S'\}\;(G_R\alpha_R + G_S\alpha_S + Z_{T+1}\gamma) = 0.$$

Postulating this condition to be valid for all possible regression coeficients we come to

$$(I-A)G_R' = BG_S'.$$

This equation has a solution for I-A if

$$BG_S'(I-P_R) = 0 \ ; \ P_R=G_R(G_R'G_R)^{-1}G_R' \ .$$

Assuming that there is no pooling of R-units that can be obtained by a pooling of S-units (except a pooling of all units which is always possible because of $G_R\iota_R = G_S\iota_S = \iota_N$) we are assured that the rank of the matrix (G_R, G_S) is exactly R+S-1, thus the maximum rank possible for the two grouping matrices is attained. Then we get

$$\left.\begin{array}{l} B = b\iota_N'G_S(G_S'G_S)^{-1} = b\iota_S' \\ I-A = b\iota_S'G_S'G_R(G_R'G_R)^{-1} = b\iota_R' \end{array}\right\} b\varepsilon R^R$$

and come to

$$(25) \quad \check{y}_{R,T+1} = \hat{y}_{R,T+1|R} - b(\hat{y}_{1,T+1|R} - \hat{y}_{1,T+1|S}), \quad b\varepsilon R^R.$$

so that it remains to determine the Rx1 vector b.

3.3. Discussion

Not going into further details concerning the determination of b+) we finally want to remark that it is at a glance rather disappointing that we can improve the R-predictions only by considering the difference between the respective aggregated predictions. But we recognize that we can compare both the R- and the S-predictions only via their 1-predictions. But by imposing additional restrictions on the R- and S-specific level parameters and therefore weakening the identification difficulties as well as by taking the advantage of possible R- and S-structural dependencies ($rk(G_R, G_S) < R+S-1$) the use of the S-predictions is no longer limited to the derived 1-prediction. By considering the artificial latent variables

$$\tilde{u}_{S,T+1} = \hat{y}_{S,T+1|S} - G_S'G_R\alpha_R^* - G_SZ_{N,T+1}\gamma$$

+) see: Reeh, K. (1976) "On the problem of combining prediction grouped in different ways", paper presented at ESEM 1976

and their conditional expectations

$$E(\tilde{u}_{S,T+1} \mid Z_{N,1},\ldots,Z_{N,T+1}) = G_S'(I-P_R)G_S\alpha_S$$

we can see that it is possible to add the S-predictions to the R-prediction model if the conditional expectations of the artificial latent variables are zero. Naturally this condition is met if we consider $\iota_S'\tilde{u}_{S,T+1} = \tilde{u}_{1,T+1}$ because of $\iota_S'G_S(I-P_R)G_S\alpha_S = 0$. But it is met for all S-predictions if we restrict the S-specific level parameters α_S by $\alpha_S = \iota_S\alpha$ because of $G_S'(I-P_R)G_S\iota_S\alpha = 0$. These two examples indicate both possibilities for extending (or limiting) the use of the S-predictions and therefore enlarging the empirical basis for the R-predictions.

In conclusion we can remark that it is worth looking for a suitable way to use other related predictions based either on an external or internal specification.

References

Chow, G.C. and Lin, An-loh (1971) "Best linear unbiased interpolation, distribution and extrapolation of time-series", Review of Economics and Statistics, 335-41

Haitovsky, Y. (1973) "Regression Estimation from Grouped Observations", Charles Griffin & Co. Ltd., London

Reeh, K. (1975) "Different ways of using external aggregate predictions", Forschungsberichte aus dem Institut für Statistik und Wissenschaftstheorie, Universität München, Serie Oe. Nr.4

Reeh, K. (1976) "On the problem of combining predictions grouped in different ways", Forschungsberichte aus dem Institut für Statistik und Wissenschaftstheorie, Universität München, Serie Oe. Nr.7; paper presented at ESEM 1976 in Helsinki

Schneeweiß, H. (1974) "Ökonometrie", 2. verbesserte und erweiterte Auflage, Physica-Verlag, Würzburg-Wien

Theil, H. (1963) "On the use of incomplete prior information in regression analysis", Journal of the American Statistical Association, 401-14

Theil, H. and Goldberger, A.S. (1960) "On pure and mixed statistical estimation", International Economic Review, 65-78

On a Flexibility Theorem of Diewert

by G. Uebe

0. Abstract

In a most recent publication Diewert (Diewert 1976) shows that any linear homogeneous, twice continuously differentiable, positive function f(x) defined over an open subset of the positive orthant in n-dimensional space can be approximated conveniently by a quadratic mean of order r. Due to linear homogeneity this result can be sharpened to a corresponding approximation by a subclass of the approximating function. In order to appreciate the application of this approximation, the quadratic mean of order r is reviewed and related to the general theory of homogeneity.

1. Statement of Problem

Let f(x) be any linear homogeneous, twice continuously differentiable, positive function, defined over an open subset of the positive orthant in n-dimensional space:

$$f : \mathbb{R}^n_+ \to \mathbb{R}^1_+, \quad x = f(v), \quad \lambda f(v) = f(\lambda v), \quad \lambda \geq 0. \tag{1}$$

Let g(r,a,v) be the quadratic mean of order r defined by

$$g : (\mathbb{R}^1_+ \times \mathbb{R}^M \times \mathbb{R}^n_+) \to \mathbb{R}^1_+, \quad x = g(r,a,v), \quad n \leq M \leq (n+1)n/2$$

$$g(r,a,v) = \left(\sum_{i=1}^{n} \sum_{j=1}^{n} a_{ij} \, v_i^{r/2} \, v_j^{r/2}\right)^{1/r}, \qquad r \neq 0. \tag{2}$$

Define

$$\frac{\partial f(v)}{\partial v_j} =: f_j(v) =: f_j, \quad \frac{\partial g(r,a,v)}{\partial v_j} =: g_j(r,a,v) =: g_j \qquad j = 1,2...n \tag{3}$$

$$\frac{\partial^2 f(v)}{\partial v_i \partial v_j} =: f_{ij}(v) =: f_{ij}, \quad \frac{\partial^2 g(r,a,v)}{\partial v_i \partial v_j} =: g_{ij}(r,a,v) =: g_{ij} \qquad i = 1,2...n, \; j = 1,2...n. \tag{4}$$

Proposition 1 (Diewert 1976, Theorem (4.3)):
For any point v^* there exists an n(n+1)/2-dimensional parameter vector a such that

$$f(v^*) = g(r,a,v^*) \tag{5.1}$$

$$f_j(v^*) = g_j(v^*) \quad \forall j \tag{5.2}$$

$$f_{ij}(v^*) = g_{ij}(r,a,v^*) \quad \forall i,j. \tag{5.3}$$

Proposition 1 is a nontrivial second order differential approximation: Functions f and g agree in their Taylor expansion up to second order terms.
Proposition 1 can be sharpened to

Proposition 2:
For any point v there exists an n-dimensional parameter vector a such that (5) is true. Before proving proposition 2 by strengthening the proof of proposition 1, some of the remarkable properties of functions f and g are summarized:

2. The Aggregator Function

By the quadratic mean of order r (2) a rich class of functions can be generated, each of which may possible serve as a production function:

1. Specialization of parameter r:

Subcase 1.1 r = 1. The generalized Leontief function (Type 1)

$$g(1,a,x) = \left(\sum_{i=1}^{n} \sum_{j=1}^{n} a_{ij} v_i^{1/2} v_j^{1/2}\right). \tag{6}$$

Subcase 1.2 r = 2. The quadratic mean function

$$g(2,a,x) = \left(\sum_{i=1}^{n} \sum_{j=1}^{n} a_{ij} v_i v_j\right)^{1/2}. \tag{7}$$

Subcase 1.3[1] $r \to 0$. The "translog function"

$$\lim_{r\to 0} g(r,a,x) = \left(\sum_{i=1}^{n} \sum_{j=1}^{n} a_{ij} \ln v_i \ln v_j\right). \tag{8}$$

Subcase 1.4[2] $r \to \infty$. The generalized Leontief function (Type 2)

$$\lim_{r\to\infty} g(r,a,x) = (v_k v_\ell)^{1/2} \tag{9.2}$$

$$v_k v_\ell = \underset{ij}{\mathrm{Max}} \{v_i v_j\}. \tag{9.2}$$

2. Specialization of the parameter vector a:

Subcase 2.1[3] $a_{ij} = 0,\ i \neq j\ (r \neq (0,1,2,\infty))$. The CES function

$$g(r,a,v) = \left(\sum_{j=1}^{n} a_{ij} v_j^r\right)^{1/r}. \tag{10}$$

---

1) The general translog function approximation of a function $h: \mathbb{R}^n \to \mathbb{R}$, $x = h(v)$, is given by $h(v) \approx \alpha_o + \alpha_1^T \ln v + \ln v^T \alpha_2 \ln v$, where the arrays α_o, α_1, α_2 are of dimensions 1×1, $n\times 1$, $n\times n$.

2) The derivation of (9) is analogous to one generating the ordinary Leontief function $f(v) = \mathrm{Min}\{v_1, v_2 \ldots v_n\}$ from the general CES function (e.g. Uebe, p. 97)

$$\lim_{r\to\infty} \ln g(r,a,v) = \frac{1}{2} \ln (v_k v_\ell) + \lim_{r\to\infty} \frac{1}{r} \ln\left(\sum_{i,j\neq k,\ell} a_{ij}\left(\frac{v_i v_j}{v_k v_\ell}\right)^{r/2} + a_{k\ell}\right).$$

Finiteness of the last bracket, gives (9.1).

3) The further specializations excluded by $(r \neq (0,1,1,\infty))$ are the usual subcases of the CES-class (see e.g. Uebe).

Subcase 2.2[1)] $a_{ij} = a_i a_j$ $(r \neq 0,2,4,\infty)$). The dyadic function

$$g(r,a,x) = \left(\sum_{j=1}^{n} a_j v_j^{r/2}\right)^{2/r}. \tag{11}$$

3. Homogeneity properties:

The aggregator function (2) is a case of Lau's almost homogeneity

(i) $$g(\lambda r,\lambda a,\lambda v) = \lambda^{1+1/r}\, g(r,a,v), \quad \lambda \in \mathbb{R}^1_+, \tag{12}$$

i.e., g is homogeneous of degree $1 + \frac{1}{r}$, respectively (see Uebe, p. 62 - 82)

$$g(r,a,v) \text{ is } \mathrm{hom}(1,1+\tfrac{1}{r})$$

respectively

$$g(r,a,v) \text{ is } \mathrm{Hom}(1,1;1+\tfrac{1}{r}) \tag{13}$$

(ii) $$g(r,\lambda a,v) = \lambda^{1/r} g(r,a;v)$$

respectively

$$g(r,a,v) \text{ is } \mathrm{Hom}(1,0;\tfrac{1}{r}) \tag{14}$$

(iii) $$g(r,a,\lambda v) = \lambda g(r,a,v)$$

respectively

$$g(r,a,v) \text{ is } \mathrm{Hom}(0,1;1). \tag{15}$$

(12)-(15) are another extension of Lau's proposition (Lau 1972):

Proposition 3:

Let F be a function $(\mathbb{R}^{n_1} \times \mathbb{R}^{n_2}) \to \mathbb{R}^1$, $F(z_1,z_2)$.

---

1 This function obviously is identical to subcase 2.1 by scaling of r. By direct specialization from (2) by $\left(v^{r/2} A\, v^{r/2}\right)^{1/r}$, $A = a\, a^T$, one recognizes subcase 2.2 as a subcase of functions related to a singular A. $rk(A) = rk(a\, a^T) = 1$, $n \geq 2$.

If F Hom(1,1;1), then

F Hom(1,0;k), iff F Hom(0,1;1-k).

<u>Proposition 4</u>:
Let F be a function $(\mathbb{R}^{n_1} \times \mathbb{R}^{n_2}) \to \mathbb{R}^1$, $F(z_1,z_2)$.
If F $Hom(1,1;h)$, $h \underset{(\leq)}{\geq} 1$, then

F Hom(1,0;k), iff F Hom(0,1;h-k).

The proof of proposition 4 is as for proposition 3, a straight forward use of the Euler equation. The roles of z_1 and z_2 are played by a and v (see above (13), (14), (15), $h = 1 + 1/r$, $k = 1/r$).
A further generalization of (14) - (15) is given by a re-specification of (2)

$$\tilde{g}(r_1,r_2,a,v) := \left(\sum_{i=j}^{n} \sum_{j=1}^{n} a_{ij} \, v_i^{r_1/2} \, v_j^{r_1/2} \right)^{1/r_2}, \quad r_1 \underset{<}{\overset{>}{\neq}} r_2. \tag{2)'}$$

Corresponding to (14) - (15) we have

$$\tilde{g}(r_1,r_2,a,v) \text{ is } Hom(1,0;1/r_2) \tag{14)'}$$

$$\tilde{g}(r_1,r_2,a,v) \text{ is } Hom(0,1;r_1/r_2). \tag{15)'}$$

Depending on the ratio r_1/r_2, $\tilde{g}$ has decreasing, respectively constant, respectively increasing returns to scale with respect to v.

3. The Singular Hessian Matrix of Linear Homogeneous Functions

The Euler equations describing the linear homogeneity in v of f and g are crucial for proposition 1 and 2

$$f(v) = \sum_{\forall k} f_k v_k \tag{17}$$

$$g(r,a,v) = \sum_{\forall k} g_k v_k \tag{18}$$

respectively

$$\sum_{\forall \ell} f_{k\ell} v_\ell = 0 \qquad \forall k \tag{19}$$

$$\sum_{\forall \ell} g_{k\ell} v_\ell = 0 \qquad \forall k\,. \tag{20}$$

(19) - respectively (20), however, obviously imply the singularity of the Hessian matrix with respect to v. In consequence the classical problem of production

(O1) $$px - q^T v = \underset{x,v}{\text{Max}}$$

subject to

(O2) $$x = f(v)$$

with its set of necessary and sufficient conditions

(O3) $$pf_j - q_j = 0 \qquad \forall j = 1,2\ldots n$$

(O4) $(f_{k\ell})$ strictly (!) positive definite

is not well defined. The same gap will be exploited in the following.

4. Diewert's Differential Equations

The proof of proposition 1 relies on the following set of differential equations (Diewert 1976: equations (6.6) and (6.7))

$$f_{ij} = \frac{1-r}{x} f_i f_j + \frac{r}{2} x^{1-r} a_{ij} v_i^{r/2-1} v_j^{r/2-1}, \quad i \neq j,\ i,j=1,2\ldots n \tag{21}$$

$$\sum_{j=1}^{n} a_{ij} v_i^{r/2-1} v_j^{r/2} x^{1-r} = f_i, \qquad i = 1,2,\ldots n \tag{22}$$

The a_{ij} ($(i \neq j)$, $a_{ij} = a_{ji}$) of (2) and (5) are defined by (21) and the diagonal elements a_{jj} of (2) and (5) are defined by (22).

5. Proof of the Strengthened Proposition

If equation (21) - (22) are to be integrable into (2), then the formulation is redundant, i.e. unnecessarily general than to be anticipated from (21) and (22). Multiply (21) by v_j and add, to obtain

$$\sum_{j\neq i} f_{ij}v_j = -f_{ii}v_i \qquad \text{by (19)} \tag{23}$$

$$= \frac{1-r}{x} f_i \sum_{j\neq i}^{n} f_j v_j + \sum_{j\neq i} x^{1-r} \frac{r}{2} a_{ij}\, v_i^{r/2-1}\, v_j^{r/2} \quad \text{by (17)} \tag{24}$$

$$= \frac{1-r}{x} f(x - f_i v_i) + rg_i - rx^{1-r}\, a_{ii} v_i^{r-1}. \tag{25}$$

The reformulation of the second term of the right-hand side of (24) uses the first derivative of (2),

$$g_i = \frac{1}{r}\left(x^{1-r}\frac{r}{2}\sum_{j\neq i} a_{ij}\, v_i^{r/2-1}\, v_j^{r/2} + rx^{1-r}\, a_{ii}\, v_i^{r-1}\right) \tag{26}$$

respectively

$$rg_i - rx^{1-r}\, a_{ii}\, v_i^{r-1} = \sum_{j\neq i} x^{1-r}\, a_{ij}\, v_i^{r/2-1}\, v_j^{r/2}. \tag{27}$$

As a final result we obtain from (25) a set of differential equations <u>only</u> depending on the diagonal terms, i.e. the a_{ij}, $i \neq j$, do not matter:

$$-f_{ii}v_i = \frac{1-r}{x} f_i(x - f_i v_i) + rg_i - rx^{1-r}\, a_{ii} v_i^{r-1}. \tag{28}$$

Therefore w.l.o.g. we decide to suppress the a_{ij} $(i \neq j)$. The second of the original differential equations (22) immediately turns into:

$$a_{ii} v_i^{r-1}\, x^{1-r} = f_i \;^{1)} \tag{29}$$

and the first one ((21), respectively (28)) collapses into (29), provided

---

1) The paper has a misprint f_1 instead of f_i (Diewert 1976,p.141)

(i) g_i is replaced by f_i as required by 5.2 and

(ii) f_{ii} is determined by (29).

This construction concludes the proof of proposition 2. The significance of the statement is the parameter reducing effect: Instead of n^2, respectively $n(n+1)/2$ (for symmetry) differential equations, only n have to be integrated. Reviewing the result, an alternative approach is to analyze (22), given any a_{ij} $(i \neq j)$. Multiplying by v_i and adding we obtain

$$x^{1-r}\left(\sum_{i=1}^{n} \sum_{j=1}^{n} a_{ij} v_i^{r/2} v_j^{r/2}\right) = \sum_{i=1}^{n} v_i f_i = x. \tag{30}$$

By homogeneity the right-hand side is equal to x ((17) resp. (18)), hence by (22) alone, (2) has been obtained, (21) is redundant. Or alternatively by the singularity of the Hessian of f(v), respectively g(.,.,v) ((19) - (20)) we have: If for any point $v^{(1)}$ there is one set of $(f_{k\ell})$, respectively $(g_{k\ell})$, then there are infinitely many on the ray $\mu v, \mu \geq 0$:

<u>Proposition 5</u>:
Let $v^{(1)}$ satisfy (17) - (18) and (19) - (20), respectively (21) - (22), i.e. there is one set $(a_{ij}^{(1)})$, then there are infinitely many (a_{ij})s.
The proof is to look at the ray $v^{(2)} = \mu v^{(1)}$. By linear homogeneity,

$$f^{(2)} = \mu f^{(1)}; \quad f_k^{(2)} = f_k^{(1)} \ \forall k; \quad f_{ij}^{(2)} = \frac{1}{\mu} f_{ij}^{(1)} \ \forall ij. \tag{31}$$

Hence (17) and (19) are satisfied trivially on the ray and the differential equations (21) - (22) for $v^{(2)}$,

$$f_{ij}^{(2)} = \frac{1-r}{x^{(2)}} f_i^{(2)} f_j^{(2)} + \frac{r}{2} x^{(2)(1-r)} a_{ij}^{(2)} v_i^{(2)(r/2-1)} v_j^{(2)(r/2-1)} \qquad i \neq j \tag{21'}$$

$$\sum_{j=1}^{n} a_{ij}^{(2)} v_i^{(2)(r/2-1)} v_j^{(2)r/2} x^{(2)(1-r)} = f_i^{(2)} \ \forall i, \tag{22'}$$

can be written:

$$f_{ij}^{(1)} = \frac{1-r}{x^{(1)}} f_i^{(1)} f_j^{(1)} + \frac{r}{2} x^{(1)(1-r)} a_{ij}^{(2)} v_i^{(1)(r/2-1)} v_j^{(1)(r/2-1)} \qquad (21)''$$

$$i \neq j$$

$$\sum_{j=1}^{n} a_{ij}^{(2)} v_i^{(1)(r/2-1)} v_j^{(1)r/2} x^{(1)(1-r)} = f_i^{(1)} \qquad \forall i. \qquad (22)''$$

Any $a^{(2)} = \mu a^{(1)}$, $\mu \geq 0$, will satisfy (21) and (22) for $v^{(1)}$.

6. Integration of the Differential Equations (29)

The solution of system (29), however, is the wellknown CES class of functions (see Krelle-Coenen for the original approach, or see Uebe).

So an outline of the integration is given:

For linear homogeneity of f it suffices to integrate (n - 1) of the differential equations (29), i.e. dividing by the first gradient, we have

$$a_{ii}^{-1} v_i^{1-r} f_i = a_{11}^{-1} v_1^{1-r} f_1, \quad i = (1),2,3,\dots,n \qquad (32)$$

Define the transformations

$$z_i := \begin{cases} a_{ii} \frac{1}{r} v_i^r & r \neq 0 \\ a_{ii} \ln v_i & r = 0, \end{cases} \qquad (33)$$

i.e., by

$$a_{ii}^{-1} v_i^{1-r} = \frac{\partial v_i}{\partial z_i} \qquad (34)$$

and by

$$\frac{\partial f}{\partial z_i} = \frac{\partial f}{\partial v_i} \frac{\partial v_i}{\partial z_i} = f_i \frac{\partial v_i}{\partial z_i} \qquad (35)$$

the system of differential equations (29) is turned into

$$\frac{\partial f}{\partial z_i} = \frac{\partial f}{\partial z_1}, \qquad i = 2,3...n. \tag{36}$$

One solution of (36) is

$$f = \sum_{i=1}^{n} z_i \tag{37}$$

and the general solution is

$$f = F(\sum_{i=1}^{n} z_i), \tag{38}$$

F to be determined; f and z_i given by (33).
An equivalent reformulation is

$$f = \begin{cases} \tilde{F}\left(\sum_{i=1}^{n} z_i\right)^{1/r} & r \neq 0 \\ \tilde{F}\left(\sum_{i=1}^{n} e^{z_i}\right) & r = 0. \end{cases} \tag{39}$$

Since finally f is linear homogeneous and F has one argument only,

$$f = \begin{cases} c_o\left(\sum_{i=1}^{n} z_i\right)^{1/r} & r \neq 0 \\ c_o \sum_{i=1}^{n} e^{z_i} & r = 0 \end{cases} \qquad c_o \text{ a constant.} \tag{40}$$

This, however, is the CES class of functions.

As a final point one should stress that the approximation is at a specific point v^*. Given two points, two sets of (a_{ij})s are obtained, hence for estimation the result does not seem to be particularly usefull.

References

Diewert, W.E.: Exact and Superlative Index Numbers, Journal of Econometrics, 4, 1976, 115 - 145.

Krelle, W., Coenen, D.: Ersetzung der Produktionsfunktion durch preis- und kapazitätsabhängige Produktionskoeffizienten, Jahrbücher für Nationalökonomie und Statistik, 176, 1964, 289 - 318.

Lau, L.J.: Profit Functions of Technologies with Multiple Inputs and Outputs, Review of Economics and Statistics, 54, 1972, 281 - 289.

Uebe, G., unter Mitwirkung von J. Fischer: Produktionstheorie, Springer-Verlag, Berlin-Heidelberg-New York, 1976.

AUTHOR INDEX

Subject Index

Editors

WOLFGANG EICHHORN, Institut für Wirtschaftstheorie und Operations Research, Universität Karlsruhe (TH), D-7500 Karlsruhe 1, Federal Republic of Germany.

RUDOLF HENN, Institut für Statistik und Mathematische Wirtschaftstheorie, Universität Karlsruhe (TH), D-7500 Karlsruhe 1, Federal Republic of Germany.

OTTO OPITZ, Institut für Entscheidungstheorie und Unternehmensforschung, Universität Karlsruhe (TH), D-7500 Karlsruhe 1, Federal Republic of Germany.

RONALD W. SHEPHARD, Department of Industrial Engineeering and Operations Research, University of California at Berkeley, Berkeley, California 94720, U.S.A.